101 Ways to Improve your Memory

101 Ways to Improve your Memory

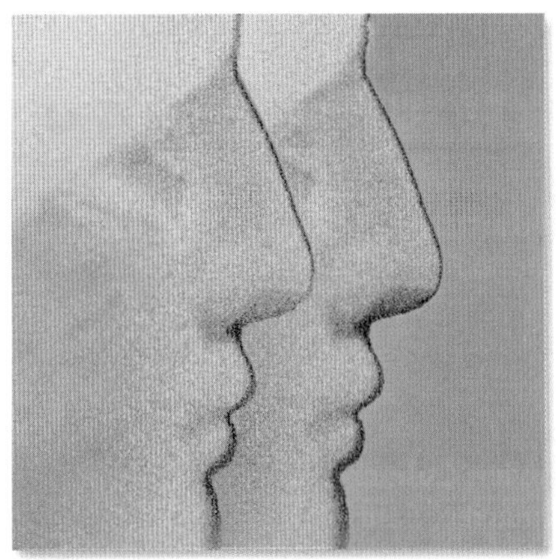

NEW YORK • HONG KONG • LONDON • MONTREAL • SYDNEY

101 Ways to Improve your Memory

was created by the Reader's Digest Association

First English language edition 2005

Original edition first published by Sélection du Reader's Digest, SA,
5-7 Louis Pasteur Avenue, 92220 Bagneux, France

We thank everyone who has contributed to the preparation and publication of this book:

The MEMORY AND LIFE ASSOCIATION,
and especially
Martine Soudani, *specialist in geriatrics*,
Yves Ledanseurs, *psychologist*.

THE CHAPTERS
were written with the guidance of
Marie-Christelle Fiorino, *clinical psychologist specialising in psycho-gerontology and medical psychology*.

EDITORIAL CONSULTANTS:
Bénédicte Dieudonné, *clinical psychologist specialising in neuropsychology*
Elsa Galan-Kouznetsov, *clinical psychologist and gerontologist*
Sophie Martineau, *psychologist specialising in geriatrics and psychotherapy*

We also thank **Régine Nuriec, Monique Tartreau and Anne-Sophie Vuillemin** for their contribution to the games component.

GAMES BOOKLETS
Editing: **Agence Media**
Creation of games modules: **Fabrice Bouvier, Colman Cohen, Philippe Fassier, Aurelien Kermarrec, Fabrice Malbert, Bernard Myers, Claude Quiec**

ILLUSTRATIONS
Laurent Audouin, Emmanuel Batisse, Philippe Bucamp, Jacqueline Caulet, Marc Donon, Philippe Fassier, William Fraschini, Sylvie Guerraz, Nicolas Jarreau, Jean-Pierre Lamérand, Patrick Lestienne, Claude Quiec, Carine Sanson

LAYOUT: **Didier Pavois**

GRAPHIC EFFECTS: **Colman Cohen**

INDEX: **Marie-Thérèse Ménager**

We also thank **Mathias Durvie, Sylvie Guerraz, Evelyne Stive, Véronique Zonca** (layout) and **Céline de Queral** (editorial secretary).

ENGLISH EDITORIAL TEAM
Editor: **Sandy Shepherd**
Art director: **Pete Bosman**
Translator: **Adré Marshall**
Games creator: **Mike Laatz**
Proofreader: **Renée Moodie**
Illustrators: **Adam Carnegie, Steven Felmore**

ISBN: 962-258-341-5

Book Code: 0411844 (E101M)
Project Code: 1544/G

Preface

You are about to pick up this book and glance through it, noting the headings, looking at the pictures and enjoying the colours ...

You will say to yourself: this book is just what I'm looking for. It deals with all my anxieties about having an unreliable memory: forgetting the name of that person I actually know very well, being unable to recall the name of that city I passed through last summer, losing track of my car keys ...

Your memory in fact permeates your whole life. You live with it from morning to night without thinking about it, just as you constantly use your arms and legs without paying attention to them – until the day you have an accident ... If one of your limbs is missing you become disabled; if your memory is faulty, it is as if your whole life is thrown off balance.

Your memory is too precious to be allowed to decline with age. It will probably change as you grow older. Certain memories from the past may become more vivid than before, and the realities of everyday life may escape you. That's the way life is – you aren't 20 for ever. But although your memory changes, it does not deteriorate.

It's up to you to do everything to ensure that your memory doesn't stop growing.There is no age limit as far as memory is concerned.Like your heart, it is intended to be there with you right up to your last breath. But you still need to look after it, to use it all the time. Memory suffers only from lack of use.

So don't hesitate any longer. Open this book wherever you choose. Start with what interests you, what attracts your attention. Then proceed gradually into new areas that are unfamiliar to you. You will be revitalised, rejuvenated and will attain a better quality of life.

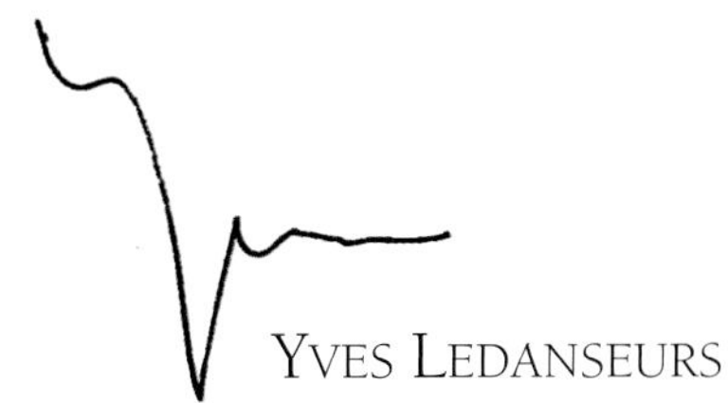

Yves Ledanseurs

Contents

How to use this book

How does the memory work?
Fascinating text helps you understand the mechanism of your memory.

Practical exercises include interpretations of results and advice on improving your memory.

Pictograms indicate an exercise.

Explanations describe the various stages in the memorisation process.

Forgetting

Paradoxically, one aspect of memorisation consists in… forgetting. In fact, it is pointless to risk saturation by trying to retain all the information that reaches you each day. This does not mean that you cannot ensure the sound functioning of your me... good 'crutches' and not trying to do several things at once. Although our desire to remembe... by our subconscious, the information suppressed is still there.

Forgetting, to prevent satu...

I would go mad if I remembered everything!

What would be the point of remembering how many red traffic lights you encountered on your way to work or school and back? Nevertheless, you certainly saw and remembered them, but only to use this information momentarily and then erase it.

The so-called normal memory erases 90-95 percent of information received in one day. This process of active forgetting, often called selective memory, is in fact a way of retaining only what is essential in the continuous flow of daily information. Without it, your memory would be saturated.

This process of active restriction does not work in the same way for everyone. Certain people are able to ...ll a great number of details. For ...ple, they will describe to you in ...hings like your ...at you were wearing ...you. This kind of ...indication of a ...mory, but it can ...he individuals ...se their relation to the ...ual impressions, and ...ir attention is focused on ...es, they are less likely to remember other information, such as the topic of conversation or the nature of the relationship.

For others, the opposite holds. They forget the physical environment of the situations they experience and are regarded as scatterbrains! Their relation with the world is probably ...d more on sentiment and ...ence and so they are ...l details.

European currencies
In 2002, 15 of the countries in the European Union (EU) adopted a common currency. Give the national currency of the 25 countries now in the EU, and indicate which have not adopted the euro.

1. Austria ....
2. Belgium ....
3. Cyprus ....
4. Czech Rep. ....
5. Denmark ....
6. Estonia ....
7. Finland ....
8. France ....
9. Germany ....
10. Greece ....
11. Hungary ....
12. Ireland ....
13. Italy ....
14. Latvia ....
15. Lithuania ....
16. Luxembourg ....
17. Malta ....
18. The Netherlands ....
19. Poland ....
20. Portugal ....
21. Slovakia ....
22. Slovenia ....
23. Spain ....
24. Sweden ....
25. United Kingdom ....

With the advent of the euro, perhaps you have started to forget these currencies. That's quite natural. The process of forgetting is at work here because this information will no longer be useful. In 20 ... a fair number of us will have partly forgotten them, except if we keep these memories alive for historical interest.

Solution p.337

Great rivers of the world
Classify these rivers in descending order according to their length.
Solution p.337

a. Ganges
b. Mississippi-Missouri
c. Amazon
d. Congo
e. Amur
f. Nile
g. Yangzi Jiang
h. Mekong

1. ......
2. ......
3. ......
4. ......
5. ......
6. ......
7. ......
8. ......

You are probably familiar with the names of these rivers, and were taught their relative length some time in your school career. But as these details are not of vital importance, you would have retained them only if they were useful – for professional reasons, for example – or if you are especially interested in geography.

Train your brain with fun exercises

Three booklets (of increasing difficulty) contain games to exercise your ability to reason and your powers of observation and concentration.

Games booklet

STRUCTURE

HIDDEN WORDS

The names of animals hidden in this grid can be discovered in several directions: horizontally or vertically, diagonally, from top to bottom or from bottom to top, from right to left and left to right. The words cross each other and the same letter may be used more than once. With the remaining letters, form the name of a hidden animal.

List of animals to find

AARDVARK, ANTLION, BUCK, BULLDOG, CHICK, DONKEY, DUGONG, ELEPHANT, FOAL, GANNET, GECKO, GIRAFFE, GOAT, GORILLA, HAMSTER, HIPPO, HUSKY, HYAENA, KITTEN, LION, MACAW, MINK, PIG, PONY, PUG, PUPPY, REINDEER, RHINO-CEROS, SHARK, SKUNK, SNAKE, TERN, WHALE

A handy index lists clearly all the games in the chapters and booklets in terms of categories and themes.

Tests evaluate your abilities and identify your strong and weak points.

Boxed tricks and tips suggest how to use your memory more effectively in your daily life.

Test Identify your crutches

Answer **YES** or **NO** to the following questions.

	YES	NO
1. I use the numbers recorded on my cellphone without learning those I call daily.		
2. I systematically make use of my address book when sending postcards to my family and friends.		
3. I make a list when buying fewer than seven products from the supermarket.		
4. I need to note down all my codes – for the front door, credit card, voicemail, cellphone…		
5. I must write down my ideas so as not to forget them.		
6. Because I often slam the door with my keys still inside, I've installed an outside handle.		
7. I regularly consult my diary to keep track of my activities.		
8. I look at the calendar more than twice a day to check the date.		
9. Before making each telephone call, I note down what I want to say.		
10. I often tie knots in my handkerchief.		
11. I write anything I'm afraid of forgetting on my hand.		
12. A white board occupies a prominent place in my kitchen.		

If you have more YES answers, don't feel guilty. We often use crutches in our daily lives and they are not necessarily a sign of mental laziness. You haven't much faith in your memory and have developed the habit of helping it. Despite that, your memory has not deteriorated, and it certainly doesn't mean there is any indication that it is not functioning properly. You must give it the opportunity to record information.

If you have more NO answers, you show confidence in your memory and are satisfied with its performance. Keep it up!

My memory and…
my shopping list

Making a shopping list does not imply that you have a lazy memory - if you don't bury your nose in it as soon as you are in the shop. It is simply making an inventory of what you want. Organising the list according to the way the goods are displayed on the shelves is a good way to remember it. Don't hesitate to read it aloud several times, and as the weeks go by you will eventually be able buy more than 30 products without systematically referring to the list. In any case, there's nothing to stop you from keeping it in your pocket and taking it out just before getting to the till to check that you haven't forgotten anything.

Test What's your

A certain number of daily habits, actions or attitudes can be a sign of minor memory problems. This questionnaire, which you must answer as honestly as possible, has been designed to help you identify them. Tick the relevant box, basing your response on your experiences during the previous month.

	NEVER	SOMETIMES	OFTEN
1. I don't concentrate for very long on what I am reading.	☐	☐	☐
2. I don't easily remember the names of people I've been introduced to.	☐	☐	☐
3. I find it difficult to put a name to a face I know well.	☐	☐	☐
4. I don't recall the names of famous people very easily.	☐	☐	☐
5. I am late for appointments.	☐	☐	☐
6. I have to resort to my diary to remember my appointments.	☐	☐	☐
7. I need a list when I go shopping.	☐	☐	☐
8. I forget what I have to do while going from one room to another.	☐	☐	☐
9. I find it difficult to remember telephone numbers I use regularly.	☐	☐	☐
10. I forget the day's date.	☐	☐	☐
11. I find it difficult to concentrate on a task for long.	☐	☐	☐
12. I have problems trying to remember where I've put my keys or glasses.	☐	☐	☐
13. I need time to adjust to any change.	☐	☐	☐
14. I forget the birthdays of my nearest and dearest.	☐	☐	☐
15. I am easily distracted by minor issues.	☐	☐	☐
16. In conversation, I struggle to find the right word.	☐	☐	☐
17. I have problems finding my way around my neighbourhood.	☐	☐	☐
18. I tend to think that my memory can mislead me.	☐	☐	☐
19. I don't find it easy to discuss a film I saw the previous day.	☐	☐	☐
20. I redo things I've already done.	☐	☐	☐
21. I forget incidents that I don't often talk about.	☐	☐	☐
22. I remember useless information.	☐	☐	☐
23. I struggle to remember the code of my bank card.	☐	☐	☐

memory like – good or bad?

	NEVER	SOMETIMES	OFTEN
24. I have difficulty remembering anything that is of no immediate interest to me.	■	■	■
25. I struggle to remember the price of the things I buy.	■	■	■
26. I quickly forget the titles of books I have just read.	■	■	■
27. I can remember no numbers whatsoever.	■	■	■
28. I take much longer than I did before to learn anything by heart.	■	■	■
29. I immediately forget what I have just watched on TV.	■	■	■
30. I find it difficult to do crossword puzzles.	■	■	■

Add up the number of points in each column, using the following scale: NEVER: 0 points, SOMETIMES: 1 point, OFTEN: 2 points.

Now enter your total number of points.

Test results

A total of 0 to 15 points

Your powers of concentration are good – unless you have somewhat underestimated your difficulties. Don't slacken though. Maintaining your physical and mental fitness is the best way to ensure that your memory keeps working well.

A total of 16 to 35 points

You have minor memory problems that should not worry you unduly. You are probably one of those people who has difficulty concentrating. To prevent these minor impediments from becoming a handicap, slow down. Take all the time you need for each task, and force yourself to do it while focusing on the task at hand without thinking about what it is to come. At the same time, find a form of relaxation that suits you, because you cannot sustain your concentration when under stress.

More than 35 points

You may have a tendency to judge yourself too severely, or to be unduly pessimistic. Nevertheless, why not take the precaution of going to see a memory consultant for a more accurate assessment of your ability? Doctors and specialist psychologists will analyse your results and advise you on the best way to address any problems you may have.

Exploring the memory

The brain and the memory

Weighing almost 1,5 kg, with an astronomical number of neurons and billions of connections, the brain – the most crucial part of your central nervous system – controls everything, from moving a little finger and solving mathematical equations to remembering happy days. But what is the connection between your brain and your memory? The brain is in fact where your memory is located, and most of your activities bring it into play. Memory forms part of your identity, your intelligence and your emotions. But where is it exactly?

That unknown entity, the brain

Test your knowledge of the brain's structure and function.

	TRUE	FALSE
1. The brain is made up of several thousand cells.		
2. You are born with a fixed number of neurons.		
3. The two hemispheres of the brain are divided into many lobes.		
4. You make use of your full complement of neurons in everyday life.		
5. Glucose is the main source of brain energy.		
6. The memory works less efficiently when you grow older.		
7. Cerebral activity continues during sleep.		
8. Stress, anxiety and fatigue affect brain function.		
9. Certain pathological conditions that affect the brain are irreversible.		
10. Memories are located in a specific part of the brain.		

1. FALSE
The brain is composed of nearly 100 billion cells, called neurons. And each neuron can rapidly form connections with 10 000 others.

2. TRUE.
The initial supply of neurons can't be replaced. At the age of 80, however, under normal health conditions, you will have lost only 10 percent. The remaining 90 percent still available does not degenerate and can establish new connections with other neurons.

3. FALSE
Each hemisphere of the brain is divided into four zones, the cerebral lobes, each of which controls specific activities. There are connections ensuring contact between these various lobes.

4. FALSE
We make use of only 30 to 40 percent of our neurons because we usually repeat the same activities. If you don't make proper use of the brain, if you underutilise or fail to stimulate it, you may experience memory problems or difficulties in finding the right word. Therefore, it is advisable to have as wide a range of activities as possible – for example, reading, writing, gardening or sport – to make your brain work in a variety of ways.

5. TRUE
The brain consumes 5 g of glucose (or sugar) an hour. To ensure an adequate supply of this fuel, you need a continuous supply of glucose in your bloodstream. So you should not exclude rapid-release and slow-release sugars from your diet.

6. FALSE
One out of two people over 50 complains of memory problems. Although it might be true that we acquire information less rapidly and find it more difficult to retrieve our memories as we get older, the ability to store new information remains unimpaired.

7. TRUE
We now know that cerebral activity is intense while we sleep. During the dream stage (or REM – Rapid Eye Movement – sleep) the brain fixes and consolidates information registered during the day.

8. TRUE
At times of stress or fatigue you will find it much more difficult to concentrate and remain alert. As a result, information reaching your memory will be less efficiently registered and thus more easily forgotten.

9. TRUE
The most widespread brain disorder is Alzheimer's disease. It is characterised by a progressive, continuous and irreversible loss of intellectual ability and is first manifested in specific memory problems. Medical treatment available at present can slow down its progress but cannot reverse it.

10. FALSE
Memories are not localised in one specific place in the brain, although we know that one section, the hippocampus, plays a key role in retrieving memories. Memory function involves different zones of the brain.

A dispersed memory

Contrary to a long-held belief, the memory is not localised in one area of the brain. Instead, it functions through networks of neurons that process and preserve different kinds of information, and which are themselves widely distributed among different zones of the brain. As soon as a piece of information has to be committed to memory, numerous connections are simultaneously activated and **a large part of the brain is involved in processing the memories.**

It is therefore wrong to speak of a memory centre. The memorisation and retrieval of information depend on different memory systems and different sensory modalities (auditory, visual, etc.). It is thus just as wrong to believe that the memory is localised in a specific area of the brain. In fact, we could say that it is 'dispersed'.

• Where are our different kinds of memory based?
As a result of scientific experiments and improved brain imaging technology, scientists are now beginning to understand which zones of the brain are involved in the process of memorisation. In summary:
– **the short-term or immediate memory** (see p.132) brings into play the cortical neuron systems (neocortex [**4**] and prefrontal cortex [**1**]), and more particularly the corticothalmic connections;
– **the semantic memory** (see p.122) requires the intervention of the neocortex [**4**], comprising the two cerebral hemispheres that cover the cortex;
– **the procedural memory** (see p.118) involves structures that are situated below the cortex, like the cerebellum [**6**] and the dentate nucleus [**5**];
– **the episodic memory** (see p.128) relies on the prefrontal cortex [**1**], as well as the hippocampus [**3**] and the thalamus [**2**], which all form part of the limbic system.

According to neurobiologists, the hippocampus plays an essential role in the memory process. Situated in the inner recesses of the brain – in the limbic system – at the same level as the temporal lobe, it ensures that connections are established between the different cerebral zones. The hippocampus plays a vital role in transferring memories from the short-term memory to the long-term memory, that is, in the consolidation of memories, which requires different parts of the brain.

We now know that damage to the hippocampus results in almost complete loss of the ability to remember new information, irrespective of whether it concerns words, faces or images.

4
1
3
2
5
6

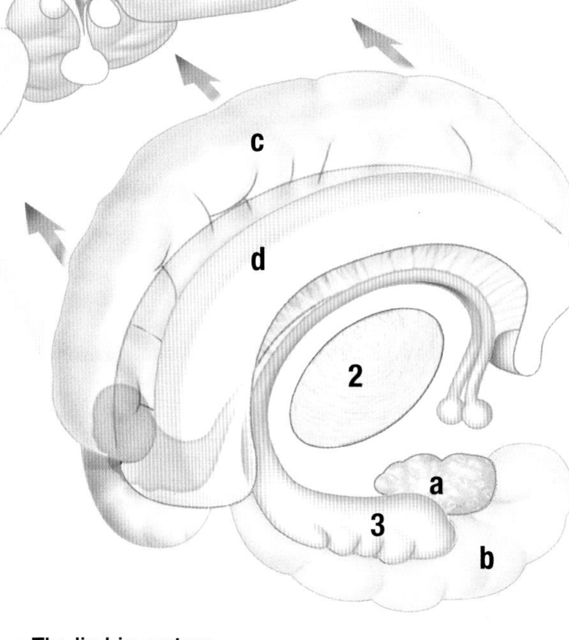

• The limbic system
consists of the hippocampus [**3**], the amygdala [**a**], parahippocampal gyrus [**b**] and the cingulate gyrus [**c**]; as for the corpus callosum [**d**], this is a part of the brain.

My memory and…
my intelligence

Intelligence is not hereditary. What does it mean to be intelligent? IQ (Intelligence Quotient) tests can be useful in evaluating intelligence, but we can't rely solely on the results of these tests. It is important to find a balance between our personal abilities and our environment. Having a good memory, being psychologically well balanced, astute and resourceful – these are important qualities that can't be measured by an IQ test.

Exploring the memory

• Tracking the course of a visual memory

First of all, the visual information strikes the retina and is transformed into nerve impulses. It then takes a few millionths of a second to proceed to the visual projection areas situated in the occipital cortex. This information will then be processed in several different ways, depending on its specific qualities (form, colour and movement).

The information will be kept temporarily in the hippocampus where it will be compared with earlier data from different areas of the cortex. Finally, depending on its value, it will either be forgotten or else stored and consolidated. The positive or negative emotional value of the information determines how we register and store it.

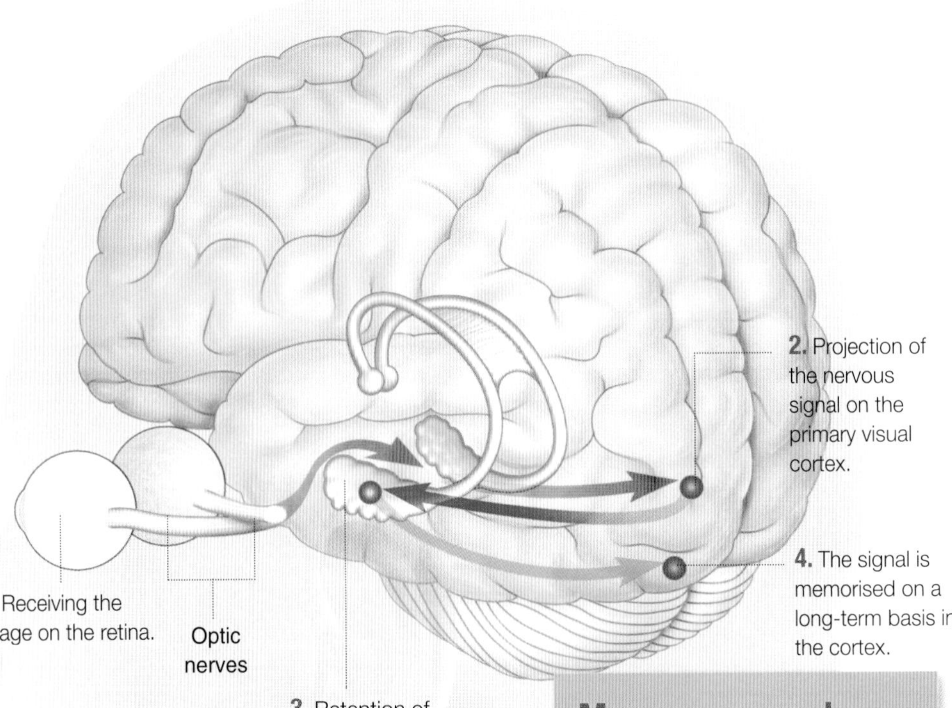

My memory and...
my parents

Memory is not part of a gene pool or genetic heritage transmitted from parent to child. And neither is Alzheimer's disease! Many people over the age of 50 are concerned and consult a specialist if one of their relatives has suffered from a disease affecting the memory. This kind of disorder is not passed on from one generation to the next. If, nevertheless, you want reassurance, consult a specialist or contact a relevant organisation about it.

Brainy words jumbled up

Put the letters of the following words in order to uncover words in the vocabulary of the brain.

TEDERNID ....

GIMENNES ....

OXOTRENCE ....

YSSAPEN ....

MADALYGA ....

SPAPUMOCIPH ....

CALICOTIP ....

EROUNN ....

CIMBLI ....

OBEL ....

SHERHEPEMI ....

EPTARILA ....

Solution p.332

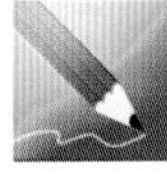

Rebus

Identify what it is that our brains need in order to function.

Solution p.332

Memory problems

Amnesia is the most common memory problem, but there are also less common disorders, such as hypermnesia, paramnesia and ecmnesisa.

- **Amnesia** is the inability to learn anything new, and is manifested in an inability to remember everyday events. The intelligence remains intact, as does the ability to acquire new visiospatial and cognitive skills – in other words, your spatial awareness and learning skills are not impaired. A typical example is hippocampal amnesia caused by damage to or disease of the Papez circuit (which links the hippocampus and the amygdala to the hypothalamus). Amnesia can also result from damaged or diseased blood vessels, diseases such as Alzheimer's, head injuries, neurosurgical operations or heart failure, and is usually irreversible.

- **Retrograde amnesia** takes the form of an inability to remember events occurring before the illness. It is often accompanied by **anterograde amnesia**, which makes the problem worse by hindering the consolidation of old memories. The time span affected by this form of amnesia can range from a few days to several years. In most cases, the store of memories is not lost but they are inaccessible because they can't be retrieved. This form of amnesia results from electric shocks or injury, and can range from Korsakoff's psychosis or Alzheimer's disease to less serious conditions.

- **Total amnesia** combines the inability to learn anything new with the impossibility of accessing knowledge predating the outbreak of the illness. It can be linked to extensive damage to the cortex and is associated with dementia, as is Alzheimer's disease.

- **An amnesiac fit, or blackout** is a short attack of amnesia that strikes people suddenly between the ages of 50 and 70 years. It is often brought on by an emotional shock, and entails forgetting all new information as well as a retroactive amnesia of several hours to several days. The episode lasts from four to six hours and starts tailing off after 24 hours.

Lacunar amnesia, the failure to recall the moments immediately preceding the episode as well as the episode itself, persists.

The most likely cause of an amnesiac fit seems to be a blood vessel spasm accompanying a migraine. The blackout is believed to originate in the hippocampus (which causes problems with encoding and consolidation). If it recurs (as happens in 15-25 percent of cases) the possibility of blood clots or blocked arteries, or even epilepsy, should be investigated.

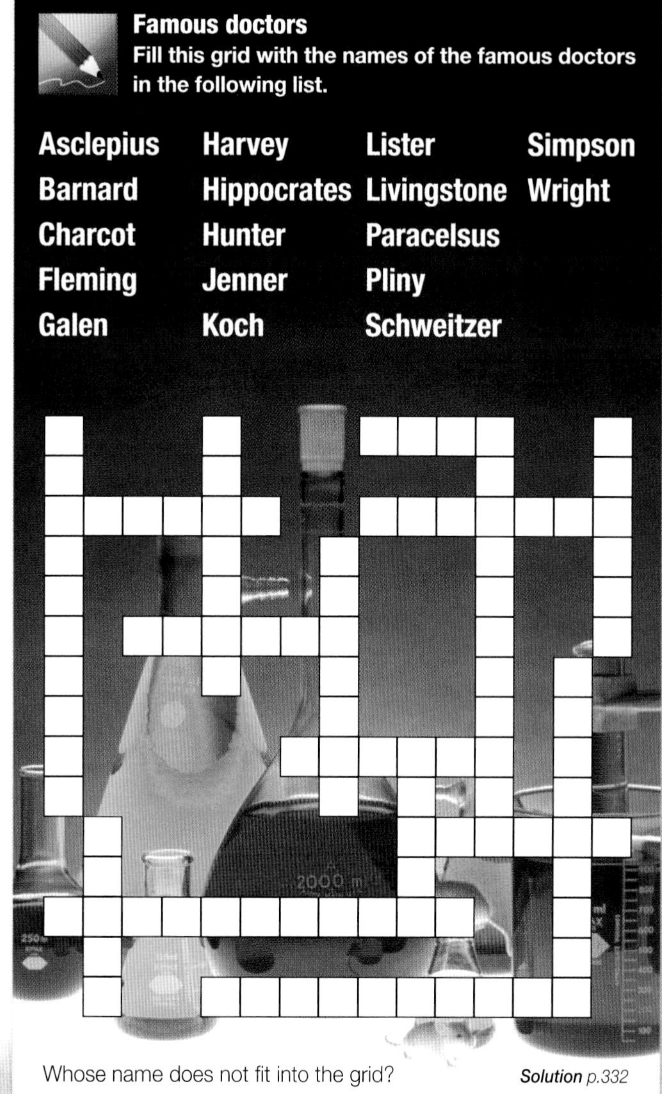

Whose name does not fit into the grid? *Solution* p.332

- **Hypermnesia** refers to a prodigious capacity for remembering facts in one field (recalling pages from the telephone directory, or long lists of names, for example). It bears no relation to intellectual level and can be permanent or temporary. In the latter case, it occurs during epileptic fits and at times of intense emotion and is accompanied by the phenomenon of reliving events from the past.

- **Paramnesia** refers to illusions generated by the memory: the impression of déjà vu (you've seen this before), déjà vécu (you've lived through this before), or conversely a sense of being in a strange environment. Brief paramnesic episodes can occur during epileptic crises of the temporal lobe.

- **In ecmnesia,** you relive slices of the past as though they were happening in the present. Ecmnesia is characteristic of Alzheimer's disease.

Memory and illness

• **Alzheimer's disease,** the most common complaint affecting the central nervous system, is characterised by a progressive and irreversible decline in mental ability. It is also a disease of the memory, and the first symptom is an inability to memorise new information and thus to recall it. The term hippocampal attack is used because both sides of the hippocampus (left and right) are affected. The disability then spreads to other mental functions, reducing patients to a state of complete dependence on their circle of family and friends. At this stage the term 'dementia' is used. Many neurons disappear in specific areas of the brain, starting with the hippocampus, and this loss is accompanied by a reduction in the supply of acetylcholine, a neurotransmitter involved in the process of memorisation. Treatment to counteract this reduction is much more effective if introduced before the disease has reached an advanced stage.

• **Atherosclerosis** is a common cerebral complaint which affects the blood vessels supplying the heart, kidneys, limbs and brain. It causes cholesterol, or fatty deposits, to collect on the walls of the arteries, scarring and calcifying them, which narrows the arteries. The blockage can lead to a progressive or sudden reduction in the blood supply to the brain and the risk of an ischaemic stroke. In other instances, the blood vessel wall may rupture, causing a cerebral haemorrhage (haemorrhagic stroke, or aneurysm). The symptoms vary, depending on the position and extent of the lesions. They can be manifested in a temporary or permanent loss of certain functions, such as the ability to walk and the ability to speak.

Even the smallest amount of damage to a cerebral artery can have irreversible effects. A bilateral lesion of the posterior communicating artery will result in anterograde amnesia accompanied by communication problems and retrograde amnesia. Tobacco, alcohol, a sedentary lifestyle, high cholesterol, hypertension and diabetes are recognised risk factors in this disease. Prevention includes a healthy lifestyle, cutting down on smoking and alcohol, a regular check on triglycerides and cholesterol levels, as well as adequate physical exercise.

Normal | **Diseased**

Alzheimer's Disease

The principal cause of dependency in the developed world, it affected 18 million people worldwide in 2000. It may affect 34 million in 2025.

CVA

Cerebral vascular accidents (aneurysms or strokes) affected more than 20.5 million people in 2001, according to the WHO. Some 5.5 million cases were fatal.

Toxins

Medications, alcohol and recreational drugs produce cerebral lesions (cocaine abuse is illustrated here).

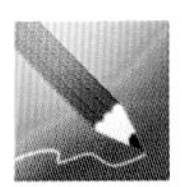

Rebus

Discover a scientific fact concerning the function of the brain.

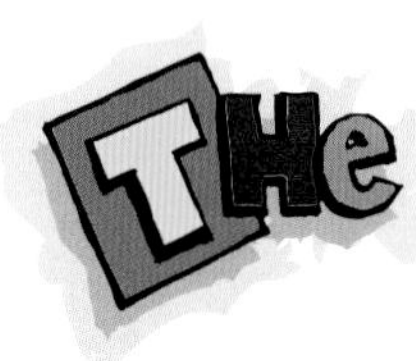

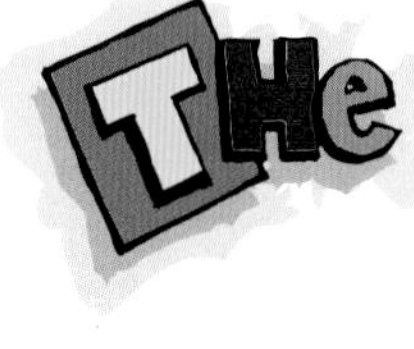

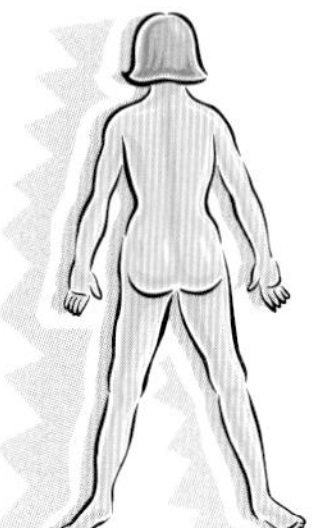

Solution p.332

• **Parkinson's disease** results from the loss of neurons in an area of the brain known as the substantia nigra, which controls motor movement and produces the neurotransmitter dopamine. The reduction in the supply of this neurotransmitter leads to shaking, muscle rigidity and slowing down of intellectual and motor activity. A deterioration of the mental faculties can follow in 30 to 40 percent of cases as the disease runs its course. Information and events are retained, but they are apparently recalled very slowly and with great difficulty, so it would be wrong to use the term amnesia here. The treatment currently used is dopamine therapy, which minimises the results of losing neurons by restoring the dopamine balance in this vital area.

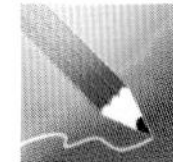

In the labyrinth of the brain

Find the only path through this maze to connect the two red arrows.

Solution p.332

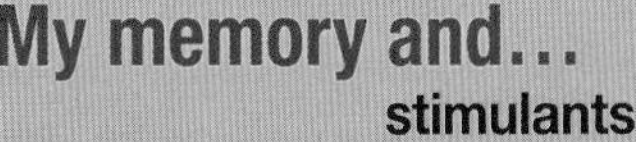

My memory and... stimulants

Pharmacies and health shops are the greatest suppliers of pills or magic potions for the memory. What can we say about these medicines supplied without prescription and which are claimed to improve your memory or even prevent any disorders in this area? The sad truth is that the memory pill does not exist. The 'magical cures' advertised usually contain a certain amount of vitamins, including Vitamin C – which is supposed to revitalise the body and improve the circulation of the blood – and minerals, usually derived from an exotic plant with reputedly magical powers (such as ginkgo biloba, jojoba, ginseng, soya, pawpaw ...). Many of these have been proven to have no effect whatsoever.

• **Korsakoff's psychosis** is found in people who drink excessive amounts of vodka, and in chronic alcoholics. It starts at the age of about 55 and includes anterograde amnesia, temporal-spatial disorientation, delusions and impaired recognition. A retrograde gap covering anything from several months to many years can precede the onset of the disease. Added to this are confusion, problems with balance and walking, and an ocular-motor paralysis.

The onset of this syndrome is sometimes insidious, the only symptom being a peripheral neuropathy. Reasoning ability is unaffected. This rare amnesiac disease has its origin in a deficiency of thiamine associated with alcoholism, which disrupts the supply, absorption and utilisation of vitamin B_1, with a drop in the levels of vitamin PP (nicotinamide) and folic acid. The lesions mainly involve the frontal lobe. It is treated by providing a substantial amount of Vitamin B_1, but the results are not exactly conclusive.

Memory and depression

Even though people suffering from chronic depression do not exhibit the same memory problems as those who suffer from pathological cognitive deterioration, they experience difficulty in remembering recent events. Their lack of motivation and energy resulting from their depressive state makes them less likely to make the necessary effort to encode new data. And because they don't register the information properly they are unable to recall it. Depression also tends to reduce performance levels in general by compromising the ability to register and process information. This creates selective recall, in accordance with the negative mood or attitude of the sufferers.

We now know how to distinguish between the effect of depression on the memory and the effect of pathological disorders such as Alzheimer's disease. Depression is characterised by a generally low level of motivation, leading to serious attention deficit problems, whereas Alzheimer's is a disease of the memory as such, which causes pathological changes in the encoding, storing and retrieval of information. When people recover from or are treated for depression, they regain their intellectual abilities.

Depression

Depression, a disease that affects about 1 in 10 people worldwide, according to WHO figures, is treated with psychotropic drugs.

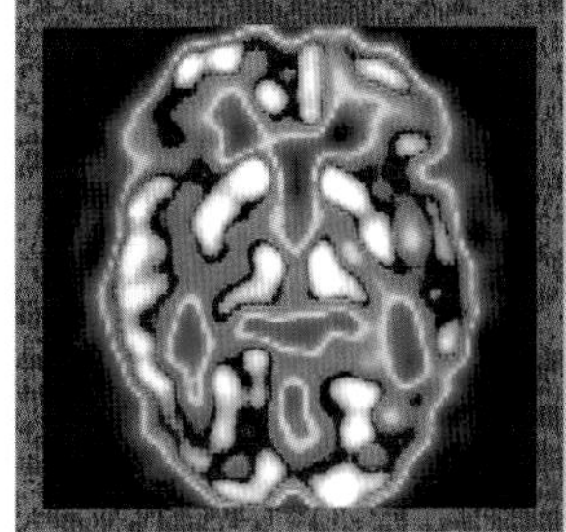

The five senses

Sight, smell, taste, touch and hearing – the five senses are channels through which information from the external world flows into your brain. It is through the senses that all data is registered and gradually accumulates to become the rich and fertile ground that constitutes your memory. According to Saint Augustine, the senses are 'privileged portals' leading to the various rooms in the 'palace of memory'.

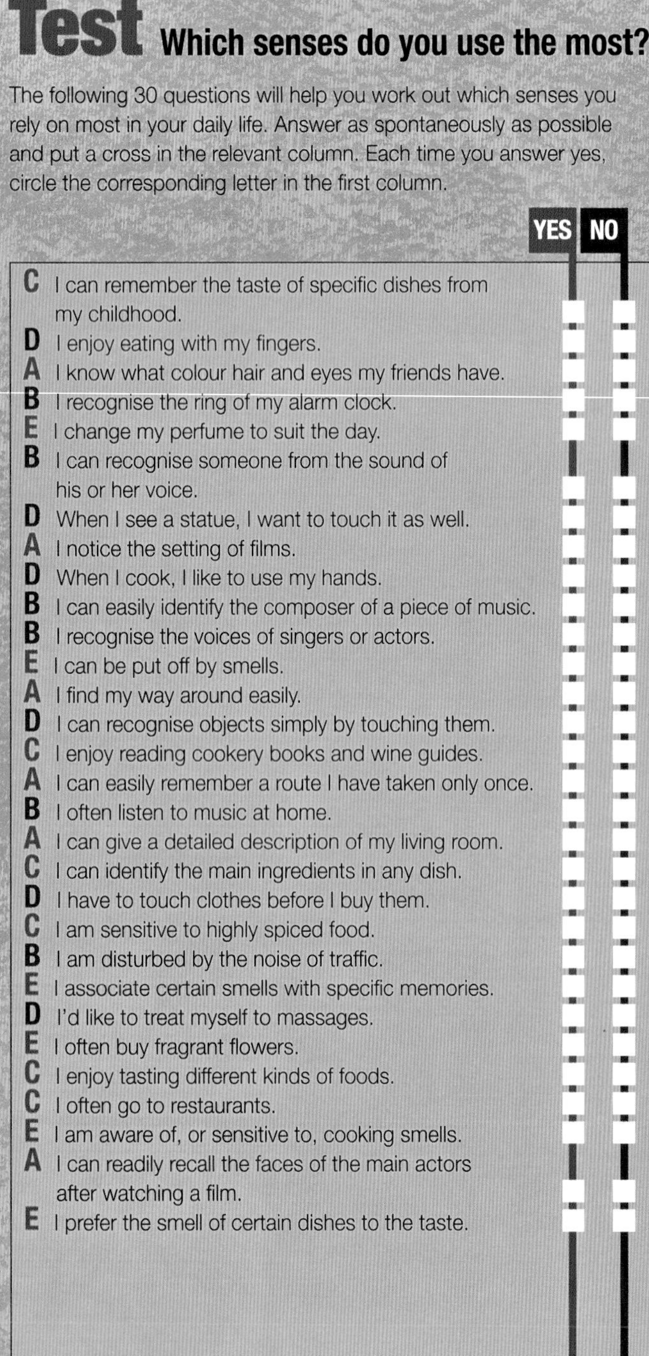

Test Which senses do you use the most?

The following 30 questions will help you work out which senses you rely on most in your daily life. Answer as spontaneously as possible and put a cross in the relevant column. Each time you answer yes, circle the corresponding letter in the first column.

		YES	NO
C	I can remember the taste of specific dishes from my childhood.		
D	I enjoy eating with my fingers.		
A	I know what colour hair and eyes my friends have.		
B	I recognise the ring of my alarm clock.		
E	I change my perfume to suit the day.		
B	I can recognise someone from the sound of his or her voice.		
D	When I see a statue, I want to touch it as well.		
A	I notice the setting of films.		
D	When I cook, I like to use my hands.		
B	I can easily identify the composer of a piece of music.		
B	I recognise the voices of singers or actors.		
E	I can be put off by smells.		
A	I find my way around easily.		
D	I can recognise objects simply by touching them.		
C	I enjoy reading cookery books and wine guides.		
A	I can easily remember a route I have taken only once.		
B	I often listen to music at home.		
A	I can give a detailed description of my living room.		
C	I can identify the main ingredients in any dish.		
D	I have to touch clothes before I buy them.		
C	I am sensitive to highly spiced food.		
B	I am disturbed by the noise of traffic.		
E	I associate certain smells with specific memories.		
D	I'd like to treat myself to massages.		
E	I often buy fragrant flowers.		
C	I enjoy tasting different kinds of foods.		
C	I often go to restaurants.		
E	I am aware of, or sensitive to, cooking smells.		
A	I can readily recall the faces of the main actors after watching a film.		
E	I prefer the smell of certain dishes to the taste.		

You have mostly YES answers

You do not disregard your senses but make full use of them in every situation. As a result, you can rely on them in memorising things.

You have mostly NO answers

You favour certain senses to the detriment of others and remember things primarily through the medium of those senses. This does not imply an inferior process of registration, but rather that the data is perhaps less firmly fixed in that you have processed only part of the information.

You have about the same number of A, B, C, D and E replies

Your senses are not mutually exclusive but work together. Note that the senses can be trained at any age and by getting to know our strong and weak points we can work on improving them. The more thoroughly we process information we want to remember – by sight, sound, and when appropriate by touch, taste and smell – the more effectively it will be retained.

You have at least 5 A's

You definitely tend to use your sight to memorise information.

You have at least 5 B's

Your auditory sense predominates, perhaps without your realising it. You are one of those people who are impressed by film scores, for example, and pay them more attention than other people do.

You have at least 4 C's

You are rather more on the gourmet side, with those who take great pleasure in savouring fine delicacies. The memory of a particular meal or special dish probably leads you back to its context and even enables you to revive many other associated memories. This is the process immortalised by Marcel Proust: the taste of the madeleine dipped in tea evoked a host of other buried memories.

You have at least 4 D's

You favour touch, which can evoke many memories; it is also often associated with intimate relationships. It is one of the senses that retain their sensitivity the longest. We can see this demonstrated in the case of babies who go to sleep quietly when they are cuddled and caressed, and very old people who can only communicate with the world around them though this sense.

You have at least 4 E's

You make great use of your sense of smell, which is often associated with taste. In your case, smells are most likely to evoke a host of memories of everyday life.

Biology of the five senses

In the centre of the human body there is a vast cord of nerves with extensions designed to capture the messages continuously circulating around the body. And this 'capture' is carried out by the senses.

Each of the senses is adjusted to a certain range of wavelengths. These waves will be captured by different organs – of sight, hearing, taste or smell – depending on the particular circumstances. They can also be picked up by an organ that covers the whole body and activates the sense of touch – the skin. **The information carried by your senses is recognised, continuously analysed and processed by specialised areas of the brain.** It is called exteroceptive when it is received from outside. But you can also capture information coming from inside the body, like pain or pleasure. This is called interoceptive information.

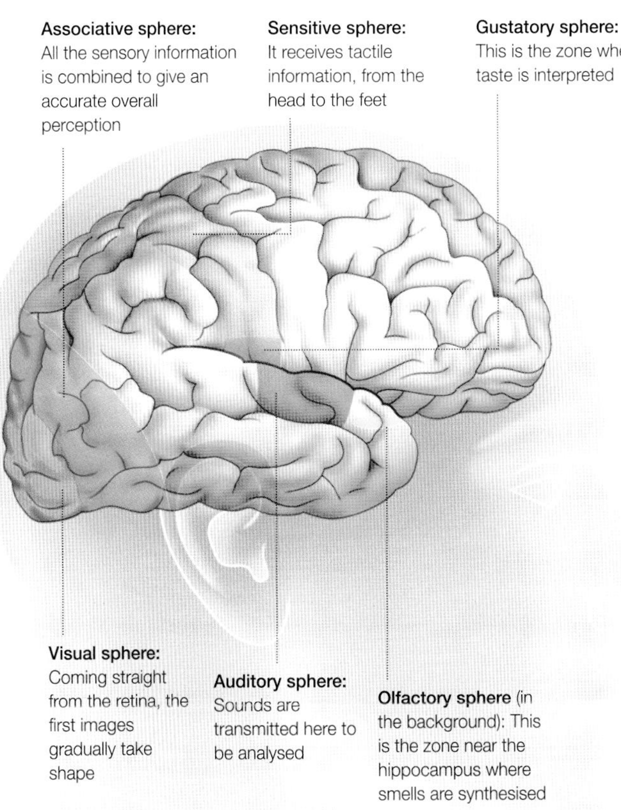

Touch

This is the first sense you use: the foetus experiences its surroundings through contact with the walls of the maternal womb. This sense is also the very first means of communication with the outside world.

The sense of touch makes use of a great variety of receptors (Meissner's corpuscles, Pacini's corpuscles and Merkel's corpuscles) distributed all over the skin. These receptors react to stimulation, change or repeated pressure. There are on average 50 per square millimetre of skin, but they are unevenly distributed. A great number are concentrated on the fingertips, for example, making very delicate tactile perception possible.

Sound

Hearing is the second sense to be aroused in the foetus, which can hear noises and recognise some low sounds *in utero*. Transmitted by vibrations in the air, sound is first of all a wave that passes through the external ear and makes the tympanum vibrate like the skin of a drum. This vibration sets the ossicles of the middle ear in motion. These in turn activate the cilia (microscopic hairs) of the internal ear and transform the vibrations into electrical impulses, which are sent to the brain.

Smell

Chronologically, this is the third sense to enter your life. At birth, a baby is already able to recognise its mother's smell. An adult will be able to distinguish on average more than 10 000 different smells – without necessarily being able to identify them, however. This sense is entirely dependent on breathing, because you smell while you inhale.

The volatile molecules of specific odours permeate the nasal passages behind the bridge of the nose. These molecules are then absorbed by about five million cilia of the receptor cells in the nasal passsages. These cilia send signals to the olfactory bulb in the brain, which divides them into families of smells – floral, musky, resinous, foul-smelling, bitter, acid, etc.

Taste

Throughout your life, great moments will inevitably lead to a meal. The sense of taste uses some 10 000 tastebuds in your mouth, detectors of flavours that are relayed by smell. These tastebuds are renewed every 10 days until the end of your life. Each one of them contains 50 or so cells that transmit to the neurons in your brain information corresponding to very precise categories: salty, sour, sweet, bitter.

Sight

Your brain receives 80 percent of its information from the sense of sight, even though it is the least developed of the senses in babies. Sight is usually the most utilised of your senses, sometimes to the detriment of the others.

The adult eye registers millions of items of information every day, in the form of light that is reflected from objects and penetrates the eye as far as the retina. Travelling at a speed of 300 000 kilometres per second, the light wave first passes through the cornea, which is protected by the conjunctiva and covers the iris. Then it goes into the opening in the centre of the eye, the pupil, before passing through the lens which can change its curvature through the action of the ciliary muscle. Finally, it passes through the vitreous humour (constituting 80 percent of the volume of the eye) to finish its journey at the back of the ocular globe, where the retina is situated. The optic nerve then conveys the light wave to the brain, taking a fraction of a second to reach this destination.

The 800 000 fibres of the optic nerve transmit such a concentrated flow of information to the brain that they are considered to be the densest channel of communication in the Universe.

The acuity of your senses is not predetermined. As soon as you become acutely aware of your perceptions and sensations, the senses can be **worked on and finely honed.**

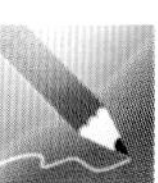

Sounds that surround us

Classify these sounds in terms of their intensity on a scale of 1 to 8.

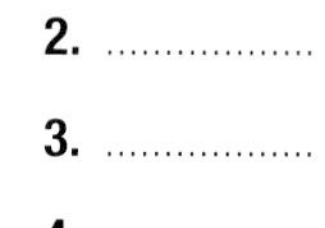

a. A cellphone ringing

b. A motorbike accelerating

c. A coffee grinder

d. An aircraft taking off

1. ....
2. ....
3. ....
4. ....
5. ....
6. ....
7. ....
8. ....

Solution p.332

e. A glass breaking

f. A door slamming

g. A bicycle bell

h. Birdsong

Hearing, and sensitivity to sounds, varies from one person to the next. Thus music lovers all have differing ideas on the ideal volume at which to listen to music. The classification used in the answer pages here might therefore differ from yours.

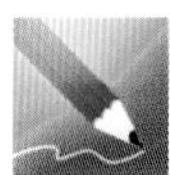

Spot the 7 differences

There are seven differences between these two photos. Can you find them?

Solution p.332

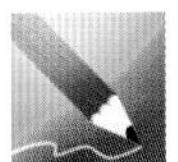

Associate the smells
Dig deep into your memory to find links between these kinds of smells and events or emotions you have experienced.

Chlorine

Burning Body odour Musk Fruit

Iodine Sulphur

Cleanliness

Ammonia

Flowers

Caramel

Mould

Rotting fish

Smells stimulate all the senses. The more highly developed your sense of smell, the more alert your senses will be. Try to copy animals, which have retained an excellent sense of smell, by going beyond merely visual and /or auditory perception to enable your brain to respond to all aspects of the information reaching you. When choosing a melon, for example, don't restrict yourself to just looking at it – smell it.

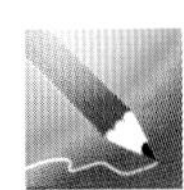

A world of flavours
Find the culinary speciality in which the following spices or herbs predominate.

1. Cinnamon	A. Couscous	1........
2. Saffron	B. Thai green curry	2........
3. Basil	C. Goulash	3........
4. Garlic	D. Paella	4........
5. Nutmeg	E. Spice cake	5........
6. Cumin	F. Pizza	6........
7. Chilli	G. Béarnaise sauce	7........
8. Coriander	H. Béchamel sauce	8........
9. Paprika	I. Quesadillas	9........
10. Tarragon	J. Pesto	10........
11. Oregano	K. Aioli	11........

Solution p.332

Taste also stimulates the appetite. The tastier a dish is, the more you will enjoy it. Apply this principle to all your dishes and you will notice that even people with the smallest appetite will come back for more.

Touch and sensation
Touch can arouse a variety of sensations depending on what you are touching. Entertain yourself by imagining what could arouse the following kinds of sensations; the objects could be either animate or inanimate things (a minimum of four)
Example: feeling something soft and squishy = **dough**

Soft....................................
....

Slimy..............................
....

Textured...........................
....

Smooth............................
....

Rough...............................
....

Solution p.332

The sensory memory: an emotional memory

Sensory activity is the source of your memory, which would not exist without it. **What you call your tastes – in fact, your preferences – are the product of a long personal history of sensory experience, which you have forgotten.** This forms the fabric of your primary sensations and associated emotions that constitute your very being and still colour your sensations and emotions today. **Your whole body is a living record of sensations** from your past that you have either enjoyed and sought for or else hated, feared and avoided.

Taste

You are not born with specific taste preferences. Choices made for you in childhood by those around you, together with your own experiences, influence your sense of taste. If you don't like bananas, for example, could it be that it is associated in your memory with the mashed banana of your childhood, which quickly turned brown? And any event commemorated with a meal, which appeals to the sense of taste, will be more firmly engraved on the memory. In short, your taste is culturally determined.

Touch

With the sense of touch, we go right back to the start of life and the source of memory. Our way of experiencing touch and interacting physically with others is rooted in our early sensations of life in the uterus and the physical relationship we have with our mothers, and accounts for much of our behaviour as adults, particularly in the realm of sexual relations.

The absence of touch, that is the absence of contact with others, is the most profound form of loneliness. The lack of the stimulation afforded by touch can have serious consequences, ranging from losing the joy of living to depression.

Smell

Smell, which is a very primitive form of communication, is also closely associated with the emotions. **Smells always have an emotional dimension**: we either like or dislike them, and, like taste, they evoke memories. Certain smells you can think of will inevitably open the door to pleasant and unpleasant memories – the smell of hot chocolate, of meat cooking on a barbecue, or even … that of the dentist's surgery. Even if attempts are made to control smells, we can still literally be led by the nose, which can influence us in unexpected ways. Shopkeepers understand this all too well – they use artificial scents such as the smell of fresh bread or flowers to encourage people to buy these goods.

Sight

Sight enriches your relation with the world around you. Through your sight, you register millions of facts. Memories of the faces, colours and objects around you exemplify the capacity of your visual memory. We all need to see something to retain and remember it – but some people are more dependent on this method of recall. And yet, even this particular form of memory is selective, because it is linked to your own areas of interest. Some people remember faces more easily, whereas others remember colours or landscapes. At the same time, we prefer to look at something that is a source of pleasure, curiosity, novelty or fear. An image charged with emotion is more easily remembered than a banal and habitual one.

Hearing

The sense of hearing is the one most used in communication. It is vital to be able to listen to conversation, music or the song of birds. The auditory memory is also charged with emotion. Think of the memory of a film score accompanying a particularly dramatic scene, or that of a parent's voice, filled with tenderness, linked to key moments in your childhood. And when you sing to yourself in the bath or shower, for example, this is the auditory memory at work once more. You have, often unknowingly, registered a collection of sounds that comes back to you. For musicians, of course, a good auditory memory is crucial. Without it, a musician would find it impossible to play the right notes and a cacophony of false notes would result.

Touché – spot on!

The sense of touch is distributed all over the skin. Its importance is even stressed in various expressions we use, such as 'to get under someone's skin'. In the same way, we say that we are 'touched by someone' or 'something'. Find 10 expressions in which the words skin and/or touch – or variations of these words – feature.

Example : to have a thick skin.

Solution p.332

1. ....
2. ....
3. ....
4. ....
5. ....
6. ....
7. ....
8. ....
9. ....
10. ....

Holiday memories

Give examples of holiday memories pertaining to each of your five senses.

Example: the sound of waves crashing on a beach outside your window at night, the taste of a local cheese in a cheese factory, the sights of a souk in Marrakech with its colourful display of exotic goods, the smell and vivid colours of a spice market.

Sights ....

....

Sounds ....

....

Tastes ....

....

Smells ....

....

Touch ....

....

The ideal wardrobe

Look at these clothes for a minute, then cover the picture and try to recall the maximum number of details. Advice: classify them first in terms of categories – for example, colours, short or long sleeves, and prints. It's up to you to organise the way your memory works.

My memory and... a number code

To remember a number code, such as that of a bank card, you need to put several senses to work simultaneously. A certain movement – your finger typing the code on the keyboard – should be accompanied by a word, which involves a mental operation. So, for a code that includes a letter of the alphabet, you change that letter into a name or other meaningful word. For example, A=Anabelle. Then you link the four digits that usually follow to a well-known event. For example, 1945 = end of the Second World War. Finally, type in the number, because it is important to watch the way your finger moves over the keyboard, while saying the code (softly) to stimulate your auditory sense. You will know your code perfectly within a week.

When sight and memory are superimposed

Read this text:

'Adoncricg to a sudty dnoe at the Uvinertisy of Cmabrigde, the oedrer of ltteers in a wrod is not itmoprnat, the olny tnihg of itpomcnarte is taht the frist and the lsat wrdos are in the rghit pclae. The rset can be in taotl dedsiror and you wlil slitl be albe to raed tehm whotiut any plorebm. Tahst bausece the haumn biran deos not raed ervey ltteer ilstef but the wrod as a wolhe.'

You will be astonished to notice that the visual memory of the whole word takes precedence over the word as written here. The image you carry of the word in your memory is enough for you to find the word that makes sense immediately.

Although it is true that the visual sense is well developed in humans, it is often difficult to register all the details when there is not much time available for observation. This is worth thinking about. We should have reservations about the viability of certain identikits and descriptions in criminal cases ...

Ageing of the senses: inevitable?

Because sensory activity is the essential means of contact with the world around you, any reduction in the acuity of one or other of the senses entails the risk of impoverishing that relation, which would result in a diminished enjoyment of life as well as a drop in the level of neuron stimulation. The neurons would then become used to restricted perception, and this would inevitably affect your memory.

Faced with any memory problem, then, you need first to question whether your senses are functioning adequately. How can you remember anything if you haven't heard it clearly? How can you construct a mental image of anything if you haven't seen it clearly?

• **Of all the five senses, sight is the one that deteriorates most rapidly.** As you grow older, the eye takes much longer to adjust to sudden changes in brightness. At 80, your eyes need eight times as much light to have the same experience of luminosity. You can adapt perfectly well to this change, by using halogen lamps, for example, which you can regulate to produce bright light for reading and a more subdued form of lighting for the room.

Myopia (short-sightedness), astigmatism and presbyopia (long-sightedness) – which appear between the ages of 40 and 50 and increase over the years – can usually be corrected very successfully by wearing glasses or contact lenses. Surgical correction of myopia has become a very common operation, which changes the life of many myopic people. As for cataracts, they usually start between the ages of 70 and 80. They are caused by the lens becoming progressively more opaque, which leads to a sensation of reduced luminosity or even fogginess. Surgery is also widely used for this condition today.

• **Hearing often deteriorates gradually from the age of about 50,** a tendency which is more marked in men than in women. At first, it is the high-pitched sounds (high frequency) that are more difficult to catch, and then the deeper, low-frequency sounds. Losing the ability to hear high-pitched sounds (a condition called presbyacousia) is bound to change your perception of voices. The people affected are often unaware of the deterioration of their hearing but it influences their behaviour and the nature of their social interactions. The hard of hearing speak loudly and often ask others to repeat what they have said. Many of them, to avoid embarrassment, shun social occasions and tend to isolate themselves. This has drastic consequences for the quality of their social life and also for their memories, which will be deprived of adequate stimulation.

It is therefore very important to adjust to this situation and compensate for faulty hearing. If you often ask people to repeat what they have said, if you turn up the sound on the TV, if you struggle to follow a conversation in a noisy place,

Test your observation skills

Look at the faces below for one minute, and then cover them and answer the following questions.

consult an ENT (ear, nose and throat) specialist without delay. This specialist will identify the problem and prescribe the most appropriate treatment: medication, a hearing aid or even physiotherapy. Thanks to progress in technology, the new hearing aids are giving very satisfactory results, but they often have a negative image with the general public. Don't hesitate to seek professional advice from the best person, who will advise you, provide you with information and accompany you when you go to acquire this new 'crutch'. For instance, you should be able to try out a hearing aid at home for several weeks before making the final purchase. And get used to stimulating your visual sense by watching the lips of people talking to you – you will then be able to see as well as hear what they are saying!

• **The olfactory sense can also become less keen, and this is often accompanied by a loss of taste** and diminished pleasure in eating. In fact, as we grow older we find food blander and less appetising. Sometimes a loss of interest in smell can indicate a lack of interest in life and even mild depression. This detachment from the outside world cannot but affect the memory function.

• **The sense of touch can also deteriorate over time** even if the cutaneous (skin) receptors remain intact. It is more likely that the transmission of tactile perceptions to the central nervous system could be defective. Several studies have shown that the pain threshold affecting the surface of the skin is higher in older people. This is something that should not be ignored, even though a pain threshold does vary from one person to the next.

It is thus essential to check regularly to see if your senses are all in good working order, and to do everything possible to ensure that they are functioning as well as can be expected. If need be, you should also adjust your social behaviour and in particular make sure that you don't withdraw from the world because of problems that are not really very serious.

1. How many men and women are there?
2. How many of the characters are wearing glasses?
3. How many women are wearing earrings?
4. How many of the characters are wearing a hat?
5. How many characters are shown in profile?
6. How many of the characters are wearing green?

What you see is greatly influenced by your preferences. If you find a face attractive or if it is very different from that of others, your eye will tend to be drawn to it and so you pay more attention to it. Be aware of this tendency, which can lead to other details, probably just as interesting, being ignored.

Poem with holes

Read aloud this extract from the poem entitled *The Walrus and the Carpenter*, written by Lewis Carroll, and see if you can fill in the gaps or invent words to fill the holes.

The Walrus and the Carpenter

The ... was shining on the sea,
Shining with all his ..... :
He did his very best to ....
The billows smooth and ...... –
And this was ... , because it was
The ...... of the night.

The .... was shining sulkily,
Because she thought the sun
Had got no .... to be there,
After the ... was done –
'It's very .... of him,' she said
'To come and spoil the ... !'

The ... was wet as wet could be,
The ..... were dry as dry.
You could not see a ..... , because
There was no ..... in the sky:
No ..... were flying overhead –
There were no ..... to fly.

The Walrus and the Carpenter
Were walking close at .... :
They .... like anything to see
Such quantities of ....
'If this were only .... away,'
They said, 'it would be ..... !'

'If seven ..... with seven mops
..... it for half a year,
Do you suppose,' the Walrus ....,
'That they could get it .....?'
'I doubt it,' said the Carpenter,
And shed a ...... tear.

Solution p.332

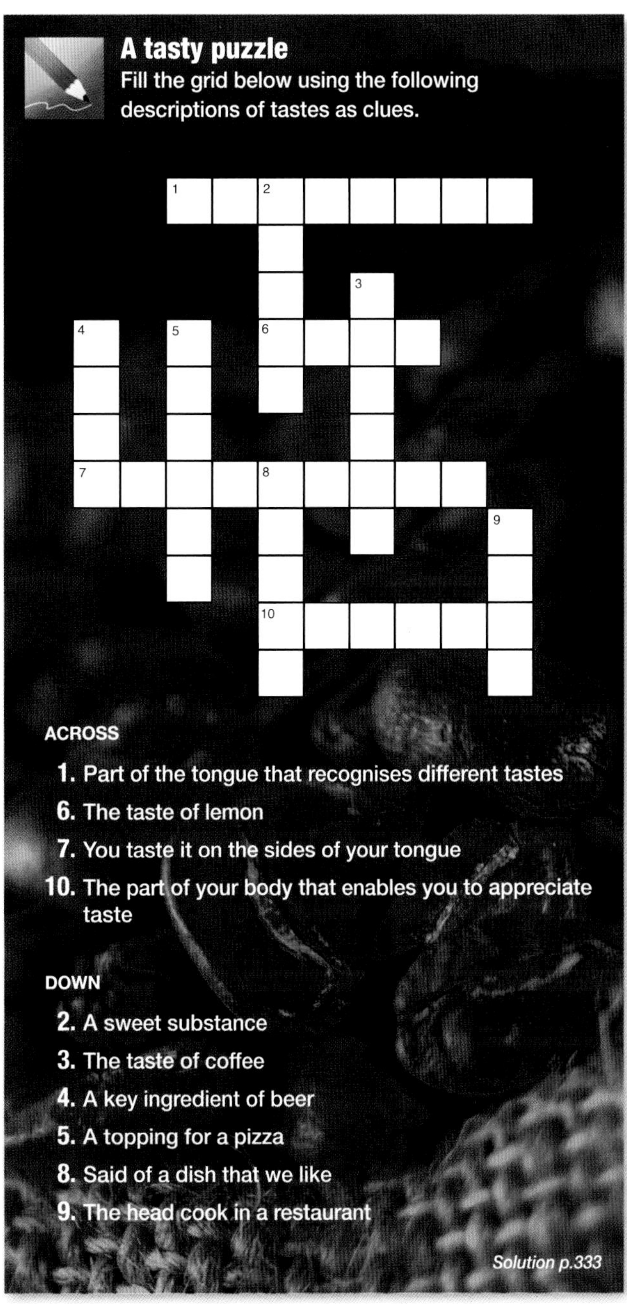

A tasty puzzle

Fill the grid below using the following descriptions of tastes as clues.

ACROSS

1. Part of the tongue that recognises different tastes
6. The taste of lemon
7. You taste it on the sides of your tongue
10. The part of your body that enables you to appreciate taste

DOWN

2. A sweet substance
3. The taste of coffee
4. A key ingredient of beer
5. A topping for a pizza
8. Said of a dish that we like
9. The head cook in a restaurant

Solution p.333

Memorising information

The process of receiving information and then recalling it from your memory is a complex mental operation. Receiving, coding, fixing and consolidating information are essential stages in this process. It is useful to understand the workings of this wonderful instrument, the memory, in order to make full use of its potential.

The memory function

Memory is a function that involves the full participation of the whole human body. In every act of memory the sensory, cognitive and emotional spheres are also all involved. So sensations and feelings are therefore just as important for your memory as reason and reflection.

Just as the black box on an airliner records and retains what is said between the pilots and the air-traffic controllers during a flight so that this information may be reproduced when required, so memorisation consists of receiving information, keeping it intact and being able to recall it at will. The smooth progression of these three stages is, however, subject to certain conditions that in reality are not always fully met.

The ingredients for good reception

Receiving information depends firstly on the efficient functioning of your senses – sight, hearing, smell, touch, taste. Often, your difficulty in remembering things can be explained by examining how the information was entered into that 'black box'. It is hard to remember something you have not seen or heard clearly. In fact, nothing can be engraved on your memory if your senses are not alert. So instead of blaming your memory, you need to train your sensory apparatus.

On the other hand, a well-functioning sensory system isn't everything. Another important ingredient is concentration, which is determined by factors such as interest, curiosity and a relatively calm emotional state. Receiving information effectively depends on your having the right frame of mind and not having the reception process disrupted.

When reading is disrupted...

1. Start reading the following text at a leisurely pace, trying to remember as much as possible.

In the 1890s, several inventors, including Thomas Alva Edison, succeeded in recording movement. But the Frenchman Louis Lumière is credited with perfecting the system of capturing movement on film. Even today our cameras still function in the same way. The only change is in the number of images per second – from 16 to the 32 images we have now. In 1895, Lumière patented a cinematograph, a camera that could also double as a projector. And so cinematography was born. This system makes use of the phenomenon that enables us to watch a film, which is called retinal persistence. In the same year, Lumière made his first film, *Workers Leaving the Lumière Factory*, which was shot at the gates of his own factory at Lyon-Monplaisir. This was the first motion picture in history.

2. At this point, stop reading and look closely at the picture opposite.

Monuments in mirror image

Look for the mistake that has slipped into the mirror images of each of the following monuments.

Two images can seem to be visually identical even though they actually have slight differences. This is a problem not of poor vision but of 'lazy' concentration. When we look at something, we unconsciously make elements alike so as to group them for easier memorisation. This reduces the diversity of our mental images, which also diminishes our powers of perception.

Solution *p. 333*

3. Now start reading again:

On December 28, 1895, the first commercial cinematographic screening was held in the cellar of the Grand Café on the Boulevard des Capucines in Paris, and his film featured on the programme. Louis, assisted by his brother Auguste, carried out various research projects on sound recording, relief photography and colour. From 1896 on, he organised teams of photographers to travel the world and record on film the first news bulletins of historical events, such as the coronation of Tsar Nicholas II. In addition, Louis directed 60 films and produced about 2 000.

4. Now answer the following questions:

- What are the first names of the Lumière brothers? ....
- In what year was cinematography invented? ....
- How many images per second were initially used? ....
- Where did the first commercial cinematographic screening take place? ....
- What was one of the first news events filmed by the cinematograph? ....
- What is the name of the phenomenon that makes it possible for us to watch a film? ....

You have probably discovered how diverting your attention to the photo during your reading of the text interfered with your assimilation of the text in its entirety. Simply using your eyes is not enough. One little distraction makes it impossible to remember everything in what you are reading.

Encoding and fixing

Like Hansel and Gretel, my brain scatters clues liberally!

All the information you receive is first transformed into 'brain language'. This is a biological process called encoding, which feeds information into the memory system. During encoding, **new information is placed in relation to everything already stored in your memory**. It is associated with, or 'given' a specific code, which could be a smell, an image, a snatch of music, or a word – any signifying element or marker which enables it to be recalled. If the word 'lemon' was encoded in relation to 'fruit', 'acidic smell', 'round', or 'yellow', one of these markers would enable it to be found if you could not recall it spontaneously. When the information you receive contributes something new, your brain creates new codes to place it in relation to other data it has already stored. The efficiency of the recovery, or recall, process depends on how thoroughly the information has been encoded, and on the organisation of the data and its free association. Because this mechanism uses the rich and fertile ground of our past (which is like a kind of potting compost), it is different for each individual and unique in the way it functions. Encoding potential, however, is limited by the absorption capacity of the brain – a maximum of five to seven items of information at any one time (see p.34).

Information, then, changes in status from a sensory image, received from the outside, to a mental image, the product of a transformation stimulated by an activity specific to the brain. This information is fixed in us in varying degrees of strength and durability.

- Short-term retention involves information from everyday life which has to be retained only for the duration of the task to be done – shopping, telephone calls, etc.
- Normal or medium-term retention comes into play for information that entails a certain degree of concentration, has grabbed our attention and that we would possibly like to pass on. It varies according to individual capacity, the time of day, how well trained we are and also the emotional content of the information. Normal retention is what we use most frequently. Its potential varies, and no-one knows its precise limits.
- Long-term retention engraves certain kinds of knowledge deeply in our memory without our being aware of doing anything in particular to achieve this. Emotionally intense events or situations often form the basis of an indelible memory. Their emotional charge makes us tell other people about them – and that consolidates them even further in our memory. We are not in control of this kind of memory... Buried messages, ostensibly long-forgotten, can resurface at any moment: in a dream, revived by a specific smell, etc.

My memory and... my diary

It is not enough to simply note an appointment or a task in your diary in order for your memory to register automatically. Although the act of writing it down is indeed a good way of fixing information, you need to reinforce it. Open the diary once a day, take the time to visualise its contents and see the appointments or tasks to be done in the context of a week or fortnight's activities. In this way you can use a diary intelligently, without it becoming a substitute for memory.

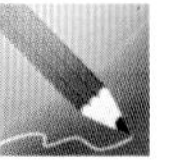

The weight of words, the impact of pictures...
See if you can identify the products that correspond to the following slogans.

It's the real thing

Because I'm worth it

Let your fingers do the walking

Coffee at its best

Vorsprung durch Technik

Kills Bugs Dead

Sch.... you know who

57 VARIETIES

All the news that's fit to print

All these slogans – and the products they promote – are no doubt familiar to you. Allow your memory free rein ...What is it in these little phrases that aroused a response in you? What images, words, atmosphere or feelings do you associate with them? Advertisers understand well the concerns and interests of their target market. They are particularly good at playing on emotion and creating an atmosphere, thus opening the door to a multitude of personal associations. Potential customers identify themselves with the situation depicted, the words and images are engraved on their memory with surprising ease, and so they rush out to buy the product!

We remember them still

Work out who the personalities are, traditionally associated with the following objects. Example: a white dress lifted by a gust of air reminds us of Marilyn Monroe.

Solution p.333

The stars of show-business, who appear frequently in the media, often have a look or object with which they are associated. As for historic personalities, it is their popularity or their influence on history that is the origin of a strongly fixed memory of them. Whether they are loved or detested, they don't leave us indifferent and are the object of numerous personal associations.

The recurring object with which each of these personalities is associated becomes a strong symbol: this supplementary association facilitates the recall of information.

Put a tiger in your tank

Don't leave home without it

'They're grrrrr-eat!'

Solution p. 333

Voluntary fixing, or consolidation

In my head, I arrange pieces of information … and I repeat them!

In some instances a mental image acquires an indelible position in the memory as a result of its strong emotional charge. In others, you have to consolidate information in some way if you want to retain it over a long period. The process of consolidation entails the considered organisation of your stock of knowledge. The new item of information has to be classified in an appropriate place, as if you were filing it in a large filing cabinet. How you sort it depends on the category in which you classify the information – meaning, shape, etc – or its inclusion in a plan or story, or the associations it evokes. So the word 'crane', for example, could be classified in the category 'bird' but could also be associated with construction, building, machinery, etc. But you might classify it differently, because **no** two people will ever store the same piece of information in the same way.

When you file something away you probably place it in front of the other items in the file. Similarly, your continuously active memory stacks up new information in front of old. So much new information eventually accumulates that your 'crane' file is buried. It will only come back to the front of the file if it is used again. If not, it will be relegated to the back like any forgotten object. So to ensure effective consolidation, it is not enough simply to organise the data. The information must be repeated four or five times in the first 24 hours and then fairly regularly thereafter to prevent its being forgotten. If this task of repetition is properly carried out, a well-consolidated mental image can be recalled from memory on demand.

Recovering information

A name escapes you? Don't get worked up – just look for clues!

Recovering information entails retrieving information that has been committed to memory. It is usually at this point in the process of remembering that you may encounter problems, with that irritating feeling of having the word at the tip of your tongue! The information is stored in your memory but is inaccessible – even though you are certain you do know it. Experience has shown that it is better not to keep trying. It is usually when something associated with the desired information happens to come to your attention that you can recover it.

When you recall an item of information on demand, this is referred to as spontaneous recall – the rapid recitation of the titles of three of Aesop's fables, for example. But if you are asked to mention those fables featuring a hare, rats and a fox, the process at work here would be triggered recall. These animals, which served as vehicles of association during the encoding process, subsequently become triggers in the process of recall.

The more emotionally charged the memories, the more the salient details are laden with personal associations and the more triggers of recall there are. You can remember many more vivid details of the significant events in your life – graduation, the birth of children, etc. – than of events of cultural importance in which you are not personally involved. It is these details that make so-called episodic memory (see p.128) so rich.

On the other hand, a process of recognition is at work when you correctly choose the right answer when presented with several possibilities. For example, which of the following titles is that of a well-known Aesop fable? *The Hare and the Stork*, *The Dog and the Wolf*, *The Fox and the Crow*?

Triggered recall and recognition produce the best results – more items of information are recalled, and these prove to be more vivid and precise.

When you struggle to recall data, it is pointless to question why the information has been temporarily lost. Rather, look at the method used in recording it: was the information sufficiently well processed – through association, organisation and structure – to ensure that it was effectively committed to memory? If not, the traces that serve as triggers will be inadequate to ensure an easy passage back into the conscious.

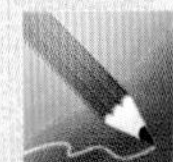

The letter chase

Change only one letter in each of the following words in order to arrive at a new word. Give yourself 15 minutes.

Example : for **pass**, by replacing an **s** with a **t**, you get **past**.

The quicker you do this, the more you exercise your faculty of recall of information, and you will improve your verbal fluency.

post	....	**cream**	....	**induct**	....
hallow	....	**invert**	....	**break**	....
fixed	....	**tickle**	....	**friction**	....
gullet	....	**wallet**	....	**bout**	....
gross	....	**dally**	....	**access**	....
fern	....	**indent**	....	**deride**	....
pure	....	**port**	....	**prone**	....
main	....	**painting**	....	**elope**	....
circus	....	**hominy**	....	**canal**	....
true	....	**attitude**	....	**implore**	....
grand	....	**pose**	....	**dotage**	....
lathe	....	**hollow**	....	**cortex**	....
cruet	....	**mouth**	....	**harp**	....
marinate	....	**flower**	....	**revere**	....
turner	....	**pest**	....	**ramble**	....
vest	....	**collusion**	....	**concert**	....
suite	....	**forewind**	....	**dough**	....
latin	....	**scarf**	....	**quite**	....
ooze	....	**mission**	....	**place**	....
crude	....	**provision**	....	**revel**	....
miscount	....	**forage**	....	**cling**	....
button	....	**infect**	....	**verge**	....

Solution p.333

My memory and...
my daily tasks

When you're doing one job and then start another, and then forget to return to the first, your memory is not really the problem. It is rather your lack of confidence in it, your fear of forgetting, which impels you to undertake too much at once. This haste is also an indication of a lack of organisation and concentration. Plan your day in terms of your availability and don't hesitate to write down what you have to do. Most importantly, take your time and don't overtax yourself. Without stress and fatigue we can do much more than we think!

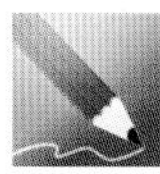

Mock exam

You have 10 minutes to find 30 words beginning with the letter **A**: 5 first names, 5 plants, 5 animals, 5 countries, 5 cities in the world and finally, 5 celebrities. Do the same with the letters **E**, **M** and **P**.

Be methodical – think of the letters of the alphabet that could follow the first letter – and don't be put off by the stress imposed by the time limit. You could play this game alone or with several others, and further extend the game to include any other letters, or groups of letters (Pi, Mo, Dr...).

	Name	Plant	Animal	Country	Town	Célebrity
A	....	....	....	....	....	....
	....	....	....	....	....	....
	....	....	....	....	....	....
	....	....	....	....	....	....
	....	....	....	....	....	....
E	....	....	....	....	....	....
	....	....	....	....	....	....
	....	....	....	....	....	....
	....	....	....	....	....	....
	....	....	....	....	....	....
M	....	....	....	....	....	....
	....	....	....	....	....	....
	....	....	....	....	....	....
	....	....	....	....	....	....
	....	....	....	....	....	....
P	....	....	....	....	....	....
	....	....	....	....	....	....
	....	....	....	....	....	....
	....	....	....	....	....	....
	....	....	....	....	....	....

This mini-test is a good way to put your memory to work and stimulate verbal fluency. The unimpeded flow of words in the brain is an indication of rapid association. Remembering then becomes much easier.

The four basic operations

In certain subjects, like arithmetic, the memory sometimes becomes lazy through lack of practice. And a calculator is so very useful! The four basic operations of arithmetic are always retained in our memory, but we need to appeal to this memory more insistently. Do the following exercises, mentally or in written form.

1 536 + 541 = ...

18 659 + 3 874 = ...

59 246 + 66 666 + 8 756 = ...

589 – 821 = ...

5 896 – 4 172 = ...

698 324 – 8 753 = ...

147 x 654 = ...

5 891 x 258 = ...

47 985 x 4 658 = ...

583 ÷ 52 = ...

4 627 ÷ 111 = ...

31 772 ÷ 32,5 = ...

Solution p.333

Stick-on syllables

By combining the following phonetic syllables, find 15 types of birds. So that you don't omit any, cross out the syllables as you match them up. Your memory will automatically make the link between the syllables and your stock of vocabulary.

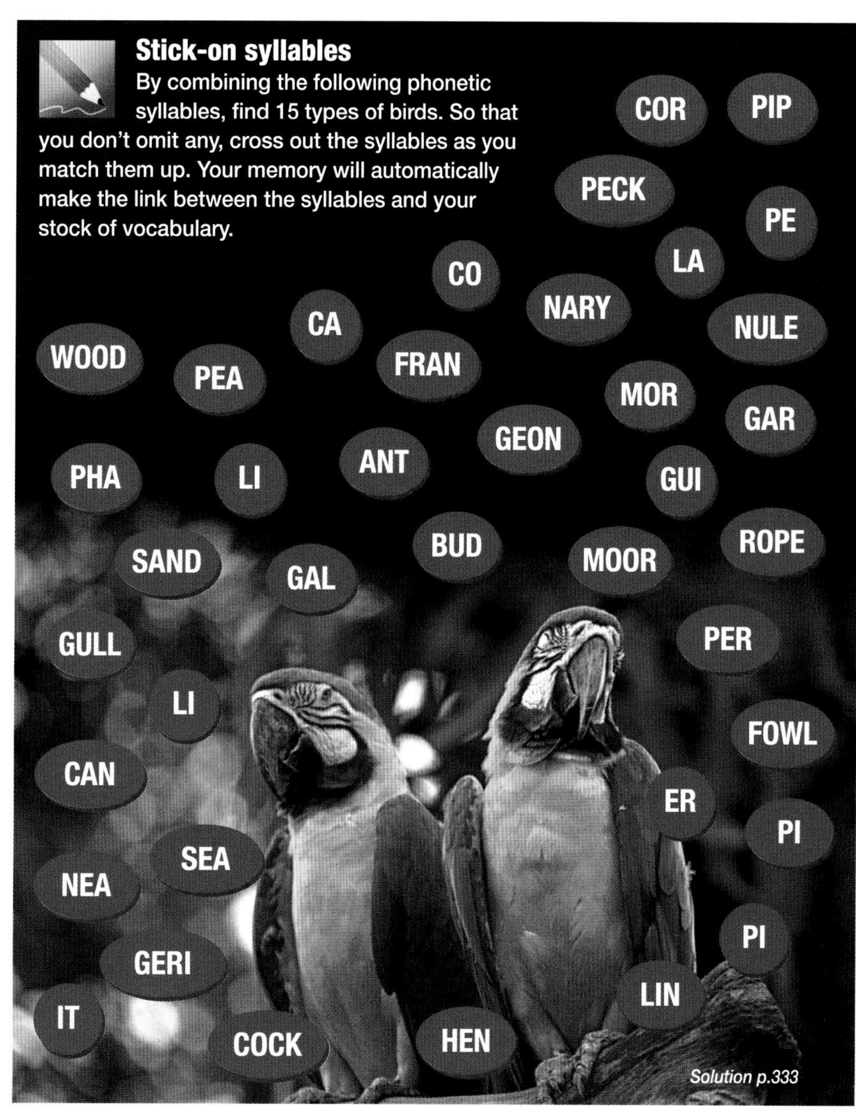

Solution p.333

A measure of memory

The immediate retention of a phone number or the details of a conversation comes under the control of the short-term memory, which is essential in everyday life. The measure of this memory is called the span.

An average of seven items

While watching the news on television, I can usually remember no more than seven items of information at a time.

In 1956, while he was studying the capacity of the short-term memory, the American researcher George Miller discovered the phenomenon of the memory span. The span determines the storage capacity of this memory function, or the number of items of information that it can retain for a limited period, up to three minutes. This capacity differs little from one individual to the next, varying between five and nine elements. The average span is seven elements, which Miller described as a magic number, like other symbolic numbers, such as the seven days of the week, the Seven Wonders of the world, the seven-branched candelabra, etc. Everyone can gauge their own word span (the number of words in a list that can be retained), phrase span (number of words that can be remembered in a text), number span (how many numbers can be remembered in a series) and their own visual span (the number of images, objects or people recalled).

It can be perfectly normal to have a larger span in some of these areas than in others. Accountants and maths experts will feel comfortable with the number span, because their ability to memorise numbers is regularly exercised. People working in the field of literature will definitely be more at ease with their span of words or phrases, because their interest in literature will stimulate this. And photographers, artists and those interested in pictures will have a greater advantage in the visual span, as they have a well-honed eye. Our memory is thus better in areas which interest us, because we have exercised it in these areas throughout our lives.

Test your word span

Read the following 16 everyday words carefully.

Bag	**Plant**	**Tree**	**Window**
Car	**Candle**	**Chair**	**Photo**
House	**Cat**	**Lamp**	**Rose**
Piano	**Table**	**Shoe**	**Pen**

Then cover the list, and in 10 seconds write below all the words you remember, in any order.

1.	**9.** ....
2.	**10.** ....
3.	**11.** ....
4.	**12.** ....
5.	**13.** ....
6.	**14.** ....
7.	**15.** ....
8.	**16.** ....

Count the words you remembered in this first attempt. ....

Five minutes later, without looking at the list, write the words below, in any order, as before.

1.	**9.** ....
2.	**10.** ....
3.	**11.** ....
4.	**12.** ....
5.	**13.** ....
6.	**14.** ....
7.	**15.** ....
8.	**16.** ....

Count the words you've written down during this second exercise. ....

Go back to the original list and correct your two attempts at recollection. Compare your results.

If you have less than seven correct words, don't panic! We don't all have the same power of recall. Even if this list contained 20 or 30 words, your rate of recollection would still be about seven, because the span remains the same.

The possible difference between your two scores will reveal the kind of concentration you applied to the exercise. You could have simply 'photographed' the words without paying any particular attention to them. In this case, your second score will naturally be worse than your first. On the other hand, it will remain the same after five minutes if your concentration was sustained while you were reading. The quality of your span therefore depends on the intensity of your concentration.

A few minutes later, all this information could vanish. This is because we use our short-term memory when we need to retain information that must be used immediately. Afterwards, this information will be forgotten if we don't have a special interest in retaining it.

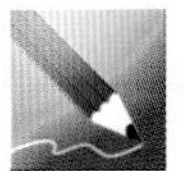

Test your phrase span

Read this text carefully, then hide it.

'From his lodge went Hiawatha,
Dressed for travel, armed for hunting;
Dressed in deer-skin shirt and leggings,
Richly wrought with quills and wampum;
On his head his eagle feathers,
Round his waist his belt of wampum,
In his hand his bow of ash-wood,
Strung with sinews of the reindeer;
In his quiver oaken arrows,
Tipped with jasper, winged with feathers'

Henry Wadsworth Longfellow (1807-1882)

... and fill in the missing words.

'From his lodge went ....,
Dressed for ...., armed for ....;
Dressed in .... shirt and leggings,
Richly wrought with .... and ....;
On his head his .... feathers,
Round his .... his belt of ....,
In his hand his bow of ....,
Strung with .... of the ....;
In his .... oaken ....,
Tipped with ...., winged with ....'

If you have filled in at least seven words your span is good. If have remembered less than this, you are not attentive enough.
When you have to remember phrases, you need to understand the sense of what you are reading. We memorise in particular the words that are important in the significance of the phrase as well as those that have a particular resonance within us and which stimulate emotions.

The span of the auditory memory

Listen attentively to a news flash lasting about five minutes, on the radio or on TV, but without looking at the screen. Then note down all the news items you have remembered, and attempt to set them down in the order in which you think they were read. Check your notes by listening to the next news bulletin.

If you repeat this exercise regularly, you could train yourself to listen more attentively and improve your auditory memory as well as your span of phrases.

My memory and...
playing games in the car with children

To keep children occupied during long car trips, you need a variety of simple verbal or visual games. Here are some examples:

- Verbal games: Find words based on certain clues: eg, objects of the same colour; words beginning with a specific letter of the alphabet or words referring to the same topic; sing old songs or learn new ones ... Starting a story and asking the children to finish it is also a good way to get their imagination working.
- Visual games: Look out of the window and describe the countryside in as many ways as possible; invent first names and names beginning with the first letter of the number plates of the cars you see (eg: GP General Problem); identify the different models of cars you see.

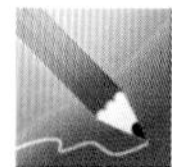

Test your number span

Before starting this exercise, make sure you have something with which you can cover up the lines of numbers. Uncover the first line and read the digits one at a time. Cover them again and in the space opposite write down those you remember. When you've done that, move to the following line and repeat the exercise to the end.

542 ....

036 ....

6092 ....

9518 ....

64296 ....

74281 ....

548263 ....

395762 ....

0151237 ....

1963751 ....

75826364 ....

65293760 ....

563214870 ....

284610359 ....

5632897401 ....

8593264017 ....

Now check your answers. The last line of digits that you have correctly noted down will give you your number span. For example, if your mistakes start at line 13, then you have a digit span of 8 (line 12 has 8 digits).

We tend to remember numbers only if they interest us for a special reason, if they have an emotional connotation or if we can associate them with something familiar to us. Such a figure would be the age of someone close to you, your graduation day, the birth of a child, your postal code, etc. If they don't evoke anything in particular and remain abstract entities, without associations that make them easy to remember, it would be difficult, if not impossible, to recall them. This could explain why the number span is lower in some people than in others and, more generally, why a fair number of people feel a certain resistance, if not blockage, when it come to numbers.

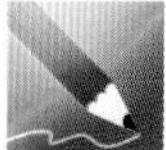

Test your visual span

Look carefully at all these pictures, going from left to right. Then cover them and write down the name of each object in the space opposite.

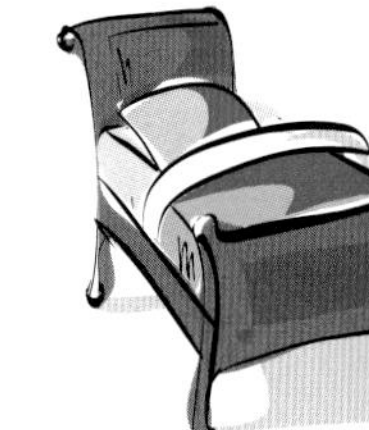

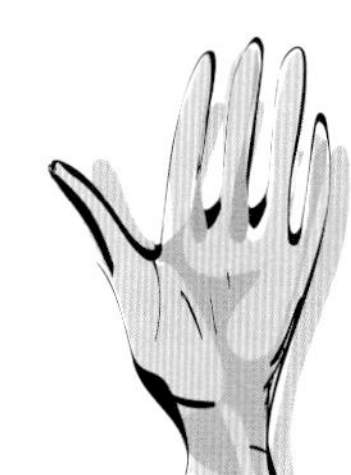

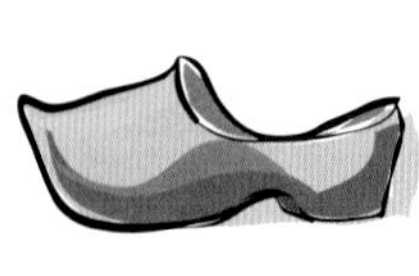

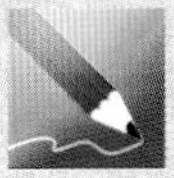

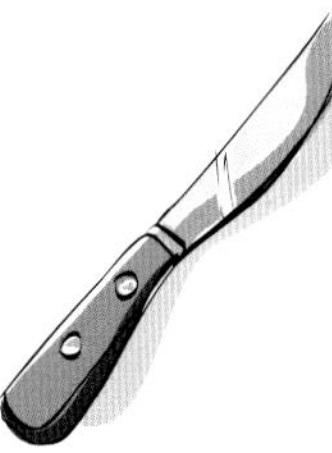

1. ....
2. ....
3. ....
4. ....
5. ....
6. ....
7. ....
8. ....
9. ....
10. ....
11. ....
12. ....
13. ....
14. ....
15. ....
16. ....
17. ....
18. ....
19. ....
20. ....

When drawing is also involved

Look carefully at these cards, then cover them and draw them again in the order in which they were displayed.

A new element comes into this exercise: it is not just about remembering the cards in the right order, but also drawing them. In addition to your visual memory, your drawing ability is now called upon. So you have two simultaneous tasks, which makes the memory's operations more complicated.

Check the words you have written down. How many of the words correspond to the pictures? Note how much you score in the visual span.

Generally, better results are obtained for the visual span than for the other spans. It ranges from 7 to 11, which gives an average of 9 elements. In fact, 70 percent of information is absorbed primarily through the visual sense. This phenomenon is more pronounced in our society, where the visual image is becoming increasingly more predominant. It is particularly noticeable in children who develop large visual spans when they regularly devote a great deal of time to video games.

My memory and...
radio news bulletins

Why do we often remember news on the radio more clearly than news on TV?

On the radio, the news is generally presented in a shorter way and the news items are formulated more succinctly than on TV, without embellishments. The news items are thus easier to remember. Conversely, the images on the TV news can distract your attention from the main news events.

Attention

We frequently complain about our poor memories, but it is often our attention that is at fault. When you take notice of something, when you pay close attention to it, all your intellectual and psychological resources are engaged. And you need a deliberate act of will for the images you perceive to become inscribed in your brain and to be recalled when they are required.

Test Do you have trouble paying attention?

The aim of this questionnaire is to help you identify any problems you might have with attention and concentration and how frequently they occur. Answer the following questions, putting a cross in the relevant box. Then add up your points using the following scale: :

NEVER: 0 points **OFTEN: 2 points**
RARELY: 1 point **VERY OFTEN: 3 points**

	NEVER	RARELY	OFTEN	VERY OFTEN
1. I listen to music while reading a book or a magazine.				
2. At home, I don't really notice when any ornament has been moved.				
3. I find it difficult to ignore noises around me.				
4. I habitually do several things at once.				
5. I feel tense for no reason.				
6. Noises around me disturb me.				
7. I do things very quickly.				
8. I don't know how to remember important things.				
9. I feel tired.				
10. I have problems with sleep.				
11. I eat too quickly.				
12. I take little interest in what is going on around me.				
13. I prefer to stay at home rather than undertake any new activities.				
14. My eyesight seems to have deteriorated.				
15. I am a scatterbrain.				
16. I have problems remembering important issues.				
17. I don't spend much time on myself.				
18. I am not well organised.				
19. I don't take the time to pay close attention to what is happening around me.				
20. I am not interested in learning anything new.				
21. I have the impression that my hearing is not as good as it was.				
22. I take tranquillisers to relax and to help me sleep.				
Total of points obtained:				

You have less than 30 points

You are generally attentive and concentrate on what you are doing, but you don't always listen when people speak to you. Don't worry, however; you are capable of handling complex situations and harnessing all your resources. Nevertheless, if you are slightly uncertain about your ability to remember, consider whether you have problems at the moment that might perhaps be unsettling you.

You have between 30 and 44 points

You often experience the frustration of wondering what you came to do or fetch in a particular room, but you find the answer very quickly. You are perhaps one of those people who allow themselves to be disturbed very easily and are sometimes distracted by trivial things. Always try to mobilise all your attention when wanting to remember something important, and don't allow yourself to be distracted by what is going on around you!

You have between 45 and 66 points

You are no doubt going through a difficult time. Your everyday life is weighing you down and your ability to pay attention is affected. You have a tendency to want to do everything yourself instead of selecting and delegating, especially as you're rather a perfectionist. You are easily distracted by noise, the demands of others, fatigue, overwork and stress, and you are floundering under the burden of your worries. You might also be taking some medication that doesn't agree with you. Above all else, make the time to stop and take stock. Don't skimp on time spent sleeping or having meals. Don't give up what you feel is vital to your stability. Allow yourself time to do things properly, without rushing. If you need reassurance or feel that you can't cope on your own, feel free to discuss it with those closest to you or consult your doctor.

Paying attention: no half-measures

Firstly, all my senses must be alert. Secondly, I must make a conscious decision to remember.

Paying attention (from the Latin *ad tendere,* meaning 'reaching towards'), **means mobilising all your senses to seize or take mental possession of your environment**. So it is in the first place an act of perception. This task is an extremely demanding one, because paying attention half-heartedly is not really paying attention. To ensure that your attention is focused on something, you must exercise your whole faculty of perception.

When you have perceived something, the information has definitely reached your brain, but everything that has been perceived is not necessarily worth remembering. Perception becomes close and searching attentiveness, capable of committing something to memory, when you are **determined to retain the information**, when the information arouses your **personal interest** or when it has to be **conveyed** to someone else. All your minor everyday problems of forgetfulness are not memory problems but problems of attention. As long as your perception remains on the superficial level, it is impossible to remember what is going on around you.

Nature has designed us well: this seeming failure of attention is really a way of protecting us against an over-abundance of unwanted information, with which we are continuously bombarded. The exercises prepared for you in this book will essentially put your visual attentiveness to work. But attention can take on as many forms as there are senses – it can be also be auditory, gustatory, olfactory and tactile.

My memory and... new technology

The computer, DVDs, Internet, cellphone... They are invading our world, but don't hold out against them, and more especially, don't panic about not understanding them. Don't focus on methods of using them that seem impossible for you to remember. Ask for repeated demonstrations of how to use this equipment. Note down in your own words, step by step, how to get it going and familiarise yourself with your new tool by repeating the operations several times.

Know your herbs

These herbs are used in the kitchen. If you've looked at them carefully before you may be able to identify them.

Solution p.333

Misleading numbers

Look at the space below. Which digit recurs most frequently?

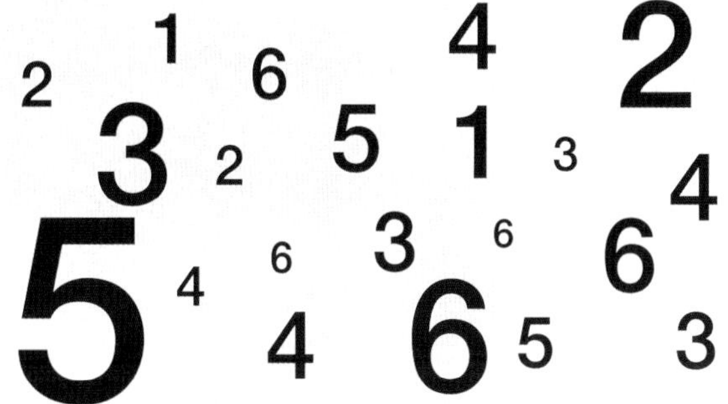

Solution p.333

Here size influences perception. The biggest digits are perceived and decoded first by your brain because they attract attention. You then take note of number. We always see large objects first and the rest seem to be secondary. Advertisers know this well, which is why they always enlarge what will entice their customers (tempting appearance, special offers, etc) and show unappetising information, such as conditions of sale, in a reduced size.

Missing letters

Look at the square opposite.

Can you work out in one minute which one of these squares numbered 1 to 6 does not contain any of the letters on the first square?

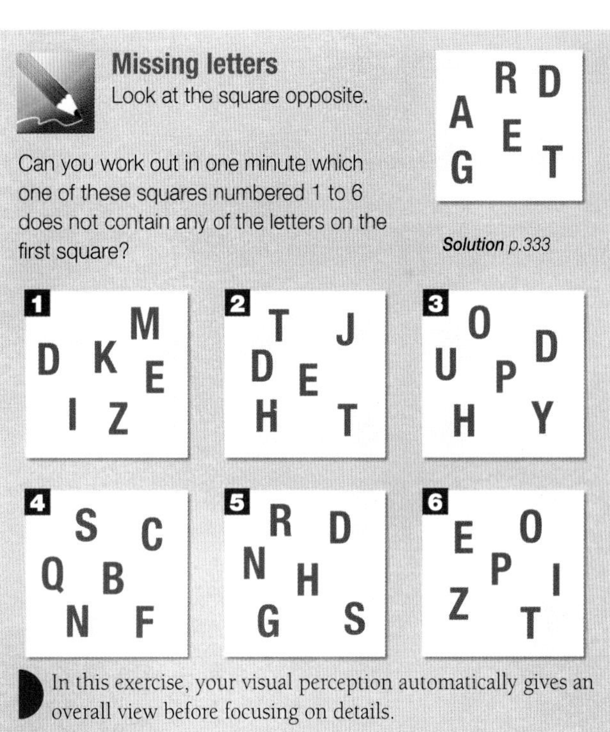

Solution p.333

In this exercise, your visual perception automatically gives an overall view before focusing on details.

You've got them all right? Bravo! But you are probably a chef, a horticulturist or a gardener You didn't get any right? That's normal. Like most of us, you eat these herbs without really looking at them carefully. In fact, it is impossible to retain all that reaches our eyes and ears. Even if we begin to remember these items of information when we perceive them, they are only properly structured afterwards.

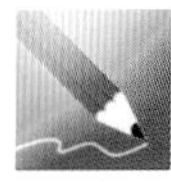

Hotchpotch

1. How many triangles, squares and rectangles can you see?

2. How many numbers do you see?

3. How many squares can you see?

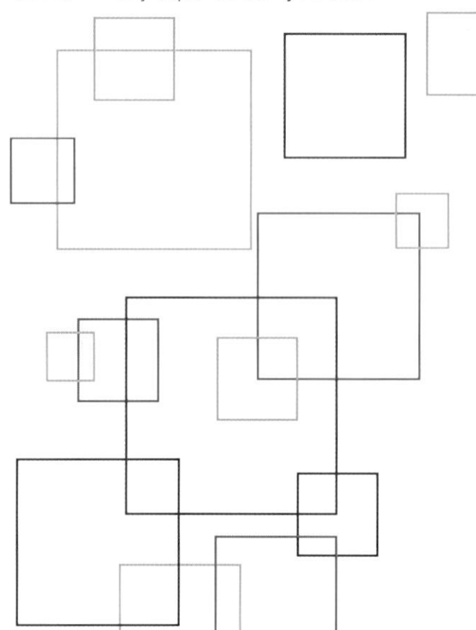

Solution p.333

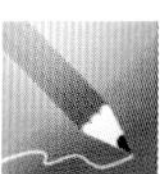

Spot the 7 differences

There are seven differences between these two photographs. Can you find them?

Attention profiles

We don't all have the same kind of attention span. We are not all equally attentive and we don't all pay attention in the same way. Your approach to taking in information is influenced by your education, but also depends on your personality, principal interests and attitude to the world.

The following attention profiles, although stereotypical, do nevertheless give you some idea of the differences.

- **Those who pay meticulous attention** display excessively attentive behaviour: everything arouses their interest; everything can or must be remembered, at the risk of overloading the memory with worthless details. They do not pay attention selectively.

Those who fit into this category tend to be perfectionists, punctilious and endowed with a very good memory. They will draw your attention to a bit of fluff on your pullover, or will remember in great detail facts which you don't consider important. They also tend to expect others to have the same kind of exhaustive non-selective memory. People who pay meticulous attention to

My memory and… films

You like going to the cinema and watching films on TV, but you can't remember what you have seen, even if you enjoyed it. Don't worry, that's perfectly normal. When you are a spectator, you are essentially passive and don't exercise your critical faculties much, if at all. If you want to remember a film, start adopting an active approach as soon as the final credits start: summarise the film, recall the scenes you liked or found shocking, evaluate the acting of the characters…And don't forget to discuss it with your friends.

Solution p.334

everything have huge reserves of information in their memories but don't make much use of it. Not much of this information will be really useful to them because it is difficult for them to select what they find really interesting.

- **Those who have a particular interest in specific fields** focus their attention on one or more centres of interest. Their attention is put to good use, is efficiently deployed in the areas concerned, and they are only slightly interested in other things, if at all. People with a focused interest will tend to try to impress others with the extent of their knowledge of selected subjects. Their attention is selective but of a high standard, as is their memory.
- **Those who are inattentive** generally don't take much interest in their environment. They often seem to have their heads in the clouds and tend to lose or forget things. They don't really listen to others and might ignore social conventions. This lack of interest in the environment often goes with an excessive interest in themselves and their feelings. Such people rarely go into anything in depth and have memories that are narcissistic and patchy. This conduct occurs frequently in some adolescents.

You probably recognise aspects of yourself in each of these profiles. What is important is to remain flexible, well focused on selected areas of interest but open-minded and able to cope with new demands and challenges. This approach will guarantee successful memorisation.

Test How much attention do you pay to your environment?

1. You use things all the time. Do you know the brands of these objects? Do this test unaided, without looking around you and without moving around. Your replies must be as spontaneous as possible.

In the bathroom

Soap ....
Toothpaste ....
Eau de toilette or perfume ....
Shampoo ....
Razor ....
Toothbrush ....
Toilet paper ....

In the kitchen

Coffee ....
Oil ....
Biscuits ....
Tea ....
Sugar ....
Salt ....
Mustard ....
Mineral water ....
Pasta ....
Dishwashing liquid ....
Scourer ....
Oven ....
Fridge ....

Elsewhere in the house

Washing machine............
Television ....
Camera ....
Music centre ....
Iron ....
Hair dryer ....

2. Can you name five shops or supermarkets near your home?

....
....
....

3. Do you know the makes of car ...

- of 3 of your family members?:

....
....

- of 3 neighbours or friends?:

....
....

If you have left more than 10 questions unanswered, or made more than 10 mistakes, you do not focus on appearances. Objects interest you only because they are functional and useful. You couldn't care less about the minor differences between brands or their aesthetic appeal. You probably throw them out readily when they no longer serve their purpose.

If, on the contrary, you have more than 10 right answers, you are among those who take more of an interest in objects, their shape and their qualities. You probably don't like throwing them away even when they are worn out. You probably love adverts and everything new. You could be emotionally attached to your material possessions.

Attention and reading

Reading demands **good eyesight**, of course, but also **comprehension**. It is a form of visual attentiveness to both the shape and sense of the words.

Whatever the shape of the letters, your attention is focused primarily on the meaning of the text rather than the typographic elements or correct spelling. And it is because a text makes sense that you can remember it.

On the other hand, when you see a text in a language you are unfamiliar with, you can pay attention only to the appearance of the words, to their shape. You couldn't really call this reading, and it would be impossible to remember the text.

The letter E

Circle all the E's in the following text by George Eliot, from *Adam Bede,* 1905. Then count them.

'The afternoon sun was warm on the five workmen there, busy upon doors and window-frames and wainscoting. A scent of pine-wood from a tent-like pile of planks outside the open door mingled itself with the scent of the elder-bushes which were spreading their summer snow close to the open window opposite; the slanting sunbeams shone through the transparent shavings that flew before the steady plane, and lit up the fine grain of the oak panelling which stood propped against the wall. On a heap of those soft shavings a rough grey shepherd-dog had made himself a pleasant bed, and was lying with his nose between his fore-paws, occasionally wrinkling his brows to cast a glance at the tallest of the five workmen, who was carving a shield in the centre of a wooden mantelpiece. It was to this workman that the strong barytone belonged which was heard above the sound of plane and hammer singing –

"Awake, my soul, and with the sun
Thy daily stage of duty run;
Shake off dull sloth ..."

Here some measurement was to be taken which required more concentrated attention, and the sonorous voice subsided into a low whistle, but it presently broke out again with renewed vigour –'

***Solution** p.334*

If you have followed the instructions and concentrated on looking at the shape of the letters, you haven't really read the text. You couldn't answer a question on the text, because the task you were set precluded comprehension.

Police mystery

Read this text attentively, but only once. To mobilise your attention, take a real interest in what you are reading, ask yourself questions as you read, identify the main points and summarise it orally.

'Hands in the air! Everyone! Come on, faster than that!' shouts the detective in the felt hat as he enters the Sportsman's Bar.

He is addressing four men in particular, seated at a table with two glasses of wine and two glasses of beer with foam overflowing onto the table. The detective trains his gun on them. They comply. In the street outside, the sirens of police cars suddenly wail. It is two o'clock in the morning and the bar is still open.

The whole police operation was set in motion five minutes earlier. According to a tip given by an informer, a witness in a case of drug trafficking, who was due to appear in court that very morning, was to be liquidated at the bar. The police didn't know who the killer was. They set a trap in the bar, with the witness as bait. He was one of the four men. So was the alleged killer, who had just joined the group. But just before entering the bar, he had become suspicious and threw his gun into the opening of the nearest manhole.

The detective interrogates the four men in the presence of the owner of the bar. Here are their replies:

1. 'I've been here for an hour and I won my round of beer in a game of poker.'

2. 'I'm being ripped off – I'm losing non-stop.'

3. 'I came in 20 minutes ago to drink a small glass of beer,' he says with foam on his lips. 'It's the only bar in this area where the beer is so good.'

4. 'I am quietly drinking a glass of wine. Don't disturb me!' He is anxious. A bead of sweat stands out on his forehead.

The detective notices a telling detail. The killer has just revealed himself.

Now answer the following questions:

- What is the name of the bar?
  ....
- What is the detective wearing?
  ....
- At what time does the action take place?
  ....
- What detail did the detective notice – who is the killer, and why?
  ....

***Solution** p.334*

Attention based on visual perception

Paying attention through visual perception demands both good eyesight and the ability to orient yourself visually and locate objects in space. This kind of attention is required when you are looking at a collection of objects placed in relation to each other in a defined setting or frame. Your eye usually carries out a sweeping movement across the whole picture before targeting particular elements and establishing their relative position in the organisation of space. Perception can differ, however, from one person to the next. When looking at a series of objects in a photo, for example, some people will initially pay attention to the frame and will even describe it first, whereas others will be attracted first to the objects themselves. Either way, your attention will be aroused only if you want to remember something.

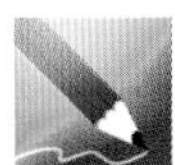

Watch those letters!

1. Look carefully at the letters written in the square below.

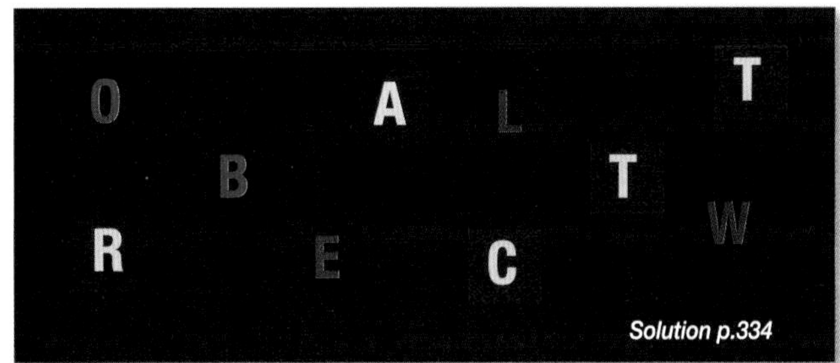

Solution p.334

2. Cover them and answer the following questions.
– Which letters are written in a square and what word can you make with them?
– Which letters are not written in a square and what word can you make with them?

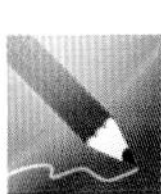

The cat in the garden

1. Look closely at this picture for three minutes, and then cover it.

2. Without referring back to the picture or having another peep at it, put as many items as possible back in their right place on the blank picture.

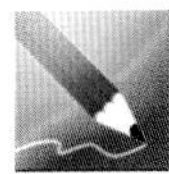

Missing shapes

Look at these completed lines of geometric shapes for a minute, and then cover them and fill in the missing shapes in the line below.

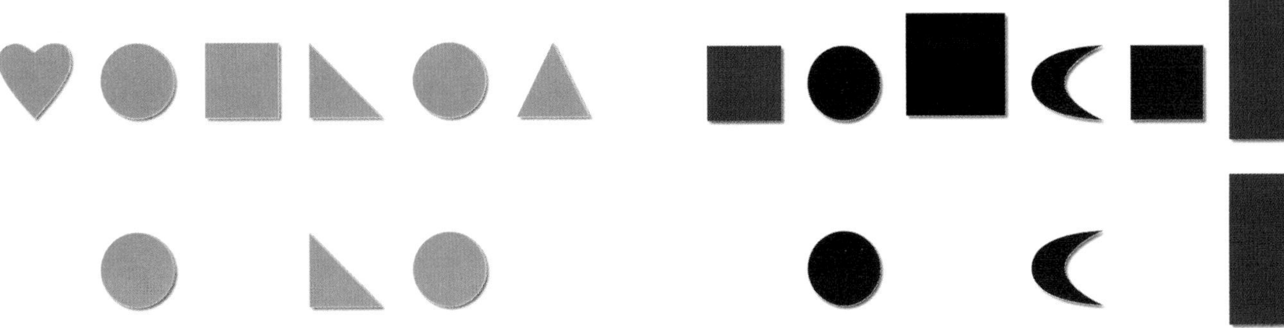

In this exercise, a sequence of geometric shapes forms a whole pattern. You had to register the order in which they appear, that is, see them in relation to each other, in order to remember them.

Attention helpers

Simply wanting to pay attention is not enough. Remember … at school you thought you were really paying attention during some lessons, but you retained virtually nothing. In the past, you tried desperately to remember your physics courses. To no avail. So, how do we explain this?

At the age of 88, the French explorer Paul-Emile Victor explained the secret of his extraordinary vitality in this way: 'I never go to sleep at night without first planning my little source of enthusiasm for the following day.' In maintaining his interest in the little everyday sources of happiness, the elderly explorer had found one of the key ingredients of a high level of attentiveness. There are others as well. And their combination is the only guarantee of a high level of attention.

Interest This is what gets your attention going at the outset. Anything that doesn't interest you, or doesn't arouse any emotion, usually fails to grab your attention.

Personality Personalities susceptible to anxiety or stress suffer from an overabundance of thoughts and distracting preoccupations. Being absent-minded is also a disadvantage. Character traits like open-mindedness and an optimistic attitude constitute the best conditions.

Enjoyment This increases the level of attention paid to anything that stimulates it.

Motivation The prospect of attaining a goal, of succeeding, or developing your potential, automatically makes you more attentive.

Vigilance A state of calm, detached alertness favours sustained attention over a long period, and you can remain open to new demands without fatigue.

Curiosity This stimulates the attention. The more curious you are about your environment and life in general, the more your attention is stimulated.

If only one of these factors is absent, your attention will be less than perfect. Even when all these factors do pertain, memorisation does not necessarily follow: in addition, you need the will to remember.

Concentration This enables you to focus your attention on selected material without being easily distracted. But note that concentration has its limits. We all differ as far as the intensity and duration of our concentration is concerned, and it also varies at different times in our own lives.

Emotions Both positive and negative emotions get your attention going automatically and make it more intense: the fear of losing one iota of information forces you to pay attention as long as possible.

Environmental factors When the environment is favourable – without auditory or visual disturbance – your attention improves and can be focused without risk of distraction.

Attention distractors

Circumstances do not always make it easy for you to maintain a high degree of attentiveness. Think of all the difficulties you may have to contend with in your daily life: fatigue, stress, the effects of certain medication, a poor lifestyle, illness … These are certainly the primary obstacles to being attentive. When you are not able to cope with these minor problems, then more insidious impediments can make their appearance in the form of certain ways of behaving or reacting to your environment. And these tend to be perpetuated.

- **Switching off and being under-stimulated** can result if you don't pay enough attention to your environment. We have a tendency, for various reasons, to leave our 'reserves of attention' underused.

- **Under-utilisation** results mainly from a chronic lack of effort. Laziness creeps in and ends up impairing your capacity to pay attention, which becomes ever more difficult to rouse. This is what happens when, for example, you have to undertake new training and adapt to the discipline of study years after completing your formal education.

- **Loss of concentration and lack of focus** result from under-utilisation. If you don't develop the habit of steadily applying your mind to something, it will become even more difficult to focus it for any length of time.

- **The absence of curiosity, wishes and projects** is perhaps attention's greatest enemy. When you have a particular project to carry out, or something you really want, this, together with curiosity about the world around you, is the best guarantee that you will maintain high levels of attention and consequently will remember information effectively.

To remember longer: the ADA

'I'm parking in Ferdinand Street, opposite the baker's, behind a yellow car.' By saying this to myself when I park there this morning, I will ensure that I will find the car this evening!

Repeatedly losing familiar objects and forgetting a task you have been asked to do are among the most common complaints about the memory. The same pattern repeats itself: you are in a hurry, tired or irritated, you think you have registered something properly and paid enough attention to it, but you forget just as quickly.

A moderate degree of attention does not guarantee long-lasting memorisation. You pay attention while crossing the road but do not retain a detailed memory of crossing it unless some reckless driver gives you a fright; you pay attention to mess on the pavement, but you remember it only if you step on it! By the same token, concentrating on an action to understand it or do it does not necessarily ensure that you will remember it. You must therefore give your experiences and your activities some **ADA**, that is, **an additional degree of attention.** This simply means directing your attention for longer than usual on memorising the task to be done or the object to remember in order to retain it more effectively. How does this work? By **ensuring that this process does not happen virtually automatically,** because this would preclude the degree of attention necessary for retention.

Take, for example, the action of locking your front door, something you probably have to check often afterwards because you do it without really paying attention – almost automatically. Introducing ADA means stimulating your attention by watching yourself lock the door and reinforcing this action by formulating it in your head or saying it aloud ('I'm locking my door.') Here there is auditory reinforcement of the visual perception. Writing down what you want to remember is another way of applying ADA.

Attention with ADA is active attention, directing your attention, and stems from a desire to apply definite ways of remembering. Here attention becomes a real factor in memorisation. Most of our difficulties arise not from a faulty memory but from too little ADA.

My memory and...
my food on the stove

Who has never forgotten a pot that is cooking on the stove? In case your attention is demanded elsewhere at the crucial moment when you need to switch off the stove, take the precaution of setting your timer as soon as you place any pan on the ring.

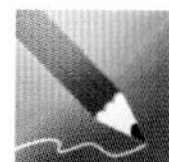

The map of the neighbourhood

Look carefully at this map for one minute. You have to replace the shops and administrative services on a blank map. Train your attention by formulating what you can see.

Example: the baker is next door to the grocer; the two are situated top left on the map.

Now cover the labelled map and put your own labels onto the blank one below.

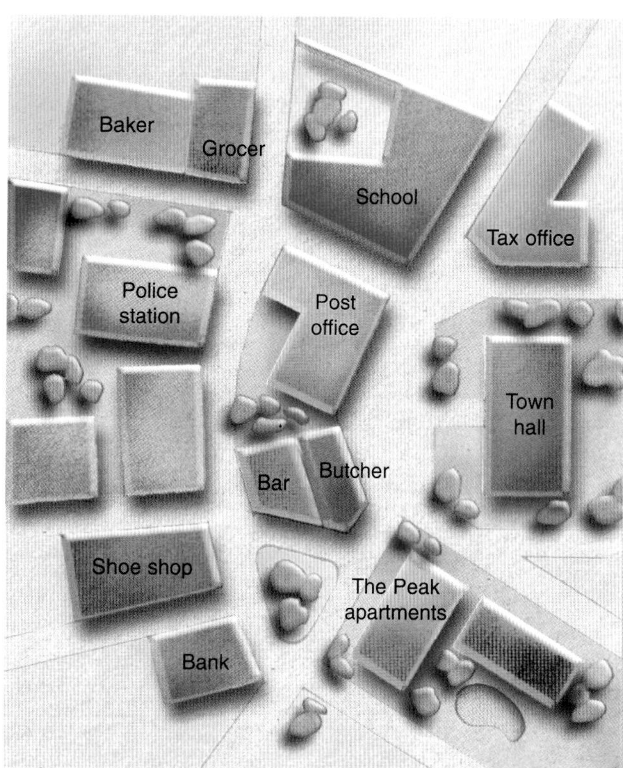

The right place

These three exercises of increasing difficulty will demand all your attention. You are required to identify forms and colours (the number of squares, the number of triangles, etc.) and locate them on the blank grid. You will remember their positions more easily if you can find and formulate some underlying principle of organisation.

1. Look carefully at the grid below. You have three minutes to memorise these geometric shapes. Make use of their position on the games board and/or the figures that they make. Then cover the grid on the left and fill in the shapes on the grid on the right.

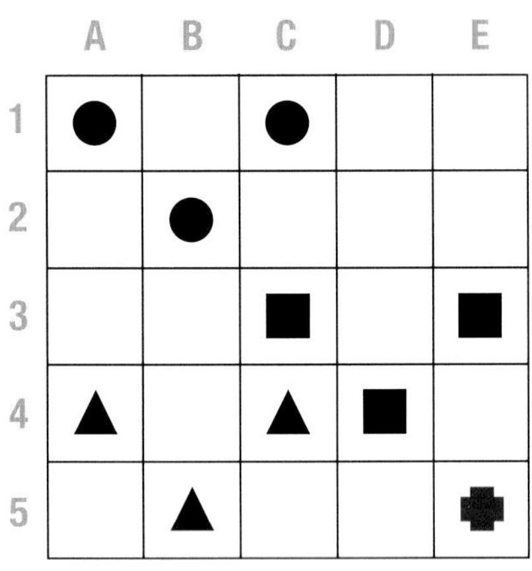

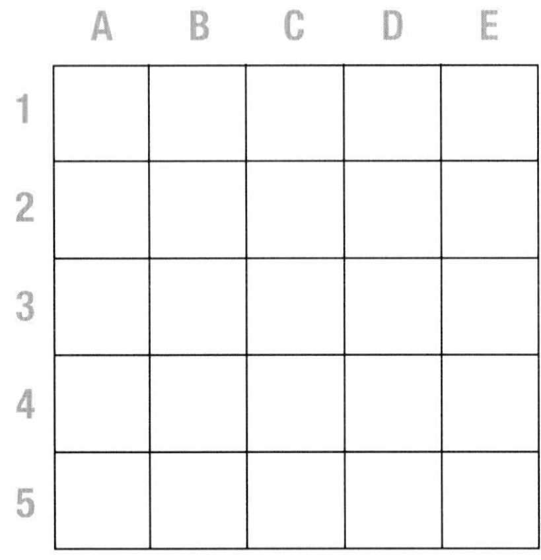

2. This exercise is identical. You must memorise the shapes in three minutes, but this time the basic grid is diamond-shaped and you can no longer use digits and numbers to help you remember their position.

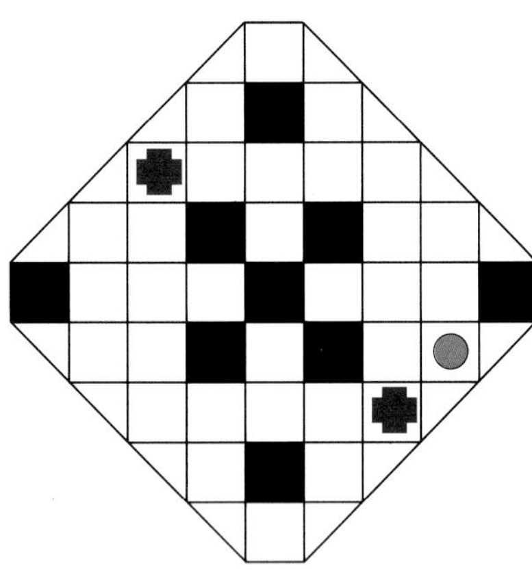

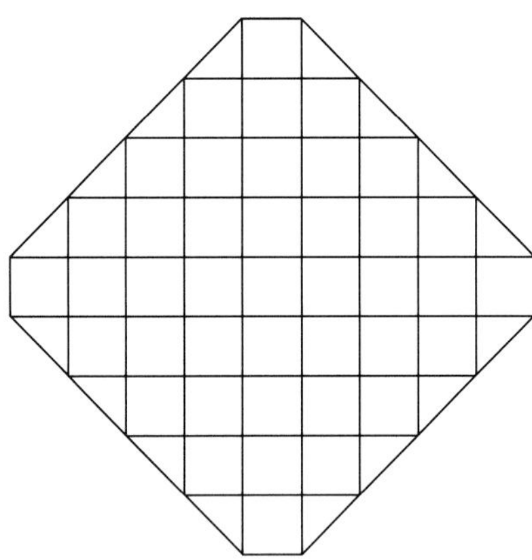

3. The exercise is even more complicated because it is made up of circles. Take as much time as you need.

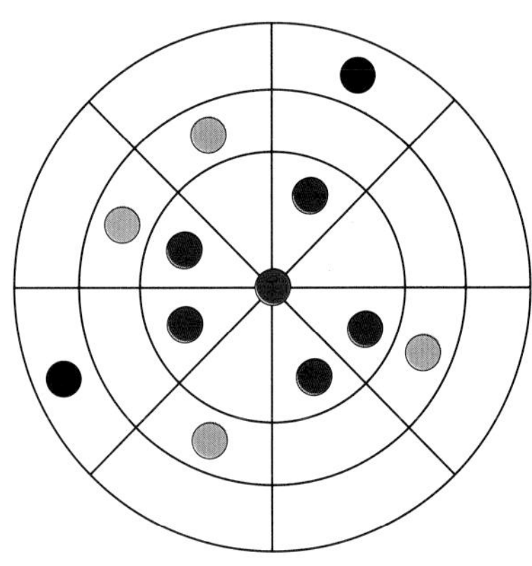

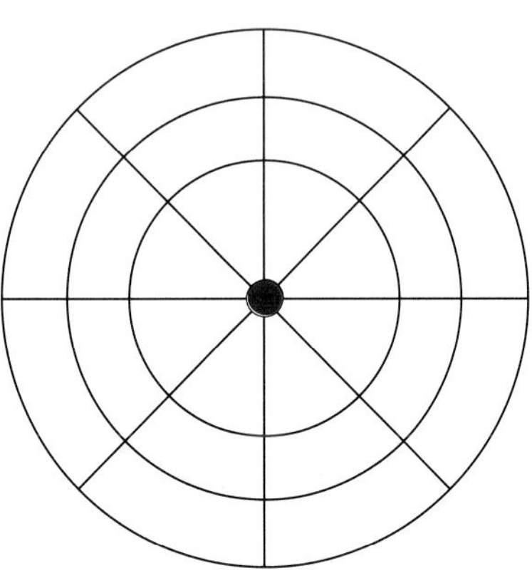

Life-long attentiveness

It's useless trying to pay attention if I can't stop and rest!

We all have our own techniques or recipes for keeping our attention in an alert state, with greater or lesser degrees of success. Fatigue, stress or mild depression can, however, make you lose confidence. And when you reach a mature age you can from time to time have the impression that you are left behind by the sheer volume of technological progress and development in the world. This is when you start agonising about your inability to adapt quickly enough. Your capacity for paying attention seems to be failing you. Is your memory under threat?

Sound self-knowledge – knowing your own pace, when you are most alert, your ability to concentrate and your preferences and limitations, as well as being aware of the different stages of attention – is the best way to maintain high levels of attentiveness throughout life. Imagine the **three stages of attention** as a roller-coaster: a rapid, keen rise in attention levels, stimulated by the factors mentioned above; the high point of the attention span, when it is intensely active for a certain time, and then the fall in attention as

Thread these beads

Look at these 11 beads. You must remember both what they look like and where they are positioned.

Advice: This exercise is very difficult if you don't find a way of making some kind of sense of the way the beads are threaded. Each bead can, for example, represent an object (bead 1: viewfinder of a camera; bead 2: a bowling ball; bead 3: wheel; bead 4: hailstone; bead 5: cat's eye; bead 6: ball of red thread, etc) which can feature in a story: the camera viewfinder was damaged by a bowling ball as round as a wheel and as cold as a hailstone. But suddenly a cat that was playing with a ball of red thread ...

fatigue sets in. A phase of rest follows (from a few seconds to several minutes) before the cycle is set in motion again.

With advancing age, stress or fatigue, your attention needs **longer and more frequent phases of rest** to be as good as before. To reactivate your attention, detach yourself from the object under review so that you can take it up again more successfully with renewed resources later. Doing several things at once also becomes more difficult as you get older because you are more susceptible to distraction (see p.142) and your brain is saturated more quickly.

My memory and...
where I parked my car

Enormous underground or open-air car parks can be like a veritable maze. Never leave your car in a hurry, without taking your bearings (the colour of the floor, the number of your parking space, your position opposite the entrance or the exit, any billboards ...). Notice on which level or in which part of the parking garage you have parked your car (2nd underground, level 1, west park ...). And if this information is not directly accessible, ask someone in the vicinity. Finally, if you have misgivings, note the number of your place on the ticket or on a piece of paper.

Golden rules to ensure lively attention

To retain your self-confidence while accepting that you are growing older, it would be useful to remember some sound principles.

- **Remain alert.** To do this, keep an open mind and be ready to learn something new. And when you have to register new information, make an effort to rid yourself of all intrusive worries so that you can concentrate better.
- **Keep up your interests and curiosity in a number of areas.** No age limit applies here. Nothing is uninteresting in itself; it's up to you to decide whether or not to find it interesting. Giving up certain interests does not imply lapsing into a state of indifference. But you must find others to replace them and maintain your faculties in an alert state.
- **Make plans and carry them out.** Any project enables you to develop or progress, and gives life a meaning, even if it changes or develops into something else, or does not come off. This always motivates you to be attentive because it keeps you open to the outside world.
- **Maintain or create stimulating new contacts with others.** You can stimulate your attention considerably by keeping up a good network of social relations. Selecting one or two centres of interest that involve meeting other people is also a good way to create new networks that are just as stimulating.
- **Communicate, and pass on information.** Sharing with others something you have remembered, learned or experienced needs mental preparation. This, together with the desire to convey something to others, is a good way to stimulate your attention and your memory.

Take all the time you need to find a strategy and then cover the beads.

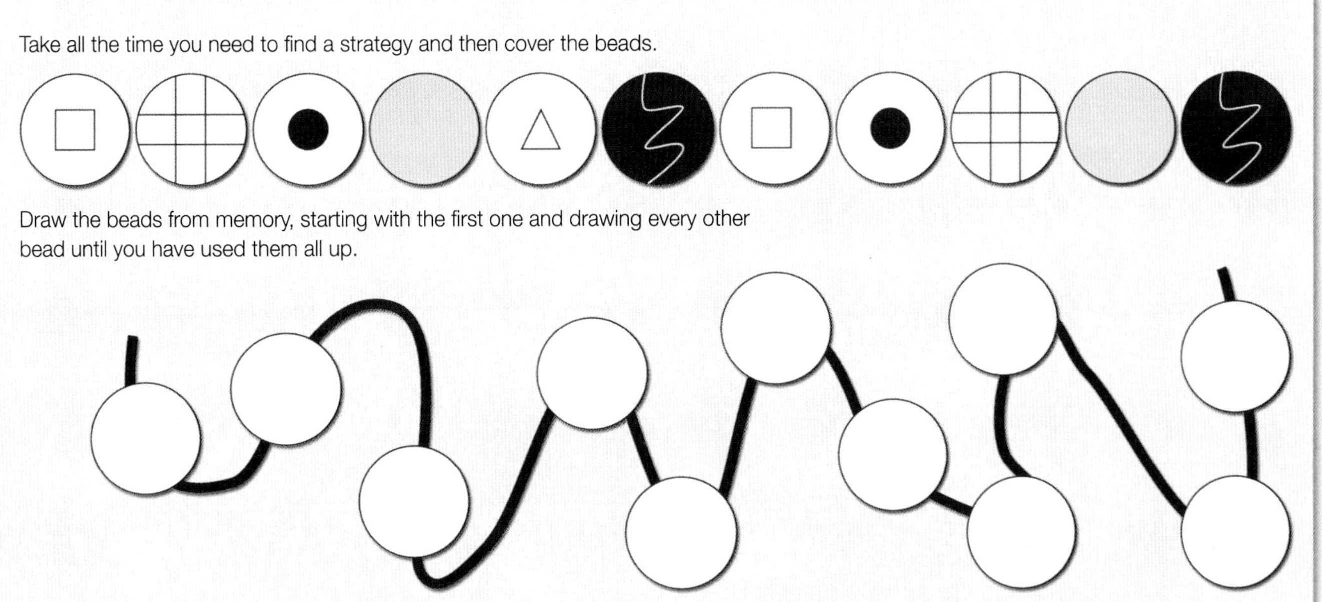

Draw the beads from memory, starting with the first one and drawing every other bead until you have used them all up.

Attention and concentration

Certain activities demanding great manual precision or deep, careful consideration need your full concentration. As soon as you lose concentration, you lose the thread of what you had started working on and might even have to start all over again. What exactly is concentration, and what is the link between concentration and attention? Is it an ability you can develop or improve?

Paying attention is not enough

If I am really concentrating, the sky could fall on my head and I wouldn't notice!

Concentration is vital whenever a task – whether physical or mental – demands a certain effort on your part. Attention and concentration are closely linked. To define **concentration**, you could say that it is **the most intense form of attention.** You have to pay attention to achieve real concentration. So attention always precedes concentration.

On the other hand, you can pay attention to an item of information without necessarily concentrating on it to the exclusion of all else. So, for example, you can listen attentively to a conversation and be aware of what is going on around you.

A student studying course material needs to pay attention to what he or she is reading but also needs to concentrate to retain all the information for a long time. As for really top-class sportsmen and -women, they are able to concentrate so intently on what they are doing that they attain a state of detachment from everything around them, from any auditory, visual or tactile distractions.

Concentration span, like attention, **varies from one person to another.** It depends on biological conditions, the time of day, your mental and physical wellbeing, what is happening in your life and most especially on how interested you are in completing the task or project .

In addition, you need to consider the part played by your habits of concentration. Some people will be used to concentrating for long periods in a noisy environment, whereas others need peace and quiet. But you can change your habits and learn to concentrate in almost any conditions.

Despite these variations, **everyone can improve their ability to concentrate** by spending a little more time on each task. This rather more specific kind of exercise is more gratifying, of course, when the activity is a pleasant one. Don't forget that if you have neither interest nor motivation, failure is never far off. When the task in itself is unappealing, you must find some kind of positive motivation or even promise yourself a reward – one square of chocolate if you are a chocoholic trying to lose weight, for example – in order to encourage yourself to concentrate on the task at hand.

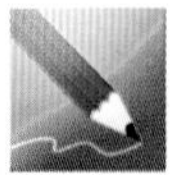

Reading and colour

Do these three exercises from left to right.
Concentrate hard and try to play as quickly as possible.

Say the colours of these fruit drops aloud.

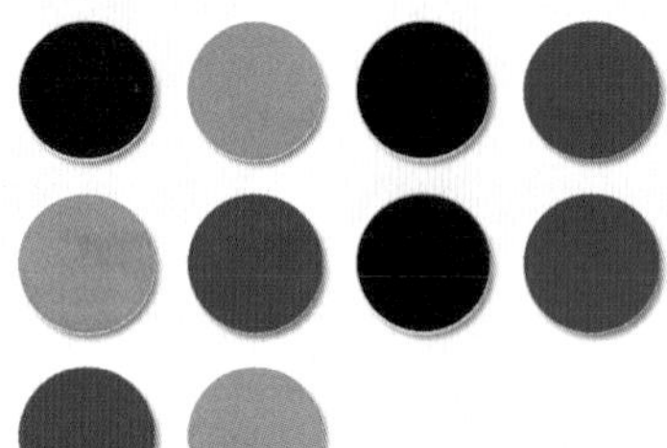

Read the following words aloud.

Blue Red Green Red
Green Blue Red Blue
Red Green Blue Green
Red Red Blue

Say aloud what colour the following words are.

Red Green Blue Green
Green Blue Red Blue
Green Red Blue Red
Green Blue Blue

You probably found the last exercise particularly difficult. This is because it brings together two contradictory kinds of information: one from reading the words and the other from recognising the colours.

The first is processed by the left side of the brain, whereas the second is processed by the right side of the brain. Reading can happen automatically, as advertisers understand only too well. So, you will first read the word (red, for example) before perceiving and verbalising the colour of the ink (green). And you have to make a great effort of concentration and attention to stop the first item of 'read' information from imposing itself. If you really concentrate you will be able to perform this exercise more and more quickly.

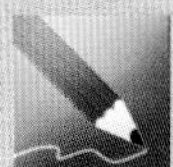

Searching for small words

In the following text by Lewis Carroll, an extract from *Alice's Adventures in Wonderland*, circle all the commas, cross out the definite and indefinite articles (the, a) and underline the co-ordinating conjunctions.

(,) ~~the~~ but

'Get to your places!' shouted the Queen, in a voice of thunder, and people began running about in all directions, tumbling up against each other; however, they got settled down in a minute or two, and the game began. Alice thought she had never seen such a curious croquet ground in her life; it was all ridges and furrows; the croquet balls were live hedgehogs, and the mallets live flamingoes, and the soldiers had to double themselves up and stand on their hands and feet, to make the arches.

The chief difficulty Alice found at first was in managing her flamingo: she succeeded in getting its body tucked away, comfortably enough, under her arm, with its legs hanging down, but generally, just as she had got its neck nicely straightened out, and was going to give the hedgehog a blow with its head, it *would* twist itself round and look up into her face with such a puzzled expression that she could not help bursting out laughing: and when she had got its head down, and was going to begin again, it was very provoking to find that the hedgehog had unrolled itself, and was in the act of crawling away: besides all this, there was generally a ridge or furrow in the way wherever she wanted to send the hedgehog to, and, as the doubled-up soldiers were always getting up and walking off to other parts of the ground, Alice came to the conclusion that it was a very difficult game indeed.

The players all played at once without waiting for turns, quarrelling all the while, and fighting for the hedgehogs; and in a very short time the Queen was in a furious passion, and went stamping about, and shouting, 'Off with his head!' or 'Off with her head!' about once a minute.

Alice began to feel very uneasy: to be sure she had not as yet had any dispute with the Queen, but she knew that it might happen any minute, 'and then,' thought she, 'what would become of me? They're dreadfully fond of beheading people here; the great wonder is, that there's any one left alive!'

She was looking about for some way of escape, and wondering whether she could get away without being seen, when she noticed a curious appearance in the air: it puzzled her very much at first, but after watching it a minute or two she made it out to be a grin, and she said to herself, 'It's the Cheshire Cat: now I shall have somebody to talk to.'

'How are you getting on?' said the Cat, as soon as there was mouth enough for it to speak with.

Solution p.334

Like the exercise in shapes, below, it is easier to proceed in stages: circle the commas, then strike through the articles and finally underline the conjunctions. When you carry out these three tasks simultaneously, line by line, it creates a break in your automatic search, which decreases your concentration.

Watch those shapes!

This exercise, which demands great precision, brings both attention and concentration into play.

1. Examine all the signs pictured here.
2. Then, as quickly as possible,

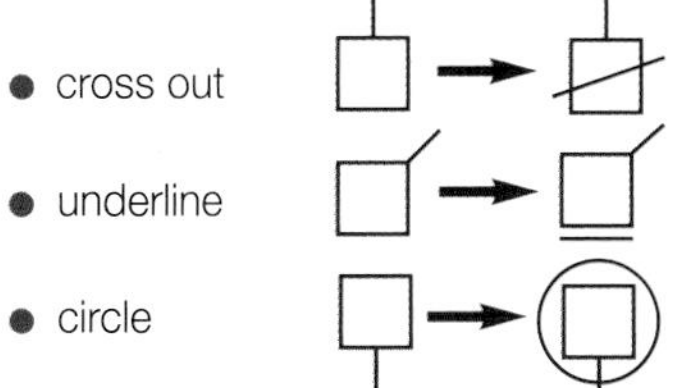

3. Count each kind of sign. You can do this in three stages.

Solution p.334

My memory and... crosswords

Crosswords are an excellent form of solitary entertainment and a good way to get your own personal dictionary working. Regular practice will promote mental fluency, and you will find words coming ever more freely to mind. Filling that grid as quickly as possible is not, therefore, the aim of the game. Do crosswords that are right for your level, and instead of getting stuck on a word you are sure you know, continue, pausing regularly for a few seconds to revitalise your attention.

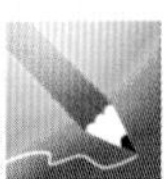

A kitchen under the microscope

1. Look carefully at this picture for 30 seconds and then cover it.

2. Now answer the following questions

1. How many bottles are on the shelf above the refrigerator?

2. What dish is being cooked in the oven?

3. What is the time shown on the clock?

4. How many fridge magnets are there on the refrigerator door?

5. Can you make coffee in this kitchen? What utensils would you use?

6. How many windows are there in the room?

7. What objects are lying on the table beside the fruit bowl?

8. What colour is the oven glove?

9. There is a pot on the gas stove: what colour is it?

The pull of the black hole

Find the only path connecting the two arrows. You may not take two crossroads of the same colour successively.

The maze is another classic game testing visual attentiveness and concentration. It is difficult to complete the puzzle if you are interrupted while in progress. You will not be able to memorise a maze, but the more mazes you do, the more proficient you will become. This is a special form of mental gymnastics, in which, like all forms of gymnastics, you will achieve better results the more you practise.

Solution p.334

Odd one out

1. Look at these fruits for 30 seconds and then cover them.

2. Which of the nine fruits is the odd one out? *Solution p.334*

My memory and... video games

Video games, which have for a long time been disparaged by teachers and parents, are now considered a good tool for developing and maintaining a child's visual concentration – in moderation. The army also uses video games for this purpose. And more and more adults are devoting their time to this pastime! But video games provide a refuge from the stress of life and they can become addictive. Some players become almost hypnotised and their lives become focused on these games. They tend to ignore their fundamental needs for sleep and food, for example, become irritable and lose their ability to interact with others.

Dining with friends

Three couples get together to organise an evening with friends. As there will be many guests, they have decided to share the work of preparing or buying the various items for the meal. You have to determine who will be preparing what.

In each horizontal row, the number on the left indicates how many of the dishes will be prepared by the cooks, and the figure on the right tells you how many of these dishes are recorded under the name of the right person.

Don't do this logigram if you are tired, because it needs sustained concentration. Choose a time when you feel relaxed and can think clearly. And, most especially, take time to understand, analyse and organise your ideas. You might want to note them down on a piece of paper.

	Vincent	Laura	Paul	Sophie	Matthew	Charlotte	
2	chocolate eclairs	roast beef	salad	apple tart	soufflé	courgette gratin	0
2	lamb stew	ratatouille	roast beef	asparagus	apple tart	grilled cheese	0
1	apple tart	bruschetta	soufflé	meat pie	courgette gratin	roast beef	1
2	courgette gratin	couscous	soufflé	roast beef	chocolate eclairs	apple tart	2
0	cake	soup	mashed potatoes	meat pie	macaroni cheese	ratatouille	0
2	asparagus	apple tart	salad	couscous	courgette gratin	sweets	2
1	soup	cake	macaroni cheese	grilled cheese	mashed potatoes	ratatouille	1
3	couscous	lamb stew	sweets	asparagus	chicken	mashed potatoes	0

Solution p.334

The letter chase

Change one letter in each of these words so that each new vertical column has a group of words on the same theme (one theme per series).

Set 1		Set 2	
CARE	....	BIND	....
DISH	....	ALOUD	....
SOCKS	....	PLANT	....
LATER	....	GUN	....
BENCH	....	MOAN	....

Solution p.334

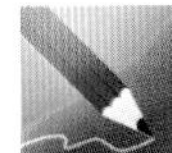

Close-up

Identify the person, animal or object our designer has had fun transforming.

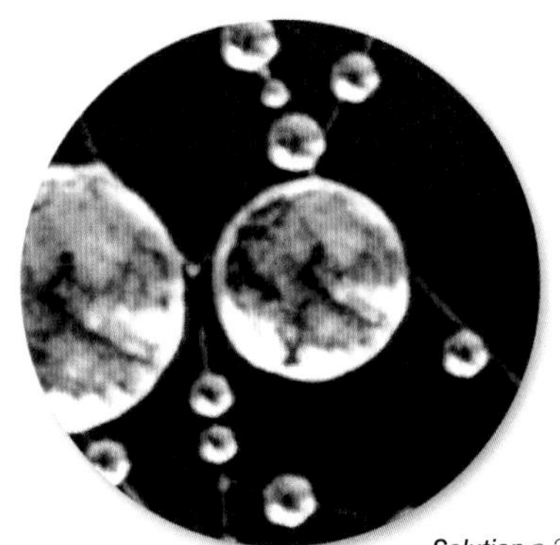

Solution p.334

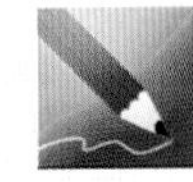

Caterpillar

Move from one word to the next by replacing the letters indicated and changing the order of the letters.

	CAPABLE
- B + S	....
- A + U	....
- P + S	....
- L + R	....
- C + D	....
- R + M	....
- U + A	....
- D + G	....
- A + E	MESSAGE

Solution p.334

Family problems

1. Read this little family history very attentively.

Luke and Jean had six children: Mary, Antoinette, Alexander, Paul, Caroline and Bernard.
Mary married Hugh, and they had three children: Christine, Michael and Andrew. Christine in her turn produced two children, Michael had one, and Andrew four.
Antoinette didn't marry but she had two daughters, who gave birth to five little boys.
Alexander had twins with Lisa, one of whom fathered a daughter called Charlene, like Paul. Caroline, a mother three times over, is also a grandmother of three. She will be a great grandmother within a few months. As for Bernard, he has just become a great grandfather for the seventh time. This is makes him very happy, as he has only two children and two grandchildren.
To the great regret of some people, the great-grandchildren of Luke and Jean have at present produced only twice as many children as all their parents combined.

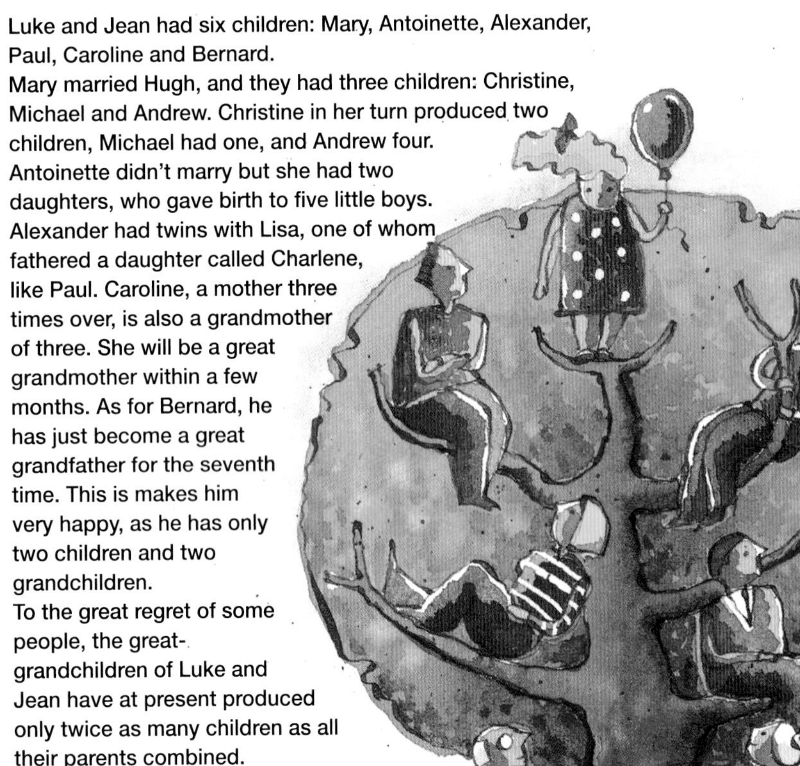

2. Reread the text so that you understand and can remember all the lines of descent. You could draw a family tree to help you visualise it all clearly.

3. Now work out how many children there are in each generation:
- that of Luke and Jean's children;
- that of their grandchildren;
- that of their great-grandchildren;
- and finally, that of their great-great-grandchildren.

Solution p.334

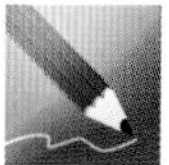

No real concentration without relaxation

This is an exercise using visualisation that will help you reach a calm, relaxed state by concentrating on a candle flame. Creating a mental image of the flame slows down the influx of distracting thoughts and enables you to attain a sense of wellbeing and awareness of your body.

Absorb the text below as thoroughly as you can because this will enable you to go through all the stages without having to open your eyes. Otherwise, you may lose the benefit afforded by complete relaxation.

Prepare yourself

1. Settle down in a quiet place, where you feel comfortable.

2. Light a candle and place it about one metre in front of you. Sit cross-legged on the floor (put a small cushion under you if necessary) or on a chair, in a comfortable position, your back straight against the back of the chair and your legs apart and relaxed.

If the seated position isn't comfortable straight away, stretch out on the floor first for five minutes if conditions permit. Close your eyes and call to mind each part of your body in turn so that you can then relax that part. Breathe calmly and deeply while you work your way through your whole body.

Relax

3. Remain in this position, with your eyes closed, for several minutes, being aware of your body and its stability. Be aware of the rhythm of your breathing, which becomes more calm and regular.

4. Now focus on the flame. If your thoughts try to move in other directions, bring them slowly back to the flame. Relax your facial muscles.

5. Close your eyes slowly.

6. Breathe deeply, paying attention to your breathing, and feel your stomach rising and falling as you inhale and exhale. This abdominal breathing encourages relaxation.

Take your time breathing in and out slowly, and let yourself slip into this regular rhythm as though you're being rocked on the waves. Repeat silently to yourself 'I am calm, I am relaxing', until you feel completely calm. If you still feel some tension in your muscles, make use of this rhythmic breathing to help you relax them. Feel a sense of calmness flow into you.

Concentrate

7. Conjure up in your mind a picture of the flame. Remain focused on its never-ending movements. It occupies your whole mind. It is as though you are hypnotised by its dancing motion and by its colours. When a thought comes to mind again, let it come, then let it be consumed by the flame.

8. Let the flame come closer, approaching your face, look at it again and feel its warmth spreading though you. Keep in contact with these sensations, in a silent inner calmness.

Loosen up

As soon as you feel weary, or thoughts enter your mind once again, let the mental image of the flame fade away. Start moving your muscles and your limbs slowly, one by one. Stretch slowly, yawn if you want to, and finally open your eyes again

Make use of this exercise whenever you feel the need to relax and you can slip away to a quiet place. If you aren't used to this type of exercise, set aside 15 minutes. With a little practice you will experience the feeling of relaxation more profoundly and you will spend more time doing this exercise. **The sense of calm relaxation it achieves will promote good concentration.**

Imagination, the source of memory

Your imagination is involved in every act of memorisation, because it is the source of all your mental images. Its creative power is expressed further in the efficient way it uses resources stored in your memory while also basing its activities on a good grasp of reality. But it can also be influenced by your desires and frustrations. So be careful of giving free rein to the uncontrolled imagination – it can lead you off course, into errors of judgement and disappointment!

The imagination feeds on memory

When I imagine, I draw from my memory

This is how the 18th-century French writer, Voltaire, defined the imagination: 'It is the power every sentient being knows he possesses to represent concrete objects within his mind. This faculty depends on the memory. We see people, animals, gardens: we receive these perceptions through our senses; our memory retains them; our imagination puts them together.'

Modern psychology confirms this view. Your imagination contributes to the formation of mental images that feed your memory. It is said to have a **reproductive function**, in that it draws on previous remembered experiences. But it also has a **creative function** in that it rearranges stored data to generate new combinations, or it transforms images derived from past experiences to create completely new connections. In short, it works on the **material already stored in the memory** but is capable of **completely new creations**: when you conjure up an unknown animal in your imagination, you are putting together certain features belonging to animals you are already familiar with.

So the really creative imagination requires, first, a sound perception of data, then a well-stocked memory, the ability to call up easily and quickly any of this store of information, and finally the power to produce really innovative combinations. And this creative power is still grounded in **the effective organisation of knowledge stored in the memory**. In science, a hypothesis can lead to a discovery only if it is based on a careful analysis of observed phenomena and a mastery of existing knowledge. In politics, it is essential to have a good understanding of the present in order to form a vision for the future and implement a plan of action. This ability to **project future developments from a present situation** underlies the most significant new interventions.

A masterpiece of the imagination results not only from bringing together diverse materials but also from **combining them to create a new 'truth'**.

Exercise your sensory memory

- **Touch:** relive the sensations produced by a texture that you like, as if you were touching it; do the same with a texture you dislike. Note your impressions.
- **Hearing:** imagine, or recreate in your mind, words spoken by another person. Note what you feel.
- **Sight:** choose a story that has impressed you and visualise certain scenes from it.
- **Smell:** select a perfume or a smell that you like and relive the sensations the fragrance arouses in you as though it filled your nostrils.
- **Taste:** think of dishes you have never tasted and try to imagine the taste they might have. It would be best to have the chance to taste them subsequently!

The imagination is always based on some sensory activity. Well-honed perception makes memorisation more effective and enhances the power of evocation.

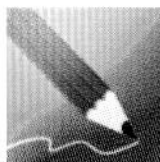

Play at being creative
Conjure up a mental image of each of these objects, their shapes, colours, etc. Become a potter, cabinet-maker, fashion designer, florist or graphic artist. Don't hesitate to vary the combinations of elements to arrive at different images. You could also draw them if you like.

A teapot

A chair

A dress

A bouquet of flowers

A book cover

A flying machine

If the creators of these items were to produce them as real objects, their creativity would not be expressed only in juxtaposing the different elements they have available in their memory. If they took, for example, the shape of the back of one chair, the style of the legs of another, and the seat dimensions of a third, they would not necessarily end up with a chair you could sit on! It's by making use of their know-how and experience in the way they combine them that they could really create a new chair which would be an expression of their imagination.

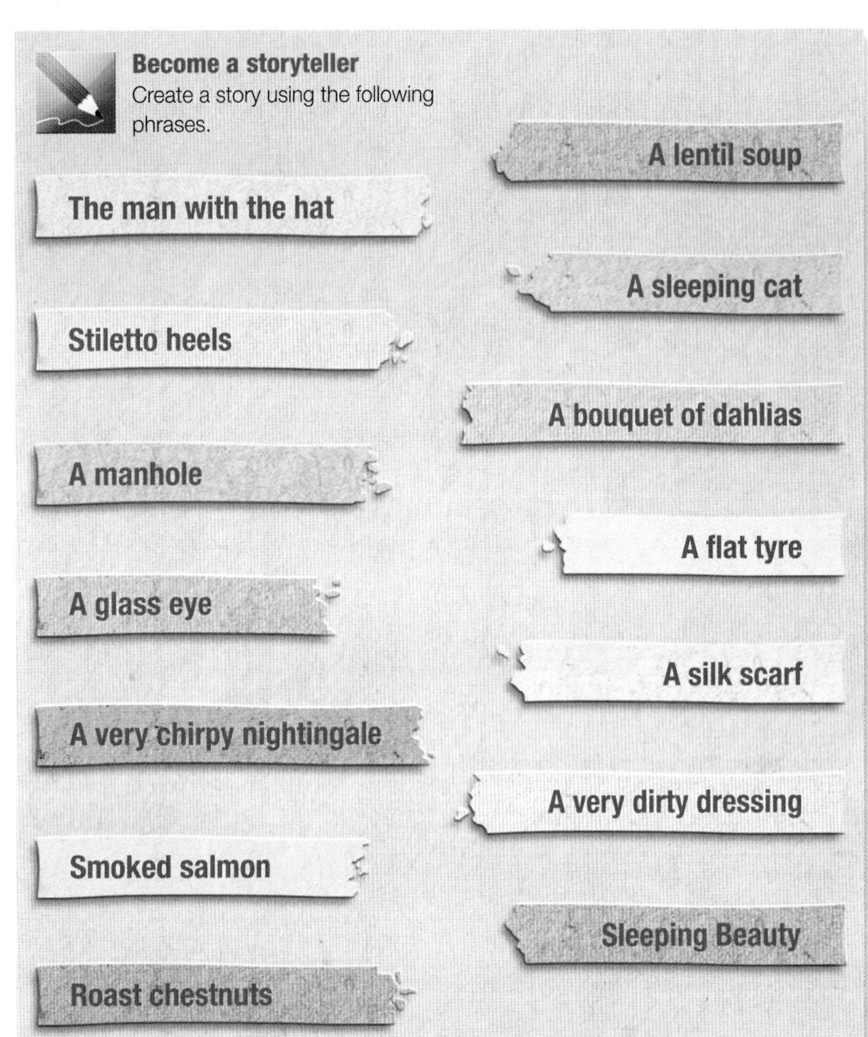

The free flights of the imagination

'The lunatic, the lover, and the poet
Are of imagination all compact.'

The power of the imagination is not the sole preserve of great creators, artists or inventors. The child who fantasises, the adolescent who dreams of the future, the reader who visualises the heroes and the setting of a novel … all are using their imagination. Reading (which encourages your mind to roam freely and conjure up rich mental images of a variety of characters, landscapes or atmosphere), writing and your interest in and curiosity about the world around you, all stimulate the productive activity of the imagination. But your creations of the imaginary world are also fed by your desires, your fantasies and your frustrations. Imagining always implies a perception of the incompleteness of the real world as well as the possibility of devising new versions that could be more satisfying because they would correspond more closely to your wishes. This explains why reality often disappoints your expectations, as in the case of the screen adaptation of a novel, a meeting with someone you have only ever corresponded with, or any other situation which is first imagined and then materialises.

This compensatory role of the imagination, which could well incite you to action, also has its drawbacks – an evasion of reality and a certain indulgence in living in a dream world. Your imagination can play tricks on you, falsify perception and lead you to mistake your fantasies for reality. The unbridled imagination is thus a source of illusion and disappointment. It can end up by falsifying or distorting reality, as can be seen in cases of daydreaming, madness and mythomania (compulsive fabrication).

My memory and… stories

Stories are a vital source of nourishment for the imagination. Children are very fond of them and easily project themselves into their own tales. Adults probably tend not to tell themselves stories to the same extent, because it is important for them to be more firmly rooted in reality. But inventing stories for young children – constructing a plot, embellishing it with anecdotes and bringing the characters to life – is a good way to stimulate your memory and imagination.

Imaginary drawing

At first glance, this drawing seems incomprehensible. What do you see in it? Give an explanation in about 10 lines.

When we are confronted with images without an immediately recognisable meaning, we delve into our imagination for the answers. What we then see – or believe we see – reveals not only our habitual mode of feeling, thinking and acting, but also what we have previously felt and experienced, or even our subconscious. The way our imagination works reveals what we are. Psychologists thus make use of visual aids – pictures, photos and diverse documents – through which individuals can project themselves as they think they are and the way others behave, or ought to behave, towards them. These tests using projection are designed to help understand the personality of individuals, their stability and way of understanding their behaviour. The Rorschach inkblot test is the most famous test using projection.

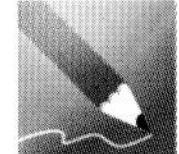

The island tower

Make up a story of about 15 sentences based on this picture. Do the exercise on your own or with others.

Why do we all formulate different stories? Because we each have our own perception of reality, our own wishes and fears, our own personal emotions and changing moods.

The theme of the image itself is not necessarily a source of inspiration: you must be able to identify with what you imagine about it and project yourself into the story for your imagination to generate rich associations in the mind.

The Lady is a Tramp

Read carefully the words of this song made famous by Frank Sinatra, while mentally visualising the story that is being told. Imagine the person of the Lady, the way she looks, the way she behaves. Make her come alive in your imagination. Write a portrait of her in a few lines and, if you'd like, draw her.

She gets too hungry
For dinner at eight.
She likes the theatre
And never comes late
She'd never bother
With people she'd hate
That's why the lady is a tramp

Doesn't like crap games
With barons and earls.
Won't go to Harlem
In ermine and pearls.
Won't dish the dirt
With the rest of those girls.
That's why the lady is a tramp.

She loves the free fresh
wind in her hair
Life without care
She's broke and it's OK
Hates California,
it's cold and it's damp
That's why the lady is a tramp.

She gets too hungry
For dinner at eight
She loves the theatre
But never comes late
She'd never bother
With people she'd hate
That's why the lady is a tramp.

Doesn't like dice games
With sharpies and frauds
Won't go to Harlem
In Lincolns or Fords
Won't dish the dirt
With the rest of those broads
That's why the lady is a tramp

She loves the free fresh
wind in her hair
Life without care
She's broke but it's oke
Hates California,
it's cold and it's damp
That's why the lady,
That's why the lady
That's why the lady is a tramp

(by Richard Rodgers and Lorenz Hart)

In cases where you can't lean on a memorised visual support (that's to say an element that you have already seen), the imagination makes up for the gap by creating a mental image. It is often like this when you regularly hear of someone without ever seeing him or her. The appearance that you imagine may be very far from reality. In the absence of an exact perception or of the knowledge of ideas, the imagination is often the source of errors and prejudice.

Exercise your imagination frequently

Imagining can help me find a solution to my problems

We know children have plenty of imagination. Think of the excuses they sometimes fabricate to get themselves out of trouble! They also find this faculty useful when creating imaginary worlds, where they integrate and transform elements drawn from reality in a harmonious new mixture, sometimes to the extent that they can no longer distinguish the real from the false.

Generally speaking, the adult world relegates the imagination to the world of childhood. The Western rationalist tradition, particularly, is suspicious and readily critical of the creations of the imagination – that 'mistress of error and falsity', according to the French philosopher Pascal – which, by deflecting us from the world as it is, may make us ineffectual.

But, by offering us new combinations of elements drawn from the real world, our imagination allows us to project ourselves into the future. It may distract us momentarily from the real world, but it also enables us to return to it with new insight. All of us would benefit from maintaining the inventiveness of childhood through creative games, in order to develop our capacity to find original responses to new problems. It is through creativity that society evolves, develops and makes progress.

The Association of Senior Improvisers, a group of retirees in Montreal, Canada, have discovered an excellent way to preserve and develop the imagination: different workshops – on the imagination, quick thinking and body language – enable them to bring their talent for improvisation to the fore. There are already several teams of six players each who form part of the Association.

Sound effects ...

All the objects and animals given below produce specific sounds. Look for them in your personal bank of sounds, and then imitate them. Here is an example of how sound effects are used in poetry, in an extract from *Summer Remembered*, by the American poet Isabella Gardner:

The pizzicato plinkle of ice in an auburn uncle's amber glass
The whing of father's racquet and the whack
Of brother's bat on cousin's ball
And calling voices calling
Voices spilling voices ...

A chicken – Hot oil in a frying pan

Opening an envelope

A galloping horse – A peacock

A walking stick on a wooden floor – **A kitten**

A farting cushion – A diamond on glass

Paper tearing – A rattle

A Big Wheel at a fair – **A branch breaking**

A fire alarm – A glass breaking on the floor

A door slamming – Footsteps in the snow

An electric toothbrush – **A lawnmower**

This is a game children often play, because their inventiveness is not shackled by convention, nor do they worry much about the opinion of others. Reactivating your spontaneity is a good way to break down the barriers that inhibit your creativity.

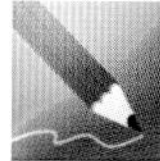

My hymn to love

Imagine the declaration of love a young man might make to the beautiful woman he is in love with. Use the following words:
Heart, always, family, passion, jewel, dream, happiness, princess, wife, forever, pearl, crazy

heart family passion always jewel DREAM happiness crazy princess wife forever PEARL

The feeling of love is held to be a powerful vehicle of the poetic imagination. You have to admit that it's quite a challenge: to seduce someone by surprising him or her, and finding the best ways to express your love. For those who know how to write, words are an infinite source of symbolic, metaphoric and even fantastic associations.

My memory and...
the names of animals

Where exactly do pet owners find the names they give to their dogs and cats? This is a good example of the links between imagination and memory. Although many family pets carry the names of their illustrious precursors (Lassie, Rintintin, Old Yeller, Jock ...), the choice of some other names can be understood only when they are seen as embodying the personal memories or even the subconscious desires of the pets' owners.

Imaginary dialogue

In 10 minutes, complete the following sentences so as to produce a meaningful dialogue.

J: It is thanks to his ....

M: It's not impossible that ....

J: As you like, but I ....

M: Think of your ....**, otherwise**..........

J: With this .... **You'll see, it'll be much better.**

M: If you believe that .... **I'll certainly try.**

J: They went ....**, they have** ....
.... **then** ....

M: Above all, don't add anything more ....

J: I prefer .... **to** ....**of all the colours.**

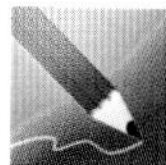

Phrases on demand

Take 10 minutes to imagine each of the following sentences :

- a sentence including **3 words starting with ex- ;**
- a sentence including **2 negatives;**
- a sentence including **3 words starting with imp-.**

Many of us have experienced the blank page syndrome. Our ideas either don't materialise or seem banal, and our vocabulary seems impoverished and ill-suited to express any subtlety of thought.

The more you write using your imagination, the more easily it will be trained and will function when needed. Your writing will show it: your thoughts will flow more easily and you will acquire increased verbal dexterity.

The museum. Study this scene closely and find the characters, animals and objects depicted on the opposite page.

Games booklet 1

MIXED PROVERBS — GENERAL KNOWLEDGE

The words making up three proverbs have been mixed up. Find the original proverbs by sorting out the confused tangle of words below.

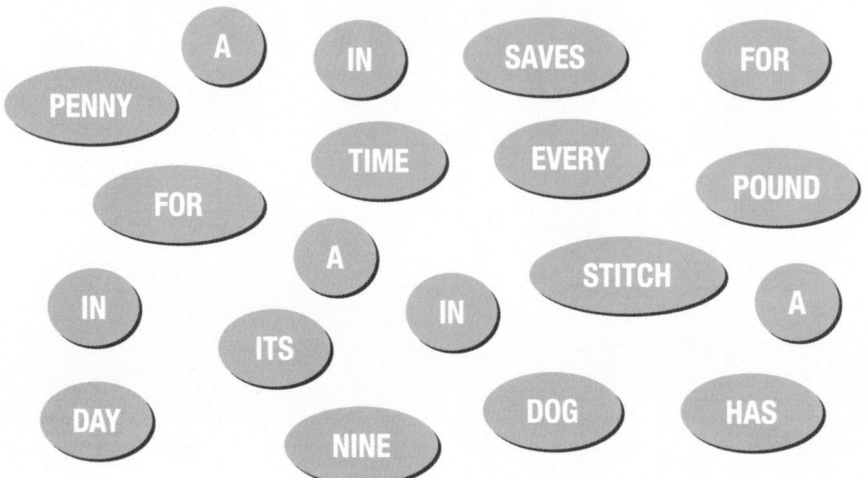

1. ....
....
....

2. ....
....
....

3. ....
....
....

MISSING ADDRESSEES — CONCENTRATION

Look at these envelopes for 30 seconds, then hide them

Amelia Durrant	John Taylor	Vivian Burton
Valerie Singleton	Bernard Routledge	Esther Rose

From memory, write the names of the addressees on the envelopes below, in the order in which they appear above.

NUMBER PYRAMID — LOGIC

Each brick in the pyramid represents the sum of the two bricks just below it. Fill in the rest of the pyramid with the aid of the numbers already in place.

117
☐ ☐
47 ☐ 10
☐ ☐ ☐ ☐
7 ☐ 6 ☐ 2

PROBLEM — LOGIC

Five years ago, my brother was exactly twice the age I was then. And in eight years' time, the combined age of the two of us will be 50. How old do you think I am?

SPOT THE 7 DIFFERENCES

CONCENTRATION

There are seven differences between these two pictures.
Can you find them?

ANAPHRASES

STRUCTURE

Use all the letters indicated in colour to form anagrams that complete the sentence in a way that makes sense.

1. N S O A E C

.... can be paddled on rivers, lakes or ....

2. A N E S T E R

Visitors to .... countries often look in .... for their .... embassy.

3. R O A D A B

Passengers climb .... before going ....

REBUS

ASSOCIATION

Find here the title of an Oscar-winning film.

SHADOWS — SPACE

Which of these shadow shapes represents the mirror image of the character?

PROGRESSIVE QUIZ — GENERAL KNOWLEDGE

Try to go as far as you can in this quiz – it becomes progressively more difficult. Theme: **the sea**.

1. What expression is used to describe someone who can walk steadily on the deck of a ship in motion?

2. What do we call the exceptionally high and exceptionally low tide that occurs twice a month?

3. Which sea, in fact a salt lake, is the largest inland sea in the world?

4. Which sea between Greece and Turkey is named after the father of Theseus, who drowned himself there when he thought his son had been devoured by the Minotaur?

5. The Dead Sea lies 390 m below sea level: true or false?

6. Which canal gave the Mediterranean its pre-eminent position in world navigation?

7. Which sea separates the Arabian Peninsula from the African continent?

8. What is the name given to the horizontal line on a ship's hull that indicates how fully it can be loaded?

9. What is the other name for a paper nautilus?

10. Which sea skirts the east coast of India?

WORD PAIRS — ASSOCIATION

Memorise these six pairs of words for a few minutes. Then cover them and answer the following questions.

Showers – Rain
Letter – Stamp
Sunshade – Sun
Beaver – Dam
House – Residence
Broth – Soup

Questions

1. Which word is Stamp associated with? ....
2. Is the word Umbrella on the list? ....
3. Which word is paired with House? ....
4. Is Letter before or after Dam? ....
5. Which word is associated with Broth? ....
6. Which word is in the plural and which other word is it associated with? ....

LETTER SEQUENCES — LOGIC

Complete the following sequences by studying the relative distances between the letters or their shape.

1. Y V R M .....
2. A E F H I K L M N T .....

HIDDEN WORDS

STRUCTURE

The names of animals hidden in this grid can be discovered in several directions: horizontally or vertically, diagonally, from top to bottom or from bottom to top, from right to left and left to right. The words cross each other and the same letter may be used more than once. With the remaining letters, form the name of a hidden animal.

List of animals to find

AARDVARK	GANNET	KITTEN	RHINO-CEROS
ANTLION	GECKO	LION	SHARK
BUCK	GIRAFFE	MACAW	SKUNK
BULLDOG	GOAT	MINK	SNAKE
CHICK	GORILLA	PIG	TERN
DONKEY	HAMSTER	PONY	WHALE
DUGONG	HIPPO	PUG	
ELEPHANT	HUSKY	PUPPY	
FOAL	HYAENA	REINDEER	

T	A	O	G	M	G	O	D	L	L	U	B
E	F	F	A	R	I	G	U	P	A	R	U
R	E	C	N	C	I	O	E	K	O	H	C
N	A	L	N	P	H	R	N	C	F	I	K
W	R	E	E	D	N	I	E	R	K	N	R
A	G	R	T	P	M	L	C	B	U	O	A
A	N	E	A	Y	H	L	A	K	P	C	V
K	O	T	K	B	I	A	S	O	U	E	D
R	G	S	L	O	P	O	N	O	P	R	R
A	U	M	N	I	P	Y	A	T	P	O	A
H	D	A	N	D	O	N	K	E	Y	S	A
S	W	H	A	L	E	N	E	T	T	I	K

THE RIGHT TIME

LOGIC

Taking into account that two of these watches are a quarter of an hour out and that a third is fast, find the watch giving the right time.

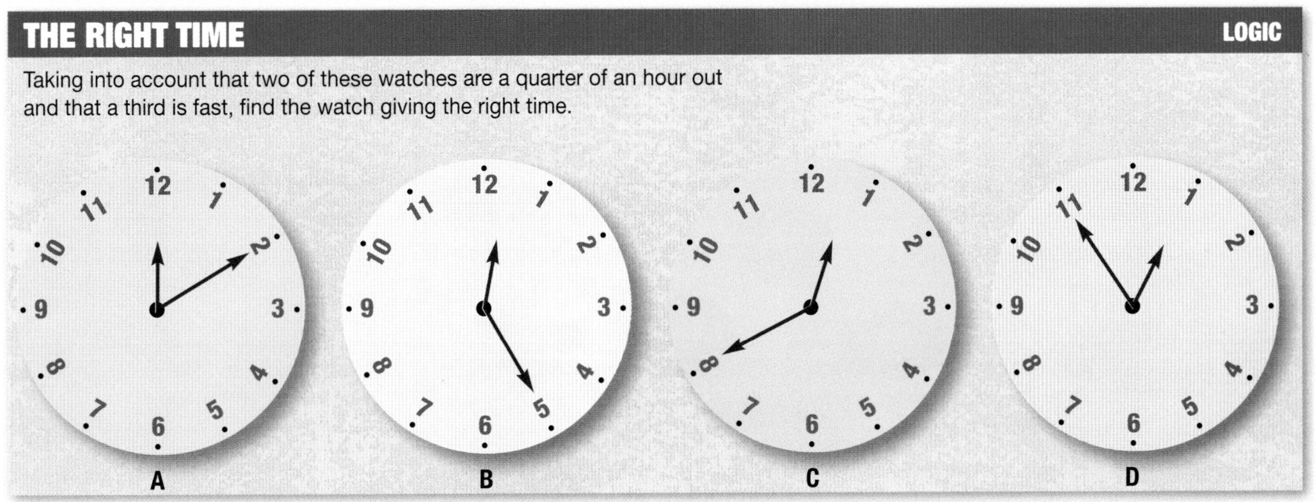

ANAGRAMS

STRUCTURE

Find the floral anagrams of the following words.

PROBLEM

LOGIC

The three scales below are balanced.

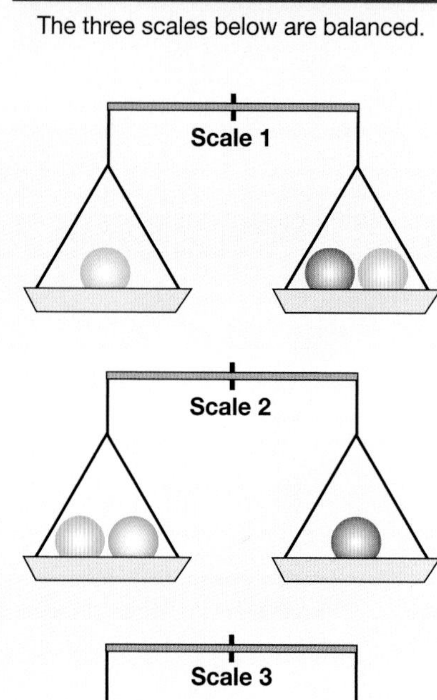

How many yellow balls do you need to place in the left pan to balance the red ball?

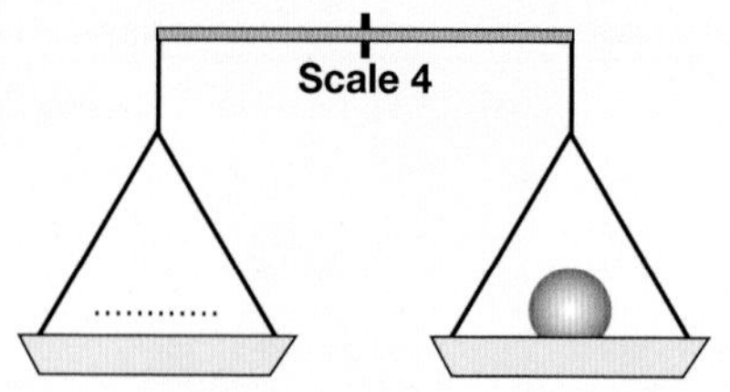

MIXED QUOTES

GENERAL KNOWLEDGE

The words making up three famous quotes have been mixed up. Unscramble the mess and reform the sentences.

DO EVERY HIS AND EXPECTS

DUTY HORSE IT MAN

KINGDOM YET TO FOR

A ENGLAND MOVES MY

1. ....

....

....

2. ....

....

....

3. ....

....

....

HOMOGRAPHS — LANGUAGE

Homographs (from the Greek *homos*, meaning 'similar', and *graphein*, meaning 'write') are words with exactly the same spelling but having a different sense, like badger (to pester) and badger (the animal). Find the homographs that complete the following sentences.

1. The woman with _ _ _ _ _ _ _ hair paid a _ _ _ _ _ _ _ price for entrance to the _ _ _ _ _ _ _ .
2. After trimming the hedges and sweeping up the _ _ _ _ _ _ _ _, the gardener _ _ _ _ _ _ _ _ .
3. Turning _ _ _ _ _ _ _ _ into the main road to reach the highway was the _ _ _ _ _ _ _ _ decision.
4. Because he disliked the intense heat and dryness of the _ _ _ _ _ _ _ _, the soldier decided to _ _ _ _ _ _ _ _ .

ONE TOO MANY — CONCENTRATION

Look at these books for 30 seconds, and then cover them up.

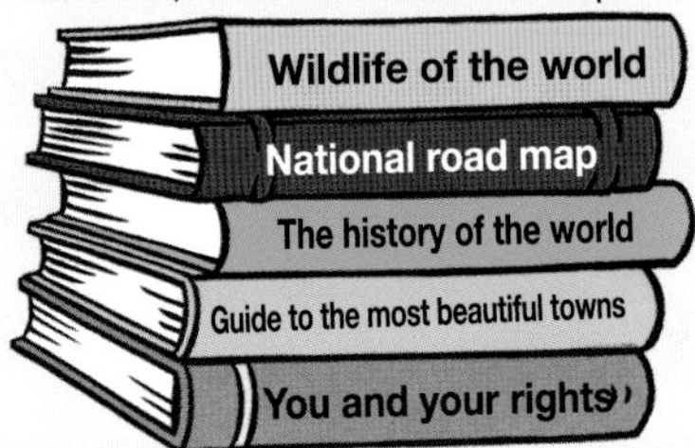

Which one has been added?

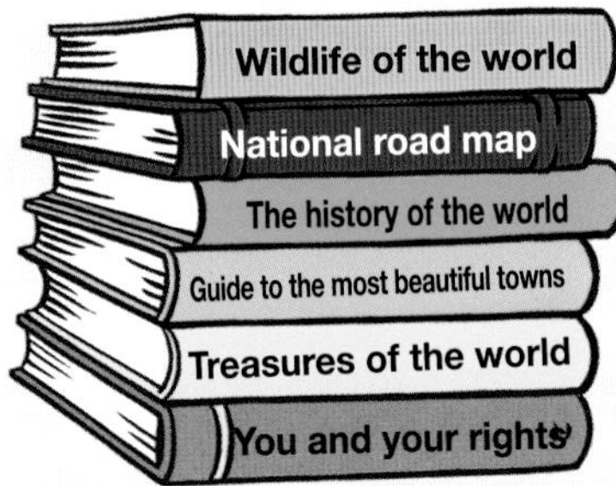

PROBLEM — LOGIC

1. Lawrence and Laura have exactly the same amount of pocket money. How much should Lawrence give Laura so that she will have one dollar more than him?

2. Sacha tells me that she has two coins worth 1,10 dollars in her pocket, and that one is not a 1 dollar coin. It's impossible! Does she think I'm a fool?

STICK-ON WORDS — STRUCTURE

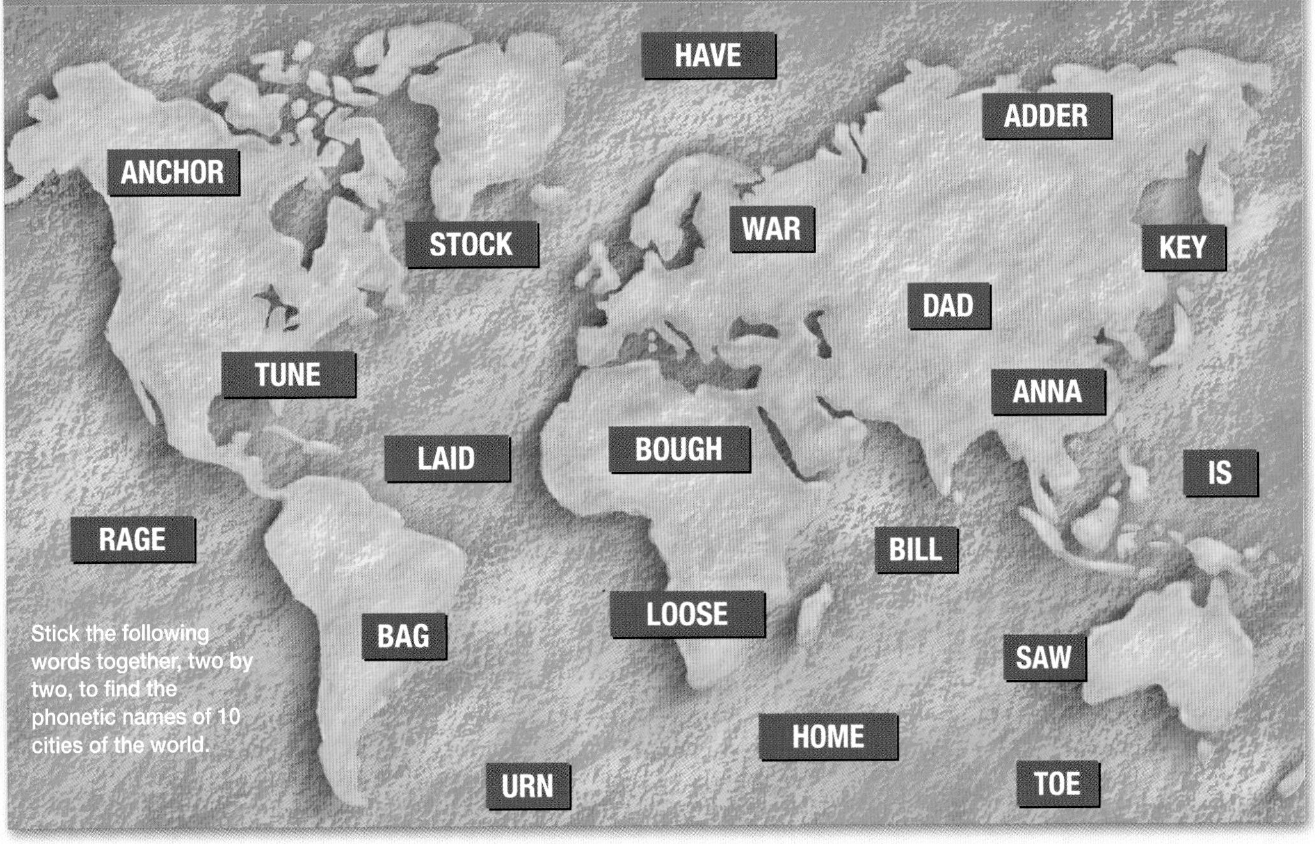

HAVE ADDER ANCHOR STOCK WAR KEY DAD TUNE ANNA LAID BOUGH IS RAGE BILL LOOSE BAG SAW HOME URN TOE

Stick the following words together, two by two, to find the phonetic names of 10 cities of the world.

KNOW YOUR WORLD

SPACE

Find 20 of the states that make up the United States, using the following clues and the locations as marked on the map.

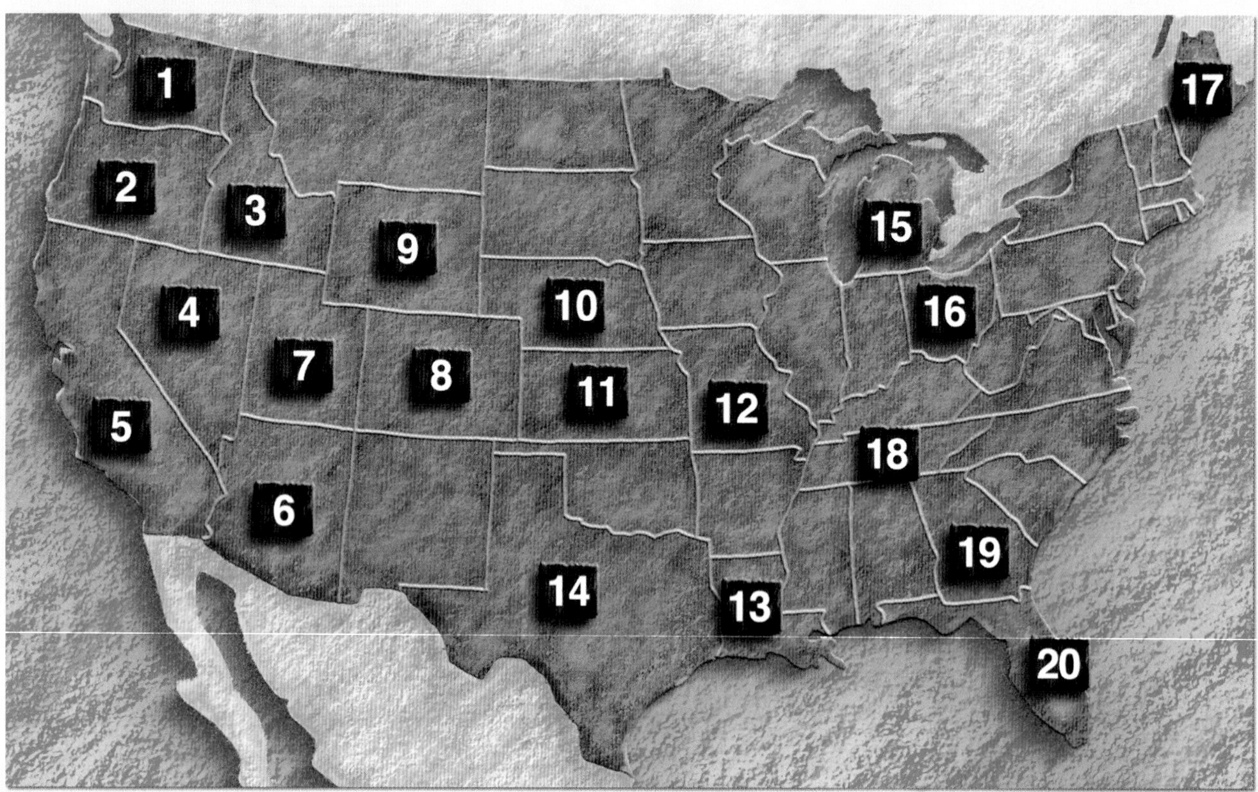

1. I am not the capital of the United States, and yet...

2. My name has six letters and has been given to a pine tree that comes from this area.

3. I feature in the name of a film that features River Phoenix and Keanu Reeves: *My own private* ....

4. My capital is Carson City, but my most famous town is Las Vegas.

5. I am home to San Francisco and Los Angeles.

6. My name starts with the same phonetic pronunciation as that of a famous Potter, minus the H.

7. My phonetic spelling is 'you tar'.

8. Anagram found in the phrase 'Much ado with color'.

9. My name begins with two of the last letters of the alphabet.

10. My name ends in the same way as that of the coldest state in the USA, situated in the north-west.

11. Dorothy, in *The Wizard of Oz*, lived here.

12. I am a river with its source in the Rocky Mountains and a state with a girl at its beginning.

13. I am the setting for New Orleans, a birthplace of jazz.

14. If you reverse my two vowels, I become identical to taxes!

15. I am surrounded by three large lakes, one of which carries my name.

16. If you write the letters of my name in a special way, my name can also mean ten minutes past midnight.

17. If you subtract an e, my name can mean 'central'.

18. Memphis, Nashville and Davy Crockett have made me famous.

19. My climate is less extreme than that of my Caucasian namesake.

20. My beaches and the Everglades, Cape Canaveral, Orlando and Miami make me a unique tourist destination.

OVERLAPPING SHAPES

CONCENTRATION

How many squares can you see?

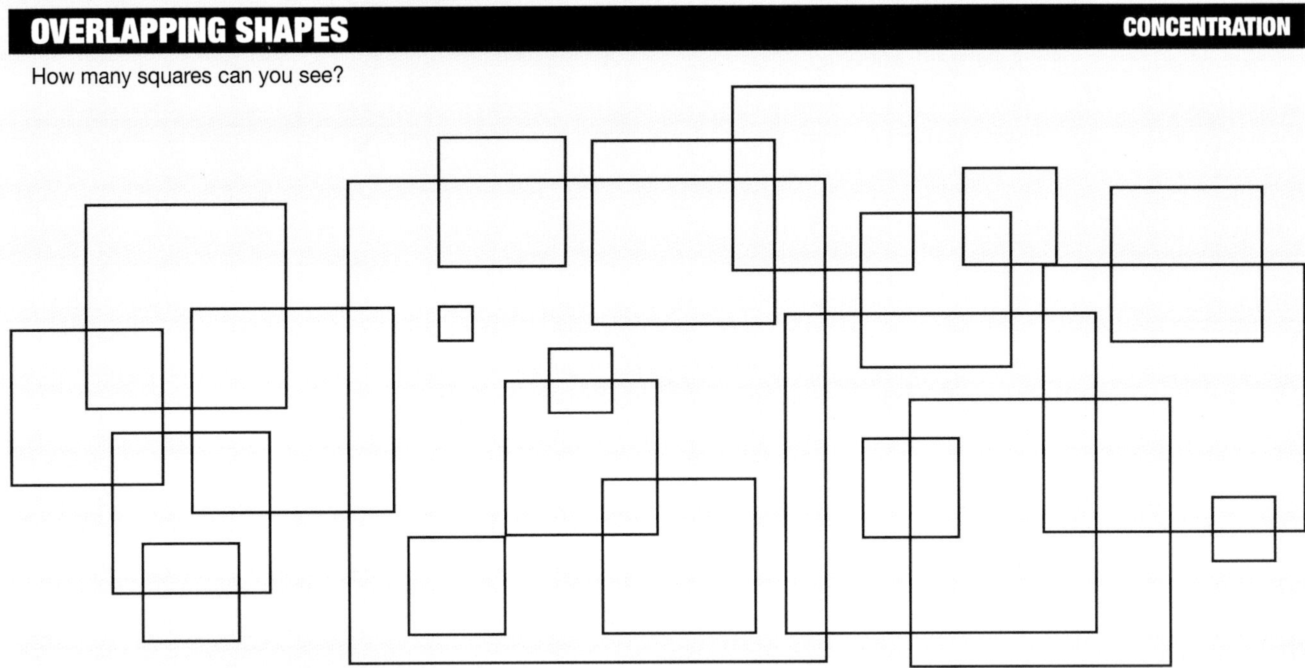

REBUS

ASSOCIATION

Work out from the visual code a well-known saying from one of Aesop's fables.

ANAGRAMS

STRUCTURE

Find the animals hiding within the following anagrams.

1. **SHORE** ....
2. **BRAZE** ....
3. **FLOW** ....
4. **DOING** ....
5. **PAROLED** ....
6. **TOAST** ....
7. **CORONA** ....
8. **TORTE** ....
9. **LOOPED** ....
10. **BARGED** ....

ZIGZAG WORDS

STRUCTURE

The French towns and cities hidden in this grid can be found in every direction: horizontally, vertically, from top to bottom and from bottom to top, from right to left and left to right. The words are also arranged in zigzag fashion (see the example of BIARRITZ), but they never cross and the same letter is used only once. With the remaining letters you may, by a miracle, find the mystery town.

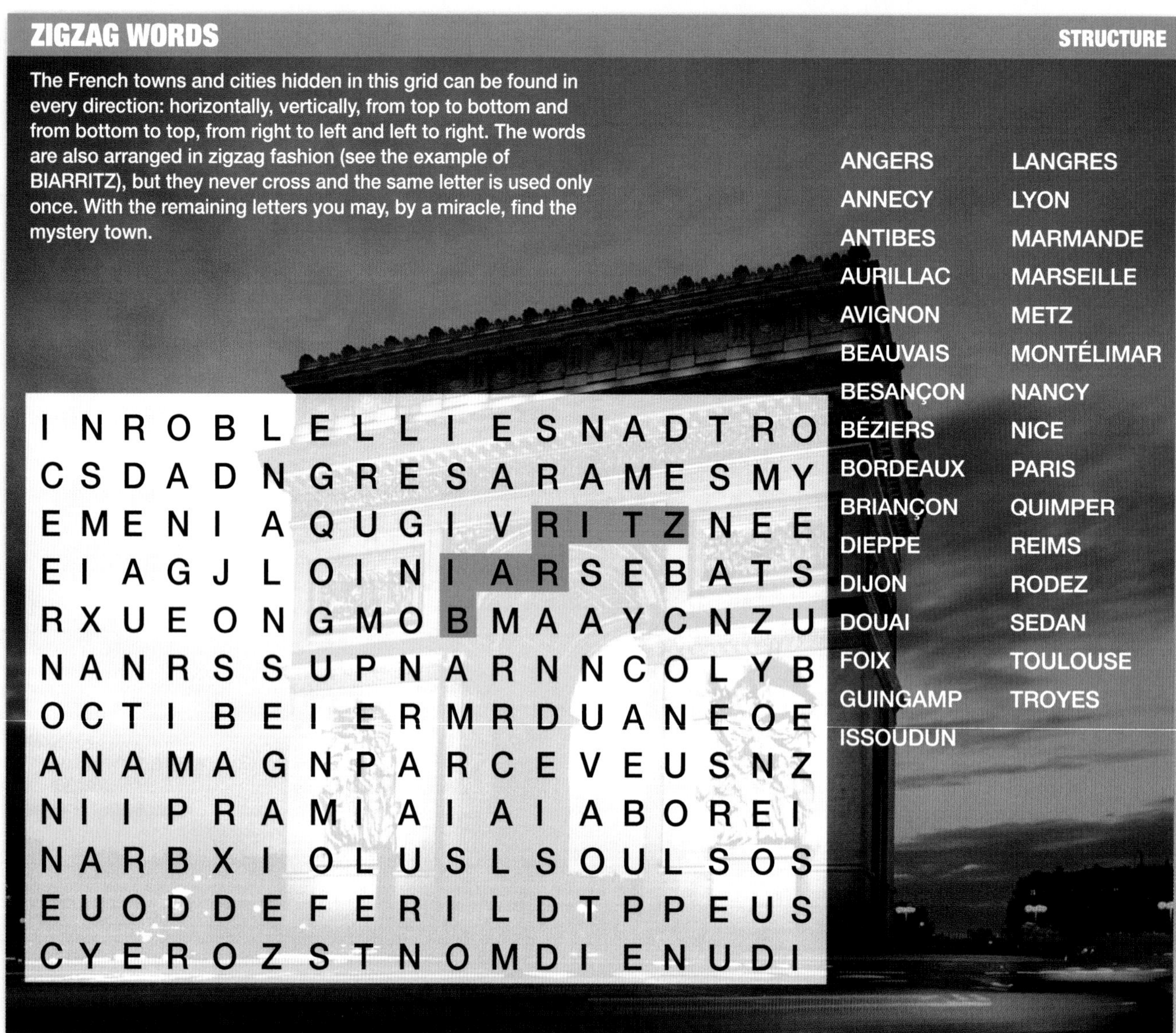

ANGERS
ANNECY
ANTIBES
AURILLAC
AVIGNON
BEAUVAIS
BESANÇON
BÉZIERS
BORDEAUX
BRIANÇON
DIEPPE
DIJON
DOUAI
FOIX
GUINGAMP
ISSOUDUN
LANGRES
LYON
MARMANDE
MARSEILLE
METZ
MONTÉLIMAR
NANCY
NICE
PARIS
QUIMPER
REIMS
RODEZ
SEDAN
TOULOUSE
TROYES

HISTORICAL LANDMARKS

TIME

Try to link these 10 historical events with the right date.

The battle of Waterloo	A	A.........	1	1500
The voyage of the *Mayflower*	B	B.........	2	1776
The raid on Pearl Harbor	C	C.........	3	1947
The discovery of Brazil	D	D.........	4	1620
The treaty of Versailles	E	E.........	5	1815
The battle of Hastings	F	F.........	6	1453
American War of Independence	G	G.........	7	1666
Independence of India	H	H.........	8	1919
The Great Fire of London	I	I.........	9	1066
End of the Hundred Years War	J	J.........	10	1941

WORD HOLES

LANGUAGE

Find the consonants that will enable you to complete the following words.

1. _ E _ E _ _ I _ I _ _
2. _ A _ A _ A _ I A
3. _ O _ O _ E _ O U _
4. _ I _ _ I _ _ I _ E
5. _ A I _ _ _ A _ E
6. _ _ I _ E _ I O _

MISSING SHAPES — CONCENTRATION

Look at this sequence of shapes for 30 seconds, then cover it.

  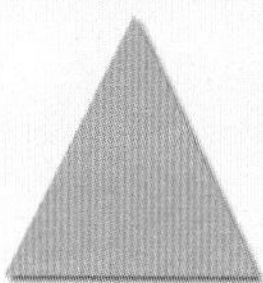   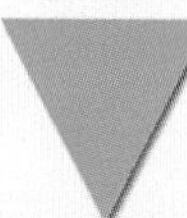

Without checking, fill in the three missing shapes to complete the sequence below and make it identical to the one above.

MATCHING UP — ASSOCIATION

Try to associate these 10 words with their language of origin from an etymological point of view.

Boycott	A	A.........	1	Afrikaans
Blackball	B	B.........	2	Greek
Trek	C	C.........	3	Malay
Compound	D	D.........	4	Irish
Thug	E	E.........	5	Scottish
Slogan	F	F.........	6	Chinese
Hypocrite	G	G.........	7	German
Autodafé	H	H.........	8	Portuguese
Mah-jong	I	I.........	9	Hindi
Dollar	J	J.........	10	English

CUT-UP LETTERS — STRUCTURE

Take out one letter from each of the words in the grid so that the remaining letters form an existing word. Place the deleted letters in the box at the end of the line to read vertically the name of a painter.

P	A	D	D	L	E	D	
S	E	R	I	O	U	S	
C	H	A	R	M	E	D	
M	A	I	M	I	N	G	
S	H	A	V	I	N	G	
D	E	S	C	E	N	T	
C	O	R	O	N	E	R	

CHALLENGE — CONCENTRATION

Look at the list of words below for several minutes and then try to write down as many as you can remember in the next minute. You are putting your short-term memory to work here. To extend the exercise, repeat it 10 minutes later without looking at the list again. Compare your results. The scores usually drop dramatically, and certain classic mistakes can be made. (see solution).

List of words to remember

Flask	Suitcase
Parmesan	Biscuit
Brochure	Seat
Curtain	Eagle
Goblet	Cupboard
Cellphone	Television

1. In the first minute

....

....

....

....

....

....

2. 10 minutes later

....

....

....

....

....

....

STICK-ON WORDS

STRUCTURE

Rearrange the following words, sticking them together two by two to obtain the phonetic names of 10 famous writers.

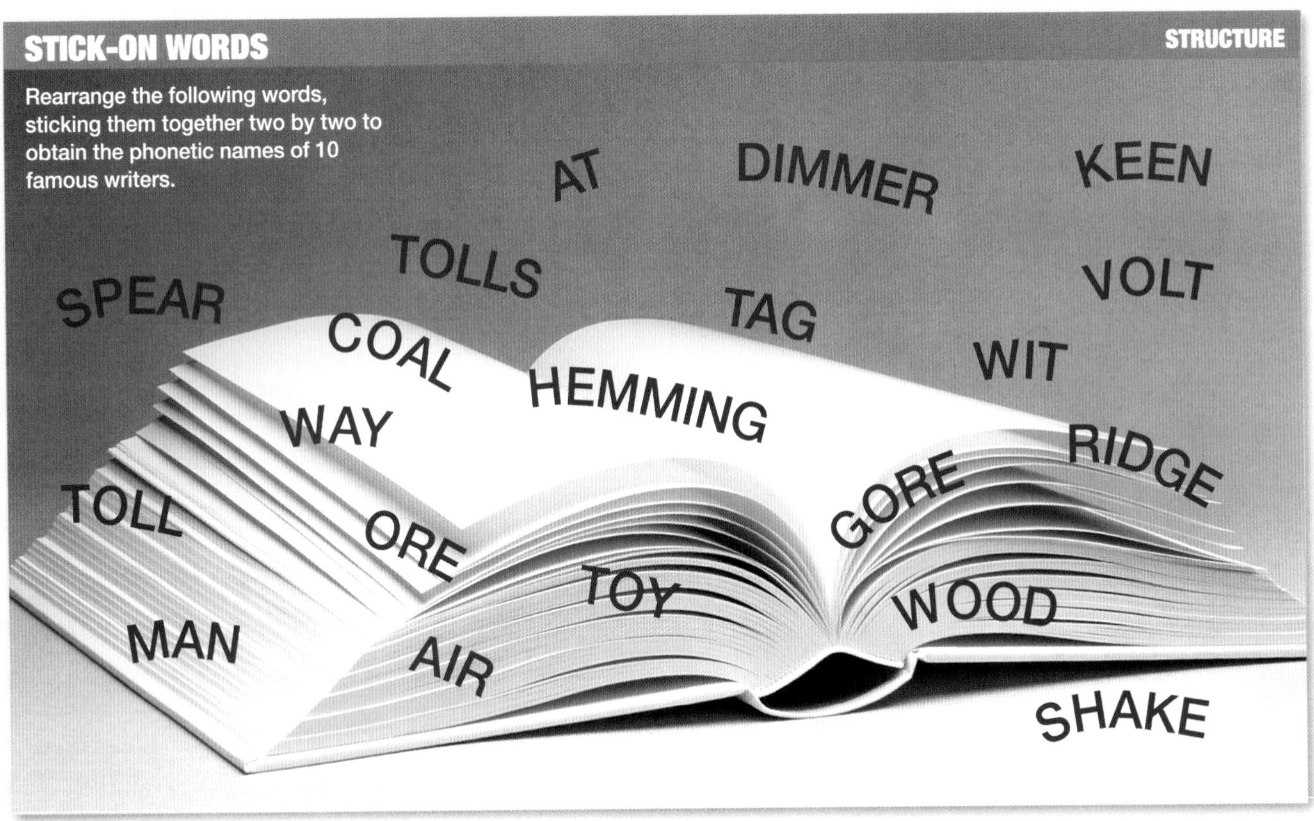

MATCHING UP

ASSOCIATION

Try to associate these 10 personalities to their year or century of birth.

- **A** Galileo
- **B** Alexander the Great
- **C** Marco Polo
- **D** Louis XIV
- **E** Christopher Colombus
- **F** Baudelaire
- **G** Einstein
- **H** Confucius
- **I** Napoleon
- **J** Pontius Pilate

A.........	F.........
B.........	G.........
C.........	H.........
D.........	I.........
E.........	J.........

1	2	3	4	5	6	7	8	9	10
551 BC	356 BC	1st century AD	1254	1450	1564	1638	1769	1821	1879

BEADS

CONCENTRATION

Look at these beads for a few minutes and then cover them up.

Try to draw them in the right order on the string.

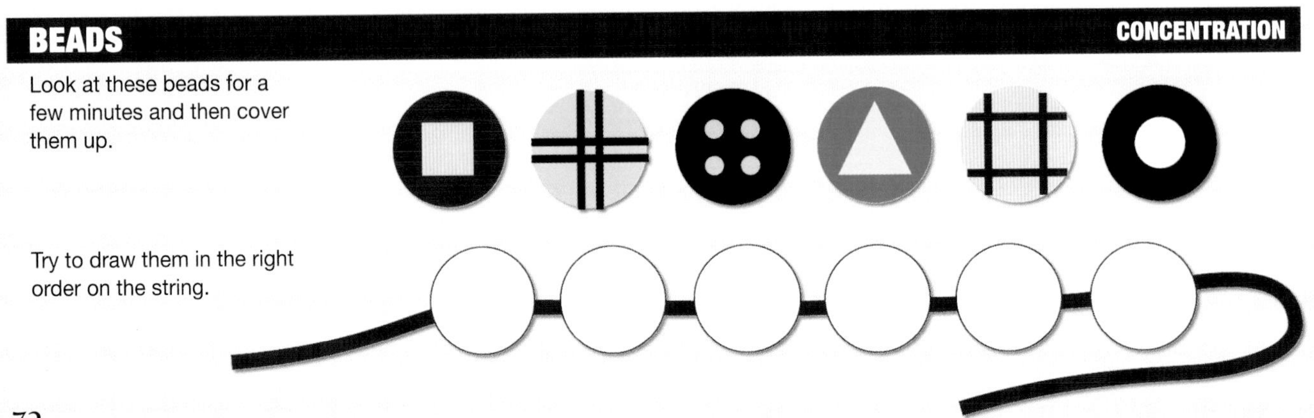

WHICH COMES NEXT?

LOGIC

Which of these three musical instruments completes the logical sequence?

MYSTERY PHRASE

CONCENTRATION

Read the following quote:

'Tlak to a man auobt hslmeif and he wlil letisn for hruos.'

You have probably noted that, even though the letters are not in the correct order, you have been able to understand the phrase, more or less. Can you identify the rule for the spelling?

LOTTO

LOGIC

Make up the total of 49 with these 16 lotto numbers by placing each one in a box with the same shape as that in which it is written.

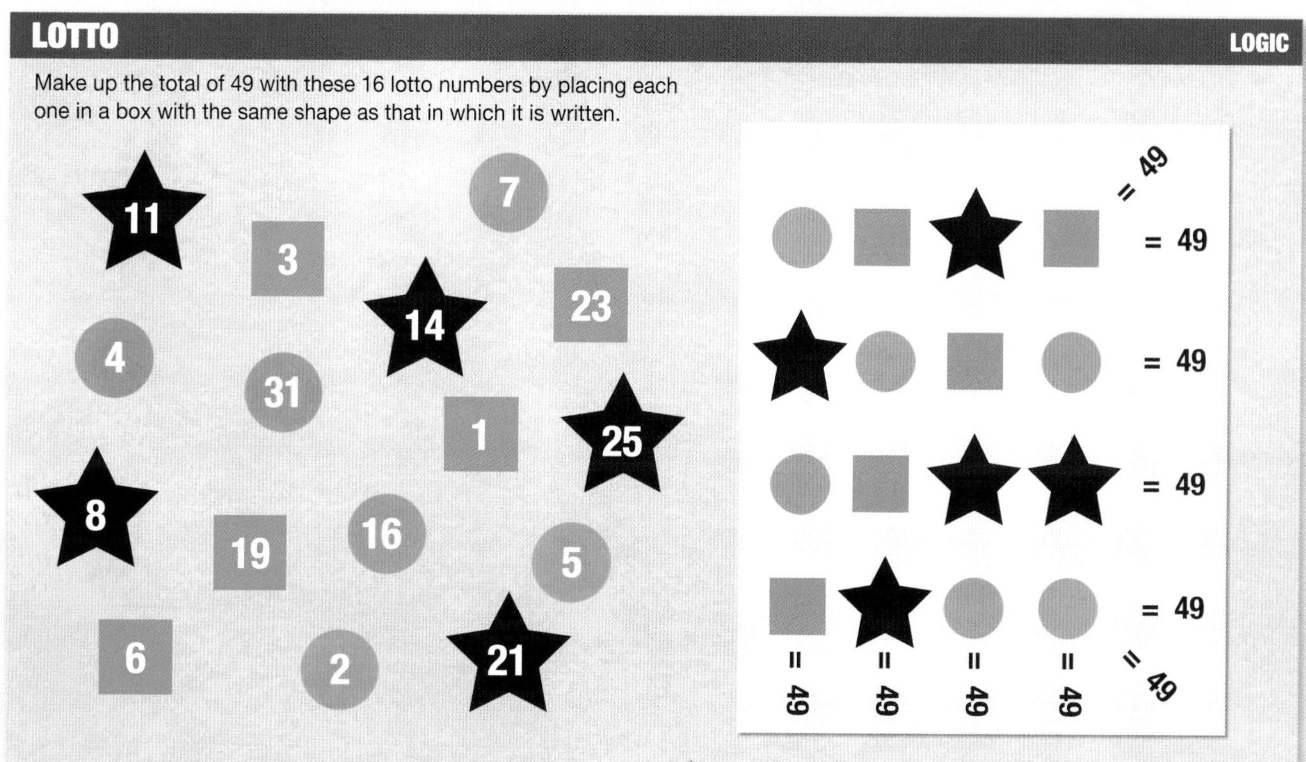

MYSTERY WORDS

With the help of a sheet of paper, which you slide down the page slowly, uncover one by one the clues that will help you identify these personalities. The aim is to recognise them using the least number of clues.

Who am I?

1. I was born in New York in 1937.
2. My father was an actor and I made my stage debut with him. My brother and niece are also actors.
3. I protested against the Vietnam War and was thereafter named Hanoi Jane.
4. I won Oscars in 1971 for my part in *Klute*, and in 1980 for my role in *Coming Home*.
5. In the 1980s I ushered in the age of aerobic fitness when I devised a fitness programme.
6. I was married to the media mogul Ted Turner.

A. ....

Who am I?

1. I was born in Marseille on June 23, 1972.
2. My initials are formed from the same, but very rarely used, letters.
3. I started my professional career in Cannes.
4. I received a red card in the 1988 World Cup when playing against Saudi Arabia.
5. All the same I was the top scorer in the same year.
6. People call me Zizou.

B. ....

Who am I?

1. I was born in England in 1965.
2. I have been writing since I was five, and my first story was called *Rabbit*.
3. As a young mother, I would write in restaurants to keep warm while I wrote.
4. I sold my first novel, published in 1997, for about $4,000.
5. The key character in my books is a young wizard.
6. I am now one of the wealthiest writers in the world.

C. ....

CRYPTOGRAM

ASSOCIATION

Decode this quote by Napoleon Bonaparte by choosing a letter that corresponds to the relevant symbol. To help you, certain letters have already been decoded.

__ I __ __ O __ __   __ __   __ __ __   V __ __ __ __ __ __

__ __   P __ __ __   E __ __ __ __ __   __ __ __ __

__ __ __ __ L __   __ __ __ __   __ __ C __ __ __ __

__ __   __ __ __ __ __   __ __ __ __

A	G	N	S
C	I	P	T
D	L	R	U
E	Y	H	O
V	F		

IDIOMATIC TRIPLETS

LANGUAGE

Find the word that is common to the three in each sequence and which forms an idiom.

Example: hide, dog, stand – **hair.**

1. Tough, class, caught
   ....
2. Mind, dozen, bad
   ....
3. Breath, clear, up
   ....
4. Bird, bite, mouth
   ....
5. Cloth, hatchet, meat
   ....
6. Shot, horse, in
   ....

GENERAL KNOWLEDGE

Who am I?

1. I was created for the public on November 18, 1928.
2. I would have been called Mortimer if the wife of my creator had not intervened.
3. Originally I had five fingers, but my designers wanted to remove one.
4. I made my first appearance in *Steamboat Willie*.
5. I am a personality owned by Walt Disney.
6. A detective mouse, I have a fiancée called Minnie.

D. ....

Who am I?

1. I was born in 1958 in Michigan.
2. My first album, *Holiday*, debuted in 1983.
3. I played the role of Eva Peron in the film *Evita*.
4. I have just published two children's books.
5. My husband, British film director Guy Ritchie, calls me Madge.
6. I am the most successful female solo artist ever, having sold 120 million copies of my albums by November 2000.

E. ....

MATCHES — LOGIC

Move five matches so as to make three squares of the same size.

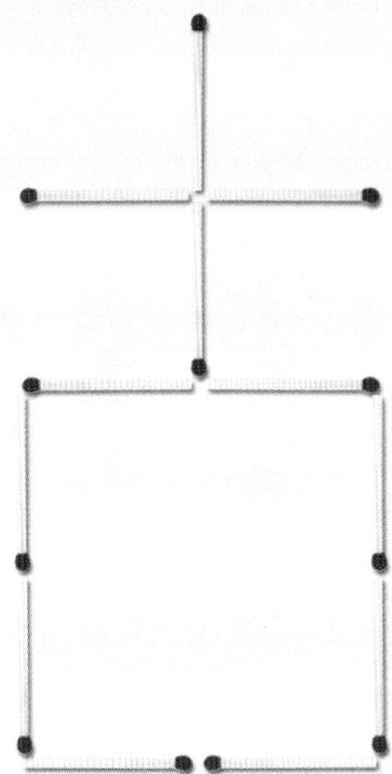

ROSETTE — STRUCTURE

Fill the flower by forming words from the jumbled-up letters below. Always write your solutions starting from the outside of the flower and working in towards the centre. Be careful – certain letters make several anagrams, only one of which will be correct and allow you to complete the grid with crossed words that make sense.

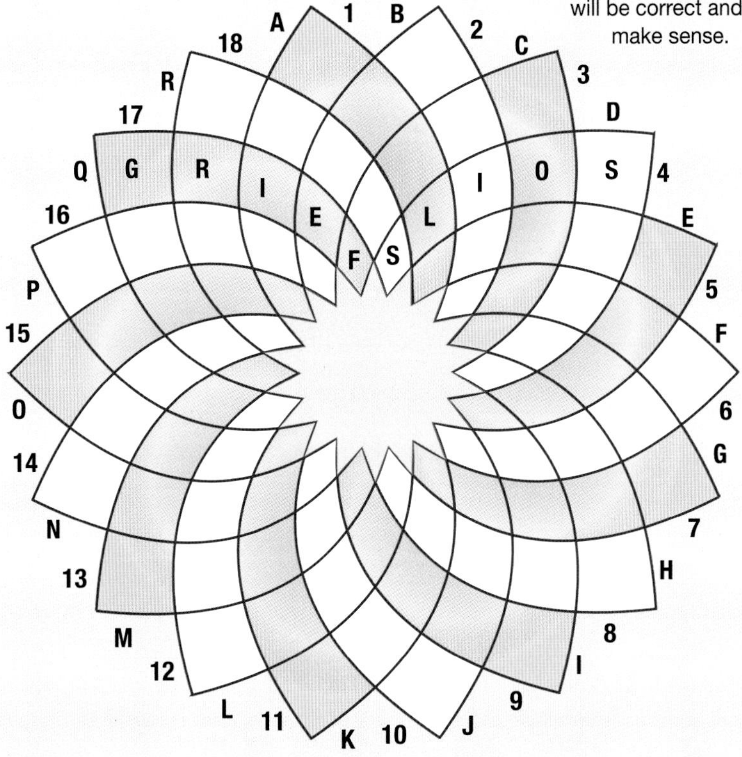

Clockwise :

A. LAISM
B. RIETB
C. OKOSB
D. PSNAS
E. LKTEN
F. SSRAT
G. ATSES
H. STLEO
I. VELOS
J. ASTBE
K. OUDCL
L. HSNOE
M. TRKIC
N. TDRIE
O. ATGRE
P. EPSRS
Q. FERIG
R. EXSOB

Anticlockwise:

1. IOSMT
2. XESTA
3. FRIEB
4. LOISS
5. BSNOK
6. AKENS
7. PSETS
8. SELSA
9. ARSTT
10. OTSBO
11. CSELL
12. ESVLA
13. TSEHO
14. TUTRO
15. DGNRI
16. PCERI
17. KREGE
18. ADBRE

GUIDED TOUR

CONCENTRATION

Look carefully at this map of a specific district. Try to memorise the position of the monuments, public places and the names of streets and squares. Then cover the map and try to fill in all these items on the blank map below.

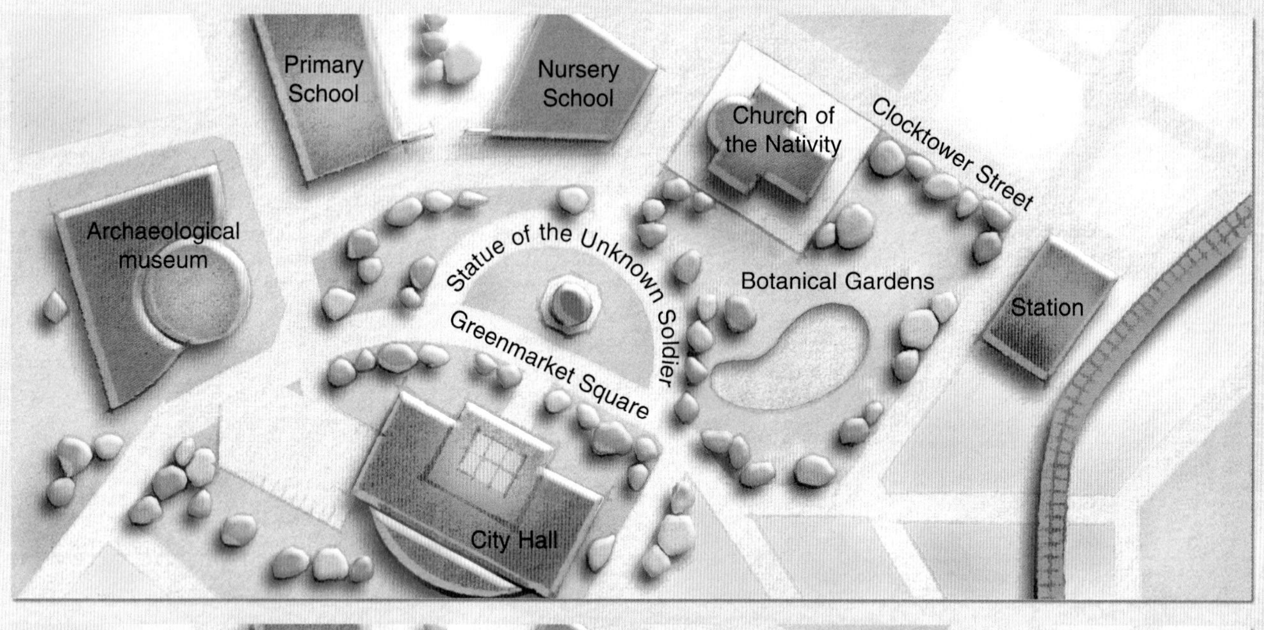

REBUS

ASSOCIATION

Read the symbols phonetically to find the title of a classic film.

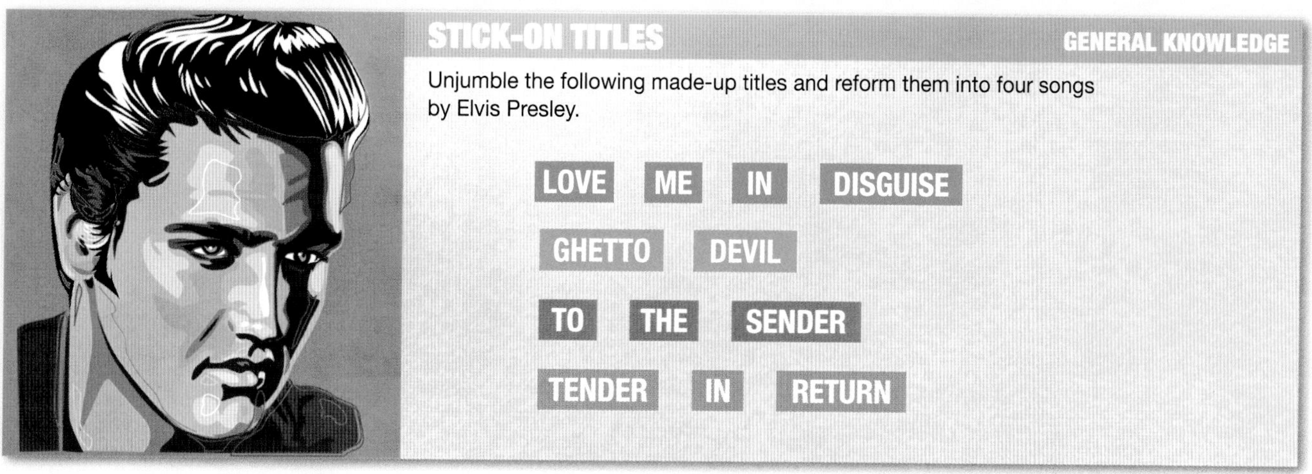

STICK-ON TITLES

GENERAL KNOWLEDGE

Unjumble the following made-up titles and reform them into four songs by Elvis Presley.

LOVE ME IN DISGUISE

GHETTO DEVIL

TO THE SENDER

TENDER IN RETURN

WHICH COMES NEXT?

LOGIC

Find the card that completes this logical sequence, both horizontally and vertically.

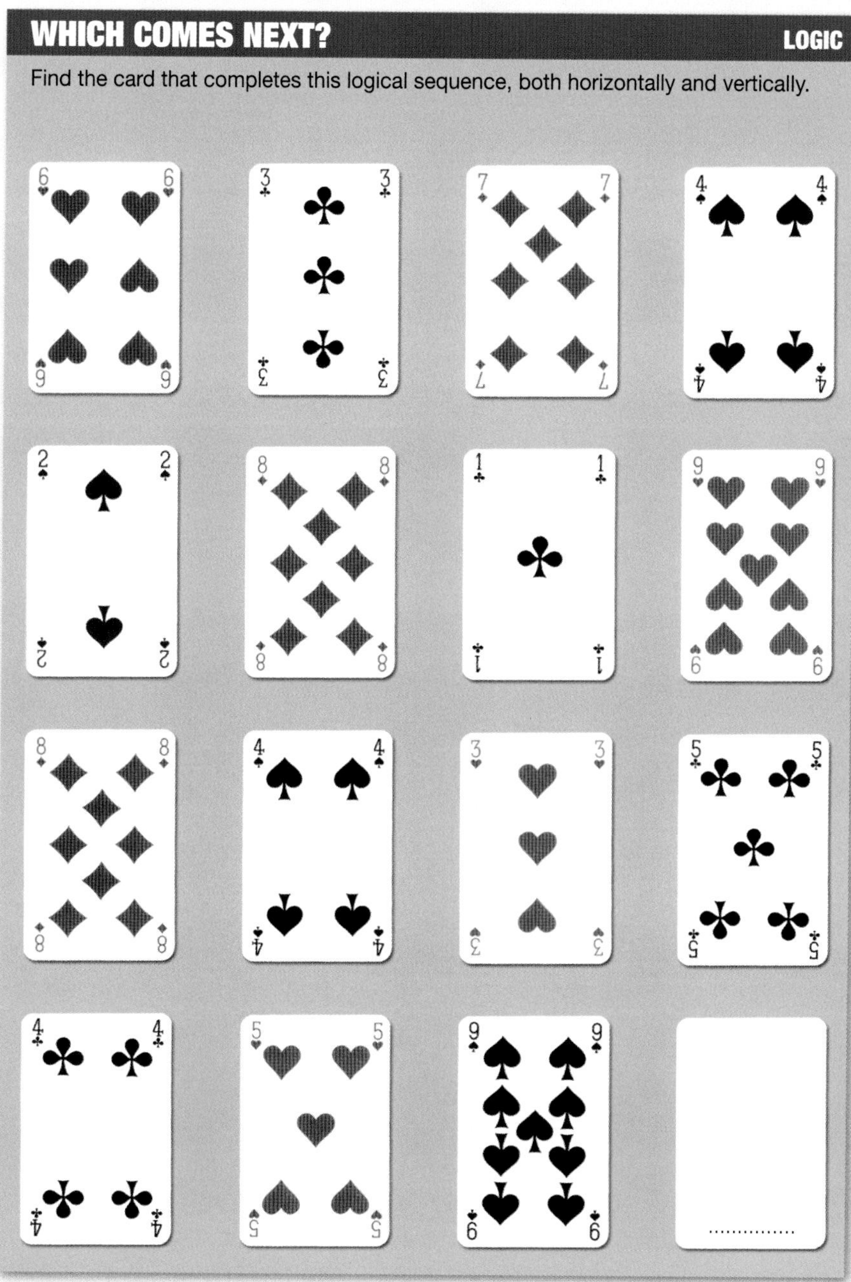

LADDER

STRUCTURE

With the help of these six crosswords, reconstruct the ladder grid forming words that have to do with health.

TEST YOUR OBSERVATION SKILLS

CONCENTRATION

Look at this picture by Georges de la Tour for a few minutes and then try to answer the 10 questions without looking at the illustration.

Questions

1. What card is the man to the left of the picture holding behind his back?
2. In which hand is the woman on the left holding the glass of wine she is bringing to the table?
3. One of the characters is holding spades: true or false?
4. What do you see on the table?
5. Is the woman wearing a pearl necklace shown in profile or from the front?
6. In which hand is the woman facing us holding her closed hand of cards?
7. The two men are looking at each other: true or false?
8. In which direction is the woman with the red headdress looking?
9. What adorns the hair arrangement of two of the characters?
10. The costume worn by the man on the right is decorated with red ribbons: true or false?

BROKEN SEQUENCES

STRUCTURE

Six words have had one or more syllables removed. Using those that are given below, make the words whole again. Be careful – several solutions are possible but only one combination will enable you to complete all the words.

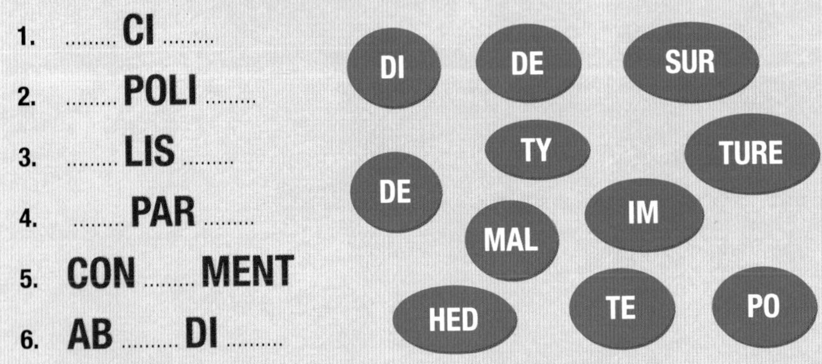

WORD HOLES

LANGUAGE

By replacing each space with a letter, find six words that start with I, keeping to the same structure.

2. I _ _ Q _ _ L _ _ Y
3. I _ S _ L _ _
4. I _ _ E _ _ M
5. I _ L _ M
6. I _ Y _ _

THE RIGHT TIME

LOGIC

1. Find the clock giving the right time, taking into account that one of the clocks is 7 hours fast while another is 7 hours slow.
2. Same question, but this time one of the clocks is 5 hours slow and another 5 hours fast

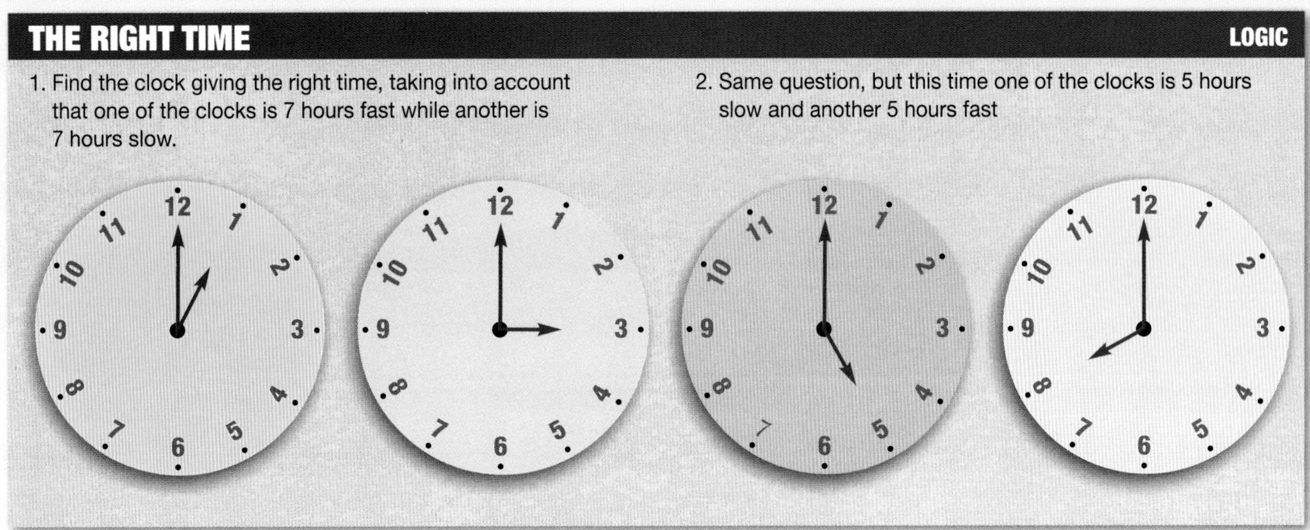

MAZE

SPACE

Find the path that connects the arrow to the logo at the base of the parasol.

CATERPILLAR

STRUCTURE

Progress from CHESS to BOARD in this 'caterpillar' by making the indicated substitution (for example, D replaces C on the first line) and by changing the order of the letters. You will probably come across several possible words.

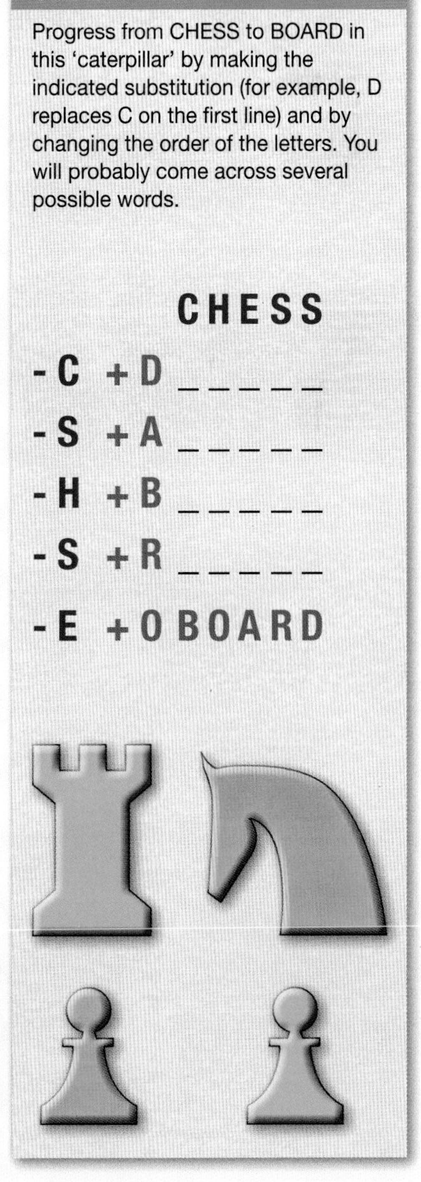

BOXED WORDS

SPACE

Place the names of the film stars into the crossword grid.

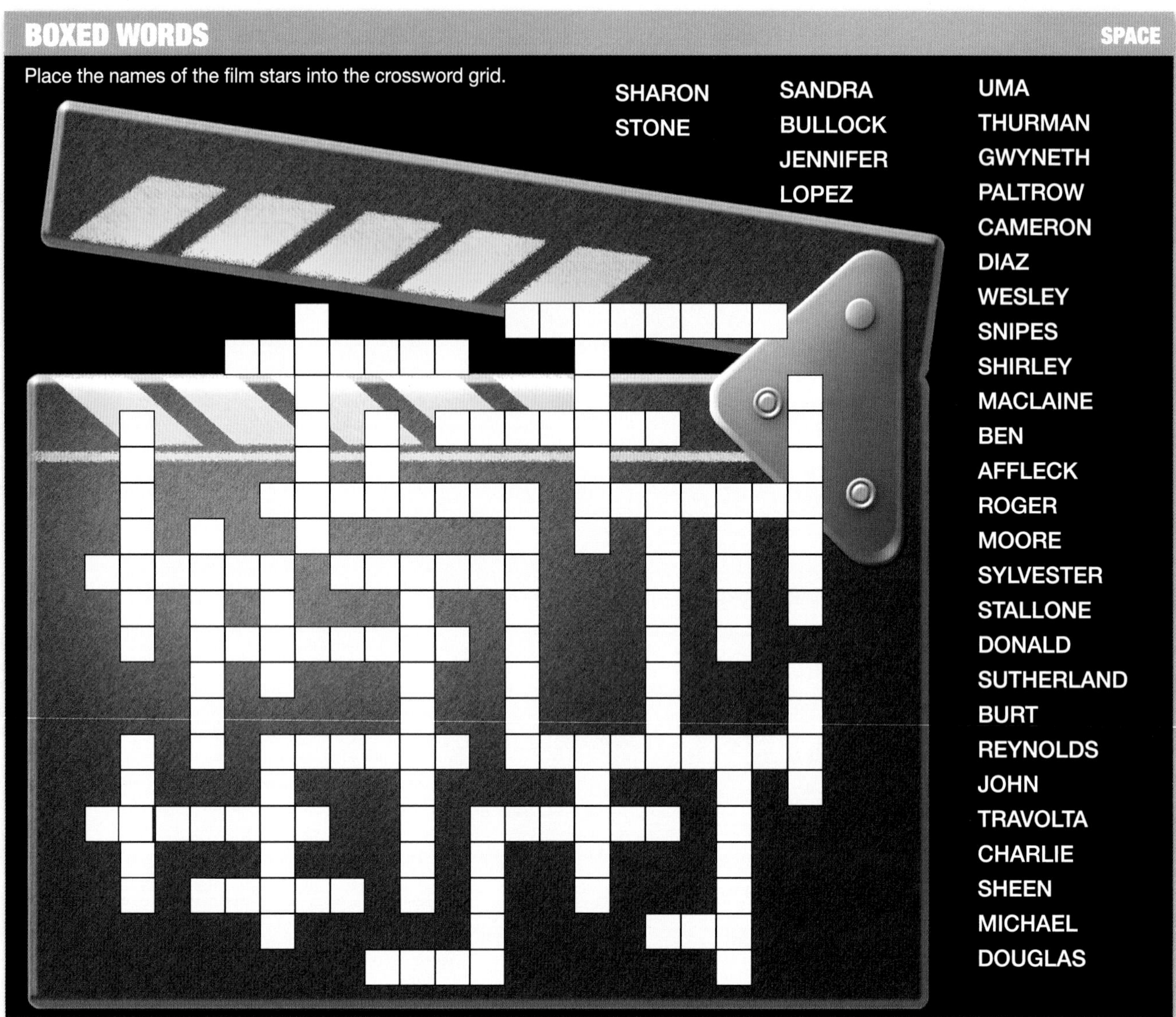

HOMOPHONES

LANGUAGE

Homophones (from the Greek *homos*, 'similar' and *phoneo*, 'speak') are words pronounced in the same way but with a different sense, such as pear, pair, pare ... Find the homophones that complete the following sentences.

1. She felt dizzy watching the _ _ _ _ wheel and _ _ _ _ through the air.

2. Driving through the thick _ _ _ _ they could not see any landmarks and so they _ _ _ _ _ _ their turning.

3. The racegoers shouted so loudly for their _ _ _ _ _ to win that within a few minutes they had become _ _ _ _ _ _.

4. The magician's _ _ _ _ _ _ _ of hand was not swift enough and I detected the _ _ _ _ _ _ movement that made the handkerchief disappear.

DRAWING FROM MEMORY — CONCENTRATION

Look at this selection of birthday cakes for 30 seconds and then cover the picture.

From memory, draw the right number of candles on each cake.

BONUS LETTER — STRUCTURE

Use the letters of the root word on the left and add the bonus letter (in this case, P) to form, in rearranging the letters, a new word that relates to the clue on the right.

			Clue
1. **ARK**	+ P	....	Open land
2. **SORT**	+ P	....	Game
3. **ROAST**	+ P	....	Priest
4. **ANTLER**	+ P	....	Garden pot
5. **REALIST**	+ P	....	Pillar
6. **ATELIERS**	+ P	....	Lustrous

LOOPY LETTERS — STRUCTURE

Put the letters on each line in the right order to give you the names of two visionary scientists. One will read in the traditional way, from left to right, and the other from right to left.

N T I E E I S N

F L I K N R A N

NUMBER PYRAMID — LOGIC

Each brick in the pyramid of numbers represents the total of the two numbers in the bricks immediately below it. Complete the pyramid, with the aid of the numbers already in place.

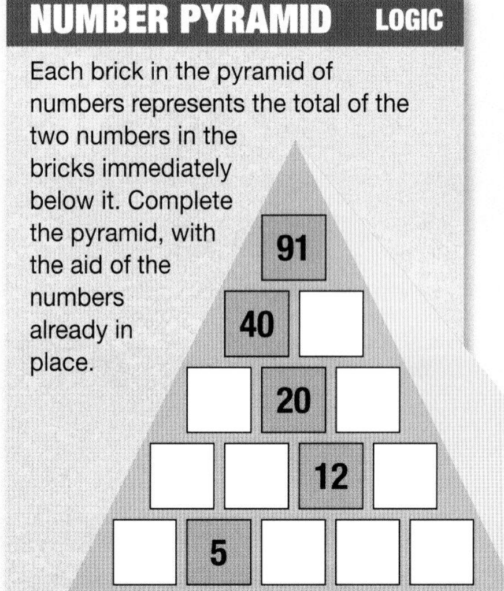

PROBLEM — LOGIC

- A train leaves station A at 8 h 06 and travels non-stop to station B at a constant speed of 75 km/h.
- Another train leaves station B at 8 h 12 and stops at 11 stations for one minute, but travels at 150 km/h between the stations.
- Taking into account that C is one third of the way between these two stations, and closer to A, which train will be further away from A when they pass each other?

GEOMETRIC SEQUENCES
LOGIC

In each series, find the numbered geometric figure that continues the sequence.

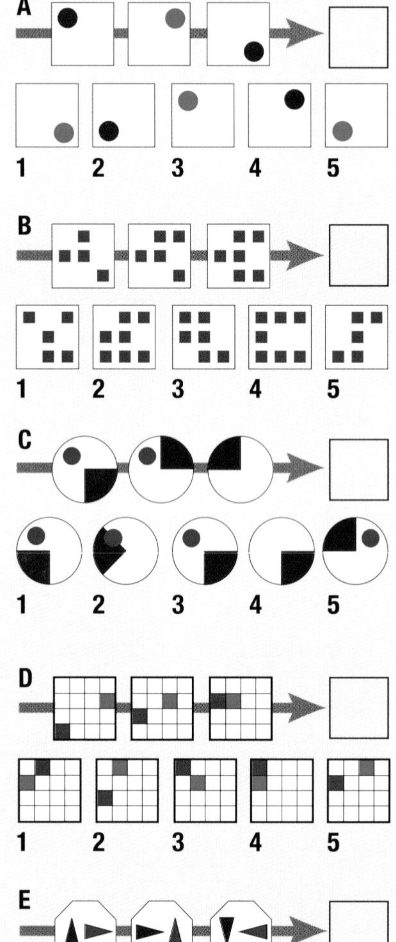

JUMBLED WORDS
STRUCTURE

Unscramble six names of film stars which have been joined up two by two.

BASOGATRAITRE
1

BLARNACANSTEDOR
2

PRACEDIFONORD
3

ESCALETTERS
STRUCTURE

Add the letters indicated one by one to form new words.

RUE

+T _ _ _ _

+N _ _ _ _ _

+E _ _ _ _ _ _

+I _ _ _ _ _ _ _

+D _ _ _ _ _ _ _ _

+L _ _ _ _ _ _ _ _ _

POINTS IN COMMON
ASSOCIATION

For each of the following series of words, find one word that relates directly to each of the three words in the series.

1. **drop – crocodile – duct** ....
2. **weather – hair – practice** ....
3. **glass – throat – paper** ....
4. **lie – goods – sale** ....

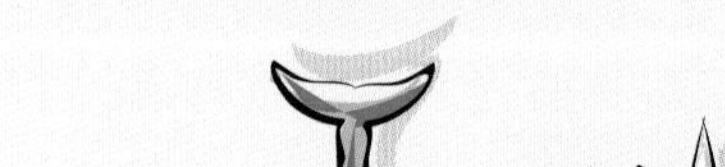

5. **north – level – love** ....
6. **pearl – pod – capital** ....

ONE TOO MANY
CONCENTRATION

Look at these three bottles for 30 seconds and then cover the picture.

Which one has been added?

THE RIGHT PLACE

CONCENTRATION

Look at these acrobats for several minutes, then hide them.

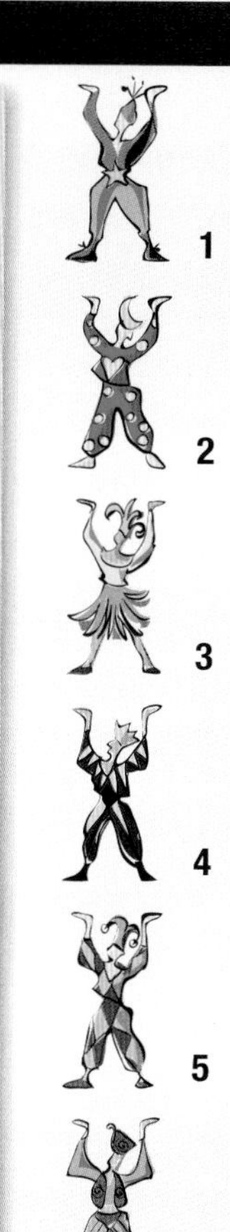

Here are the six acrobats you saw earlier. Put them back in their places, writing their numbers in the relevant boxes.

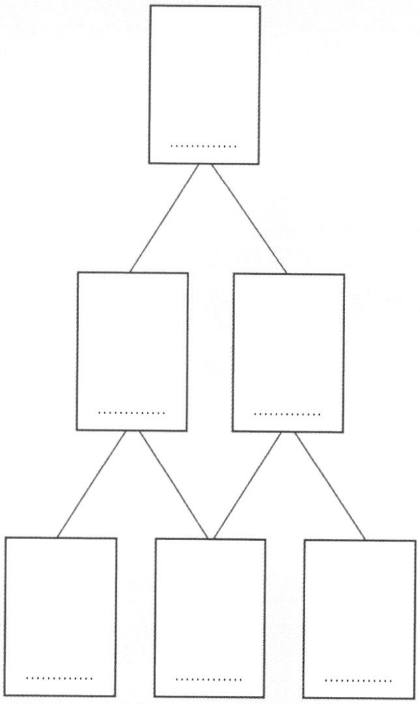

SUPERIMPOSITION

CONCENTRATION

Imagine that the discs below are made of glass. Find the three you must superimpose to make figure A. You need not turn the discs, and certain identical colours can be superimposed.

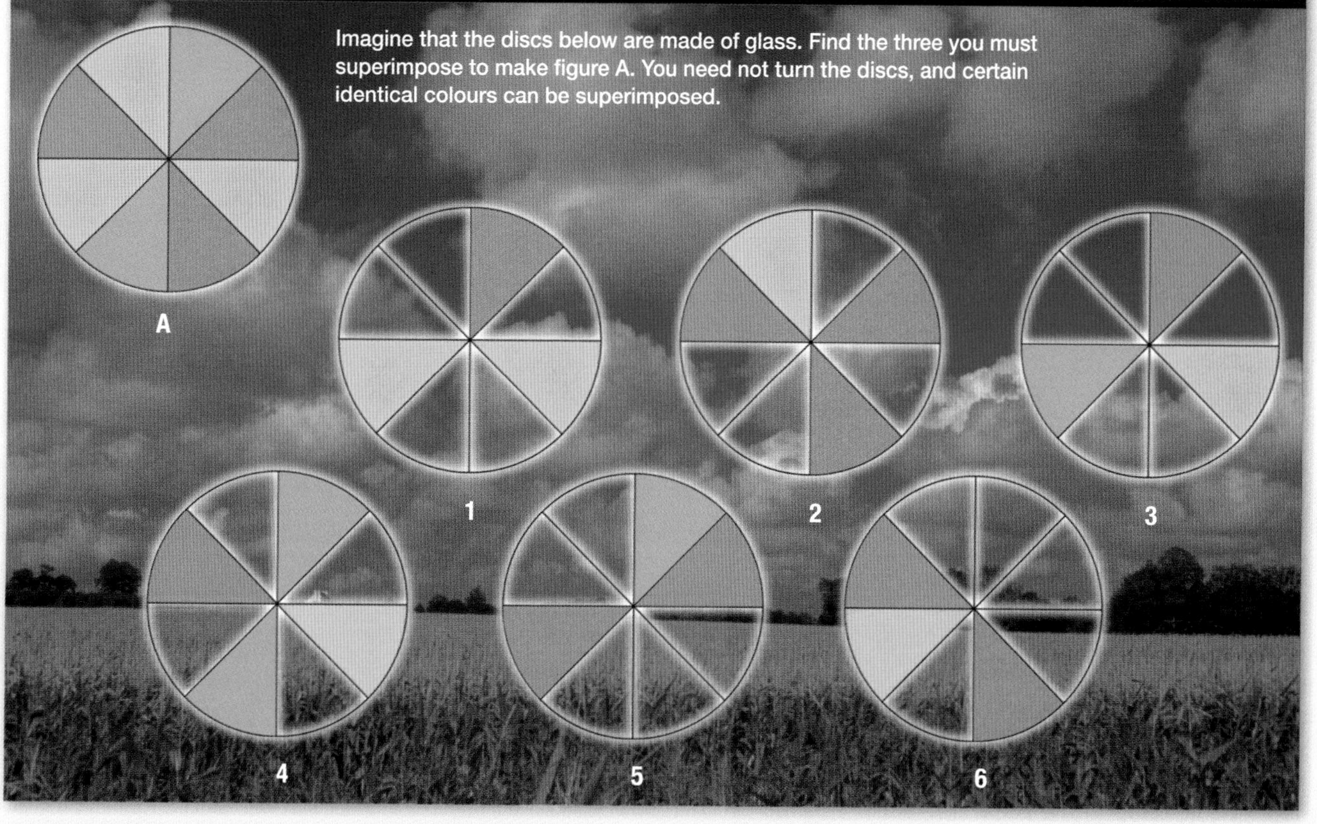

A

1 2 3

4 5 6

IDIOMATIC TRIPLETS

LANGUAGE

Find the word that is common to the three in each sequence and which forms an idiom.

Example:
hide, dog, stand – **hair.**

1. Safe, devil, late

....

2. Workman, penny, news

....

3. Bark, bullet, hand

....

4. Stone, water, sweat

....

5. Giveaway, loss, doornail

....

6. Grain, earth, wound

....

TEST YOUR OBSERVATION SKILLS

CONCENTRATION

Look at this sequence of pictures for a few minutes, and then try to answer the 10 questions without looking at the illustrations.

1

2

3

4

5

6

7

8

Questions

1. In which picture does the waiter drop his table napkin for the first time?
2. What is the blonde woman doing when the waiter comes to take a chair in picture 2?
3. The waiter is carrying an empty tray in his left hand when he picks up the napkin: true or false?

4. What colour are the clothes worn by the woman in the first picture?
5. How many chairs are used by the characters?
6. In how many pictures are all the characters visible simultaneously, even if partially?
7. Only one of the three characters represented in the sketches remains the same throughout the story. Which one?
8. In one picture, the ceiling light is switched off: true or false?
9. The waiter's napkin appears in seven of the eight pictures: true or false?
10. Where is the napkin in the last picture?

IDENTIKIT

LOGIC

Identify the flag by a process of elimination, with the help of the clues given below, in the order in which they appear.

1. The mystery flag is not square in shape.
2. It is not composed of five colours (white is considered a colour).
3. If the flag has a black area, that area is not the same size as another area of a different colour on the flag.
4. It is not a two-coloured flag with the two coloured areas of the same size.
5. The flag does not consist of exactly three triangles.
6. It does not have an identical inverted shape of another colour.
7. The flag is not made up of four quadrilaterals.
8. Of the flags remaining, the mystery one has areas of differing shapes.

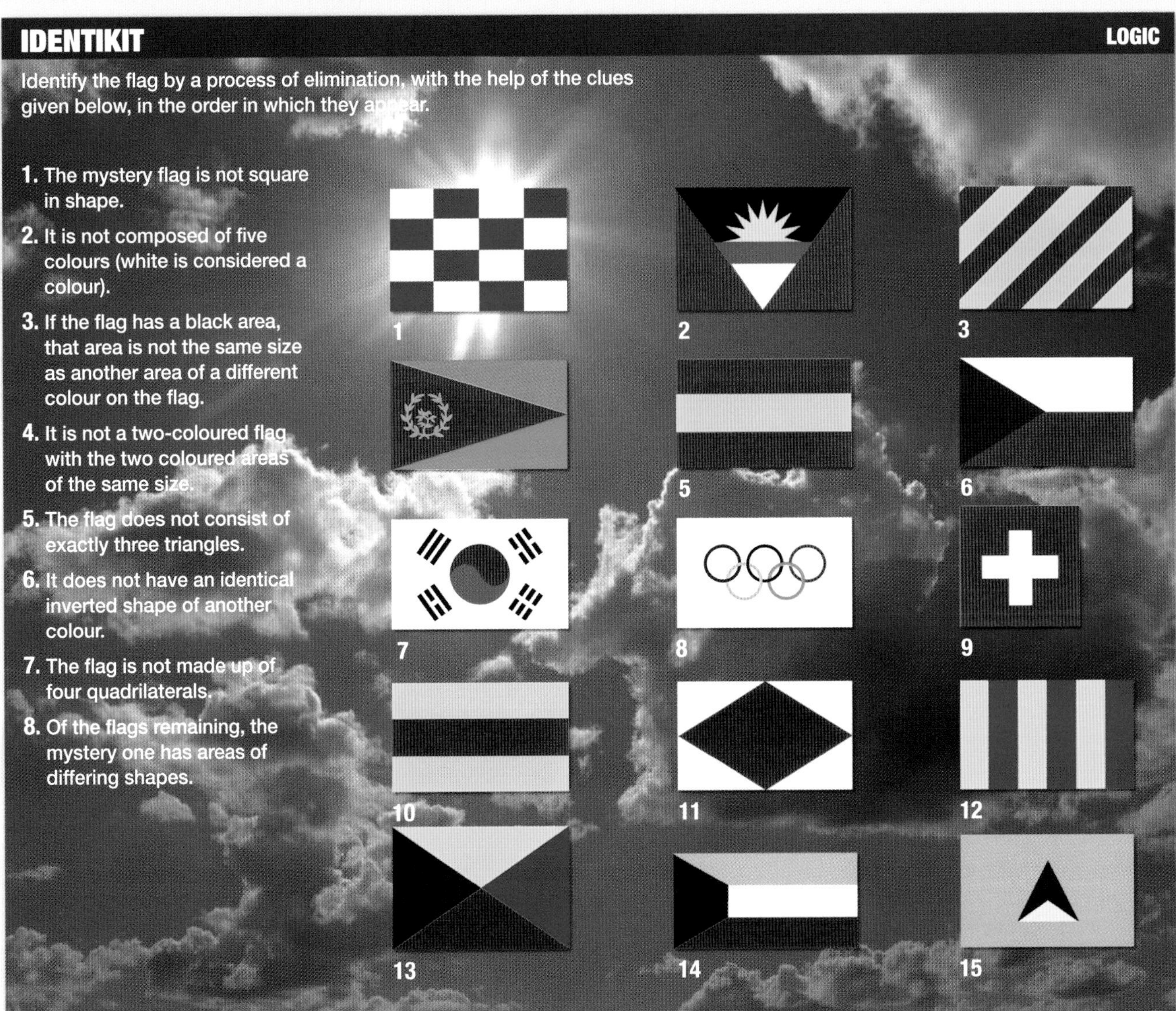

SANDWICH

STRUCTURE

By completing the horizontal words find a well-known Latin expression in the vertical middle column Sometimes, several words may be possible, but only one will lead you to the solution. The first column gives you a clue.

C	O		K	S
E	N		C	T
L	U		C	H
E	X		E	L
B	L		N	D
R	I		E	R
A	M		S	S
T	R		S	S
E	M		E	T

MATCHING UP

ASSOCIATION

Try to link each of the following 10 African countries with its capital.

Senegal **A**	A	**1**	Bamako
Chad **B**	B	**2**	Addis-Ababa
Angola **C**	C	**3**	N'Djamena
Mali **D**	D	**4**	Windhoek
Togo **E**	E	**5**	Nouakchott
Mauritania **F**	F	**6**	Lome
Morocco **G**	G	**7**	Tripoli
Libya **H**	H	**8**	Dakar
Ethiopia **I**	I	**9**	Luanda
Namibia **J**	J	**10**	Rabat

MYSTERY WORDS

Identify these mystery words by using a sheet of paper to uncover the clues one by one. The aim is to get the answer with the aid of the minimum number of clues.

What am I?

1. When I am not proper that does not imply that I am indecent.
2. I change in certain contexts.
3. I have family connections.
4. I am completely common, whether male or female.
5. I try to stick when I belong to an artist.
6. When I am scientific, I often sound as if I am of Latin origin.

What am I?

1. I waited for one hundred years after the French Revolution before standing up.
2. I like exhibiting myself, I was born for that.
3. I bear the name of my maker.
4. I am both in the city and not far from the Fields.
5. I am, in my own way, an iron lady.
6. I have received more than 200 million visitors since I was built in Paris.

What am I?

1. My rings are not found on your finger.
2. I can live in a building, or travel by car, by train, by plane ...
3. My voice can be personalised.
4. My name refers to both an object and a means of attaining it.
5. I used to be black, but now I come in a variety of colours.
6. I am asked to remain silent in public places if I am mobile.

A. ....

B. ....

C. ....

TEST YOUR OBSERVATION SKILLS

ATTENTION

Look at this wedding scene for several minutes, then try to answer the 10 questions without looking at the illustration.

Questions

1. What animal appears under the rope, on the left?
2. What is the person on the left, in a red jacket and white shirt, holding?
3. Most of the people on the right of the scene are musicians: true or false?
4. A stork is perched on its nest in the background: true or false?
5. Is the person watching the scene from the window at the top right of the picture a woman or a man?
6. A little girl is throwing rice at the bride: true or false?
7. What level do the pants of the groom come up to?
8. The hem of the bride's dress is red: true or false?
9. There is a violinist in the scene: true or false?
10. Where is the signature of the painter?

GENERAL KNOWLEDGE

What am I?

1. I am taken as an example to show how perfectly something can fit.
2. I am sometimes put in a compartment or cubby-hole.
3. I am usually met on the tips of your fingers.
4. I can be thin or well-padded.
5. I never leave prints.
6. I am thrown down to start a duel, not like the towel or sponge that signifies defeat!

D. ....

What am I?

1. I can be intermediate between a Kingdom and an Order.
2. I am more often second than first.
3. If people say you have me, you are pleased.
4. In the plural, I can have a scholarly sound.
5. I have inspired people like Marx, but not Groucho!
6. I am traditionally upper, middle and lower.

E. ....

PROBLEM — LOGIC

It is midday. My friend has just left and has arranged to meet me at the New Wave cinema when the small hand on my watch has gone around 10 times.

What time will it be when I meet him?

SYNONYMS — LANGUAGE

Synonyms (from the Greek *sun*, 'with', and *onoma*, 'name') are words that have a similar or very close meaning, like light, faint, pale. Find eight synonyms for the word 'heavy' corresponding to the clues.

1. **C _ _ _ _ _ _ _ _ T**
   (for a weighty person)
2. **S _ _ _ _ Y**
   (for a turbulent sea)
3. **L _ _ _ _ N**
   (for a gloomy sky)
4. **O _ _ _ _ _ _ _ _ E**
   (for a silence)
5. **S _ _ _ _ _ _ _ _ _ L**
   (for an investment)
6. **V _ _ _ _ _ N**
   (for a gangster)
7. **C _ _ _ _ _ _ _ D**
   (for traffic)
8. **L _ _ _ E**
   (for a meal)

HISTORICAL LANDMARKS — TIME

Link these celebrities, two by two:
the rule is that they were born in the same year.
Then try to order them from the oldest to the youngest.

Bill Gates	Elvis Presley
Aung San Suu Kyi	Ayn Rand
Julie Andrews	Maya Angelou
Jean-Paul Sartre	Bruce Willis
Che Guevara	Steve Martin

ONE WORD TOO MANY — LOGIC

In each of the following series of words, take out the word that has nothing in common with the others.
Identify a common geographical or historical thread, as well as additions or subtractions, to find the odd one out.

1. **SENILE RHINESTONE DONKEY AURAL INDUSTRY PAPER**
2. **STUART TUDOR WINDSOR SMITH BRUCE PLANTAGENET**
3. **SUPERIOR HURON VICTORIA ERIE MICHIGAN ONTARIO**

LOGIGRAM **LOGIC**

At the races

A large number of punters are waiting at Ascot for the results of the forecast betting on five horses. But the commentator is tantalising them by releasing the information bit by bit. With the help of the clues below, establish the place won by each of the five horses at the finish, its number and the colour of its silk. The horses are: Lake Kazakh, Lady Heels, Peacemaker, Pull-in and Sounds OK.

Clues

1. It was a photo-finish, and difficult to sort out the identities of the three winning horses. After careful consideration, it was announced that the blue silk had passed the post just behind no 10, but just in front of a horse whose silk wasn't yellow.
2. No 15, Peacemaker, didn't win, but it was one place ahead of the horse with the grey silk.
3. The sum of the numbers of the last two horses in the first five gives the number of the winner, which is not Lake Kazahk.
4. The horses whose names begin with the same letter are separated by two places.
5. Number 5 finished two places behind the red silk.

Solution table

When one of the clues allows you to eliminate an alternative, write N at the relevant intersection and write O at the intersection of the eliminated horse.

		Silk					Number					Place				
		BLUE	GREY	YELLOW	RED	GREEN	5	8	10	13	15	FIRST	SECOND	THIRD	FOURTH	FIFTH
Horse	LAKE KAZAKH															
	LADY HEELS															
	PEACEMAKER															
	PULL-IN															
	SOUNDS OK															
Place	FIRST															
	SECOND															
	THIRD															
	FOURTH															
	FIFTH															
Number	5															
	8															
	10															
	13															
	15															

Performance table

HORSE	LAKE KAZAKH	LADY HEELS	PEACEMAKER	PULL-IN	SOUNDS OK
PLACE					
NUMBER					
SILK					

GAMES BOARD

CONCENTRATION

Look at the board on the left and note where the dark squares and triangles are placed. Cover it and fill in the missing squares and triangles on the blank board.

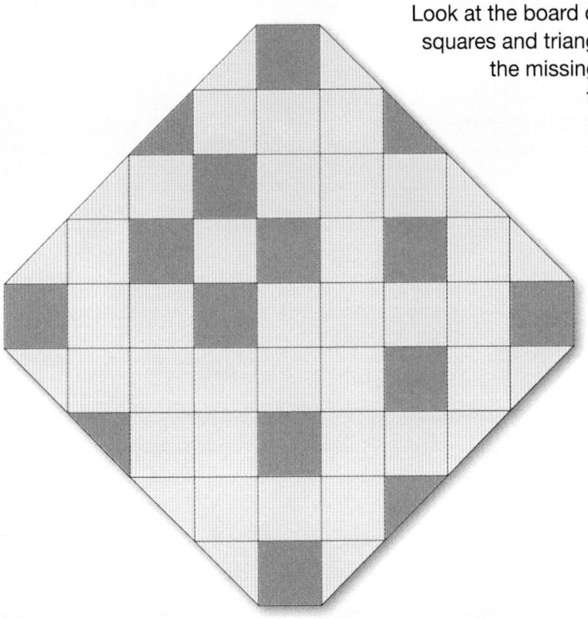

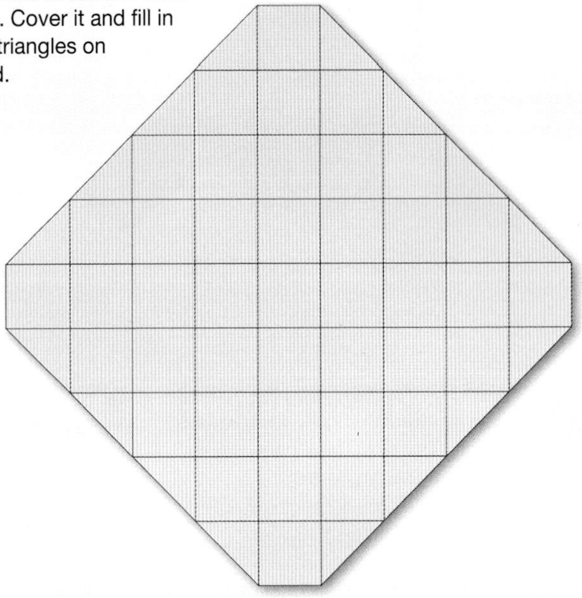

CRYPTOGRAM

ASSOCIATION

Decode this quote by Leonardo da Vinci by choosing for each symbol one of the letters that corresponds to it.

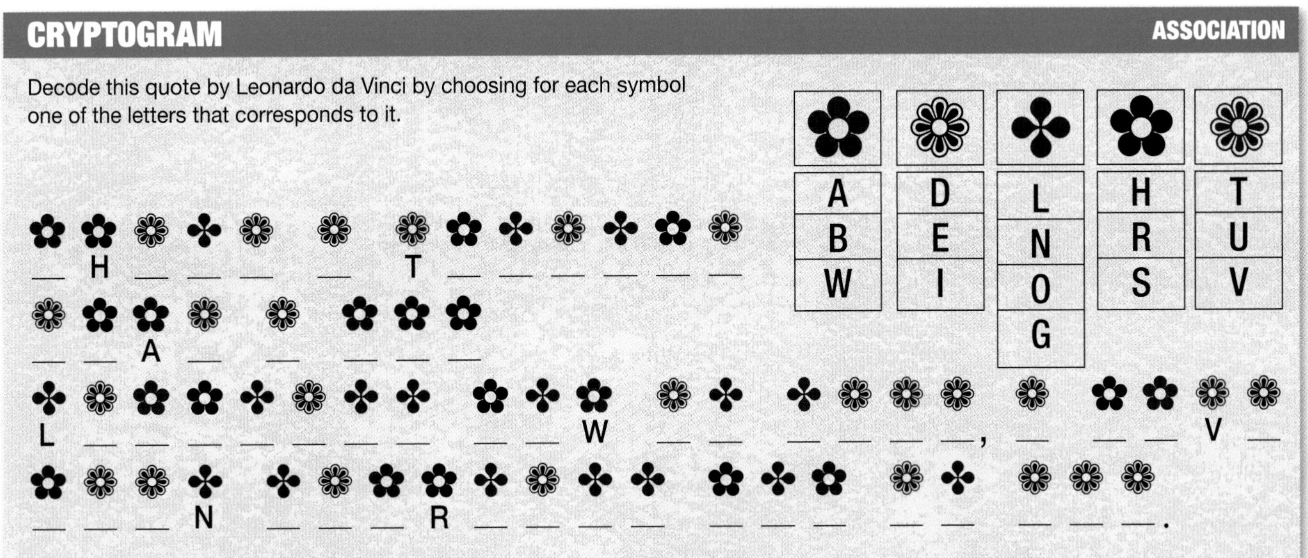

ONE WORD TOO MANY

LOGIC

In each of the following series of words, take out the one that doesn't have the same thing in common as the others do. Look closely at the letters that make up each word, and at possible additions or subtractions.

1. **BLOWER BRACKET BLAST BORDER BOOT BALLOT**

2. **HAND SANDER VERTICAL WREST DUCK UNDER**

3. **KAYAK RACECAR RADAR CIVIC LEVEL SNOWFLAKE**

CUBES — STRUCTURE

Form the names of three African countries, each time choosing a different letter from one of the sides of the cubes.

1. .... 2. .... 3. ....

PARONYMS — LANGUAGE

Paronyms (from the Greek *para*, 'beside', and *onoma*, 'word') are words having a very similar form but a totally different sense, like collision and collusion (a secret agreement). Find the paronyms that complete the following sentences.

1. When the border dividing the country came into _ _ _ _ _ _ it was to _ _ _ _ _ _ many families tragically by splitting them apart forever.
2. Before a crowd of scientists, the _ _ _ _ _ _ _ meteorologist announced the _ _ _ _ _ _ _ _ danger of a new heat wave linked to global warming.
3. The teacher said she would _ _ _ _ _ _ any excuse from her pupils _ _ _ _ _ _ those that explained why their work was late.
4. Taking drugs for recreational purposes is _ _ _ _ _ _ _ _ _ _ but taking those a doctor has _ _ _ _ _ _ _ _ _ _ to treat an illness is quite acceptable.

NUMBER SEQUENCES — LOGIC

Complete the logical sequence of these numbers

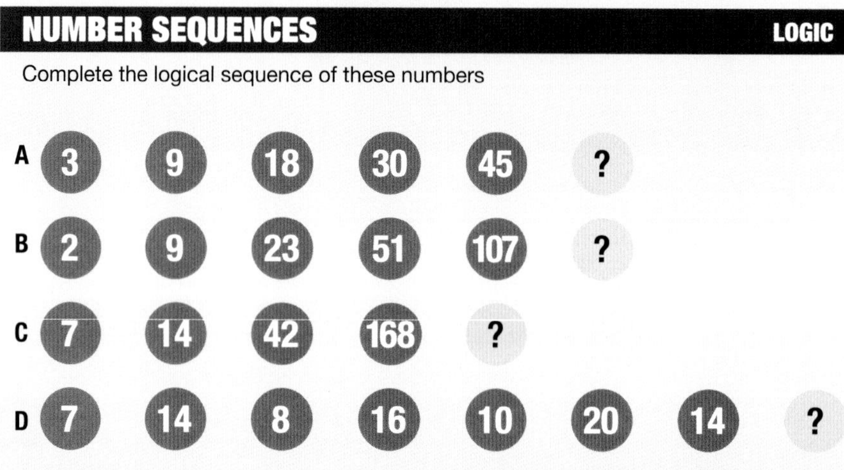

MIRROR IMAGES — SPACE

Draw these images as seen in a mirror.

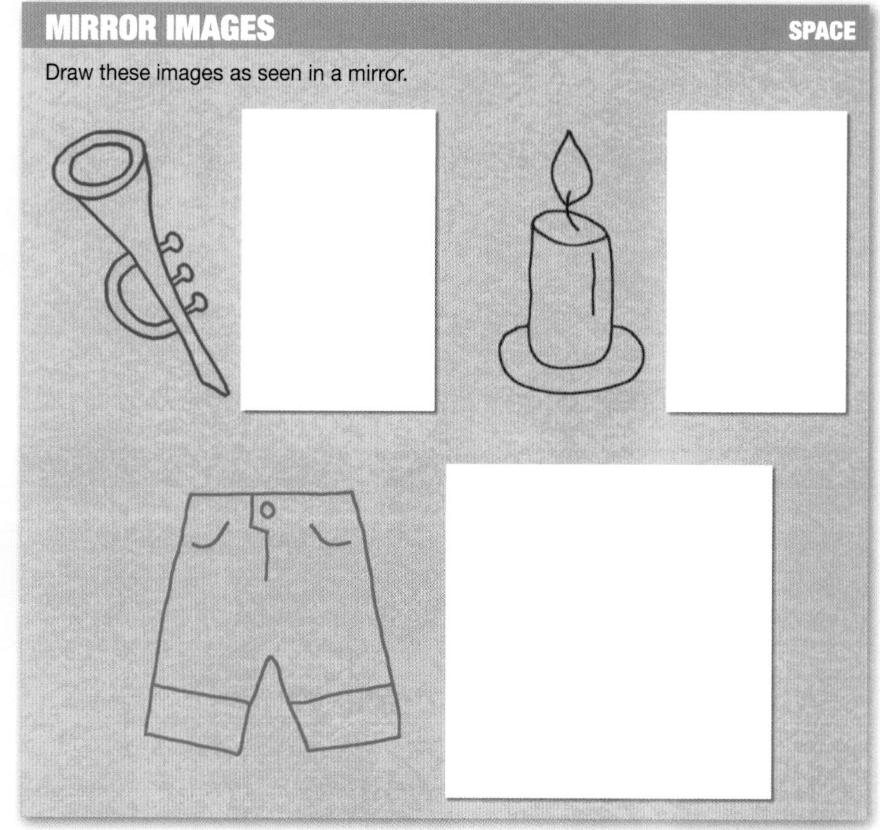

BOXED WORDS

SPACE

Fill the grid with all the names of the following birds.

CANARY
EAGLE
EMU
FALCON
GROUSE
HAWK
MYNAH
OSTRICH
OWL
PARROT
QUAIL 
ROOSTER
SEAGULL
SPARROW
STARLING
SWAN
TERN
THRUSH
TOUCAN
VULTURE

THE RIGHT PLACE

CONCENTRATION

Look carefully at this collection of hats and then cover the pictures.

Using the appropriate numbers, put the three hats on the left in the right place to restore their former layout.

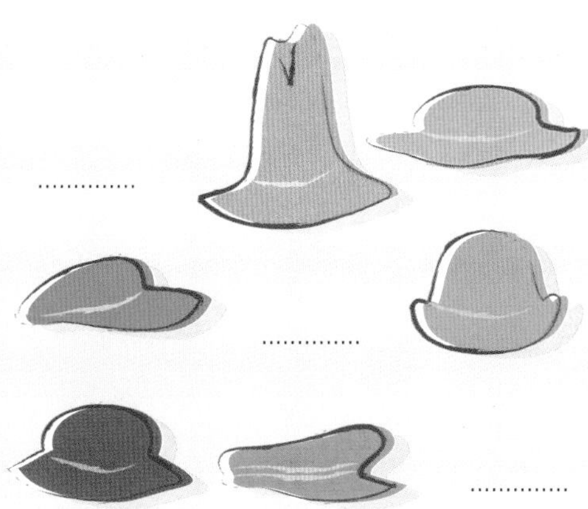

MISSING SHAPES — CONCENTRATION

Look carefully at this line of images for a few minutes and then cover it.

Draw the missing images from memory so that the line of images is correctly reproduced.

....  .... 

NUMBER SEQUENCES — LOGIC

Complete the logical sequence of the following numbers, taking due note of the geometric shapes associated with them.

A 6 12 24 29 58 63 ?

B 8 16 61 122 221 ?

C 2 — 5 — 8 — 33 — ?

POINTS IN COMMON — ASSOCIATION

For each of these series of three words, find a word that links directly to those in the series.

1. **fair – cheese – car** ....
2. **trigger – soup – barber** ....
3. **bicycle – petrol – shoe** ....
4. **eye – pine – love** ....
5. **boxer – insect – kite** ....
6. **civilisation – chorus – morning** ....

PROVERBS — LANGUAGE

Find six well-known proverbs from the explanations below. The letters of one word from each proverb are given in brackets.

1. The goal excuses the actions committed to attain it. **(EFIIJSTUS)**

....

2. There is always a good side to a bad situation. **(EILVSR)**

....

3. Those who are alike seek each other's company. **(AFEETRH)**

....

4. Something is lovely only when the person looking at it thinks it is. **(YTABEU)**

....

5. Doing nothing leads to mischievous thoughts. **(DLIE)**

....

6. One should not form an opinion of people based on their appearance. **(EVCOR)**

....

PAIRING UP

ASSOCIATION

Look carefully at these 12 photographs for a few minutes.
Group them in pairs to remember them more easily. Cover them, and then try to recall them.

1. ....
....
2. ....
....
3. ....
....
4. ....
....
5. ....
....
6. ....
....

MOCK EXAM

GENERAL KNOWLEDGE

Find a word starting with each syllable in each of the eight categories. If you are able to fill at least half the panels you have obtained 50 percent and have therefore passed your exam. But you have to complete this exam in 10 minutes and you cannot use the same word more than once.

	CO	RE	PA	MA	FI	GI
Actor (male)						
Known brand						
Item of clothing						
Title of a song (without the article)						
A girl's first name						
A quadriped animal						
A historical personality						
A flower or plant						

BROKEN SEQUENCES — STRUCTURE

Six words have had one or more syllables removed. Using those that are given below, make the words whole again. Be careful – several solutions are possible but only one combination will enable you to complete all the words.

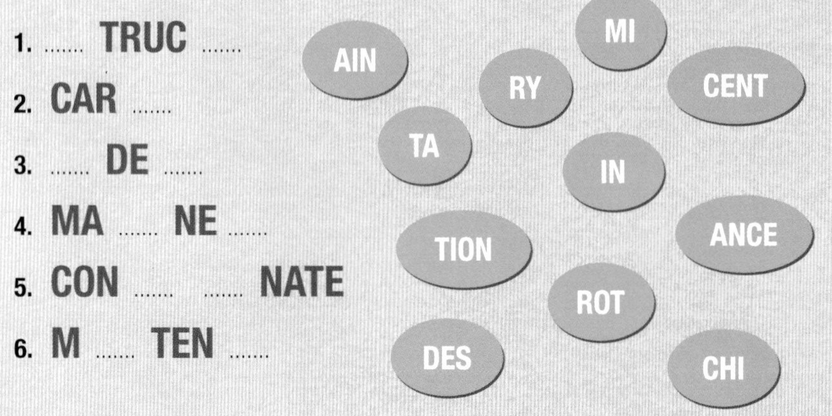

HAPPY ENDINGS — ASSOCIATION

Find 10 words ending in –CLE and directly linked to the clues given. There is one letter per dash.

1. Piece of writing ➤ _ _ _ _ C L E
2. Shoulder bone ➤ _ _ _ _ _ C L E
3. Historical record ➤ _ _ _ _ _ _ C L E
4. Means of transport ➤ _ _ _ _ C L E
5. Marine crustacean ➤ _ _ _ _ _ C L E
6. Male organ ➤ _ _ _ _ _ C L E
7. Piece of matter ➤ _ _ _ _ _ C L E
8. Spike of ice ➤ _ _ _ C L E
9. Geometrical shape ➤ _ _ _ C L E
10. Limb of a sea creature ➤ _ _ _ _ _ C L E

LOOPY LETTERS — STRUCTURE

Put the letters in each line in the right order to give you the names of two female singers. One will read in the traditional way, from left to right, and the other from right to left.

IDENTIKIT

Mrs Brown has been robbed by a bag-snatcher. She goes to the police station and, confronted with six suspects, must identify the criminal. As she is unwilling to identify him directly she says to the police officer:

NUMBER PYRAMID — LOGIC

Each brick in the pyramid represents the sum of the two bricks just below it. Fill in the rest of the pyramid with the aid of the numbers that are already in place.

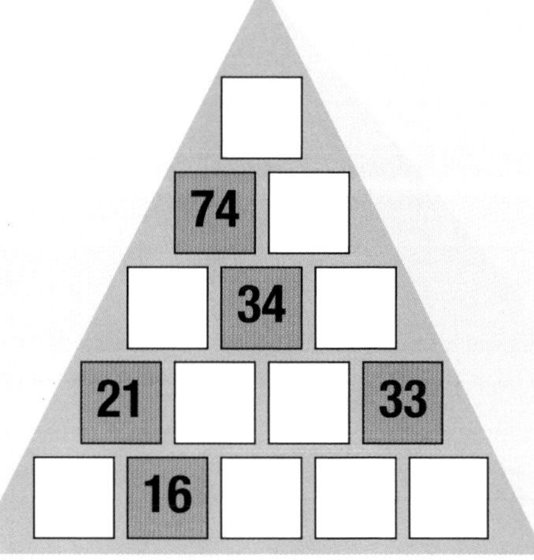

LOGIC

'Of the suspects with at least two of these three characteristics – spectacles, moustache and beard – the guilty man is the one who is smiling, has a side parting, and is not wearing a chain bracelet.' Will this suffice for the police officer to arrest the unscrupulous individual?

TRUE OR FALSE

GENERAL KNOWLEDGE

Try to work out if the following claims concerning famous paintings and artists are true or false. Circle the letters beneath T and F that correspond to your answers, and then reorder the letters you have circled to create the name of an artist.

_ _ _ _ _ _

	TRUE	FALSE
1. You would need 87 copies of the *Mona Lisa,* by Leonardo da Vinci, to cover *The Raft of the Medusa*, by Géricault.	R	S
2. *The Mona Lisa* was stolen in 1911 and found again in 1913.	I	E
3. Picasso would have been 100 years old in 2004.	G	N
4. The tomb of Gauguin is one of the most visited in the Père-Lachaise Cemetery in Paris.	P	E
5. A fresco covers the cooling tower of the Cruas nuclear power station in the Ardèche, France.	O	T
6. Rembrandt, in contrast to Van Gogh, died an enormously wealthy man, in 1669.	I	R

MAZE

SPACE

Find the only path between the two 1 euro coins touching the frame, ensuring that the path passes only over overlapping euros and cents.

WORD PAIRS

ASSOCIATION

Memorise these six pairs of words for a few minutes and then cover them and answer the six questions.

Idiot – Imbecile

Camel – Burden

Charming – Prince

Village – Hamlet

Duke – Baron

Stupid – Dopey

Questions

1. How many names of Snow White's dwarves are on the list?

....

2. Which word is associated with Hamlet?

....

3. Which title proves to be Charming?

....

4. Name the two words starting with a vowel.

....

5. What is the word Cretin linked to?

....

6. Which animal is mentioned in this list?

....

THEMATIC CROSSWORD — GENERAL KNOWLEDGE

All the names that make up this grid are those of breeds of dogs. Certain key letters have been revealed in order to guide you. Are you able to identify all these dogs?

ITINERARY — STRUCTURE

Complete the following geographical names horizontally to obtain vertically, in the first and last columns, an Eastern European town and an American state.

	O	P	E	K	
	S	R	A	E	
	W	A	N	D	
	T	H	E	N	
	E	W	A	R	
	N	K	A	R	

GAMES BOARD — CONCENTRATION

Look at this games board for a few minutes to memorise the way the shapes on it are distributed. Cover it up and then fill in the shapes in the right place on the blank board.

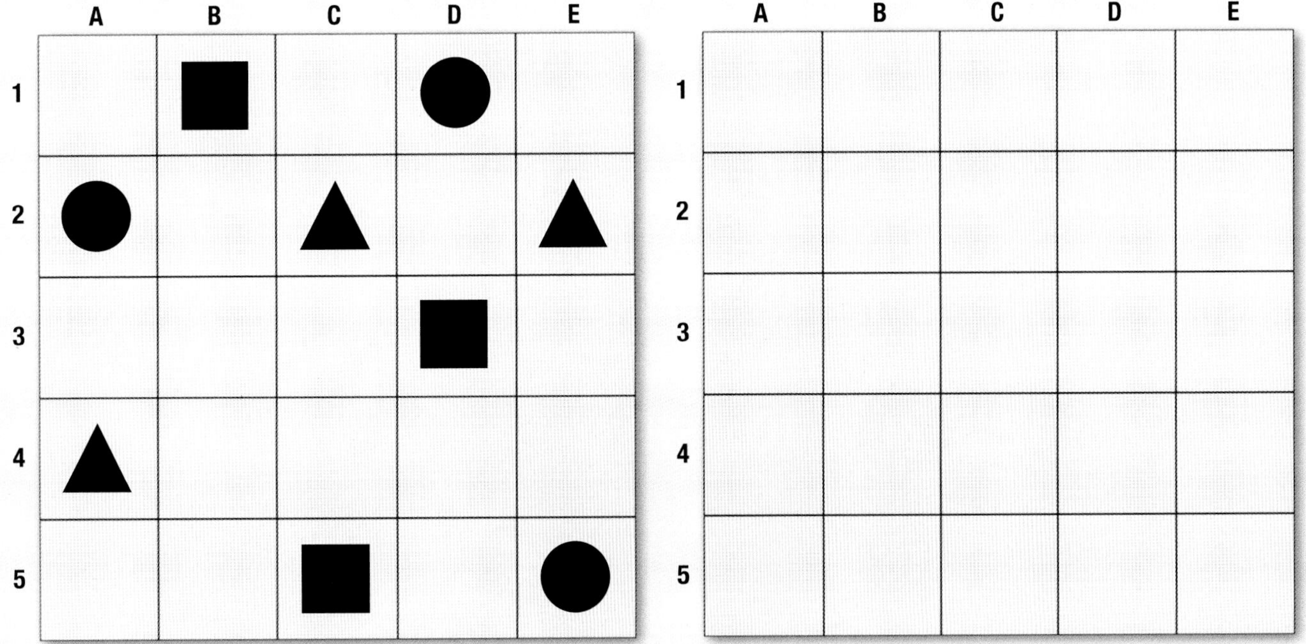

THEMATIC CROSSWORD

GENERAL KNOWLEDGE

Complete this thematic crossword with the help of the following clues.

ACROSS
1 The main product of apiculture (5)
3 A pointed, venomous organ serving to kill rivals (5)
5 Secreted by glands, it forms the cells that make a honeycomb (3)
6 A social insect, the only one domesticated apart from the silkworm (3)
7 The name of a colony of tens of thousands of individuals (5)
9 Sought after for its rejuvenating properties (5, 5)
10 The female who dominates the colony and produces 3 000 eggs a day (5)

DOWN
1 The home of the colony (4)
2 This insect has two of these, composed of 3 000 to 8 000 simple ones (4)
4 They go from flower to flower collecting this (6)
5 The sterile individual that ensures the nutrition and defence of the colony (6)
6 Mistakenly, it attempts to reproduce during the nuptial flight (9)
8 The powder that draws this insect to flowers (6)

MAGIC SQUARE

LOGIC

Here is a magic square made up of five rows. Fill in the missing numbers from 1-9 to make the sum of 65 for each vertical, diagonal and horizontal line.

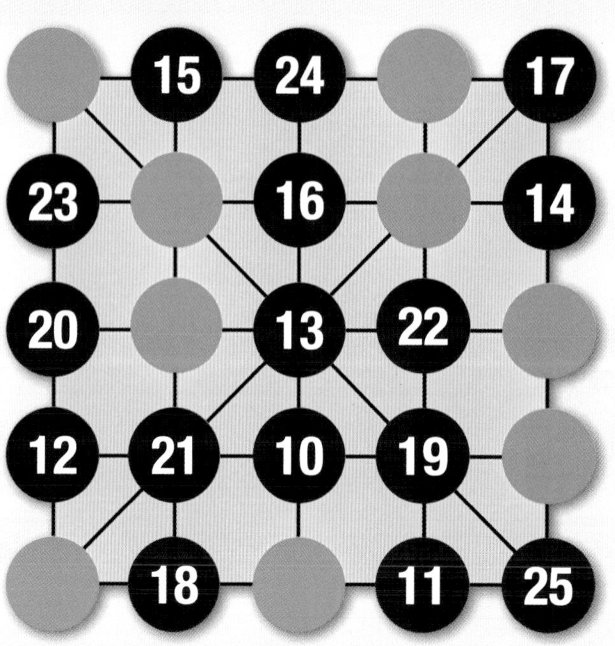

CLOSE-UP

CONCENTRATION

Identify the object, animal or character that our designer has had fun transforming.

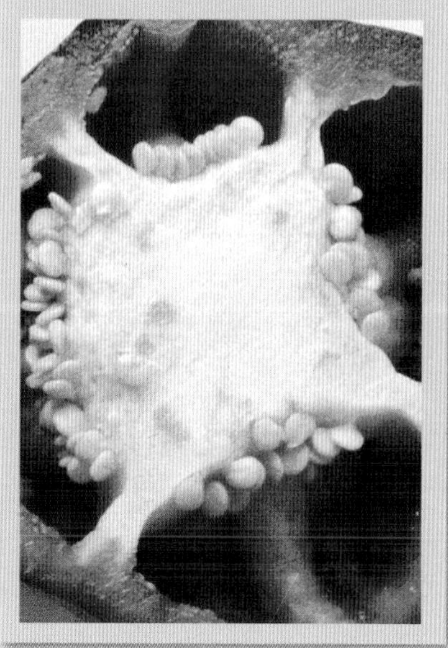

PROBLEM — LOGIC

A sweet-shop attracts all the neighbourhood children. It sells lollipops, toffees and boiled sweets in flavours that can't be found elsewhere.

- Lucy bought four lollipops, three toffees and two boiled sweets for two dollars.
- Kevin took six toffees and one lollipop or the same price.
- Anna chose ten boiled sweets, one lollipop and one toffee; she also paid two dollars.

What is the price of the sweets as sold by the shop?

Boiled sweet ....

Toffee ....

Lollipop ....

SANDWICH — STRUCTURE

Move all the letters below to the empty spaces in the grid to the right, to obtain nine horizontal words. If you have chosen correctly you will discover vertically the titles of two songs by the Beatles.

List of letters to use:

A A D E E E
E L N N N P
R S T Y Y Y

F	L		P	A		E	R
C	H		A	P		S	T
D	I		T	A		C	E
A	T		O	R		E	Y
A	M		T	H		S	T
C	I		C	U		A	R
M	E		I	T		T	E
D	I		G	O		A	L
A	N		W	H		R	E

ITINERARY — STRUCTURE

Complete the following geographical names horizontally to obtain, vertically, in the first and last columns, a Central American country and an American state.

	O	L	A	N	
	N	K	A	R	
	A	S	H	I	
	R	A	K	A	
	U	S	C	A	
	R	A	B	I	

SPOT THE 7 DIFFERENCES — CONCENTRATION

There are seven differences between these two pictures. Can you find them?

OVERLAPPING SHAPES — CONCENTRATION

Look at this picture: which shape recurs most frequently? You must respond in under 30 seconds and without taking notes.

HISTORICAL LANDMARKS — TIME

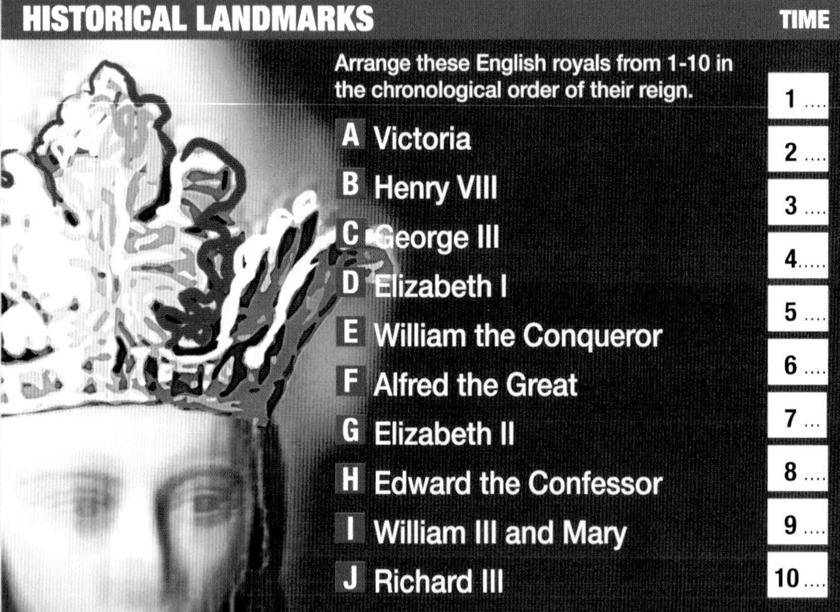

MEMORY TEST — CONCENTRATION

Look carefully at these seven objects for 30 seconds, and then cover them.

Can you name them, using their initials to help you?

J ....

B ....

S ....

B ....

T ....

K ....

C ....

CUBES — STRUCTURE

Form the names of three great cricket players by taking a different letter from the side of each cube.

1. ....

2. ....

3. ....

ODD ONE OUT — LOGIC

Establish the link between all these creatures and then identify the odd one out.

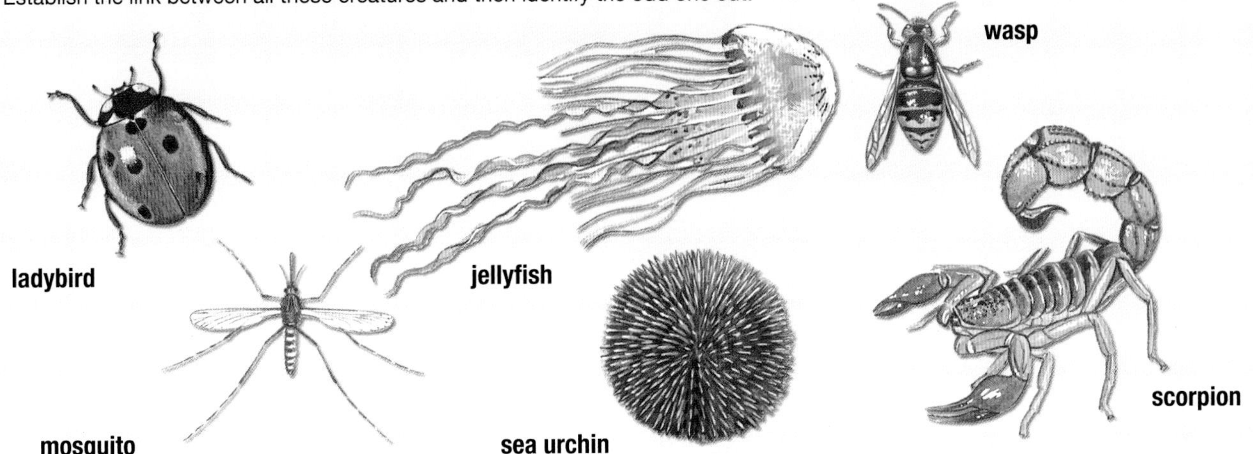

MATCHES — LOGIC

Move only one match to change the five squares into six squares.

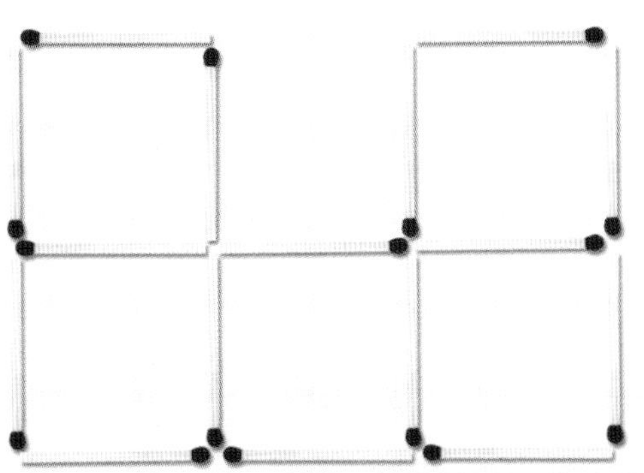

PROBLEM — LOGIC

The scores on a dart board get higher from the outside to the centre: 1, 3, 7, 15 and 25 points.
Roland has six darts and manages to make 102 points. Can you list all the ways in which he could have obtained this score, and work out which places on the target he didn't hit?

HAPPY ENDINGS — ASSOCIATION

Find 10 words ending in -ORE and directly associated with the clues given (there is one letter per dash).

1. Sign ➤ _ _ _ _ _ _ ORE
2. Oral culture ➤ _ _ _ _ _ ORE
3. Love madly ➤ _ _ ORE
4. Investigate ➤ _ _ _ _ ORE
5. Large quantity ➤ _ _ _ ORE
6. Take no notice of ➤ _ _ _ ORE
7. Meat-eater ➤ _ _ _ _ _ _ ORE
8. Earlier than ➤ _ _ _ ORE
9. Skin ulcer ➤ _ _ _ _ ORE
10. Coastline ➤ _ _ ORE

SPEED LIMIT OF 90!

LOGIC

Reach 90 with these sixteen numbers by placing each one in a box identical to the one it appears in.

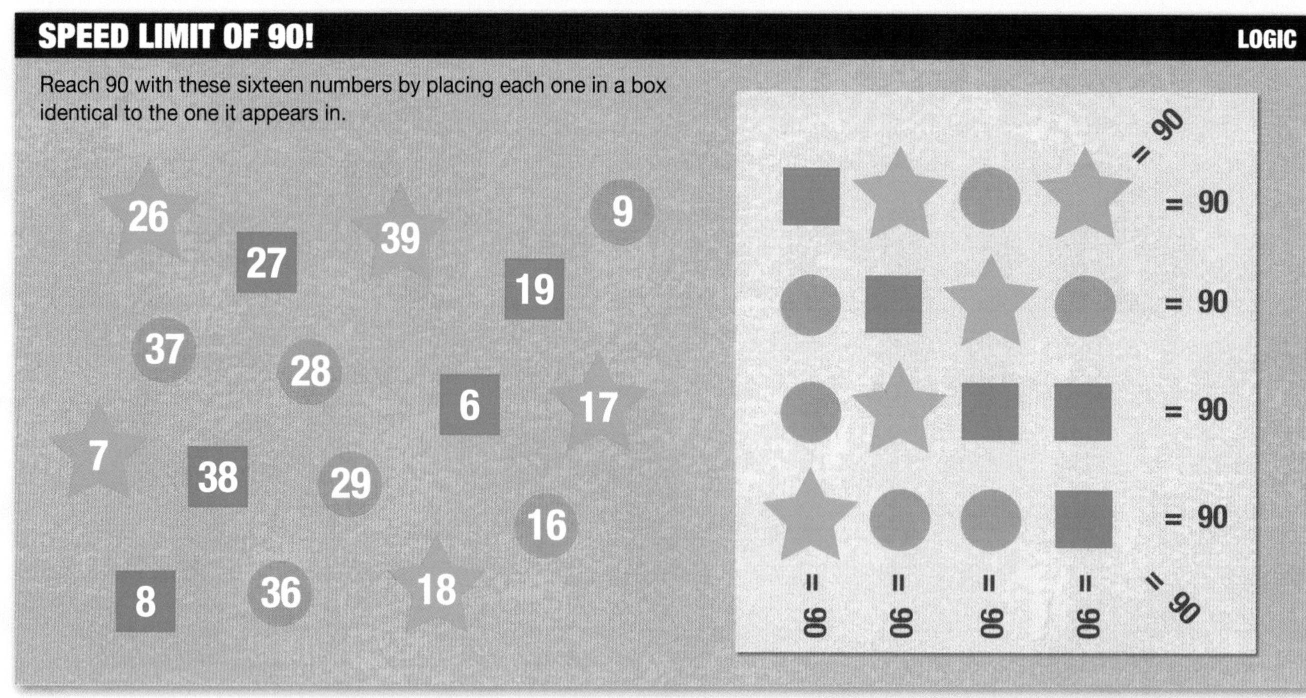

POINTS IN COMMON

ASSOCIATION

For each of these series of words, find one word that links to the three others.

1. **soap – sea – beer** ....
2. **rainbow – dive – light** ....
3. **degree – music – adult** ....
4. **dancer – asterisk – sun** ....
5. **rib – lift – canary** ....
6. **stage – bird – chair** ....

MAGIC SQUARE

LOGIC

On this box are superimposed three rows of three circles, the central one of which contains the number five. Using a range of numbers from 1 to 9 fill in the circles in such a way that each line of three circles, vertical, diagonal and horizontal, adds up to the number 15. You will have to feel your way through this puzzle.

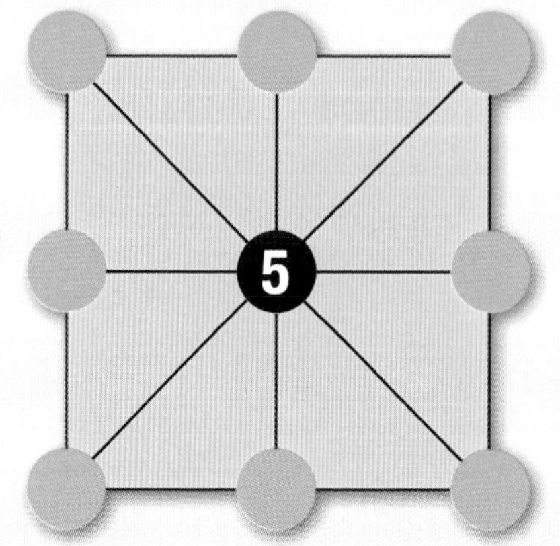

DRAWING FROM MEMORY

CONCENTRATION

Look carefully at these drawings. Close your eyes and try to visualise them in relation to each other. If you forget one of them, look at it again to consolidate the image.

Cover the pictures and try to draw them all from memory.

ODD ONE OUT

LOGIC

Spot the odd one out in this series of ten animals.

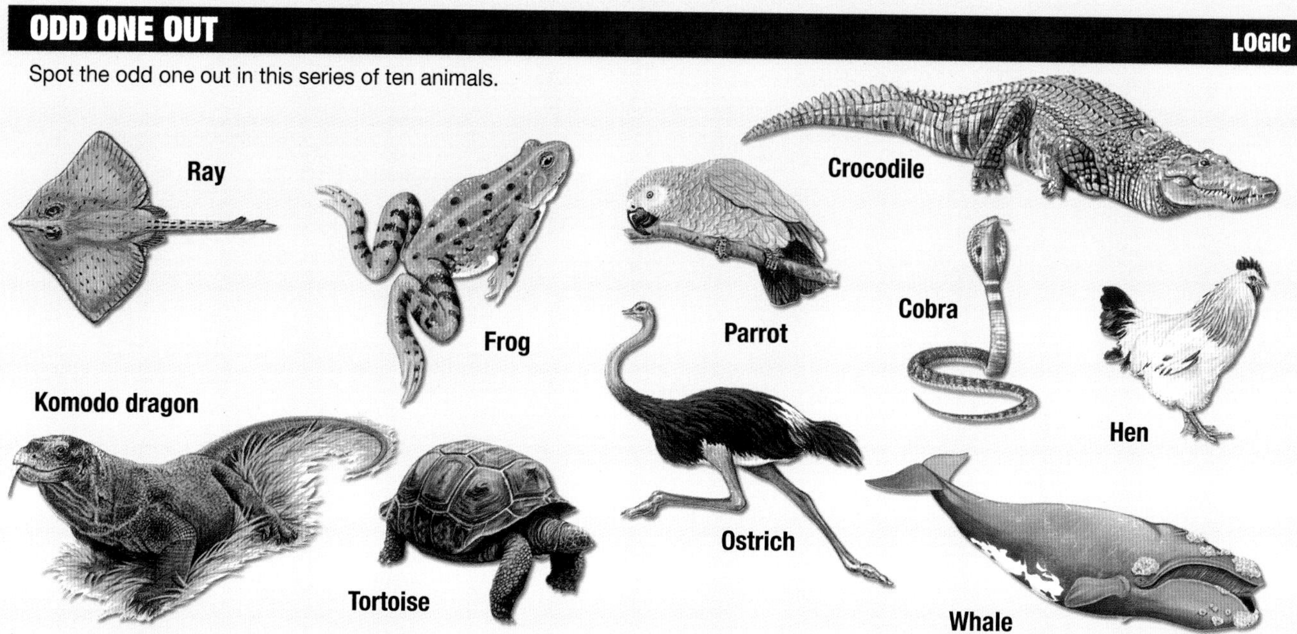

CODE-BREAKER

CONCENTRATION

Here is the basis of Morse code

A .-	I ..	Q --.-	Y -.--
B -...	J .---	R .-.	Z --..
C -.-.	K -.-	S ...	. .-.-.-
D -..	L .-..	T -	, --..--
E .	M --	U ..-	? ..--..
F ..-.	N -.	V ...-	: ---...
G --.	O ---	W .--	- -....-
H	P .--.	X -..-	' !

1. Can you decode this quote by Samuel Johnson ?

- .... . / - .-. ..- . / .- .-. - / --- ..-. /
-- . -- --- .-. -.-- / .. ... / - .... . /
.- .-. - / --- ..-. / .- - - . -. - .. --- -.

2. Can you code this quote by Kahlil Gibran?
Yesterday is but today's memory, tomorrow is today's dream.

....

....

....

ANAPHRASES

STRUCTURE

Use all the letters given in colour to form anagrams that complete the sentence in a sensible way.

1. G A I I N S R
.... and ....are two words that both mean 'moving upwards'.

2. D E R S P I A
The inventor of disposable .... should be ....for saving parents from the .... of endless laundering.

3. U Y D T I N
Those who practise .... are unlikely to have .... cupboards.

PAIRING UP — CONCENTRATION

Look at these five pairs of photos carefully for a few minutes, and then cover them.

Here is one half of each pair. Can you remember what the other half is?

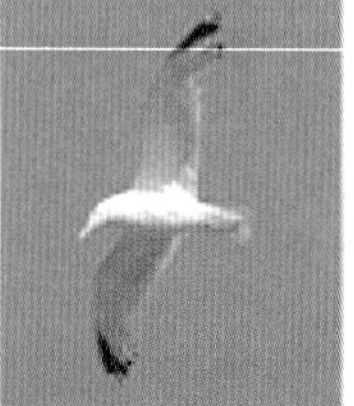

PUZZLE — SPACE

Look at this figure.

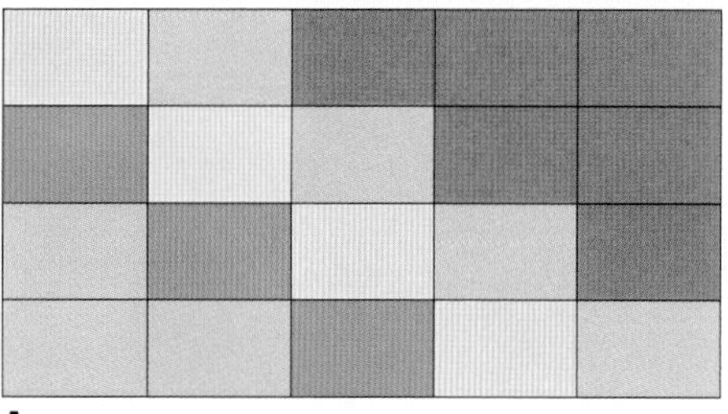
A

Which three of the numbered pieces below should you put together to make figure A? (Don't superimpose or modify the shape of the pieces.)

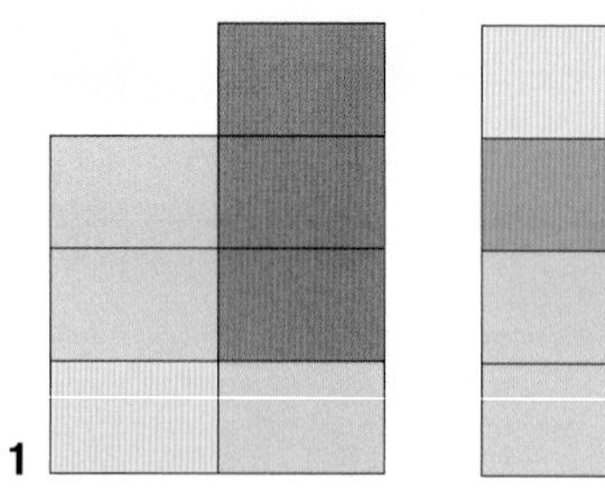

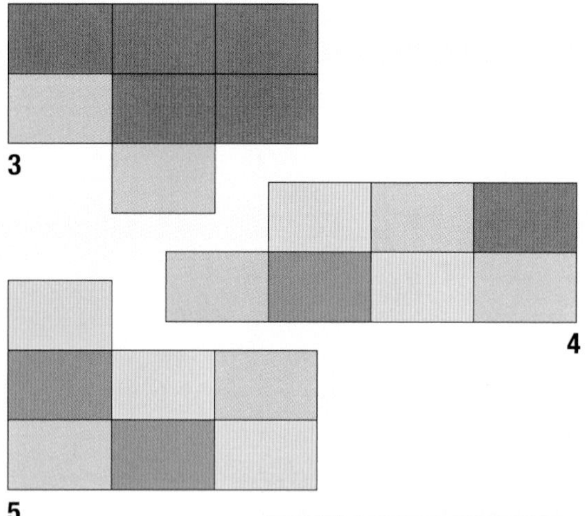

ODD ONE OUT — LOGIC

Spot the odd one out in this sequence of numbers.

3 5 7 11 13 17 19 21 23

Solutions

Pages 62-63

MIXED PROVERBS

1. Every dog has its day
2. A stitch in time saves nine
3. In for a penny in for a pound

NUMBER PYRAMID

The fourth number at the base of the pyramid must be a low number, or else you couldn't get 10 on the third level. So put 1 between 6 and 2. And going up: 6+1=7, and 1+2 =3 at the end of the second level. In the same way, to get 117 at the top, you add 47, 10 and twice the missing number on the third level: 117-47-10=60 and 60÷2=30. So 30 goes between 47 and 10. You can then place 47+30=77 and 30 +10 =40 on the fourth level. On the second level, you get 30-7=23 and 47-23=24. At the base, you end up with 24-7 or 23-6=17.

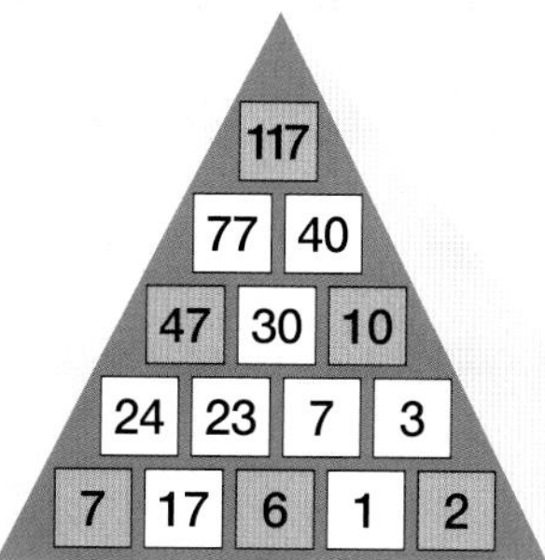

PROBLEM

If x is the age of the younger brother five years ago, the older brother was then 2 x. Today, they are respectively x + 5 and 2 x + 5. In eight years' time, they will be x +13 and 2 x +13. This makes a total of 3 x +26. For 3 x + 26 to equal 50, x must equal 8. So the child who is speaking is 13 today (8 + 5).

SPOT THE 7 DIFFERENCES

ANAPHRASES

1. Canoes, oceans
2. Eastern, earnest, nearest
3. Aboard, abroad

REBUS

American Beauty, directed by Sam Mendes, starring Kevin Spacey, Annette Bening, Thora Birch, Wes Bentley and Meena Suvari. (1999) (A – mare – reek – can – butte – ee)

Pages 64-65

SHADOWS

Shadow no.4.

PROGRESSIVE QUIZ

1. Having one's sea legs
2. Spring tide
3. The Caspian Sea
4. The Aegean Sea
5. True. It is in fact a lake, the most salty in the world (30%)
6. The Suez Canal
7. The Red Sea
8. Plimsoll line
9. Argonaut
10. The Gulf of Oman

WORD PAIRS

1. Letter
2. No
3. Residence
4. Before
5. Soup
6. Showers, rain

LETTER SEQUENCES

1. G: you go back 3 letters, then 4, then 5. The following is 6 letters before M.
2. V: it is a sequence of letters that, when written in capital form, need no rounded shape.

HIDDEN WORDS

The name of the hidden animal is BABOON.

THE RIGHT TIME

Watch B shows the right time: 12h 25. Watches A and C are out by a quarter of an hour (12h 10 and 12h 40) and watch D is half an hour fast (12h 55).

Pages 66-67

ANAGRAMS

1. Crocus
2. Lotus
3. Rose
4. Aster
5. Mimosa
6. Primrose
7. Gentian
8. Gardenia
9. Scilla

PROBLEM

Five yellow balls.
On scale 2, three reds = three yellows + three blues. Now, three blues equal two greens (scale 3). And two greens equal two reds + two yellows (scale 1). So three reds equals three yellows + two reds + two yellows. If you take two reds from each pan, what remains is one red = three yellows + two yellows, that is, five yellows.

MIXED QUOTES

1. 'My kingdom for a horse': quote from *Richard III* by Shakespeare.
2. 'And yet it moves': Italian astronomer Galileo accused of heresy.
3. 'England expects every man to do his duty': Admiral Horatio Nelson.

HOMOGRAPHS

1. Fair
2. Leaves
3. Right
4. Desert

PROBLEM

1. He needs to give her only 50 cents. Lawrence will have 50 cents less, Laura 50 cents more, the difference between what they have being one dollar.
2. It's possible: one 1 dollar coin and one coin of 10 cents, which is not one dollar.

STICK-ON WORDS

ANCHOR, RAGE (Anchorage)
HAVE, ANNA (Havana)
STOCK, HOME (Stockholm)
BAG, DAD (Bagdad)
ADDER, LAID (Adelaide)
TUNE, IS (Tunis)
WAR, SAW (Warsaw)
KEY, TOE (Quito)
LOOSE, URN (Lucerne)
BILL, BOUGH (Bilbao)

Pages 68-69

KNOW YOUR WORLD

1. Washington
2. Oregon
3. Idaho
4. Nevada
5. California
6. Arizona
7. Utah
8. Colorado
9. Wyoming
10. Nebraska
11. Kansas
12. Missouri
13. Louisiana
14. Texas (Taxes)
15. Michigan
16. Ohio (0 H I0)
17. Maine
18. Tennessee
19. Georgia
20. Florida

OVERLAPPING SHAPES

There are 32.

REBUS

Misfortune is the true test of friendship
(The Travellers and the Bear)
(miss – four – tune – is – the – true – test – of – friend – ship)

ANAGRAMS

1. Horse
2. Zebra
3. Wolf
4. Dingo
5. Leopard
6. Stoat
7. Racoon
8. Otter
9. Poodle
10. Badger

Pages 70-71

ZIGZAG WORDS

The town is LOURDES.

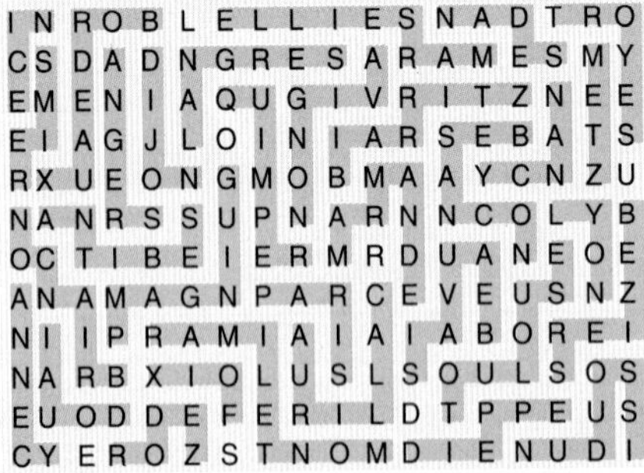

HISTORICAL LANDMARKS

A5 – B4 – C10 – D1 – E8 – F9 – G2 – H3 – I7 – J6

WORD HOLES

1. Serendipity
2. Macadamia
3. Homogenous
4. Discipline
5. Fairytale
6. Criterion

MATCHING UP

A4 (from Charles *Boycott*, land agent in Ireland whose tenants refused to communicate with him after he wouldn't lower rents) – B10 (from *black ball*: symbol of an opposing vote) – C1 (from *trek*: 'draw', referring to the oxen drawing a wagon on a long journey) – D3 (from *kampong*: 'village') – E9 (from *thag*: 'thief') – F5 (war cry) – G2 (from *hupocrisi* : 'mimic') – H8 ('act of faith') – I6 ('I win') – J7 (from *Taler*, short for *Joachimstaler*: coin made from metal mined in Joachimstal).

CUT-UP LETTERS

You could take out :
P (Addled) – I (Serous) – C (Harmed) – A (Miming) – S (Having) – S (Decent) – O (Corner).
The name of the painter is PICASSO.

CHALLENGE

If you have remembered more than half the words in one minute, well done ! If you have trouble remembering three of them 10 minutes later, this is normal. It is also possible that you have said or written glass for goblet, cheese for Parmesan, bird for eagle … The memory retains the sense of words, not their form.

Pages 72-73

STICK-ON WORDS

TOLLS, TOY (Tolstoy)
VOLT, AIR (Voltaire)
WIT, MAN (Whitman)
AT, WOOD (Atwood)
TOLL, KEEN (Tolkien)
SHAKE, SPEAR (Shakespeare)
HEMMING, WAY (Hemingway)
COAL, RIDGE (Coleridge)
GORE, DIMMER (Gordimer)
TAG, ORE (Tagore)

MATCHING UP

A6 – B2 – C4 – D7 – E5 – F9 – G10 – H1 – I8 – J3

WHICH COMES NEXT?

The illustrated words have been classified according to their first letter in inverse alphabetical order: zebra, Yorkshire, xylophone, whisky. The fifth word must therefore start with V, and among the proposed instruments (piano, trombone, violin) it can only be violin.

MYSTERY PHRASE

The quote is: 'Talk to a man about himself and he will listen for hours.' (Benjamin Disraeli)
The first and the last letters of each word are the only ones in the right place.

LOTTO

Pages 74-75

MYSTERY WORDS

A. Jane Fonda
B. Zinedine Zidane
C. J.K. Rowling
D. Mickey Mouse
E. Madonna

CRYPTOGRAM

History is the version of past events that people have decided to agree upon.
Napoleon Bonaparte

IDIOMATIC TRIPLETS

1. Act
2. Half
3. Air
4. Hand
5. Man
6. Dark

MATCHES

The blue-tipped matches have stayed in place.

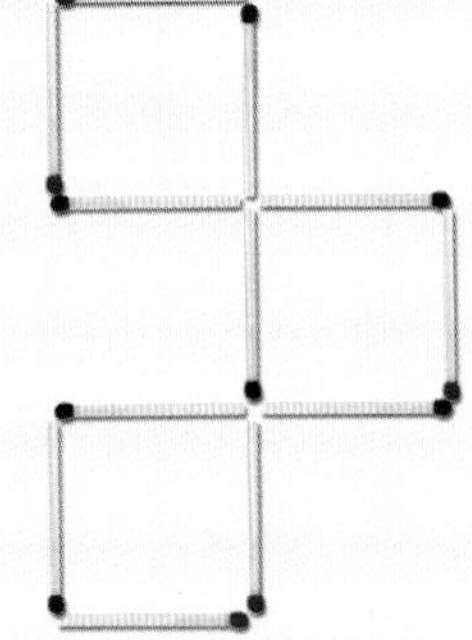

ROSETTE

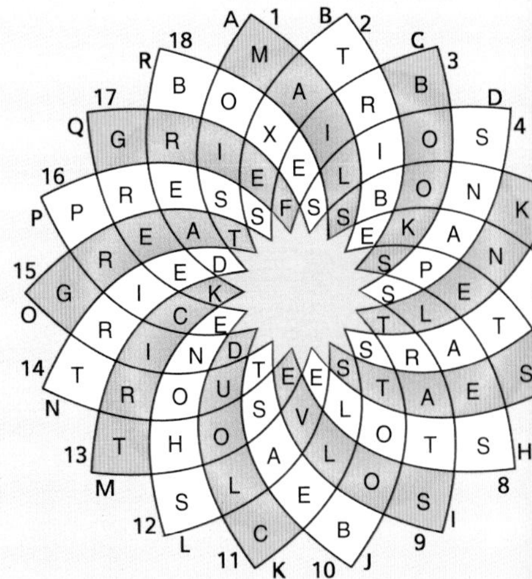

Pages 76-77

REBUS
Once upon a time in the west, by Sergio Leone
(one – sup – honour – time – in – the – west)

STICK-ON TITLES
1. In the ghetto
2. Return to sender
3. Devil in disguise
4. Love me tender

WHICH COMES NEXT?
The 2 of diamonds completes this sequence of cards vertically and horizontally. To find the suit you have to note that the four suits (hearts, spades, diamonds, clubs) appear once on each line and in each column, with red and black alternating. As for the number, this becomes obvious once you have worked out that the sum of the value of the cards is 20 in both directions.

LADDER
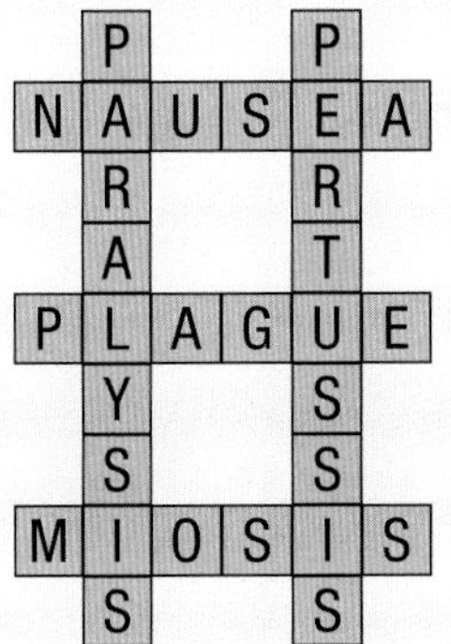

Pages 78-79

TEST YOUR OBSERVATION SKILLS
1. A red ace
2. The right hand
3. False
4. Gold coins
5. Facing forward
6. Her left hand
7. False
8. To the left
9. Feathers
10. True

BROKEN SEQUENCES
1. Decimal
2. Impolite
3. Polished
4. Departure
5. Condiment
6. Absurdity

WORD HOLES
1. Iceberg
2. Inequality
3. Insular
4. Interim
5. Islam
6. Idyll

THE RIGHT TIME
1. The clock registering 8 o'clock matches all the conditions. The one reading 1 o'clock is 7 hours behind, and the one reading 3 o'clock (pm) is 7 hours fast.
2. The answer is once again the clock showing 8 o'clock. The clock that reads 1 o'clock (pm) is 5 hours fast and the one reading 3 o'clock is 5 hours slow.

MAZE

CATERPILLAR
CHESS
SHEDS
SHADE
BASED
BEARD
BOARD

Pages 80-81

BOXED WORDS
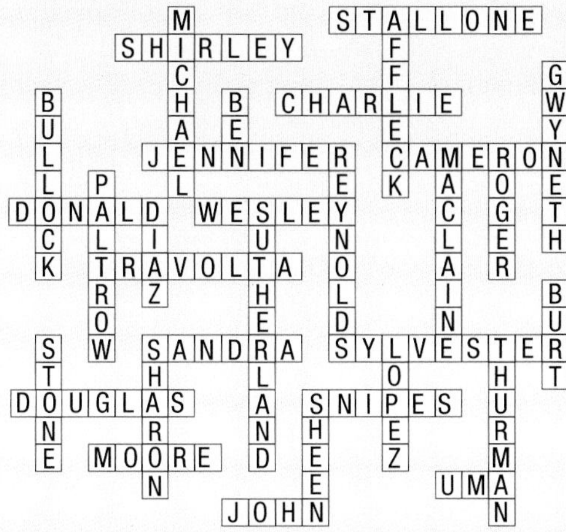

HOMOPHONES
1. Tern, turn
2. Mist, missed
3. Horse, hoarse
4. Sleight, slight

BONUS LETTER
1. Park
2. Sport
3. Pastor
4. Planter
5. Pilaster
6. Pearliest

LOOPY LETTERS
E I N S T E I N
N I L K N A R F

NUMBER PYRAMID
Start at the top and work your way down: 91-40 = 51 which you place next to 40. Then 40-20 = 20 which you place on the left in the third row, and so on.

91				
40	51			
20	20	31		
12	8	12	19	
7	5	3	9	10

PROBLEM
Put away your calculator! When they cross they will be the same distance away from this station.

Pages 82-83

GEOMETRIC SEQUENCES

A. Figure 5: the coloured dot moves from one corner to the other in a clockwise direction and alternates between red and green.
B. Figure 2: each figure repeats the previous configuration and adds a square.
C. Figure 1: the red segment makes a quarter turn in an anti-clockwise direction. The blue dot doesn't move, but is hidden when the red segment moves across it.
D. Figure 4: each coloured square moves one place each time in a specific direction. The blue moves up, the green towards the left
E. Figure 2: the red triangle turns 90 degrees each time in a clockwise direction. The blue triangle does the same thing in the opposite direction.

JUMBLED WORDS

1. Bogart – Astaire
2. Brando – Lancaster
3. Pacino – Redford

ESCALETTERS

RUE
+T TRUE
+N TUNER
+E TUREEN
+I RETINUE
+D REUNITED
+L INTERLUDE

POINTS IN COMMON

1. Tear
2. Fair
3. Cut
4. White
5. True
6. Seed

SUPERIMPOSITION

Discs 2, 4 and 6

Pages 84-85

IDIOMATIC TRIPLETS

1. Better
2. Bad
3. Bite
4. Blood
5. Dead
6. Salt

TEST YOUR OBSERVATION SKILLS

1. The third one.
2. She is lighting her neighbour's cigarette
3. False: the tray is laden
4. Blue
5. Five
6. Three: pictures 5, 6 and 7
7. The character in the middle, with the scarf
8. False: it is switched on throughout
9. True: all except the first
10. On the back of the chair in which the waiter is sitting.

IDENTIKIT

Mystery flag

SANDWICH

CARPE DIEM ('seize the day'), the slogan of those who celebrate life.

C	O	C	K	S
E	N	A	C	T
L	U	R	C	H
E	X	P	E	L
B	L	E	N	D
R	I	D	E	R
A	M	I	S	S
T	R	E	S	S
E	M	M	E	T

MATCHING UP

A8 – B3 – C9 – D1 – E6 – F5 – G10 – H7 – I2 – J4

Pages 86-87

MYSTERY WORDS

A. A name
B. The Eiffel Tower
C. The telephone
D. A glove
E. Class

TEST YOUR OBSERVATION SKILLS

1. A dog
2. A pistol
3. True
4. True
5. A woman
6. False
7. Above the knee
8. False
9. Yes, to the right, in a black hat.
10. Bottom left.

HISTORICAL LANDMARKS

Jean-Paul Sartre and Ayn Rand (1905) – Maya Angelou and Che Guevara (1928) – Julie Andrews and Elvis Presley (1935) – Aung San Suu Kyi and Steve Martin (1945) – Bill Gates and Bruce Willis (1955)

PROBLEM

Midday. It will be midday again, but five days later, because the little hand tracing the hours completes two revolutions per day.

SYNONYMS

1. Corpulent
2. Stormy
3. Leaden
4. Oppressive
5. Substantial
6. Villain
7. Congested
8. Large

ONE WORD TOO MANY

1. This series contains the names of rivers of the world (Nile, Rhine, Don, Ural, Indus) except PAPER, which doesn't contain letters referring to a river.
2. These are the surnames of British royals, except for SMITH.
3. These words all refer to the Great Lakes of North America, except for VICTORIA which is in Africa.

Pages 88-89

LOGIGRAM

At the races

According to clue 3, the winner is number 13 (5+8) or number 15 (5+ 10).
Clue 2 eliminates number 15 as the potential winner. Therefore number 13 won the race.
Numbers 5 and 8 are in the two last places.
Numbers 10 and 15 are either second or third.
Number 15, Peacemaker, is three places away from the other horse which also has a name beginning with P (Pull-In), according to clue 4.
Peacemaker therefore can't be third (Pull-In would be last or sixth!) Number 15 is therefore second, and Pull-In, three places behind, is fifth. So number 10 is third. The horse with the blue silk is therefore fourth (first clue). The horse with the grey silk is just behind Peacemaker, that is, third (clue 2).
The horses with the names beginning with L (Lake Kazahk and Lady Heels) must therefore be first and fourth, because the P's are second and fifth. So the third is Sounds OK.
Lake Kazahk did not win (clue 3). He therefore came fourth, and the winner is Lady Heels.
Number 5 did not come fifth, otherwise the red silk would be third (clue 5), but the third is in grey. So number 5 is fourth and number 8 fifth. The red silk is thus second. By a process of elimination, the yellow, which is

not last (clue 1) is first, whereas the last of the first five is wearing the green silk.

Performance table

HORSE	LAKE KAZAKH	LADY HEELS	PEACEMAKER	PULL-IN	SOUNDS OK
PLACE	fourth	first	second	fifth	third
NUMBER	5	13	15	8	10
SILK	blue	yellow	red	green	grey

CRYPTOGRAM

While I thought that I was learning how to live, I have been learning how to die.

Leonardo da Vinci

ONE WORD TOO MANY

1. You can remove the initial letter B and still read an existing word (lower, racket, last, order, allot), except for BOOT.
2. Each of the words can be lengthened with –LING (handling…), except for VERTICAL.
3. Each word is a palindrome (they read the same from left to right and right to left), except for SNOWFLAKE.

BOXED WORDS

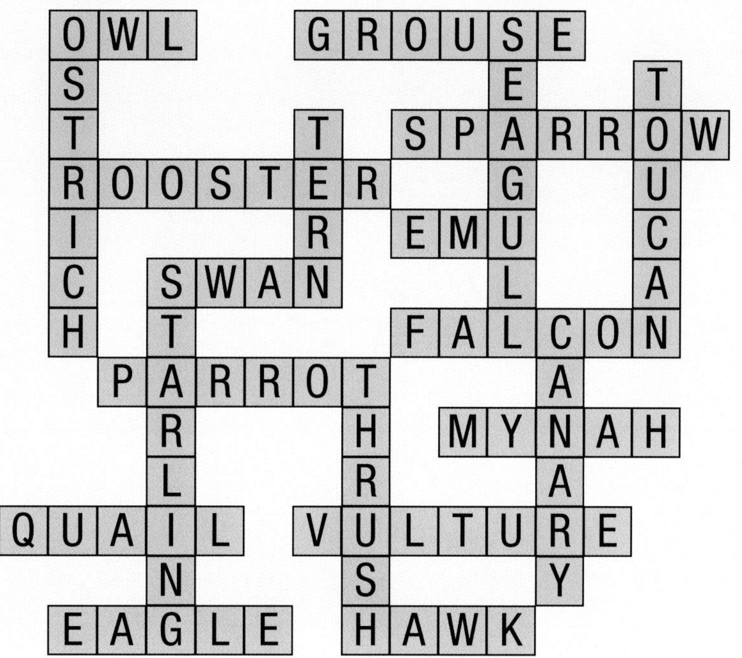

Pages 90-91

CUBES

Burundi – Namibia – Senegal

PARONYMS

1. Effect, affect
2. Eminent, imminent
3. Accept, except
4. Proscribed, prescribed

NUMBER SEQUENCES

A. 63; you add 6, then 9, 12, 13, 15.
The next is 45 + 18.

B. 219; you multiply by 2 and add 5.
The next is 107 x 2 +5.

C. C. 840; you multiply by 2, and then by 3, by 4….
The next is 168 x 5

D. D. 28; you multiply by 2 and subtract 6 alternately. The next is 14 x 2.

MIRROR IMAGES

Pages 92-93

NUMBER SEQUENCES

A. 68: In a circle, you multiply by 2; in a square, you add 5. The next one is 63 + 5.

B. 122: a triangle multiples by 2, a star reverses the meaning of what is written. So 221 is written from right to left and you get back to 122.

C. 62: multiply by the number of sticks above the line, and subtract the number of sticks below. The next is 33 x 2 -4.

POINTS IN COMMON

1. Wheel
2. Hair
3. Pump
4. Apple
5. Fly
6. Dawn

PROVERBS

1. The end justifies the means.
2. Every cloud has a silver lining.
3. Birds of a feather flock together.
4. Beauty is in the eye of the beholder.
5. The devil makes work for idle hands.
6. Never judge a book by its cover.

PAIRING UP

1. Skier and mountain
2. Sea and surfer
3. Kangaroo and giraffe
4. Medicines and doctor
5. Tower of Pisa and Eiffel Tower
6. Bread and cheese

MOCK EXAM

Examples of solutions :

CO Connery, Coca-Cola, coat, *Copacabana (Barry Manilow)*, Colleen, coati, Cook (Capt. James), coconut palm

RE Redford, Renault, redingote, *Red sails in the sunset*, Renée, reindeer, Reagan, red-hot poker

PA Pacino, Pac-man, pants, *Paloma blanca*, Patricia, panda, Paganini, papyrus

MA Martin (Steve), Marmite, mackintosh, *Mandy*, Maya, macaque, Mao Tse Tung, macadamia

FI Fishburne, Fiat, fichu, *Fifty ways to leave your lover*, Fiona, Fennec, Fibonacci, fig

GI Gibson, Gillette, gilet, *Gimme Gimme Gimme* (ABBA), Gillian, giraffe, Gilbert (Sir Humphrey), ginger

Pages 94-95

BROKEN SEQUENCES

1. Destruction
2. Carrot
3. Indecent
4. Machinery
5. Contaminate
6. Maintenance

HAPPY ENDINGS

1. Article
2. Clavicle
3. Chronicle
4. Vehicle
5. Barnacle
6. Testicle
7. Particle
8. Icicle
9. Circle
10. Tentacle

LOOPY LETTERS

E	D	I	T	H	P	I	A	F
S	S	O	R	A	N	A	I	D

IDENTIKIT

Mrs Brown's description fits only suspect number 3.

NUMBER PYRAMID

Start with 74. 74-34 = 40, to the left of 34. Then 40-21 = 19 to the right of 21, 34-19 = 15 to the right of 19. The numbers at the bottom are thus 21-16 = 5 on the left, then 19-16 = 3 in the middle; then, 15-3 = 12 and 33-12 = 21 in the right-hand corner. Still on the right, on the third level, you will have 33+15 = 48; on the fourth level you will have 34+48 = 82 and so, at the top, 82+74 = 156.

156
74 82
40 34 48
21 19 15 33
5 16 3 12 21

TRUE OR FALSE

1. True (R)
2. True: by an Italian named Peruggia (I)
3. False: he was born in 1881 (N)
4. False: he died on the Marquesas Islands and lies not far from the singer Jacques Brel (E)
5. True (O)
6. False : he died bankrupt (R)

With these six letters you can form the name of RENOIR.

Pages 96-97

MAZE

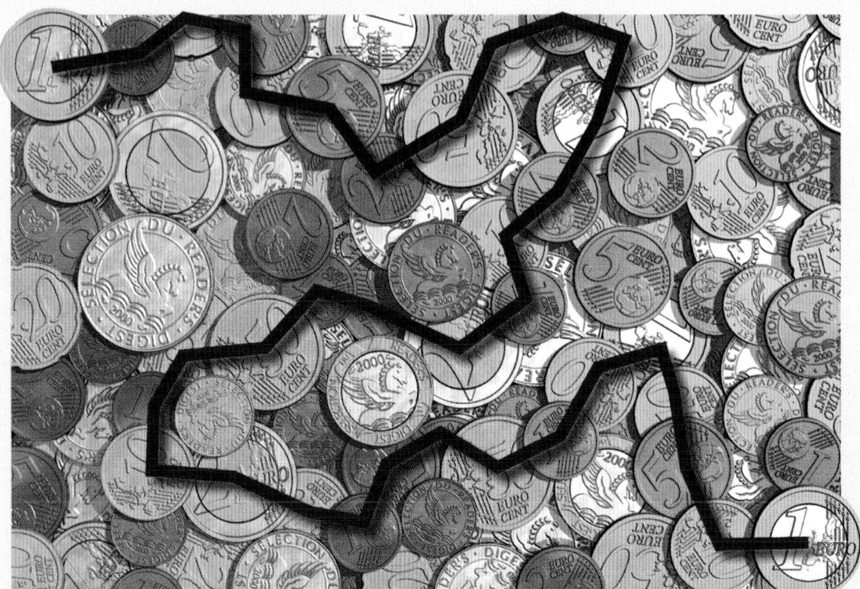

WORD PAIRS

1. Only one, Dopey
2. Village
3. Prince
4. Idiot, Imbecile
5. It's a trick question. Cretin isn't on the list
6. Camel

THEMATIC CROSSWORD

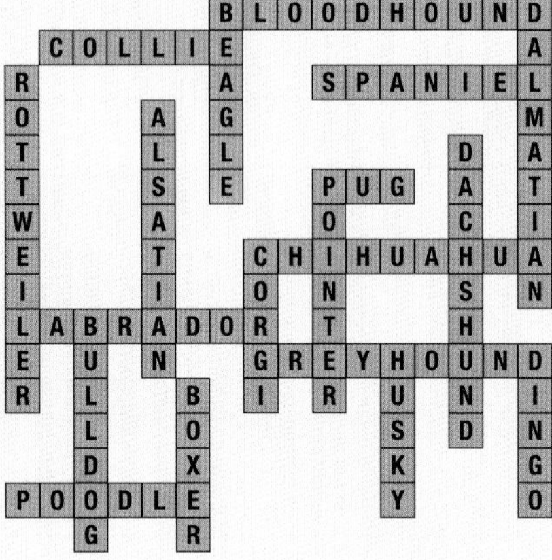

ITINERARY

TIRANA – ALASKA

T	O	P	E	K	A
I	S	R	A	E	L
R	W	A	N	D	A
A	T	H	E	N	S
N	E	W	A	R	K
A	N	K	A	R	A

Pages 98-99

THEMATIC CROSSWORD

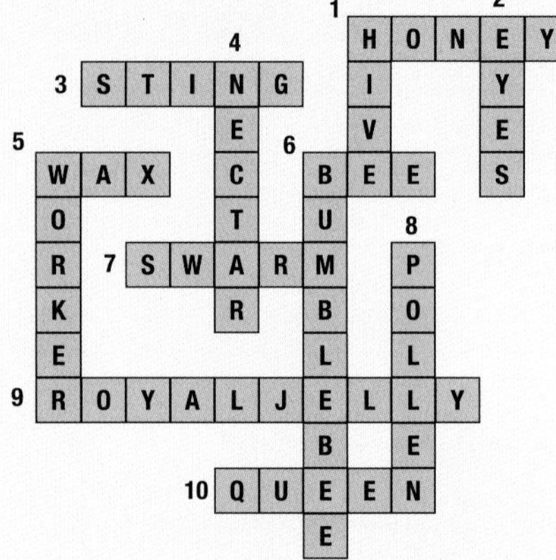

MAGIC SQUARE

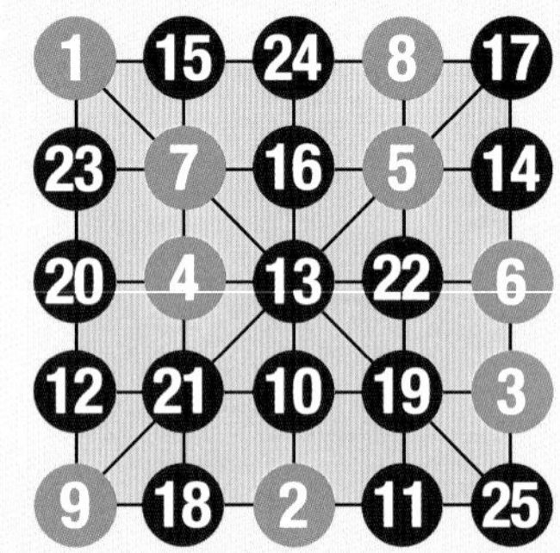

Note also that if you draw an x (for example, on 1, 7, 13, 20 and 24) or a + (for example, on 15, 7, 4, 23 and 16) on five numbers on the grid, the sum of these five numbers is still 65!

CLOSE-UP

A sweet red pepper

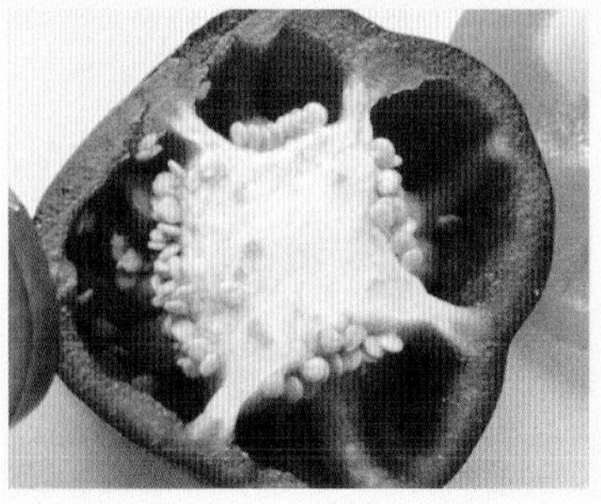

PROBLEM

You can deduce from the combined purchases of Anna and Kevin that 10 boiled sweets are equal to 5 toffees. Simplified, this means that 2 boiled sweets = 1 toffee. So what Lucy bought could be seen as 4 lollipops + 4 toffees = 2 dollars, in which case 1 lollipop =1 toffee = 0, 50 cents. Because 6 toffees + 1 lollipop = 2 dollars, 5 toffees = 1,50 dollars.
So you can work out that:
Boiled sweets: 15 cents
Toffees: 30 cents
Lollipops: 20 cents

SANDWICH
YESTERDAY – PENNYLANE

F	L	Y	P	A	P	E	R
C	H	E	A	P	E	S	T
D	I	S	T	A	N	C	E
A	T	T	O	R	N	E	Y
A	M	E	T	H	Y	S	T
C	I	R	C	U	L	A	R
M	E	D	I	T	A	T	E
D	I	A	G	O	N	A	L
A	N	Y	W	H	E	R	E

ITINERARY
PANAMA – DAKOTA

P	O	L	A	N	D
A	N	K	A	R	A
N	I	S	H	I	K
A	R	A	K	A	O
M	U	S	C	A	T
A	R	A	B	I	A

SPOT THE 7 DIFFERENCES

Pages 100-101

OVERLAPPING SHAPES
The square (7 squares, 4 circles, 4 triangles)

HISTORICAL LANDMARKS
1F. Alfred the Great (871-901)
2H. Edward the Confessor (1042-1066)
3E. William the Conqueror (1066-1087)
4J. Richard III (1483-1485)
5B. Henry VIII (1509-1547)
6D. Elizabeth I (1558-1603)
7I. William III and Mary (1689-1694)
8C. George III (1760-1820)
9A. Victoria (1837-1901)
10G. Elizabeth II (1953-)

CUBES
Ponting – Ganguly – Kirsten

MEMORY TEST
Jam – Bowl – Shirt – Butter dish – Teaspoon – Kettle – Coffeepot

ODD ONE OUT
The ladybird is the only animal that doesn't sting.

MATCHES
Four of the original squares are still in place, but two new squares have been created, four times larger than the original ones, made up of the two tiers on the left or the two tiers on the right of the figure. So the total is now 6 squares.

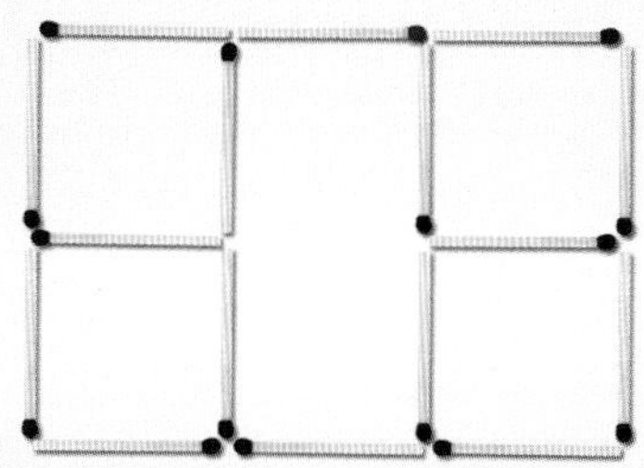

HAPPY ENDINGS
1. Semaphore
2. Folklore
3. Adore
4. Explore
5. Galore
6. Ignore
7. Carnivore
8. Before
9. Bedsore
10. Shore

PROBLEM
1. Four times 25, twice 1.
2. Twice 25, three times 15, one 7.
3. He didn't hit the 3.

Pages 102-103

SPEED LIMIT OF 90!

POINTS IN COMMON
1. Foam
2. Sky
3. Major
4. Star
5. Cage
6. Wings

MAGIC SQUARE
This solution is one example, but there are several other possible solutions.

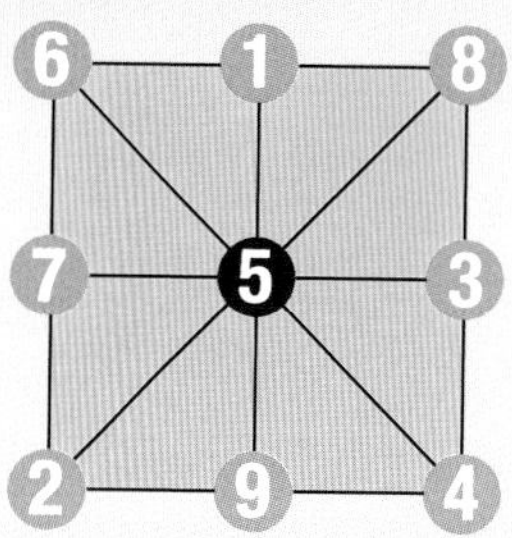

ODD ONE OUT
The odd one out is the whale, which, unlike the other animals, is not oviparous (oviparous animals reproduce by laying eggs).

CODE-BREAKER
1. The true art of memory is the art of attention.
2. --.- ..- .- -. -.. / --- -. / -. . / ... .- .. - / .-. .. . -. / .--. .- .-. .-.. . --..-- / .. .-.. / ..-. .- ..- - / .- ...- --- .. .-. / -.. . / .-.. ' .- -- -... .. - .. --- -. .-.-.-

ANAPHRASES
1. Raising, arising
2. Diapers, praised, despair
3. Nudity, untidy

Page 104

PUZZLE
Pieces 2, 4 and 6.

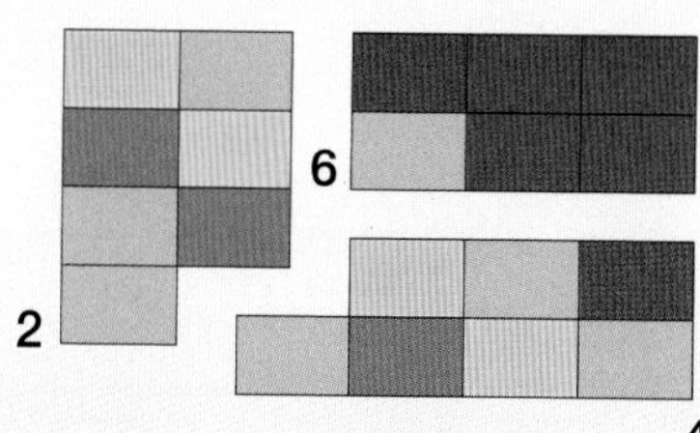

ODD ONE OUT
They are primary numbers, with one exception. The odd one out in this sequence is number 21, which is divisible by 3 and 7. To realise this, you had to note the odd numbers missing between 3 and 23: 9 (3 x3) and 15 (5 x 3).

Memory in all its forms

Forms of memory

Even if scientists have succeeded in deciphering the most important aspects of the mechanism of memory and producing a kind of map of its different forms, they are still far from a full understanding of all its complexity.

Short-term and long-term: a ceaseless to and fro

❶ When the **sensory receptors** take in new data, the information is received and retained for a short time – from a few fractions of a second to several seconds – in the sphere of memorisation that corresponds to each of the senses (sight, smell, touch, taste and hearing) and which constitutes **sensory memory.**

❷ Information that attracts attention or arouses interest is transferred to the **short-term memory**. This guarantees immediate access – from a few seconds to about two minutes – to information that has just been stored in the sensory memory.

❸ The transfer to **long-term memory** is made only if the information has been subjected to a deliberate act of concentration and if it has been repeated often enough. In the absence of such a process of consolidation it will be forgotten.

❹ Your **long-term memory** thus enables you t remember, or to recognise, information that has been acquired a few minutes, hours, or years before. It comprises:

- **episodic memory**, which stores the sequence of 'life events' that make up your autobiography (see p.128);
- **procedural memory**, which stores information enabling you to carry out activitie requiring automatic movements, such as riding a bicycle (see p.118);
- **semantic memory**, which is your reservoir of knowledge about the world (see p.122).

❺ The transfer to the **short-term memo** is carried out when you use information stored on a permanent basis for specific tasks. This is what happens, for example, when you prepare a dish from memory a fe days after having the recipe explained to you to remember the ingredients and instruction without taking notes you must have ha a particular interest in that recipe and been strongly motivated

My memory and…
my next holiday

Preparing for a holiday is a way of keeping your memory in good shape: it works much harder than you imagine when you take an interest in the geography, language and culture of a country, with travel books, guides and brochures on hand as back-up material. Time spent on research into the best offers – detailed descriptions of services provided, comparisons of price etc. – makes your memory function more quickly. This stimulation, which lasts during and after the holiday, gives many travellers the impression of a resurgence of vitality. Yes, holidays do indeed help to keep you young!

Memory and the learning process: explicit and implicit memory

I know where and how I learned to ride a bicycle, but then when did I learn to speak?

All your experience, from cradle to grave, can be considered as a learning process in the sense that it influences everything that happens subsequently. Just as a child behaves differently once it has learned to walk or to read, adults change their mode of being after every experience, whether it be a year of study or the break-up of a relationship.

The list of learning experiences is thus infinite. If some kinds continue throughout life – learning to love, for example, or learning to be independent, it is still possible to identify the major events in your personal journey through life. The first serious relationship with a lover is a key stage in learning about the realm of love relationships, just as the first year at college, far from your parental home, can represent a stage in the acquisition of independence. The many diverse learning experiences that are milestones in your life contribute, then, to the development of your personality.

The ability to remember **events concerned with acquiring knowledge**, or the specific circumstances surrounding them, constitutes **the explicit memory**. An example is when you say, 'I remember learning to play the piano with Mrs Mitchell when I was in grade 6; she was a wonderful teacher.' So the explicit memory enables you to recall information at will and to identify where and how you acquired it.

By contrast, **the term implicit memory is used when something is learned without remembering the context** in which this took place or the experiences and stages in the course of this acquisition of knowledge. This memory, which **stores the unconscious knowledge that enables you to apply your skills, is omnipresent in your everyday life**. It is evident in most of your behaviour: you act without even realising that a certain activity, which you take to be spontaneous, is really under the control of your memory. But you can't explain its origin nor its function. You can't verbalise or explain this memory (you can't say 'I remember ....') but it **enables you to act without asking yourself questions**.

In a lecture given in 1993, this is how the French psychiatrist and gerontologist, Dr Louis Ploton, explained how the phenomena of unconscious memorisation and unconscious transmission come into play in connection with relationships with others: 'What happens between people when they meet cannot be completely reduced to what they convey in a verbal exchange. I don't know what I am communicating to you unawares, and I don't know what you are communicating to me about yourself unawares. Perhaps we spend our energy hiding things from ourselves and trying to hide them from others while they are aware of them and will make use of them without realising it ...'

The two forms of memory that assist you in learning, **the explicit and implicit memory, both form part of your long-term memory.**

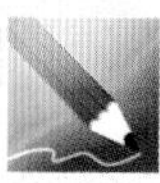

Unconscious memorisation

Read the following short text very carefully:
(extract from *The Prophet*, by Khahil Gibran, 1923)

Then a woman who held an infant in her arms said to him, Speak to us of our children;
And he said:
Your children are not your children
They are the sons and daughters of Life's longing for itself:
They come through you but not from you,
And though they are with you yet they belong not to you.
You may give them your love, but not your thoughts,
For they have their own thoughts.
You may house their bodies, but not their souls,
For their souls dwell in the house of tomorrow,
Which you cannot visit, not even in your dreams.
You may strive to be like them, but seek not to make them like you
For life goes not backward nor tarries with yesterday.
You are the bows from which your children as living arrows are sent forth.
The archer sees the mark on the path of the infinite, and He bends you with His might that His arrows may go swift and far.
Let your bending in the Archer's hand be for gladness;
For even as he loves the arrow that flies
So He loves also the bow that is stable.

Now tick off on this list the words that find resonance in you, or that evoke memories.

car	visit	window
box	child	bows
infant	dreams	life
paper	sun	bench
printer	path	motorbike
infinite	cassette	house

It is quite likely that most of the words you ticked came from the text; in particular, infant – visit – child – dreams – path – bows – life– house – infinite. That is one of the effects of the implicit memory. Memorisation takes place without your knowing it, and you don't remember having learned anything in particular. Nevertheless, you see the results of this activity. You can't say how and what you have learned, or in what circumstances, but you have nevertheless absorbed information without being aware of it.

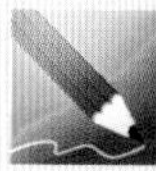

To the tune of rock 'n roll

Link each of these singers or groups to one of their hit tunes:

1. Beach Boys	**a. Another Brick In The Wa**
2. Beatles	**b. Blowing In The Wind**
3. Chuck Berry	**c. Blueberry Hill**
4. Bee Gees	**d. Good Vibrations**
5. Louis Prima	**e. Help!**
6. Rolling Stones	**f. I'm Just a Gigolo**
7. Fats Domino	**g. Light My Fire**
8. Doors	**h. Love Me Tender**
9. Elvis Presley	**i. Massachusetts**
10. Police	**j. Mrs Robinson**
11. Pink Floyd	**k. Rock Around The Cloc**
12. Bob Dylan	**l. Roll Over Beethoven**
13. Simon and Garfunkel	**m. Roxanne**
14. Bill Haley	**n. Satisfaction**

Solution p.3

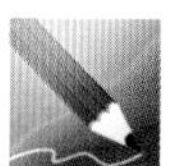

The right definition

Here are the names of some lesser-known experts followed by several possible definitions of their activities. Tick what seems to be the right definition.

Solution p.334

A. A cruciverbist is:
1. Someone who gets to the crux of a problem
2. A crossword puzzle enthusiast
3. Someone who makes crucifixes

B. A conchologist is :
1. A chestnut eater
2. A member of the Big Nose Society
3. A shell expert

C. A lepidopterist is:
1. An expert on leopards
2. A butterfly expert
3. An acrobat

D. A numismatist is:
1. A supplier of car tyres
2. A doctor who specialises in chest complaints
3. An expert on coins

E. A prestidigitator is:
1. Someone who enjoys prestigious gatherings
2. A conjuror
3. A typist who can type extremely quickly

F. A sommelier:
1. A wine steward
2. Someone who walks in his sleep
3. A resident of the Somme region.

In this exercise, the question contains a word that does not necessarily figure in your repertoire of names of well-known jobs or professions. With the help of the clues provided in the proposed definitions, by association of ideas and deduction you will arrive at the right answer. The unfamiliar word will be classified in your semantic memory and put in relation to similar items of information already there.

1.	8. ......
2.	9. ......
3.	10. ......
4.	11. ......
5.	12. ......
6.	13. ......
7.	14. ......

What you are asked to do here is to form associations between the data recovered from your memory. You associate each singer or famous group with a specific repertoire of song titles, tunes, words, or sometimes memories. This exercise therefore calls into play your semantic memory or, at times, your episodic memory.

Changing words

Here is an anagram of a famous historical person, the French emperor Napoleon. The second phrase is formed with the letters of his name and makes reference to an event in his life.

NAPOLEON BONAPARTE
NO PEON APART ON ELBA

The second anagram has a historical foundation: after Napoleon was forced to abdicate as emperor he was sent into exile on the island of Elba.
Using the words below, create a series of anagrams (find new words without adding or removing any letters).

REGIME = ...	**PART** = ...	**CAUSE** = ...
SPACE = ...	**DIRE** = ...	**RENAL** = ...
AMEND = ...	**RAGE** = ...	**EAGER** =........................
PIER = ...	**DRAIN** =........................	

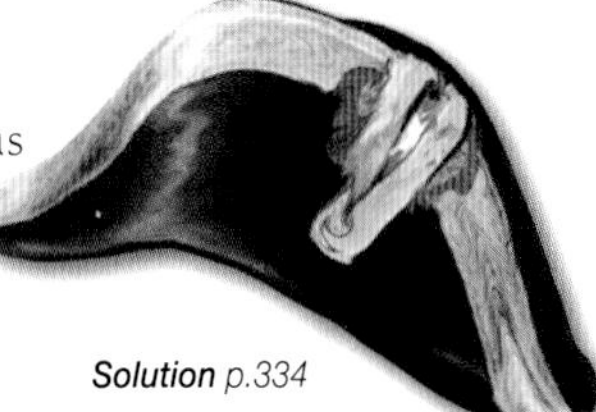

This exercise puts your mental flexibility to work, that fabulous capacity to transform one piece of information into another, from the same elements. Your semantic memory helps you here in the sense that it contains your vocabulary and provides you with clues to construct new words.

Solution p.334

Street scene

Find at least 20 words starting with **ma-** which appear or which are referred to in the picture to the right.
Think of the things presented in the picture and also, by association of ideas, words that are related to the scene.

1.	11. ....
2.	12. ....
3.	13. ....
4.	14. ....
5.	15. ....
6.	16. ....
7.	17. ....
8.	18. ....
9.	19. ....
10.	20. ....

Solution p.334

This exercise sets your verbal fluidity to work. The images serve as clues to transfer the words stocked in your long-term memory – the semantic memory – to your short-term memory.

Procedural memory

Certain movements are never forgotten; our actions in certain contexts become automatic. The same applies even if there has been an interruption of several years. This extraordinary kind of memory, this automatic functioning, is what is called procedural memory.

The automatic functioning of procedural memory

I'll never forget how to ride a bicycle!

Fortunately, many of our everyday activities do not require reflection or any real effort of memory. Dressing, washing, eating – all these everyday skills are acquired at an early age. Similarly, the skills involved in driving a car, riding a bicycle, or doing the work of an artisan or someone on an assembly line are learned once and for all. These actions become automatic. That is the main task of procedural memory, or habitual memory, which **stores the series of movements making up the physical knowhow associated with automatic mental functions.**

The functioning of procedural memory, which is part of the long-term memory, relies on a conditioning process that results from repetition and training. **Reflex actions are indelibly inscribed in our memory.** They are never forgotten, except in the case of an accident or illness that damages or changes certain parts of the brain. Even if there is a long break – during which you do not do any cycling, for example – you will not lose the necessary skills.

But procedural memory is not only expressed in the realm of physical activities. Gut reactions in response to the use of certain words can also be regarded as automatic mental reflexes where any act of reflection seems absent, if not impossible. This is what happens, for example, when you experience involuntary shudders or other reactions of disgust, and give vent to cries of 'How horrible!' or similar expressions of anguish, or even take flight when confronted with the sight or even the mention of certain essentially inoffensive animals, such as mice, insects or reptiles.

Finally, procedural memory also promotes the development of the automatic mental functions that come into play in rote learning.

My memory and... the highway code

Learning to drive, and learning the rules of the road, is based on common sense and automatic reactions. Driving reinforces the theoretical knowledge of the rules. In the course of time, drivers forget the theory but become increasingly more confident on the road. They combine their driving expertise with the visual decoding of obstacles and signs and finding the right direction. But the rules are not immutable; you need to update your knowledge to acquire new reflex actions.

All those insignificant actions ...

List in the space below the actions that you usually carry out automatically, without thinking.

1. In the realm of housework (movements you make when rinsing the dishes, for example)

....

....

....

....

....

2. In your professional capacity (the action of opening letters, for example)

....

....

....

....

....

3. In your leisure activities (strokes of a brush on canvas, for example)

....

....

....

....

....

Write with your eyes shut

Close your eyes and write any sentence you like in the space below.

....

....

Learning to write is one of the most important learning activities of childhood. You probably hardly remember the steps in the process whereby you acquired the necessary automatic movements – for the formation of letters, words and then sentences – but they are firmly fixed in your procedural memory thanks to constant repetition and practice. In this exercise, the words are put together mentally in a sentence that guides your hand: your writing hand retains its agility even when your eyes are closed.

Memory of spaces

Do this little experiment.
– At night, place any object you choose on a piece of furniture or even on the floor in one of the rooms of your house.
– Move to the opposite side of the room and switch the light off. The room must be completely dark.
– Grope your way towards the object.
Did you have problems finding the object?
What can you deduce from this experiment?

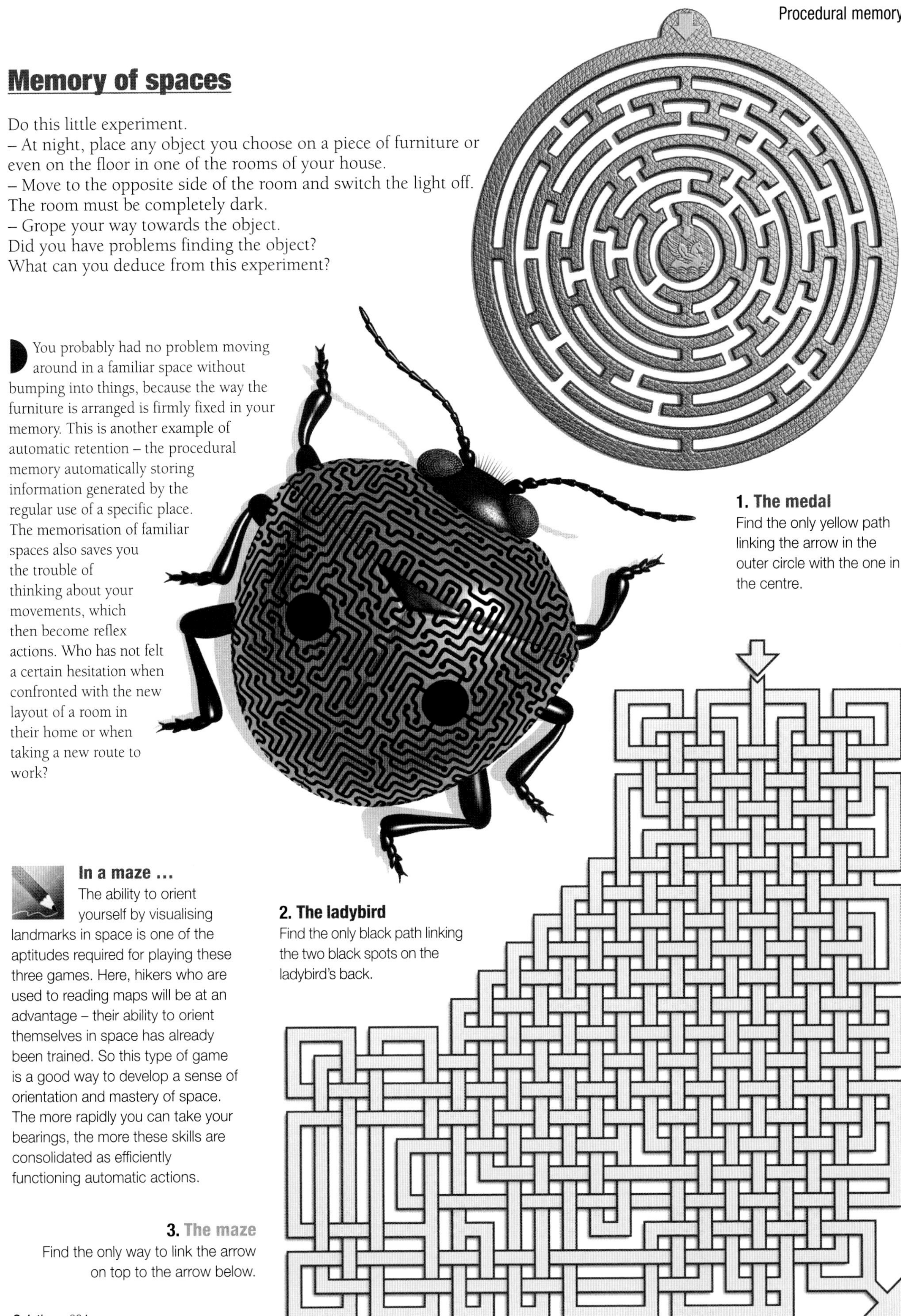

You probably had no problem moving around in a familiar space without bumping into things, because the way the furniture is arranged is firmly fixed in your memory. This is another example of automatic retention – the procedural memory automatically storing information generated by the regular use of a specific place. The memorisation of familiar spaces also saves you the trouble of thinking about your movements, which then become reflex actions. Who has not felt a certain hesitation when confronted with the new layout of a room in their home or when taking a new route to work?

1. The medal
Find the only yellow path linking the arrow in the outer circle with the one in the centre.

In a maze ...
The ability to orient yourself by visualising landmarks in space is one of the aptitudes required for playing these three games. Here, hikers who are used to reading maps will be at an advantage – their ability to orient themselves in space has already been trained. So this type of game is a good way to develop a sense of orientation and mastery of space. The more rapidly you can take your bearings, the more these skills are consolidated as efficiently functioning automatic actions.

2. The ladybird
Find the only black path linking the two black spots on the ladybird's back.

3. The maze
Find the only way to link the arrow on top to the arrow below.

Solution p.334

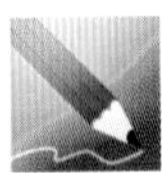

One line is enough

Draw the following figures in one go, without lifting your hand. First establish where to begin and end each figure. Then trace the path with your finger before using a pencil.

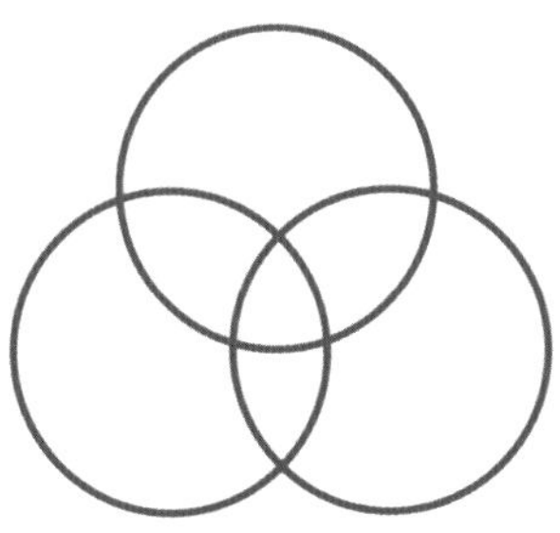

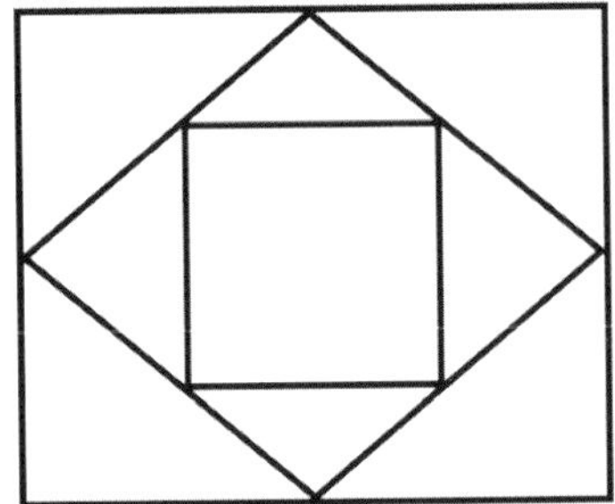

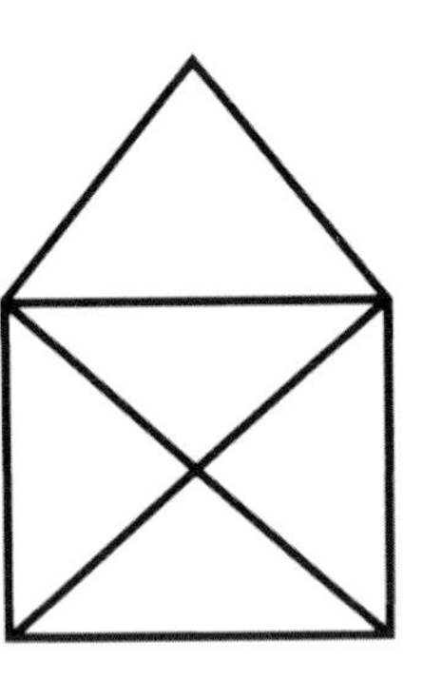

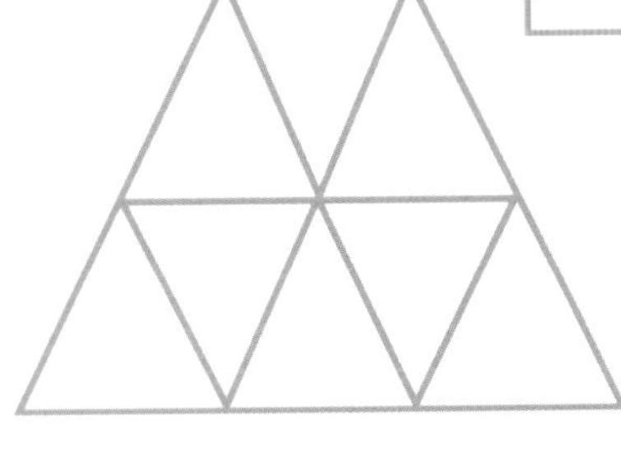

Solution p.335

Here, you must first think about the layout of the figures before copying the drawing. But then it becomes an automatic process: holding a pencil and drawing straight or curved lines to create geometric figures is something we do without thinking.

The right reflection

Which of these 6 silhouettes matches the cowboy below?

In this exercise testing visual perception, your eyes first scrutinise the character referred to, then flit between that form and each of the others, making comparisons. When performing these visual manoeuvres you don't have to stop and consciously consider that what was on the left will be on the right, and vice versa. This happens automatically.

Solution p.335

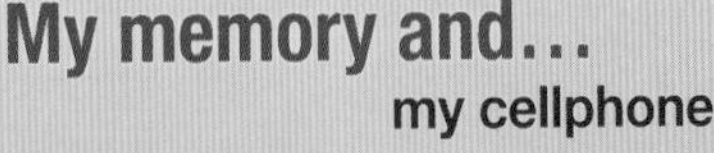

My memory and...
my cellphone

Cellphones are so easy to use they encourage laziness! Because a cellphone can have an electronic list of 100 numbers, there is no point in trying to remember some of them. Its personalised ring tone creates a kind of conditioned reflex and encourages concentrated listening, certainly, but the ability to immediately transmit the information received by pushing a button for another phone call frees you from making the effort to remember it long enough to convey the information later. So don't use your cellphone as your sole means of communication; your memory could really suffer as a result.

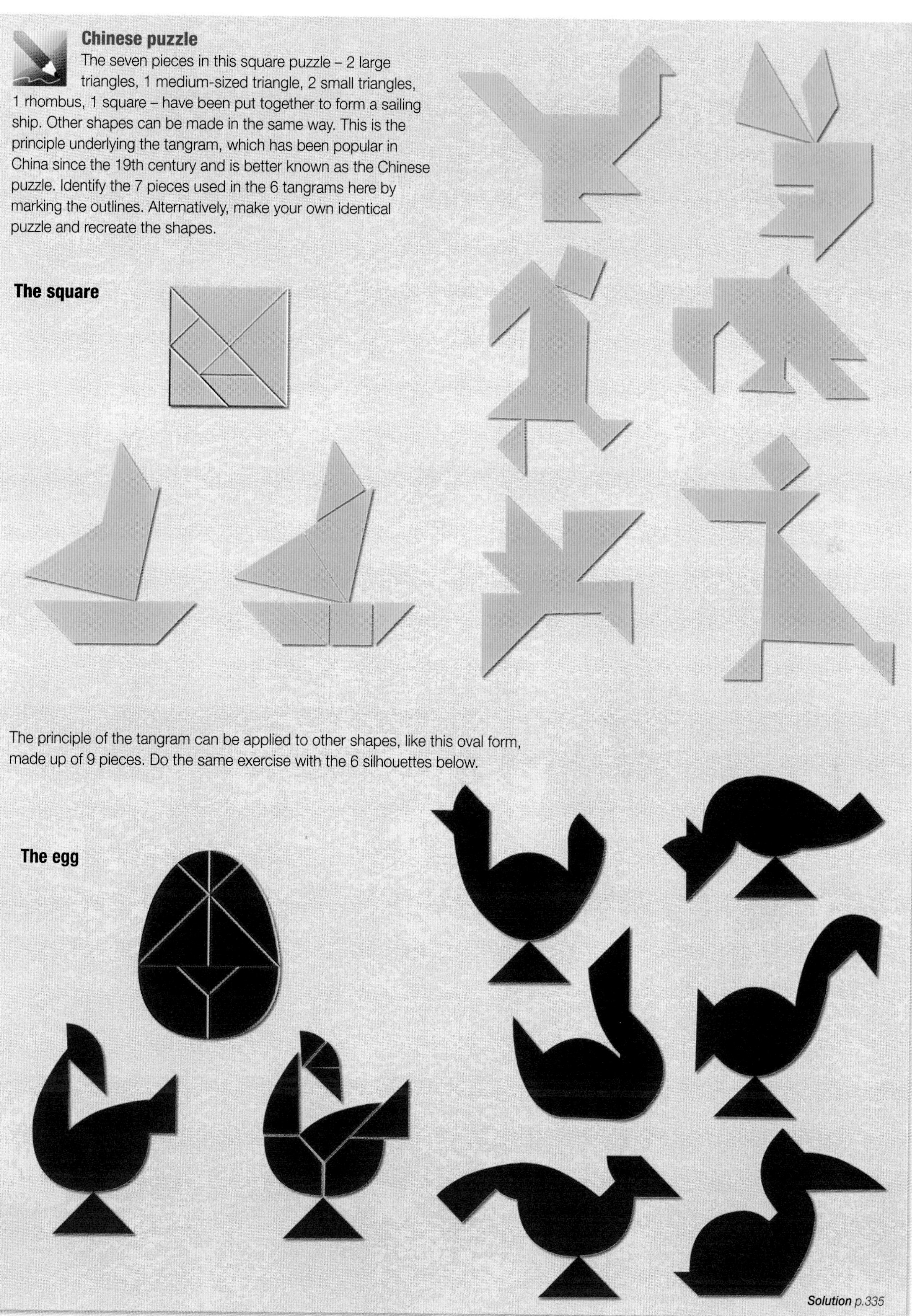

Chinese puzzle

The seven pieces in this square puzzle – 2 large triangles, 1 medium-sized triangle, 2 small triangles, 1 rhombus, 1 square – have been put together to form a sailing ship. Other shapes can be made in the same way. This is the principle underlying the tangram, which has been popular in China since the 19th century and is better known as the Chinese puzzle. Identify the 7 pieces used in the 6 tangrams here by marking the outlines. Alternatively, make your own identical puzzle and recreate the shapes.

The square

The principle of the tangram can be applied to other shapes, like this oval form, made up of 9 pieces. Do the same exercise with the 6 silhouettes below.

The egg

Solution p.335

Semantic memory

Semantic memory stores knowledge and organises it to make it meaningful. This constitutes your general cultural knowledge. It also gives you mastery of language, words and concepts.

A reservoir of knowledge

Semantic memory is a vast reservoir of knowledge. It stores all that you have learned about the world around you. It can be imagined as a gigantic spider's web made up of millions of interconnections: this is the knowledge stored up since childhood. All the pieces of information are thus interlinked to form the network of the web. All newly acquired knowledge – every new interconnection – is inevitably linked up to all the knowledge already there.

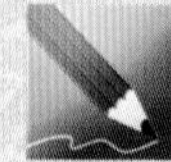

The big quiz

Entertain yourself by testing your general knowledge with these 50 questions.

History and geography

1. Who was the famous Carthaginian general who invaded Italy over the Alps using elephants?

a. Attila
b. Alexander
c. Hannibal
d. Xerxes

2. In AD 79, which city was completely destroyed by the eruption of Mount Vesuvius?

a. Rome
b. Milan
c. Pompeii
d. Tivoli

3. What was the name of the Suffragette who threw herself under the King of England's horse?

a. Emily Pankhurst
b. Florence Nightingale
c. Emily Hobhouse
d. Virginia Woolf

4. Who wrote a diary about her childhood experiences under the Nazi occupation in Amsterdam?

a. Alice Liddell
b. Anne Frank
c. Antonia Byatt
d. Alice Walker

5. Who was the tutor of Alexander the Great?

a. Plato
b. Cicero
c. Euripides
d. Aristotle

6. What organisation was founded by Henry Dunant in 1863?

a. The Salvation Army
b. Médecins du monde
c. The Red Cross
d. The Hospice movement

7. Which one of these presidents of the USA was not assassinated?

a. Lincoln
b. Garfield
c. Kennedy
d. Franklin D. Roosevelt

8. On what island did Napoleon die?

a. Elba
b. Guernsey
c. St Helena
d. Jersey

9. On August 6, 1945, a bomber took off to drop the first atom bomb on Hiroshima. What was the bomber called?

a. *Enola Gay*
b. *Fat Man*
c. *Little Boy*
d. *Good Molly*

10. Who was the first Prime Minister of France's Fifth Republic?

a. François Mitterrand
b. Michel Debré
c. Jacques Chirac
d. Pierre Granier-Deferre

11. First it was known as Byzantium, then it was called Constantinople. What is it's name today?

a. Samarkand
b. Teheran
c. Istanbul
d. Smyrna

12. Burkino Faso is the present name of the latter day:

a. Upper Volta
b. Rhodesia
c. New Guinea
d. Ethiopia

13. Where is Austerlitz situated?

a. In Denmark
b. In Germany
c. In Austria
d. In the Czech Republic

14. What is the name of the highest waterfall in the world?

a. Angel Falls
b. Niagara Falls
c. Victoria Falls
d. Iguaçu Falls

15. Where is the biggest gulf in the world?

a. Mexico
b. France
c. Saudi Arabia
d. Japan

Art and literature

16. Some of his photographs – *Rue Mouffetard*, *Dimanche sur les Bords de la Marne* (*Sunday on the banks of the Marne*) – are considered to be major works of the 20th century. Who is this famous photographer?

a. Robert Doisneau
b. Édouard Boubat
c. Man Ray
d. Henri Cartier-Bresson

17. He started making films in 1925 and established himself as a genius of the cinema. Among his most famous films is *Rebecca.* Who is he?

a. Luis Buñuel
b. Alfred Hitchcock
c. Orson Welles
d. Jean Renoir

18. Who is the famous film director and actor we associate with *The Immigrant*, *The Gold Rush*, *Limelight* ...?

a. Orson Welles
b. Tom Hanks
c. Charlie Chaplin
d. Alfred Hitchcock

19. Who plays the part of Harry Potter in the film series?

a. Rupert Grint
b. Daniel Radcliffe
c. Orlando Bloom
d. Viggo Mortensen

20. Who wrote the trilogy on which the *Lord of the Rings* films are based?

a. A A Milne
b. J K Rowling
c. J R Tolkien
d. Philip Pullman

21. What famous picture was stolen from the Louvre on August 21, 1911?

a. *The Bathers*
b. *Mona Lisa*
c. *Le Moulin de la Galette*
d. *The Sunflowers*

22. Who painted *The Waterlilies?*

- **a.** Manet
- **b.** Monet
- **c.** Gauguin
- **d.** Van Gogh

23. What is the name of the American painter famous for his *Portrait of the Artist's Mother* (1872)?

- **a.** Audubon
- **b.** Whistler
- **c.** Rockwell
- **d.** Turner

24. Called to Rome by Pope Julius II, this famous Renaissance artist painted the frescoes of Genesis on the ceiling of the Sistine chapel. Who was he?

- **a.** Raphael
- **b.** Michelangelo
- **c.** Botticelli
- **d.** Piero della Francesca

25. Picasso's painting, *The Demoiselles d'Avignon,* originally had a different name. What was it?

- **a.** The young women in spring
- **b.** The philosopher's brothel
- **c.** Lady's choice
- **d.** Nudes

26. Which of these symphonies was not written by Mozart?

- **a.** The Linz symphony
- **b.** The Heroic symphony
- **c.** The Prague symphony
- **d.** The Jupiter symphony

27. A long-running television programme featured the tangled lives and loves of a wealthy family in Texas. What was it called?

- **a.** *Dallas*
- **b.** *The Bold and the Beautiful*
- **c.** *Dynasty*
- **d.** *Days of our Lives*

28. Four young self-taught musicians from Liverpool formed a group called The Quarrymen. By what name did they become famous throughout the world?

- **a.** The Rolling Stones
- **b.** The Beatles
- **c.** The Supremes
- **d.** The Who

29. A character in a 20th-century play declares: 'Hell is other people'. Who was the playwright?

- **a.** Eugene Ionesco
- **b.** Sam Shepard
- **c.** Jean-Paul Sartre
- **d.** Arthur Miller

30. Who was the Australian author of *The Tree Of Man* (1955), who won the Nobel Prize for Literature in 1973?

- **a.** Katherine Mansfield
- **b.** Patrick White
- **c.** Mathew Peake
- **d.** Colleen McCollough

31. Which Shakespearean character meets his father's ghost?

- **a.** Hamlet
- **b.** Othello
- **c.** Macbeth
- **d.** Henri V

32. In which Agatha Christie novel does the detective Hercule Poirot first appear?

- **a.** *Ten Little Niggers*
- **b.** *Death on the Nile*
- **c.** *The Mysterious Affair at Styles*
- **d.** *The Mousetrap*

33. What was the pseudonym of Eric Blair?

- **a.** George Orwell
- **b.** Henry Miller
- **c.** Somerset Maugham
- **d.** Kingsley Amis

34. Which English writer is featured in the Pulitzer-prize winning novel *The Hours*?

- **a.** Katherine Mansfield
- **b.** Virginia Woolf
- **c.** Mrs Dalloway
- **d.** Sylvia Plath

35. Her only novel is *Wuthering Heights*. Who was she?

- **a.** Emily Brontë
- **b.** Margaret Mitchell
- **c.** Anaïs Nin
- **d.** Virginia Woolf

36. Which French literary masterpiece begins: 'For a long time, I used to go to bed early' ?

- **a.** *In Remembrance of Things Past*
- **b.** *The Human Comedy*
- **c.** *The Red and the Black*
- **d.** *Madame Bovary*

37. Which famous English political figure won the Nobel Prize for Literature in 1953?

- **a.** Clement Attlee
- **b.** Neville Chamberlain
- **c.** Winston Churchill
- **d.** Harold Macmillan

Science and technology

38. In about 1826, who produced the first photographs by perfecting the use of a diaphragm?

- **a.** Nicéphore Niépce
- **b.** The Lumière brothers
- **c.** William Hamilton
- **d.** Nadar

39. What is the name of the technique used in medicine to obtain images by subjecting the body to a magnetic field and studying the variations in signals emitted by resonating elements?

- **a.** A scanner
- **b.** Radiography
- **c.** Scintigraphy
- **d.** MRI

40. In about 200 BC he invented a hydraulic lift system using an endless screw which is still used today. Name him.

- **a.** Archimedes
- **b.** Euclides
- **c.** Ptolemy
- **d.** Parmenides

41. He claimed that the Earth revolved around the Sun and the Moon around the Earth. Who was he?

- **a.** Nicolas Copernicus
- **b.** Giordano Bruno
- **c.** Johannes Kepler
- **d.** Galileo

42. In 1897, this engineer designed an engine in which combustion was produced by heating fuel vapour through compression in the cylinder. What was his name?

- **a.** Gottlieb Daimler
- **b.** Carl Benz
- **c.** Rudolph Diesel
- **d.** Enzo Ferrari

43. When did the first commercial jet airliner, a Boeing 247, come into service?

- **a.** 1933
- **b.** 1935
- **c.** 1955
- **d.** 1957

44. Which medical doctor and biologist discovered the TB bacillus in 1882?

- **a.** Louis Pasteur
- **b.** Alexander Fleming
- **c.** Robert Koch
- **d.** Edward Jenner

45. In 1687, he formulated the universal theory of gravity. His name?

- **a.** René Descartes
- **b.** Isaac Newton
- **c.** Galileo
- **d.** Christiaan Huygens

46. How many equal angles are there in an isosceles triangle?

- **a.** 2
- **b.** 3
- **c.** 0
- **d.** 4

47. What is used in the manufacture of aluminium?

- **a.** Iron
- **b.** Bauxite
- **c.** Limestone
- **d.** Cobalt

48. How many planets are there in our Solar System?

- **a.** 10
- **b.** 7
- **c.** 12
- **d.** 9

49. What was the first substance used to anaesthetise a patient?

- **a.** Ether
- **b.** Chloroform
- **c.** Cocaine
- **d.** Alcohol

50. In 1967, who performed the first successful heart transplant?

- **a.** Luc Montagnier
- **b.** Christiaan Barnard
- **c.** Christian Cabrol
- **d.** Claude Pasteur

Solution p.335

It's never too late to learn

Contrary to what many people believe, the ability to learn has no age restriction. Your memory can absorb new information at any stage of life, whether it be a new subject or a new language.

Countries and capitals of the ex-USSR

1. Look carefully at the map opposite. Repeat to yourself the names of all the countries while visualising where they are found on the map. Do the same for the names of the capital cities. Then cover the map.

2. Fill in the names of each country on the blank map below.

3. Fill in the names of all the capital cities on the map below.

In order to absorb this geographical information you organised it quickly into categories (countries, cities). This method of retention is all the more interesting in that the same method is used when your stock of information is organised in your memory. In fact, the spider's web of semantic memory cannot be reduced to a mere accumulation of interconnections. The new facts are not linked to already existing knowledge in a haphazard fashion. They are structured, organised into a hierarchy and categorised so as to be slotted into the existing store of knowledge, rather as goods are arranged on the shelves of a shop. As you grow older, your memory simply needs more time to record information, but that does not change in the slightest its ability to retain information. What is important is not to skimp on the repetition necessary to ensure that the information is firmly fixed (see p.234).

Finding the words, giving them meaning

I can't remember a word if I don't know what it means!

All knowledge, all information, involves a close association between words and their meaning, between the container and the content. The one does not go without the other. Everything concerning the form of a word, or the container, constitutes one of the facets of either semantic or lexical memory. **Memorisation depends on these two factors, the form and the meaning of words.**

When you wish to remember a word whose meaning you know, your semantic memory will put it in relation to other words of similar meaning. The word 'islet', for example, will be linked to the word 'isle' and 'island'. It is thanks to this semantic closeness that you will remember it. At the same time, you will remember the form of the word, that is, the way it is written. On the other hand, when faced with a word whose meaning you don't know, it is your lexical memory that will initiate the process of memorisation: you will associate it with words with the same form. However, if you really want to remember it, you should look up the meaning of an unknown word in a dictionary.

When you concentrate on retrieving information, your memory will therefore explore these two parallel paths, examining the container as well as the content. **The shape of words must make sense for the words to be retrieved by your memory.** If you know what you want to say but the word escapes you – commonly known as having the word on the tip of your tongue – this is a breakdown in vocabulary: it concerns your lexical memory. But if you know a word but can't remember its meaning, your memory of the content is failing you. In both cases it will be difficult for you to find the right answer. **A good semantic memory guarantees mastery over words and language.**

My memory and...
lectures

Listening to a lecture is a good way to acquire new information on any subject of your choice. Start by reading about the subject and then attend lectures that are easy to follow. Observe the following rules for good memorisation.

- Do not neglect to take slow-release sugars in your diet: your brain will then function without slowing down.
- Sit as close as possible to the lecturer in case he or she uses diagrams or photographs.
- Make rough notes of the main points during the lecture.
- Make a summary soon after the lecture or discuss what you learned with someone else.
- Finally, to minimise the risk of confusion, try not to attend more than two lectures a week.

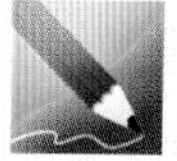

Poly-? Ante- ? Semi- ? Pre ?

In this exercise, your lexical memory is primarily brought into play. It is the form of the first part of the word that will lead you to a new word with a specific meaning.

Find 10 words starting with **poly**.	Find 10 words starting with **ante**.	Find 10 words starting with **semi**.	Find 10 words starting with **pre**.
poly	**ante**	**semi**	**pre** ....
poly	**ante**	**semi**	**pre** ....
poly	**ante**	**semi**	**pre** ....
poly	**ante**	**semi**	**pre** ....
poly	**ante**	**semi**	**pre** ....
poly	**ante**	**semi**	**pre** ....
poly	**ante**	**semi**	**pre** ....
poly	**ante**	**semi**	**pre** ....
poly	**ante**	**semi**	**pre** ....
poly	**ante**	**semi**	**pre** ....

Solution p.335

Cities of Britain

You have probably known some of the names of British cities since your first years at school. At that time of your life, the semantic memory develops the fastest.

But the letters of some of these cities have been mixed up. Unscramble them to find their correct order in five minutes, then mark the cities on the map. To ensure that you can keep to the time llimit, remind yourself quickly of the names of the cities. You will fill them in much faster if you do.

1. TMOYPULH	**9. GRICEDAMB**
2. TREXEE	**10. HABRIMMING**
3. SMORTTHOUP	**11. PLOVEROIL**
4. STROBIL	**12. STENCHMARE**
5. SEWNASE	**13. ROKY**
6. STEGCOUREL	**14. GRINDUBEH**
7. FRODOX	**15. CANELWEST**
8. DONNOL	**16. NEEBEARD**

Solution p.335

Extra clues

To recall various forms of knowledge, you can rely on **visual clues**, that is, to a mental image (see p.204). This image can enable you to retrieve the elusive word or information. At other times, **verbal clues** will predominate. Whether you choose the visual or verbal channel in the process of retrieving memory depends on your individual aptitude. Some people are more comfortable with images, others with words.

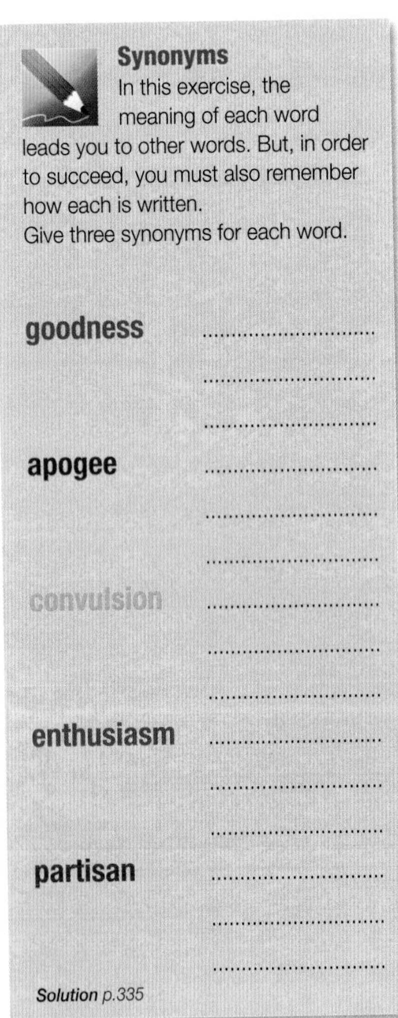

Synonyms

In this exercise, the meaning of each word leads you to other words. But, in order to succeed, you must also remember how each is written.

Give three synonyms for each word.

goodness ....
....
....

apogee ....
....
....

convulsion ....
....
....

enthusiasm ....
....
....

partisan ....
....
....

Solution p.335

Mystery words

With the help of six clues, find out what is hidden in these sentences. Be careful – the clues could be visual or verbal (puns). When each new clue is given, your memory will look for information that seems to correspond to the clue in that sentence. Each piece of information will gradually join the other clues to create or activate a network leading to the mystery word.

A: What am I?

1. Lying side by side with my kind, I have a pink head.
2. If you strike me, my head turns white.
3. Whether venerated or feared, I represent progress.
4. When you blow on me, my head turns black.
5. Whether Swedish or Spanish, I always have the same shape.
6. I can be replaced by something more modern, the cigarette lighter.

B: What am I?

1. I am the salt of the earth.
2. I can measure time.
3. I can be stored in a silo.
4. I can fall to dust.
5. I can measure sense.
6. I am also found in the sea.

C: What am I?

1. I set the tone, even though I am not talkative.
2. I am rectangular, but replace a fair number of round objects.
3. My chip is not off the old block.
4. Must you be reminded when I am exhausted ?
5. I am coveted by collectors; I like being decorated.
6. I am as easy to find as a stamp.

The flags of Europe

Which country does each of these flags belong to? Do this exercise on your own or with others.

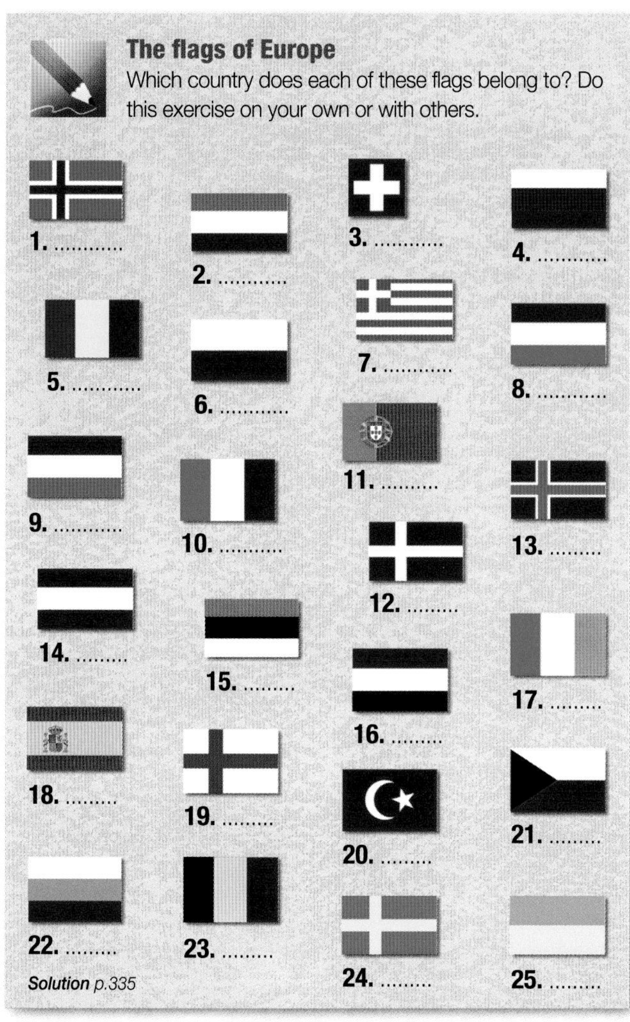

Solution p.335

History and chronology

Place the following important events in world history on the chronological chart. First fill in the dates you know as reference points.

1. **The Wall Street Crash**
2. **The Great Flu Epidemic**
3. **Hong Kong is handed back to China**
4. **First flight by the Wright brothers**
5. **Bay of Pigs invasion**
6. **Fall of the Berlin Wall**
7. **First man on the Moon**
8. **San Francisco Earthquake**
9. **First and last flights of Concorde**
10. **Winston Churchill became Prime Minister**

2000 ....
... .
... .
... .
... .
1950 ....
... .
... .
... .
... .
1900 ....

Solution p.335

The reference points on a chronological chart can facilitate the retrieval of information. By positioning yourself in relation to these points you can deduce the dates of lesser-known events.

The aim of this game is to find the solution with the aid of as few clues as possible. You can also have several players. Then give each player points according to how many clues were needed to find the solution.

6 points for the first clue
5 points for the second clue.
4 points for the third clue.
3 points for the fourth clue
2 points for the fifth clue.
1 point for the sixth clue.

D: What am I?

1. I made my first appearance in 1927.
2. I am brilliant and much sought after.
3. I am celebrated each year, in at least 23 copies.
4. My name is also a first name.
5. Despite numerous attempts I am rarely given to France.
6. I am symbolised by a gilded statuette.

E: What am I?

1. I am a man.
2. I am a woman.
3. I am neither a man nor a woman.
4. I am dark in colour.
5. The sun and the light are my friends.
6. My rate of motion depends on others.

F: What am I?

1. I run on the spot.
2. I stop without having moved.
3. Although I climb, I never run down.
4. I am the enemy of laziness.
5. Whether manual or battery-operated, I depend on people.
6. Thanks to me, time passes.

G: What am I?

1. If you find the path, I am revealed to you.
2. You can either keep me or share me.
3. But if you decide to share me, I disappear.
4. In my case, silence is golden.
5. I am a real treasure.
6. You could pay a heavy price for betraying me.

H: What am I?

1. Without me, cathedrals would collapse.
2. With me, you can escape.
3. I am the solution.
4. I am a precious asset when entering paradise.
5. I am useful to musicians.
6. Losing me could cost you dearly.

Solution p.335

Episodic memory

The memory of ordinary everyday events and the memory of crucial moments making up your life history both form part of what is called episodic memory, which is peculiar to each individual. It enables us to live from day to day, but also to weave the threads of our autobiography.

Memory of a day, memory of a life

What moves me is engraved in my memory.

When you look back at a specific day in your life, or reconsider your whole life as such, what do you see? **A succession of experiences, a great variety of different episodes.** All this material, consisting of so many scattered fragments, makes up your personal history, your episodic memory.

Why have you recorded and stored some events rather than others? Because of their emotional import. The emotional resonance they evoked in you – pleasure, satisfaction, excitement, displeasure, anxiety, uneasiness, irritation, anger, or any other emotional state – precipitated the subconscious, automatic retention of many related bits of information about the circumstances in which the experience took place: the time of year, the place, the setting of the action or encounter (including olfactory or visual elements), the atmosphere and the facial appearance or behaviour of another person.

The process of recalling a specific memory depends on a similar mechanism. It entails a simultaneous resurfacing of the significant event, the emotions associated with it – 'I remember the face of my Latin teacher, the one who was so hard on me' – and, simultaneously, the context. In everyday life, the same process is at play in the incidental memorisation, and thus the recollection, of more structured information, such as a conversation or the contents of a television programme.

The function of episodic memory is in a sense that of **sorting and differentiating one moment from another according to a specific context,** so that these memories can enable you to function from day to day – to think of what you have to do, but also be sure that you have taken the pot off the stove after making lunch! A similar management process takes place on a larger scale, that of life itself. Episodic memory is **that taut thread linking events in the experience of each individual and imposing coherence and meaning**. Everyone, thus, creates their own unique sequence of memories.

This explains why you are able to situate yourself in time, without necessarily being precise about place – you are not necessarily able to assign the place a name and geographical location, but it is retained as a visual impression in your memory – or the date: the events of your life are organised in chronological order, with a 'before' and 'after'. As you grow older, episodic memory functions at full capacity. Who has not felt the need to take stock of the events of their life? Who does not have an aged parent who draws constantly on memories of the past?

Throughout life, the influence of this memory is considerable. Its supply of information enriches your knowledge of the world and augments your semantic memory (see p.122).

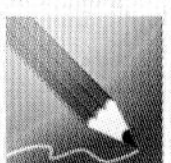

My abiding memories

So many things happen in one day! And the richness of each personal history is made up of so many varied events. Think about these experiences for a few minutes by considering the following questions:

1. Who phoned you today and yesterday? What did you talk about?
2. When and where did you spend your last holiday? What did you do? Which places did you visit? What are your most vivid memories?
3. What were you doing on the following days: **July 14, 2003? December 31, 2002? September 11, 2001? August 11, 1999 (eclipse of the Sun)?**
4. There are things you enjoyed in some circumstances and hated in others. What are they? For example, a school subject you liked in one teacher's class and detested in another.
5. A birthday is often a memorable day. Can you recall specific moments or events associated with particular birthdays?
6. Religious holidays are another time of intense experience. What characterised the celebrations of your childhood? Where did you celebrate them? Who was usually present? What rituals did you observe?
7. Finally, the long holidays of your childhood. What special events do you recall?

My memory and... my medication

When you have to take medicine several times a day, it's your episodic memory that makes these actions part of the daily routine by according a special space for them. Your mind and body rapidly make the required adjustment to this routine. If you forget to take the medicine once or twice, it is most probably because that day was different in some way or because you were psychologically or physically upset that day. Don't worry, relax, and tomorrow you won't forget!

Train your episodic memory

- **At the end of every day:**
  - take the time to recall the most memorable moments of the day;
  - clarify the context in your mind – place, time, setting, attitude of those present, atmosphere (tense, relaxed), feelings about your interaction with others (anxiety, enjoyment of the conversation, irritation, etc.) You might find it helpful to record your memories in a logbook.
- **When there is a family reunion or a gathering of friends:**
  - talk about shared experiences;
  - contextualise your memories in time and space;
  - search your memory to recall as many details as possible.
- **Sit down somewhere in a place you do not often visit:**
  - learn a poem or any other short text that appeals to you;
  - two days later, sit down in a familiar place and, as an aid to recollection of the words learned, visualise the environment associated with that learning exercise. This spontaneous recall is also one of the functions of episodic memory.

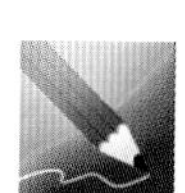

Well-known television programmes

The programmes on the following list have been landmarks in the history of television. You might have found them interesting, amusing, annoying, even revolting, but you probably did not feel indifferent. That, precisely, contributed to the workings of your episodic memory, which probably stored away not only the event and your reactions, but also a mass of related information. What were you doing when these programmes were first shown on television? Where were you? Was it before or after a certain episode in your life? Using the context in which you were first exposed to each of these programmes as a point of reference, arrange them in chronological order in terms of your own experience and then rearrange them in the order in which they were aired.

1. **Friends**
2. **Frasier**
3. **Coronation Street**
4. **Sex and the City**
5. **Seinfeld**
6. **The Weakest Link**
7. **Dallas**
8. **Absolutely Fabulous**
9. **The Oprah Winfrey Show**
10. **The Muppet Show**
11. **Big Brother**
12. **Baywatch**
13. **The Late Show with David Letterman**
14. **Who wants to be a Millionaire?**
15. **Cheers**
16. **Charlie's Angels**
17. **Will and Grace**
18. **Everybody loves Raymond**

Solution p.336

Two comic actors and their films

Peter Sellers and Robin Williams, two monumental figures in the history of comedy, acted in the 10 following films. Your episodic memory no doubt registered the story and some of the scenes in certain films, but it also registered a mass of supplementary information like the music or dialogues.
How old were you when these films were first shown?
Did you find these films entertaining, interesting, thought-provoking? Use all these factors to help you match the right actor to the right film.

1. **The Fiendish Plot of Dr Fu Manchu**
2. **The Fisher King**
3. **The Party**
4. **Mrs Doubtfire**
5. **The Pink Panther**
6. **Aladdin**
7. **What's new Pussycat?**
8. **Dr Strangelove**
9. **Good Morning, Vietnam**
10. **Dead Poets' Society**

	Sellers	Williams
1.		
2.		
3.		
4.		
5.		
6.		
7.		
8.		
9.		
10.		

Solution p.336

A habit doesn't make a monk

Every era produces a unique style of clothing and a panoply of beauty accessories. Order the following 12 items from the oldest to the most recent.

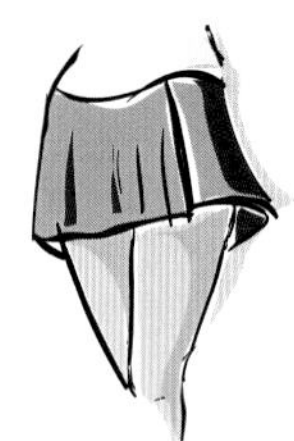

a. The miniskirt

b. Spectacles

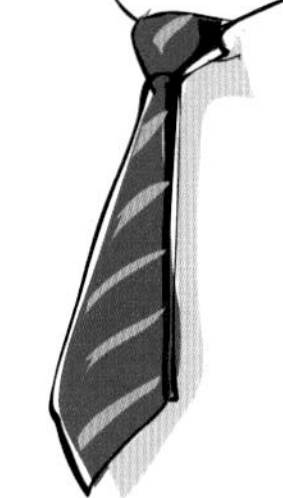

c. The necktie

d. The stiletto heel

e. The bracelet watch

f. Rubber boots

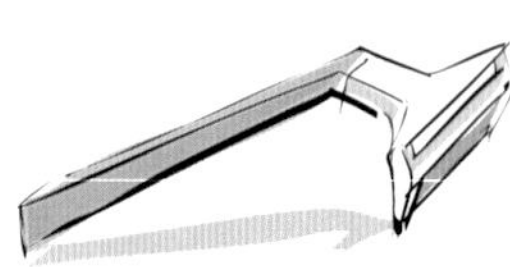

g. The disposable razor

h. The tailored suit

i. Nail polish

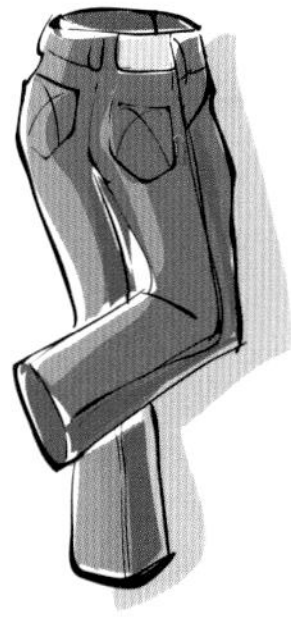

j. Blue jeans

k. The zip

l. The macintosh

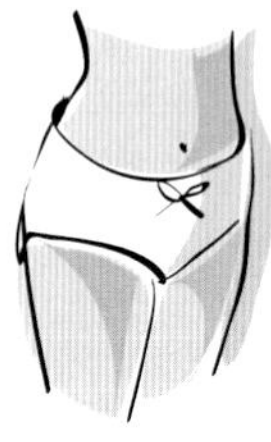

m. Briefs

n. Nylon stockings

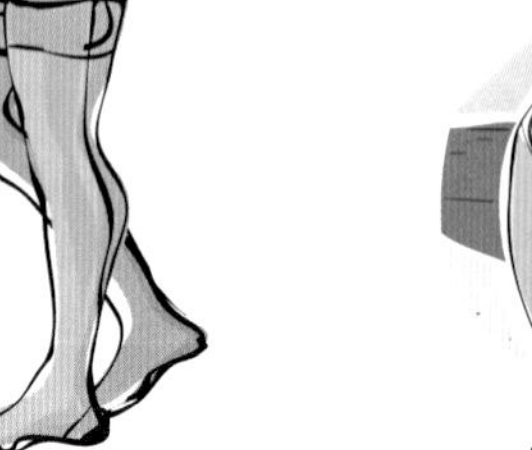

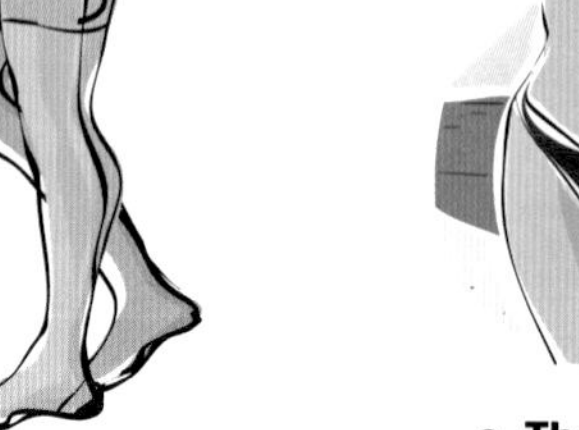

o. The bikini

Solution p.336

1. ....

2. ....

3. ....

4. ....

5. ....

6. ....

7. ....

8. ....

9. ....

10. ....

11. ....

12. ....

13. ....

14. ....

15. ....

My memory and…
my daily routine

Our lives can seem monotonous to us at times. Our capacity for reflection is dulled, little seems to motivate us. Everybody experiences these states of mind. At any stage of life we need a little fantasy, novelty or a project to make us feel fully alive. You should therefore be wary of routines that you adopt to secure your peace of mind; you should make an effort to keep your interest alive. Every day, give yourself a small unexpected treat, or do something new. And take note that, unfortunately, when everyday life seems dreary to you, your memory, deprived of stimulation, tends to suffer as a result.

Heard on the radio

In groups of two or more, recall the names of radio stations of today and yesterday. In each round, all have a turn until you run out of ideas. The last person to give the name of a radio station wins.

Why do you choose to tune in to a certain radio station? Because your parents listened to it, because it's fashionable or because it is to your taste (in terms of topics presented, style of presentation, type of music played, etc). One or other of these factors – or all three – influenced the choice of a radio station at specific times. So a subtle correspondence is often established between a radio station and a period of your life.

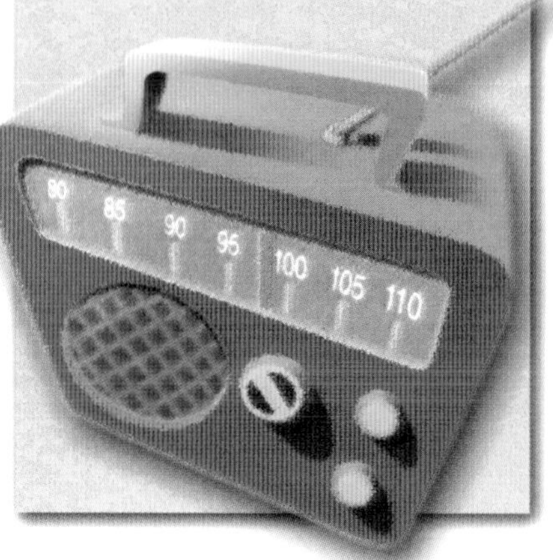

The three phases of memory

The length of time in which information is retained by the memory is classified into the subdivisions of sensory memory, short-term memory and long-term memory. Childhood memories are regarded as belonging to the long-term memory, and experiences of only a few minutes ago as being part of the short-term memory. But this classification has only a theoretical value, becauses the perception of time is essentially subjective.

Sensory memory

We all have memories that are closely associated with smells, tastes, tactile sensations, sounds … As an organism, the human body is rather like a large radar system which, through the medium of the senses, captures all the information coming in from the environment. The brain, through the nervous system, receives and translates data into its own language. This first recording is the sensory memory, which consists of **visual, auditory, gustatory, olfactory and tactile memories.** It is important to stimulate this memory because it is the first stage in the acquisition of information, coming before short-term memory.

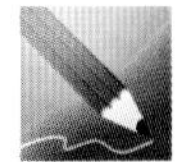

Training keen perception

1. Sit down in a comfortable chair at home
– Listen attentively to all the noises around you, identifying them and listening to each separately.
– For five minutes, look carefully at the objects surrounding you, one by one. Concentrate on noticing details – the size, shape, colour.
2. Repeat this exercise for a fortnight in different places – your workplace, a shop – choosing a time when you can concentrate intently on this activity.
3. Repeat the experiment when walking in town or out in the country.

The essence of an apple …

1. Look carefully at an apple. What colour is it? Yellow, red, green?
2. Pick it up, feel it, stroke it. What does it feel like? Is it smooth, rough, wrinkled…?
3. Lift it to your face and smell it. What do you smell? The scent of the orchard, of the undergrowth?
4. Put it to your mouth and bite into it with relish, then taste it slowly. What is it like? Firm, floury, juicy …? What does it taste like? Sweet, with a honey flavour?
5. Listen … What noise do you hear when you bite into the fruit? And when you chew a piece?

It is difficult to spontaneously make a fine distinction between our various perceptions. From the dawn of humanity, the need for us to adapt to a changing environment in a sense programmed us for an overall awareness of our surroundings, because only this could enable us to react appropriately in the event of danger. Information of this nature is thus forgotten very easily. A conscious decision to focus our attention is necessary for this reflex action to be replaced by **selective perception.** Then objects, colours, shapes and smells can be perceived with greater intensity. They take on a concrete presence, while clearly defined images are being formed in the brain. Sensory memory is then working at full capacity. In the sensory realm, as in many other areas, training produces surprising results. Do you know, for example, that in the depths of a forest the untrained ear distinguishes no more than four bird calls, while the finely trained ear of the ornithologist can distinguish more than ten? **Perception can thus be stimulated**, brought into play regularly, if you concentrate on paying attention to your surroundings. And the more finely your perception is honed, the more receptive the senses become.

But **sensory memory is very susceptible to interference,** to those disturbances that disrupt an activity and distract your attention. A few seconds of distraction is enough to erase information, thus precluding the process of mental repetition that is essential for memorisation. Information disappears just as easily if you don't consider it worth retaining. In spite of the ephemeral nature of perception, you would be surprised by the precision of some of your sensory memories, which are reminiscent of images captured on film. It is through the activity of your sensory memory that this whole process of memorisation is launched: the information, finely and attentively perceived, is rapidly recorded in the short-term memory. It also has a good chance of being firmly fixed in your long-term memory.

Details that jar your senses

Sharpen your visual perception by looking carefully at this picture. The room has only a superficial semblance of reality: 16 anomalies have slipped in – incongruous shapes, impossible positions and other aberrations.

Solution p.336

Short-term memory

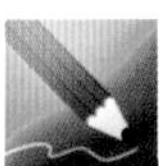

Geometric figures

Look carefully at the drawing for 30 seconds, then cover it and reproduce it from memory.

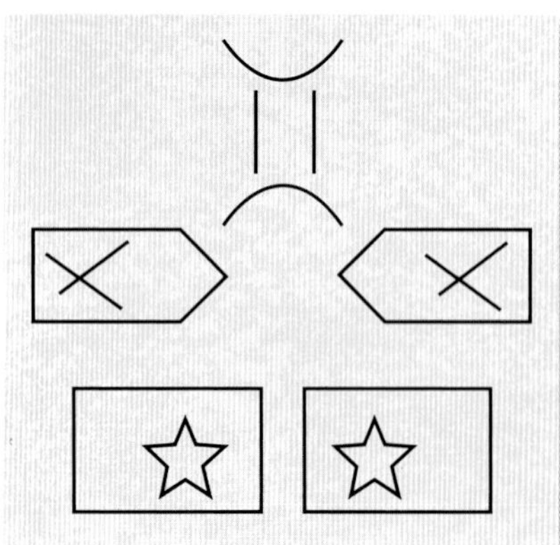

You have just put your short-term memory to work on the visualisation of shapes. Coming after sensory memory, this is the second stage in the process of memorisation. Short-term memory is essentially a **practical memory**, which is immediate and is manifested in all your everyday actions: you remember the ingredients of a dish you are preparing just after reading the recipe, a telephone number seen in the telephone directory long enough to ring it up, an address you have just heard long enough to write it down, etc. The fundamental characteristic of this memory is its volatility.

Your short-term memory functions to **enable you to carry out immediate tasks that will soon be forgotten**. It is measured in minutes (a maximum of three) or even seconds.

Short-term memory has a **limited recording capacity**: it can retain only a few items of information at a time – with a maximum of seven. This is what is known as the **span** (see p.34). It is without doubt for a very particular reason that it possesses a 'filter mechanism' – this allows it to eliminate all extraneous facts that are not vital for carrying out a given task. This filtering function is moreover exercised in all situations of daily life: it prevents you from being constantly overwhelmed by a never-ending flow of information. Thanks to the filter, you do not memorise the faces of all the passers-by in the street, nor all the sounds you hear in the course of the day. The filter eliminates all information that does not appear to be essential, allowing you to focus on a particular task.

Cryptogram 1. Decipher the following two proverbs. Each letter is replaced by a symbol. When you have completed the decoding, wait for two minutes before doing exercise 2, opposite.

G = ♣ I = ➡ M = ➤ T = ♥

First proverb

....

....

Second proverb

....

....

....

Solution p.336

2. Cover the left-hand side and then work out which letter corresponds to which symbol.

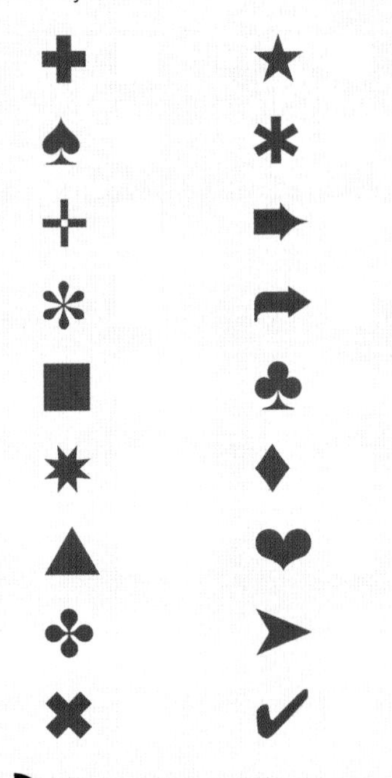

This exercise must have seemed very demanding. It demonstrates how difficult it is for the short-term memory to exceed the limit of elements retained by the memory span and also to retain this data for more than a few minutes.

Four lovely ladies
Look attentively at these four women for 30 seconds and memorise their first names. Then cover the picture and answer the questions that follow.

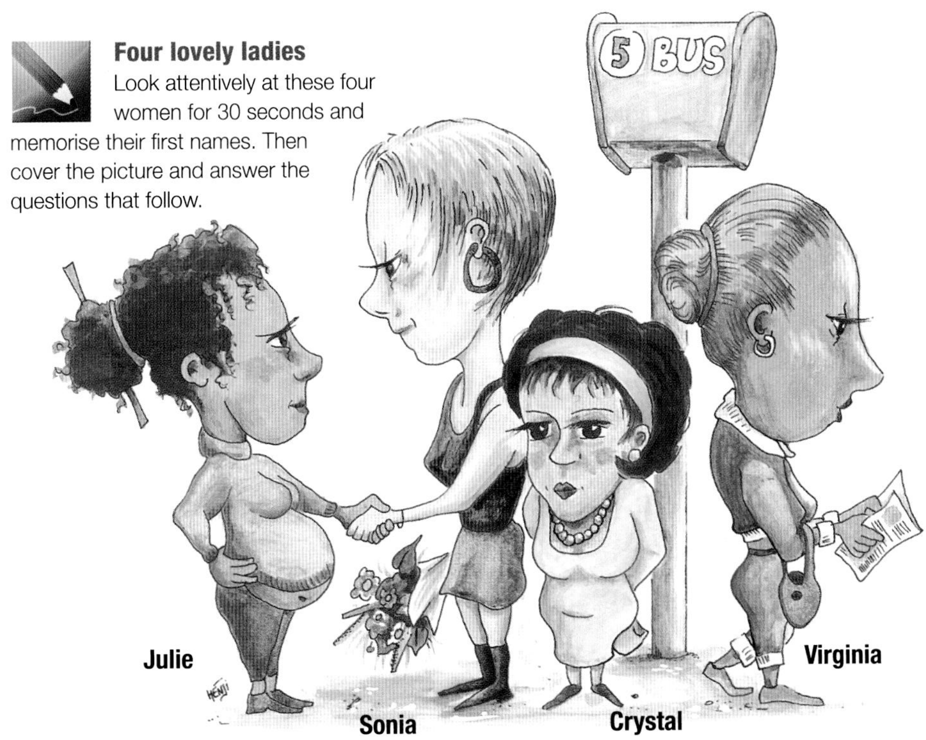

1. What is the name of the pregnant woman? ....
2. Which one is wearing a dress with long sleeves? ....
3. Who is wearing a necklace? ....
4. Do they all have chignons? ....
5. What is Virginia holding? ....
6. Are all four women blondes? ....
7. Two women are looking to the right and two others towards the left. Can you say which? ....

The working memory

A peculiarity of the short-term memory is its ability to change to working mode as soon as a task demands the rapid memorisation of abstract information – as in, for example, mental arithmetic, ideas, concepts.

Mental arithmetic
Without using a calculator, do the following sums

769 + 586 = ...

698 + 524 = ...

587 + 269 + 874 = ...

356 + 587 + 214 = ...

1005 + 33 + 646 = ...

994 + 136 + 428 = ...

650 + 123 + 541 = ...

421 + 789 + 666 = ...

***Solution** p.336*

When doing each sum, the immediate operations you have carried out are held in your working memory long enough for the completion of the task, in this case finding the total, then they rapidly disappear.

To carry out this mental operation, you also had to know how to do addition! Another function of the working memory is to recall skills learned a long time before and stored in the long-term memory for specific tasks. When students amass facts in order to pass an exam, the interaction of newly learned pieces of information and those acquired earlier enables them to give appropriate answers on D-day. A few months later they will be unable to answer these questions.

Long-term memory

Your long-term memory is capable of retaining a multitude of items of information accumulated in the course of your life. This virtually **unlimited storage capacity** allows everyone to store up the learning experiences of childhood and knowledge of the world subsequently acquired through learning and direct personal experience.

For decades, research has been carried out into the organisation and functioning of this amazing mental reservoir that is essential to life. It has thus been possible to establish the following sub-categories of memory: **episodic memory** (see p.128), **semantic memory** (see p.122), **procedural memory** (see p.118), and **implicit and explicit forms of memory** (see p.115).

Although the potential of long-term memory is the same for all people, the capacity to initially retain and then later retrieve information varies from one individual to the next.

The class photo
1. Find one of your old class photographs and then, without initially looking at it, try to recall the names and faces of your classmates. Write the names of those you remember on a sheet of paper.

2. Now, looking at the photograph, can you remember more of them? Write all the names you have recalled on the silhouettes in this picture.

3. How many names did you recall?
before looking at the photo:
....
looking at the photo:
....

The Owl and the Pussy-Cat...

Whether you learned it at school or heard it some time later, you certainly know some lines from *The Owl and the Pussy-Cat,* a well-known poem by Edward Lear. From memory, try to complete these few verses.

The Owl and the Pussy-cat went to ....
In a beautiful pea-green.........
They took some.........
and plenty of money
Wrapped up in a .... note
The Owl looked up to the .... above
And .... to a small guitar,
'O .... Pussy! O Pussy, my love,
What a .... Pussy you are,
You are, You are!
What a .... Pussy you are!'

Pussy said to the .... ,
'You elegant .... !'
How charmingly .... you sing!
'O let us be......... ! too long we have .... :
But what shall we do for a .... ?
They .... away for a year and a day

To the land where the .... grows
And there in a wood a .... stood
With a .... at the end of his nose,
HIs nose, His nose,
With a .... at the end of his nose.

'Dear Pig, are you .... to sell for a ....
Your ring?' Said the Piggy, '.........'
So they took it away,
and were .... next day
By the .... who lives on the ....
They dined on .... and slices of ....
Which they ate with a .... spoon
And hand in hand , on the edge of the ....
They danced by the light of the moon,
The moon, The moon,
They danced by the light of the moon.

My memory and... curiosity

Admittedly, curiosity can be considered a bad fault. On the other hand, it is a real asset in improving our powers of memory. Being curious indicates that one has developed a wide range of interests. This is the best way to keep the memory in good shape. By contrast, focusing on one or two exclusive areas of interest is not of much benefit to the memory. It is certainly a good thing to have a special hobby but be careful – you must also know how to be a bit of a jack of all trades!

Why have you remembered most of the poem? Perhaps you recited it in class? You could be either congratulated or criticised! If the poem does not remind you of anything in particular, perhaps it arouses in you a general feeling of pleasure or nostalgia. And why did you remember one particular class in the exercise with the class photo? Did the sight of those faces enable you to recall more names? And anecdotes?

Two people linked by shared experiences will not have retained the same memories. Whether it is knowledge gleaned from books, the recollection of an event or a specific life experience, **the mode of retention is as personal as the mode of recall.** Because your memory depends on the imposition of order for long-lasting retention, any attempt to **impose structure on the information** will favour the transfer from sensory memory to short-term memory, then to long-term memory and ultimately to its consolidation in this memory. It guarantees a swift and effective **process of recall.**

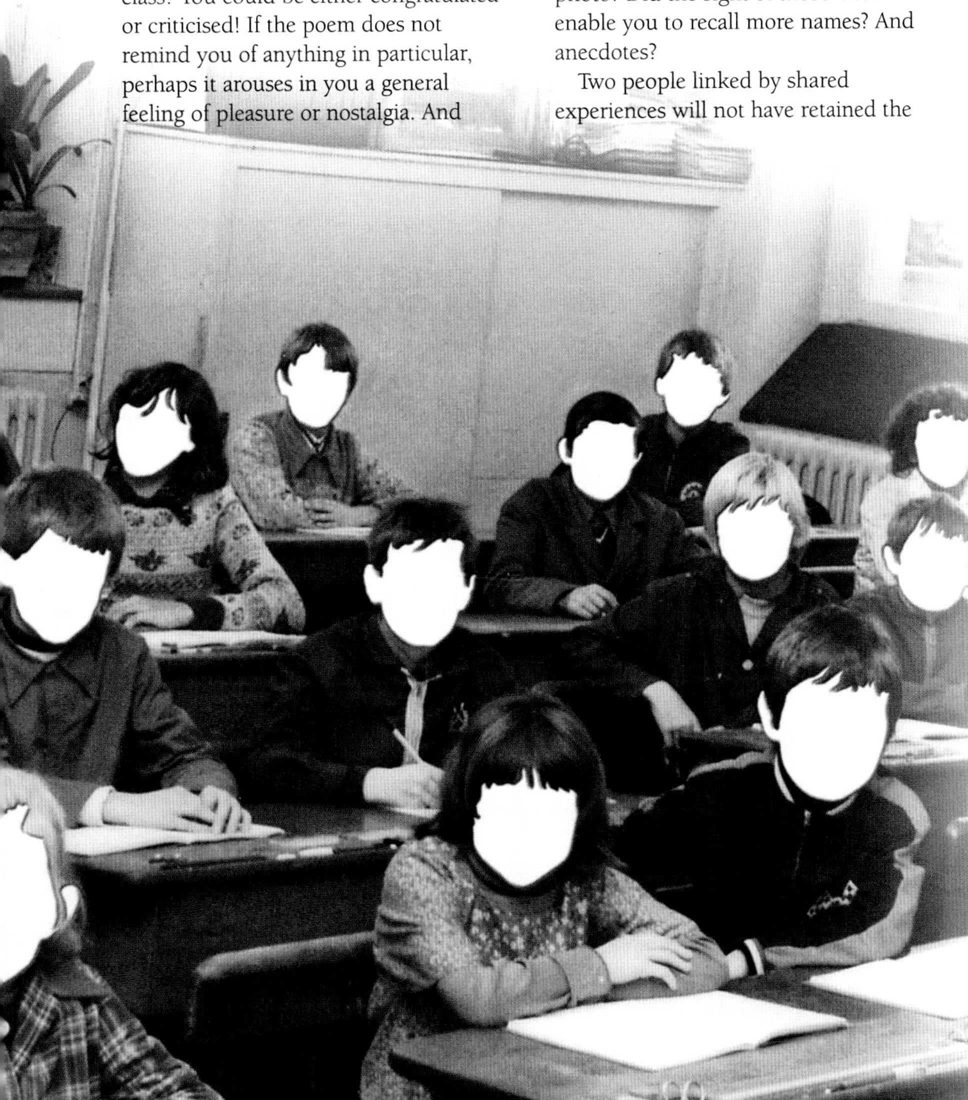

But the process of recording in the long-term memory does not always depend on the will. Most often it is **the emotional colouring of the event,** whether pleasant or unpleasant, that determines the engraving of a lasting memory. Another factor is the degree of **interest and attention** you paid to an item of information or an event in your life. All these aspects also play a part in the speed of recovery of a memory. This explains why certain memories considered beyond recall can easily come back to you in response to sensory stimulations – a sound, a taste, a picture, certain words, or an atmosphere ... which constitute so many factors that can trigger a recollection. The story of Proust's madeleine (which evokes a world of childhood memories when he dips it in a cup of tea years later) is precisely that.

Songs and words

Find the words or titles of songs containing the following words or themes.

For example, the word **night** is found in: In the Middle of the **Night** – Silent **Night** – **Nights** in White Satin.

Paris

....

Sun

....

Love

....

Colours

....

Names of cities

....

Thanks to what is usually a pleasant atmosphere in which a song is heard, some of the words in the song are deeply embedded in our memory without our realising it.

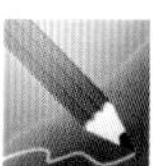

Perfume, hippopotamus, catastrophe and nectarine

The words making up our vocabulary are inscribed in our memory on a long term basis. In a maximum of eight minutes, find five words beginning with **per**-, **hippo**-, **cata**- and **nec**-.

Per	**Cata** ....
Per	**Cata** ....
Per	**Cata** ....
Per	**Cata** ....
Per	**Cata** ....
Hippo	**Nec** ....
Hippo	**Nec** ....
Hippo	**Nec** ....
Hippo	**Nec** ....
Hippo	**Nec** ....

A hairy story

It is often thanks to our visual perception that certain memories are firmly fixed in our memory. Hair colour, for example, is a defining feature to which our memory of people we have met is attached. Name five celebrities or well-known personalities whose hair is obviously blond, red or black.

Blond hair	Red hair	Black hair
1.	1.	1. ....
2.	2.	2. ....
3.	3.	3. ....
4.	4.	4. ....
5.	5.	5. ....

Footloose

We rarely forget the meaning of everyday words or expressions. This is because language depends on semantic memory, a sub-category of long-term memory. Find as many words and expressions as possible containing the word 'foot'.

1. ....
2. ....
3. ....
4. ....
5. ....
6. ....
7. ....
8. ....
9. ....
10. ....
11. ....
12. ....
13. ....
14. ....
15. ....

Forgetting

Paradoxically, one aspect of memorisation consists in … forgetting. In fact, it is pointless to risk saturation by trying to retain all the information that reaches you each day. This does not mean that you cannot ensure the sound functioning of your memory by using good 'crutches' and not trying to do several things at once. Although our desire to remember is sometimes thwarted by our subconscious, the information suppressed is still there.

Forgetting, to prevent saturation

I would go mad if I remembered everything!

What would be the point of remembering how many red traffic lights you encountered on your way to work or school and back? Nevertheless, you certainly saw and remembered them, but only to use this information momentarily and then erase it.

The so-called normal memory erases 90-95 percent of information received in one day. This process of active forgetting, often called selective memory, is in fact a way of retaining only what is essential in the continuous flow of daily information. Without it, your memory would be saturated.

This process of active restriction does not work in the same way for everyone. Certain people are able to recall a great number of details. For example, they will describe to you in minute detail things like your hairstyle and what you were wearing when they met you. This kind of recall is not an indication of a prodigious memory, but it can indicate that the individuals concerned base their relation to the world on visual impressions, and because their attention is focused on appearances, they are less likely to remember other information, such as the topic of conversation or the nature of the relationship.

For others, the opposite holds. They forget the physical environment of the situations they experience and are regarded as scatterbrains! Their relation with the world is probably based more on sentiment and personal experience and so they are less interested in physical details.

European currencies

In 2002, 15 of the countries in the European Union (EU) adopted a common currency. Give the national currency of the 25 countries now in the EU, and indicate which have not adopted the euro.

1. Austria ....
2. Belgium ....
3. Cyprus ....
4. Czech Rep. ....
5. Denmark ....
6. Estonia ....
7. Finland ....
8. France ....
9. Germany ....
10. Greece ....
11. Hungary ....
12. Ireland ....
13. Italy ....
14. Latvia ....
15. Lithuania ....
16. Luxembourg ....
17. Malta ....
18. The Netherlands ....
19. Poland ....
20. Portugal ....
21. Slovakia ....
22. Slovenia ....
23. Spain ....
24. Sweden ....
25. United Kingdom ....

With the advent of the euro, perhaps you have started to forget these currencies. That's quite natural. The process of forgetting is at work here because this information will no longer be useful. In 20 years, a fair number of us will have partly forgotten them, except if we keep these memories alive for historical interest.

Solution p.337

Great rivers of the world

Classify these rivers in descending order according to their length.

Solution p.337

a. Ganges
b. Mississippi-Missouri
c. Amazon
d. Congo
e. Amur
f. Nile
g. Yangzi Jiang
h. Mekong

1. ......
2. ......
3. ......
4. ......
5. ......
6. ......
7. ......
8. ......

You are probably familiar with the names of these rivers, and were taught their relative length some time in your school career. But as these details are not of vital importance, you would have retained them only if they were useful – for professional reasons, for example – or if you are especially interested in geography.

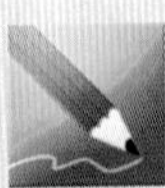

Words ending in -tle, words ending in -oot

In three minutes, find as many words as possible ending in -tle and -oot. Simple words, and those frequently used, will spring to mind first. However, you'll have to make more of an effort to track down words that do not form part of your everyday vocabulary.

Words ending in -tle

....

....

....

....

....

....

....

....

....

Words ending in -oot

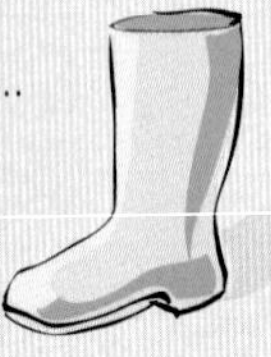

....

....

....

....

....

....

....

As in the preceding exercise, the process of forgetting affects words you do not commonly use. To develop a rich vocabulary, carry out this exercise regularly, varying the endings of the words you search for (eg, using endings such as -cide, -amy, -age, et, or even words starting with mon-, man- etc).

Solution p.337

My memory and… the word on the tip of my tongue

This situation is not uncommon: you know the word but it won't come to mind (or off your tongue). You then feel embarrassed, or even ridiculous. Relax, it is perfectly normal for words to come less rapidly than thoughts, and the less you talk, the more you are likely to encounter this problem. It can be overcome by using a more expanded vocabulary and by making a habit of finding synonyms. It is also advisable to control the rush of disordered thoughts and to concentrate on talking slowly and calmly.

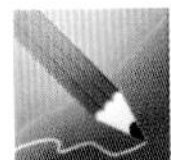

When remembering becomes pointless

1. **Do you remember...** your very first telephone number?
2. **Do you remember...** the registration number of your first car?
3. **Do you remember...** the address of your oldest child's paediatrician?
4. **Do you remember...** the code number of your first bank card?
5. **Do you remember...** the first film you ever saw at the cinema?
6. **Do you remember...** the date of your first day at work?

You most probably had great difficulty in finding answers to the first four questions, and that is to be expected. What would be the use of storing in your memory the registration number of your first car? Our memory serves to retain facts that are useful to us in our everyday life, but 90 percent of this material is destined to be actively eliminated so that we can carry out our different daily tasks without cluttering up our 'memory apparatus'.

But you did perhaps recall the date of your first day at work or the title of your first film, probably because these were important milestones in your life and possibly because you talk about them.

Good and bad crutches

My fridge is covered with Post-it notes! Are they really necessary?

Imagine that you set off to do your weekly shopping, and try to draw up a mental list of all the goods you need. This memory exercise is our daily lot. What do you do next? Write a shopping list?

Faced with the various tasks of everyday life, we tend to resort to crutches (a scrap of paper, note, Post-it, notice board …). Are they good memory aids, or do they end up destroying the memory? Should we try to do without them?

A good crutch enables us to do what we could never manage without it. Is it reasonable, or even realistic, to believe that we could recall everything contained in a diary or an address book? That would be a gross overestimation of the power of memory. The diary and address book are good tools allowing us to function from day to day without overloading the memory.

On the other hand, **a crutch becomes harmful when it leads us to underutilise our memories.** So when we systematically resort to opening an address book to look up a familiar telephone number, this deprives the memory of vital mental gymnastics and can lead to laziness that could in due course have a negative effect on our personal independence.

Test Identify your crutches

Answer **YES** or **NO** to the following questions.

	YES	NO
1. I use the numbers recorded on my cellphone without learning those I call daily.	☐	☐
2. I systematically make use of my address book when sending postcards to my family and friends.	☐	☐
3. I make a list when buying fewer than seven products from the supermarket.	☐	☐
4. I need to note down all my codes – for the front door, credit card, voicemail, cellphone ...	☐	☐
5. I must write down my ideas so as not to forget them.	☐	☐
6. Because I often slam the door with my keys still inside, I've installed an outside handle.	☐	☐
7. I regularly consult my diary to keep track of my activities.	☐	☐
8. I look at the calendar more than twice a day to check the date.	☐	☐
9. Before making each telephone call, I note down what I want to say.	☐	☐
10. I often tie knots in my handkerchief.	☐	☐
11. I write anything I'm afraid of forgetting on my hand.	☐	☐
12. A white board occupies a prominent place in my kitchen.	☐	☐

If you have more YES answers, don't feel guilty. We often use crutches in our daily lives and they are not necessarily a sign of mental laziness. You haven't much faith in your memory and have developed the habit of helping it. Despite that, your memory has not deteriorated, and it certainly doesn't mean there is any indication that it is not functioning properly. You must give it the opportunity to record information.

If you have more NO answers, you show confidence in your memory and are satisfied with its performance. Keep it up!

Who am I? Identify each of these celebrities by making use of the clue provided. This will be a word associated with the character or his or her work ... This crutch will help you reactivate your memory.

Solution p.337

Figaro

....

Flying machine

....

Freedom

....

Stratford

....

Polonium

....

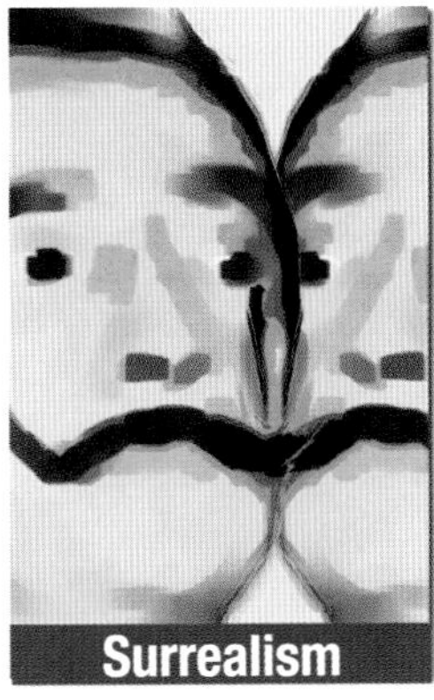
Surrealism

....

Gettysburg

....

Dr Gachet

....

Mazurka

....

The calendar crutch
The calendar often serves as a crutch to remind us of dates to celebrate, or meetings. Fill in the following religious and public holidays on the calendar.

Christmas

Labour day/Worker's day

Thanksgiving

Diwali

Armistice day

Ramadan

Eid ul-Fitr

Hannukah

All Saints eve

Day of the dead

New Year's day

Easter Sunday

Ascension day

Pesach

Independence day

Good Friday

Hallowe'en

Guy Fawkes

St Valentine's day

Next, fill in the birthdays of 10 of your close relatives or friends.
This exercise will enable you to establish points of reference that will make you less reliant on your calendar in future.

January

1
2
3
4
5
6
7
8
9
10
11
12
13
14
15
16
17
18
19
20
21
22
23
24
25
26
27
28
29
30
31

Febr

1
2
3
4
5
6
7
8
9
10
11
12
13
14
15
16
17
18
19
20
21
22
23
24
25
26
27
28
29

July

1
2
3
4
5
6
7
8
9
10
11
12
13
14
15
16
17
18
19
20
21
22
23
24
25
26
27
28
29

Aug

1
2
3
4
5
6
7
8
9
10
11
12
13
14
15
16
17
18
19
20
21
22
23
24
25
26
27
28
29
30
31

Solution p.333

Interruptions and multi-tasking

When someone talks to me, I lose track of what I'm doing!

When you are busy with a task, noises around you, or someone's unexpected arrival, or any other disturbance can make you lose track of what you had started doing. The information vanished because this interruption interfered with the functioning of your short-term memory, which demands undivided attention. This is not really forgetting as such, but **the absence of memorisation because of a momentary distraction.**

Similarly, when you are obliged to interrupt what you are doing to carry out another task simultaneously, the memorisation process is impeded. Who hasn't often been distracted while going to another room to fetch something? This information is retained in your memory from 30 to 90 seconds, enough time to carry out your task. If you have to answer the telephone during this time or if someone asks you something – another short-term demand – you definitely run the risk of finding yourself in the room in question asking yourself, 'What did I come here to fetch?' You were put in a multi-tasking situation – obliged to do several things at the same time.

Keeping your tasks separate, even the least demanding ones, and doing them one after the other, **reduces the risk of failure**. You can use this handy little set response: 'Just wait a few seconds until I've finished what I'm doing.' And drop the idea that you can respond to several demands at once, even to please others.

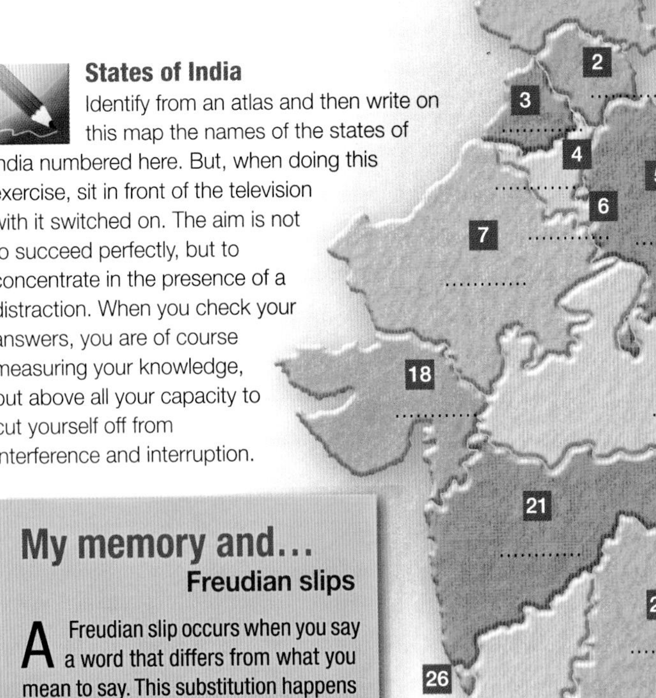

States of India

Identify from an atlas and then write on this map the names of the states of India numbered here. But, when doing this exercise, sit in front of the television with it switched on. The aim is not to succeed perfectly, but to concentrate in the presence of a distraction. When you check your answers, you are of course measuring your knowledge, but above all your capacity to cut yourself off from interference and interruption.

My memory and...
Freudian slips

A Freudian slip occurs when you say a word that differs from what you mean to say. This substitution happens frequently and often passes unnoticed. And yet it reveals an unconscious desire and gives others an inkling of what you really think. These little language errors are not really examples of forgetting but rather pointers to what is really going on inside your mind.

Reading and counting simultaneously

Read this text (an extract from Voltaire's *Candide*) while counting silently to yourself at the same time. Then answer the questions without looking back at the text.

The whole little community entered into this admirable project; everyone started exercising their talents. The little piece of ground brought in plenty. It is true that **Cunégonde** was, in fact, very ugly; but she became an excellent confectioner; **Paquette** did embroidery; the old woman looked after the linen. Even brother **Giroflée** helped; he was a very good carpenter, and even became an honest man; and **Pangloss** often declared to **Candide**: 'All events are linked in the best of all possible worlds: for if you had not been chased away from a splendid castle by hefty kicks in the backside for the love of Miss Cunégonde, if you had not been put before the Inquisition, if you hadn't travelled all over America on foot, if you hadn't given the baron a good blow with your sword, if you hadn't lost all your sheep from the good country of Eldorado, you would not be here eating crystallised lemon and pistachio nuts.' 'That is well said,' replied Candide, 'but we must cultivate our garden.'

Questions

1. What are the names of the characters mentioned in this text?..........................
2. Where did Candide lose all his sheep?..
3. What number had you reached by the end of the text?......................................
4. What is Candide eating? ....

It is more than likely that you couldn't answer any questions if you were counting at the same time. And that is because you were multi-tasking ...

Irrespective of your performance, you must realise that very few people are really capable of doing many things at once, and results obtained when different actions are carried on simultaneously are often unsatisfactory. It is better to complete one task at a time and do it successfully than to try to do too many different things at once.

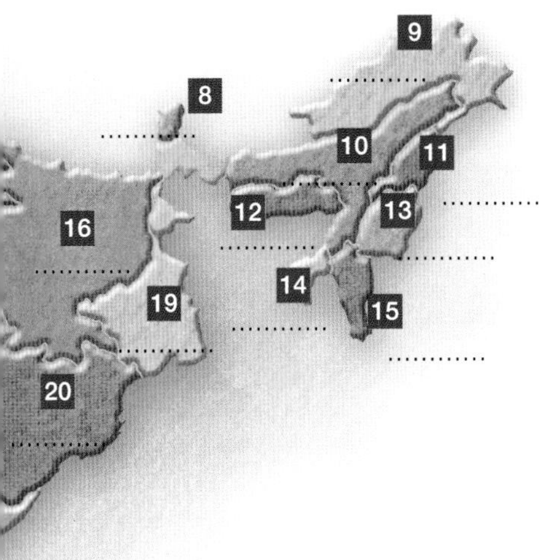

Solution p.337

Hidden objects

Ten faces – human and animal – are hidden in this famous picture of the *Mona Lisa*. You will have to look at the picture from all angles to find some of them.

It is not only the visual effect or perspective that makes it difficult for you to identify these hidden objects at first glance. You first have an overall view, which does not focus on details, and then you recognise what is immediately identifiable. This is the normal way memory functions. You have to make a special effort to suppress your awareness of the primary sense of the image so as to allow other shapes with no direct link to the principal subject to emerge.

Solution p.337

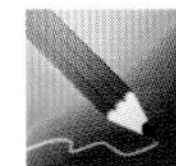

Fishing for words

You have three minutes to find as many words as possible in each of the following categories. You can play on your own or with others, with each player taking a turn to answer.

1. **Names of countries in alphabetical order**
2. **Names of supermarkets**
3. **Exotic dishes**
4. **Painters**
5. **Musical instruments**
6. **Breeds of dogs**

The fewer distractions you are subjected to, the greater your chances of doing well in this exercise. If doing it on your own, for example, don't switch on the radio. If there are several players, you won't be able to avoid being distracted by the replies of the other players; you could then work on your ability to concentrate and check whether you allow yourself to be easily distracted – by repeating the answer given by others, or by forgetting the answer you were planning to give.

Repression

I often forget my dental appointments … I know very well that it's not by accident!

When a little girl whose mother forces her to take dancing lessons often forgets to turn up at the class, you can't help suspecting that this is not simply absent-mindedness but an unconscious strategy to avoid an activity she dislikes: a way of opposing her mother without coming into open conflict with her. The child has experienced not a lapse of memory but **an act of repression**.

From the time of Sigmund Freud we have known that one part of us wants to forget the things that upset us. In fact, it is a matter of **unconsciously wanting to forget something, usually to avoid an unpleasant situation or realisation.** Repression is a mechanism to ensure a sound psychological state. Without it, the coherence of the personality is at risk of being seriously undermined by internal conflicts that are difficult to understand and to control.

You could be surprised at times by lapses of memory that on the face of it seem incomprehensible, such as forgetting an important meeting. You do not then question yourself unduly but curse your memory for letting you down. But bear in mind that repression is also at work in this instance.

It is also possible that you find using certain objects unpleasant, and that certain words are difficult to say. They are the visible part of an iceberg of anxiety and collective and personal fears that we bury deep inside ourselves. But these fears can resurface when the object is before you, or when you hear the word said. And you don't know why.

Finally, there are certain activities that disturb you, perhaps without your knowing the reason why. It is likely that this uneasiness can be linked to a negative or traumatic experience in the past, which you have repressed.

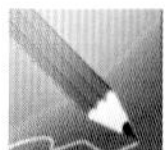

Why did I forget?

Try to remember. One day, you were surprised when you forgot something obvious, or important, or even habitual. For example, an appointment with the doctor, a final exam, or a favour you were meant to do for a best friend. First, recall the exact context of that lapse of memory. Then give honest answers to the following questions.

1. **Was I worrying about whatever I forgot?**
2. **Did I really want to carry out that task?**
3. **Did that lapse of memory eventually enable me to avoid an undesirable situation or conflict?**

Test Those words that disturb us

1. Tick the relevant boxes in the following chart as spontaneously and truthfully as you can.
2. Read the psychologists' comments, and then refer to the analysis of the results.

		Do not bother me at all	Bother me slightly	Bother me a great deal	I avoid saying them
Frightening creepy-crawlies	cockroach				
	spider				
	mouse				
	rat				
	snake				
Shunned by society	lunatic				
	nazi				
	jobless				
The body and its ills	mucus				
	excrement				
	cancer				
	Aids				
	handicap				
Sex and taboos	sex				
	penetration				
	orgasm				
	erection				
Facing death	tomb				
	death				
	die				
	mourning				

ain words to do with animals, society, the body, illness or death
e us uncomfortable. We sometimes even find it difficult to say
e words

at do the psychologists think about this?

ds concerning animals are sometimes fraught with fear, loathing and misconceptions.
kroaches and spiders are small, come out at night, and often live in insalubrious places teeming
germs: they embody an invisible danger. Rats and mice are also associated with squalor and
gienic conditions. As for the snake, a cold-blooded animal, it is traditionally a sexual symbol,
also embodies evil or sin. All these associations are generally disturbing. We suppress them
otect ourselves, but we can be overcome by fear when the words carrying these associations
up, especially when they are augmented by unpleasant more personal impressions that are
lly connected with fears these animals might have aroused in us in childhood.

tics are isolated; society considers lunatics to be beyond the realm of the normal. Nazis are
imously condemned. As for the jobless, they are still often considered to be worthless.
e words are laden with significance, conveying social disapproval, if not rejection, and prey
ne collective imagination. It is the suppressed fear of being similarly ostracised by society
resurfaces in the discomfort aroused by these words.

body and its ills never leave us indifferent. Illness reminds us of
ragility of life. This range of words carries the weight of our
ential anguish, confronting us with what we essentially are, with
eality of our material being. This implicit awareness, which is
n repressed, can resurface in our consciousness as a feeling of
siness when these words are mentioned.

ng about sex is still taboo, even though our society claims to be
ated in this respect. Although religious prohibitions and our own
al sense of propriety both play a part, it is really fear of our own
tions and those of others that comes to the fore in this difficulty with
ds relating to sex.

odern society, death is increasingly placed at a distance and no longer
s part of the continuity of life. This fear is conveyed so strongly in these
ds that it becomes crucial to repress it, to exorcise our anguish. But it
pears in the difficulty we experience in saying these words, so that some
ple then have recourse to euphemisms such as 'the departed', 'he has
sed away', 'he has left us', etc.

Analyse your results

Write down the number of crosses you made in each section.

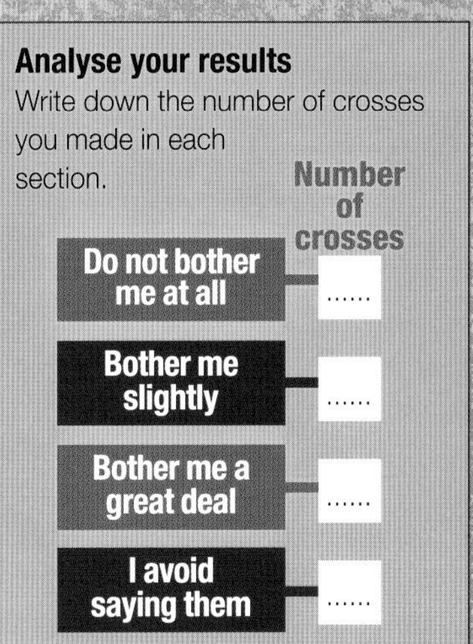

If most of your crosses are in the 'Do not bother me at all' column, you are comfortable with this vocabulary, but be careful of distancing your self too much from your emotions.

If most of your crosses are in the 'Bother me slightly' column, you are aware that certain words trouble you, but you are quite prepared to use them if necessary. You are well balanced and you accept reality.

If most of your crosses are in the 'Bother me greatly' column, you need to question yourself further. You can't content yourself with simply acknowledging that these words disturb you or displease you. Perhaps you should learn to verbalise your emotions more and overcome any reluctance to confide in others.

If most of your crosses are in the 'I avoid saying them' category, you have a real block where certain words are concerned. Perhaps this is a momentary reaction. It is no doubt a protective mechanism adopted to preserve your mental balance.

If your replies are evenly distributed refer back to each comment and try to analyse the words that disturb you most.

How do you perceive danger on the road?

Here are 20 road signs indicating danger, prohibition and obligation, and all of them advising caution. Classify them in descending order in terms of your perception of the relative risk. This exercise can be done on your own or with other players; in the latter case, you will not fail to notice differences in approach between the various participants.

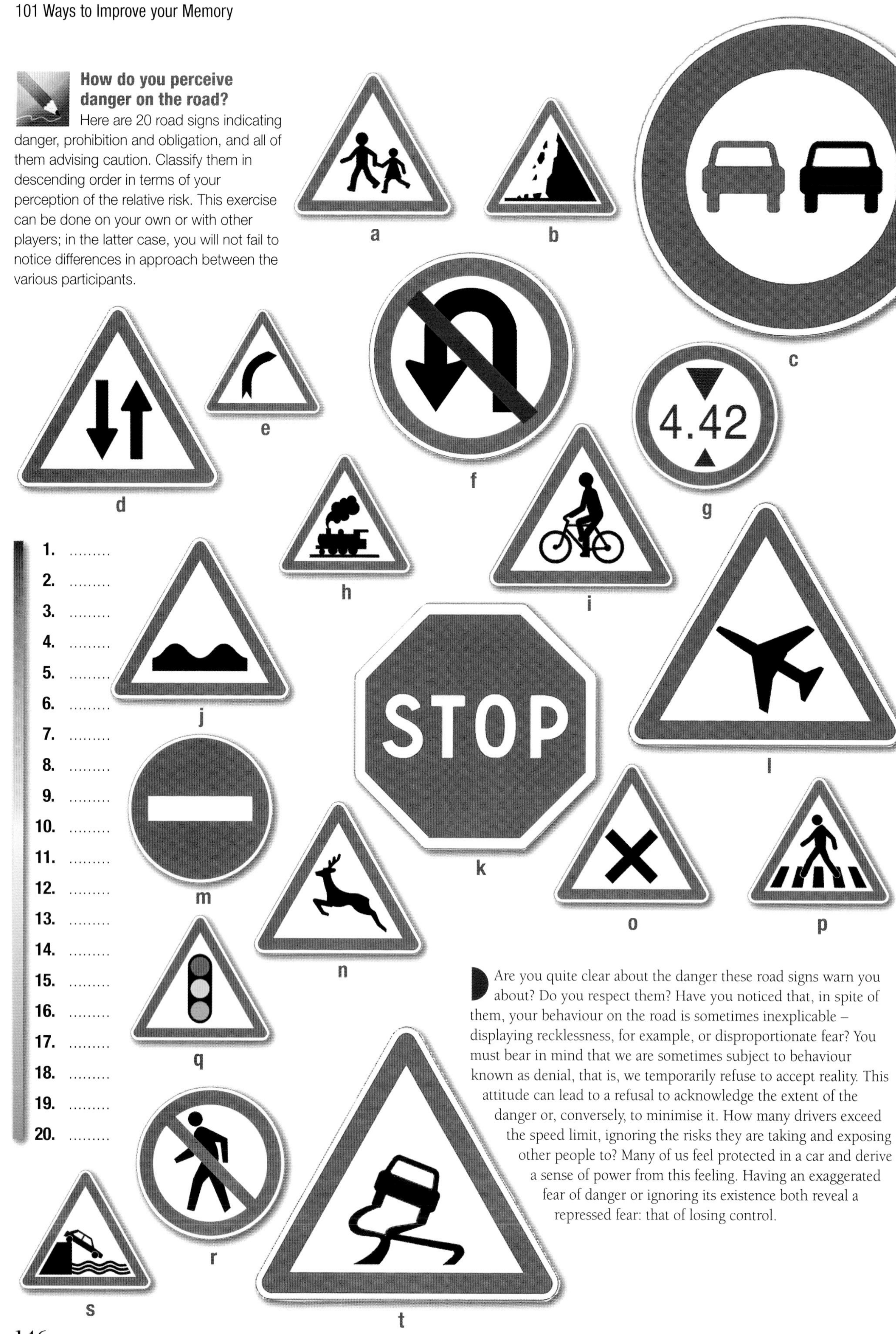

1. ....
2. ....
3. ....
4. ....
5. ....
6. ....
7. ....
8. ....
9. ....
10. ....
11. ....
12. ....
13. ....
14. ....
15. ....
16. ....
17. ....
18. ....
19. ....
20. ....

Are you quite clear about the danger these road signs warn you about? Do you respect them? Have you noticed that, in spite of them, your behaviour on the road is sometimes inexplicable – displaying recklessness, for example, or disproportionate fear? You must bear in mind that we are sometimes subject to behaviour known as denial, that is, we temporarily refuse to accept reality. This attitude can lead to a refusal to acknowledge the extent of the danger or, conversely, to minimise it. How many drivers exceed the speed limit, ignoring the risks they are taking and exposing other people to? Many of us feel protected in a car and derive a sense of power from this feeling. Having an exaggerated fear of danger or ignoring its existence both reveal a repressed fear: that of losing control.

When it is impossible to forget

Although your memory actively erases short-term memories, you retain long-term information in your memory unknowingly, and do this on a continuous basis.

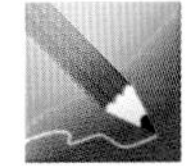

Wright or wrong?
The words below possibly contain errors. Give the right spelling where necessary.

1. **dinamite** ....
2. **recieve** ....
3. **seperate** ....
4. **definately** ....
5. **hopefull** ....
6. **truely** ....
7. **biseps** ....
8. **therefor** ....
9. **pschycology** ....
10. **epitomy** ....
11. **apostrophe** ....
12. **vacilate**......................

Solution p.337

My memory and...
my shopping list

Making a shopping list does not imply that you have a lazy memory – if you don't bury your nose in it as soon as you are in the shop. It is simply making an inventory of what you want. Organising the list according to the way the goods are displayed on the shelves is a good way to remember it. Don't hesitate to read it aloud several times, and as the weeks go by you will eventually be able buy more than 30 products without systematically referring to the list. In any case, there's nothing to stop you from keeping it in your pocket and taking it out just before getting to the till to check that you haven't forgotten anything.

You probably found that little exercise quite easy. Even if the exact spelling doesn't come back to you straight away, you can certainly sense when something isn't quite right! You would in fact find it very difficult to forget your spelling. Throughout childhood, you integrate your experiences of the world by putting things into words. Language (the meaning of words, spelling, and images associated with words) is embedded in your memory and shapes your views of the world and your relations with others. In short, it structures your personality. This is a cognitive learning process.

Certain events in your personal life also shape you, and you cannot forget them. They involve major changes in your life – separation, job loss, death of a loved one ... When you suffer such a loss, what do you experience?

Here your memory sets out to work through the process of grieving. This intense, private process is an activity that makes the memories associated with the loss less painful. It takes place in five stages, in the course of which the process of separation is followed by one of reconstruction.

- **Shock.** Following immediately after the loss, it has a paralysing effect on your whole psycho-emotional state, and is sometimes accompanied by a denial of reality – 'No, it's not true!'
- **Realisation and mentally coming to terms.** You are overwhelmed by memories associated with your loss. The irrevocability of the loss is accepted. This stage is characterised by the search for explanations and the need to understand; this is when you ask 'Why?' and declare 'If only I had done this or that ...'
- **Assimilation.** This is when you tend to idealise and recall all the good memories. The feelings of guilt and anger subside, the pain is more diffused, and depression might set in, thus allowing the beginning of a progressive detachment from what has been lost.
- **Re-engagement or the search for possible alternatives.** If the image of what has been lost is positive enough, you will be able to re-engage with the present and turn back to the outside world.
- **Readjustment or reconstruction.** The wound heals, and your energy can once more be directed towards living. This process of working though grief demands a great deal of energy. Your ability to remember present information can be affected by it. It is nevertheless thanks to this process, which enables you to internalise the loss and make it bearable, that you can carry on living.

The theatre. Study this scene closely and locate the characters, animals and objects depicted on the opposite page.

Games
booklet 2
Solutions 194
zzz

MIXED PROVERBS

GENERAL KNOWLEDGE

The wording of three proverbs has been jumbled up.
Untangle them to find the original proverbs.

LOOK A WORTH THE SAFE
THAN THE HAND LEAP
BIRD YOU IN TWO BUSH
SORRY IN IS BETTER BEFORE

1. ....
....
....

2. ....
....
....

3. ....
....
....

BIB OF THE DAY

CONCENTRATION

Look at these bibs carefully for a few minutes and then cover them.

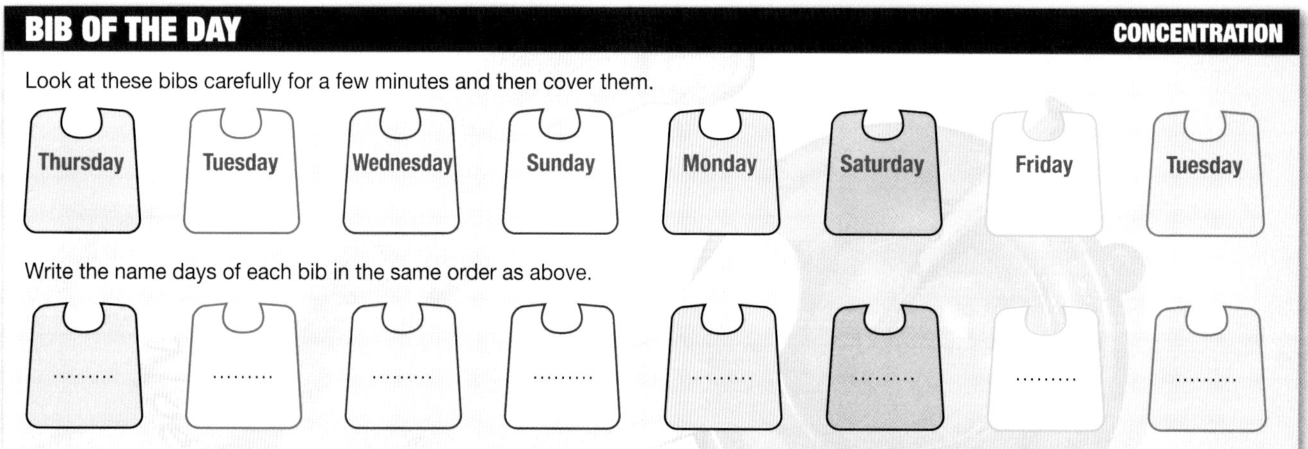

Write the name days of each bib in the same order as above.

BRAIN TEASER

LOGIC

You are travelling to see a friend. You remember the number of the house, 13, but have forgotten the name of the street. Using the following clues, in numerical order, find the right address by a process of elimination.

Clues

1. There is no apostrophe on the street sign.
2. There is not more than one T in this address.
3. The name is that of an important historical personage.
4. The number of letters on the sign is greater than 15.
5. Every vowel appears in this address.

ANAGRAMS — STRUCTURE

Find the names of the musical instruments contained in these anagrams.

1. **MASCARA** ....
2. **GROAN** ....
3. **RELY** ....
4. **ASTIR** ....
5. **UNDERARMS** ....
6. **INTEGRAL** ....
7. **INSTEP** ....
8. **BULGE** ....
9. **ABUT** ....
10. **SHORN** ....

HISTORICAL LANDMARKS — HISTORY

These 16 events can be linked in pairs (they took place in the same year). Can you pair them correctly?

A Earthquake in Armenia: 55,000 dead.
B Ben Johnson is convicted on drug charges.
C UNESCO is founded.
D The start of Prohibition in the United States.
E The start of the Second Reich under Bismarck.
F George Washington becomes the first president of the USA.
G End of the Ming Dyasty in China.

H Olympic Games in Moscow.
I The first July 14 celebration in France.
J French designers Réard and Heim invent the bikini.
K The death of Beethoven.
L The death of Steve McQueen.
M The birth of Fellini.
N The Great Chicago Fire.
O The birth of Stradivarius .
P The launch of the *Standard* newspaper in England.

.... / ....
.... / ....
.... / ....
.... / ....
.... / ....
.... / ....
.... / ....
.... / ....

TARGET — CONCENTRATION

Look at the target on the left for several minutes and memorise the distribution of the shaded areas. Cover it, and then fill these in on the target on the right.

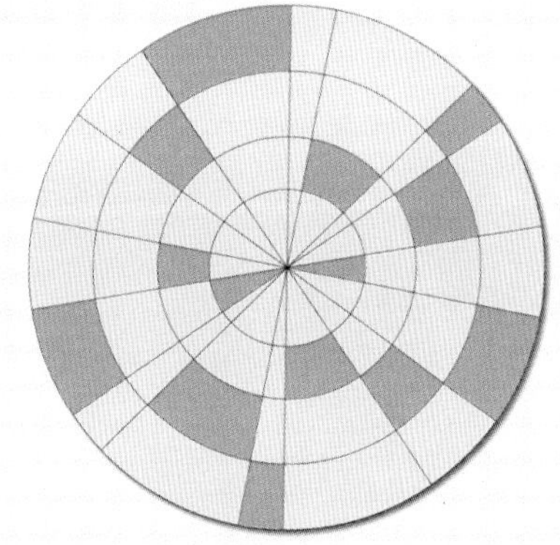

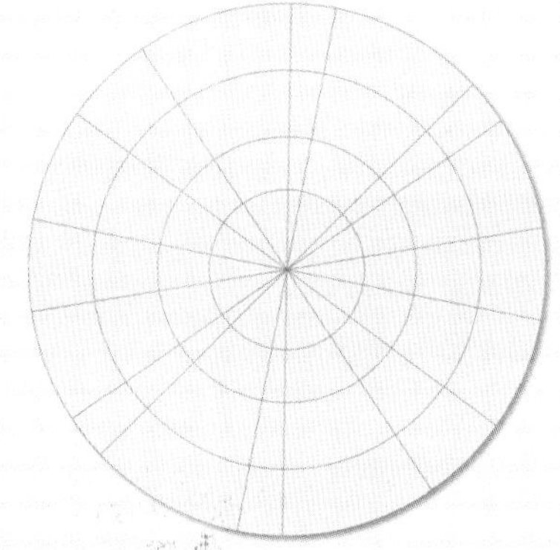

SPOT THE 7 DIFFERENCES — CONCENTRATION

There are seven differences between these two photos. Can you find them?

PROGRESSIVE QUIZ — GENERAL KNOWLEDGE

Try to go as far as you can with this progressive quiz about Aesop and his fables.

1. What nationality was Aesop?
2. In which century did he live?
3. In which fable do we read 'The reason of the mightiest is always the best'?
4. In *The Crow and the Pitcher* how did the crow get to the water deep inside the pitcher?
5. Finish this phrase from *The Grasshopper and the Ants:* 'Don't put off for tomorrow ...'.
6. In which fable do we read: 'Slow and steady wins the race'?
7. In *The Fisherman and the Little Fish* the little fish asks the fisherman to throw him back into the water and not to catch him until he grows bigger. What is the moral of the story?
8. In which fable do we read: 'They are too sour ...'?
9. Which animal of the fields invites his town relation to visit?
10. Which bird whose name is made up of three letters ties peacock feathers to its tail?

PUZZLE — SPACE

Make two circles, a blue and a yellow one, using three out of the four pieces in each exercise.

1.

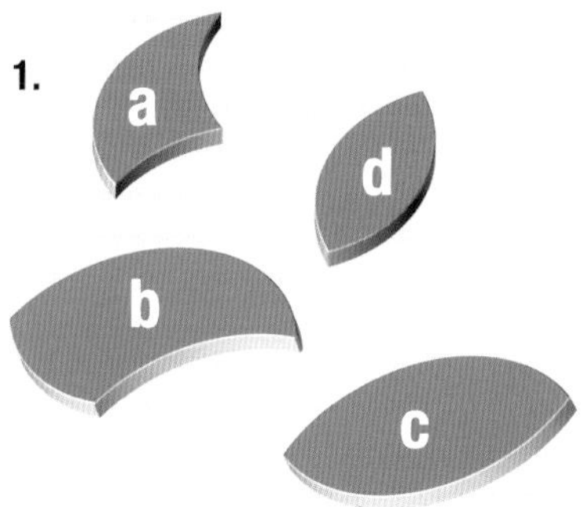

2.

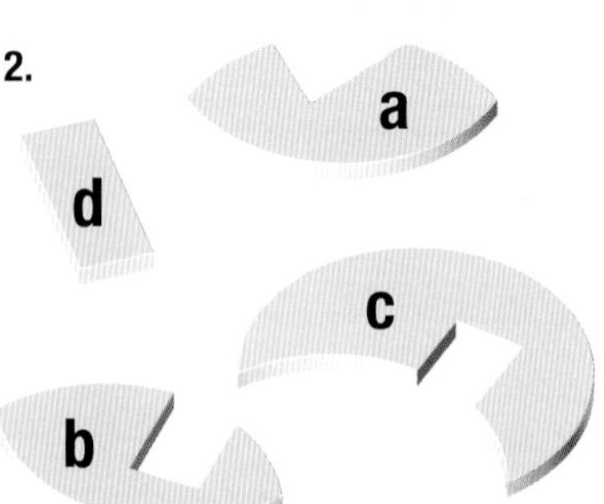

STICK-ON WORDS — STRUCTURE

Stick the following words together in pairs to make the phonetic names of nine cities.

NUMBER PYRAMID — LOGIC

Each brick in a number pyramid represents the sum of the two bricks immediately below.

Question

What identical number must be placed in each box at the base of this pyramid to arrive at the number 320 at the top?

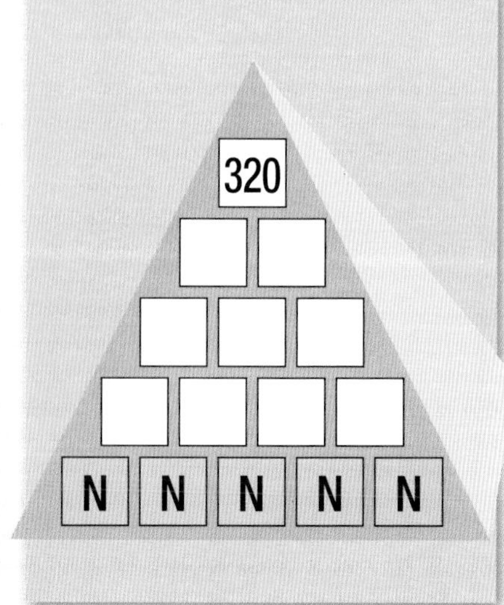

PAIRING UP

ASSOCIATION

Look at these 10 pairs of photos for several minutes and then cover them.

Can you put the pairs together again?

Answers

...... and ......
...... and ......
...... and ......
...... and ......
...... and ......

SHADOWS

SPACE

Which of these shadows is the reverse image of the group of animals?

SANDWICH

STRUCTURE

Complete the five-letter horizontal words to find, in the middle column, Mark Twain's description of Wagner's music. Several solutions are possible, but only one will take you to the correct quote.

C	A		A	L
A	D		P	T
H	U		C	H
B	I		E	S
P	E		K	S
A	C		E	S
M	I		E	S
A	C		E	D
S	T		L	E
C	A		A	L
S	L		P	S
M	A		C	H
B	A		E	D
C	L		V	E
M	O		S	E
B	I		D	S
H	I		E	S
B	A		K	S

ONE TOO MANY

CONCENTRATION

Look carefully at these eight calendars for a few minutes and then cover them.
Which one has been added?

Which calendar did not appear before?

THE RIGHT PLACE

CONCENTRATION

Look at the cars in the parking bays for 45 seconds, and then cover the picture.

Put each car back in its place.

1 2 3 4 5 6 7 8

ZIGZAG WORDS

STRUCTURE

The names of the composers hidden in this grid can be read in all directions: horizontally or vertically, up or down, from right to left or the other way round. The words are arranged in zigzag patterns, but never cross, and each letter can be used only once. With the remaining letters, you can form the name of a composer born in Cologne who subsequently acquired French nationality.

BACH
BEETHOVEN
BERG
BERLIOZ
BIZET
BRAHMS
COUPERIN
DEBUSSY
HAYDN
LALO
LISZT
LULLY
MACHAUT
MAHLER
MONTEVERDI
PERGOLESI
PROKOFIEV
PURCELL
RAVEL
ROSSINI
SALIERI
SCARLATTI
SCHOENBERG
SCHUBERT
SCHUMANN
STRAUSS
STRAVINSKY
VIVALDI
WAGNER

```
M I R E I S Y K H O V E N N T O A H
O S C H L A T S T H C A F O E D Y S
Z A R U B E R N E E B B P M V N U S
B I T E B H C I V E C R U R E R A R
F Z G R N A A M A L L S S O D D E T
L E T Y E U P N R T S I A M E I B S
A L O L O T E R G Z I N H U B I E R
R L U L H C S L O O I E L S V D L G
E N B I T T A E S I L R Y S I V A S
A G A W S C L O R C R E B Z T A H M
M U H C S A R K P R E L I S L R B H
A N N V E I F O N I P U O C E V A R
```

POINTS IN COMMON

ASSOCIATION

For each of these series of words, find the word that links the three others to form a compound word.

1. Clover
   Seasons
   Quarters
   ....

2. Bus
   Orchestra
   Electricity
   ....

3. Sandwich
   Actor
   Fist
   ....

4. Round
   Cut
   Tiger
   ....

5. Cow
   Teeth
   Shake
   ....

6. Hour
   Wine
   Window
   ....

BROKEN SEQUENCES

STRUCTURE

Six words have had two syllables lopped off. Piece them together again, using the syllables provided. Note that there are sometimes several possible solutions, but only one combination will enable you to complete all the words.

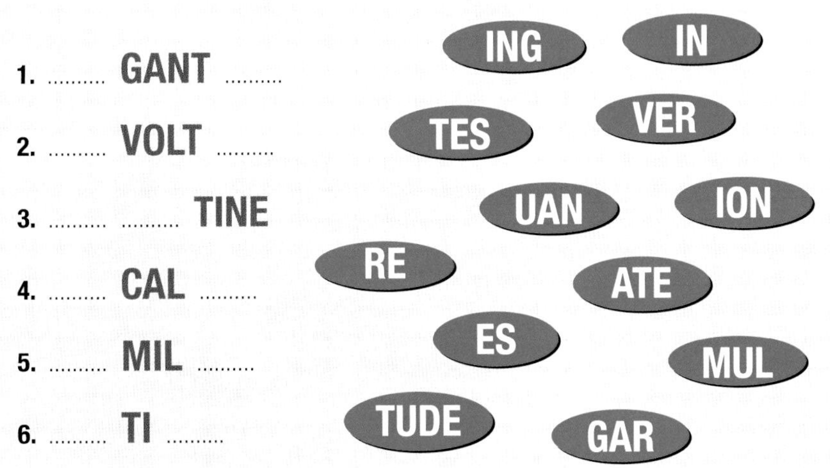

BOXED WORDS — SPACE

Fit the names of all the following mythological figures into the grid.

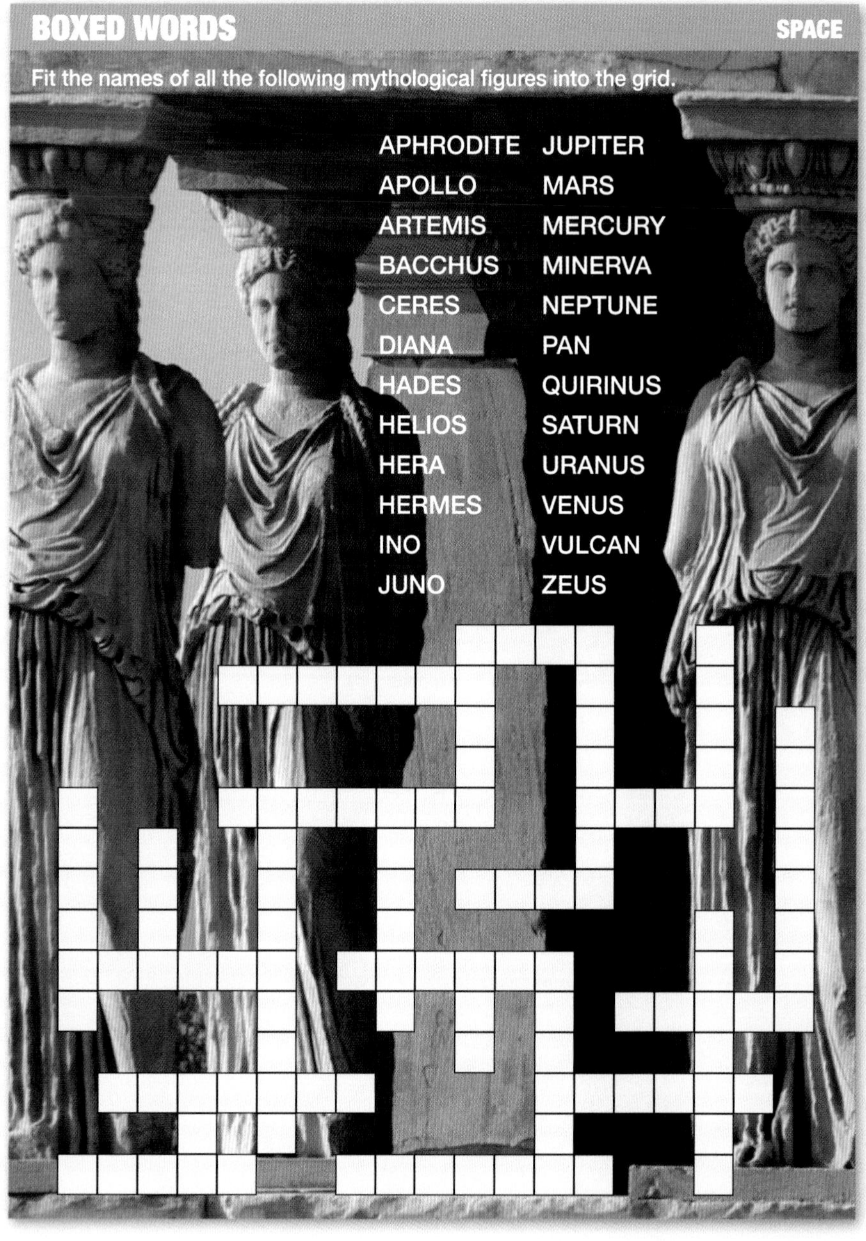

APHRODITE	JUPITER
APOLLO	MARS
ARTEMIS	MERCURY
BACCHUS	MINERVA
CERES	NEPTUNE
DIANA	PAN
HADES	QUIRINUS
HELIOS	SATURN
HERA	URANUS
HERMES	VENUS
INO	VULCAN
JUNO	ZEUS

ESCALETTERS — STRUCTURE

Form new words by adding the letters provided, one by one. Several solutions are possible.

RAT

+E _ _ _ _

+I _ _ _ _ _

+P _ _ _ _ _ _

+S _ _ _ _ _ _ _

+A _ _ _ _ _ _ _ _

+D _ _ _ _ _ _ _ _ _

CATERPILLAR — STRUCTURE

Go from VAMPIRE to DRACULA in this caterpillar by replacing letters in the manner indicated (for example, L replaces M in the first line) and by changing the order in which the letters appear.

VAMPIRE

-M +L _ _ _ _ _ _ _

-V +C _ _ _ _ _ _ _

-P +D _ _ _ _ _ _ _

-E +A _ _ _ _ _ _ _

-I +U DRACULA

BROKEN SEQUENCES — STRUCTURE

Six words have had two or more syllables lopped off. Piece them together again, using the syllables provided. Note that there are sometimes several possible solutions, but only one combination will enable you to complete all the words..

1. .... TRI ....
2. .... TY
3. .... QUA ....
4. .... DI ....
5. DIA ....
6. .... TER ....

LI, CAP, HAN, RIC, MET, IN, TY, BER, LO, NI, ET, GUING, CIOUS

HIDDEN WORDS — STRUCTURE

The names of 30 colours hidden in this grid can be read in any direction: horizontally or vertically, diagonally, from the top down or in the opposite direction, from right to left or the opposite. Words can cross and the same letter can be used several times. With the letters left over, you can make a word describing several shades of the same colour.

Y	D	N	U	G	R	U	B	W	B	G	B
O	D	L	A	R	E	M	E	H	N	R	L
C	E	R	I	S	E	W	R	I	C	E	A
R	E	D	R	U	S	T	U	T	R	Y	C
I	A	L	B	R	O	N	Z	E	E	L	K
M	T	O	C	I	R	P	A	L	A	A	N
S	N	G	R	E	E	N	L	I	M	E	A
O	E	I	E	V	I	O	L	E	T	T	T
N	G	D	U	R	W	I	N	D	I	G	O
A	A	A	T	U	R	Q	U	O	I	S	E
J	M	P	U	R	P	L	E	K	N	I	P
O	R	A	N	G	E	N	O	O	R	A	M

APRICOT	EMERALD	MAROON	TAN
AZURE	GOLD	MAUVE	TEAL
BLACK	GREEN	ORANGE	TURQUOISE
BRONZE	GREY	PINK	VIOLET
BURGUNDY	INDIGO	PURPLE	WHITE
CERISE	JADE	RED	YELLOW
CREAM	LIME	ROSE	
CRIMSON	MAGENTA	RUST	

MATCHING UP — ASSOCIATION

Try to match each animal with the word describing its call.

Crow	A	A.......	1	Gobble
Eagle	B	B.......	2	Cry
Cicada	C	C.......	3	Screech
Frog	D	D.......	4	Yap
Gull	E	E.......	5	Croak
Goose	F	F.......	6	Honk
Fox	G	G.......	7	Squeak
Tawny owl	H	H.......	8	Caw
Marmot	I	I.......	9	Drone
Turkey	J	J.......	10	Hoot

JUMBLED WORDS — STRUCTURE

Identify the three comedians whose names have been jumbled up in the words below.

NERDYFLISJEER
1

KRISTOWANNANO
2

BILDWOOPHOGGER
3

ODD ONE OUT — LOGIC

Which is the odd one out?

A

B

C

D

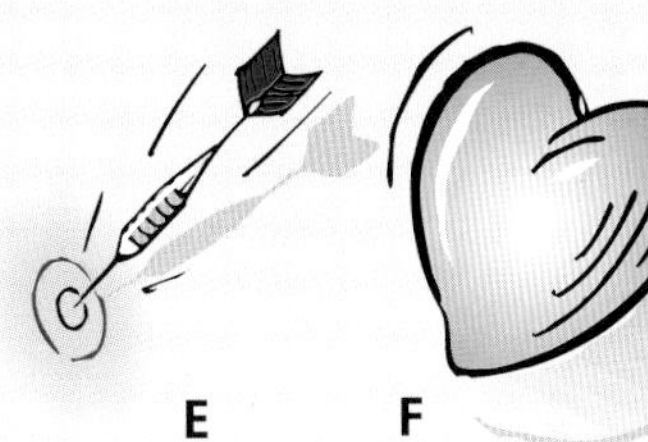
E F

CUBES

SPACE

1. The diagram below represents one of the cubes opened out. Which is it? There are two possibilities.

2. Two cubes can be made from the unfolded diagram below. Which ones?

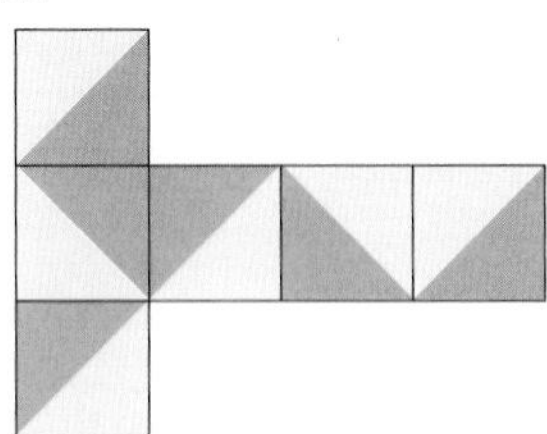

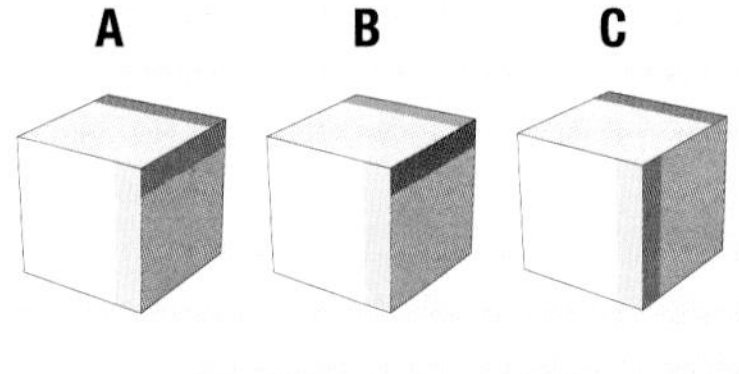

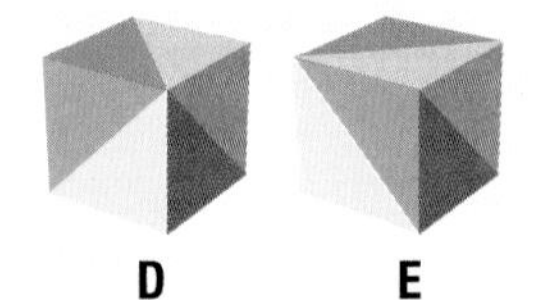

3. Two cubes can be made from the unfolded diagram below. Which ones?

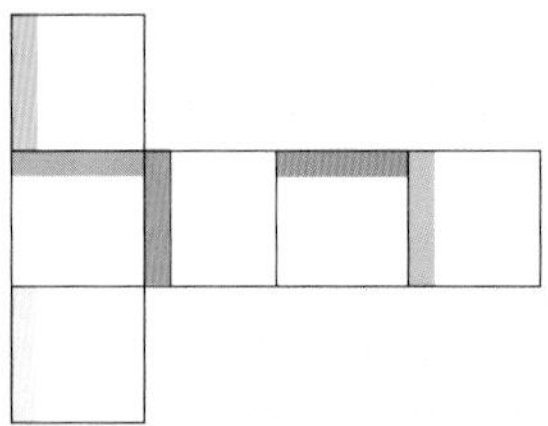

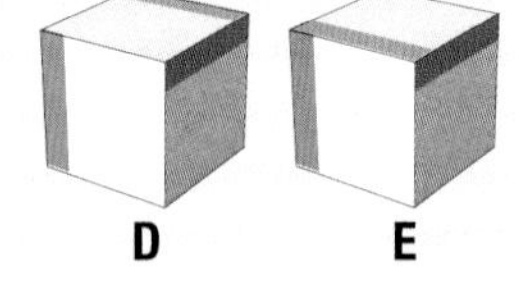

ANAGRAMS

STRUCTURE

Find the islands for which the following words are anagrams:

1. Traumas ....
2. Englander ....
3. Sh ....
4. Hordes ....
5. Thorn ....
6. Erect ....
7. Transmits ....
8. Smoker ....
9. Adorns ....
10. Romance ....

THE RIGHT TIME

LOGIC

At the time registered by all these clocks, it is 13 hours in Paris. One clock is in Los Angeles, one in Beijing, a third in Rio and a fourth in Sydney. Which clock is in which city?

LOTTO — LOGIC

Make a total of 49 in all directions with these 16 Lotto numbers by placing each one in the right matching shape. Hint: the sum of the four numbers in the centre also equals 49.

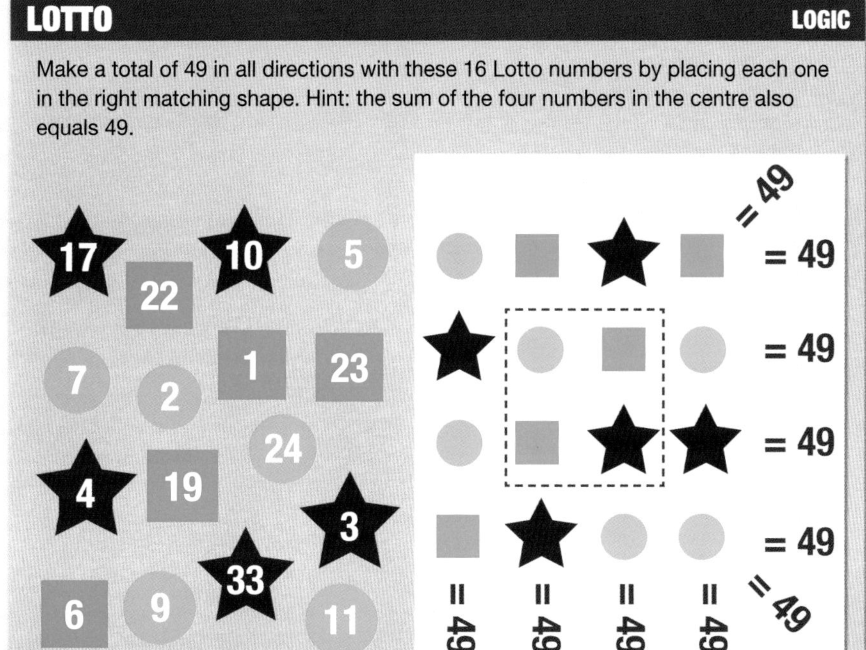

WORD HOLES — LANGUAGE

Replace the dashes with letters to change these ciphers into ordinary words.

1. TH_RE___E
2. F___OUR
3. F___IV___E
4. S__I_X
5. SEVE__N__
6. E___IGHT

MATCHING UP — ASSOCIATION

Match each English monarch with his or her nickname or surname.

Ethelred II	A	A	1 The Confessor
Edward	B	B	2 Lionheart
Edward I	C	C	3 Rufus
Mary I	D	D	4 Bolingbroke
Richard	E	E	5 of Orange
Henry IV	F	F	6 Longshanks
William I	G	G	7 Bloody
William II	H	H	8 The Unready
William III	I	I	9 The Sailor King
William IV	J	J	10 The Conqueror

MISSING LETTERS — STRUCTURE

Replace all the available letters in the grid to make six words that read horizontally.
If you've made the right choices, you will find the names of two works by James Michener, read vertically.

A N O I A W P A
H I L D

E	M		A	T		I	C
G	L		S	S		R	Y
A	L		E	Y		A	Y
C	H		P	L		I	N
A	M		E	S		A	C
F	I		E	L		T	Y

PUZZLE — SPACE

Which piece must be fitted to the first in each case to make a square?

1.

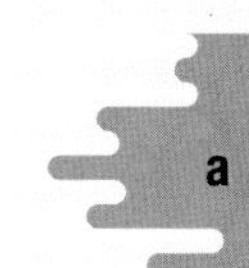

a b c d e

2.

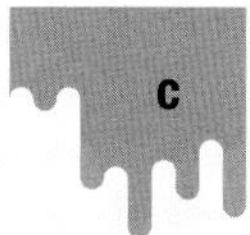

a b c d e

THEMATIC CROSSWORD

Fill in the thematic grid with the help of the following definitions.

Across:

1. A card game with counting combinations. (8)

4. To bet either or both hands against the dealer's hand. (8)

6. A game played with cues and numbered, coloured balls. (4)

8. Another word for draughts. (8)

10. Seven cards of the same rank. (7)

11. A game played with fifteen red balls, six balls of other colours and a white cue ball (7)

12. A card game with groups of three cards. (5)

15. Also known as blackjack. (7)

17. 48 cards, all higher than 8. (8)

19. A game played with wooden blocks with dots. (8)

20. A card game for four players, in two partnerships. (5)

21. A betting game with several variations. (5)

22. Contract is one variation of this game. (6)

Down:

2. Also known as pontoon (9).

3. A game with a cue ball and two black balls (9).

5. Checkmate is the object (5).

7. This game involves drawing pictures (10).

9. The aim is to buy as many houses and hotels as you can. (8)

11. A word game with lettered square pieces. (8)

13. A strategy game based on general knowledge. (10)

14. You play this game by yourself. (9)

16. A ball and wheel decide your luck in this game. (8)

18. Use the clues to find out if it was the butler who killed the colonel. (6)

CRYPTOGRAM — ASSOCIATION

The letters of the mystery quotation have been classified into four categories, each corresponding to a different coloured triangle. Try to decipher it with the aid of the letters that are already in place.

◥	◣	◤	◢
R	A	D	L
S	E	H	N
T	I	W	U
V	O	B	

T_ L__E __ H____S W_

L___E B___N_ __ N__

__ D__

PROBLEM — LOGIC

You have 76 biscuits to feed every day to 14 animals belonging to your neighbours, who are on holiday. There are only dogs and cats, and the dogs each eat two biscuits more than the cats. Taking into account that there are no biscuits left at the end of your round, and that all the animals have eaten, what could be the proportional distribution of biscuits among the dogs and cats you fed?

BEADS — CONCENTRATION

Look carefully at these eight beads for a few minutes, and then cover them.

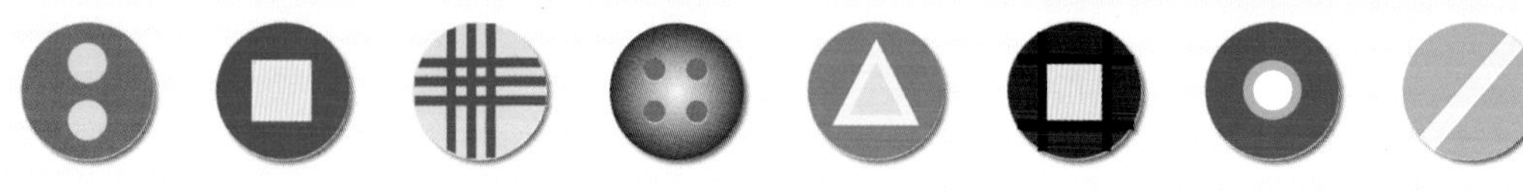

Try to draw them in the right order on the thread.

GENERAL KNOWLEDGE

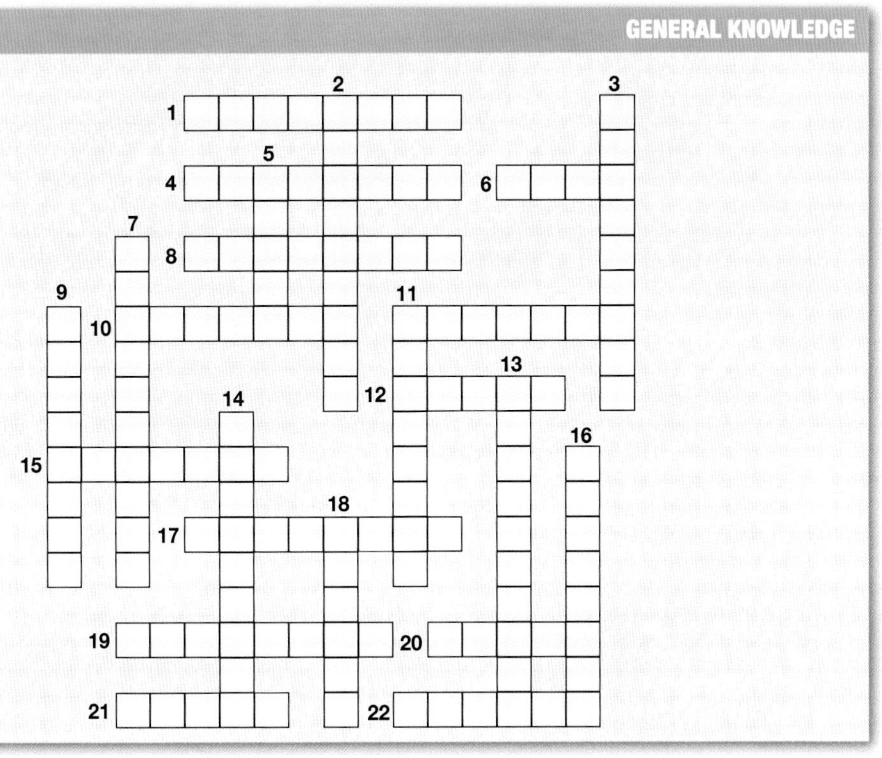

POINTS IN COMMON

ASSOCIATION

For each of these series of words, find one word which has something in common with the three others.

1. Shower Pink Beetle ....
2. Dollar Ireland Chlorophyll ....
3. Komodo St George Fly ....
4. Slap Meal Laugh ....
5. Ear Beat Roll ....
6. Stone Eye Boundary ....

ROSETTE

STRUCTURE

Complete this rosette puzzle by forming words from the letters below. Always write your answers from the outside in towards the centre. Be careful – in some cases, several anagrams are possible, but only one will allow you to complete the grid with the words being read both ways.

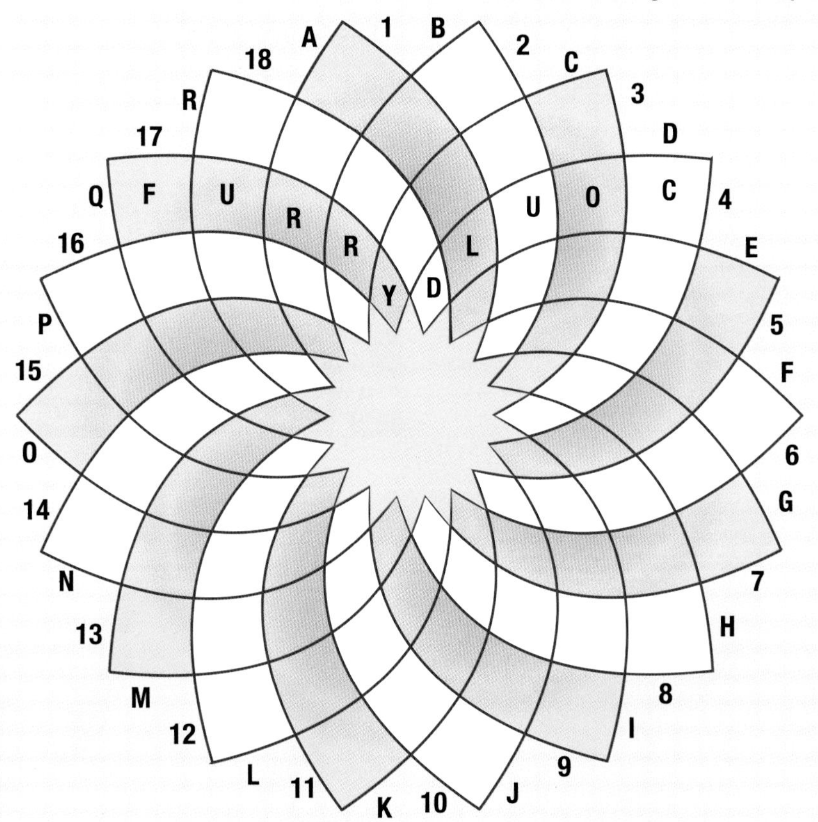

Clockwise:

A. ELTLS
B. DNWOU
C. NIDOG
D. NUTOC
E. TRUCO
F. SECIL
G. RHACI
H. NEEVS
I. PORES
J. AKESM
K. SNAPT
L. SODAT
M. HTOTO
N. STOCA
O. SLEFE
P. BNIDL
Q. RRUYF
R. LIDUB

Anticlockwise:

1. RUNST
2. RIDEW
3. ODLLY
4. UDLOC
5. SNOCI
6. NUDOS
7. GNLUC
8. THIRS
9. CARTE
10. VEMIO
11. PERAP
12. KENAT
13. OTNSE
14. STACO
15. FOSOD
16. ABEST
17. SHEFL
18. LITBU

STICK-ON TITLES

GENERAL KNOWLEDGE

Unscramble the following mixed-up titles and stick them together again to make the titles of four real songs composed by John Lennon.

Night Ticket to Forever

Hard Mystery

Tour Strawberry Fields

A Magical Day's Ride

1. ....
....

2. ....
....

3. ....
....

4. ....
....

MAGIC SQUARE

LOGIC

Here is a way of completing a magic square with an uneven number of boxes – in this case, seven. You start by putting 1 in the centre of the top row. Then you continue by moving up and towards the right (thus, diagonally) while respecting the following rules:

- When you reach one of the sides, you continue in the direction of the box that would be there if you added a square (see the transition from 1 to 2, from 4 to 5, from 10 to 11, from 12 to 13); you then copy this same number (2, 5, ...) at the other end of the column or line.
- When a box that should be filled is already occupied, you then fill the box immediately below the one that has just been filled (look at the passage from 7 to 8), then resume the normal progression along the diagonal. If you reach the top or right side of the square, write the following number in the box below, in the same way.

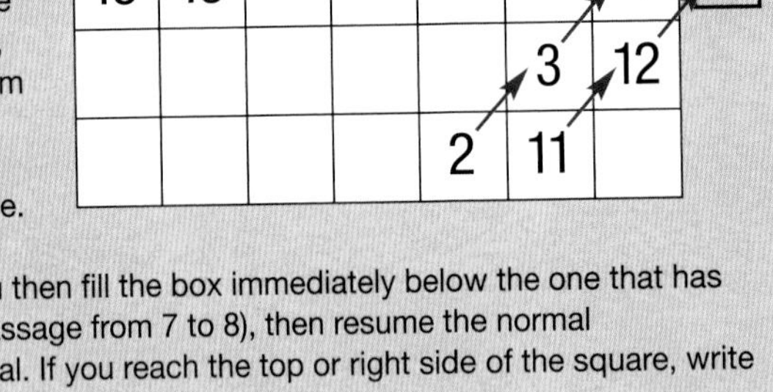

Following these rules, will you succeed in completing this magic square? The sum of each line, column or major diagonal is 175.

HIDDEN OBJECTS

CONCENTRATION

To save the princess, the knight must find six objects: a key, a shoe, a hammer, a watch, a bottle and a saw.

ODD ONE OUT

LOGIC

Which is the odd one out?

Emu

Penguin

Cassowary

Ostrich

Auk

BOXED WORDS

SPACE

Put all the fruit names below back in the right boxes.

APRICOT	LIME	PINEAPPLE
AVOCADO	LYCHEE	PLUM
BANANA	MANGO	TANGERINE
CHERRY	MELON	WATERMELON
DATE	MULBERRY	
FIG	NECTARINE	
GRANADILLA	OLIVE	
GRAPE	ORANGE	
LEMON	PEAR	

SPOT THE 7 DIFFERENCES

CONCENTRATION

There are seven differences between these two photos.
Can you find them?

TEST YOUR OBSERVATION SKILLS — CONCENTRATION

Look at these four menus for several minutes, and then cover them and answer the questions.

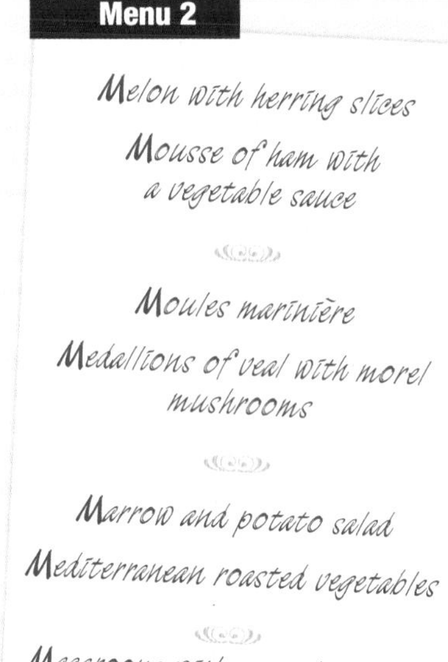

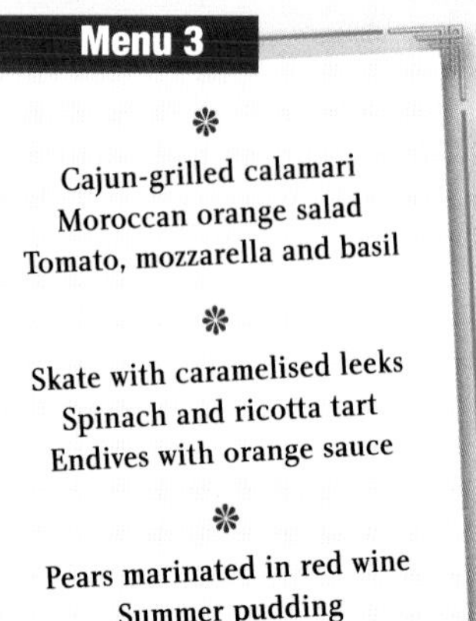

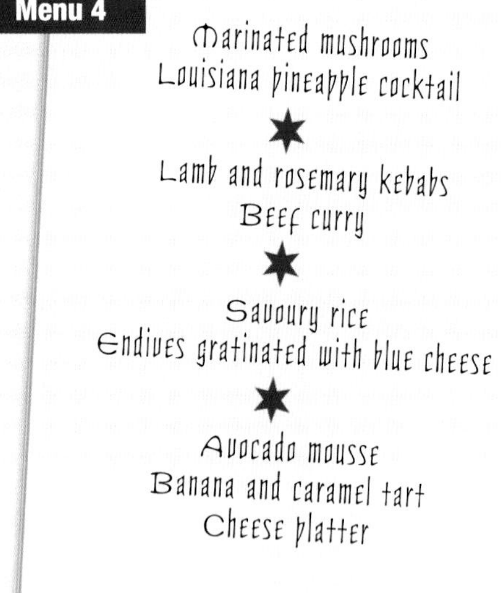

Questions

1. Which letter do all the courses offered in menu 2 start with?
2. Where does the pineapple cocktail in menu 4 come from?
3. How many sauces are served with the asparagus in menu 1?
4. What kind of mushrooms are served with the veal in menu 2?
5. What kind of stewed fruit is offered in menu 3?
6. Which two vegetables are offered with a cheese topping in two different menus?
7. Which fruit, prepared in the Moroccan way, is offered as a first course?
8. What are the herrings served with?
9. Which symbol is used to demarcate the courses in menu 4?
10. In which menu does the term caramelised appear?
11. Which dish has the shortest name on all these menus?

HOMOPHONES — LANGUAGE

Find the homophones (words with the same pronunciation but a different meaning) that complete the following sentences.

1. An overfilled backpack will ______ you down on a hike and will seem to get heavier along the _____.
2. The letter she ________ from New York to London didn't cost her a ________ because her sister took it with her on her flight.
3. As the little child stood up after smelling the ______ it looked as if her nose had been dusted with yellow _____.
4. The king's unhappy _________ started with 100 days of relentless ________ and costly floods.

OVERLAPPING SHAPES

CONCENTRATION

How many circles do you see?

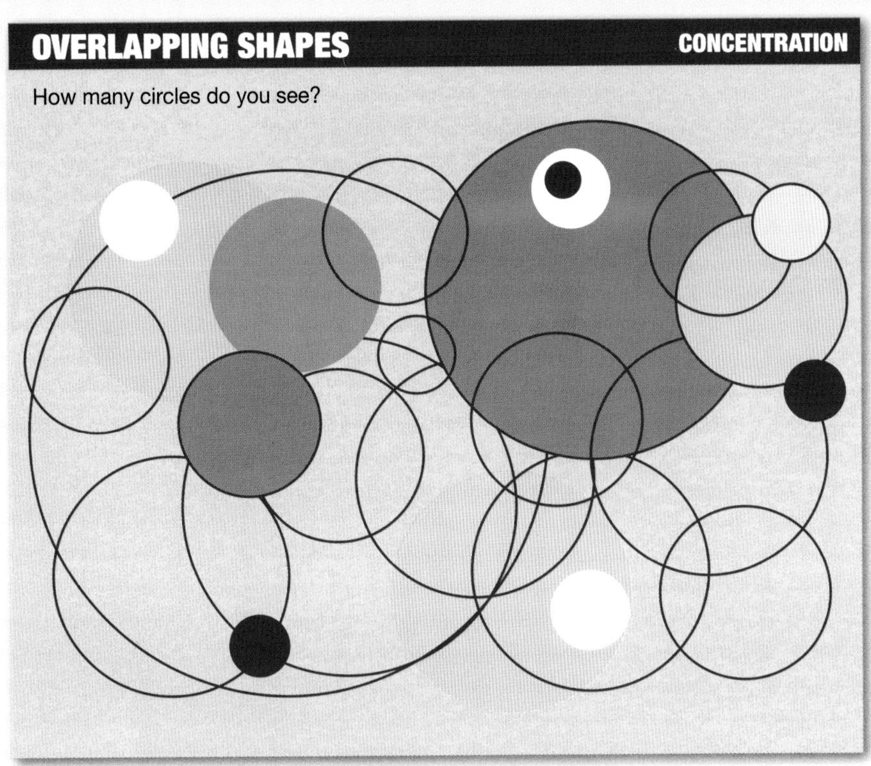

ANAPHRASES

STRUCTURE

Use all the letters in brackets to make anagrams which will complete the sentences in a meaningful way.

1. **(ARESOHCTR)**
   From the wagon, which was being pulled by a _________, the driver could hear an _________ playing.

2. **(NOCETDIIMA)**
   The __________ of the human race was prevented by the use of __________.

3. **(IAECONTXIT)**
   Drugs can __________ and lead to __________ of the nervous system.

CUBES

SPACE

1. These three drawings are views of the same cube. What colour is the side opposite the red side?

2. These three drawings are views of the same cube. What colour is the side opposite the yellow and green side?

LOOPY LETTERS

STRUCTURE

Work out the order in which to arrange the letters in each line so as to read, horizontally, the names of two games; one will read in the traditional way, from left to right and the other from right to left.

HISTORICAL LANDMARKS

TIME

Are these statements true or false?

1. The use of papyrus in Egypt predates the Iron Age in the Near East. .... True False
2. The Greek mathematician Pythagoras was the contemporary of Jesus Christ. .... True False
3. Copernicus formulated the hypothesis that the Earth revolves around the Sun. But Aristarchus of Samos made the same claim in the third century BC, that is, 18 centuries before Copernicus! .... True False
4. Dogs were first domesticated in 200 BC. .... True False
5. Antiquity refers to the period from 600 BC. .... True False
6. Ptolemy taught people the use of fire in the second century BC. .... True False

GUIDED TOUR

CONCENTRATION

Look carefully at this map of central Beijing and then cover it.

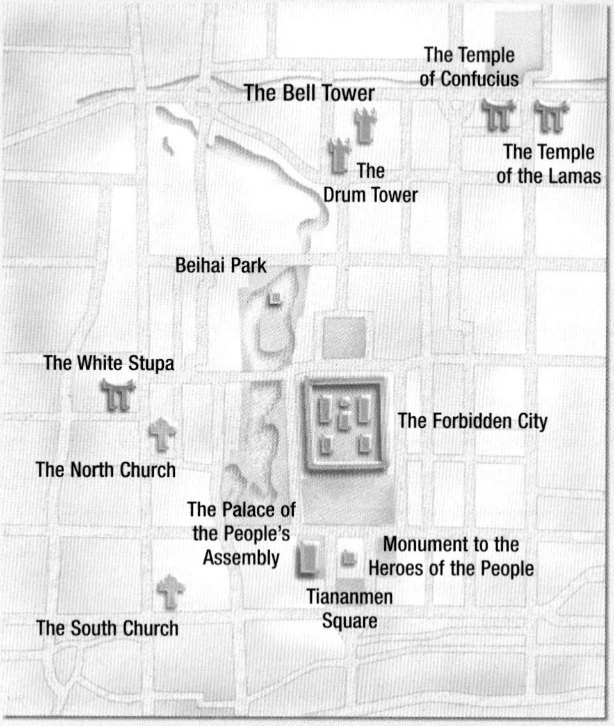

The Temple of Confucius
The Bell Tower
The Temple of the Lamas
The Drum Tower
Beihai Park
The White Stupa
The Forbidden City
The North Church
The Palace of the People's Assembly
Monument to the Heroes of the People
Tiananmen Square
The South Church

Position the following landmarks:

1. The Forbidden City
2. The South Church
3. The North Church
4. The White Stupa
5. Tiananmen Square
6. Monument to the Heroes of the People
7. The Palace of the People's Assembly
8. Beihai Park
9. The Bell Tower
10. The Drum Tower
11. The Temple of Confucius
12. The Temple of the Lamas

CHALLENGE

CONCENTRATION

Look at these groups of words for several minutes. You then have one minute to recall as many as you can. To extend the exercise, wait for 10 minutes and then try again without checking the list.

Work
Novel
Story

Computer
Rocking-chair
Walkie-talkie

Portal
Mortal
Chortle

Miniature
Duckling
Little girl

Wolf
Dachshund
Sheep

1. First try: ....

2. 10 minutes later: ....

MISSING SHAPES — CONCENTRATION

Look carefully at this series of images for a few minutes and then cover it.

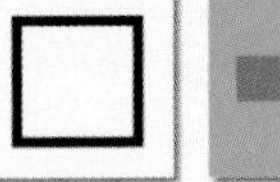

Draw all the missing figures from memory, so that the line of images below is identical to the original.

MATCHES — LOGIC

Here is a dustpan made out of matches, which contains dust. How can you get the dust out of the pan by moving only two matches while ensuring that the shape of the dustpan is retained?

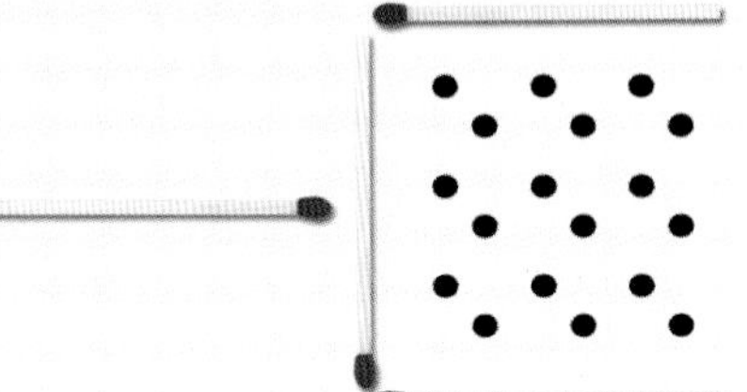

ANAGRAMS — STRUCTURE

Find the parts of the body contained in the following anagrams.

1. INKS ....
2. SNIPE ....
3. VILER ....
4. FRINGE ....
5. EARTH ....
6. KEEN ....
7. BELOW ....
8. ELATION ....
9. BAREST ....
10. BREAD ....

MAZE — SPACE

Turn the handle (top left) in the direction indicated by the arrow and then work out which way the indicator (bottom right) will move – to the left or to the right?

LOGIGRAM — LOGIC

BLA BLA BLA

The parents of five rather talkative teenagers are monitoring their telephone calls. They start timing the moment the girls call their best friends and prepare to present them with the bill as soon as they have hung up. With the help of the following clues, establish the names of the five friends that Catherine, Charlotte, Isabelle, Louisa and Maria are phoning, their topic of conversation and the length of the call.

Clues

1. Two of the friends talking to each other have names beginning with the same letter. Their call lasts exactly half the time taken by Ciara and her friend to discuss fashion.
2. Charlotte is a chatterbox, but her friend, whose name is the shortest of all, cut the conversation short. This was the 'shortest' conversation.
3. The wide-ranging discussion about going to the movies took Louisa less time than Suzie needed for confidential disclosures about her dogs.
4. Maria wasn't the most garrulous. But the discussion about the maths homework took more than three quarters of an hour. The parents couldn't scold their daughter, however, because it was time well spent.

Answer grid

When a statement enables you to eliminate one possibility, place N in the appropriate place, and Y when the opposite holds.

		Duration					Subject					Friend				
		24 min	54 min	1 h 12	1 h 48	2 h 06	Dogs	Films	Boys	Maths	Fashion	Anne	Cynthia	Natasha	Suzie	Ciara
Teens	Catherine															
	Charlotte															
	Isabelle															
	Louisa															
	Maria															
Friends	Anne															
	Cynthia															
	Natasha															
	Suzie															
	Ciara															
Subject	Dogs															
	Films															
	Boys															
	Maths															
	Fashion															

Table of responses

Teen	Catherine	Charlotte	Isabelle	Louisa	Maria
Friend					
Subject					
Duration					

MISSING SHAPES — CONCENTRATION

Look at this series of geometric shapes for a few minutes, and then cover it.

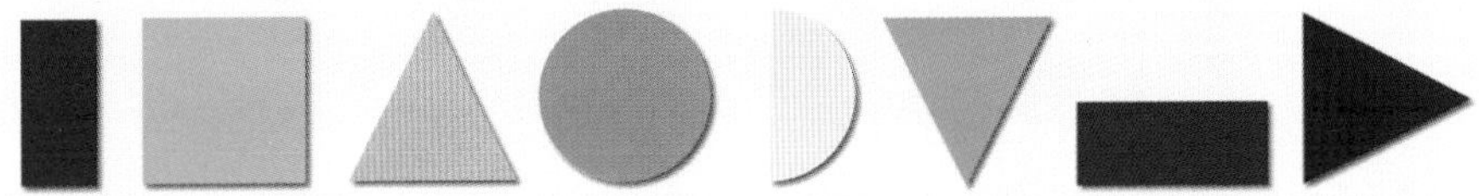

Complete the sequence below by drawing the missing shapes from memory.

PUZZLE — SPACE

In each case, make a square out of three pieces.

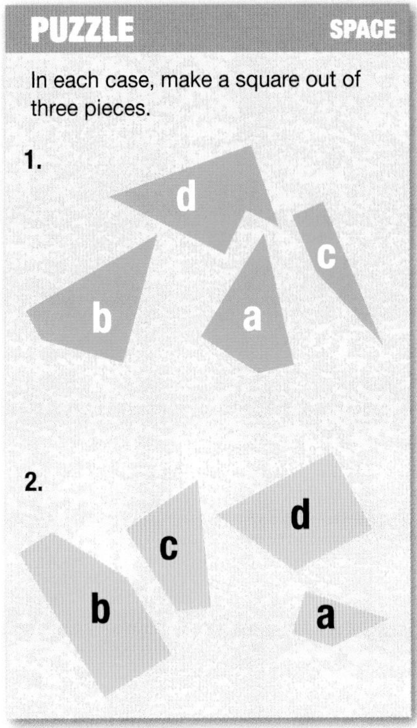

BONUS LETTERS — STRUCTURE

Using the first word and the bonus letter (in this game, P), form a new combination of letters to create a new word that corresponds to the clue.

Starting word	+ P	New word	Clue
1. ONE	+ P	....	Not closed
2. LEAD	+ P	....	Foot lever
3. DARES	+ P	....	Curtains
4. POSTER	+ P	....	A plug
5. REPRISE	+ P	....	To sweat
6. CORNIEST	+ P	....	An examiner

LOOPY LETTERS — STRUCTURE

Work out the order in which the letters on each line must be arranged horizontally so as to spell the names of two literary genres. One word is read from left to right and the other from right to left.

CRYPTOGRAM — ASSOCIATION

Decode the mystery quotation by replacing the flowers with the corresponding letters. It will help if you start with vowels. E has already been positioned.

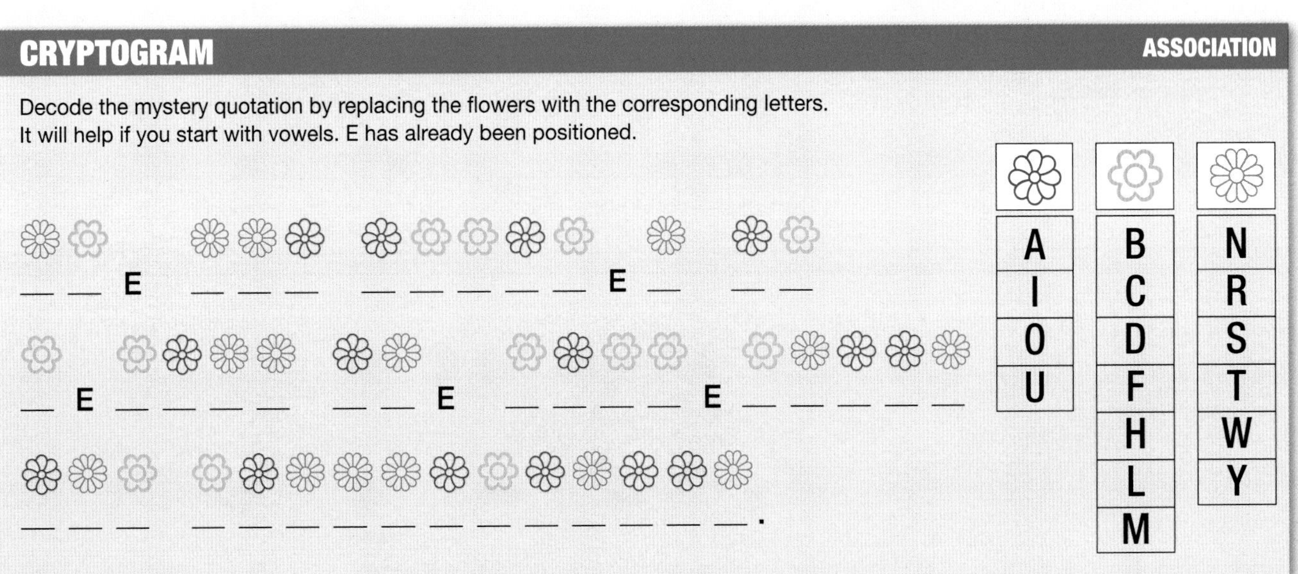

ANAPHRASES

STRUCTURE

Use all the letters between the brackets to make words that will complete the sentence and give it a meaning.

1. (ECREIP)
According to the ______, you should ______ the potatoes before baking them.

2. (AEGIIMNR)
When my friend says he sees colours and shapes when he has a _______, I think of him as a great _______.

3. (CLARITE)
The journalist wrote an _______ about the pianist's magnificent _______.

CUT-UP LETTERS

STRUCTURE

Cross out one letter in each of the eight horizontal words in the grid below, so that the remaining letters form a word. Place the deleted letter in the space at the end of each line to form a word, read vertically, which is the name of a web that first made its appearance in 1974 and has been spreading ever since.

W	A	I	V	I	N	G	
D	I	N	N	E	R	S	
S	T	A	Y	I	N	G	
A	P	P	E	A	L	S	
R	A	M	B	L	E	D	
B	A	N	K	E	R	S	
C	R	E	A	T	E	D	
T	A	N	G	L	E	D	

GEOMETRIC SEQUENCES

LOGIC

In each case, find the correct numbered figure to continue the sequence.

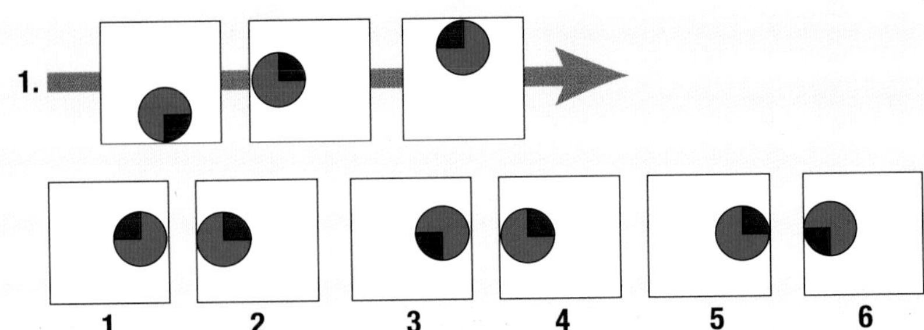

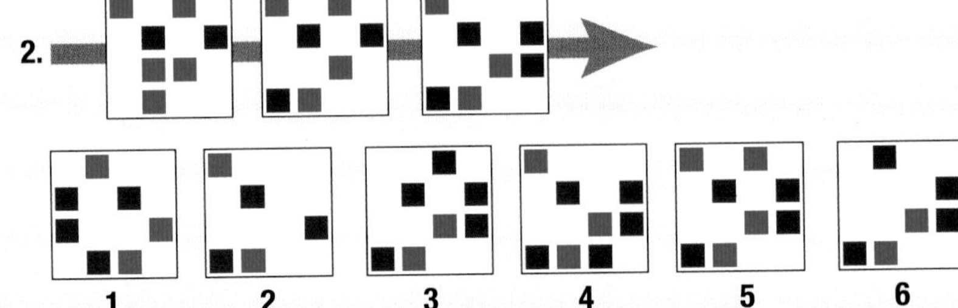

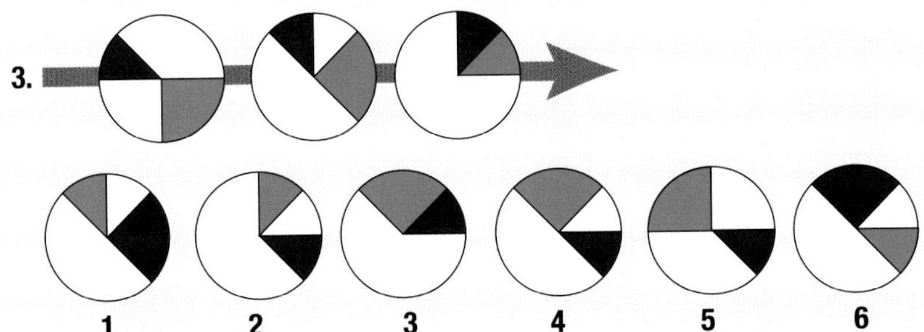

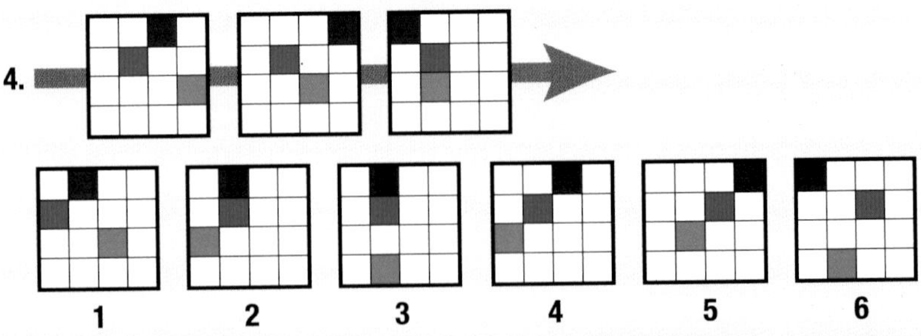

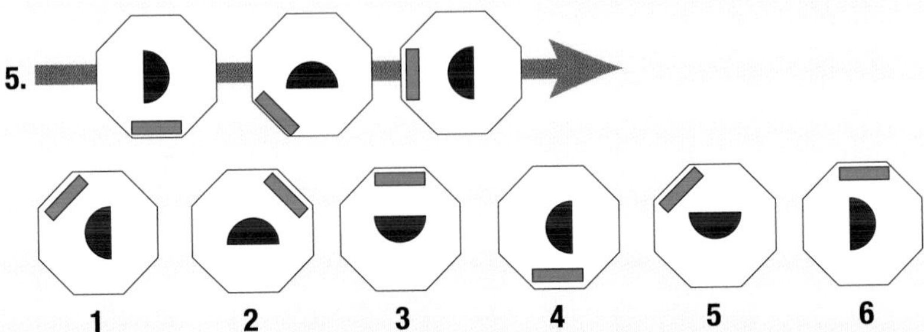

WORDS IN THE PICTURE

LANGUAGE

Find at least 20 words beginning with the letters Pl that refer to either an object or an idea featured in this picture.

HISTORICAL LANDMARKS

TIME

Classify these 10 historical events in chronological order, ending with the most recent.

	Event		
A	Battle of Waterloo	1	....
B	Conflict in ex-Yugoslavia	2	....
C	Hundred Years' War	3	....
D	War of Secession	4	....
E	Thirty Years' War	5	....
F	First Gulf War	6	....
G	Yom Kippur War	7	....
H	Vietnam War	8	....
I	First Crusade	9	....
J	First World War	10	....

POINTS IN COMMON

ASSOCIATION

Find a word that relates to each of the three words in the following series.

1. Computer
   Field
   Cheese
   ....
2. Cheque
   Toe
   Cigarette
   ....
3. Bride
   Chador
   Nun
   ....
4. Sound
   Tar
   Black
   ....
5. Picnic
   Currency
   Case
   ....
6. Spoon
   Dust
   Punch
   ....

MYSTERY WORDS

Using a sheet of paper, uncover the clues to each mystery character one by one, and try to identify them using the minimum number of clues

Who am I?

1. I am a writer and was awarded the Noble Prize for literature in 1907.
2. I was born in Bombay in 1865.
3. In my books I often describe my childhood in the colonies.
4. My son, John, for whom I wrote a famous poem, died in battle before he turned 18.
5. The title of this poem is *If*.
6. I am the author of *The Jungle Book*.

Who am I?

1. I was an actress and photographer's model.
2. I was born in Los Angeles in 1926.
3. My first names were really Norma Jean.
4. Three men took me to the altar, among them Joe di Maggio and Arthur Miller.
5. I was dated by an American president to whom I famously sang *Happy Birthday*.
6. I starred in *Gentlemen Prefer Blondes*.

Who am I?

1. I was born in 1946 in Cincinnati, Ohio.
2. I shot to stardom between 1971 and 1975 thanks to two films with titles of four letters each.
3. I have been the director or producer of numerous films with animals as main characters.
4. My divorce proved to be the most expensive in the world.
5. I received 11 Oscar nominations for *The Color Purple*.
6. My cinema creations include *ET* and *Indiana Jones*.

A. ....

B. ....

C. ....

TEST YOUR OBSERVATION SKILLS

CONCENTRATION

Look at this picture for a few minutes and then cover it and answer the questions.

Questions

1. What three sums are written on the blackboard?
2. Is there a washbasin in the classroom?
3. The teacher is wearing a skirt. True or false?
4. How many tables are there?
5. How many coats and hats are hanging on the pegs to the right of the picture?
6. There is a picture of the sun hanging on the wall. True or false?
7. The child in the bottom right-hand corner of the picture is crying as he looks at his picture. True or false?

GENERAL KNOWLEDGE

Who am I?

1. I was born on October 28, 1955, in Seattle and studied at Harvard.
2. In 1995 I published *The Road to the Future* in which I expressed my views on the future of information technology in society.
3. I have already given more than three thousand million dollars to charity.
4. I am familiar with many more language systems than living languages.
5. In 1975, I changed the name of my company, Traf-O-Data, and I invented Basic.
6. The new name of that company is Microsoft.

D. ....

Who am I?

1. I was born in London in 1934.
2. My mentor was the anthropologist Louis Leakey, for whom I worked as an assistant in Ethiopia.
3. I set up the Gombe Wildlife Research Institute in Tanzania.
4. I received the Albert Schweitzer award in 1987, the Kyoto prize for science in 1990 and I am a Dame of the British Empire.
5. I count chimpanzees among my best friends.
6. I am a primatologist and conservationist.

E. ....

SYNONYMS — LANGUAGE

Find eight synonyms for the word 'plain' using the clues given and the letters provided as guidelines.

1. **T_ _ _ _ _** (treeless area with frozen subsoil)
2. **F _ _ _** (level tract of land)
3. **P _ _ _ _ S** (treeless area in South America
4. **P _ _ _ _ _ E** (fertile but unforested area of US Midwest)
5. **R _ _ _ E** (flat grazing land in North America)
6. **S _ _ _ _ _ A** (African grassland with trees and shrubs)
7. **S _ _ _ _ E** (flat grassland in Russia)
8. **V _ _ _** (open grassland in southern Africa)

HISTORICAL LANDMARKS — TIME

Place the names of the personalities below in the right place on the chronological chart by filling in the relevant letter in each square.

A Alexander the Great
B Attila the Hun
C Buddha
D Caesar
E Charlemagne
F Clovis I
G Confucius
H Frederick of Barbarossa
I Gengis Khan
J William the Conqueror
K Henry VIII
L Joan of Arc
M Machiavelli
N Mohammed
O Nebuchadnezzar II
P Nero
Q Ramses II
R Jean Calvin
S Solomon
T Socrates

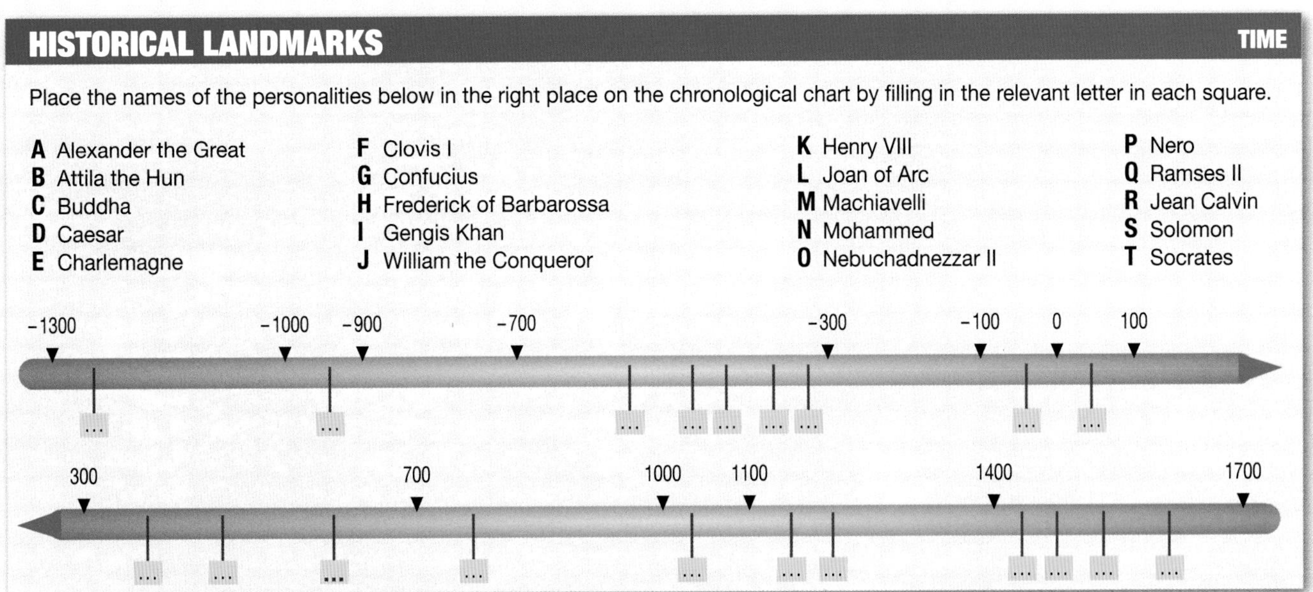

ONE WORD TOO MANY — LOGIC

In each of the following series of words, cross out the word that does not have the same special feature as the others in the series. Pay special attention to the letters making up each word, as well as any possible additions or substitutions.

1. **Age Angle Athlete Corn Shelf Ton**
2. **Baguette Torte Challah Focaccia Naan Pitta**
3. **Apple Forest Mint Olive Vermilion Viridian**

KNOW YOUR WORLD

SPACE

Find the names of 20 towns or cities, countries, landscape features, rivers and seas in central and Balkan Europe with the aid of the clues given below and the map to the right.

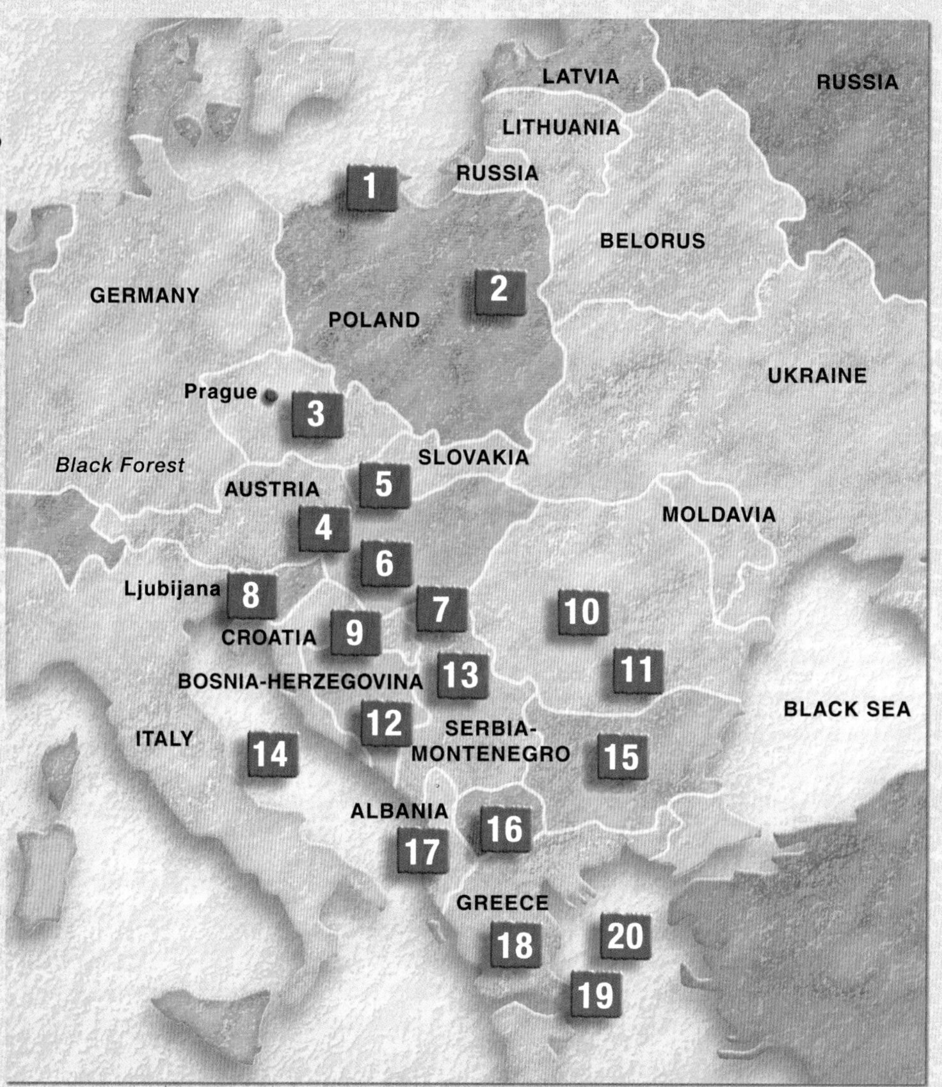

1. I am situated on the Baltic Sea and have been a free city since 1918. My corridor was a source of great dissension.
2. I am the capital of my country and there is a pact named after me, signed in 1955, which concerns a military alliance of the Soviet Union with other countries.
3. I am a country of 10 million inhabitants. My highest peak, at 1 602 metres, is in the Mountains of the Giants in Bohemia.
4. I am a circular mountain chain, my highest peak is 2 655 metres, and I harbour vampires, so they say...
5. I am the capital of Slovakia.
6. My flag is made up of three horizontal stripes: red, white and green. My currency is the forint.
7. From the Black Forest to the Black Sea, I measure 2 850 km in length.
8. My capital is Ljubijana, and I gained my independence in June 1991.
9. I am the capital of Croatia and my name begins with the two letters that are farthest apart in the alphabet.
10. I am a country of 237 000 square km and my name harbours that of a citizen of a great empire.
11. I am the capital of the aforementioned country. Don't confuse me with the capital of a neighbouring country which has a name similar to mine.
12. I was the Olympic city in 1984, then the site of violent confrontations that started in May 1992.
13. I am the capital of my country, and my first four letters are also the first four letters of a country bordering France.
14. I bathe the west coast of this region but also the east coast of Italy.
15. I am a country with a predominantly orthodox and Slavic population, and my capital is reminiscent of a woman's name.
16. My capital is Skopje. Gourmets will find that my name reminds them of a term sometimes found on the menu.
17. I am the capital of my country and had to accommodate a huge influx of refugees from Kosovo.
18. I am a city in Greece, the ancient capital of a Latin kingdom. I am also written with THES in front of my name.
19. I am the harbour of Athens.
20. I am a sea named after a father who mistakenly believed his son died in Crete.

HOMOGRAPHS

LANGUAGE

Find the right pairs of homographs (words with the same spelling as another but having a different origin and meaning) to complete the following sentences.

1. You may get into trouble if you _____ a tent on a cricket _____.
2. In a fast lift, it takes only a ______ to get to the ______ floor.
3. Members of every ____ are likely to compete in the ____.
4. The nurse _____ a bandage round the limb, to cover the _____.

HISTORICAL LANDMARKS

TIME

Classify these eight inventions in chronological order, starting with the oldest.

Morse code

Iron

Sundial

Parachute

Microwave oven

Calculator

Artificial heart

Barcode

0 123 479 4

1. ....
2. ....
3. ....
4. ....
5. ....
6. ....
7. ....
8. ....

DRAWING FROM MEMORY

CONCENTRATION

Look closely at these drawings. Close your eyes and try to visualise their shapes and positions in relation to each other.

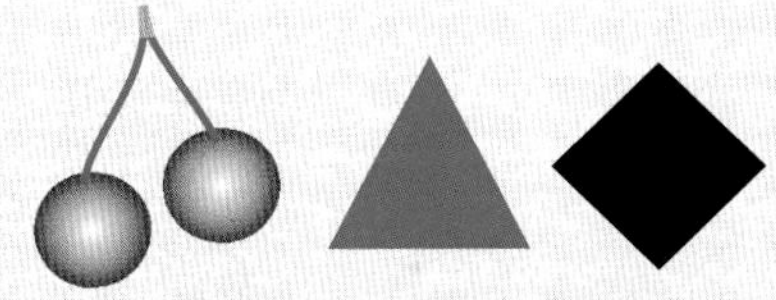

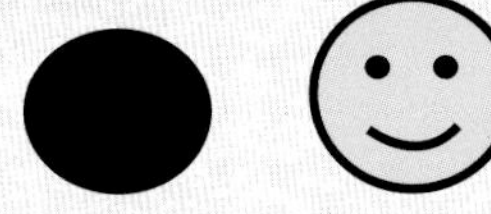

If you forget one of them, look at it closely again in order to fix it in your memory.

Cover the pictures and try to reproduce them from memory.

PUZZLE

LOGIC

1. How many months of the year have 31 days? How many have 28?
2. Mrs Martin is writing a postcard to someone whose sister she is, but the recipient is not her sister. Is that possible?
3. In the United States, can a man receive an inheritance from his widow's sister?

PERFECT COPIES?

Which two of these texts are identical in wording?

A

Roast peaches with strawberries.

Switch the grill on. Grease an oven dish and sprinkle it with sugar. Place the peach halves in the dish, open side up. Sprinkle with the rest of the sugar, blobs of butter and almonds. Arrange 100 g of strawberries around the peach halves. Grill for 5 min. Garnish each half peach with one strawberry and serve.

B

Roast peaches with strawberries.

Switch the grill on. Grease an oven dish and sprinkle it with sugar. Place the peach halves in the dish, open side up. Sprinkle with the rest of the sugar, blobs of butter and almonds. Arrange 100 g of strawberries around the peach halves. Grill for 5 mins. Garnish each half peach with 1 strawberry and serve.

C

Roast peaches with strawberries.

Switch the grill on. Grease an oven dish and sprinkle it with sugar. Place the peach halves in the dish, open side up. Sprinkle with the rest of the sugar, blobs of butter and almonds. Arrange 100 g of strawberries around the peach halves. Grill for 5 min. Garnish each half peach with 1 strawberry and serve.

IDENTIKIT

LOGIC

Seven is a lucky number, they say … But not at the casino in Manchoville! Posters bearing the faces of these seven women are stuck up all over town. They are suspected of cheating at roulette. There were three of them in the scam and one of them was even carrying a gun. With the help of these statements made by three witnesses, find the three swindlers and identify the one who was armed.

'The two accomplices who were wearing earrings had blonde hair.'

'The only one of the three swindlers who was carrying a gun had dark hair.'

'The only swindler wearing a necklace was also wearing earrings.'

1

2

3

4

5

6

7

IDIOMATIC TRIPLETS

LANGUAGE

In each line, find a term that goes perfectly with the three words to form a commonly used expression.

Ex: hide, dog, stand – **hair**.

1. **Life, hair, writing**

   ....

2. **Ball, way, light**

   ....

3. **Deep, jerk, bend**

   ....

4. **Worm, keeper, shelf**

   ....

5. **Bag, grill, doubles**

   ....

6. **Jump, water, board**

   ....

CONCENTRATION

D

Roast peaches with strawberries.

Switch the grill on. Grease an oven dish and sprinkle it with sugar. Place the peach halves in the dish, open side up. Sprinkle with the rest of the sugar, blobs of butter and almonds. Arrange 100 g of strawberries around the peach halves. Grill for 5 min. Garnish each half peach with 1 strawberry and serve.

E

Roast peaches with strawberries.

Switch the grill on. Grease an oven dish and sprinkle it with sugar. Place the peach halves in the dish, open side up. Sprinkle with the rest of the sugar, blobs of butter and almonds. Arrange 100 g of strawberries around the peach halves. Grill for five minutes. Garnish each half peach with 1 strawberry and serve.

F

Roast peaches with strawberries.

Switch the grill on. Grease an oven dish and sprinkle it with sugar. Place the peach halves in the dish, open side up. Sprinkle with the rest of the sugar, blobs of butter and almonds. Arrange 100 g of strawberries around the peach halves. Grill for 5 min. Garnish each peach half with a strawberry and serve.

ROSETTE

STRUCTURE

Fill in this rosette with words made out of the letters below. Write the answers from the outside of the flower towards the centre. Note that in some cases there are several possible anagrams, but only one will allow you to complete the grid in both directions.

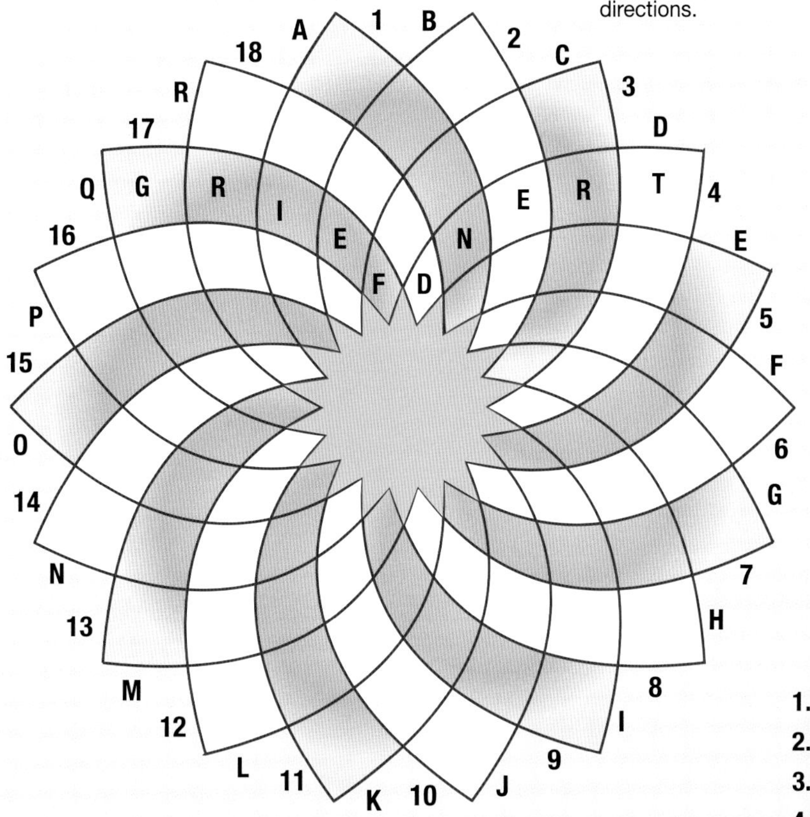

Clockwise:

A. HINAC
B. MEEHT
C. ZYARC
D. SIRTE
E. KESSD
F. GOSNS
G. ILNAS
H. ITSTW
I. TATOS
J. SATNL
K. LSOEC
L. BVARE
M. ODSFO
N. CLSUB
O. AGSSR
P. CANER
Q. RFIEG
R. OBERD

Anticlockwise:

1. OCSIN
2. ETREH
3. HFIEC
4. NDTRE
5. AMARD
6. SIZEE
7. SNOEY
8. ATNSK
9. STIGW
10. LOISS
11. SCASL
12. BSTLA
13. RNOFT
14. TCOSA
15. LGVEO
16. RCDUE
17. ABGRS
18. BRSAS

SUPERIMPOSITION — CONCENTRATION

Which numbered fragments can be superimposed on grid A? The pieces must be used as they are, without being turned.

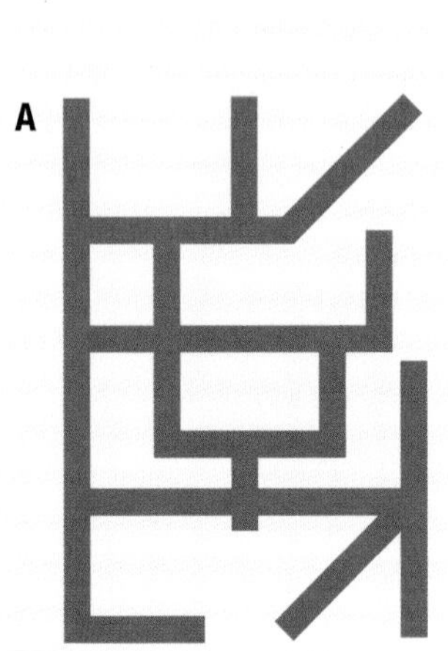

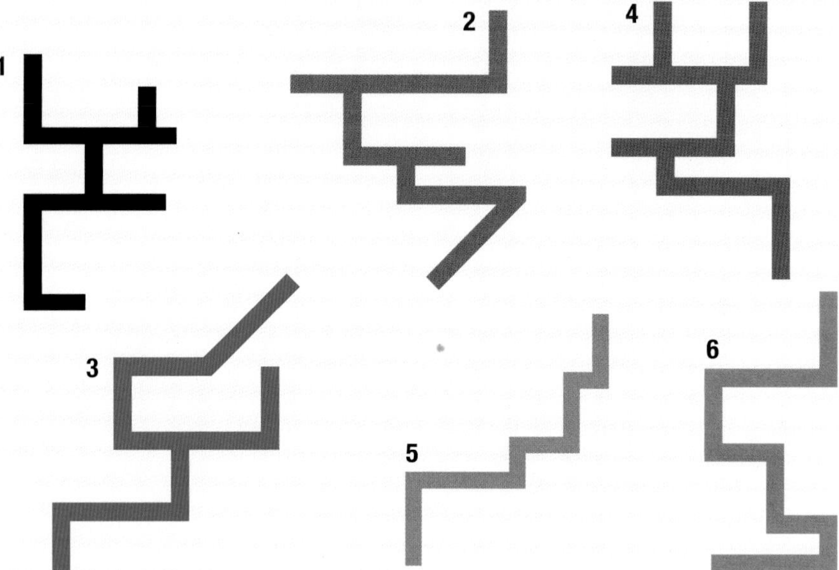

HISTORICAL LANDMARKS — TIME

Here is a list of eight films and eight film stars. Match the year to the film that won the Oscar for Best Picture and the actress who was awarded the Oscar for Best Actress, leading or supporting.

Films			Actress		
1. *The Silence of the Lambs*	1939	....	A. Jodie Foster	1939	....
2. *Driving Miss Daisy*	2001	....	B. Vivien Leigh	2001	....
3. *A Beautiful Mind*	1991	....	C. Shirley MacLaine	1991	....
4. *Chicago*	1996	....	D. Jessica Tandy	1996	....
5. *Shakespeare in Love*	1989	....	E. Catherine Zeta-Jones	1939	....
6. *The English Patient*	1983	....	F. Gwyneth Paltrow	1983	....
7. *Terms of Endearment*	1998	....	G. Jennifer Connelly	1998	....
8. *Gone with the Wind*	2002	....	H. Juliette Binoche	2002	....

CLOSE-UP — CONCENTRATION

Identify the person, animal or object featured in this close-up.

ONE WORD TOO MANY — LOGIC

In each of the following series, cross out the word that does not have the same special feature as the others in the series. Take into account the letters forming each word and any possible additions or substitutions.

1. **Actor Apple Ever Lawless Lopped Right**
2. **Combatant Flammable Flute Proliferation Resident Sense**
3. **Abcess Bijou Chintz Defile Effort Griddle**

MIXED QUOTES

GENERAL KNOWLEDGE

The words making up three quotations have been jumbled up. It's up to you to disentangle them and reconstruct the original quotations, attributed to Churchill, Stalin and Eisenhower.

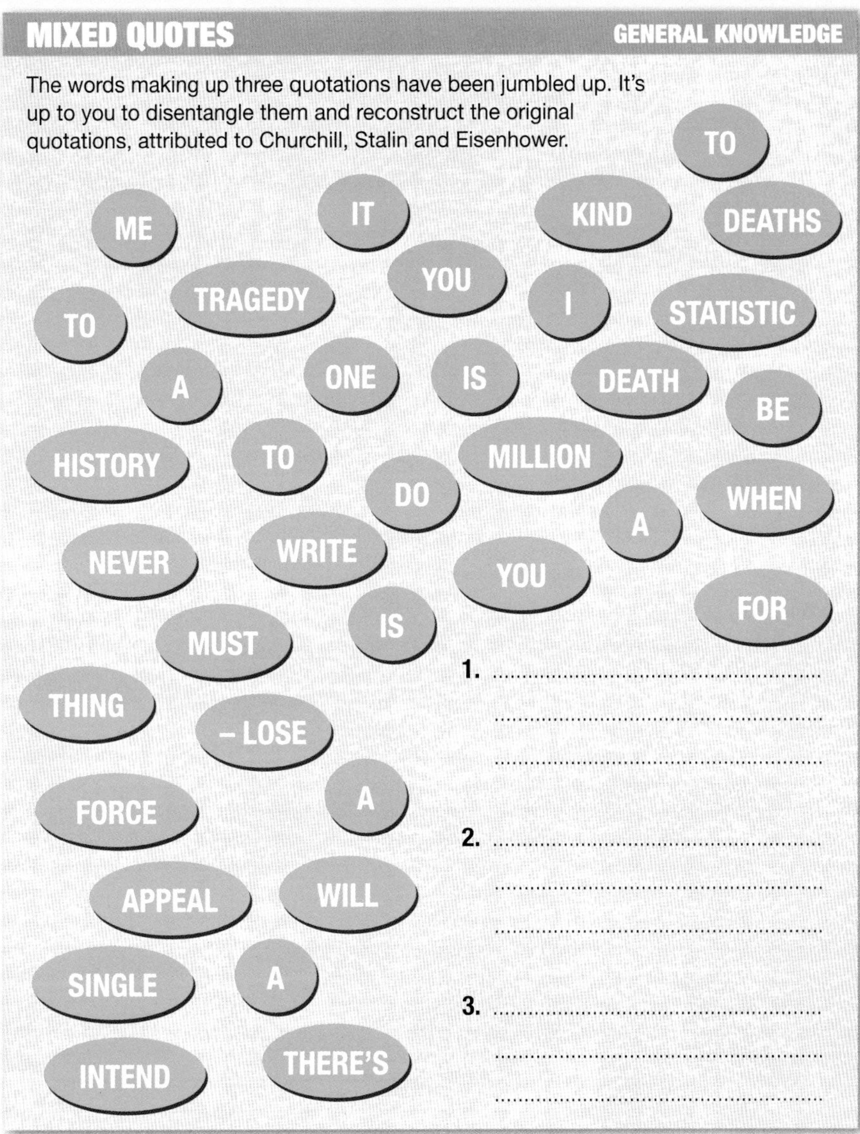

1. ....

2. ....

3. ....

SUPERIMPOSITION

CONCENTRATION

Imagine that the cut-out shapes below are made of cardboard. Find the three you need to superimpose to create figure A, and work out the order in which they must be superimposed.

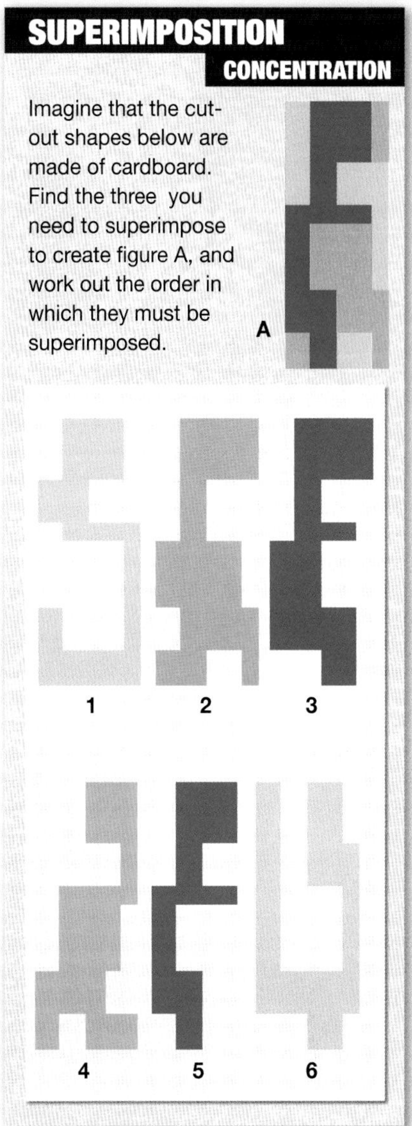

ONE TOO MANY

CONCENTRATION

Look closely at these nine characters for several minutes, and then cover them.

Which one did not appear above?

LOGIGRAM

LOGIC

HOLIDAYS IN ASIA

Five holidaymakers who are sports enthusiasts have decided to enjoy their favourite activity in Asia. Using the clues given below, you must find the destination chosen by Alexander, Alicia, Audrey, Marina and Oliver, the sport they participated in and the cost of their stay.

Clues

1. Of the three tourists with first names beginning with the same letter, the one who went to Thailand paid as much for the holiday as the other two combined paid for theirs. None of these three sports enthusiasts went on the catamaran.

2. The two skiers together spent as much as Oliver and the person who went to Indonesia combined. Oliver spent the most of all four tourists mentioned in this clue.

3. The paraglider spent less than the person who discovered the attractions of Vietnam, but more than the young woman who chose bungee jumping.

4. Marina didn't go to Myanmar. Audrey spent less in Malaysia than Alexander, who did not go water skiing.

Anwer grid

When a statement allows you to rule out one possibility, put N in the relevant block, but put Y if the opposite holds.

		Cost					Sport					Country				
		$1 400	$1 600	$2600	$3000	$4200	Catamaran	Jet-ski	Paragliding	Bungee jumping	Water skiing	Myanmar	Indonesia	Malaysia	Thailand	Vietnam
Tourist	Alexander															
	Alicia															
	Audrey															
	Marina															
	Olivier															
Country	Myanmar															
	Indonesia															
	Malaysia															
	Thailand															
	Vietnam															
Sport	Catamaran															
	Jet-ski															
	Paragliding															
	Bungee jumping															
	Water skiing															

Answer form

Tourist	Alexander	Alicia	Audrey	Marina	Oliver
Country					
Sport					
Cost					

HAPPY ENDINGS — ASSOCIATION

Find 10 words ending in -INE which have a direct connection with the clues given (one letter per dash).

1. Put together ➤ ____INE
2. Clarify the meaning of ➤ ___INE
3. Something that is cow-like ➤ ___ INE
4. To form a mental image ➤ ____INE
5. A mechanical device ➤ ____INE
6. A periodic publication ➤ _____INE
7. A butter substitute ➤ ______INE
8. Relating to something beneath the sea ➤ ______INE
9. The backbone ➤ __INE
10. Relating to a deity ➤ ___INE

WORD HOLES — LANGUAGE

Change the names of these cities into ordinary words by replacing each dash with a letter.

1. TU_NI_S
2. ___PARIS__
3. _O_S_L___O_
4. __R_I_O
5. __R_O_ME_
6. __BER__LIN

CLOSE-UP — CONCENTRATION

Identify the person, animal or object featured here that our designer has had fun transforming.

MIRROR IMAGES — SPACE

Draw these pictures in the mirror.

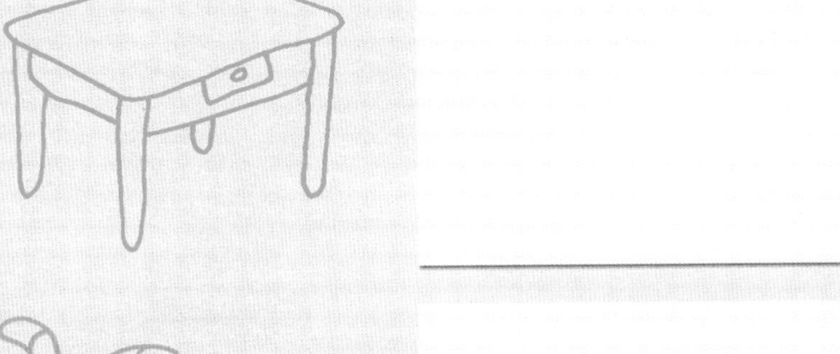

MAZE
SPACE

These two perpendicular plans, put together, form a labyrinth. You proceed along the open sections of the orange plan and along the solid paths of the blue plan. The transition from open to solid paths occurs at the vertical intersection (ignore the hidden parts). Find the only pathway from one arrow to the other.

THEMATIC CROSSWORD
GENERAL KNOWLEDGE

The names making up this grid are those of 21 winners of the Tour de France cycle race. Certain key letters have been put in place to guide you. Can you identify and fill in all the names of these champions?

SUPERIMPOSITION
CONCENTRATION

Imagine that the diagrams below are made of glass. Find the three you need to superimpose to make image A.

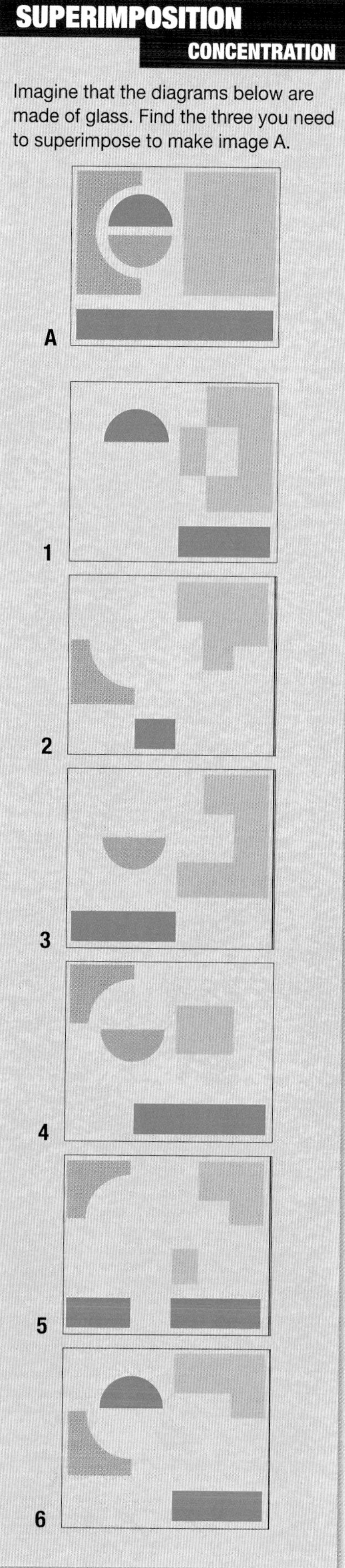

PERFECT COPIES?

CONCENTRATION

Which two photographs are exactly the same?

A

B

C

D

E

F

THEMATIC CROSSWORD

GENERAL KNOWLEDGE

With the aid of the following clues, complete this crossword puzzle based on literary themes. In most cases the names you need to find are the surnames.

Across:

1. The author of *Rape of the Lock.* (4)
2. The French Romantic writer of *The Hunchback of Notre Dame.* (4)
6. His *Woman in White* established the genre of mystery stories. (7)
8. He wrote *Tess of the D'Urbervilles.* (5)
10. Her only novel, *Gone With the Wind*, took 10 years to write, and won her a Pulitzer Prize. Who was she? (8)
12. The English poet who wrote *Paradise Lost.* (6)
14. Who wrote the play *The Beggar's Opera* on which the popular opera was based? (3)
15. To whom are the *Waverley* novels attributed? (5)
16. The name of the brother of Sherlock Holmes. (7)
17. He was P G Wodehouse's perfect butler. (6)
19. The Brontë sister who wrote *Wuthering Heights.* (5)
20. See 19 Across – her sister wrote *Jane Eyre.* (9)
22. Which English free-verse poet wrote *A Phoenix Too Frequent*? (3)
23. The deception of George Eliot and George Sand – who were they in fact? (5)
24. The creator of Perry Mason. (7)

Down:

1. The clever woman in *The Merchant of Venice.* (6)
2. Sir Thomas Erpingham appears in this Shakespeare play. (5,1)
3. The author of *Elegy Written in a Country Churchyard* (4)
4. The colour of the beard in Perrault's tale. (4)
5. The writer of *The Jungle Book.* (7)
7. This Irish playwright, who wrote *Saint Joan*, among many other notable plays, won the Nobel Prize for Literature in 1925. (4)
9. A clergyman and satirist, he lampooned political parties in *Gulliver's Travels.* (5)
11. This writer invented an imaginary valley in the Himalayas, which he called Shangri-La, so adding a new fantasy world to our vocabulary. (6)
12. Three witches feature in this play by Shakespeare. (7)
13. This English poet, who wrote *The Rime of the Ancient Mariner,* among many other poems, was said to have written under the influence of opium. (9)
15. Long John Silver is a dominant character in one of his adventure novels. (9)
16. Lord Chancellor to Henry VIII, and beheaded for refusing to recognise him as head of the Church, he wrote *Utopia.* (4)
17. Who wrote *Daisy Miller*? (5)
18. The author of *Last Days of Pompeii*. (6)
20. He wrote *To be a Pilgrim.* (4)
21. The master of nonsense verse, who wrote *The Owl and the Pussy-cat.* (4)

MYSTERY WORDS

Read the clues one by one so as to identify the mystery word as quickly as possible.

What am I?

1. There is a dolphin with a nose my shape.
2. Some people hit me, but it doesn't hurt me at all.
3. Wherever I am, there is usually cork around.
4. I can be made of leather, glass, metal or plastic.
5. I can contain liquid or gas.
6. My name comes from the Latin word *butis*, meaning a 'barrel'.

What am I?

1. I can be a person, an event or a story.
2. In past times, I was a play based on the life of Christ.
3. I am extremely popular – people love reading me.
4. I am perplexing.
5. I arouse curiosity.
6. I exist only when you can't solve me.

What am I?

1. I saved Rome.
2. People who are silly sometimes carry my name.
3. My step is anything but casual.
4. In my maternal form, children love listening to me.
5. My covering keeps you warm at night.
6. I am usually present in a less lively form at Christmas.

A. ....

B. ....

C. ....

WORD PAIRS

ASSOCIATION

Memorise these eight pairs of words for a few minutes. Use all the mnemonic techniques you can. Then cover the list and answer the six questions.

passenger – worm **glass – traveller**

locomotive – hair **automobile – bed**

sofa – vehicle **wagon – parade**

pan – paradise **seat – casserole**

Questions

1. Which word is paired with paradise? ....
2. How many words begin with the letter P? ....
3. Is the word train paired with a word associated with travel? ....
4. With which word is the only three-letter word paired? ....
5. Mention two cooking utensils on this list.
   ....
6. Which words are paired with passenger and traveller?
   ....

GAMES BOARD

CONCENTRATION

Look closely at this games board for a few minutes to memorise the figures distributed on it. Cover it, and then replace the figures in the right place on the empty board.

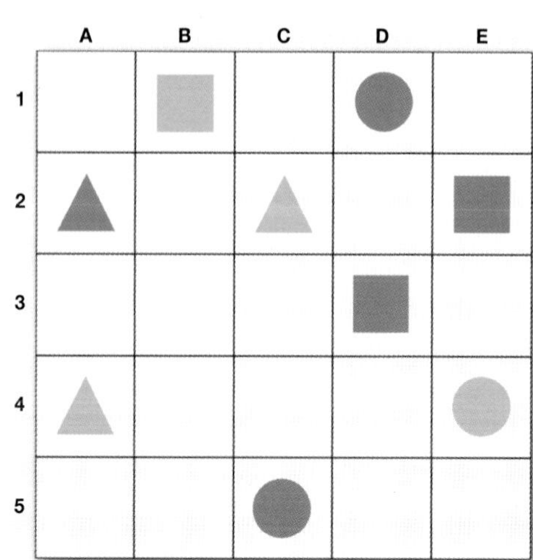

	A	B	C	D	E
1					
2					
3					
4					
5					

GENERAL KNOWLEDGE

What am I?

1. I am seen either as a form of protection or a restriction.
2. I keep things out, but also in.
3. In slang, I am a dealer in stolen property.
4. Horses jump over me.
5. You sit on me when you can't make a decision.
6. You mend me when you have fallen out with someone and want to repair the relationship.

D. ....

What am I?

1. I can be copious or sparse.
2. I am actually dead, but I can be considered to be healthy.
3. Although dead I continue to grow.
4. Some like me – others go to extreme measures to get rid of me.
5. When you split me you are being petty.
6. You have fun when you let me down.

E. ....

PROBLEM — LOGIC

The gromph and the gromphette were hybrids who lived happily in Gromphland several thousand years ago.

Taking into account that all individuals of the same sex were identical, that gromphs and gromphettes had the same total number of limbs (legs and arms) and that, when a gromph romped about with three gromphettes, there were an equal number of arms and legs in action whereas a gromphette had twice as many legs as a gromph, work out how many arms and legs the gromph and gromphette had.

RECITATION — GENERAL KNOWLEDGE

Try to remember the endings of the lines of this great classic by the Irish poet W B Yeats

The Lake Isle of Innisfree

	a.	b.	c.
I will arise and go now, and go to ....,	*the lake by the sea*	*Innisfree*	*Lough Tralee*
And a small cabin build there, of clay and	*grasses laid*	*red bricks baked*	*wattles made*
Nine bean-rows will I have there, a hive for	*the honey-bee*	*the bumble-bee*	*the carpenter bee*
And live alone in the	*bird-sweet glade*	*bee-loud glade*	*peace I've made*
And I shall have some peace there, for peace comes ....,	*to those who know*	*to the hollow*	*dropping slow*
Dropping from the veils of the morning to where ....;	*the cricket sings*	*the church bell rings*	*the quiet is king*
There midnight's all a glimmer, and noon.......................,	*a golden yellow*	*a sleepy hollow*	*a purple glow*
And evening full of	*the black starlings*	*the firefly's wings*	*the linnet's wings*
I will arise and go now, for always	*I think and pray*	*night and day*	*work or play*
I hear lake water lapping with low sounds ....;	*by the shore*	*by my door*	*in every pore*
While I stand on the roadway, or on the ....,	*edge of the bay*	*fringe of the fray*	*pavements grey*
I hear it in the	*sweet folklore*	*ears ever more*	*deep heart's core*

W B Yeats

GEOMETRIC SEQUENCES — LOGIC

In each case, use the numbered figures to continue the sequence.

A

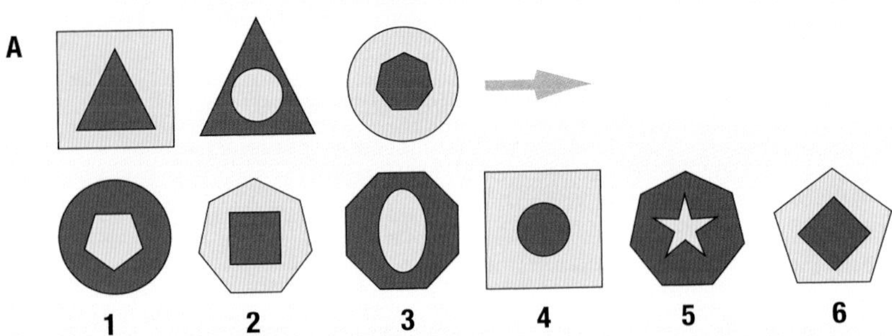

B

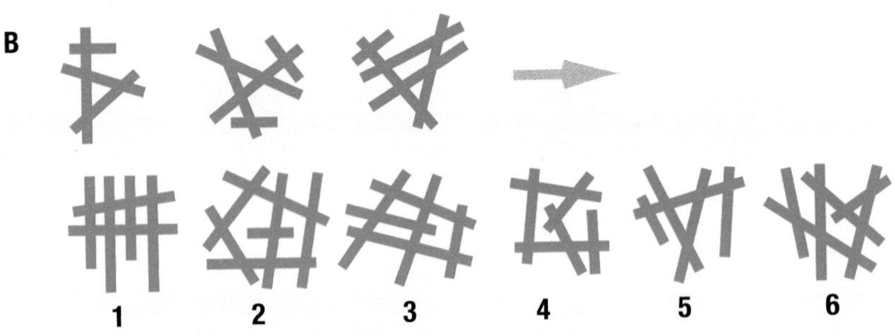

C

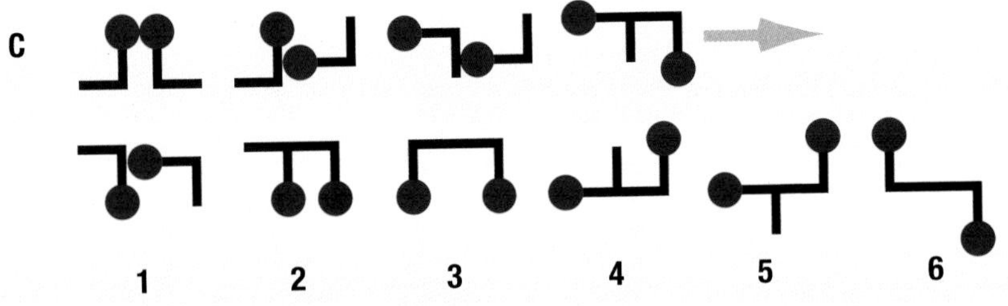

D

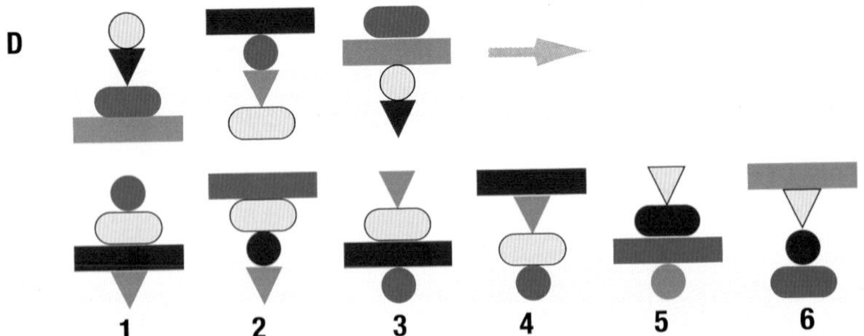

E

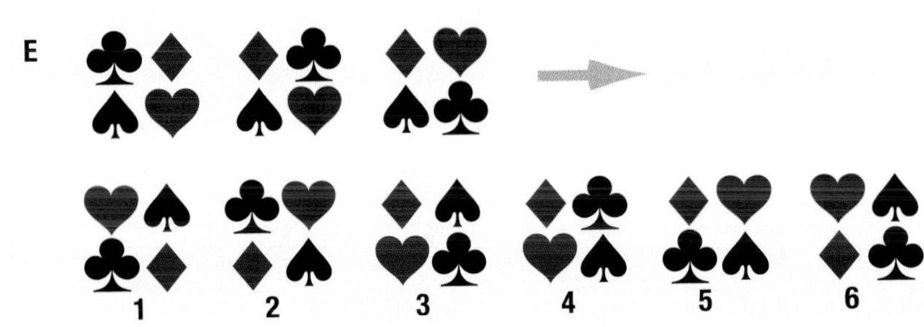

LADDER — STRUCTURE

Using the six crosspieces, reconstruct the ladder by making words associated with sport.

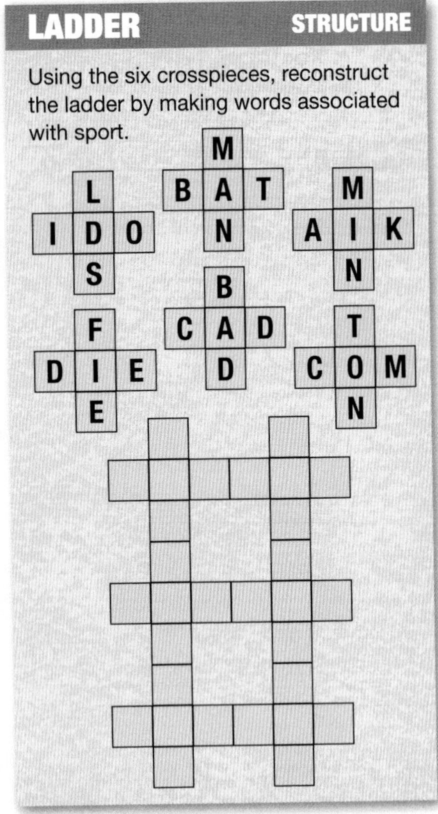

THE RIGHT TIME — LOGIC

It takes one hour to fly from Paris to London and there is a time difference of one hour, so that you take off and land at the same time. Julian has a video recorder that can be set from a distance, but the timer on his machine is one hour slow. In his London hotel, the clock (English time) is at 22h and Julian wants to record on his video player in Paris a programme that runs from 1 to 2h 30. His answer phone in Paris, which is linked to his video machine, asks him in how many minutes the programme is due to start and how long it will last. Is there at least one reply among the following answers that will make it possible for him to record the programme?

	Starts...	Duration
A.	60	90
B.	120	90
C.	90	120
D.	180	120

MATCHING UP

ASSOCIATION

Try to match up these 10 pairs of actors with one of the films they acted in.

A. Sean Connery/Jill St John ....

B. John Travolta/Olivia Newton-John ....

C. Leonardo di Caprio/Kate Winslet ....

D. Glenn Close/John Malkovich ....

E. Audrey Hepburn/Rex Harrison ....

F. Julia Roberts/Richard Gere ....

G. Anthony Hopkins/Jodie Foster ....

H. Geena Davis/Susan Sarandon ....

I. Catherine Zeta-Jones/Renee Zellweger ....

J. Vivien Leigh/Clark Gable ....

1

2

3

4

5

GONE WITH THE WIND

HOWARD DE HAVILLAND

6

7

8

9

10

TRUE OR FALSE

GENERAL KNOWLEDGE

Try to work out if the following statements about dinosaurs are true or false. Circle the letters corresponding to your answers in the relevant column, and then reorder the letters to find what the second part of the word 'dinosaur' means – 'terrible ...'.

	True	False
1. The Komodo dragon is a type of dinosaur.	B	L
2. Cro-Magnon peoples ate certain small dinosaurs.	O	Z
3. Dinosaurs laid eggs.	I	M
4. No one knows what colour their skin was.	D	H
5. Today we know of 30 species of dinosaurs.	S	A
6. Dinosaurs are referred to in the Dead Sea Scrolls.	W	R

PROBLEM

LOGIC

1. How many animals of each species did Moses load on to the ark?
2. A ladder is attached to a ship. The first rung is at the same level as the water, and the rungs are 10 cm apart. If the tide rises by 20 cm an hour, after how long will the water reach the sixth rung?
3. A smoker, horrified at the increase in the price of tobacco, hoards all his cigarette butts. He can make one cigarette out of four cigarette butts. How many cigarettes can he smoke if he uses the 15 cigarette butts he has saved? And how many will he have left?
4. Show how one taken away from 19 can give you 20.

PROGRESSIVE QUIZ — GENERAL KNOWLEDGE

Answer as many questions as you can on these female singers ranging from the 50s to the present.

1. Which Motown singer first sang *I Heard it Through the Grapevine*?
2. In 1959, which French singer had a hit on the English hit parade with the song *Milord*?
3. Which South African diva sang at President Kennedy's birthday and was the wife of Black Panther leader Stokely Carmichael?
4. Counting Crows, a US group, had a hit in 2003 with the song *Big Yellow Taxi*. Which Canadian singer first sang this song?
5. The daughter of the sitar master Ravi Shankar produced an album in 2002, *Feels Like Home*, which sold over a million copies in one week. Who is she?
6. She should be so lucky, she's gone from *Neighbour* to *Impossible Princess* in *Light Years*. Who is this Australian icon?
7. Which singer joined the Supremes after 1961?
8. In 1989, which American singer sang the *Marseillaise* in Paris at the Place de la Concorde?
9. Which Scottish pop singer changed the rules of the European Song Contest in 1969 and was married to one of the Bee Gees?
10. This US folk singer is a Quaker, and in the 60s and 70s was a civil rights campaigner.

STICK-ON WORDS — STRUCTURE

Pair up these five-letter words to form 10 new words of 10 letters.

RETRO, BARGE, AFTER, FRONT, CENTRE, SHOCK, CHAIN, FRUIT, SAWED, CHILD, BOARD, PIECE, BEACH, CAKES, GRADE, LIGHT, PROOF, GHOST, BULBS, WRITE

1. ..../..................
2. ..../..................
3. ..../..................
4. ..../..................
5. ..../..................
6. ..../..................
7. ..../..................
8. ..../..................
9. ..../..................
10. ..../..................

NUMBER SEQUENCES — LOGIC

Find the number that follows logically to complete the sequences below.

1. 1 2 5 10 20 50 100 200 ?
2. 18 63 621 2 421 2 484 ?
3. 2 6 12 20 30 42 56 ?
4. III 3 XII 4 XIV 5 XXII 6 XXVII ?*

* Note that the answer here is not 7...

PROBLEM — LOGIC

Mr Martin, Mr Lee and Mr Patel each have a dog: one has a poodle, one a Yorkshire terrier, and the third has a pitbull. To keep burglars at bay, without really resorting to lies, each one has written a sign on his door:

Only those among us who have a pitbull tell the truth

Then each man added a personal message.
On the first door, Mr Martin wrote:

Mr Patel has a Yorkshire terrier

On the second door, Mr Lee wrote:

Mr Martin has a Yorkshire terrier

On the third door, Mr Patel wrote:

Mr Lee has a poodle

So who has a pitbull?

....

PAIRING UP

ASSOCIATION

Look at these 10 pairs of objects for several minutes and then cover them.

Below is one object from each pair. Do you know what the missing object is?

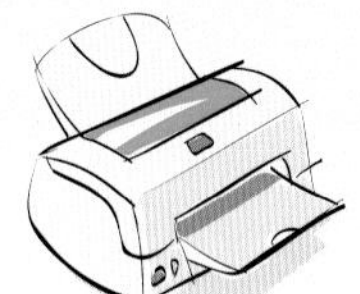

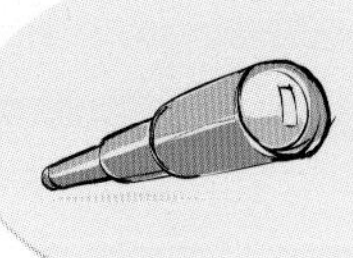

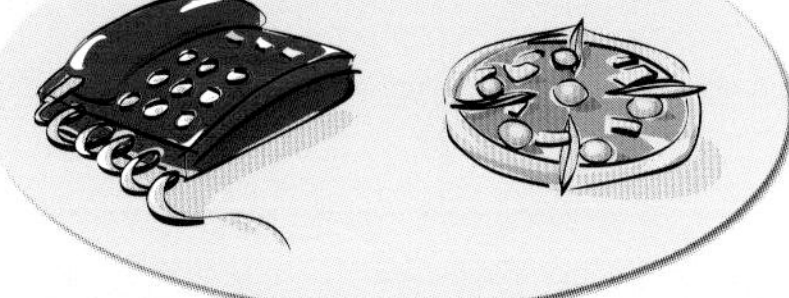

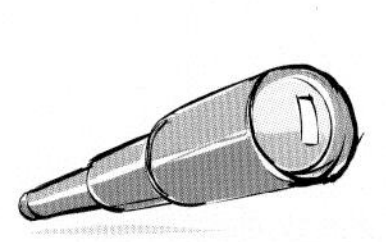

ITINERARY

STRUCTURE

Fill in the missing letters to complete, horizontally, the names of the following places. In the first and last columns a geographical point and a city in Japan will appear vertically.

	A	P	E	T	O	W	
	N	A	C	O	N	D	
	A	I	C	H	E	N	
	T	H	I	O	P	I	
	O	N	D	U	R	A	
	K	L	A	H	O	M	
	A	D	S	T	O	C	
	A	G	A	S	A	K	

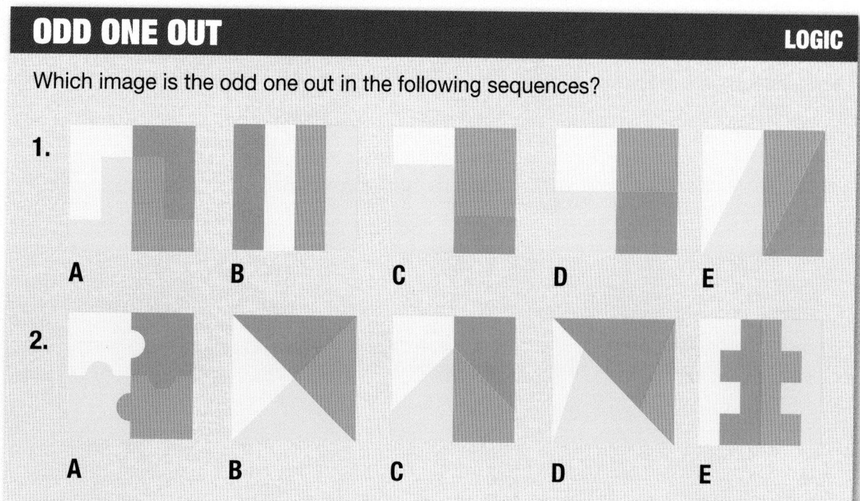

ODD ONE OUT

LOGIC

Which image is the odd one out in the following sequences?

SPEED LIMIT OF 90! LOGIC

Using these 16 digits, go up to 90 in all possible directions (including diagonally) by placing each digit in a matching shape.

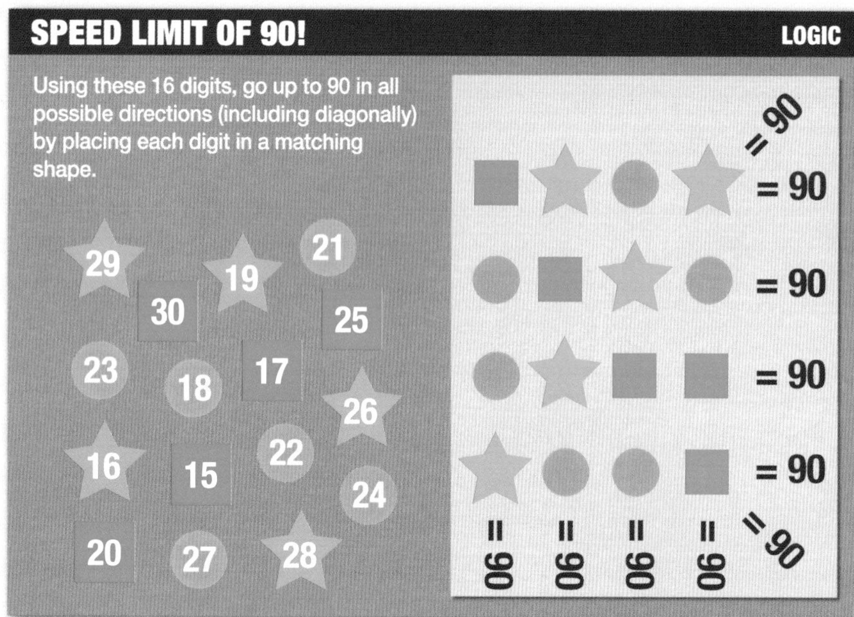

MOCK EXAM

Find a word beginning with each of the syllables in all eight categories. If you manage to fill in at least half of the spaces, you will obtain 50%, which is the pass mark! Note that you must do the test in 10 minutes and no word can be used twice.

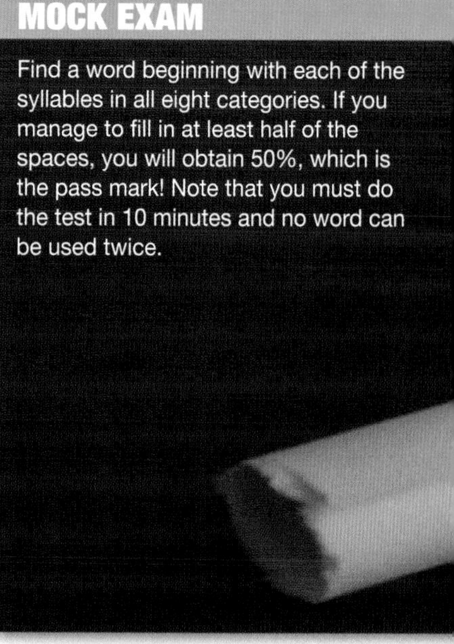

HAPPY ENDINGS ASSOCIATION

Find 10 words ending in –AVE that correspond to the clues given below (one letter per dash).

1. Conduct yourself well ➤ _ _ _ AVE
2. Courageous ➤ _ _ AVE
3. Musical interval of eight notes ➤ _ _ _ AVE
4. A surface that curves inwards ➤ _ _ _ _ AVE
5. An assembly of cardinals ➤ _ _ _ _ _ AVE
6. Smooth and sophisticated ➤ _ _ AVE
7. To interlace ➤ _ _ AVE
8. To depart ➤ _ _ AVE
9. Last resting place ➤ _ _ AVE
10. To inscribe ➤ _ _ _ _ AVE

NUMBER SEQUENCES LOGIC

Find the digit that follows logically in the sequences below:

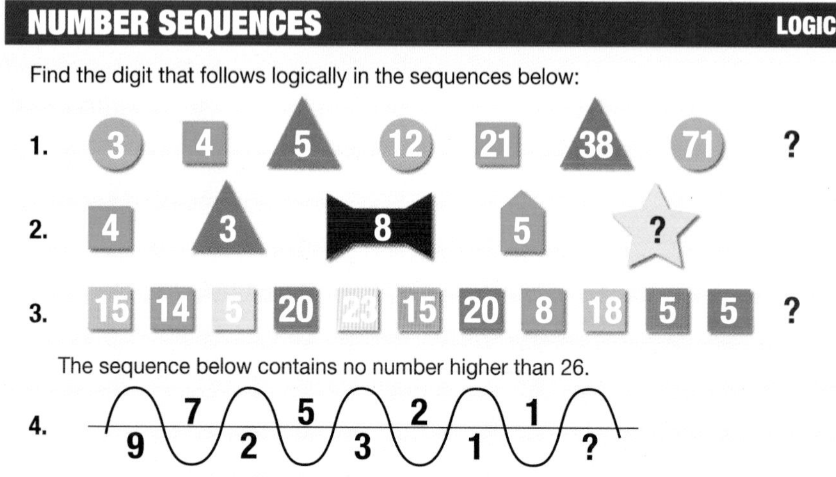

NUMBER PYRAMID LOGIC

Each brick in the number pyramid is the sum of the two bricks immediately below it. Fill in all the numbers by making use of those already in place.

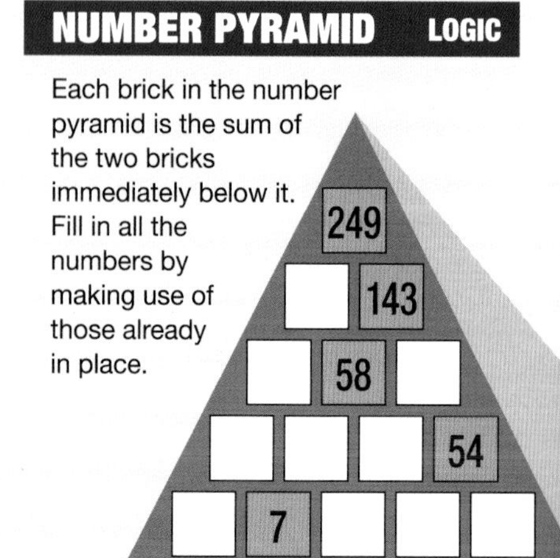

GENERAL KNOWLEDGE

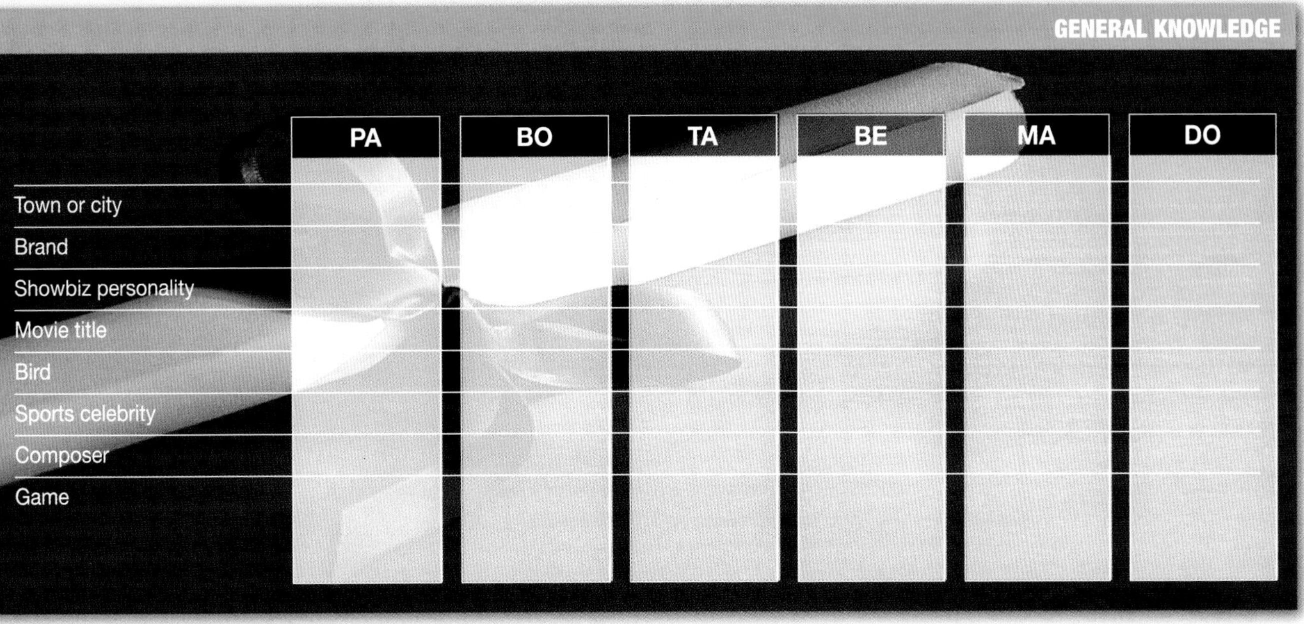

	PA	BO	TA	BE	MA	DO
Town or city						
Brand						
Showbiz personality						
Movie title						
Bird						
Sports celebrity						
Composer						
Game						

PARONYMS — LANGUAGE

Paronyms are words that are similar in form but different in meaning (example – collision and collusion). Find the paronyms that complete the following sentences.

1. It is not advisable to swim in the sea with any sort of bleeding ______ on your skin where sharks are ______ since they are likely to be attracted to the blood.
2. While on __________ he saved a child from a house fire and so discovered his ___________ as a firefighter.
3. People often confuse the word ________, which is a hypothesis or supposition based on incomplete evidence, with the word _______, which describes a combination of events at a given time.
4. The ________ for her cooking course including making a medieval ________.

PROBLEM — LOGIC

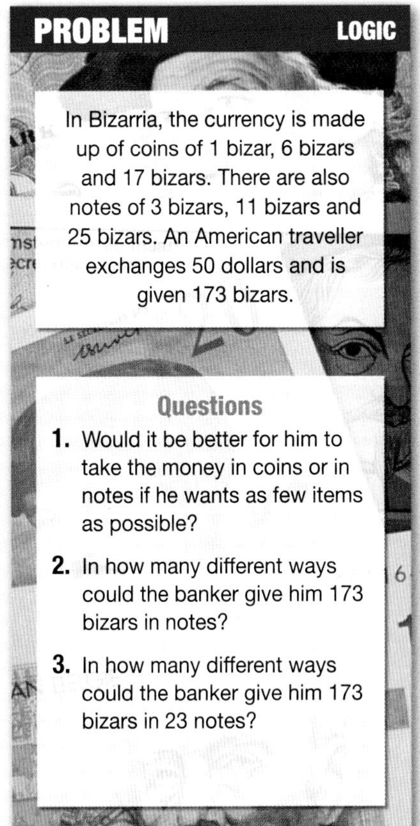

In Bizarria, the currency is made up of coins of 1 bizar, 6 bizars and 17 bizars. There are also notes of 3 bizars, 11 bizars and 25 bizars. An American traveller exchanges 50 dollars and is given 173 bizars.

Questions

1. Would it be better for him to take the money in coins or in notes if he wants as few items as possible?
2. In how many different ways could the banker give him 173 bizars in notes?
3. In how many different ways could the banker give him 173 bizars in 23 notes?

ESCALETTERS — STRUCTURE

Form new letters by adding the letters given below, one at a time. Several solutions are possible.

T I P

+S ____

+E _____

+R ______

+E _______

+C _________

+K __________

MATCHES — LOGIC

Can you obtain the number 11 by adding 3 matches to this number 6? (All operations are permissible.)

CUBES — STRUCTURE

Using a different letter each time from one of the sides of these cubes, form the names of three female mystery writers.

1. ....
2. ....
3. ....

CUBES
STRUCTURE

Using a different letter each time from one of the sides of these cubes, form the names of three Presidents of the United States.

1. .... **2.** .... **3.** ....

TRUE OR FALSE
GENERAL KNOWLEDGE

Try to work out if the following statements about dietetics are true or false. Circle the relevant letter matching your response under True or False, and the six letters obtained will spell the name of the first substance that acts on the starch in your food and changes it into sugars.

	True	False
1. Honey provides more energy than sugar.	G	 A
2. Fish and meat contain on average the same amount of protein.	L	 T
3. Margarine contains less fat than butter.	A	 S
4. Brown sugar is better for your health than white sugar.	A	 V
5. Parsley is very rich in iron.	A	 F
6. Too much lemon is harmful to your bones.	O	 I

POINTS IN COMMON
ASSOCIATION

Find the word that links the three words on each line forming a compound word.

1. Park, bearing, point
....

2. Cup, nose, fish
....

3. Paper, flower, street
....

4. Fingers, knife, cup
....

5. Master, ache, over
....

6. Vault, north, position
....

ITINERARY
STRUCTURE

Fill in the names of these places horizontally to discover vertically two places on opposite sides of the English Channel.

	U	T	O	
	S	A	K	
	A	I	R	
	E	L	F	
	K	E	N	
	Y	O	N	

MOCK EXAM
GENERAL KNOWLEDGE

Find a word beginning with each of the syllables in all eight categories. If you manage to fill in at least half he spaces, you will have obtained 50%, which is the pass mark! Note that you must do the test in 10 minutes and no word can be used twice.

	CA	PO	SH	GA	GO	DE
Singer or band						
Brand						
Word of 8 letters with 6 consonants						
Song title						
Town or city						
Four-legged animal						
Writer						
Word referring to currency or money						

GEOMETRIC SEQUENCES

LOGIC

In each of the following sequences, figure a is to figure b what figure c is to figure 1, 2, 3, 4, 5 or 6.

A

a b c

1 2 3 4 5 6

B

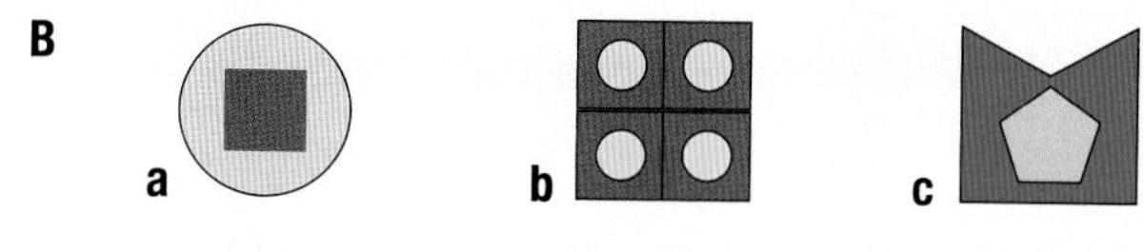

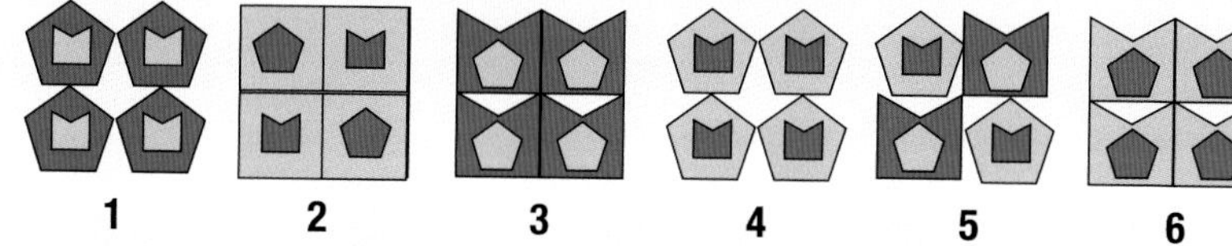

C

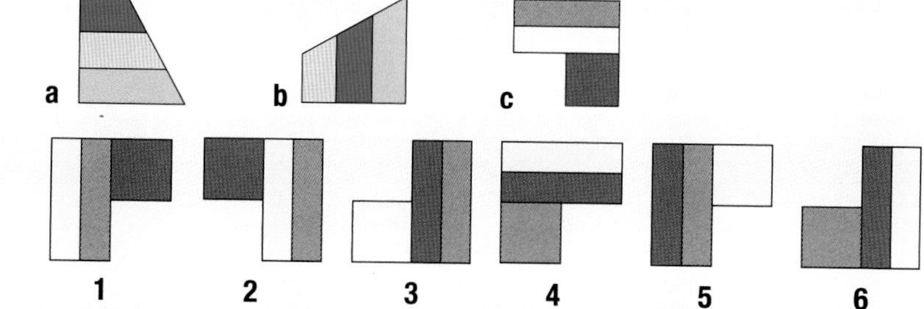

D

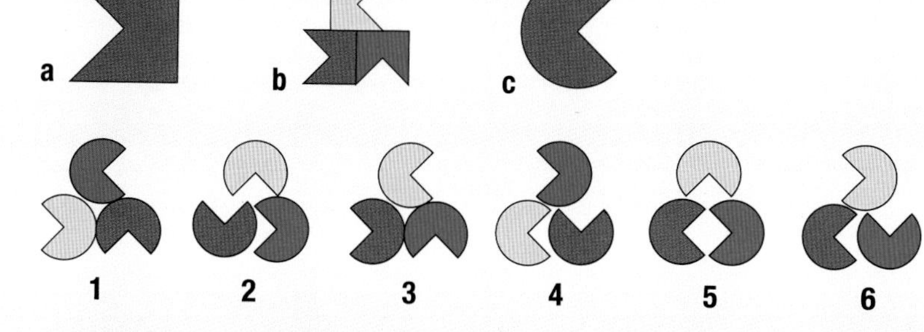

E

a b c

1 2 3 4 5 6

CUT-UP LETTERS

STRUCTURE

Cross out one letter in each of the nine words in the grid, ensuring that the remaining letters still constitute an existing word. Rewrite the rejected letters at the end of each line to spell the name of someone who in 1564 decided that the first day of the year would henceforth be January 1 instead of March 25, as Christian tradition had previously decreed.

B	A	C	K	I	N	G	
C	H	A	M	B	E	R	
B	O	A	R	D	E	R	
R	E	P	O	R	T	S	
F	I	L	L	I	N	G	
G	R	E	A	T	E	R	
D	E	S	C	E	N	T	
N	E	I	T	H	E	R	
I	N	D	E	X	E	D	

CATERPILLAR

STRUCTURE

Move from ADVANCE to RETREAT in this caterpillar by carrying out the series of substitutions indicated (for example, R replaces N in the first line) and by modifying the order in which the letters are written.

		ADVANCE
-N	+R	_ _ _ _ _ _ _
-V	+S	_ _ _ _ _ _ _
-A	+R	_ _ _ _ _ _ _
-C	+T	_ _ _ _ _ _ _
-S	+E	_ _ _ _ _ _ _
-D	+T	RETREAT

Solutions

Pages 150-151

MIXED PROVERBS

1. Look before you leap.
2. Better safe than sorry.
3. A bird in the hand is worth two in the bush.

BRAIN TEASER

Clue no. 1 eliminates Alexandra's Hill and Bishop's Rise.
Clue no. 2 eliminates Victoria Street and Fifteenth Street.
Clue no. 3 eliminates Parliament Hill, Piper Place, Deer Park Road, Azalea Avenue, Sandpiper Walk, Rhododendron Drive and Kennington Lane.
Clue no. 4 eliminates Rhodes Drive and Albert Avenue.
Clue no. 5 eliminates Mahatma Gandhi Mews. It is therefore 13 Washington Avenue that you need to go to.

ANAGRAMS

1. Maracas
2. Organ
3. Lyre
4. Sitar
5. Snaredrum
6. Triangle
7. Spinet
8. Bugle
9. Tuba
10. Horns

HISTORICAL LANDMARKS

1644 : G/O (Ming Dynasty, Stradivarius)
1789 : F/I (Washington, French Revolution)
1827 : K/P (Beethoven, *Standard* newspaper – later to become the *Evening Standard*)
1871 : N/E (Chicago Fire, Bismarck)
1920 : M/D (Fellini, Prohibition)
1946 : C/J (Unesco, bikini)
1980 : H/L (Moscow, McQueen)
1988 : A/B (Armenia, Johnson)

SPOT THE 7 DIFFERENCES

Pages 152-153

PROGRESSIVE QUIZ

1. Greek
2. The 6th century BC.
3. *The Wild Ass and the Lion*
4. He placed stones in the water to raise its level.
5. '... what you should do today.'
6. *The Hare and the Tortoise.*
7. A little thing in hand is worth more than a great prospect.
8. *The Fox and the Grapes.*
9. The country mouse.
10. The jay.

PUZZLE

1

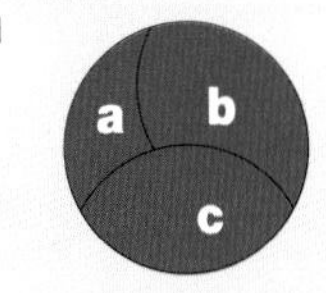

2

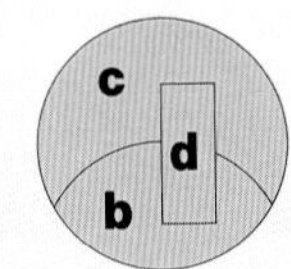

STICK-ON WORDS

Bang, Cock (Bangkok) – Sid, Knee (Sydney) – Bomb, Bay (Bombay) – Bay, Route (Beirut) – Wind, Hook (Windhoek) – Bore, Dough (Bordeaux) – Bell, Fast (Belfast) – Canter, Berry (Canterbury) – Whinny, Peg (Winnipeg).

NUMBER PYRAMID

Since the numbers at the base are identical, let us call them N, for example.
You then get the following pyramid.
In order for 16 x N to equal 320, N must be equal to 20.

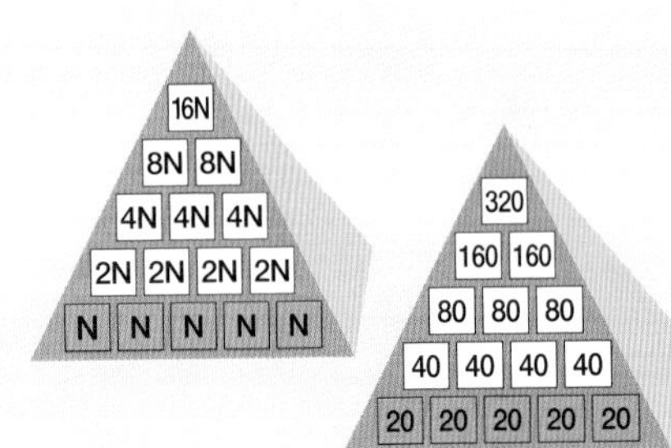

SHADOWS

It's no. 5.

SANDWICH

Mark Twain's description of Wagner's music.

C	A	B	A	L
A	D	E	P	T
H	U	T	C	H
B	I	T	E	S
P	E	E	K	S
A	C	R	E	S
M	I	T	E	S
A	C	H	E	D
S	T	A	L	E
C	A	N	A	L
S	L	I	P	S
M	A	T	C	H
B	A	S	E	D
C	L	O	V	E
M	O	U	S	E
B	I	N	D	S
H	I	D	E	S
B	A	S	K	S

Pages 154-155

ZIGZAG WORDS

Offenbach

POINTS IN COMMON

1. Four
2. Conductor
3. Ham
4. Paper
5. Milk
6. Glass

BROKEN SEQUENCES

1. Gargantuan
2. Revolting
3. Intestine
4. Escalate
5. Vermilion
6. Multitude

Pages 156-157

BOXED WORDS

ESCALETTERS

R A T
+ **E** T E A R
+ **I** I R A T E
+ **P** P I R A T E
+ **S** T R A I P S E
+ **A** P A R A S I T E
+ **D** A S P I R A T E D

BROKEN SEQUENCES

1. Intriguing
2. Liberty
3. Loquacious
4. Handicap
5. Diametric
6. Eternity

CATERPILLAR

V A M P I R E
P R E V A I L
R E P L I C A
D E C R I A L
R A D I C A L
D R A C U L A

HIDDEN WORDS

The hidden word is RAINBOW.

MATCHING UP

A8 – B3 – C9 – D5 – E2 – F6 – G4 – H10 – I7 – J1.

JUMBLED WORDS

1. Jerry Seinfeld
2. Rowan Atkinson
3. Whoopi Goldberg

ODD ONE OUT

D, the parrot. The names of the other objects or the idea they evoke ends with the syllable 'art' (art, tart, smart, dart, heart).

Pages 158-159

CUBES

1. B and C
2. B and D
3. A and D

ANAGRAMS

1. Sumatra
2. Greenland
3. South
4. Rhodes
5. North
6. Crete
7. St Martins
8. Skomer
9. Andros
10. Menorca

THE RIGHT TIME

It is 4h in Los Angeles, 9h in Rio de Janeiro, 20h in Beijing and 22h in Sydney.

LOTTO

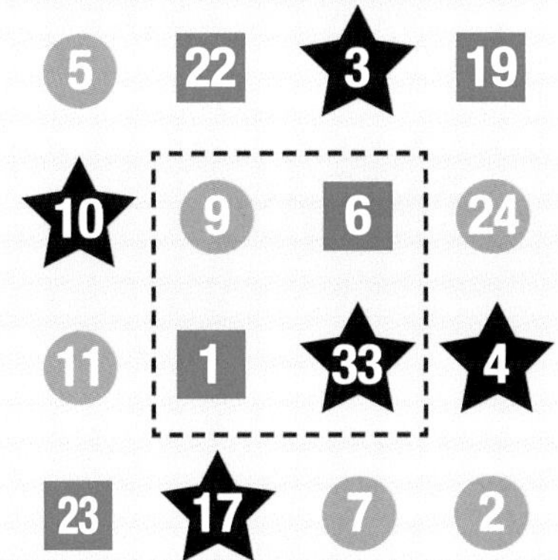

WORD HOLES

1. Therefore
2. Flavour
3. Forgivable
4. Sphinx
5. Severance
6. Eyesight

MATCHING UP

A8 – B1 – C6 – D7 – E2 – F4 – G10 – H3 – I6 – J9.

MISSING LETTERS

Poland and *Hawaii*, two works by James Michener.

E	M	P	A	T	H	I	C
G	L	O	S	S	A	R	Y
A	L	L	E	Y	W	A	Y
C	H	A	P	L	A	I	N
A	M	N	E	S	I	A	C
F	I	D	E	L	I	T	Y

PUZZLE

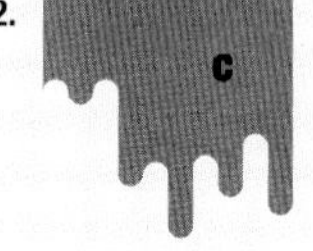

Pages 160-161

THEMATIC CROSSWORD

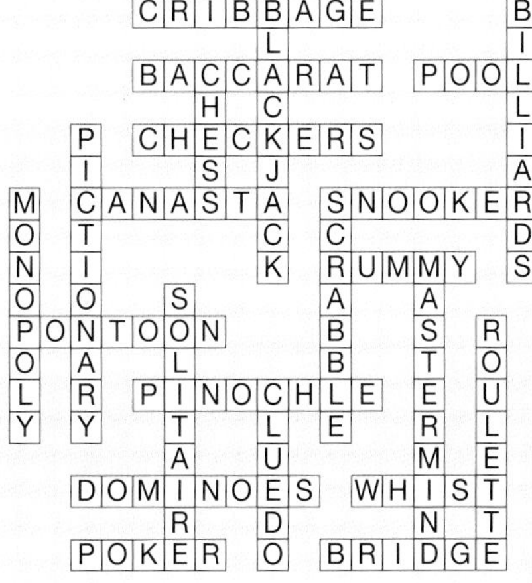

CRYPTOGRAM

To live in hearts we leave behind is not to die.
Thomas Campbell
Hallowed Ground.

PROBLEM

Let x be the number of cats, y the number of dogs and n the number of biscuits.
We know that $x + y = 14$ and that $nx + (n + 2) y = 76$.
$x = 14 - y$ and $n (14 - y) + (n + 2) y = 76$.
You can deduce from this that $2y = 76 - 14n$, so that $y = 38 - 7n$.
For the values of n = 1, 2 or 3, y is more than 14, which is impossible.
For n = 4, we find that y = 10 and so x = 4.
And for n = 5, you get y = 3 and x = 11.
So 10 dogs have each eaten 6 biscuits and 4 cats have each eaten 4 biscuits, or 11 cats have each eaten 5 biscuits and 3 dogs 7 biscuits.

POINTS IN COMMON

1. Rose
2. Green
3. Dragon
4. Hearty
5. Drum
6. Wall

ROSETTE

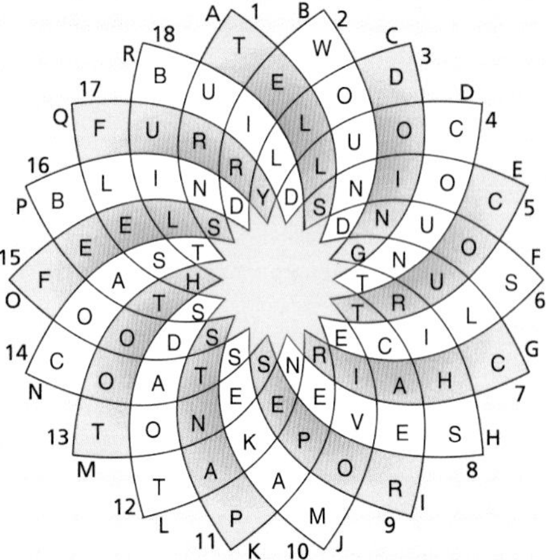

Pages 162-163

STICK-ON TITLES

1. *Strawberry Fields Forever*
2. *Ticket to Ride*
3. *A Hard Day's Night*
4. *Magical Mystery Tour*

MAGIC SQUARE

	31	40	49	2	11	20	
30	39	48	1	10	19	28	30
38	47	7	9	18	27	29	38
46	6	8	17	26	35	37	46
5	14	16	25	34	36	45	5
13	15	24	33	42	44	4	13
21	23	32	41	43	3	12	21
22	31	40	49	2	11	20	

HIDDEN OBJECTS

ODD ONE OUT

All of them are birds, but only the auk can fly.

BOXED WORDS

M		D	A	T	E				N		A	P	R	I	C	O	T
U				A		L	I	M	E		V						
L	E	M	O	N		Y			C		O		G	R	A	P	E
B		A		G		C			T		C		R				
E		N		E		H		B	A	N	A	N	A			C	
R		G		R		E			R		D		N			H	
R		O	L	I	V	E			I		O	R	A	N	G	E	
Y				N					N				D			R	
	P	I	N	E	A	P	P	L	E			F	I	G		R	
	L						E						L			Y	
	U					W	A	T	E	R	M	E	L	O	N		
	M	E	L	O	N		R						A				

SPOT THE 7 DIFFERENCES

Pages 164-165

HOMOPHONES

1. Weigh, way
2. Sent, cent
3. Flower, flour
4. Reign, rain

OVERLAPPING SHAPES

26 circles.

ANAPHRASES

1. Carthorse, orchestra
2. Decimation, medication
3. Intoxicate, excitation

CUBES

1. Yellow.
2. Orange and green.

LOOPY LETTERS

HISTORICAL LANDMARKS

1. True: 3 000 BC for papyrus, 1 200 BC for the Iron Age.
2. False: he was born almost six centuries before Christ.
3. True: he even correctly estimated the size of the Moon.
4. False: domestication of the dog began about 14 000 BC
5. False: it starts around 3 000 BC, but the epoch of Greek thought began around 600BC and ended in about AD 500.
6. False: he developed mathematics and astronomy. Don't confuse him with Prometheus who in Greek myth introduced fire to people.

Pages 166-167

CHALLENGE

If you have remembered half the words, or more, in one minute, then congratulations! A few minutes later it is normal that you would remember a little less. You possibly wrote down 'machine' for 'computer' or 'book' instead of 'novel', because your memory has fixed the sense of the words and not their form. It has produced the most common word for the memorised object.

MATCHES

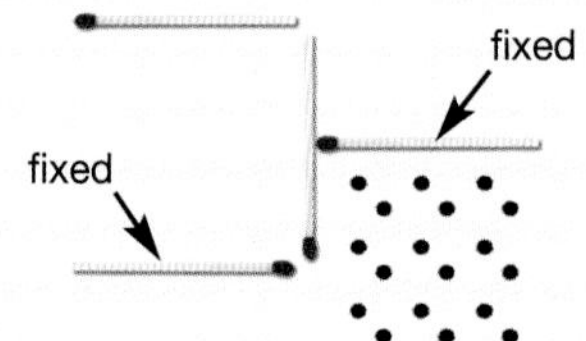

ANAGRAMS

1. Skin
2. Spine
3. Liver
4. Finger
5. Heart
6. Knee
7. Elbow
8. Toenail
9. Breast
10. Beard

MAZE

Pages 168-169

LOGIGRAM

Clue 1: looking at the initials of their names, we know that Cynthia has spoken to either Catherine or Charlotte. Cynthia's conversation lasted 54 minutes; Ciara's (2 x 54 = 108 minutes = 1 h 48) was about fashion.
Clue 2 : the friend whose name is shortest is Anne. Her conversation with Charlotte lasted 24 minutes (the shortest of them). Therefore Catherine called Cynthia.
Clue 3 : Louisa didn't speak to Cynthia or Anne (clues 1 and 2), or even to Ciara, who was discussing fashion, or Suzie, who was talking about dogs. So by elimination, Louisa phoned Natasha. They talked about films. The lengths of conversation not yet identified are 1h 12 and 2h 6. So it must have been Louisa's that lasted 1h 12, which is less than Suzie's, in which she talked about dogs for 2 h 6.
Clue 4 : Charlotte spoke for 24 minutes, Catherine for 54 and Louisa for 1h 12. Maria therefore chatted for 1h 48, less than Isabelle who was the most talkative. The doggy conversation lasted 2h 6, the one on fashion 1h 48, and the one about films 1h 12. Maths therefore occupied Cynthia and Catherine for 54 minutes on the telephone (more than 45 minutes), while 24 minutes was enough for Anne and Charlotte.

Table of answers

Teen	Catherine	Charlotte	Isabelle	Louisa	Maria
Friend	Cynthia	Anne	Suzie	Natasha	Ciara
Subject	Maths	Boys	Dogs	Films	Fashion
Duration	54 min	24 min	2h 6	1h 12	1h 48

PUZZLE

1.

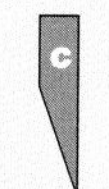

2.

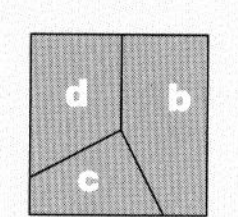

BONUS LETTERS

1. Open
2. Pedal
3. Drapes
4. Stopper
5. Perspire
6. Inspector

LOOPY LETTERS

CRYPTOGRAM

The two offices of memory are collection and distribution.

Samuel Johnson.

Pages 170-171

ANAPHRASES

1. Recipe, pierce
2. Migraine, imaginer
3. Article, recital

GEOMETRIC SEQUENCES

1. **Figure 3:** the circle moves clockwise from the middle of one side to another and itself does a quarter turn at each stage in an anticlockwise direction.
2. **Figure 3:** each figure is the same as the last but with one extra red square and minus one blue square.
3. **Figure 3:** the red section turns an eighth in a clockwise direction; the green sector equally does an eighth of a turn but in the opposite direction. When they meet the red covers the green.
4. **Figure 2:** the little red and green squares move to the next box each time; when they reach the edge of the big square, they move to the opposite edge in the next figure. Red: moves horizontally to the right. Green: moves horizontally to the left. The blue square doesn't move.
5. **Figure 5:** the green rectangle moves clockwise from one edge to the next. The red hemisphere turns 90° anticlockwise eat each stage.

CUT-UP LETTERS

You could remove:
I (Waving) – N (Diners) – T (Saying) – E (Appals) – R (Ambled) – N (Bakers) – E (Crated) – T(Angled) : Internet.

WORDS IN THE PICTURE

Here are a few examples: picnic, picnic basket, picnic blanket, pizza, pie, piece (of pie), pips (in the watermelon), pink, pirate, picture, pilot, pinniped (the seal), pincers, pinch, pinstripes, pince-nez, piscatory (place for fishing), pig, pile, pilchards, pigeons

HISTORICAL LANDMARKS

1. First Crusade (1096)
2. Hundred Years' War (1337)
3. Thirty Years' War (1618)
4. Battle of Waterloo (1806)
5. War of Secession (1861)
6. First World War (1914)
7. Vietnam War (1954)
8. Yom Kippur War (1973)
9. First Gulf War (1990)
10. Conflict in ex-Yugoslavia (1992)

POINTS IN COMMON

1. Mouse
2. Stub
3. Veil
4. Pitch
5. Basket
6. Bowl

Pages 172-173

MYSTERY WORDS

A. Rudyard Kipling.
B. Marilyn Monroe.
C. Steven Spielberg.
D. Bill Gates.
E. Dame Jane Goodall.

SYNONYMS

1. Tundra
2. Flat
3. Pampas
4. Prairie
5. Range
6. Savanna
7. Steppe
8. Veld

HISTORICAL LANDMARKS

In the order of the bar graph:
Q Ramses II (– 1304/– 1236)
S Solomon (– 970/– 931)
O Nebuchadnezzar II (– 605/– 562)
C Buddha (– 560/– 480)
G Confucius (– 552/– 479)
T Socrates (– 470/– 399)
A Alexander the Great (– 356/– 323)
D Caesar (– 100/– 44)
P Nero (37/68)
B Attila the Hun (395/453)
F Clovis I (465/511)
N Mohammed (570-632)
E Charlemagne (742/814)
J William the Conqueror (1028/1087)
H Frederick of Barbarossa (1122/1190)
I Gengis Khan (1167/1227)
L Joan of Arc (1412/1431)
M Machiavelli (1469/1527)
K Henry VIII (1491-1547)
R Jean Calvin (1509/1564)

ONE WORD TOO MANY

1. You could add 'tri-' before each word to get: triage, triangle, triathlete, tricorn, triton, except for SHELF.
2. These are different kinds of breads, except for TORTE, which is a cake.
3. Each word is a shade of green, except for VERMILION, which is red.

Pages 174-175

KNOW YOUR WORLD

1. Gdansk
2. Warsaw
3. Czech Republic
4. Carpathians
5. Bratislava
6. Hungary
7. Danube
8. Slovenia
9. Zagreb
10. Romania
11. Bucharest
12. Sarajevo
13. Belgrade (Belgium)
14. Adriatic Sea
15. Bulgaria
16. Macedonia (macedoine)
17. Tirana
18. Salonica
19. Piraeus
20. Aegean Sea

HOMOGRAPHS

1. Pitch
2. Second
3. Race
4. Wound

HISTORICAL LANDMARKS

1. Sundial (1500 BC, in Egypt)
2. Iron (China, in the 4th century)
3. Calculator (invented by Pascal, 1639)
4. Parachute (Lenormand, 1783)
5. Morse code (Morse, 1840)
6. Artificial heart (Demikhov, 1937)
7. Microwave oven (Spencer, 1945)
8. Barcode (Monarch society, 1970)

PROBLEM

1. Seven months contain 31 days but all the months contain at least 28 days.
2. Yes, if this person is her brother!
3. No, because if he has a widow it is he who is dead.

Pages 176-177

PERFECT COPIES?

C and D.

IDENTIKIT

You will have quickly identified 2 and 7, who have earrings and blonde hair. No. 2 also has a necklace. No. 3 can be deleted from those without earrings and a necklace, and having brown hair. It is no. 1 who was armed.

IDIOMATIC TRIPLETS

1. Style
2. High
3. Knee
4. Book
5. Mixed
6. Running

ROSETTE

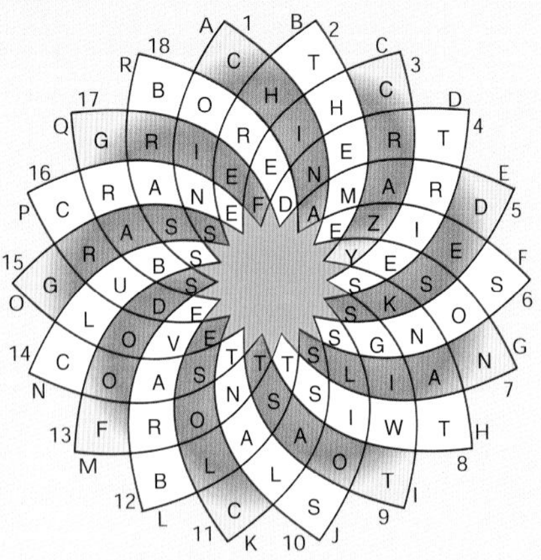

ONE WORD TOO MANY

1. Each word can be preceded by F to create a new word – factor, fever, flawless, flopped, fright – except for APPLE.
2. Each word can be preceded by NON – noncombatant, nonflammable, nonproliferation, nonresident, nonsense – except for FLUTE.
3. The initial letters of the first five words are in alphabetical order, A, B, C, D, E – except for GRIDDLE.

MIXED QUOTES

1. 'History will be kind to me for I intend to write it.' (Churchill)
2. 'When you appeal to force, there's one thing you must never do – lose.' (Eisenhower)
3. 'A single death is a tragedy, a million deaths is a statistic.' (Stalin)

SUPERIMPOSITION

The three plaques to superimpose are no. 6, then no. 2 in the middle and no. 5 on top.

Pages 178-179

SUPERIMPOSITION

Fragments 1, 2, 5 and 6.

HISTORICAL LANDMARKS

1939 **(8, B)**: *Gone with the Wind*, Vivien Leigh.
1983 **(7, C)**: *Terms of Endearment*, Shirley MacLaine.
1989 **(2, D)**: *Driving Miss Daisy*, Jessica Tandy.
1991 **(1, A)**: *The Silence of the Lambs*, Jodie Foster.
1996 **(6, H)**: *The English Patient*, Juliette Binoche.
1998 **(5, F)**: *Shakespeare in Love*, Gwyneth Paltrow.
2001 **(3, G)**: *A Beautiful Mind*, Jennifer Connelly.
2002 **(4, E)**: *Chicago*, Catherine Zeta-Jones.

CLOSE-UP

Pages 180-181

LOGIGRAM

Holidays in Asia

Clue 1: this clue concerns Alexander, Alicia and Audrey. Altogether they have spent 1 400 + 1 600 = $3 000, and 1 600 + 2 600 = $4 200. The one who spent the most did so in Thailand. It was Marina or Oliver who went on the catamaran.
Clue 2 : the only equation that applies to this clue is 1 400 + 4 200 = 2 600 + 3 000 (= $5 600). Oliver had the biggest budget of the four, so $4 200 applies to him. In contrast, the person who went to Indonesia spent $1 400. What is more, since Oliver does not start with A, the budgets of Alexander, Alicia and Audrey are therefore (without yet knowing how much each spent) $1 400, $1 600 and $3 000 ($3 000 for Thailand).
By elimination, Marina's budget is $2 600. The two ski enthusiasts (water skiing and jet-ski) have, following the clue, each spent $2 600 and $3 000.
You can deduce that it was not Marina who went on the catamaran (because she was skiing), but Oliver, for $4 200.
Clue 3 : with what you've just established, this clue shows the the holidays devoted to paragliding cost $1 600 and that the female fan of bungee jumping (Alicia or Audrey) spent only $1 400 (in Indonesia).
Clue 4: this last clue enables you to

conclude that Marina (with a budget of $2 600) did not go to Myanmar or Indonesia ($1 400), or to Thailand ($3 000), or to Malaysia (Audrey). Marina therefore chose Vietnam. The woman whose name begins with A and who spend $1 400 in Indonesia is thus Alicia. Audrey paid $1 600 for her stay in Malaysia and Alexander $3 000 for his Thai holiday, while Oliver was in Myanmar. Finally, clue 4 allows you to conclude that it was Marina who went water skiing whereas Alexander preferred jet-ski.

Table of answers

Tourist	Alexander	Alicia	Audrey	Marina	Oliver
Country	Thailand	Indonesia	Malaysia	Vietnam	Myanmar
Sport	Jet-ski	Bungee jumping	Paragliding	Water skiing	Catamaran
Cost	$3 000	$1 400	1$ 600	$2 600	$4 200

HAPPY ENDINGS

1. Combine
2. Define
3. Bovine
4. Imagine
5. Machine
6. Magazine
7. Margarine
8. Submarine
9. Spine
10. Divine

WORD HOLES

1. Turnips
2. Comparison
3. Consolation
4. Vertigo
5. Performer
6. Tuberculin

CLOSE-UP

MIRROR IMAGES

Pages 182-183

MAZE

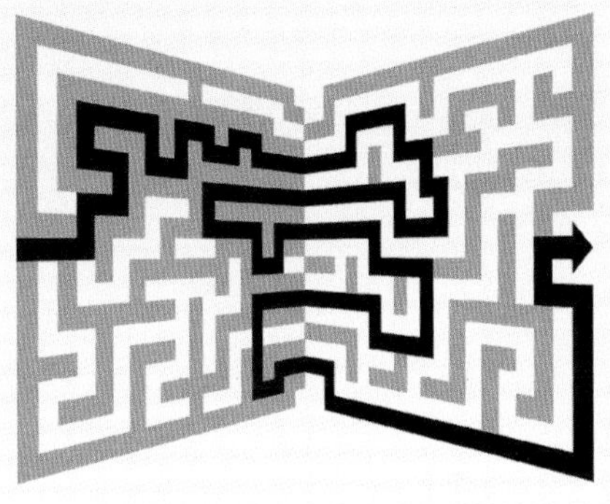

SUPERIMPOSITION

Plaques 3, 4 and 6.

THEMATIC CROSSWORD

PERFECT COPIES?

B and E.

A

C

D

F

THEMATIC CROSSWORD

Pages 184-185

MYSTERY WORDS

A. A bottle
B. A mystery
C. A goose
D. A fence
E. Hair

WORD PAIRS

Refer back to the list of words to check if you have answered correctly, but beware of the trap in question 3: the word 'train' is not in the list!

PROBLEM

If A is the number of hands of a gromph and B the number of feet, C the number of hands of a gromphette and D the numbers of feet, then you can work out the following: A + B = C + D on one hand (the same total number of limbs), A + 3C = B + 3D on the other hand (hands and feet in equal number in the grouping of 1 gromph + 3 gromphettes) and finally D = 2B (twice as many feet on a gromphette). The minimal solution for B = 1 leads to an unequal number of hands for the gromphette (1,5 !), but for B = 2 you quickly reach D = 4, C = 3 and A = 5. So the gromph has 5 hands and 2 feet, and the gromphette has 3 hands and 4 feet.

RECITATION

b: Innisfree – **c:** wattles made –
a: the honey-bee – **b:** bee-loud glade –

c: dropping slow – **a:** the cricket sings –
c: a purple glow – **c:** the linnet's wings

b: night and day – **a:** by the shore –
c: pavements grey – **c:** deep heart's core

Pages 186-187

GEOMETRIC SEQUENCES

A **Figure 5:** the shape inside the preceding figure becomes the external shape of the next.
B **Figure 6:** the number of intersections increases by 1 each time (4, 5, 6 and 7 with figure 6).
C **Figure 3:** assume that each figure is made of two modules comprising a red dot and a blue right angle. Each module alternately turns 90° anticlockwise.
D **Figure 3:** the shape at the bottom of each preceding figure moves to the top of the next, with the other shapes moving down one place. The colour of the top shape moves to the bottom and the other colours all move up one place.
E **Figure 5:** the spade moves one place each time in a clockwise direction. The symbol that was in this place moves back one space to occupy the previous position of the spade.

LADDER

	B			F	
C	A	D	D	I	E
	D			E	
	M			L	
A	I	K	I	D	O
	N			S	
	T			M	
C	O	M	B	A	T
	N			N	

THE RIGHT TIME

When it is 22h in London, it is 23h in Paris. But Julian's video recorder is in fact indicating 22h. He needs to record a programme which lasts from 1h to 2h 30, or, on his machine, from 0 hours to 1h 30. The ideal programme is therefore B. But C will also allow him to see his programme.

MATCHING UP

A5 – B2 – C3 – D4 – E7 – F8 – G9 – H10 – I1 – J6.

TRUE OR FALSE

1. False (L), the Komodo dragon is a reptile that is still alive today.
2. False (Z), the dinosaurs had disappeared long before Cro-Magnon times.
3. True (I), they were oviparous.
4. True (D), we can only imagine that they resembled the reptiles of today.
5. False (A), we know of more than 600.
6. False (R), the word dinosaur appeared in 1842.

The word dinosaur comes from the Greek '*deinos*' (terrible) and '*sauros*' (lizard). LIZARD is the word.

PROBLEM

1. None! It was Noah who took animals aboard his ark, not Moses.
2. Never! The boat will rise with the tide…
3. He uses 12 butts to make 3 cigarettes, which he smokes. Three butts are left before smoking. He now has 6. He can remake one cigarette, and he will have 2 butts left. In all he has smoked 4 cigarettes and he is left with 3 butts (the 2 he had before plus the one from the last cigarette he smoked).
4. Write 19 in Roman letters: XIX. Take one away and you are left with XX.

Pages 188-189

PROGRESSIVE QUIZ

1. Gladys Knight
2. Edith Piaf
3. Miriam Makeba
4. Joni Mitchell
5. Norah Jones
6. Kylie Minogue
7. Diana Ross
8. Jessye Norman
9. Lulu
10. Joan Baez

STICK-ON WORDS

Retro, Grade – After, Shock – Centre, Piece – Barge, Board – Beach, Front – Chain, Sawed – Child, Proof – Fruit, Cakes – Ghost, Write – Light, Bulbs.

NUMBER SEQUENCES

1. This is a sequence of values of coins and notes in euros. It is followed by the 500 € note.
2. The number is multiplied by 2 and then the digits are inverted (2 x 18 = 36, becomes 63 ; 2 x 63 = 126, becomes 621…). The next will be 2 x 2 484 = 4 968 inverted, which becomes 8 694.
3. The sequence is 1 x 2, 2 x 3, 3 x 4, 4 x 5, 5 x 6, 6 x 7, 7 x 8. It is completed by 8 x 9 = 72.
4. The number that follows the Roman number is that of the number of matches needed to make it. For XXVII, you would need 8.

PROBLEM

If Mr Martin has a pitbull, Mr Patel has a Yorkshire terrier and Mr Lee a poodle, then Mr Patel is telling the truth? Impossible. If Mr Patel has a pitbull, then Mr Lee has a poodle and Mr Martin has a Yorkshire terrier, so Mr Lee is telling the truth: equally impossible. So Mr Lee has the pitbull, Mr Martin the Yorkshire terrier and Mr Patel the poodle. Don't ring Mr Lee's bell!

C	A	P	E	T	O	W	N
A	N	A	C	O	N	D	A
P	A	I	C	H	E	N	G
E	T	H	I	O	P	I	A
H	O	N	D	U	R	A	S
O	K	L	A	H	O	M	A
R	A	D	S	T	O	C	K
N	A	G	A	S	A	K	I

ITINERARY Cape Horn, Nagasaki

ODD ONE OUT

1. C ; **2.** D
In both cases, the odd figure is not made up of 4 equivalent shapes.

Pages 190-191

SPEED LIMIT OF 90!

HAPPY ENDINGS

1. Behave
2. Brave
3. Octave
4. Concave
5. Conclave
6. Suave
7. Weave
8. Leave
9. Grave
10. Engrave

NUMBER SEQUENCES

1. Each shape contains the sum of the numbers in the three preceding shapes (eg: 71 = 12 + 21 + 38); so the next will be 21 + 38 + 71 = 130. The geometric shapes appear in a repeated pattern, so 130 will be in a square.
2. Each shape contains the number of sides necessary to draw it. For the star, you need 10 sides.
3. If you assume that every number corresponds to a letter of the alphabet in the same position, you will read ONE TWO THREE. The following number must therefore be 4, the position of the letter F, the initial of 'four'.
4. The following number in the crest and trough of each wave is the sum by subtraction of the two preceding numbers above and below the line. So 0 (the difference between 1 and 1) is the next number.

NUMBER PYRAMID

Start with 143. 143 – 58 = 85 to the right of 58. Then 85 – 54 = 31 to the left of 54, 58 – 31 = 27 to the left of 31. The numbers at the base are thus, to the right of the 7: 27 – 7 = 20, then 31 – 20 = 11 and 54 – 11 = 43 at the end on the right. Start at the top to finish the puzzle; on the fourth line up from the base, you have 249 – 143 = 106, on the third 106 – 58 = 48, on the second 48 – 27 = 21. The first number at the left of the base is thus 21 – 7 = 14.

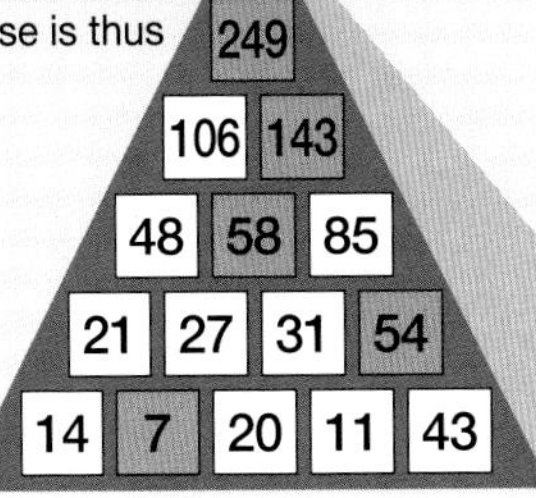

MOCK EXAM

PA Paris, Pampers, Paltrow, *Paris Texas*, parrot, Palmer, Paganini, Pacman
BO Bonn, Boeing, Bonham-Carter, *The Boys from Brazil*, booby, Boucher, Borodin, bowling
TA Tampa, Tag Heuer, Taylor, *The Talented Mr Ripley*, tailorbird, Taylor (Lawrence), Tallis, tag
BE Beijing, Bernina, Bening, *Beauty and the Beast*, bee-eater, Beckham, Beethoven, Boggle
MA Madras, Mazda, MacDowell, *Mad Max*, mallard, Mansell, Mahler, Mah-jong
DO Donegal, Dom Pérignon, Doherty, *Don't Look Now*, dodo, Doohan, Donizetti, dominoes

PARONYMS

1. Lesion, legion
2. Vacation, vocation
3. Conjecture, conjuncture
4. Syllabus, syllabub

PROBLEM

1. It would be better if he were given notes, because he will only have 11 (6 x 25, 1 x 11 and 4 x 3) whereas if he took coins he would need a minimum of 14 (9 x 17, 3 x 6 and 2 x 1).
2. Note (x, y, z) triplets of notes of 25, 11 and 3 bizars (x notes of 25, y notes of 11, z notes of 3).
   The triplet possibilities adding to 173 number 21 :
   (6 ; 1 ; 4), (5 ; 3 ; 5), (5 ; 0 ; 16), (4 ; 5 ; 6), (4 ; 2 ; 17), (3 ; 7 ; 7), (3 ; 4 ; 18), (3 ; 1 ; 29), (2 ; 9 ; 8), (2 ; 6 ; 19), (2 ; 3 ; 30), (2 ; 0 ; 41), (1 ; 11 ; 9), (1 ; 8 ; 20), (1 ; 5 ; 31) ; (1 ; 2 ; 42), (0 ; 13 ; 10), (0 ; 10 ; 21), (0 ; 7 ; 32), (0 ; 4 ; 43), (0 ; 1 ; 54).
3. In two ways (4 ; 2 ; 17) and (0 ; 13 ; 10): 4 notes of 25, 2 notes of 11 and 17 notes of 3 bizars or 13 notes of 11 and 10 notes of 3 bizars.

ESCALETTERS

T I P
+S S P I T
+E S P I T E
+R S P R I T E
+E R E S P I T E
+C R E C E I P T S
+K P I C K E T E R S

MATCHES

Position them in the mirror image of the first matches to get a roman XI !

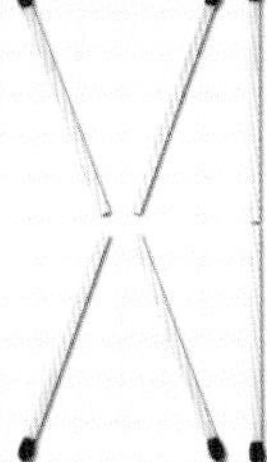

CUBES

Rendell – Fyfield – Walters.

Pages 192-193

CUBES

Carter – Reagan – Monroe

TRUE OR FALSE

1. False (A), and yet its sweetness is even greater.
2. True (L), about 20 g for every 100 g.
3. False (S), each contains about 83 % fat.
4. False (V), the colour is due only to additives and impurities.
5. True (A), six times more than spinach
6. False (I), it is rich in calcium.

The first substance that acts on the starch in your food and converts it into sugars is SALIVA.

POINTS IN COMMON

1. Ball
2. Hook
3. Wall
4. Butter
5. Head
6. Pole

ITINERARY

London – Nantes.

L	U	T	O	N
O	S	A	K	A
N	A	I	R	N
D	E	L	F	T
O	K	E	N	E
N	Y	O	N	S

MOCK EXAM

CA Callas, Cadillac, calypsos, *Calling You*, Canberra, cat, Carroll, cash
PO Police, Pontiac, polygamy, *Po' Boy*, Port Moresby, pony, Poe, pound (pony)
SH Shakira, Sharp, shackles, *She*, Shanghai, Sharpei, Shields, shekels (shillings, shrapnel)
GA Garland, Gauloises, gadgetry, *The Garden*, Galway, gavial, García Márquez, gainings
GO Gorillaz, Golf, gormless, *Goldfinger*, Goa, gopher, Gordimer, gold
DE Destiny's Child, Defy, desserts, *Devil in Disguise,* Delhi, desman, DeLillo, denarii

GEOMETRIC SEQUENCES

A **Figure 3:** the entire shape is turned on a vertical axis and the colours are inverted.
B **Figure 1:** the external shape moves to the interior and the inverse occurs. The colours are inverted. The whole shape is reduced by 50 % and repeated 4 times.
C **Figure 1:** the figure is turned 90° anticlockwise. The colour that was at the base stays the same, but the two others are inverted.
D **Figure 6:** the figure is reduced by 50 % and presented in three ways. The first stays as it was, the second turns anticlockwise 90° and is blue, the third, beneath, turns 180° and is yellow.
E **Figure 3:** the shapes and the colours are exchanged without changing position (the diamond becomes the bobbin form, and the inverse occurs, the green becomes blue, and the inverse occurs).

CUT-UP LETTERS

You could take out:
C (Baking) – H (Camber) – A (Border) – R (Repots) – L (Filing) – E (Grater) – S (Decent) – I (Nether) – X (Indeed).
You get: Charles IX of France.

CATERPILLAR

A D V A N C E
C A D A V E R
A R C A D E S
S C A R R E D
S T A R R E D
R E T R E A D
R E T R E A T

Improving your memory

Mental images

Your senses capture information which is transformed into mental images. This is how your memories are formed. You need to exercise this ability to create mental images regularly in order to improve your powers of memorisation.

Pictorial and verbal representation

First step

1. Look carefully at the nine pictures below fc
minutes and memorise them. Then cover the

Images and words

My head is full of images … and teeming with words!

What happens when information or data reaches your mind? You create mental representations of it. There are two forms of symbolic representation, one pictorial and the other verbal, which both contribute to the creation of a mental image. You usually register and recognise information **in the form of a mental picture** and simultaneously transcribe it into **verbal form**.

Being creatures endowed with language, we always put words to things. But when our experience of some new information is coloured by a strong emotion, the images imprinted on our minds are not always verbalised straight away. You see an extreme form of this phenomenon in people who have suffered a traumatic shock. They relive images and emotions over and over again but often cannot verbalise the experience for a long time afterwards.

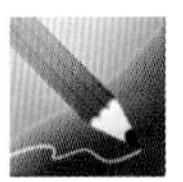

Famous people and characters

Note down all the visual and other characteristics that seem to you to represent each of the following characters.

Example: Father Christmas: white beard, red and white greatcoat, paunch, black boots, ho ho ho laughter, sledge drawn by reindeer, bell, sack bursting with presents, chimney, etc.

1. The Virgin Mary

....
....
....
....

2. Marilyn Monroe

....
....
....
....

3. Tutankhamun

....
....
....
....

4. Albert Einstein

....
....
....
....

5. Little Red Riding Hood

....
....
....
....

6. Luciano Pavarotti

....
....
....
....

7. Alfred Hitchcock

....
....
....
....

8. Julius Caesar

....
....
....
....

In this exercise, you visualised the name of each character (when you can't actually see the name before you, you might conjure up a phonetic approximation of the spelling), and then various characteristics, physical or other, contributed to the construction of a visual image. Both these aspects – verbal and iconic representation – form part of your mental image. This can be seen as incorporating your conception of the character in the absence of his or her physical being. This incredible mental activity gives symbolic reality to something you can't see before you. Either verbal or pictorial elements can predominate, depending on your knowledge of a certain subject. When you hear the name Tutankhamun, the verbal representation is probably stronger if you are not well-informed in this area. On the other hand, the pictorial representation of Father Christmas is bound to be more vivid than the verbal aspect of his image.

2. Draw them from memory in the grid below. Without doing any corrections, proceed to the second stage of the exercise.

Second step

1. Look at the pictures again for a minute, this time with their labels. Cover them again.

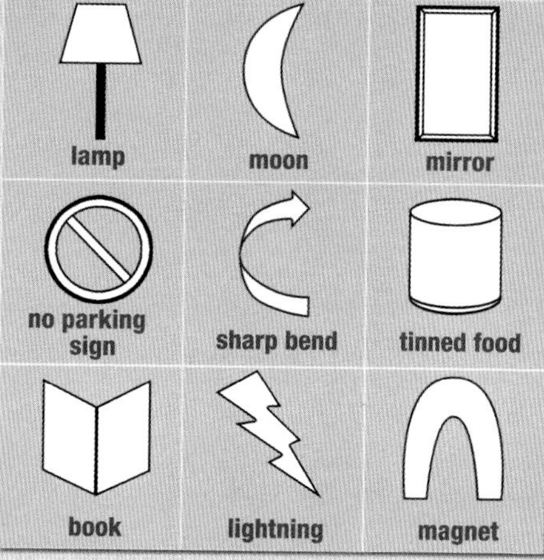

2. Draw them from memory in the grid below.

In the first part of this exercise, the information is purely visual. Pictorial representations are registered in your mind. In the second part, the data is again visual but the objects are labelled. So the mental image now has two parts, visual and verbal. You probably memorised this double representation more successfully.

Mental images, memorisation and memories

My memories are a jigsaw puzzle of mental images polished by time

Dip into your memories for a moment. You most probably have the impression of seeing a series of mental images unfolding, like photographs flitting past. When you want to retain an item of information, you rely first of all on your senses to register it. If you pay attention, you will retain not only visual but also auditory and tactile images. If you read a text you are not really interested in, without paying attention, and unmotivated by any desire to remember the contents or make use of that information in future, no mental image will be created. This information will not be committed to memory. Conversely, if these three elements are present – interest, paying attention and a wish to convey the information to others – you will form a certain number of mental images and will set in motion the process of memorisation.

The richer your mental images, the more solid the memorisation process will be. But these images are not retained in your memory in the same form, as would be the case with real photographs. They undergo a certain metamorphosis through the effects of time. When you retrieve a memory, you reassemble all these scattered elements to construct an image more or less like the original. This is how your memories are formed.

My memory and … the impression of déjà-vu

Do you wonder why you sometimes experience a fleeting impression of déjà-vu in a place you've never seen before? It's not your memory playing tricks on you, nor is it the result of mental confusion. A place you seem to recognise often has features reminiscent of some other place you have indeed visited and remember. Landscapes, in particular, are often not distinctive enough to prevent your memories of them from becoming intermingled. But the new impression usually displaces the old memories fairly quickly, and the impression of déjà-vu disappears.

A head full of images

Put a mental image to each of these words.

1. Cup	**8. Games**
2. Piano	**9. Bottle**
3. Box	**10. Lunchbox**
4. Suitcase	**11. Cushion**
5. Watch	**12. Wardrobe**
6. Painting	**13. Tie**
7. Bed	**14. Shoe**

Now write down all the words you remember, making use of all the mental images that you constructed

1.	**6.**	**11.** ....
2.	**7.**	**12.** ....
3.	**8.**	**13.** ....
4.	**9.**	**14.** ....
5.	**10.**	

The less stereotypical your representations of these words, the more evocative they will be, and the more easily you will remember them. You can enrich them with sensory associations (perfume, texture, weight, etc).

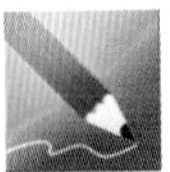

Points in common

Two words with different meanings can have one or two things in common. Find the linking word in the following word pairs by visualising each word and creating mental images of them.

Example: visualise 'pine' and 'sewing'. The element common to both is 'needle'.

The further you go in this exercise, the more you will have to enrich your mental images with additional elements. Imagine everything possible both about the object (its composition, attributes, shape, use or what it reminds you of) and the word (its use, expressions it is used in, synonyms, etc.).

Level 1

pen-octopus = ink
shoe-chair = ...
windmill-yacht = ...
zebra-op art = ...
duvet-bird = ...
spectacles-astronomy = ...
hair-tree = ...
carpet-sheep = ...
steps-mountain = ...

Level 2

mugshot-jail = criminal
disinfectant-apéritif = ...
banana-press = ...
crab-salt = ...
bicycle-cheese = ...
cock-mountain = ...
fish-caterpillar = ...
shoe-steak = ...
food-multiplication = ...

Level 3

knot-bag = husband
computer-brain = ...
phrase-money = ...
palm-calendar = ...
butterfly-tank = ...
peak-syringe = ...
ear-carpenter = ...
elbow-thief = ...

Solution p.337

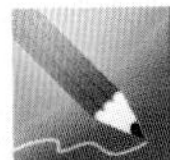

Personal and collective images

What image comes spontaneously to mind when you hear the following words? Do this exercise with several players, each answering in turn. Then compare the different mental images, establishing similarities and differences.

Dog Force
Willpower
Work
Train

My memory and ... my travels

When you find yourself in an unfamiliar place, don't panic: look carefully at your map of the town or your road atlas. Orient yourself by locating major landmarks such as the principal thoroughfares, crossroads and one-way streets, and then try to form a mental image of your surroundings. As a general rule, always start from an overall view of the map before focusing on specific details, as here too the memory needs order and structure to function most efficiently.

Building

Friendship

Communication

Flower

Hand

Car

Concrete nouns readily create a variety of mental images which vary from person to person. The word 'flower', for example, evokes for some the image of a rose, for others, a tulip or even a little girl dressed in a frilly skirt. Some words, however, produce minimal differences in representation and can be regarded as generating personal and collective mental images. The word 'cowboy', for example, for most people conjures the image of a wide-legged man in a stetson, wearing leather chaps over denim jeans, checked shirt, boots with Cuban heels and spurs and a low-slung holster with a gun in it. The creation of mental images of abstract words is more complex and unpredictable. This is why we resort to collective images with symbolic representations: a pair of scales for justice, a dove for peace, and a heart for love, for example.

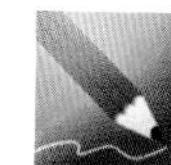

Hotchpotch of letters

Look carefully at these letters: the letters of the same colour make up a word. When you have worked out the anagrams, memorise the words, using mental images as aids, and then cover them.

O C A I N R

E T H R B

C A P N C D N

R I S A I E G

I C A B U

Now answer the following questions:

1. Which word was written in:

RED ....

GREEN ....

PINK ....

ORANGE ....

BLUE ....

2. What common theme links these 5 words?

....

Solution p.337

Colourful images

A colour can evoke mental images of specific objects and even, at times, of expressions. You have five minutes to find seven objects in each of these colours, or objects we attribute these colours to, and three expressions in which they are used.

	Objects	Expressions
White	....	....
	....	....
Yellow	....	....
	....	....
	....	....
	....	....

Solution p.338

Word pairs
Here are eight pairs of words associated at random.
You have to remember them in three stages.

Step 1: Formulate a sentence including each word pair and then create a mental image of this sentence.
Example: EDITOR/COMPUTER.
An editor works on her computer.
Close your eyes and imagine the scene.

Step 2: Complete the word pairs, and then cover them.

Step 3: Put all the word pairs back in the right place and the same order.

Step 1	Step 2	Step 3
cannon / island	.... / island	.... / ....
market / tarpaulin	market /	.... / ....
peanut / macaroon	.... / macaroon	.... / ....
violet / hat	violet /	.... / ....
song / hammer	.... / hammer	.... / ....
swing / hook	swing /	.... / ....
lid / bible	.... / bible	.... / ....
telephone / painting	telephone /	.... / ....

The placing method

The technique of 'placing' is a mnemonic strategy, or way of remembering, that is closely associated with the process of forming a mental image.

The Greek poet, Simonides of Ceos, is credited with being the first person to use the mnemonic method of organised spatial representation. He was the sole survivor when a building collapsed and buried those attending a banquet, and so it was up to him to remember where each guest was sitting so the victims could be identified. Noting how he had retained a vivid image of each person there, he then conceived the 'placing' technique.

The Roman statesman, Cicero, too made use of different areas of the forum to 'place' different sections of the speech he was preparing to deliver. He undertook a visual tour of the forum as he spoke, allocating various topics of his speech, arranged in sequence, to places along his route through different parts of the forum. This explains why he always started his speeches with the words, 'In the first place, I will talk to you about...'

As in the example illustrated on the opposite page, you can work out your own method of 'placing' by walking around your home or room.

My memory and ... my things

The placing method can be very helpful in remembering where you have put your things. If you frequently lose your car keys at home, for example, associate these keys with a place where you can always leave them – the drawer where you put your front-door keys, for example. Or, to find the umbrella that you stand near the door, create a mental image of an umbrella stand.

First stage: work out your route

- Select a certain number of 'places' – fixed items in a room – following a set path determined by the distribution of the objects in the room or rooms. Now number them. In the example provided, 'place' number 1 is the vase on the table at the entrance; 2 is the coffee table with its ceramic plate, etc.
- Choose (and don't change) the direction in which you will move around the room.
- Go over the set route in your mind, so that you can easily remember the numbered places in the right order.

Second stage: position 'things to remember' strategically along your 'route'

In your mind, place the items you want to remember on each 'object-stop', and try to establish a link between the two. At object-stop 1 (the vase on the table), we have mentally positioned a bottle of mineral water, because water is the element they have in common. At object-stop 3, the sofa in the living room, cheese is the associated object (we pose for family photos on the sofa and have to produce smiles in response to 'cheese!'). The more imaginative the link you establish between the two elements, the better you will remember them. Visualise the link clearly. Do this for all the items you have to remember.

If you have a shopping list to remember, do a mental survey of your home while visualising what you will have to buy at each stage. In the shop, you will repeat this survey in your mind to ensure that you haven't forgotten anything.

This method might seem tedious. In fact, it entails a form of mental gymnastics that is quite demanding but does enable you to remember a great many items – far more than is usually possible. You can make use of this mental survey in many ways, to remember all kinds of things (for example, words, books, shopping lists, stages of a journey, tasks to be done, etc).

Rooms/ objects-stages	My shopping list
1. Entrance/vase	Mineral water
2. Living room/table with earthenware plate	Apples
3. Living room/sofa	Cheese
4. Living room/red armchairs	Tomatoes
5. Living room/desk	Envelopes
6. Kitchen/ sink	Sponge
7. Kitchen/ table	Paper towel
8. Kitchen/ fridge	Eggs
9. Bedroom/ white bedlinen	Milk
10. Bedroom/ carpet	Ham
11. Bathroom/ radio on wash stand	Batteries
12. Laundry room/ washing machine	Washing powder

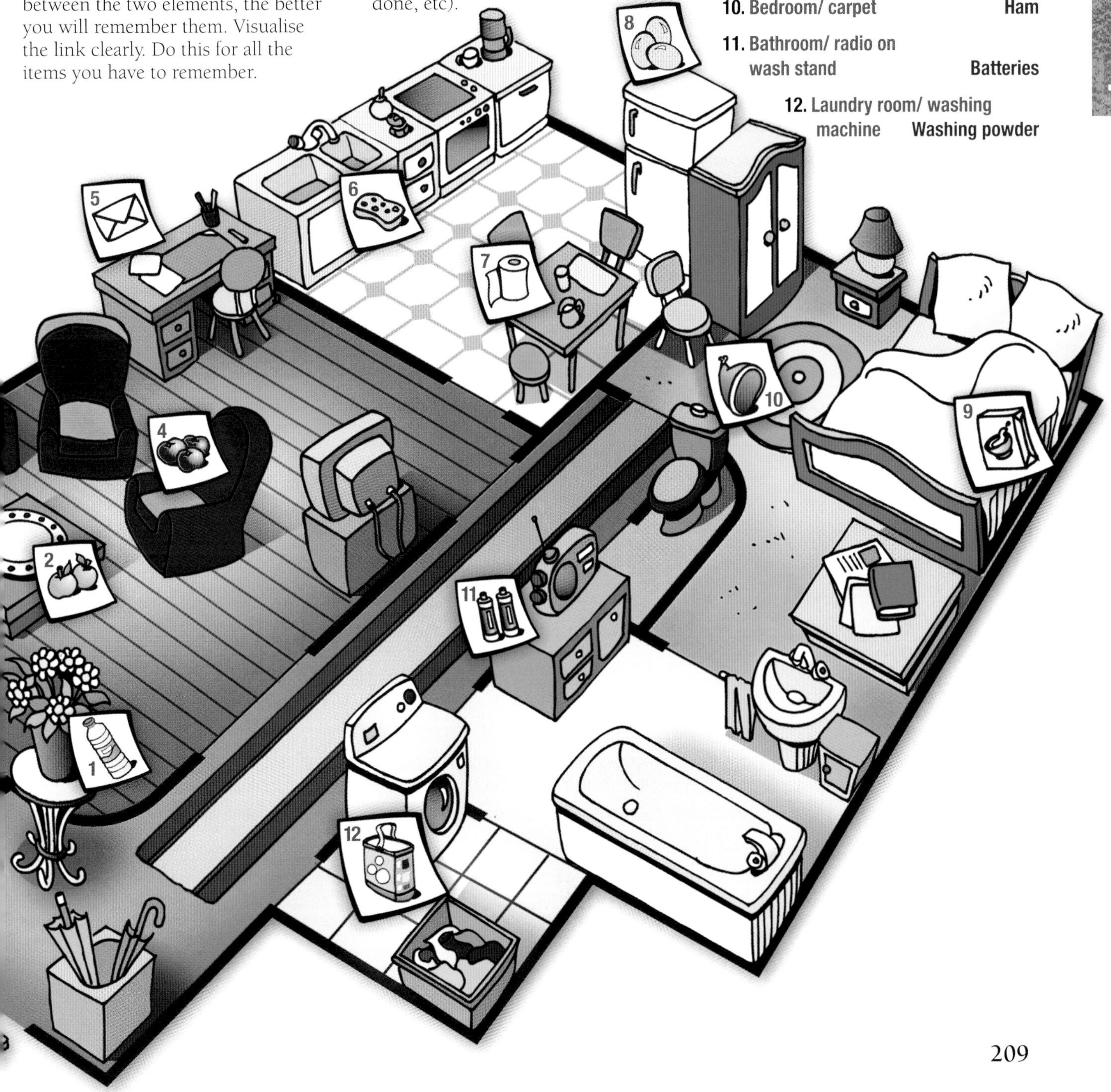

Improving your memory

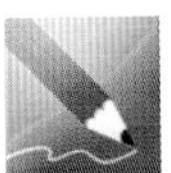

The apartment

1. Look at the picture on the right and memorise it using the placing strategy. Describe the apartment aloud, in great detail, pinpointing all objects and establishing links between them and fixed items – create points of reference if there are not enough of them – and construct a mental image for each of these associations. Mark out the apartment in squares, as if you were an interior decorator, and work out a route.

2. Close your eyes and visualise the apartment with all its accessories: revisit it mentally.

3. Cover the picture and then move immediately to the next picture.

4. Look at the new picture and list five displaced objects, five newly introduced objects, and five missing objects.

1. Displaced objects

....

....

....

....

....

2. Added objects

....

....

....

....

....

3. Removed objects

....

....

....

....

....

Solution p.338

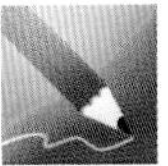

20 names for a champion

Three or four participants can play this game.

1. Each player makes a mental list of five famous people.
2. The first player says his or her five names very slowly. The others have three minutes in which to memorise them using the placing method. They must mentally create a route around the room establishing a link between each of the five names and an object in the room. All the players must remember these first five names. Next, the second player has a turn to give his or her five names. Continue until all players have had a turn.
3. When all the players have contributed their five names, each player has to write down on a piece of paper as many names as he or she can remember. Give each player one point per name recalled, with a bonus of 10 points for the player who remembers the names in their original order. The winner is the player who achieves the most points.

Tip: when applying your mnemonic placing technique, you can allocate names to places throughout the room for each series of names, or you can restrict yourself to a small section of the room at a time.

A tour of your neighbourhood

Write two lists of 10 words each.
To memorise these 20 words, work out a route around your neighbourhood where you will choose 10 reference points. Link each one with one word from list 1 and one from list 2. Reread everything, then put the exercise aside.

List 1	List 2
1.	1. ....
2.	2. ....
3.	3. ....
4.	4. ....
5.	5. ....
6.	6. ....
7.	7. ....
8.	8. ....
9.	9. ....
10.	10. ....

Three or four hours later,

try to rewrite both lists and then record the number of words you remembered in the table at the end of this exercise.

List 1	List 2
1.	1. ....
2.	2. ....
3.	3. ....
4.	4. ....
5.	5. ....
6.	6. ....
7.	7. ....
8.	8. ....
9.	9. ....
10.	10. ....

24 hours later,

try once again to rewrite the lists. Note the number of words you have remembered.

List 1	List 2
1.	1. ....
2.	2. ....
3.	3. ....
4.	4. ....
5.	5. ....
6.	6. ....
7.	7. ....
8.	8. ....
9.	9. ....
10.	10. ....

One week later,

do it again. Try to recall the words on both lists. Note how many words you remembered.

List 1	List 2
1.	1. ....
2.	2. ....
3.	3. ....
4.	4. ....
5.	5. ....
6.	6. ....
7.	7. ....
8.	8. ....
9.	9. ....
10.	10. ....

Number of words recalled	List 1	List 2
The same day	....	....
The next day	....	....
A week later	....	....

The use of the placing method almost certainly enabled you to remember a great number of words. Through the connections established between the reference points and the words you had to remember, you could structure the information by means of a guiding thread, so facilitating the retrieval process as well. Even if this method differs from your usual approach, try it. It will exercise your powers of association and visualisation.

Logic and structure

Not everyone can think logically. And we don't all have the same logical ability. Nevertheless, the memory has everything to gain from the process of reflection and reasoning that enables you to find coherence in words, figures and images. By structuring your mental activity intelligently, you present your memory with what it needs: order.

Test Are you more intuitive or more logical?

Answer the following questions by circling the letter that fits you best.

1. When you meet someone for the first time ...
- **a.** You keep track of your emotions, both positive and negative.
- **b.** You prefer to get to know them better before forming an opinion.

2. Which game would you rather play?
- **a.** Monopoly
- **b.** Scrabble

3. When looking at a work of art ...
- **a.** Your impressions are enough for you.
- **b.** You feel the need to understand it.

4. When you buy books, you prefer ...
- **a.** Novels
- **b.** Essays

5. When you have a dish to prepare ...
- **a.** You improvise a little
- **b.** You follow the recipe scrupulously

6. Products are on promotion at the supermarket ...
- **a.** You simply walk past
- **b.** You let yourself be tempted.

7. You are walking around an unfamiliar town ...
- **a.** You wander at will, guided by inspiration.
- **b.** You prefer to walk with a map or guidebook in your hand.

Count the number of a. answers and b. answers.

*** At least 5 a's.**
You are one of those who rely primarily on intuition when they have important decisions to take. Let us hope for your sake that it continues to guide you well. But don't forget also to weigh the pros and cons, as intuition can sometimes be misleading!

*** At least 5 b's.**
Unlike people who rely on intuition, you need to analyse, to consider things before taking a decision, because you don't like to feel deprived of your reasoning ability. You prefer to be rational at the expense of your creativity. But be careful – don't try to master every situation at all costs. Accept the unexpected. The brain is an organ that needs flexibility to function to the best of its ability.

*** The numbers are balanced (4 a's and 3 b's or 3 a's and 4 b's).**
Your wish to understand your environment so as to be best adapted to it has not closed the door to your desires and your enjoyment of the unexpected. You can 'let yourself go' in the right circumstances. This is likely to give rise to internal conflict, but it's worth it.

One or many forms of logic?

My way of reasoning differs from my friend's. It doesn't matter, if we both find the right answer!

Being logical implies **reasoning according to certain rules.** Both deduction (where a conclusion is drawn from a collection of premises) and induction (where general principles are drawn from particular cases) enable you to find appropriate solutions to a fair number of problems. Since the first half of the 20th century, when psychology set out to explain and measure intelligence, the primary focus for measuring IQ (Intelligence Quotient) has been testing logical and structuring ability.

Mathematics traditionally embodies this capacity to **think logically.** Numerous studies in this field have demonstrated that we don't all set out with the same resources. Some have great ability in this area, others have less: not everyone is endowed with a flair for maths!

It is during childhood that the basic elements of logic are acquired. **All forms of logic are derived from a specific learning process** – such

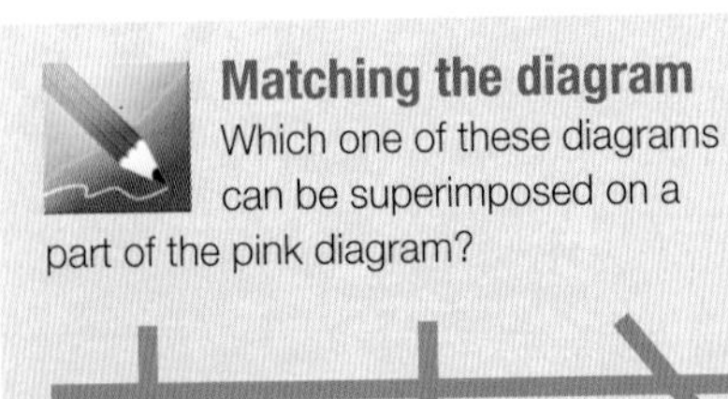

Matching the diagram
Which one of these diagrams can be superimposed on a part of the pink diagram?

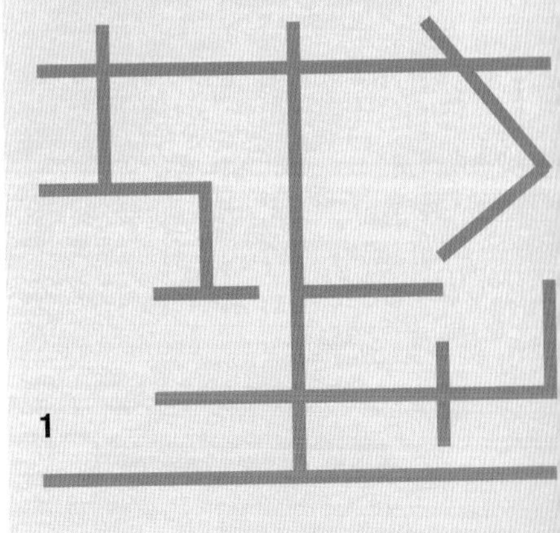

My memory and...
complicated words

Why are complicated and technical words so difficult to remember? Because you probably don't hear them frequently. In order to remember them, look up their meaning and if possible write down their definitions in simple language, in your own words. Then find a possible synonym, a more accessible one. Finally, find an opportunity to use them in conversation!

as language, construction games, reading, arithmetic, etc. – hence the vital role of teachers.

As a child, then as an adolescent, you imitate your mode of reasoning and develop your ability to think rationally in the framework of various disciplines, each of which is based on a set of established rules on which a specific logic is founded – the logic of language, construction, numbers, etc. The degree to which you are comfortable with each of these disciplines depends on the way in which they were inculcated.

This basic knowledge of rules and methods is subsequently further expanded through your first contacts with the realities of the professional world and then by lessons acquired though your life experience. And so, faced with a task to accomplish, you use all the knowledge you have acquired to find your **own personal organisational logic.** In everyday life, various trains of thought can bring us to the same result. Everyone has thus forged their own logic and way of resolving problems. Any method will appear coherent to the person adopting it, even though it can seem peculiar to others.

The following exercises are designed for you to apply and develop various forms of logic.

Discs

Which discs need to be superimposed to make the one in the centre? ?

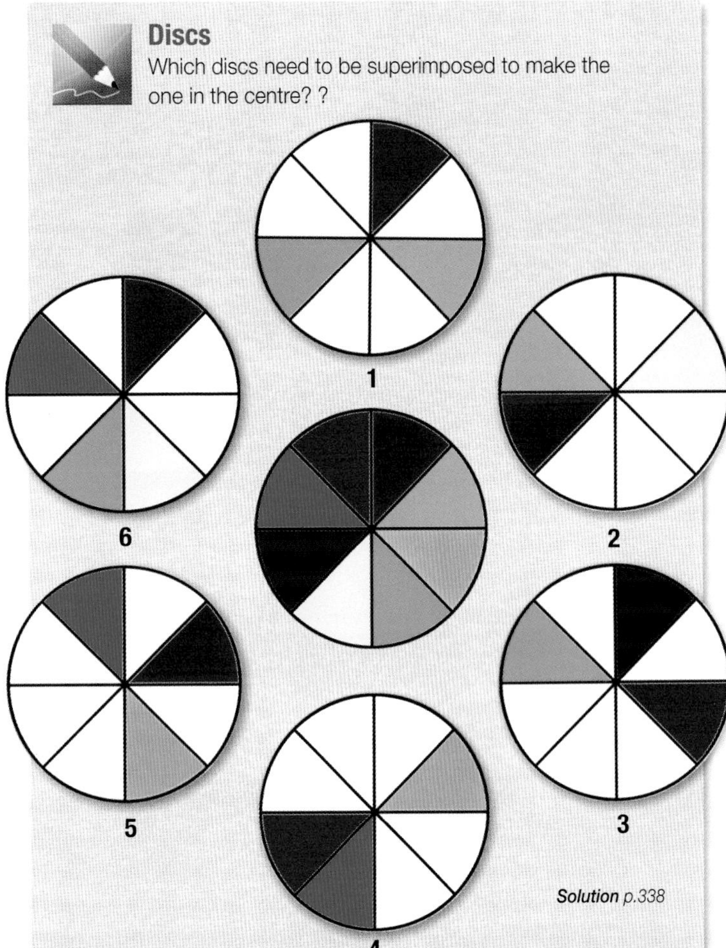

Solution p.338

These two exercises are designed to make you put into practice that ability to compare and match shapes – to visualise basic shapes, and by deduction identify the right and wrong pieces – that is acquired in early childhood. When a child tries to put a cube in a square hole, it is this kind of logic that is being developed. The perception of forms precedes the logic of construction that the child will apply later by creating basic shapes out of building blocks or anything else.

Solution p.338

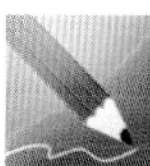

The dance of the cubes

The following shapes are made up of cubes piled one on top of the other. Look at them carefully and count the number of cubes. Watch out – some of them are hidden!

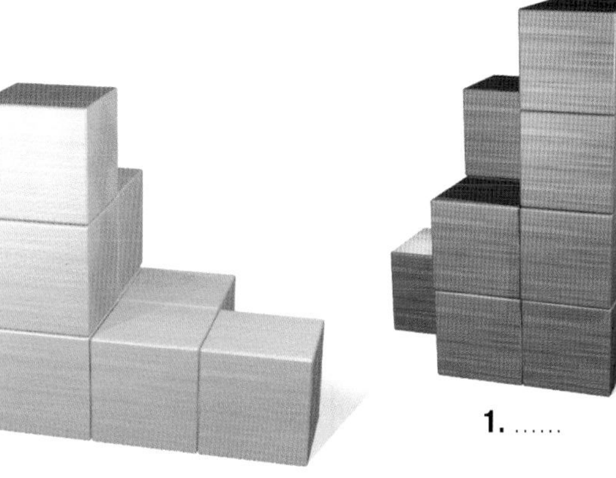

1. ......

Example : 8 cubes

2. ......

This exercise demands the neurological maturity that enables you to form a mental picture of an object in three dimensions. (A child younger than eight couldn't do it.) The perception of a cube in the background enables you to deduce that another one is hidden there. Anyone who is used to working with three-dimensional spaces, an architect for example, will be perfectly comfortable with this type of exercise. But anyone could easily develop this logic of construction.

3. ......

4. ......

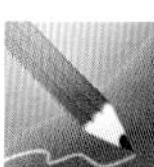

The dance of the letters

1. Going from left to right, choose one letter per cube to form the names of three Australian cities of eight letters each.

Solution p.338

2. Find the names of eight fruits that are jumbled up, two in each line.

1. **b e l n a p a n a p a** ....
2. **w a p t i r o c a p w a p** ....
3. **p e h a c r e p a** ....
4. **g o r n a m o g a n e** ....

Solution p.338

The logic of word construction comes from the early stages of learning to read and write, the same period when you acquire the ability to construct sentences. If you need to learn a foreign language that is based on Latin, like French or Italian, for example, and your own language does not have the same base, you will have to learn a different logical system of sentence construction (syntax).

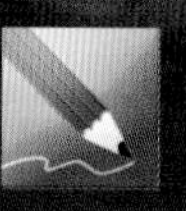

The animal world

Six animal lovers have banded together to form a zoo. Each of them has a favourite animal, which will of course be there on opening day. It's up to you to identify everyone's pet animal!

The figures on the left indicate the number of favourite animals that feature in each row. The figures on the right indicate the number of favourite animals placed under the name of the right person.
A tip to start with: cross out the animals in the fifth row, because no favourite animal features there. Then deduce ...

To complete the logigram, a classic exercise in logic that puts your powers of association and deduction to work, you need to concentrate and be constantly alert throughout. Cross out the words as you go along until the answers become obvious.

Solution p.338

5. ......

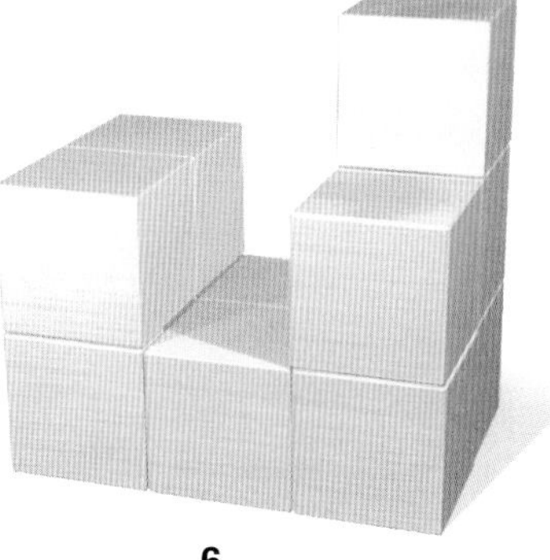

6. ......

Solution p.338

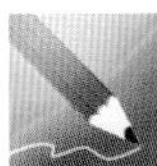

Logical sequence

In a logical sequence, you have to first establish the link between the elements and deduce a rule from that. Apply this rule and you will find the missing element.

Solution p.338

1. Complete the sequence by filling in square **D.**

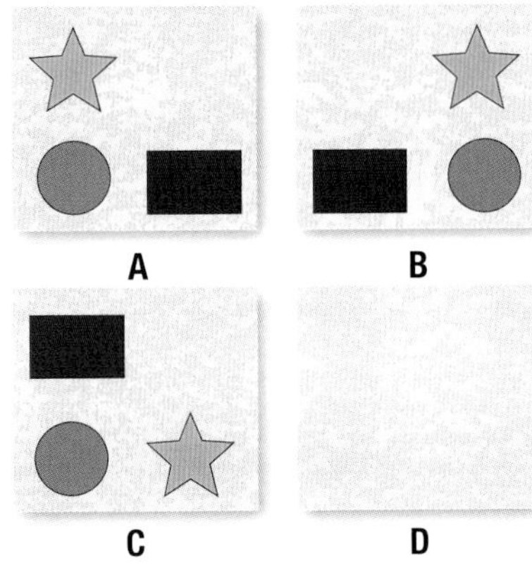

2. Six of these seven numbers have something in common. Which?

5 - 2 - 7 - 14 - 28 - 52 - 56

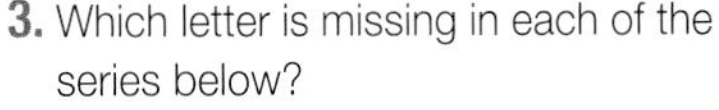

3. Which letter is missing in each of the series below?

Example: M - K - I - ...... - E

The answer is **G**: count backwards, two letters at a time:

M (L) K (J) I (H) G (F) E

1. **A - D - B - E - ......**
2. **O - P - R - ...... - U**
3. **T - ...... - R - Q - P**
4. **A - E - ...... - M - Q**
5. **A - E - B - F - C - G - ...... - H**
6. **A - E - C - F - J - H - K - ...... - M - P - T - R**

Success in the search for a logical sequence also depends on the ability and interests of each individual. The logic of forms will probably seem easier if you have good visual perception; a love of juggling with figures is necessary for finding the sequence of numbers, and a love of counting certainly helps when completing the sequence of letters.

	ERIC	LEE	MARK	LUCY	CHARLES	JUSTINE	
2	WOLF	PENGUIN	PINK FLAMINGO	DROMEDARY	POLAR BEAR	OSTRICH	2
1	ZEBRA	ELEPHANT	PARROT	TIGER	LEMUR	LLAMA	1
3	WOLF	LION	DROMEDARY	PINK FLAMINGO	OSTRICH	SEAL	2
1	GIRAFFE	ZEBRA	OSTRICH	LEMUR	LLAMA	PINK FLAMINGO	0
0	PARROT	PENGUIN	RHINOCEROS	DROMEDARY	LEMUR	TIGER	0
2	ZEBRA	TIGER	LION	PINK FLAMINGO	LLAMA	GIRAFFE	1
1	PENGUIN	PARROT	LEMUR	GIRAFFE	RHINOCEROS	TIGER	1
3	LION	GIRAFFE	ZEBRA	LEMUR	SEAL	LLAMA	0

Logic, structure and memory

I think, I understand, I reason, I find an order. That's it – I remember!

The ability to think logically is a generally recognised indication of intelligence, but does it also provide proof of a good memory?

The exercises in this module encourage you to think, to reason, to establish connections so as to find logical solutions. They seem more directed at developing the capacity for abstract thought than for memory as such. Indeed, you could show great ability in the sphere of abstract reasoning or numerical logic and have a good memory in this field while having a bad memory for other kinds of information. Conversely, you could feel perfectly confident coping with activities relying on good memory and then useless when it comes to pure logic. There again, everyone is different …

Nevertheless, the more you apply your mind, the greater your chance of understanding. And **a thorough understanding of information promotes good retention.** At the same time you are maintaining and developing your powers of concentration. Reflection and concentration combine to maintain a high level of cerebral activity. But, most importantly, **logical reasoning trains the mind to impose structure on information,** that is, to establish order and meaning according to certain rules. And **the memory needs order**. For example, without it it would be difficult for you to remember the combination of lines in the following drawing…

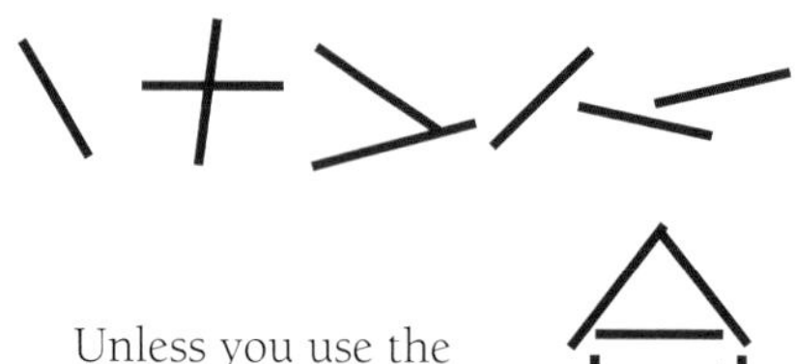

Unless you use the eight lines to compose this shape:

The same principle applies to words, images and lists. You need only find some kind of order or logic enabling you to impose structure on the information to make it meaningful. It will then be more easily retained in your memory. And if knowledge has already been stored in accordance with a sound logical system, when any new problem arises the structure of this data in the memory will be used to work out an appropriate solution. If you exercise your logical and reasoning faculty, your well-trained brain will serve you well not only in intellectual operations but also in everyday life. And your memory can only improve as a result.

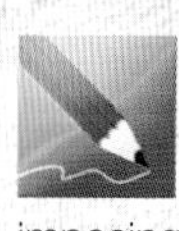

A script in images

Working out a scenario, as in making a film, implies imposing meaning on a succession of images. Using these 15 images, work out the script of a short film.

1. Write down the planned sequence of scenes.

....
....
....
....
....
....
....
....
....
....
....
....
....
....
....

From jumbled words to a sentence

Here is a collection of jumbled words from which you have to construct a sentence.

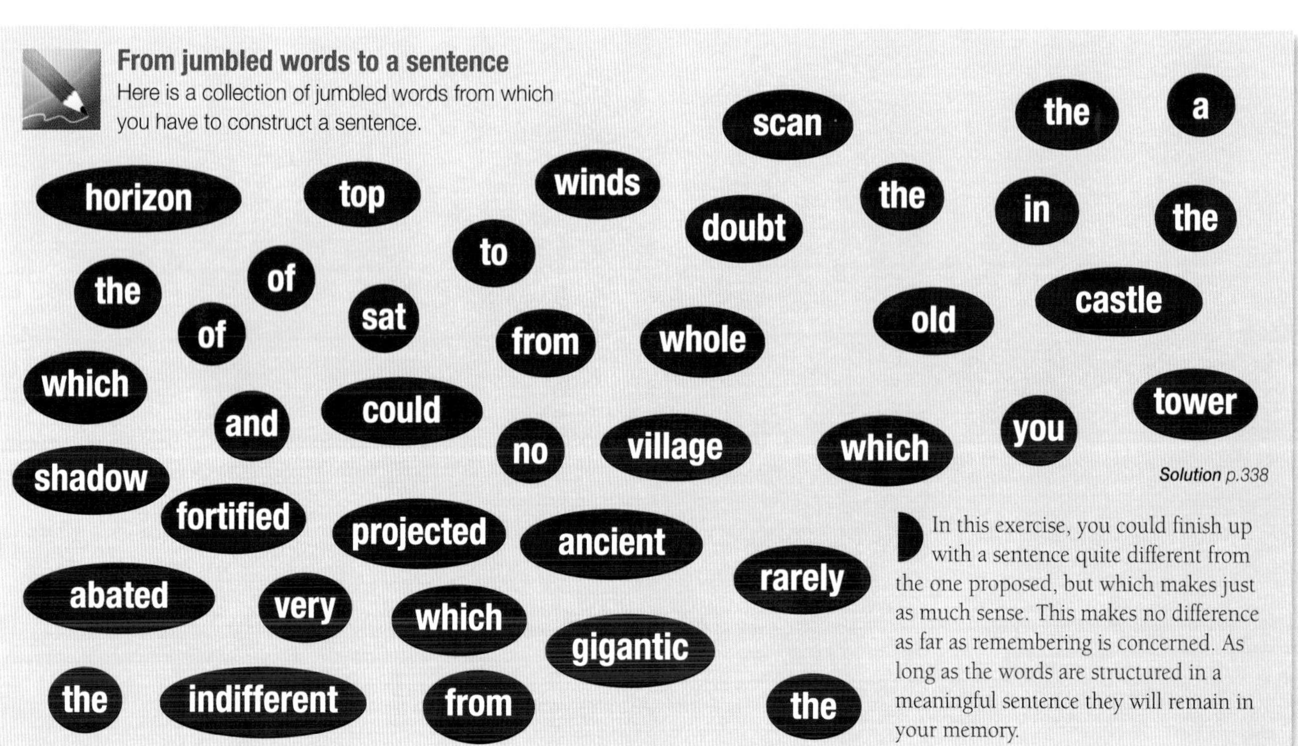

Solution p.338

In this exercise, you could finish up with a sentence quite different from the one proposed, but which makes just as much sense. This makes no difference as far as remembering is concerned. As long as the words are structured in a meaningful sentence they will remain in your memory.

2. Then cover the illustrations and your notes, and write down the names of the different objects in the order of their appearance in your story.

1. ....
2. ....
3. ....
4. ....
5. ....
6. ....
7. ....
8. ....
9. ....
10. ....
11. ....
12. ....
13. ....
14. ....
15. ....

Jigsaw puzzle

Find the nine pieces that make up this puzzle, rejecting the one that doesn't fit, and fit the pieces back in the right places.

1 2 3 4 5 6 7 8 9 10

Solution p 338

Number sequences

1. Work out the logical principle determining the sequence of these numbers and then find the seventh.

11 - 17 - 25 - 35 - 47 - 61 - ......

2. What is the missing number in this sequence?

7 - 23 - 71 - ...... - 647

3. What are the missing numbers in the empty blocks?

4. What is the missing number in this square?

2	4	5	1
7	13	14	8
9	21	16	9
9	3	2	......

Solution p.338

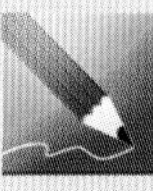

Shape sequences

1. Work out the logical principle determining the sequence of the following geometric figures and then draw the missing figures.

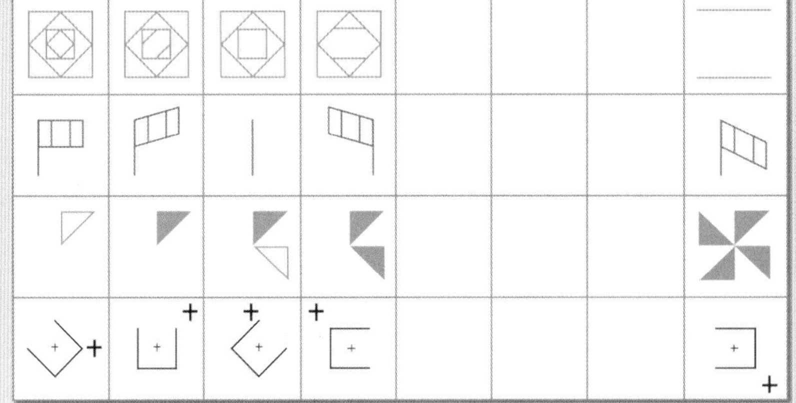

2. Look at this sequence of five cards.

Which among these four cards continues the logical sequence?

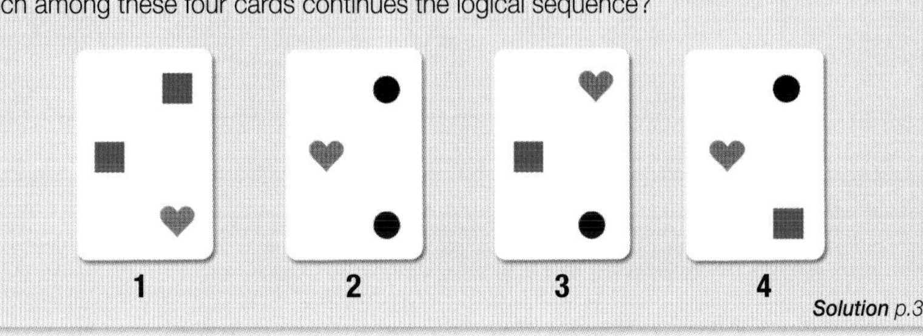

Solution p.338

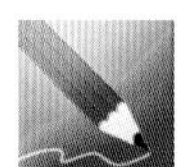

Palindromes

A palindrome is a word, a line of verse, a sentence or a combination of numbers that can be read both forwards and backwards. When making a palindrome, you need not take punctuation or spaces between words into account.

Example:
A common noun = radar
A verb = bob
A name = Eve
A town = Laval
A phrase = Able was I ere I saw Elba
A date = 10.02.2001

Now it is your turn to find two palindromes for each of these categories:

Common nouns ....
....

Verbs ....
....

Names ....
....

Towns ....
....

Phrases ....
....

Dates ....
....

Solution p.338

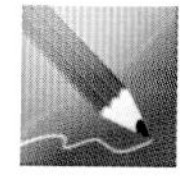

Film sequence

Find the titles of these 10 films, using the letters already in place. They are all European and American films, except for one. Which is it? Before filling in the spaces, remind yourself of the titles of great film classics.

Example:

T_ _ _ _ _ _ _ _ e o_

t_ _

r_ _ _r K_ _ _

= The Bridge on the river Kwai

Solution p.338

The sound of music ...

In his youth, Eddy was a trumpeter in four groups – the Funnies, the Jacobs, the Rockers and the Cats. Help him to remember the order in which these groups were formed and the number of musicians in each (four, five, six or seven).

Clues:

- The **JACOBS** was the biggest group and the first to appear on the scene.
- The fourth group, which was not called the **CATS,** consisted of six musicians.
- Eddy remembers that after leaving the **FUNNIES,** which had two musicians less than the first group, he joined the **CATS.**

Tip: Follow the clues step by step, making use of each piece of information. Formulate hypotheses by placing crosses in the appropriate columns: you can erase them if necessary in the course of your deductive progress.

Solution p.338

	Group 1	Group 2	Group 3	Group 4	4 musicians	5 musicians	6 musicians	7 musicians
FUNNIES								
JACOBS								
ROCKERS								
CATS								

Organising and categorising information

The semantic memory's natural organisational ability enables it to retain existing stocks of knowledge while continuing to store new information. To ensure long-term retention, you would benefit greatly if you consciously developed strategies of organisation and categorisation.

Order in everything: associate and consolidate

One of the key elements in memorisation is using a specific system to impose order on information. In this way you will link up new information more easily with knowledge that is already in place in your memory. Confronted with an influx of diverse information, you therefore need to **impose some kind of order where it is lacking.**

Grouping things together is one way to impose order. Take, for example, a telephone number made up of 10 digits: 0-1-8-5-9-6-3-2-8-7. Regrouping the digits in pairs gives you only five elements to remember, that is, 01-85-96-32-87. But you can also try a regrouping of two digits twice followed by three digits twice – 01-05-963-287 – which gives you only four elements to remember.

In the same way, when you have to remember several series of facts, it is better to start by establishing groups. If you have to name the bones of the skeleton, for example, it would be more efficient to start with the bones of the skull, then the thorax, then those of the upper limbs and so on, rather than citing them unsystematically.

What a story!

Mr. X decided to go on holiday. But he had a strange experience, which is illustrated here in a series of pictures presented in random order. You have to piece the story together so you can relate it to his sister, who has not had confirmation of his arrival at his planned holiday destination. Notice all the relevant details that will enable you to put these pictures in the right order to understand the ramifications of Mr X's curious adventure.

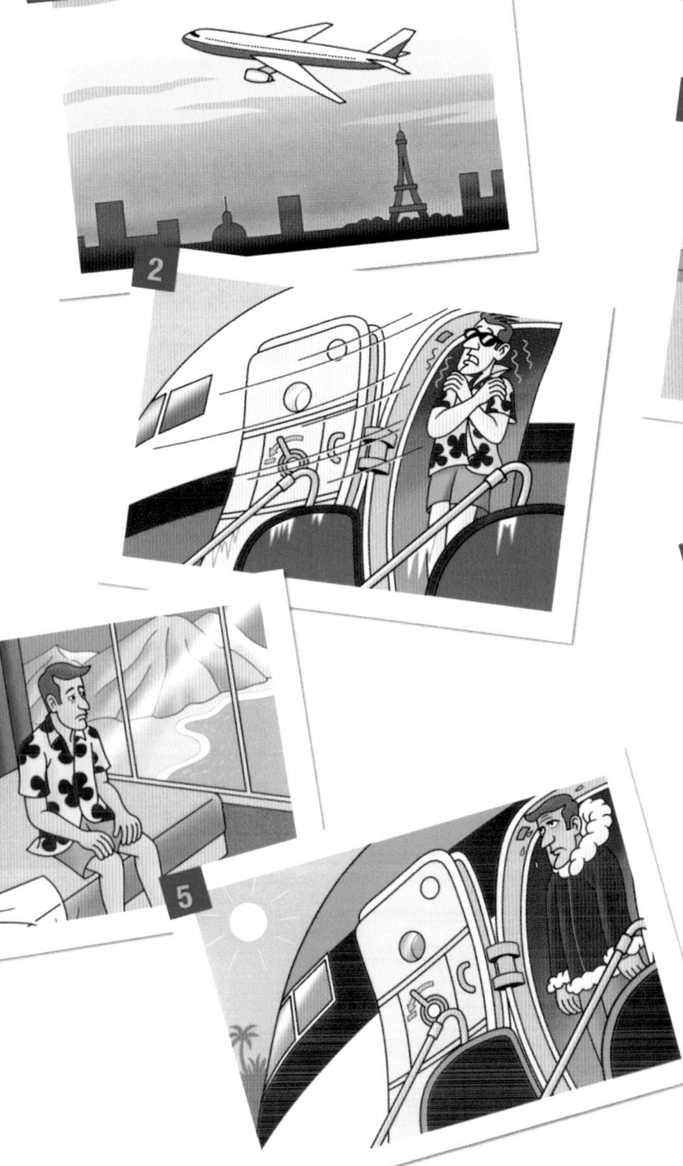

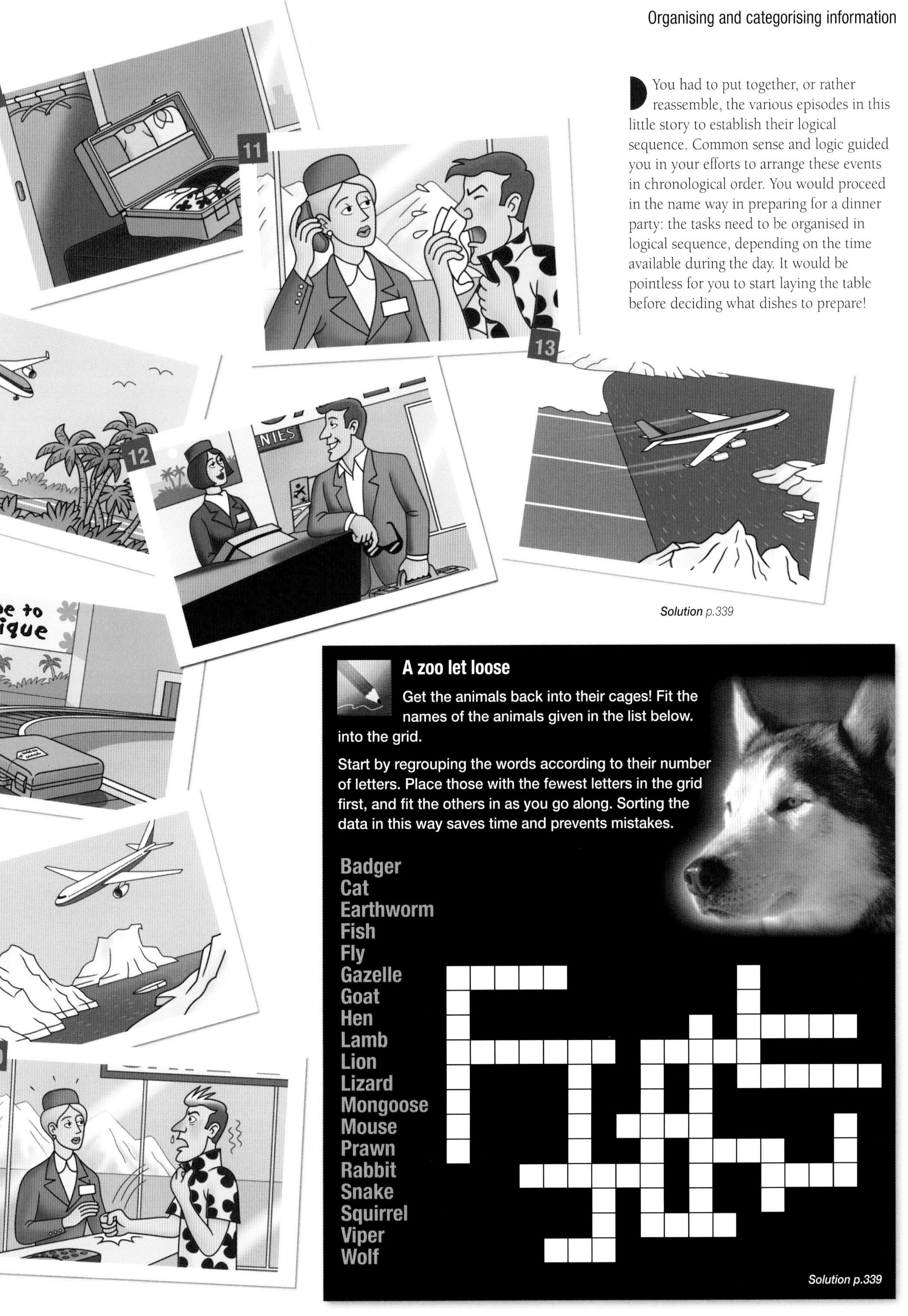

You had to put together, or rather reassemble, the various episodes in this little story to establish their logical sequence. Common sense and logic guided you in your efforts to arrange these events in chronological order. You would proceed in the name way in preparing for a dinner party: the tasks need to be organised in logical sequence, depending on the time available during the day. It would be pointless for you to start laying the table before deciding what dishes to prepare!

Solution p.339

A zoo let loose

Get the animals back into their cages! Fit the names of the animals given in the list below. into the grid.

Start by regrouping the words according to their number of letters. Place those with the fewest letters in the grid first, and fit the others in as you go along. Sorting the data in this way saves time and prevents mistakes.

Badger
Cat
Earthworm
Fish
Fly
Gazelle
Goat
Hen
Lamb
Lion
Lizard
Mongoose
Mouse
Prawn
Rabbit
Snake
Squirrel
Viper
Wolf

Solution p.339

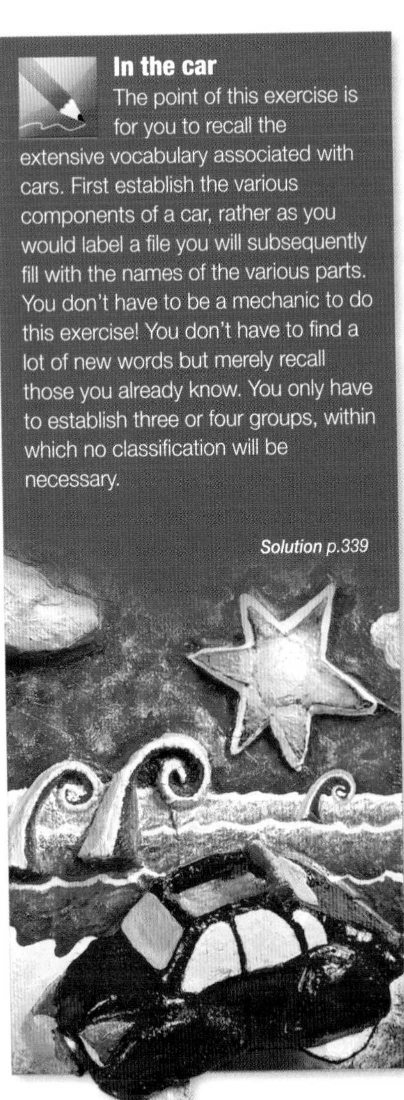

In the car

The point of this exercise is for you to recall the extensive vocabulary associated with cars. First establish the various components of a car, rather as you would label a file you will subsequently fill with the names of the various parts. You don't have to be a mechanic to do this exercise! You don't have to find a lot of new words but merely recall those you already know. You only have to establish three or four groups, within which no classification will be necessary.

Solution p.339

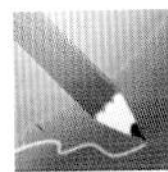

Guided tour

You have to take a friend on a tour of this area; look carefully at the map below and memorise it.

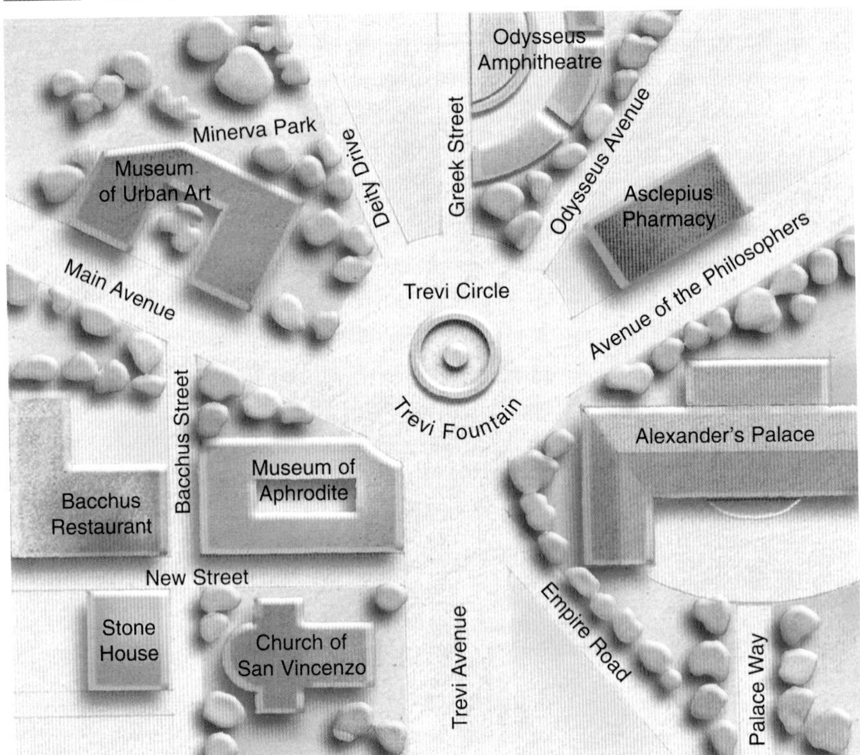

Cover the map and fill in the following places on the blank map below: **Minerva Park; Museum of Urban Art; Odysseus Amphitheatre; Asclepius Pharmacy; Trevi Circle; Alexander's Palace; Stone House; Museum of Aphrodite.**

To do this, work out a logical route that will ensure that you include everything. Constructing a visual survey of this nature is a good way to organise this kind of information and memorise it.

My memory and ... my collection

Making a collection of some sort encourages you to do research, gives you a focus and stimulates your interest in a specific subject. And whatever their age, collectors are enthusiastic about developing a really outstanding collection. This encourages them to maintain contact with their peers and meet new people. These are all positive factors, and collectors often have very good memories. So it is beneficial to pursue your interests and establish a good collection, with the proviso of course that it doesn't become your sole interest in life!

Choosing sound criteria

It is essential to choose sound criteria when you are deciding how to classify the information you want to remember. To ensure that you don't forget anything on your shopping list, for example, grouping the articles in accordance with their position on the shop shelves works well. You could also group various elements together if they are similar in nature.

If you can't establish appropriate categories you have to resort to a different mnemonic strategy. You might have to adopt criteria of varying degrees of precision depending on the kind of information you need to retain. But don't be too hard on yourself – studies of memory and categorisation have shown that it is preferable to limit yourself to seven categories.

30 words

Read this list of 30 words very carefully. Work out how to classify them in terms of certain categories and write those headings down on a piece of paper.

bread	**salad**	**trout**	**orange**
sheep shed	**kennel**	**ant hill**	**stable**
chest	**elbow**	**apple**	**foot**
den	**haunches**	**nose**	**neck**
burrow	**poultry**	**head**	**femur**
finger	**croissant**	**stomach**	**flour**
soup	**cheese**	**steak**	
pen	**tomato**	**cucumber**	

Cover this list and your notes.
Write down all the words you can remember.

You were probably surprised to find how many words you were able to remember. By establishing that certain words belong in the same subject areas you can classify them in categories. In this exercise, you can group together words referring to food, different dwellings or habitat, and parts of the human body. Putting them into three categories in this way made it easier to remember them. This method enables you to recall 16-20 words and can be used for up to 50 words. In the latter case, it is better not to have more than seven categories. If you added any words that were not on the original list, ask yourself the following questions:

- Did you read the words carefully enough, paying attention to each one and forming a mental image of the word?
- Do the words you added or left out have any particular emotional connotations for you? If so, what are they?

Points in common

1. Look at these 28 pictures. Find links between them that enable you to make seven groups of four elements sharing a common theme.

2. Now look at these 50 pictures. In one minute, and without looking back, find those that featured on the previous page.

Solution p. 339

Initials

Write coherent sentences using words starting with the following initials. Punctuation can be used.

Solution p.339

Example::

A............ **C**............ **J**............ **D**............ **F**............

Ask **C**athy, **J**ustin **D**ances **F**antastically.
Aunt **C**hristine **J**ust **D**rives **F**ast
A Currant **J**elly **D**resses up **F**ish

L............ **T**............ **E**............ **R**............ **S**............

L............ **P**............ **V**............ **S**............ **M**............

L............ **M**............ **D**............ **N**............ **C**............

M............ **C**............ **E**............ **D**............ **R**............

Manipulating language also involves organising data. You have to choose words according to a logical system, that of sentence structure. Working with the structure of your language is a useful tool for exercising your memory.

Stringing along

Make one two-syllable word by using the first syllable provided. Then use the second syllable of the word to make a new word. Once you have found the first word, your memory will recall words beginning with the second syllable. So you will be applying a phonetic system of association.

Example :

PAN	EL	➤➤➤	EL	EPHANT
CELL	....	➤➤➤	....	....
BUT	....	➤➤➤	....	....
CRI	....	➤➤➤	....	....
CAR	....	➤➤➤	....	....
GAR	....	➤➤➤	....	....
LEAD	....	➤➤➤	....	....
EN	....	➤➤➤	....	....
PA	....	➤➤➤	....	....
BE	....	➤➤➤	....	....
PRO	....	➤➤➤	....	....
ME	....	➤➤➤	....	....
SUB	....	➤➤➤	....	....
MAM	....	➤➤➤	....	....
AN	....	➤➤➤	....	....
NUM	....	➤➤➤	....	....
PLA	....	➤➤➤	....	....
CUR	....	➤➤➤	....	....
BO	....	➤➤➤	....	....

The more you practise this kind of game, the more you will revive the dormant words in your vocabulary, and the more fluent your speech will become. Words flow more easily the more you express yourself, and your vocabulary increases at the same time.

Solution p.339

Establish a hierarchy

Simply grouping information is not enough when each group comprises too many diverse elements. You then need a second level of organisation in the form of a classification of varying degrees of complexity within each group. It will be more difficult to establish relevant criteria in these circumstances. Within a very general category you could classify the data in a relatively simple way by listing items alphabetically, for example, or by a different method of classification, using **sub-categories**. This method of classification will be clearer if you use **a hierarchical system of organisation**.

In the natural sciences, for example, hierarchical classification is used to facilitate the identification of different species in the animal and plant kingdoms.

Below is an example of a simple tree diagram incorporating the following terms: dog – canary – stag – magpie – rabbit – budgie – robin – donkey – sheep – parrot – deer – vulture.

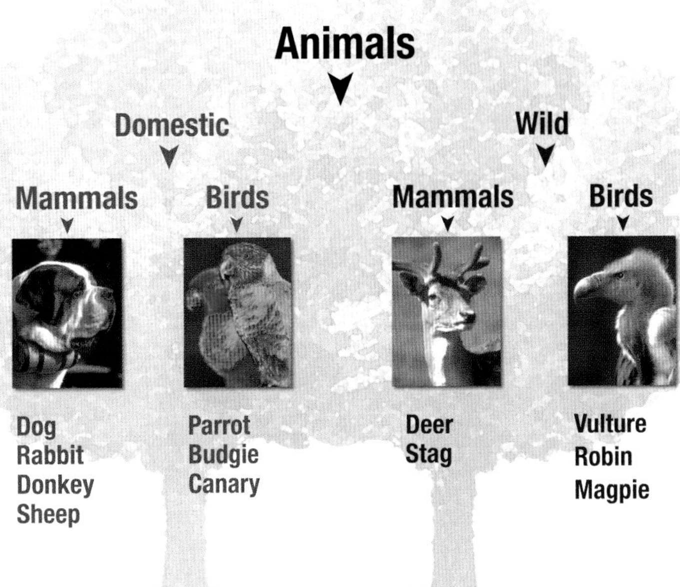

World tour

Work out a satisfactory hierarchical classification of these 36 names and note it down.

Vancouver, Beijing, Seville, Ganges, Boston, Yukon, Dallas, Kuala Lumpur, Salvador, Goa, Rio de Janeiro, Seattle, Loire, Indus, Manila, Siena, Rhine, Delhi, Montreal, St Lawrence, Valladolid, Trudeau, Assisi, De Gaulle, Guadalquivir, Durban, Mississippi, Mandela, Lagos, Colombo, Amazon, Ottawa, São Paulo, Toledo, Nice, Congo

Now cover both the list and your notes. Write down as many names as you can

Solution p.339

Using a hierarchical system to classify information considerably improves your chances of remembering it. However, you can't use this strategy for all kinds of data: you have to find appropriate criteria in each instance in order to establish a logical pyramid or tree diagram.

The more you know about a subject the easier it is to categorise material. Unless you were a geologist, you would find it difficult to classify a series of rocks using the criteria of shape, size, colour, etc.; it would be wiser to consult the mineralogical classification system and use that.

My memory and... people's faces

Many of us often cannot put a name to a face. This is usually because when you first meet the person you are not paying attention – you are looking at their clothes instead, perhaps, and you remember these instead of the name and face. Or you have no strong intention of remembering that person. When you meet people, repeat their names in your conversation with them, ask them to spell their names if they are unusual. Give them your full attention and mentally select one thing about them that is different. You are now more likely to remember them.

Highlight and summarise

Highlighting and summarising is a method of **bringing out the main points in a text** and making them easier to remember. The first stage is reading the text attentively without taking notes. You then **highlight or underline the central ideas**: this reveals the underlying structure of the whole text along with the writer's train of thought. Finally, **underlining the key words** focuses attention on the content of the crucial points and how they are developed. This approach is more demanding than learning by heart but it has proved to be effective.

When you want to remember what ground is covered by a certain book, you will find that reading the summary is a good way to obtain an overview of its principal themes and will help you understand how the key ideas are developed.

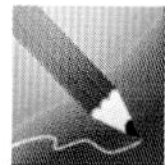

Emile or *On Education*

Read this text by the 18th-century French philosopher and educationist, Jean-Jacques Rousseau, and then, using a ruler, pencil and highlighter, apply the method described on the preceding page.

'Reading is the scourge of childhood, yet it is usually the only occupation that is given to children. At scarcely twelve years of age, will Emile even know what a book is? "But he must at least learn to read," people will say. I agree: he must learn to read, when he finds reading will be of some use to him; until then, he will only find it an ordeal…

How is it that so pleasant and useful an art has become a torment to children? Because they are compelled to acquire this skill against their will, and it is used for purposes the child doesn't understand at all. A child has no desire to perfect an art that is an instrument of torture to him; but make this instrument into a source of pleasure, and he will soon apply himself irrespective of our wishes.

People make a great fuss about finding the best method of teaching children how to read; they invent presses and cards, and turn the child's room into a printer's shop. Locke would have the child taught to read by using dice. Isn't that a wonderful invention? What a waste of time! A much more effective way, and one that is generally ignored, is to exploit the wish to learn. Give the child this incentive, then forget about your presses and your dice – any method will serve the purpose. If the interest is there, that is the great motive, the only one that will lead him further with certainty.'

Demonstration

'Reading is the scourge of childhood, yet it is usually the only occupation that is given to children. At scarcely twelve years of age, will Emile even know what a book is? "But he must at least learn to read," people will say. I agree: he must learn to read, when he finds reading will be of some use to him; until then, he will only find it an ordeal…

How is it that so pleasant and useful an art has become a torment to children? Because they are compelled to acquire this skill against their will, and it is used for purposes the child doesn't understand at all. A child has no desire to perfect an art that is an instrument of torture to him; but make this instrument into a source of pleasure, and he will soon apply himself irrespective of our wishes.

People make a great fuss about finding the best method of teaching children how to read; they invent presses and cards, and turn the child's room into a printer's shop. Locke would have the child taught to read by using dice. Isn't that a wonderful invention? What a waste of time! A much more effective way, and one that is generally ignored, is to exploit the wish to learn. Give the child this incentive, then forget about your presses and your dice – any method will serve the purpose. If the interest is there, that is the great motive, the only one that will lead him further with certainty.'

'Reading is the scourge of childhood' is the first striking idea expressed in the text. The reasons for making this statement are given in the key words underlined: 'the only occupation', while reading 'of some use' is contrasted with that which is just 'an ordeal'.

The second idea, which is the main theme of the second paragraph, is expressed in the question: 'How is it that so pleasant and useful an art has become a torment to children?' The response 'Because they are compelled' to apply themselves to something a child 'doesn't understand', suggests the consequence, a lack of interest in reading. The transition to the next main point in this paragraph follows: 'but make this instrument into a source of pleasure'.

In the third paragraph, the principal idea expressed has the ring of a conclusion drawn from reflection on the 'best method' of teaching: 'If the interest is there, that is the great motive.' And the driving force behind it all is the 'wish to learn'.

Remembering by association

In the brain, all new information is naturally related to information already in place in the memory. You can thus use this natural faculty of the mind, association, as a memorisation technique. To train your brain to do this, it is essential for you to learn how to liberate your creativity.

Memorisation and association

Making associations comes as naturally as breathing to me.

The process of memorisation always takes place in three stages: encoding, storing and retrieval (see p.28). For new information to be retained, it must first be transformed into 'brain language'. It is compared to all the other items of information already in the memory to establish whether it has already been recorded or if it contributes something really new – rather like a computer updating its files. If it does indeed represent something new, the brain will look for other information to associate it with. That is the process of encoding. Every individual's personal history provides fertile ground for this encoding process. So, each time you encounter something new, whether it be a material object or an idea, you are going to associate it automatically with what you already know. **Association is an automatic mental process.**

We are often confronted with questions we think we don't know the answers to. By setting up a network of associations with all the knowledge already at your disposal you are most likely to find answers to new questions. This ability is most obvious in people who can use their knowledge with great facility, who always know how to connect a new fact with what they already know: they have developed their natural capacity to make associations exceptionally well.

The correct distances

To classify these journeys in terms of their relative length, from the shortest to the longest, you can use your memory as a veritable bank of information and dip into it to find the answers. You are probably familiar with some of the distances involved. Using these as a base, and relating them to other facts – what you remember from school, your notions of geography, the time needed to complete these journeys, etc. – you will be able to determine their relative length in ascending order.

In France

a - Paris-Lyon	1	.....
b - Paris-Strasbourg	2	.....
c - Paris-Toulon	3	.....
d - Paris-Lille	4	.....
e - Paris-Ajaccio	5	.....
f - Paris-Nantes	6	.....
g - Paris-Marseille	7	.....
h - Paris-Bordeaux	8	.....
i - Paris-Nice	9	.....

In Europe

a - Paris-Athens	1	.....
b - Paris-Berlin	2	.....
c - Paris-Brussels	3	.....
d - Paris-Dublin	4	.....
e - Paris-London	5	.....
f - Paris-Madrid	6	.....
g - Paris-Prague	7	.....
h - Paris-Rome	8	.....
i - Paris-Helsinki	9	.....
j - Paris-Stockholm	10	.....
k - Paris-Zurich	11	.....
l - Paris-Copenhagen	12	.....

Across the world

a - Paris-Saigon	1	.....
b - Paris-Washington	2	.....
c - Paris-Moscow	3	.....
d - Paris-Marrakech	4	.....
e - Paris-Istanbul	5	.....
f - Paris-Dakar	6	.....
g - Paris-Cape Town	7	.....
h - Paris-Rio de Janeiro	8	.....
i - Paris-Baghdad	9	.....
j - Paris-Algiers	10	.....
k - Paris-Cairo	11	.....
l - Paris-Sydney	12	.....

Solution p.340

Considered associations and spontaneous associations

The associations I make are determined by my personality, my knowledge, my life experience…

Association is a mental process enabling you to establish **connections between people, objects, images, ideas, etc. which have something in common** or share one or more of the same characteristics. Put simply, when A reminds you of B, you form a link between them, and when A + B remind you of C, that means A and B have something in common with C. Some of these links are generally recognised, which means you can classify them in the following way:

Phonetic associations. Here a similarity in sound results in the words spontaneously being put together. Example: tomato and stomata.

Semantic associations. The association is made between the meaning of the word and what you know about it from your general knowledge. Example: tomato and fruit.

Metaphorical associations. B is associated with A because the meaning of B is close to that of A by virtue of a meaning being transferred by an analogous substitution. Example: tomato and shame (red as a tomato).

Logical associations. Two elements used in the same context are placed in association. Example: tomato and sauce.

Associations based on kind or type. Two items have one characteristic in common (shape, size, weight, colour, smell …) Examples: tomato and red pepper (both red in colour); tomato and grape (shape of the bunch on the vine).

Associations of ideas. Two elements are associated on the basis of a more abstract connection. Example: tomato and sun.

But you also establish links arising out of **your personal experiences and private world**
So there are therefore two more kinds of association you have to add to this list.

Subjective associations. The connection can only be understood by the person making it, because it concerns an allusion to one of their personal memories. Example: sea and angina – 'because the last time I went to the sea, I suffered from angina' …

Unconscious associations. The connection is made beyond the realm of conscious thought and its creator can't explain it.

My memory and...
my phone number

Here are a few tricks to help you memorise a 10-digit number easily.

1. Group the numbers 3 by 3 or 4 by 4. Instead of trying to remember 08 00 40 32 29, for example, try to memorise it as 0 800 403 229.

2. Associate groups of numbers with sizes, personally relevant dates, historical dates …

3. Regularly write down this number.

4. Repeat it several times, aloud and in your head, every day for the first week.

The frequent use of a number guarantees a good recollection.

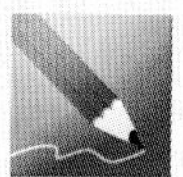

Stick-on words

Here is an exercise aimed at putting your phonetic associations to the test.

If you phonetically link the words 'ledge' and 'end' you get 'legend'. In the same way, link the phonetic words below, two by two, to create 16 new words.

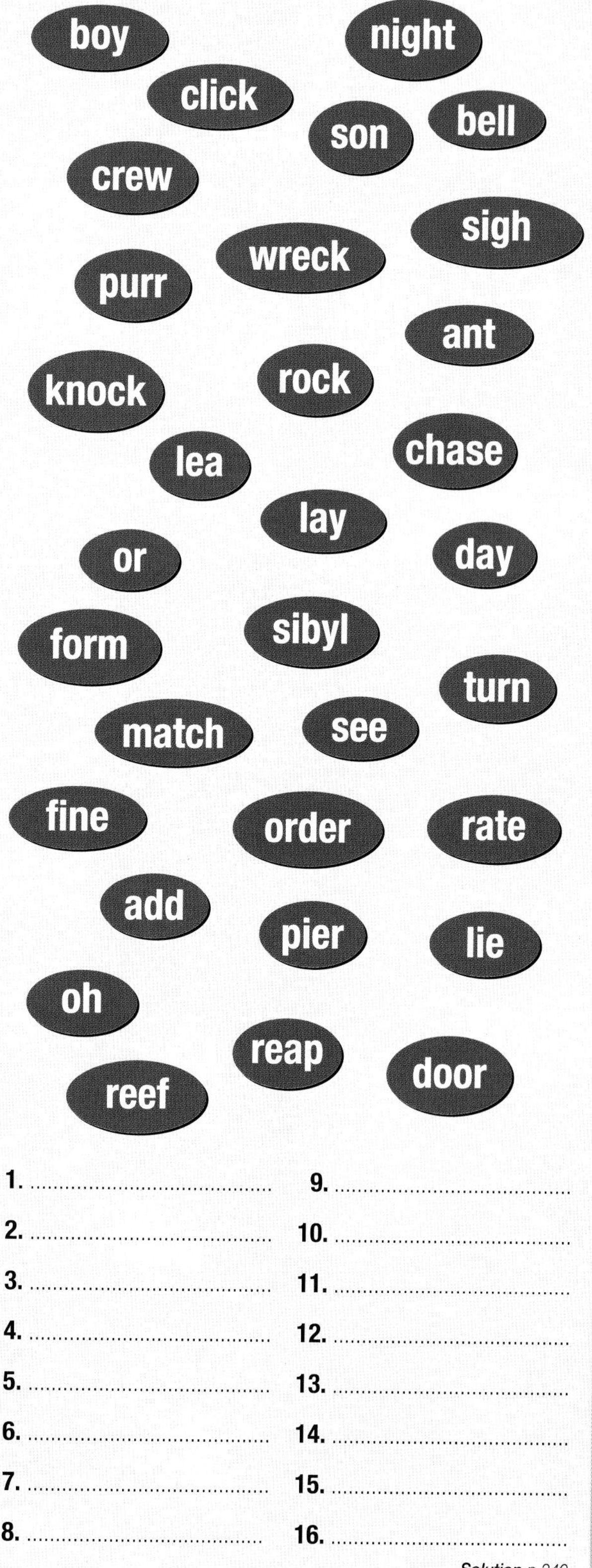

1. ....
2. ....
3. ....
4. ....
5. ....
6. ....
7. ....
8. ....
9. ....
10. ....
11. ....
12. ....
13. ....
14. ....
15. ....
16. ....

Solution p.340

Happy endings

To do this exercise, you need to associate the first word with a common or proper noun ending with **-ine** or **-ain** (phonetically). The two words should also have a link in sense or logic.
Example: the word 'navigation' could be associated to 'marine'.

doctor ....

tree ....

jump ....

read ....

dye ....

mountain ....

poverty ....

coffee ....

swimming ....

dog ....

factory ....

together ....

principal ....

agony ....

landscape ....

locomotive ....

teetotaller ....

reach ....

cheap ....

Hook ....

keep ....

arrest ....

Solution p.340

Two images, one word

Look closely at these 12 pairs of images. A connection, which may be different in nature (type, sense, logic), associates them.
This common point exists in a word. See if you can work it out!

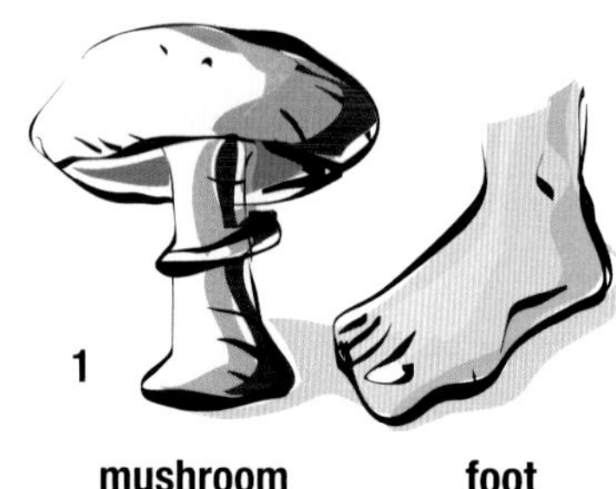

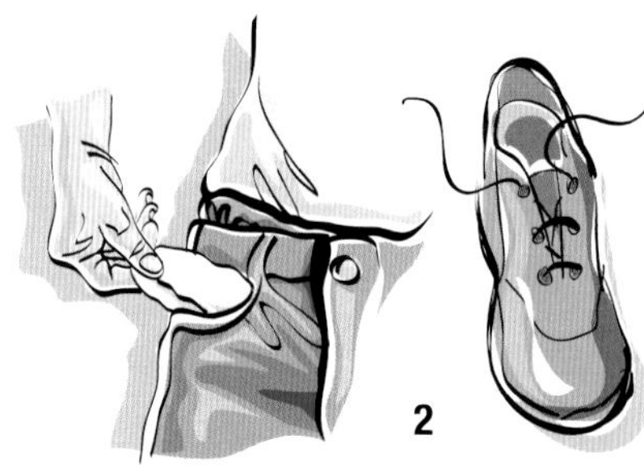

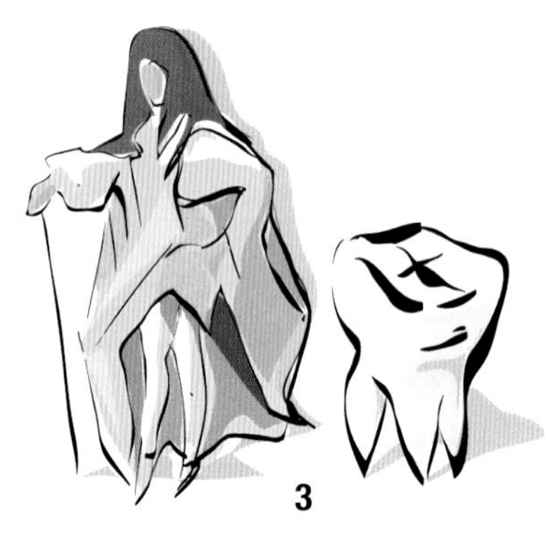

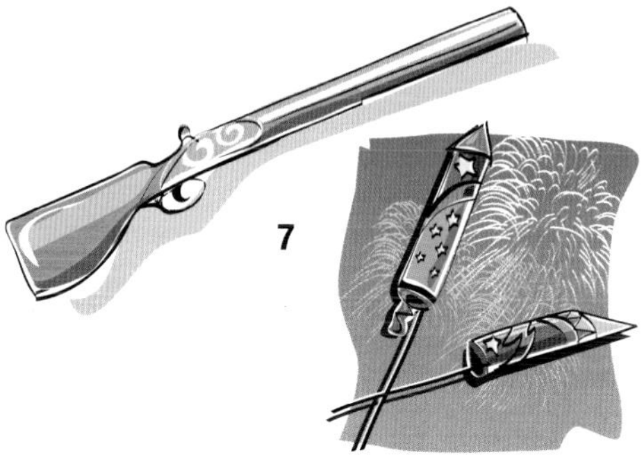

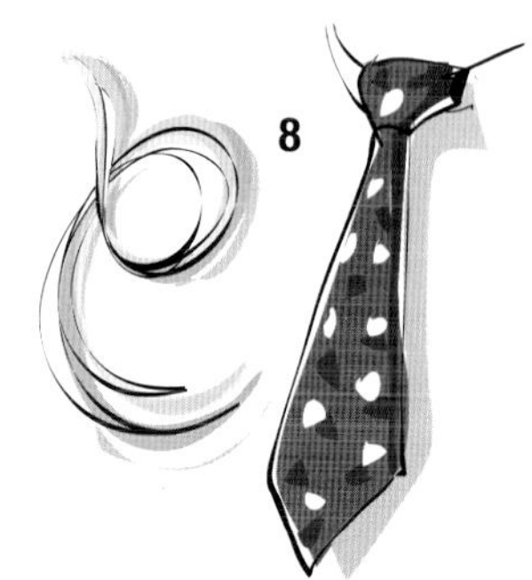

11

12

1. **fungus**
2. ....
3. ....
4. ....
5. ....
6. ....
7. ....
8. ....
9. ....
10. ....
11. ....
12. ....

Solution p.340

My memory and...
people's names

Take good note of the physical characteristics of people you meet in order to remember them – details of their faces, attitude, etc. Establish a connection between certain details and the name of a person. For example, Mr Redman might have a particularly ruddy skin, or be wearing a red item of clothing, or even have reddish hair. Or think of an aspect of their personality or hobbies. So, if Miss Gilmour likes swimming, you could associate her with a fish's gills!

To each its own references

Certain associations between words are simple and constructed with reference to physical similarities (association of type or kind) – panther/cat – or to obvious similarities in meaning (semantic association) – strawberry/fruit. Others, in contrast, arrive through cultural references which are often more complex. Panther could therefore be associated with an African-American through the Black Panther Movement, which championed the rights of African-Americans.
In the following exercise, try to find these types of associations between the words given.

Word	Simple association	Complex association
tomato	fruit, juice, sauce, salad	love (the love apple, once considered to be an aphrodisiac), *Fried Green Tomatoes* (a film by Jon Avnet) ...
taxi	....	....
nose	....	....
bicycle	....	....
phantom	....	....
sun	....	....
gold	....	....
mouse	....	....
night	....	....
plane	....	....

Solution p.340

Using your imagination to create associations

And if a bird makes me think of a hat, why not? We all have our own associations.

The mnemonic strategy of association enables you to establish links between several things while multiplying the chances of remembering them all. Regular practice will encourage the creation of links between two items of information, and the **more original they are, the better the chance that these associations will be firmly fixed in your memory.** You must therefore give free rein to your imagination and encourage the emergence of images, words and feelings that come spontaneously to mind, without censoring them. Bear in mind that **it is vital for the process of memorisation to find an association that appeals to you**, that is, the link you establish between two items must be meaningful for you personally, or arouse a specific emotion.

Memorising the right definition

Here is a list of unusual words whose meaning you have to find and remember. Do this in three stages.

1. Think about what the unknown word makes you think of (a related word).

2. Imagine your definition of this word in one sentence.

3. Look for the exact definition of this word.

Example : The word **potto.**
Associated word: **potty.**
Your definition: a state of madness.
The right definition: a short-tailed monkey with a spiny neck, related to the loris, which originates in tropical Africa.

blenny ....
drosometer ....
galatea ....
koan ....
periapt ....
ramstam ....
sciamachy ....
tetrarch ....
ventifact ....
zetetic ....

This approach, which relies on association, is a very efficient way to remember new or difficult words. When you next encounter a new word, your memory will automatically recall the word you associated with it initially and will follow this path to the right meaning, even if you had given it a different one.

Solution p.340

My memory and... dates

It is more difficult to remember a date than a word, because numbers do not take on an explicit sense. To remember dates of history more easily, for example, you need to associate them with personally relevant dates, or draw a parallel with familiar numbers (dates of birth, height, weight ...).

Another mnemonic technique is the so-called funnel approach: the date is split up into century, year, season, month and day – and then linked with various points of reference. Example: March 31, 1970. Last third of the 20th century, seven years after Kennedy's death (1963), first month of spring, last day of the month, one day before April Fool's day.

Leapfrogging over sheep

The aim of this exercise is to practise your ability to make associations by going from one word to another. The links you will thus establish are based on other words that serve as so many logical steps.

So to go from 'cat' to 'sport' in two stages, you could first associate a cat with agility, then relate agility to gymnastics, and finally, go from gymnastics to sport. In the same way, to go from 'book' to 'science', you could make the transition through 'teacher' and 'school'.

To complicate this exercise, you go from one word to the next in three, four, and finally five stages, always using this process of successive associations.

The solutions given are only there to serve as examples. Everyone must give their ingenuity and imagination free rein to encourage a personal system of associations to emerge.

In 3 stage

cigarette	**smok**
telescope	....
hairdresser	....
make-up	....
computer	....

In 2 stages

book	**cover**	**box**	**moving hous**
tea	....	....	**locomotive**
car	....	....	**funfair**
telephone	....	....	**surgery**
coffee	....	....	**beach**

In 5 stages

chain	prison	bars	iron	weapon	axe	trunk
ball	....	....	....	....	....	kitchen
door	....	....	....	....	....	feather
circle	....	....	....	....	....	sailor
animal	....	....	....	....	....	selfportrait

In 4 stages

weight	scales	zodiac	astrology	sky	star
savanna	....	....	....	....	silhouette
wrist	....	....	....	....	climate
bird	....	....	....	....	sea
news	....	....	....	....	promise

Solution p.340

fire	fireman	helmet
....	....	champagne
....	....	gardening
....	....	fish soup
....	....	cherry tree

Repetition and rote learning

At some time or other, we have all been obliged to learn things off by heart. This method is a topic of heated discussion between those who are good at it and those who aren't – with the latter protesting that it isn't fair! Anyone, however, can consolidate what they have learned by dint of repetition.

Learning by heart

Learning by heart isn't easy when you've lost the habit of using this method. This learning technique is an integral part of schooling or even tertiary education, so if you are a student in either of these categories, you will find it easy. If you are older than 40, however, your first step is to revive the use of this technique by sitting down in a quiet place where you won't be disturbed and immediately repeating several times, at a regular pace, the information you want to retain.

A trial run

Learn by heart this poem by the 18th-century

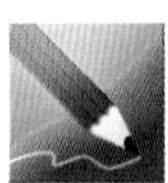

English poet William Cowper, or another that interests you, taking the time necessary. Return to the poem after two to three weeks.

Let Sleeping Cats Lie

A poet's cat, sedate and grave,
as poet would wish to have,
was much addicted to enquire,
for nooks to which she might retire,
and where, secure as mouse in chink,
she might repose, or sit and think.
I know not where she caught her trick,
nature perhaps herself had cast her,
in such a mould philosophique,
or else she learn'd it of her master.
Sometimes ascending, debonair,
an apple tree or lofty pear,
lodg'd with convenience in the fork,
she watched the gard'ner at his work;
sometimes her ease and solace sought,
in an old empty wat'ring pot,
there wanting nothing, save a fan,
to seem some nymph in her sedan,
apparell'd in exactest sort,
and ready to be borne in court.

Two weeks later, without re-reading the poem, recite it and note down what you remember.

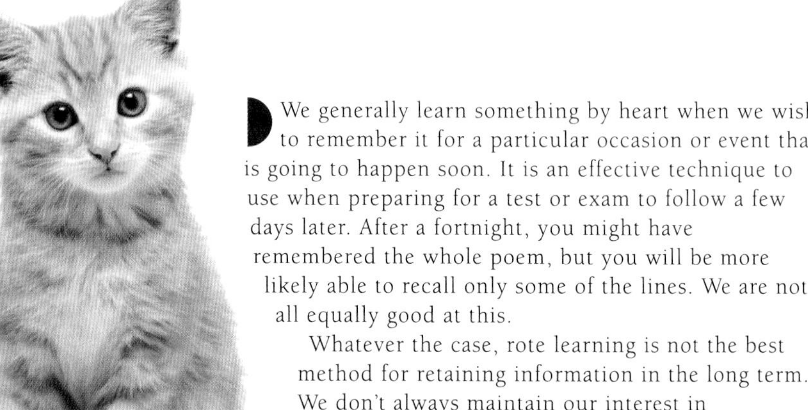

We generally learn something by heart when we wish to remember it for a particular occasion or event that is going to happen soon. It is an effective technique to use when preparing for a test or exam to follow a few days later. After a fortnight, you might have remembered the whole poem, but you will be more likely able to recall only some of the lines. We are not all equally good at this.

Whatever the case, rote learning is not the best method for retaining information in the long term. We don't always maintain our interest in everything we have learned and, furthermore, once the deadline has passed, we no longer bother to repeat what we have revised. We rarely learn something off by heart in order to recite it from memory 20 years later!

A graph of forgetfulness

Most people think that they forget slowly and surely, that the process is progressive and constant, that as time passes, the memory, rather like a leaking reservoir, empties out everything it has learned. But this is a misconception.

The first experiments into the mechanism of forgetting were carried out by a German psychologist, Herman Ebbinghaus (1850-1909). He learned a meaningless list of syllables by heart and then noted how many he remembered after a few minutes, a few hours and then a few days. From these results, he worked out a graph, called the **Ebbinghaus curve,** which shows you how your brain really forgets what it had previously stored.

The putative curve of forgetting shows the mistaken notion we generally have of the mechanism of forgetting. In reality, forgetting does not follow a linear path. It follows a logarithmic curve in slowing down: a rapid drop at first, and then a slower, more gradual drop with the

Touring England and Wales

Learn by heart this list of counties and metropoles with their number, then cover them.

01 Avon
02 Bath
03 Bedfordshire
04 Birmingham
05 Blackpool
06 Bolton
07 Bournemouth
08 Bracknell Forest
09 Bradford
10 Brighton and Hove
11 Bristol
12 Buckinghamshire
13 Cambridgeshire
14 Cheshire
15 Cornwall
16 Coventry
17 Darlington
18 Derby
19 Derbyshire
20 Devon
21 Doncaster
22 Dorset
23 Durham
24 East Riding of Yorkshire
25 East Sussex
26 Essex
27 Gateshead
28 Gloucestershire
29 Greater London
30 Greater Manchester
31 Halton
32 Hampshire
33 Hartlepool
34 Herefordshire
35 Hertfordshire
36 Isle of Wight
37 Kent
38 Kingston-upon-Hull
39 Lancashire
40 Leeds
41 Leicester
42 Leicestershire
43 Lincolnshire
44 Liverpool
45 Luton
46 Medway
47 Merseyside
48 Middlesborough
49 Milton Keynes
50 Newcastle upon Tyne
51 Newport
52 Norfolk
53 N.E. Lincolnshire
54 North Lincolnshire
55 North Somerset
56 North Tyneside
57 North Yorkshire
58 Northamptonshire
59 Northumberland
60 Nottingham
61 Nottinghamshire
62 Oxfordshire
63 Peterborough
64 Plymouth
65 Poole
66 Portsmouth
67 Reading
68 Sheffield
69 Shropshire
70 Slough
71 Solihull
72 Somerset
73 South Gloucestershire
74 South Yorkshire
75 Southampton
76 Southend-on-Sea
77 Staffordshire
78 Stockton-on-Tees
79 Stoke-on-Trent
80 Suffolk
81 Surrey
82 Swindon
83 Tyne and Wear
84 Warrington
85 Warwickshire
86 West Berkshire
87 West Midlands
88 West Sussex
89 West Yorkshire
90 Wiltshire
91 Wokingham
92 Worcestershire
93 Wrexham
94 York

Write all the missing counties and metropoles in the spaces below.

01 ....
02 ....
03 ....
04 ....
05 ....
06 ....
07 ....
08 ....
09 ....
10 Brighton and Hove
11 ....
12 ....
13 ....
14 ....
15 ....
16 ....
17 ....
18 ....
19 Derbyshire
20 ....
21 ....
22 ....
23 ....
24 ....
....
25 ....
26 ....
27 ....
28 Gloucestershire
29 ....
30 ....
....
31 ....
32 ....
33 ....
34 ....
35 ....
36 ....
37 Kent
38 ....
....
39 ....
40 ....
41 ....
42 ....
43 ....
44 ....
45 ....
46 Medway
47 ....
48 ....
49 ....
50 ....
....
51 ....
52 ....
53 ....
54 North Lincolnshire
55 ....
56 ....
57 ....
58 ....
....
59 ....
60 ....
61 ....
62 ....
63 ....
64 Plymouth
65 ....
66 ....
67 ....
68 ....
69 ....
70 ....
71 ....
72 ....
73 South Gloucestershire
74 ....
75 ....
76 ....
....
77 ....
78 ....
....
79 ....
80 ....
81 ....
82 Swindon
83 ....
84 ....
85 ....
86 ....
87 ....
88 ....
89 ....
90 ....
91 Wokingham
92 ....
93 ....
94 ....

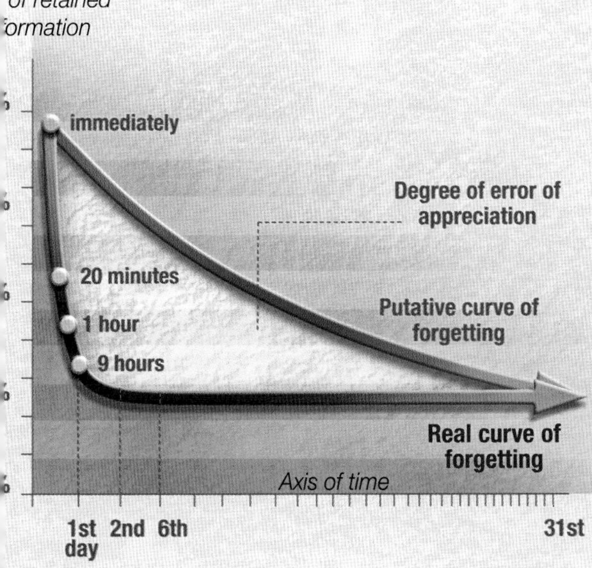

passage of time. So we start forgetting soon after we've learned something. A few hours later, we can no longer recall 70 to 80 percent at will. **The real curve of forgetting shows a very sharp drop.**

The blue section of the graph to the left reveals the **extent of this misjudgement. Being ignorant about the functioning of the memory** and the process of forgetting, **we don't make the best possible use of it** and so it works less efficiently.

To fix data firmly in your memory, you need to prevent the process of forgetting from setting in by **starting to revise straight away**. This is what is called **reinforcement time.**

Ebbinghaus also understood that certain factors influence recall and forgetting. For example, we don't memorise a list of meaningless syllables and a poem in the same way. Hence, the kind of material to be recalled, its emotional charge, and the way it was learned (for example, the use of memorisation strategies such as mental images and associations) all play a role in the retention of information.

Improving your memory

Reinforcement time: repetition

For an encoded item of information to become a lasting memory, you must contain it in a strong mental image, that is, it must be consolidated (see p.31). There are **numerous ways in which data can be consolidated:** by integrating new information with existing knowledge through a process of association (see pp.228-233), by classifying and categorising data (see pp.220-227), and by logical organisation. And in all instances a strong emotional charge promotes consolidation.

With uncomplicated data, **repetition is still the most reliable means of consolidation. Each repetition serves as reinforcement**: the information already in place is retrieved and restored to your memory, which gives it greater durability. Besides, repetition is an indication of the interest and importance you accord to an item of information, and hence the need to preserve it. There is every possible reason for the information to stay firmly in place in your memory.

If, in addition, you make extra use of your brain's resources overnight by memorising what you need to remember just **before you go to sleep**, you increase even further the probability of long-term retention. You must nonetheless recall this data immediately on waking up the following morning, before it has been displaced by other concerns.

My memory and...
learning a part in a play

Learning a part in a play can be an ordeal. Simply repeating the part word by word and learning it by rote can be tedious. To really absorb it and immerse yourself in the role, you need to understand the text and its complexities fully. Consider the meaning of the words by going over each sentence slowly, with the appropriate facial expressions and gestures. Rehearse with someone else in the play – that makes it more rewarding. Say your lines aloud, in a quiet place. Finally, every night before you go to sleep, reread the text quietly: it will be inscribed in your memory while you sleep.

Waltzing Matilda

The national song of Australia, sometimes even mistaken for its national anthem, is sung by thousands of people around the world, particularly at sporting events.

Learn one verse by heart every day. On the second day, repeat the first verse before learning the second, and so on until the fourth day. On the fifth day, recite it in its entirety. Then, continue repeating it for a month.

While learning this song, ask yourself the following questions:

1. Who wrote *Waltzing Matilda*?
2. Who or what was *Waltzing Matilda*?
3. How can the song be interpreted?
4. What is a swagman?
5. What is a squatter?

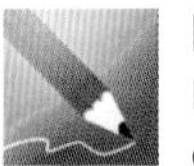

Follow this line

If you live in a big city you probably travel by underground often. And you probably know by heart the stations on the line nearest where you live. Whether you are a city-dweller or not, try the following exercise: memorise in three steps a part of the Kipling-McCowan line of the Toronto Subway. At each stage, memorise the names that are marked and then fill in the missing names. By the end, you will find that the names previously seen become easier to remember. Take your time and do the exercise a few times if you wish, building on what you have already memorised, to achieve a faultless reconstruction of the underground line.

Look closely at the stations on this line. Memorise them, then hide the first plan and complete the one below, writing in the names where words are missing.

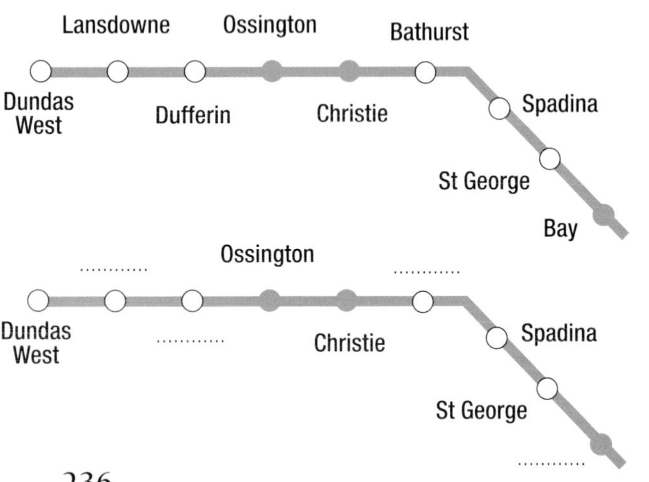

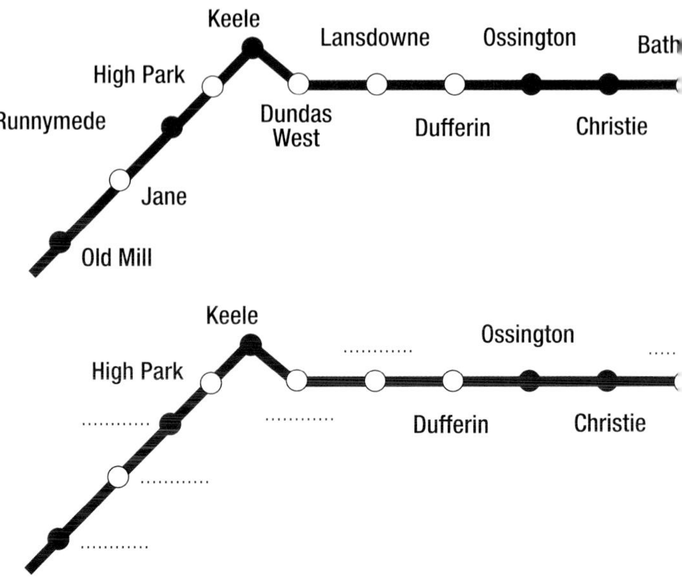

Once a jolly swagman
camped by a billabong
Under the shade of a coolibah tree
And he sang as he watched
and waited 'til his billy boiled
You'll come a-waltzing Matilda with me.

Refrain

Waltzing matilda, waltzing matilda,
You'll come a-waltzing matilda with me
And he sang as he watched
and waited while his billy boiled
You'll come a-waltzing Matilda with me.

Down came a jumbuck
to drink at that billabong
Up jumped the swagman
and grabbed him with glee
And he sang as he stuffed
that jumbuck in his tucker-bag
You'll come a-waltzing Matilda with me.

Refrain

Up rode the squatter
mounted on his thoroughbred
Up rode the troopers,
one, two, three
'Where's that jolly jumbuck
you've got in your tucker-bag?'
You'll come a-waltzing Matilda with me.

Refrain

Up jumped the swagman and
sprang into the billabong
'You'll never take me alive!', said he
And his ghost may be heard
as you pass by that billabong
You'll come a-waltzing Matilda with me.

Refrain

Learning by heart a text such as *Waltzing Matilda*, which probably contains some unfamiliar words, while at the same time making sure you understand the meaning and the context, makes it easier to remember the song in the long term.

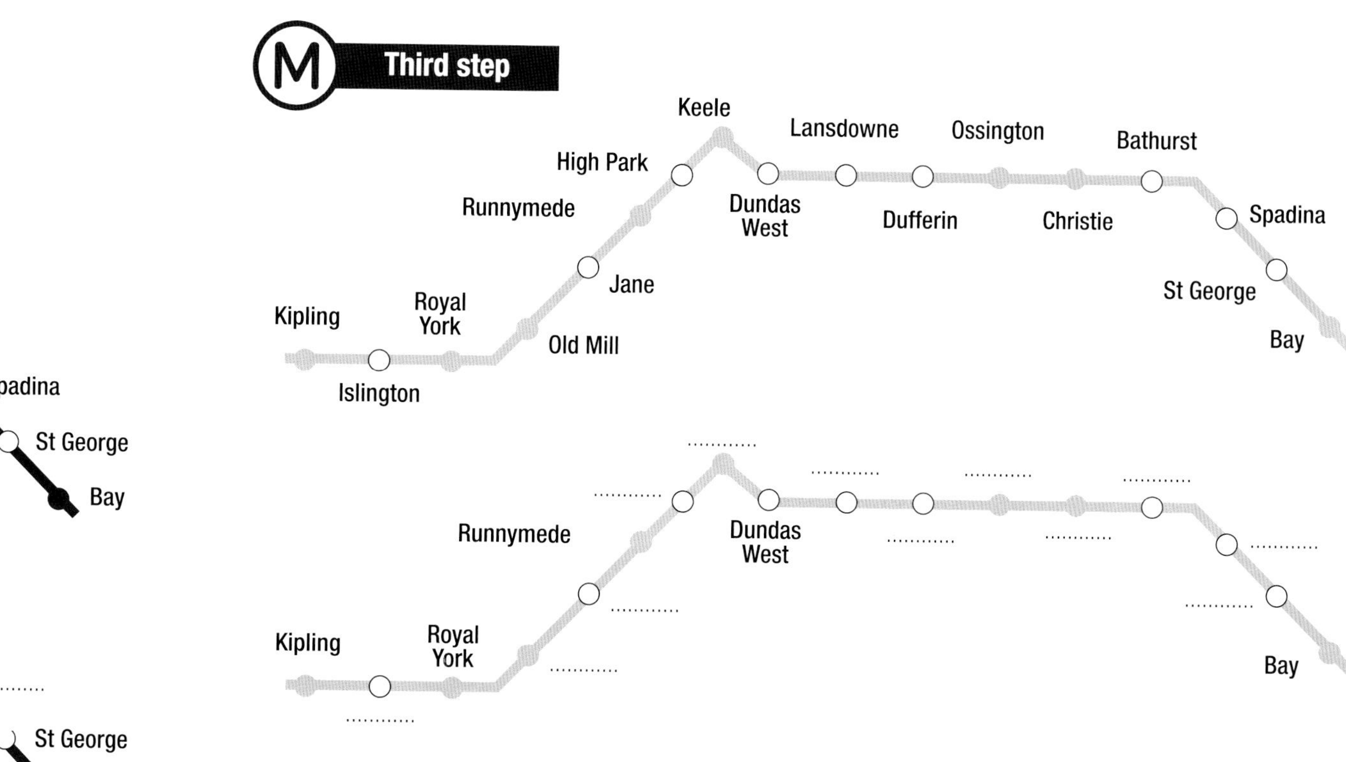

Improving your memory

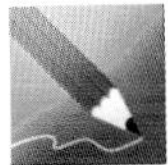

Stringing up striped socks

1. Here are 15 tricky tongue twisters demanding absolutely clear diction. Try to say them aloud, either on your own or with others. You will probably find that your pronunciation becomes rather slurred and clumsy after a while, with rather unfortunate results at times. Keep innocent ears closed!

2. Now try to remember and repeat as many of them as you can.

Seventy-seven benevolent elephants.

●

Round and round the rugged rock the ragged rascal ran.

●

Tie twine to three tree twigs ...

●

Rolling red wagons ...

●

The great Greek grape growers grow great Greek grapes.

●

I saw Esau kissing Kate,
I saw Esau, he saw me,
and she saw I saw Esau.

●

There was a fisherman named Fisher
Who fished for some fish in a fissure
Till a fish with a grin
Pulled the fisherman in
Now they're fishing the fissure for Fisher.

●

She sells sea shells by the sea shore ...

●

I saw a saw in Arkansas
That would outsaw any saw I ever saw
And if you've got a saw that will
Outsaw the saw I saw in Arkansas,
Let me see your saw.

●

Six sleek swans swam swiftly southwards.

●

Clean clams crammed in clean cans ...

She shows striped socks strung on a washing line ...

●

Six sick hicks nick six slick bricks with picks and sticks ...

●

One-one was a race horse,
Two-two was one two,
One-one won one race,
Two-two won one too.

●

Red Buick, blue Buick...

In this exercise, you will have less difficulty in recalling the words thanks to both repetition and the humorous nature of the words.

Hello!

It is very important to know certain telephone numbers by heart. The following questions will help you establish whether you have indeed memorised these numbers. Note that you must do this exercise as quickly and spontaneously as possible, without any help from others.

1. **Directory enquiries**

   ....

2. **The number to phone to report a power failure**

   ....

3. **The police or security company**

   ....

4. **Fire brigade**

   ....

5. **Ambulance**

   ....

6. **Your doctor**

   ....

7. **Poisons unit**

   ....

8. **Telephone numbers of two friends or relatives to contact in an emergency**

   ....

   ....

The WWWWHWW method

The so-called WWWWHWW method will help you remember a text more easily by giving your notes some focus and structure. Each letter of the acronym introduces a question.

Who? The subject of the action.

What? The action.

Where? The place.

When? The time, or era.

How? The means.

What for? The purpose.

Why? The reason or cause.

Apply these seven questions daily to everything you read. You will notice how much this technique improves your comprehension and hence your ability to remember. Use this approach to tell a story or else to summarise a film or exciting incident.

The causes of the war of Rion

Apply the technique of WWWWHWW to the following text.

It is the year 9600. Rion is an enormous city on the planet Rana, in the constellation of the Bear. The inhabitants, the Rionese, wish to avenge their king Taramac, for the serious crime committed against him by an inhabitant of Olys, a city on the neighbouring planet of Mirvalum. This crime was the abduction of his wife, the beautiful Persephone, by Orus, a prince from Olys.

According to the legend, it all started when, in the course of a party, the fairy Zizania flung a gold ring down in the middle of the hall, telling the guests that it would belong to the most beautiful of all the goddesses. Wisely, the guests refused to make a choice. The goddesses participating in the competition were getting impatient. Zarma, the jealous and malicious wife of Ervan, the king of the gods, Irisa, goddess of wisdom and victory, and Amoria, goddess of love and beauty, all wished to be chosen.

At last Ervan, infuriated, demanded the opinion of Prince Orus, said to be the most handsome man of his time. Each goddess attempted to secure victory by showering him with gifts. But despite their efforts, Orus crowned Amoria, who had promised him the love of the most beautiful woman in the world, Persephone of Rion – the wife of Taramac.

Orus immediately embarked for Rion, where King Taramac accorded him a gracious welcome. The prince took advantage of the momentary absence of Taramac to abduct the queen and take her to his palace in Olys. Taramac dispatched ambassadors to the old king, Orulys, the father of Orus. But to no avail: the young man was determined to keep Persephone.War was inevitable.

Now answer the questions listed below:

Who? ....

What? ....

Where? ....

When? ....

How? ....

What for? ....

Why? ....

Solution p.340

Communicate – to remember

Passing on information to others in your own words is a good way to ensure that you remember it. You remember films, books, stories, poems, etc much more successfully after formulating the contents yourself. And talking about your experiences imposes a certain coherence on your own story, imprinting it on your memory and that of others.

To communicate is to remember

I told my children the story of the film Titanic *the day after it came out. Three years later, I still remember it very clearly!*

It can happen to any of us: we see a film on TV in the evening and don't remember what it was about the next day. Some people are alarmed by this inability to remember. They are afraid their memory is failing.

Instead of over-reacting, we should ask ourselves the following question: did we really enjoy the film and find it interesting? Don't forget that wanting to remember is an essential component of successful memorisation. So if you watch a film simply to relax, without taking much interest in it, there is a good chance that you won't remember much about it. This is equally true of people who complain that they don't remember what they read the previous evening. In fact, when reading becomes just a way of putting yourself to sleep, a kind of soporific, you don't pay enough attention to what you are reading to ensure that you remember it.

Telling someone else what a film or book is about soon after seeing or reading it is an excellent way to **ensure you remember it**. You have to **structure your account of different aspects of the story**, classify them, and **select what is most significant** to make it comprehensible to the person you're talking to. This way of reworking information by talking about it makes it easier to encode. **Discussing a film or book gives impetus to your efforts to organise your ideas about the contents,** thus ensuring that it becomes firmly fixed in your memory. Besides, if you know that you will be telling other people about it, you pay more attention and really concentrate. You don't simply remain a passive consumer of the story.

In any discussion of a cultural event, the memory is a remarkable instrument of communication, which not only transmits information but also conveys a wide range of feelings and emotions. **No meaningful or dynamic communication is possible without significant interaction.** This is nothing like communicating with a computer, whose prodigious memory can only unload a huge stock of information, devoid of any feeling.

My memory and… funny stories

Telling a funny story is not always easy: you have to remember it, know how to relate it, even how to use several voices or devices, and especially you have to make it your own so as to capture the attention of your listeners. Here are a few tips on how to become a talented humorist:

1. Listen to the story several times to capture all the nuances.
2. Size up all the characters, and establish the pivotal events and the crucial details that lead up to the punch line.
3. Practise on your own and add your own words to the story. In this way, everyone will have the impression that it's your own personal creation.

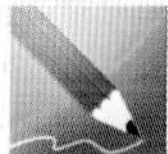

Little Red Riding Hood

Everybody knows the story of Little Red Riding Hood, by Charles Perrault. But do you remember exactly how the plot unfolds?

1. Cover the page on the right and try to write the story as if you had to tell it to a child, recounting the different stages in the story and giving as much detail as possible.

You must have noticed that in the simple act of writing the story down, basing your account solely on what you remembered, you recalled details you would possibly not have thought of spontaneously. In fact, writing it down made you concentrate and maintain your attention level. Then, in writing the story, you had to make an effort to present it in a coherent and comprehensible way. You organised it by arranging the events in logical sequence. During this process you remembered various incidents. Now test the accuracy of your rendition. How is Little Red Riding Hood described? Why does she go to see her grandmother and what does she take her? Where does she meet the wolf? Why doesn't he eat her straight away? Where does Little Red Riding Hood go after meeting the wolf? What does the wolf do to get into the grandmother's house? What does the grandmother say to let him in? Where does he hide? What does Little Red Riding Hood say to the wolf? And what does he reply? What is the moral of this story?

2. Now read the original story on the opposite page.

Once upon a time there was a little village girl, the prettiest to be seen. Her mother was devoted to her, her grandmother even more so. This good woman made her a red hood, which suited her so well that everyone called her Little Red Riding Hood. One day, her mother, who had made some cakes, said to her: 'Go and see how your grandmother is. I've heard that she is ill. Take her this cake and this little pot of butter.'

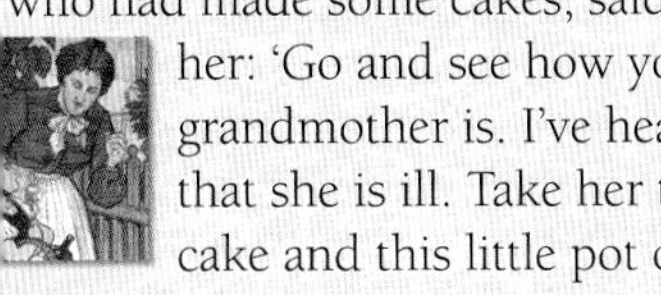

Little Red Riding Hood put the cake and little pot of butter in her basket and set off straight away for her grandmother's house in a nearby village.

While walking through the forest, she met Comrade Wolf. He was very eager to gobble her up, but didn't dare to because of the woodcutters working in the forest.

He asked her where she was going. The poor child, who didn't know it was dangerous to stop and listen to wolves, replied: 'I am on my way to see my grandmother and take her a cake and a little pot of butter from my mother.'

'Does she live far away?' asked the wolf.

'Oh yes,' replied Little Red Riding Hood, 'she lives beyond the mill you can see over there, in the distance, in the first house in the village.'

'Well,' said the wolf, 'I wish to go and see her too. I'll take this path, and you take that path, and we'll see who gets there first.'

The wolf immediately started running as fast as he could along the shortest route, while the little girl took the longer route. She didn't hurry at all. Instead, she sang and danced her way gaily along the path, and enjoyed picking flowers, chasing butterflies, and making posies of the little flowers she saw.

The wolf did not take long to reach the grandmother's house. He knocked. Knock, knock.

'Who is there?'

'It's your granddaughter, Little Red Riding Hood,' said the wolf, disguising his voice. 'I've brought you a cake and a little pot of butter from my mother.'

The good woman, who was feeling rather poorly and had taken to her bed, called out: 'Draw the bolt, and the latch will open!'

The wolf drew the bolt, and the door opened. He flung himself on the poor woman and gobbled her up in no time at all, as he hadn't eaten for more than three days. Then he closed the door and got into the grandmother's bed to wait for Little Red Riding Hood. A short while later she knocked on the door. Knock, knock.

'Who is there?'

Little Red Riding Hood, hearing the gruff voice, was afraid, but believing that her grandmother had a cold, replied: 'It's your granddaughter, Little Red Riding Hood, and I'm bringing you a cake and a little pot of butter from my mother.'

'Draw the bolt and the latch will open!'

Little Red Riding Hood drew the bolt and the door opened.

The wolf, seeing her come in, hid himself under the bedclothes, saying, 'Put the cake and the little pot of butter on the chest and come and get into bed with me.'

Little Red Riding Hood took her clothes off and prepared to get into the bed, where she was surprised to see what her grandmother looked like with no clothes on.

She said: 'But grandmother, what big hairy arms you have!'

'All the better to hug you with, my dear.'

'But grandmother, what big hairy legs you have!'

'All the better to run with, my child.'

'But grandmother, what big ears you have!'

'All the better to hear with, my child!'

'But grandmother, what big eyes you have!'

'All the better to see with, my child!'

'But grandmother, what big teeth you have!'

'All the better to eat you with!'

And with these words, that wicked wolf threw himself on Little Red Riding Hood and gobbled her all up.

Moral:
This story shows that children, especially girls
Should be careful before casting their precious pearls
Before swine. Don't ever stop and talk
To those plausible wolves, or walk
In the forest alone, without any friend.
If you do, it's likely you'll end
Like poor Riding Hood
Who, sweet, kind and good
Suffered a terrible fate at the cruel hand
Of a villain whose diabolical plot was well planned.

Little Red Riding Hood in fact symbolises a rather naïve young girl who allows herself to be hoodwinked. She is so taken in by a seemingly obliging and charming wolf that she even takes her clothes off and gets into bed with him. It is more than likely that the sexual connotations would be beyond the comprehension of a child of six to eight years, or even a little older. On the other hand, the principal theme that 'we should not listen to wolves' has strong resonances at an age when our personal security is an important issue and the need to feel safe from exploitation and predation arouses our spontaneous suspicion of strangers. This idea lingers in our memory and subsequently provides a guiding thread in recalling the logical sequence of events in the story. In addition, we have elements both verbal (the bolt, the latch) and visual (the red outfit, cake and little pot of butter), the wolf disguised as a grandmother, etc, that provide colourful images charged with dramatic intensity that are vividly imprinted on our memory.

Film fun...

- Next time you go to the movies, tell someone about the film afterwards. Try to formulate the key themes in the story, noting too the ramifications of the plot, the dramatic tension or comic elements, and try to maintain a sense of suspense so that your account will be really interesting. You will then find that you retain a vivid and detailed memory of the film.

- Watch a film with your family and then ask everyone to write down what they remember. Compare the different versions. Explore various impressions of and reactions to the film (including auditory and visual details) and what was most interesting. Discuss your responses and what each person felt about the film.

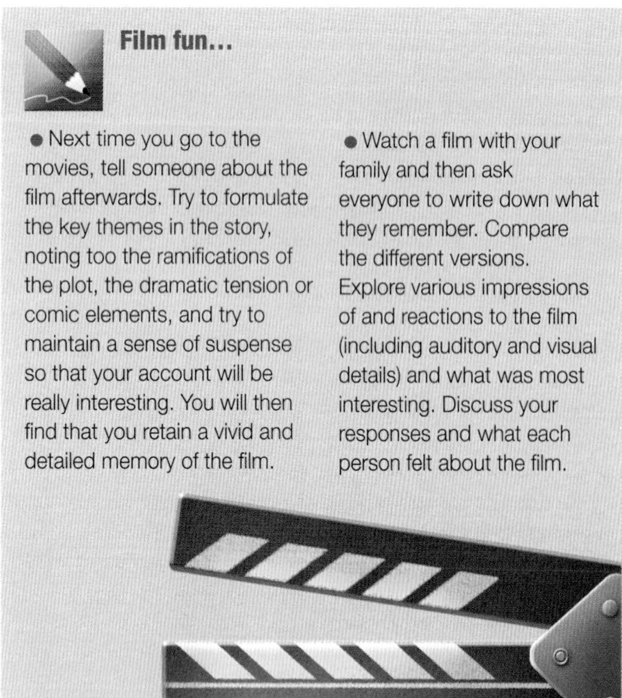

Words, words, words...

The letters of the following verbs – all synonyms of words meaning 'to talk' or 'communicate' – have been jumbled up. Can you put them back in the right order?

Example : **A T B E D E = DEBATE**

1. **SOGSIP** ....
2. **TRACTHE** ....
3. **GANWICH** ....
4. **TIGANOTEE** ....
5. **RUMRUM** ....
6. **LOMOGUNEO** ....
7. **VORCENES** ....
8. **NEMOCICUTMA** ....
9. **MISTARNT** ....
10. **FRONCE** ....
11. **LAYPER** ....

Solution p.340

The individual adds to the collective memory

Sharing your life and experiences with other people provides you with the opportunity to reconsider the story of your life. **You can select what seem to be your most important memories.** Assuring the survival of your personal story, as your ancestors formerly did, is to ensure continuity in a society where the present moment is so highly valued. The accelerated pace of history in contemporary society sometimes creates the impression that our lives are cut off from the past, that we live in a kind of frenetic flight towards the future. Many people experience this as a loss of points of reference, which can lead to a feeling of instability or insecurity. While avoiding the pitfalls of nostalgia and glorification of the past (everything wasn't necessarily better before!) we can all **participate in this constructive act of transmitting our memories**. Popular wisdom is right in claiming that we can't decide where we wish to go if we don't know where we came from.

You contribute with a **verbal account of your life,** in which you pass on your knowledge, recounting your memories and expressing your feelings. You also contribute through **what is passed on through your genes.** You need only look at members of both sides of your family to be aware of the persistence of certain physical characteristics or character traits. In addition there is **everything you communicate that transcends language**, what you convey unconsciously, by facial expressions, the way you talk, behave, or react to things.

My memory and... my private diary

Many people keep a personal and often intimate diary. This is a very good way to keep your memory in shape. Writing helps to inscribe something on your memory and is indispensable when you don't have much opportunity for oral communication. For adults, keeping a diary is a good way to keep a record of thoughts and what is happening in their life. A diary often starts off as a simple record of engagements and rapidly changes into a tool for reflection, even a collection of experiences to pass on to future generations.

All to the table!

What better time for conviviality and social intercourse than a meal? But to improve communication with all the guests, it is advisable to get to know them all as quickly as possible, to remember the names of the guests next to you and those next to them, as well as what they are talking about... Conversation becomes much easier as soon as you can place and identify everyone present.
Here is a table of dinner guests: you have to remember the surname of each one and where he or she is sitting. Take all the time you need, and then cover the picture and answer the questions opposite.

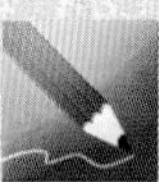

Paul Dal

What I pass on

- Pinpoint a physical characteristic in your family that has been passed on from the maternal side, and another one from the paternal side. Also find a character trait that you seem to have inherited from your forebears.
- Next, think about the memories you recount most frequently and what aspects of yourself you express at such times. Consider too what you might convey unconsciously. All the impressions you leave in the memory of others form part of your perception of yourself, just as your history does, and they contribute to the elaboration of the history of your family.

Little scraps of paper

Find the names of different kinds of paper hidden in the following anagrams, and then place them in the grid below.

ADAMHEND
CARTNIG
DYRECLEC
EDLIN
ITSUSE
LITOET
NARPGWIP
OTEN
PECRE
SWEN
WLAL

Solution p.341

Barbara Beatty

Charles Maistry

Laura Dalrymple

Christopher Whitehead

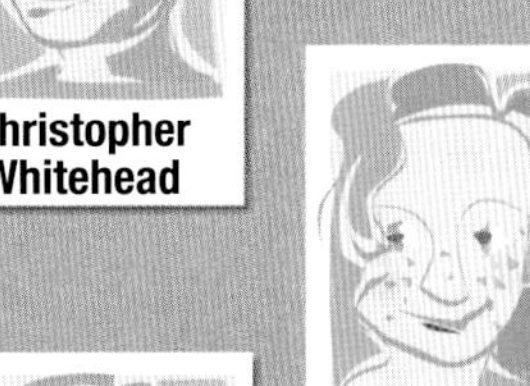
Juliet Fox

Iona Sharp

Eddy Khan

Amelia Garrick

Luke Sharp

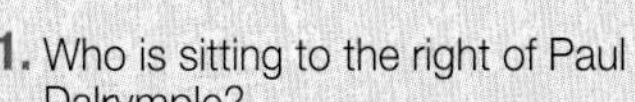

1. Who is sitting to the right of Paul Dalrymple?
2. Who is opposite Amelia Garrick?
3. Who is on Christopher Whitehead's right?
4. Who is sitting on Laura Dalrymple's left?
5. Who are the guests on either side of Juliet Fox?
6. Are there two men sitting opposite each other?
7. How many guests are there altogether around the table? Give their names.

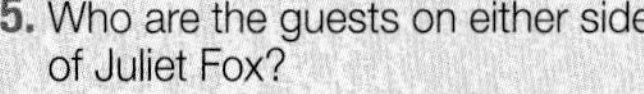

Association can be a good method to use when memorising proper names. Associate names with physical characteristics, for example (Juliet Fox – red hair, Christopher Whitehead – blond hair) or link them with information about the person (Luke Sharp is a musician).

The yacht. Look closely at this scene then find the people, animals and objects listed on the opposite page.

Games booklet 3

MIXED PROVERBS

GENERAL KNOWLEDGE

The words of three proverbs have been mixed up. Untangle them to find the original proverbs.

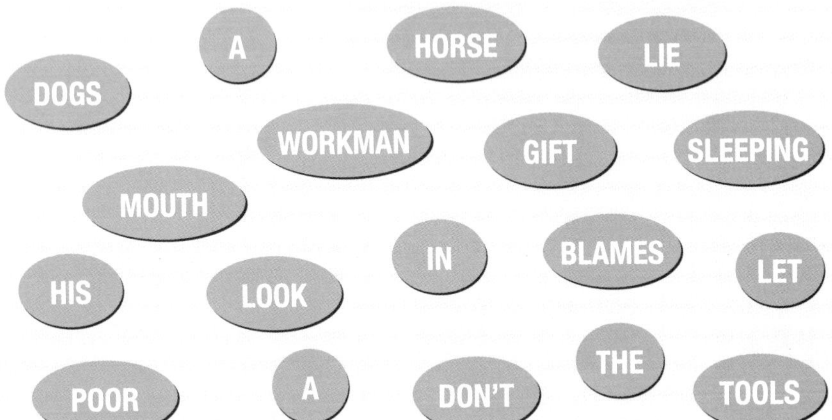

1. ....
....
....

2. ....
....
....

3. ....
....
....

BRAIN TEASER

LOGIC

Basil, Betty, Edith, Erwan, Frances and Frank make up three couples.

Put them in the right pairs with the help of the following clues:

- No couple wears the same colour clothes.
- The first names of each couple never start with the same letter.
- Frances is going out with the man in red.
- Erwan is going out with the woman in green.
- Frank and Betty, neither of whom is wearing mauve, are not dating each other.

CATERPILLAR

STRUCTURE

Move from the word CROUPIER to ROULETTE in this caterpillar by substituting the letters as indicated and changing the order of the letters.

CROUPIER

-C +S _ _ _ _ _ _ _ _

-I +T _ _ _ _ _ _ _ _

-P +T _ _ _ _ _ _ _ _

-O +E _ _ _ _ _ _ _ _

-T +C _ _ _ _ _ _ _ _

-S +L _ _ _ _ _ _ _ _

-C +O _ _ _ _ _ _ _ _

-S +T ROULETTE

MAGIC SQUARE LOGIC

This is a supermagic square with 8 rows and exceptional properties. It's up to you to complete it. We have filled in all the numbers apart from the multiples of 7 (7, 14, 21, etc) which must be filled in on the yellow circles, and the multiples of 8 (8, 16, 24, etc) which must be filled in on the blue circles. If you don't know how to start, read the extra clue.

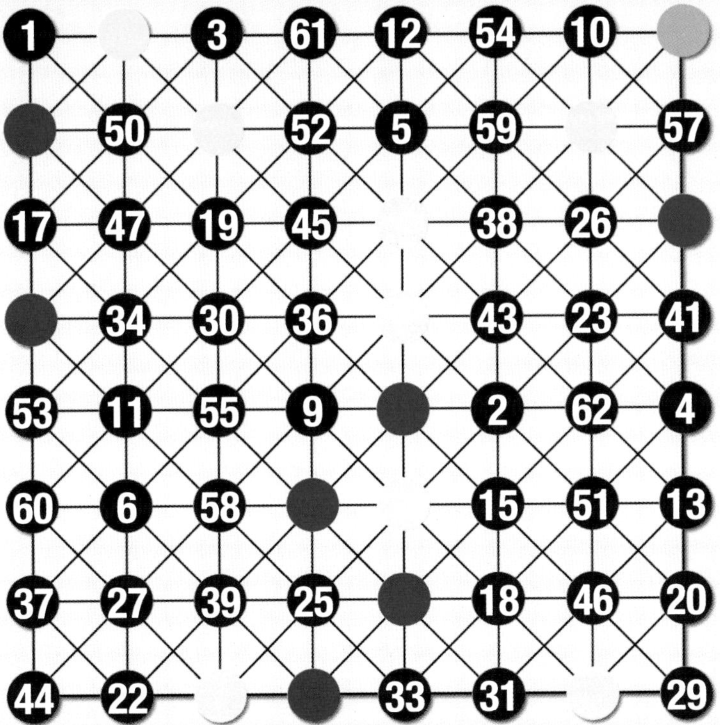

1		3	61	12	54	10	
	50		52	5	59		57
17	47	19	45		38	26	
	34	30	36		43	23	41
53	11	55	9		2	62	4
60	6	58			15	51	13
37	27	39	25		18	46	20
44	22			33	31		29

Extra clue: Note that apart from the classic properties of magic squares (the sum of each line and each diagonal is the same), in this square the same constraints hold for each square of four numbers. Now it should be easy to complete the square!

SYNONYMS LANGUAGE

With the help of the clues given, find eight synonyms of the word FLAW.

1. B _ _ _ _ _ H (a spot on the skin)
2. D _ _ _ _ T (that which prevents functioning)
3. S _ _ _ _ _ _ _ _ _ _ G (deficiency in things or people)
4. M _ R (slight defect)
5. F _ _ _ _ E (eccentricity)
6. F _ _ _ T (that which impairs excellence)
7. F _ _ _ _ _ G (undesirable characteristic)
8. I _ _ _ _ _ _ _ _ _ _ _ N (incompleteness)

HISTORICAL LANDMARKS TIME

Put these 10 presidents of the USA in the right chronological order.

A	Lyndon B. Johnson	1	....
B	Theodore Roosevelt	2	....
C	Abraham Lincoln	3	....
D	John F. Kennedy	4	....
E	Thomas Jefferson	5	....
F	Dwight D. Eisenhower	6	....
G	Bill Clinton	7	....
H	George Washington	8	....
I	Ronald Reagan	9	....
J	Harry S. Truman	10	....

MAGIC TRIANGLE LOGIC

Try to fill in all the numbers from 1 to 9 on this triangle so as to end up with the same total, in this case 20, on each of the sides. Then take it a little further by ensuring that the sum of the squares of these numbers is the same and equals 126. Proceed logically.

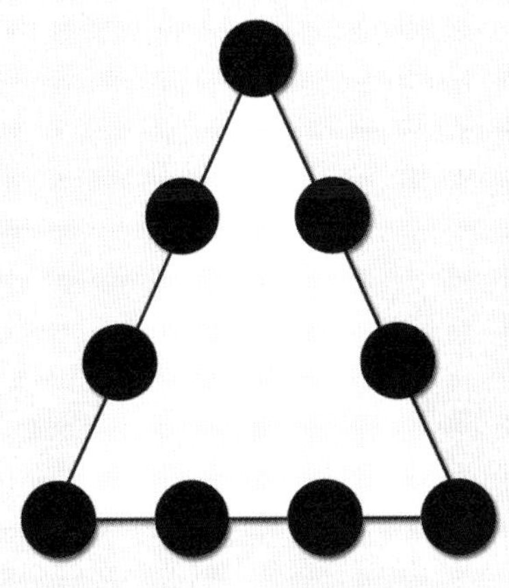

HIDDEN WORDS

STRUCTURE

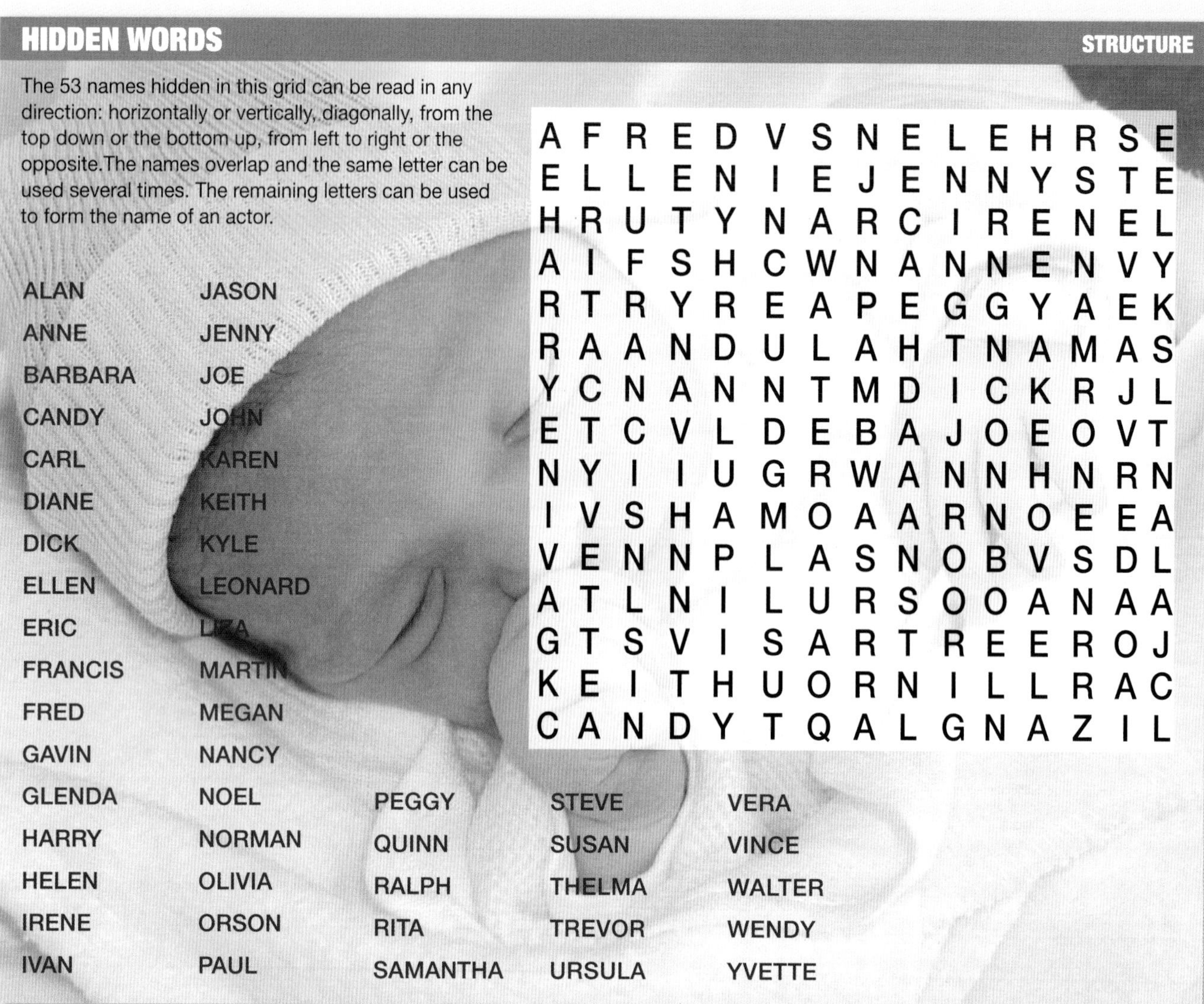

The 53 names hidden in this grid can be read in any direction: horizontally or vertically, diagonally, from the top down or the bottom up, from left to right or the opposite. The names overlap and the same letter can be used several times. The remaining letters can be used to form the name of an actor.

```
A F R E D V S N E L E H R S E
E L L E N I E J E N N Y S T E
H R U T Y N A R C I R E N E L
A I F S H C W N A N N E N V Y
R T R Y R E A P E G G Y A E K
R A A N D U L A H T N A M A S
Y C N A N N T M D I C K R J L
E T C V L D E B A J O E O V T
N Y I I U G R W A N N H N R N
I V S H A M O A A R N O E E A
V E N N P L A S N O B V S D L
A T L N I L U R S O O A N A A
G T S V I S A R T R E E R O J
K E I T H U O R N I L L R A C
C A N D Y T Q A L G N A Z I L
```

ALAN
ANNE
BARBARA
CANDY
CARL
DIANE
DICK
ELLEN
ERIC
FRANCIS
FRED
GAVIN
GLENDA
HARRY
HELEN
IRENE
IVAN
JASON
JENNY
JOE
JOHN
KAREN
KEITH
KYLE
LEONARD
LIZA
MARTIN
MEGAN
NANCY
NOEL
NORMAN
OLIVIA
ORSON
PAUL
PEGGY
QUINN
RALPH
RITA
SAMANTHA
STEVE
SUSAN
THELMA
TREVOR
URSULA
VERA
VINCE
WALTER
WENDY
YVETTE

STICK-ON TITLES

GENERAL KNOWLEDGE

Detach the words of the following made-up titles and then stick the words together to form the names of four songs sung by Patsy Cline.

SHE'S AFTER YOU

BABY'S WALKIN' BACK

MIDNIGHT IN ARMS

I GOT PIECES TO FALL

HISTORICAL LANDMARKS

TIME

Are the following statements true or false?

1. Joan of Arc lived in the 15th century. ... True False
2. Leonardo da Vinci and Christopher Columbus were contemporaries. .... True False
3. The Taj Mahal was built as a wedding present. .... True False
4. The Egyptians built Great Zimbabwe, now a ruined city. .... True False
5. Pocahontas married John Smith. .... True False
6. The Battle of Trafalgar took place after the Battle of Waterloo. .... True False

BROKEN SEQUENCES — STRUCTURE

These six words have each had one or more syllables removed. Put the words together again by using some of the syllables provided. Note that there are at times several possibilities, but only one will enable you to restore all the original words.

1. .... ME ....
2. CON ....
3. RE ....
4. .... NI ....
5. .... VA ....
6. .... TY

MA BER VED LANCHE SAN TOU A PU TO SER CER PAR

CLOSE-UP — CONCENTRATION

Identify the object, animal or person that our designer has had fun transforming.

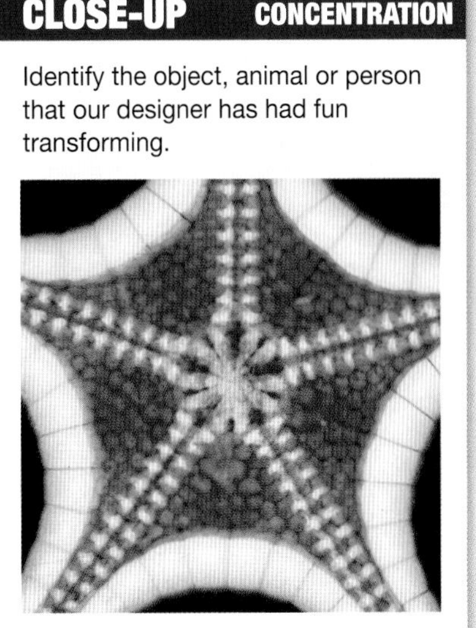

BRAIN TEASER — LOGIC

Using the following clues, allocate the headgear to the rightful owners – Richard, Victor, Matthew and Steven.

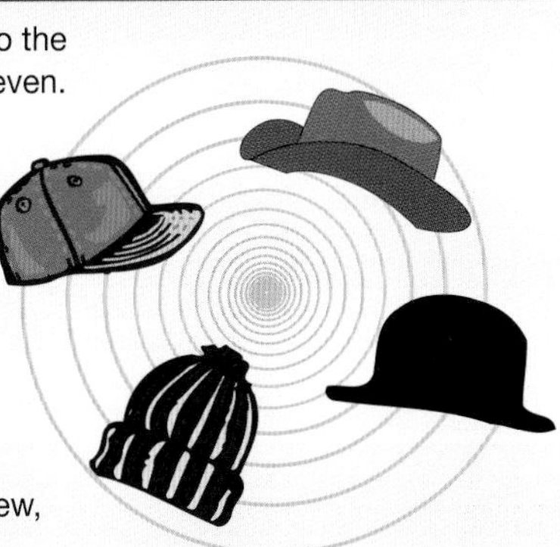

1. Victor's hat is either the cowboy hat or the woollen hat.
2. If the cap doesn't belong to Richard, the cowboy hat belongs to Matthew.
3. If the bowler hat belongs to Matthew, then the woollen hat belongs to Richard.
4. If the cap doesn't belong to Victor, then the bowler doesn't belong to Steven.
5. If the woollen hat belongs to Richard or Matthew, then the bowler belongs to Steven.

PROGRESSIVE QUIZ — GENERAL KNOWLEDGE

Try to go as far as you can in answering these questions about the Nobel prizes.

1. Who instituted the annual Nobel prizes?
2. In what year?
3. What nationality was he?
4. What was his invention that exploded onto the world in 1866?
5. In how many categories did he stipulate prizes should be awarded?
6. Which was the last category instituted after his death, in his honour, in 1969?
7. Which two men jointly won the Nobel Peace Prize in 1993?
8. Which female scientist was awarded a Nobel prize twice in her life?
9. On what date are the prizes awarded each year?
10. What is the significance of this date?

TRUE OR FALSE — GENERAL KNOWLEDGE

Try to establish whether the following statements about candles and their flames are true or false. Tick the relevant letters under T or F, and by rearranging them you will be able to make another name for animal fat used to make candles.

	Statement	True	False
1.	The word 'flame' comes from the dance 'flamenco' and refers to the leaping red edge of the dancer's skirt.	M	L
2.	The principle of a burning candle was discovered in 20 BC.	A	O
3.	A bull gave enough fat to supply a farm with lighting oil for three months in the 17th century.	T	R
4.	*Candle in the Wind* is the title of a song by Elton John, about Marilyn Monroe.	L	M
5.	'Burning the candle at both ends' means leaving all the lights on in your home.	E	A
6.	Candlewood is used as a substitute for wax to make candles.	W	S

ANAGRAMS — STRUCTURE

The following ten words are anagrams of terms used in chemistry. What are they?

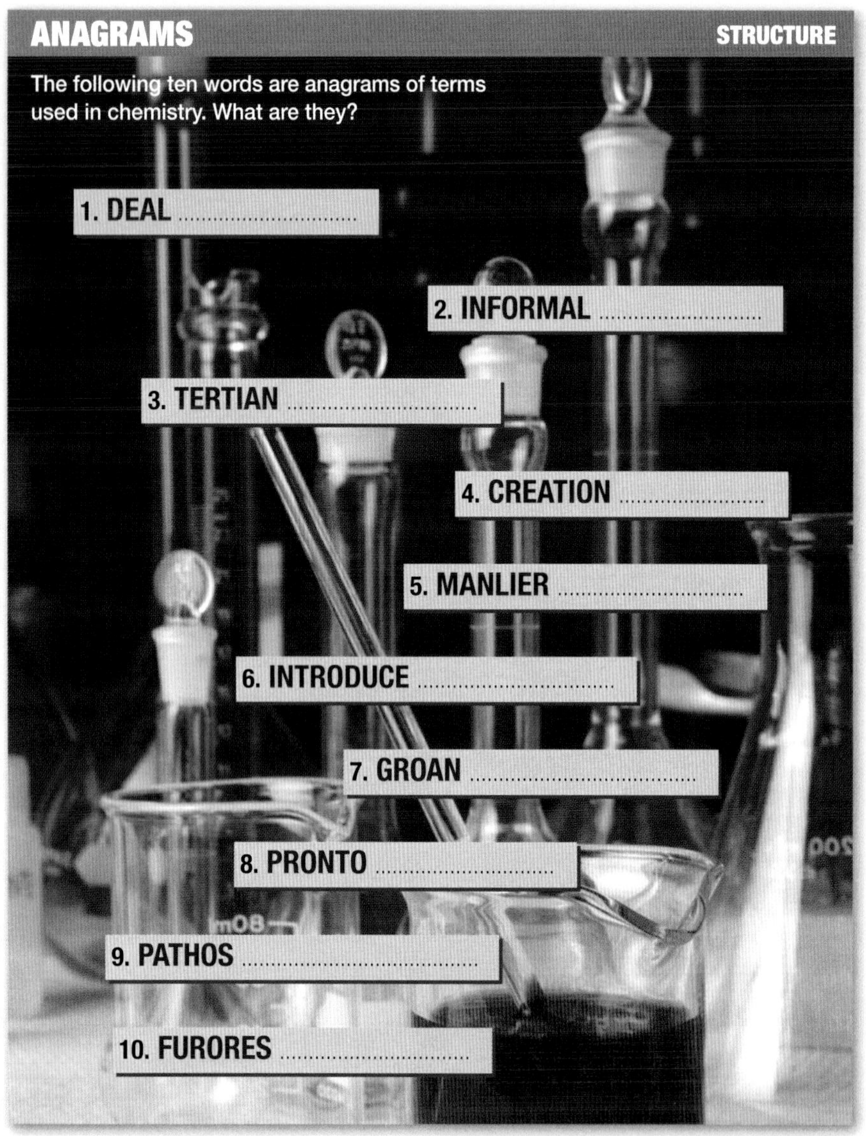

CHALLENGE — CONCENTRATION

Look carefully at this list of 20 compound words for several minutes. Cover it and see how many you can write down in one minute. You will be making your short-term memory work.

List to memorise

Vol-au-vent	April fool
Bread bin	Horse brass
Food processor	Medicine ball
Capri pants	Fair play
Scottish terrier	House style
Neck brace	Nanny goat
Hot dog	Paper nautilus
King cobra	Royal purple
Crew cut	Double bass
Bus lane	Shadow play

....	....
....	....
....	....
....	....
....	....
....	....
....	....
....	....
....	....
....	....

WHICH COMES NEXT? — LOGIC

These playing cards have been arranged in a certain order and the last card has been replaced by a joker. Can you say what this card should be?

LOOPY LETTERS — STRUCTURE

Work out the order in which these letters must be placed to spell the names of two Italian Renaissance painters. One name reads from left to right and the other from right to left. Note that one letter from each line has been switched to the other line, to make the task more difficult.

ANAPHRASES

STRUCTURE

Use all the letters given to form anagrams that will complete the sentence and give it a meaning.

1. M D I C L P E O

The person who .... the list of regulations probably had a very clear idea of how they should be .... with.

2. T D S R E E N I

The .... of the house came home rather inebriated on Friday and seemed to have difficulty as he .... the key into the lock.

3. N A D O I E T E C S R

Those who commit acts of .... are not very ....

MATCHING UP

ASSOCIATION

Try to match up each of these quotes with the country, city or state to which it refers.

Egypt	A	A.........	1	The nation's thyroid gland.
Rome	B	B.........	2	Reform is (its) second revolution.
California	C	C.........	3	That knuckle-end of England.
Venice	D	D.........	4	They do there as they see done.
London	E	E.........	5	Good Americans go to ... when they die.
Scotland	F	F.........	6	Like eating an entire box of chocolate liqueurs in one go.
Paris	G	G.........	7	A wonderful place to live – for an orange.
Athens	H	H.........	8	A roost for every bird.
New York	I	I.........	9	From whose all dateless tombs arose forgotten pharaohs.
China	J	J.........	10	The eye of Greece, mother of art.

PROBLEM

LOGIC

There I was, praying peacefully in an isolated little church in the south of France, when three men dressed in silk burst in, each man accompanied by three women. Each woman was carrying three baskets, in each of which three sacred cats were sleeping. How many living creatures were there in the church?

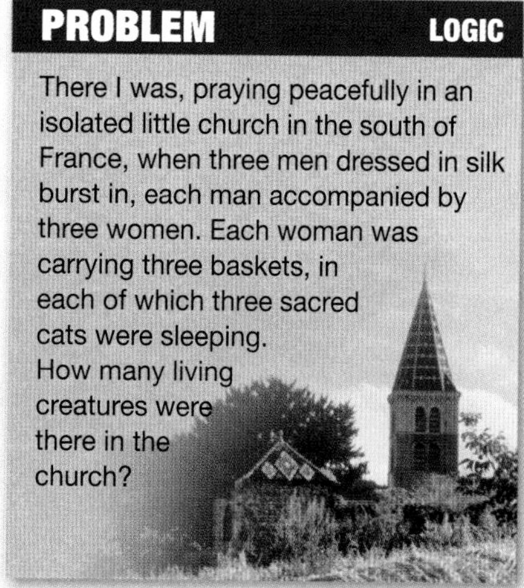

STICK-ON TITLES

GENERAL KNOWLEDGE

Separate the words of these made-up titles, then stick them together again to spell the titles of four films produced by David Lean.

ON THE RIVER LAWRENCE

OF A BRIDGE TO ARABIA

INDIA ENCOUNTER

BRIEF KWAI PASSAGE

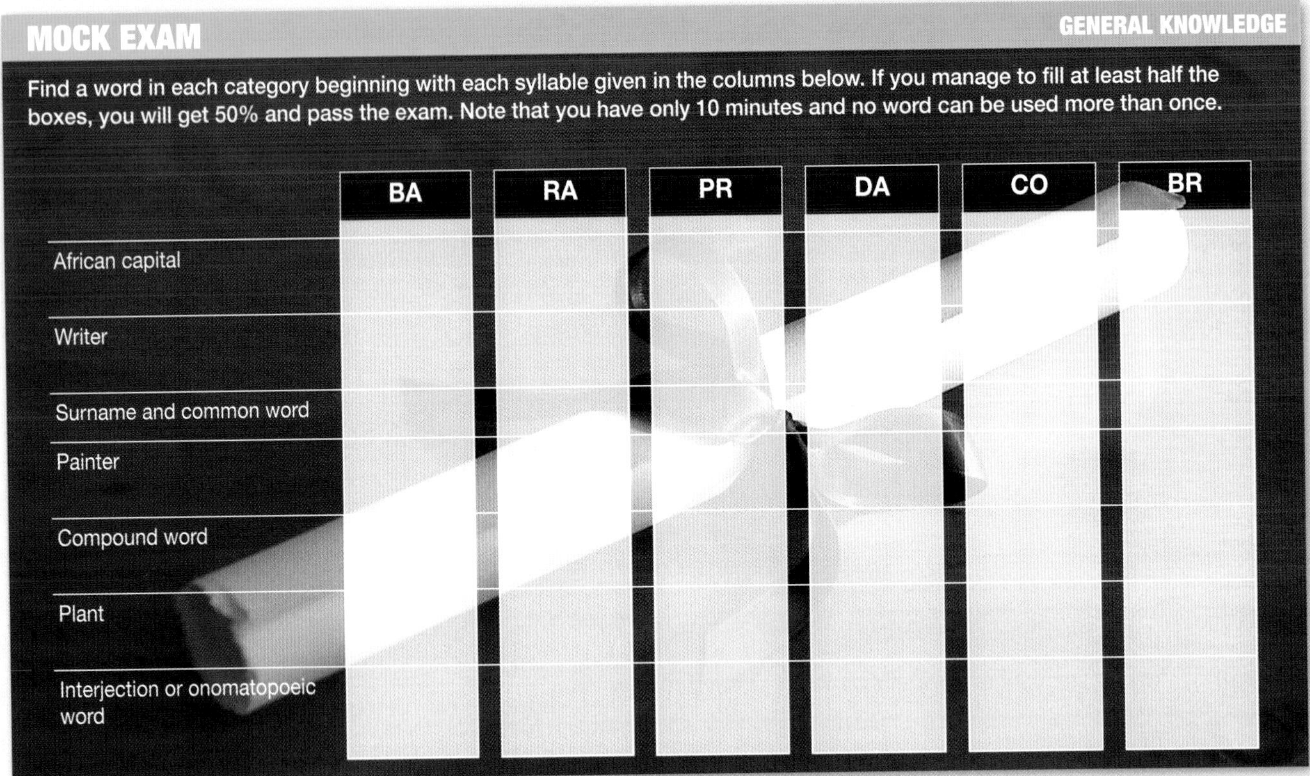

MOCK EXAM

GENERAL KNOWLEDGE

Find a word in each category beginning with each syllable given in the columns below. If you manage to fill at least half the boxes, you will get 50% and pass the exam. Note that you have only 10 minutes and no word can be used more than once.

	BA	RA	PR	DA	CO	BR
African capital						
Writer						
Surname and common word						
Painter						
Compound word						
Plant						
Interjection or onomatopoeic word						

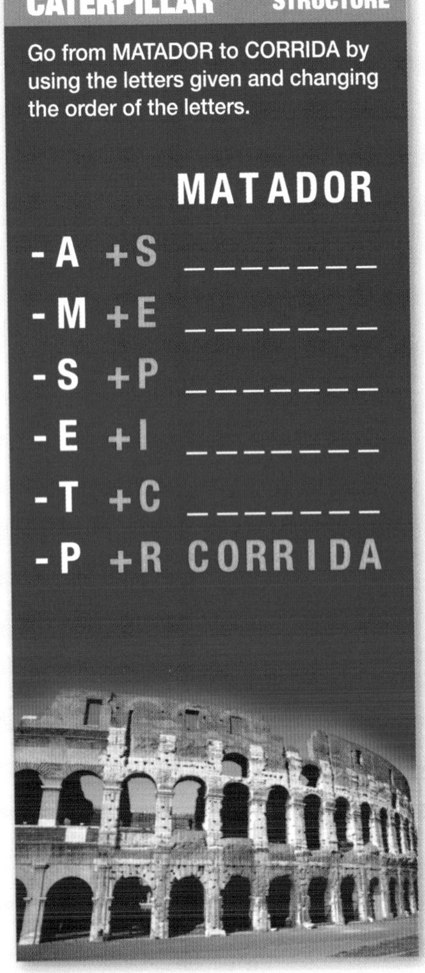

CATERPILLAR

STRUCTURE

Go from MATADOR to CORRIDA by using the letters given and changing the order of the letters.

MATADOR

- A +S _ _ _ _ _ _ _

- M +E _ _ _ _ _ _ _

- S +P _ _ _ _ _ _ _

- E +I _ _ _ _ _ _ _

- T +C _ _ _ _ _ _ _

- P +R CORRIDA

BRAIN TEASER

LOGIC

In a fencing competition, the five finalists faced each other once, and there were three possible outcomes each time: winning (W), losing (L) or a draw (D). With the help of the table below summarising the results, show who won and who lost each match, or if it was a draw.

	ARTHUR	BLAISE	CARLA	DAMIAN	EDWARD
Won	1	4	1	0	2
Lost	1	0	2	3	2
Draw	2	0	1	1	0

ARTHUR	BLAISE

CARLA	DAMIAN

EDWARD	ARTHUR

BLAISE	CARLA

DAMIAN	EDWARD

ARTHUR	CARLA

BLAISE	DAMIAN

CARLA	EDWARD

ARTHUR	DAMIAN

BLAISE	EDWARD

MIXED PROVERBS

GENERAL KNOWLEDGE

The words making up three proverbs have been mixed up. Untangle them to find the original proverbs.

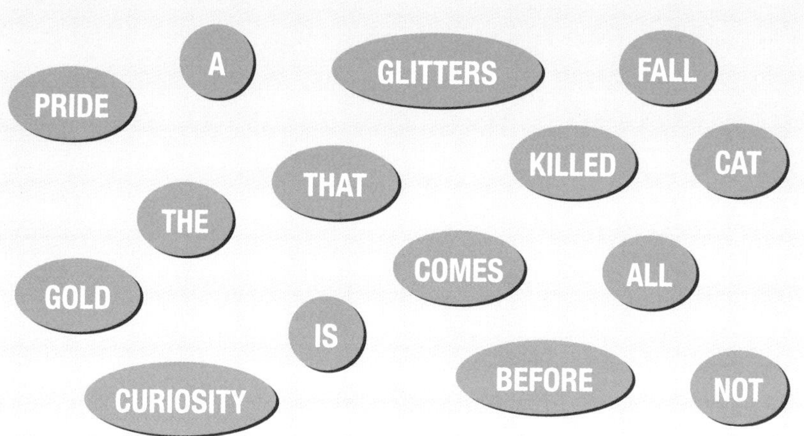

1. ....
....
....

2. ....
....
....

3. ....
....
....

ITINERARY

STRUCTURE

Fill in the names of the following geographical locations horizontally and discover the names of places, read vertically, one in Europe and one in North America.

	A	Z	
	H	Y	
	L	B	
	A	D	
	O	R	
	T	N	

CUBES

STRUCTURE

Use one letter from each face of these cubes to form the names of three literary heroes.

1. .... 2. .... 3. ....

THE RIGHT SUM

LOGIC

Using these 16 numbers, reach a total of 130 in all possible directions (including diagonally), by placing each number in a box identical to the one it is written in.

MAGIC SQUARE

LOGIC

All the numbers making up this magic square can be written in the form of y = 2+ 5x, with x varying between 0 and 24. Bearing this in mind, try to find the nine missing numbers.

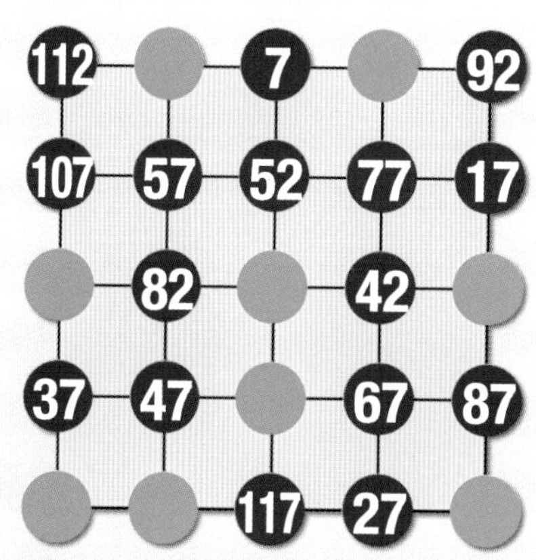

ZIGZAG WORDS

STRUCTURE

The film titles hidden in this grid can be read in all directions: horizontally and vertically, from the top down or the bottom up, from right to left or the opposite. The words can turn corners but must never overlap, and each letter can be used only once (watch out for multiple pathways). With the remaining letters you can spell out the name of one last film, launched the same year as *The Godfather*.

S	D	I	E	R	M	I	N	A	N	E	D	A	L	P	D	E	U
N	I	S	A	Y	R	E	T	T	O	R	D	T	O	M	A	G	S
I	D	S	R	A	C	S	A	N	D	S	I	H	O	A	E	R	E
S	S	A	I	W	B	U	L	T	I	N	M	E	N	E	A	A	I
I	M	R	D	I	C	O	P	A	T	I	L	R	G	C	S	E	R
N	A	E	G	C	U	M	I	N	E	G	A	C	B	N	A	A	R
E	L	R	L	U	L	D	C	E	A	T	P	D	R	I	D	P	A
N	A	C	E	T	A	R	N	I	K	I	I	R	F	B	H	O	C
I	S	I	X	A	N	A	C	U	S	E	T	A	L	A	S	C	C
H	I	E	L	C	O	R	E	L	H	G	I	H	R	O	B	O	H
C	N	O	I	K	E	U	N	A	L	A	D	I	V	M	N	W	I
O	I	S	S	A	T	D	L	O	W	N	T	T	A	A	P	O	N
D	N	U	H	G	E	I	L	R	E	D	A	A	H	N	R	T	A
N	U	N	O	R	E	W	R	N	O	E	N	D	I	V	O	A	M
A	R	A	S	T	B	M	A	A	V	C	N	E	S	E	U	N	M
M	T	A	B	T	O	C	A	S	A	A	B	Y	S	L	L	E	E

ABYSS
AMADEUS
ASSASSINS
BATMAN
BIRDCAGE
CARRIE
CASANOVA
CASINO
CHINATOWN
COPLAND
DIDIER
DIVA
DRACULA
DUNE
ELISA
EMMANUELLE
FLASHDANCE
GERMINAL
GHOST
GREASE
GREMLINS
HIDDEN
HIGHLANDER
INDOCHINE
MANHATTAN
MULAN
NIKITA
PIRATES
PLATOON
PROVIDENCE
RAMBO
RIDICULE
ROBOCOP
ROCKETEER
SUBWAY
TAXI
TERMINATOR
TITANIC
URANUS
WILLOW

PROBLEM

LOGIC

The first two scales are balanced. Will the third tip to the right or the left, or is it also balanced? (Cubes of the same colour weigh the same.)

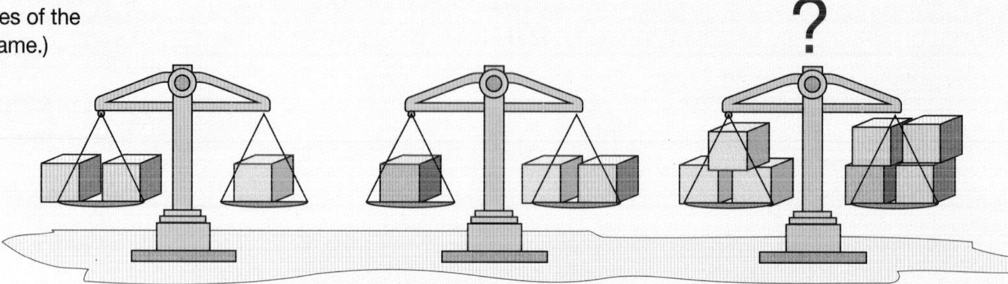

TWO MAKE A PAIR — ASSOCIATION

With the help of the definitions provided, find 10 words containing the letters DON, in that sequence.

1. A pale green colour ➤ _ _ _ _ _ _ _ _
2. This person sorts out crooked teeth ➤ _ _ _ _ _ _ _
3. The pursuit of pleasure ➤ _ _ _ _ _ _ _ _ _
4. A Renaissance sculptor ➤ _ _ _ _ _ _ _ _ _ _ _
5. A symphony by Vaughan Williams ➤ _ _ _ _ _ _ _ _ _ _ _
6. The sound made by a bell ➤ _ _ _ _ _ _ _ _ _ _ _
7. Instrument played for the tango ➤ _ _ _ _ _ _ _ _ _ _ _ _
8. Grape variety, originating from Burgundy and Champagne ➤ _ _ _ _ _ _ _ _ _ _ _
9. Poisonous plant with beautiful flowers, often pink ➤ _ _ _ _ _ _ _ _ _ _ _
10. A prehistoric reptile ➤ _ _ _ _ _ _ _ _ _

MATCHES — LOGIC

Make six triangles by moving four matches in this design of two hour-glasses placed side by side.

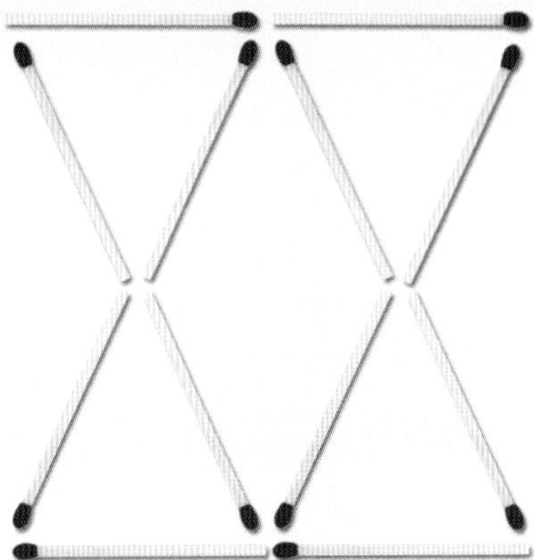

ANAGRAMS — STRUCTURE

The following 10 words are anagrams of terms associated with art. Can you work them out?

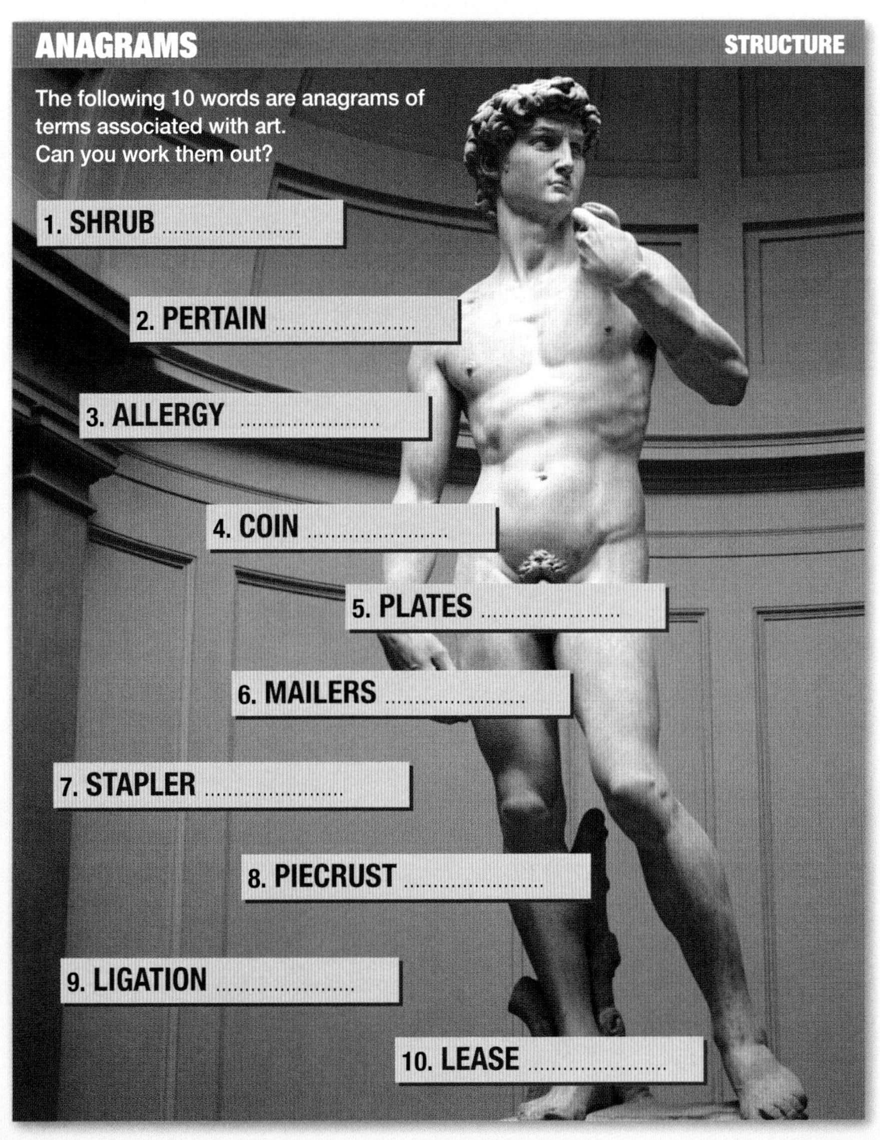

1. SHRUB ....
2. PERTAIN ....
3. ALLERGY ....
4. COIN ....
5. PLATES ....
6. MAILERS ....
7. STAPLER ....
8. PIECRUST ....
9. LIGATION ....
10. LEASE ....

HOMOGRAPHS — LANGUAGE

Find the pairs of homographs (words with the same spelling but differing in meaning) that will complete the following sentences and give them a meaning.

1. The driver turned _ _ _ _ _ _ _ _ and _ _ _ _ _ _ _ _ the highway.
2. Because he was _ _ _ _ _ _ _, he _ _ _ _ _ _ _ a hole into the plank.
3. The police officer became _ _ _ _ _ _ _ _ and blew his whistle because the pedestrian tried to _ _ _ _ _ _ _ _ the road against a red traffic light.
4. Although his camping torch was _ _ _ _ _ _ _ _ in weight, it gave off a good _ _ _ _ _ _ _ _ and allowed him to see clearly in the dark.

LOGIGRAM

LOGIC

FRIENDS OF EXOTIC PETS

In the little community of Friends of Exotic Pets, the FREP, four citizens of Animotown, Messrs Boa, Crocodile, Tarantula and Monitor, placed notices on their front doors to alert passers-by to the pets inside. But Mr Cuckoo, a great troublemaker, wickedly mixed up the notices during the night. In the morning, Cuckoo's eight sons, much more civic-minded than their father, tried to put things right. They tried to remember the information available to them so they could restore the messages on the doors of the rightful owners of the strange animals.

16 words are to be used to make four sentences.
Word 1: Boa, Crocodile, Tarantula, Monitor
Word 2: Accommodates, feeds, refuses, sells
Word 3: three, four, six, eight
Word 4: boas, crocodiles, tarantulas, monitors

Clues obtained by the Cuckoo brothers

1. Tarantula does not sell.
2. Boa and four are in the same sentence.
3. Accommodation and monitors are in the same sentence.
4. Refuse and crocodiles do not appear in the same sentence.
5. Tarantula and Crocodile are not in the same sentence.
6. Six and monitors are in the same sentence.
7. Eight and crocodiles are in the same sentence.
8. Boa and Tarantula do not offer meals or accommodation.

Table of answers

	Sentence 1	Sentence 2	Sentence 3	Sentence 4
Word 1				
Word 2				
Word 3				
Word 4				

ANAPHRASES

STRUCTURE

Make use of all the letters given here to form anagrams which will complete each sentence and give it a meaning.

1. I O R E P S I M N S

He was under the .... that he had been given .... to go home early.

2. R N U L A C E

Some people are .... about the safety of .... energy.

TWO MAKE A PAIR

ASSOCIATION

Use the following definitions to find 10 words containing the smaller word GAT.

1. Crocodile ➤ _ _ _ _ _ _ _ _ _
2. Bird found in tropical oceans ➤ _ _ _ _ _ _ _
3. A mere trifle ➤ _ _ _ _ _ _ _ _ _
4. Acting unselfishly ➤ _ _ _ _ _ _ _ _ _ _ _
5. Place of temporary purification ➤ _ _ _ _ _ _ _ _ _ _ _
6. Ground almonds in caramel ➤ _ _ _ _ _ _ _ _ _ _
7. An uninvited guest ➤ _ _ _ _ _ _ _ _
8. Airport near London ➤ _ _ _ _ _ _ _ _ _
9. Latin translation of the Bible ➤ _ _ _ _ _ _ _
10. An assembly or meeting ➤ _ _ _ _ _ _ _ _ _ _ _

MAGIC NUMBER

LOGIC

Choose a number of 4 digits, with at least 2 different digits (not 2222!). Take for example 7584. Write the digits in decreasing order, that is, **a** = 8754. Then write the digits in ascending order, that is, **b** = 4578. Then calculate **a - b**. Next, repeat the preceding operation, starting with the result of this subtraction.

Repeat this, taking different examples of numbers, and repeat the operation until you observe an interesting phenomenon that has intrigued generations of mathematicians.

HIDDEN WORDS

STRUCTURE

The 56 words concealed in this grid all have to do with music and can be read in any direction: horizontally and vertically, diagonally, from top to bottom or bottom up, from right to left and the opposite. The words overlap and the same letter can be used more than once. With the letters remaining you can make one last word that refers to an 'instrument' used in music.

A S C O N G A P O S S I Y M
C L I P T H S H A O D B A E
O V L T F L C C L R L O T R
P E I E A E A O E O I O S Y
M A L V G R T V D M T A E L
E C O C A R I N A N E N L W
T R E M O L O N A A R W M O
A E N O T R D C R D A O C L
P T A N G O C I P O N B S S
A U E O B O H I Y C S A O E
S L M U R D A U J E T O N T
P O O D D N U O S A K O A U
A E U I T R E H T I Z N T L
R E E L V I O L I N B Z A F

ACCORD
ALLEGRO
ALTO
ANDANTE
ARIA
BOW
CANTO
CELESTA
CLEF
CLIP
CODA
CLEF
CONGA
DOLBY
DRUM
ECHO
FLUTE
JAZZ
KEY
LENTO
LIVE
LUTE
LYRE
MARACAS
NOTE
OBOE
OCARINA
OPUS
PIANO
RAÏ
RAP
REEL
RONDO
SCAT
SITAR
SLOW
SNARE
SOLO
SONATA
SOUL
SOUND
TANGO
TAP
TEMPO
TONE
TREMOLO
VERDI
VIOLA
VIOLIN
VIVALDI
ZITHER

WORD PAIRS

ASSOCIATION

Memorise these word pairs for one minute. Use all the mnemonic techniques you can think of. Then cover them and answer the six questions.

Superstar – Instigator

Supplier – Accessoriser

Champion – Recreation

Incognito – Conversion

Perversion – Star

Diversion – Stardom

Drunk – Ripening

Hieroglyph – Rawness

Originator – Superbly

Egyptian – Blushing

Questions

1. Which word is coupled with the shortest word on the list?
2. Which derivative of 'version' is 'incognito' paired with?
3. Which word is paired with Egyptian writing?
4. Which word is found just before entertainment?
5. Which word is 'instigator' paired with?
6. Which words not yet cited have the same etymological derivation?

POINTS IN COMMON

ASSOCIATION

Find, for each of these series, a word that has a direct connection with the other three words.

1. line, number, call

2. field, drinking, reading

3. keeper, worm, address

4. book, brief, sad

5. cuff, second, bag

6. weight, wall, plate

HISTORICAL LANDMARKS — TIME

Place the following events in the correct chronological order.

- **A** Assassination of Caligula by the members of the Praetorian Guard
- **B** Trojan War
- **C** Carthage founded by the Phoenicians
- **D** Legendary foundation of Rome and assassination of Remus by Romulus
- **E** Assassination of Caesar and start of the third civil war
- **F** Hannibal crosses the Alps and suffers the loss of a large proportion of his army
- **G** Death of Rameses II; his son, Merenptah, succeeds him
- **H** Trial and death of Socrates

1 ....
2 ....
3 ....
4 ....
5 ....
6 ....
7 ....
8 ....

PROBLEM — LOGIC

Camilla suggests the following game to Virgil: if Virgil hits target A with his dart gun he wins 1 dollar; if he hits target B, he gets 3 dollars. But if he misses both, he must give 2 dollars to Camilla. After an hour and 70 shots, Virgil has a total of between 30 and 40 dollar. He hit target A 10 more times than he missed the targets.

A = $1 **B = $3**

How many times did Virgil hit each of the 3 zones (target A, target B and in-between) during this hour and exactly how much did he win?

POINTS IN COMMON — ASSOCIATION

Find, for each of these series, a word that can be used with the other three words.

1. **blue – honey – full** ....
2. **stop– stud – printing** ....
3. **shift – good – club** ....
4. **common – shoulder – feet** ....
5. **quick – stone – blast** ....
6. **drawing – cushion – safety** ....

BROKEN SEQUENCES — STRUCTURE

Six words have had some of their syllables removed. Put the words together again, using the syllables provided. Note that in some cases there are several possible solutions, but only one will enable you to restore all the words.

1. .... **TY**
2. **IN** ....
3. .... **INE**
4. .... **DISE**
5. **A** ....
6. .... **FEI** ....

TED, DI, BRI, RI, CEN, SAC, OC, ME, CHAR, FOR, VIA, RY, HY, SED

CATERPILLAR — STRUCTURE

Go from WORDS to SONGS in this caterpillar by substituting the letters as indicated and changing the order of the letters.

W O R D S

- O + A _ _ _ _ _ _ _

- R + N _ _ _ _ _ _ _

- A + I _ _ _ _ _ _ _

- D + G _ _ _ _ _ _ _

- W + K _ _ _ _ _ _ _

- G + S _ _ _ _ _ _ _

- K + G _ _ _ _ _ _ _

- I + O **S O N G S**

WHICH COMES NEXT? LOGIC

Find the figure that completes the logical sequence in each case.

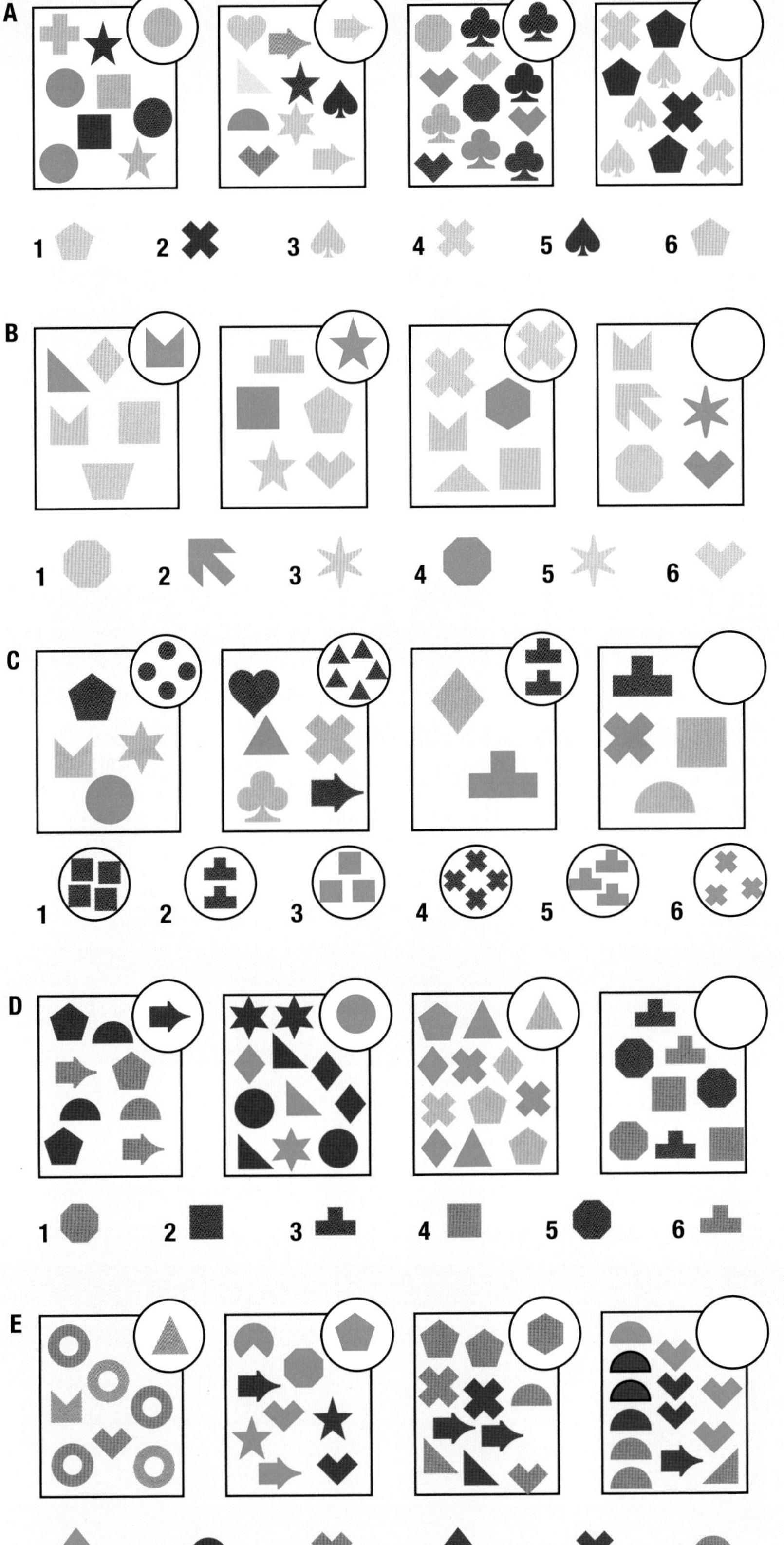

SANDWICH STRUCTURE

Complete the five-letter words written horizontally and you will find, in the third column, a proverb on foolishness. There are several possibilities at times but only one will lead you to the right proverb.

C	R		B	S
S	A		E	R
S	L		T	S
W	O		D	Y
P	A		E	R
L	E		S	E
T	E		O	R
A	D		E	R
O	T		E	R
A	L		E	N
C	A		E	S
T	I		E	R
B	L		C	K
C	A		A	L
F	E		D	S
M	A		O	R
B	E		C	H
B	I		D	S
S	C		N	E
B	A		E	D
A	R		S	E
S	H		R	T
S	E		D	S
P	A		E	R
W	H		L	E
B	O		E	D
W	A		E	R
S	P		L	L
R	I		E	R

MIXED QUOTES

GENERAL KNOWLEDGE

The words making up three quotations have been mixed up. Untangle them to find the original quotations attributed to Mao Zedong.

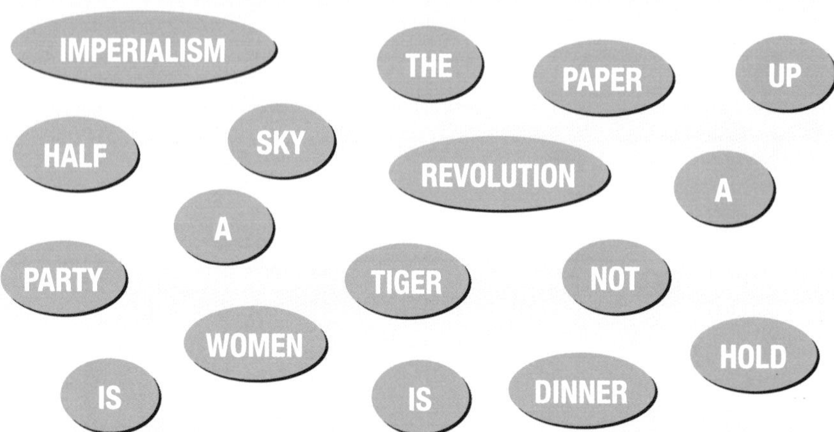

1. ....

....

....

2. ....

....

....

3. ....

....

....

WHICH COMES NEXT?

LOGIC

1. Work out what this sequence is based on.

1 4 1 5 9 2 6 5 3 5

2. Find the number that follows logically in the next sequence.

25 29 85 89 145 42 20 ?

3. Find the number that completes the following sequence as logically as possible

60 60 24 ? 52 100 10

4. Find the number that follows logically in the next sequence.

19 14 28 23 37 32 ? 41

IDIOMATIC TRIPLETS

LANGUAGE

Find the term that fits in perfectly with the three words in each line to make a common expression or idiom.

1. wisdom, saw, milk

....

2. helps, himself, taste

....

3. root, makes, talk

....

4. blind, world, way

....

5. healer, flies, tide

....

6. heads, company, tango

....

ITINERARY

STRUCTURE

Complete horizontally the names of towns, to read, vertically, the capital of the Republic of Ireland and a major city in Australia.

	O	U	G	L	A	
	R	U	G	U	A	
	A	G	H	D	A	
	E	B	A	N	O	
	V	A	N	H	O	
	E	W	Q	U	A	

ESCALETTERS

STRUCTURE

Add the letters given one by one to the root word to form new words each time. Several answers are possible.

R E D

+ **U** _ _ _ _
+ **N** _ _ _ _ _
+ **E** _ _ _ _ _ _
+ **T** _ _ _ _ _ _ _
+ **V** _ _ _ _ _ _ _ _
+ **A** _ _ _ _ _ _ _ _ _

STICK-ON WORDS

STRUCTURE

Stick these five-letter words together in pairs to form 12 new 10-letter words.

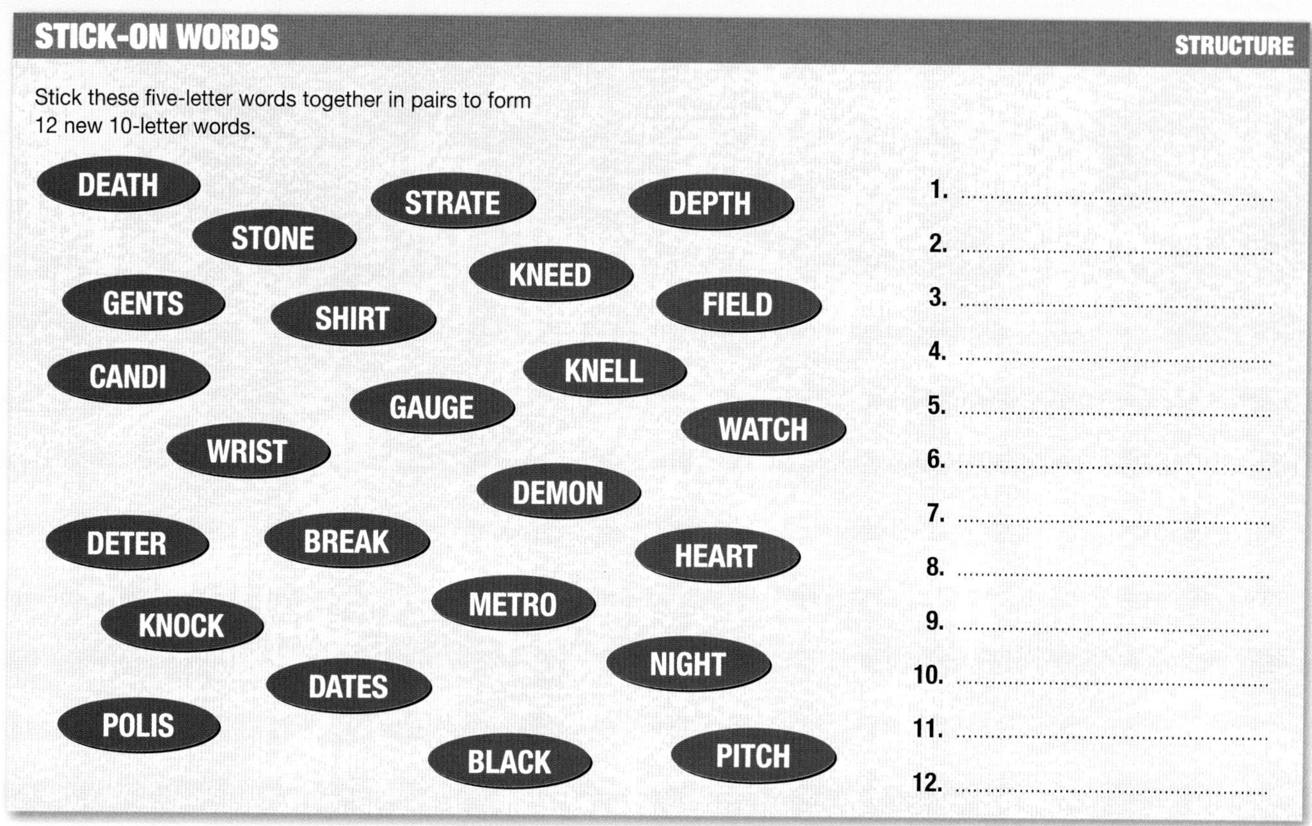

1. ....
2. ....
3. ....
4. ....
5. ....
6. ....
7. ....
8. ....
9. ....
10. ....
11. ....
12. ....

NUMBER PYRAMID

LOGIC

Each brick in the number pyramid is the sum of the two bricks immediately below.
Fill in the whole pyramid, observing the following rules:

- a, b, c, d and e are positive numbers and b is greater than a.
- a = e.
- d = b – 1.
- c = b + 1.

The apex of the pyramid (A) equals 89, 90 or 91 – which is right?

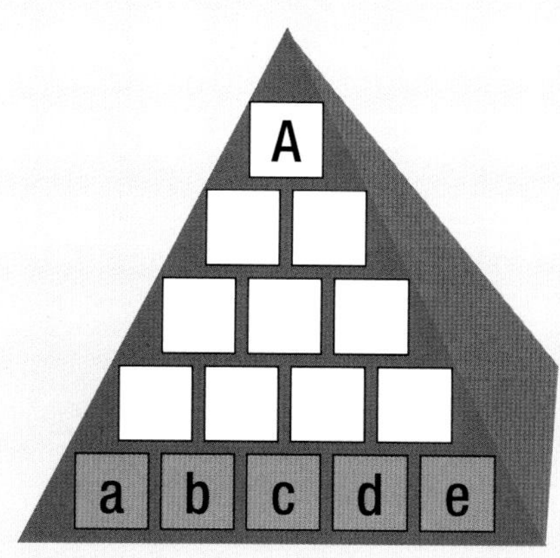

BOXED WORDS

SPACE

Put the names of these 25 singers back in the grid.

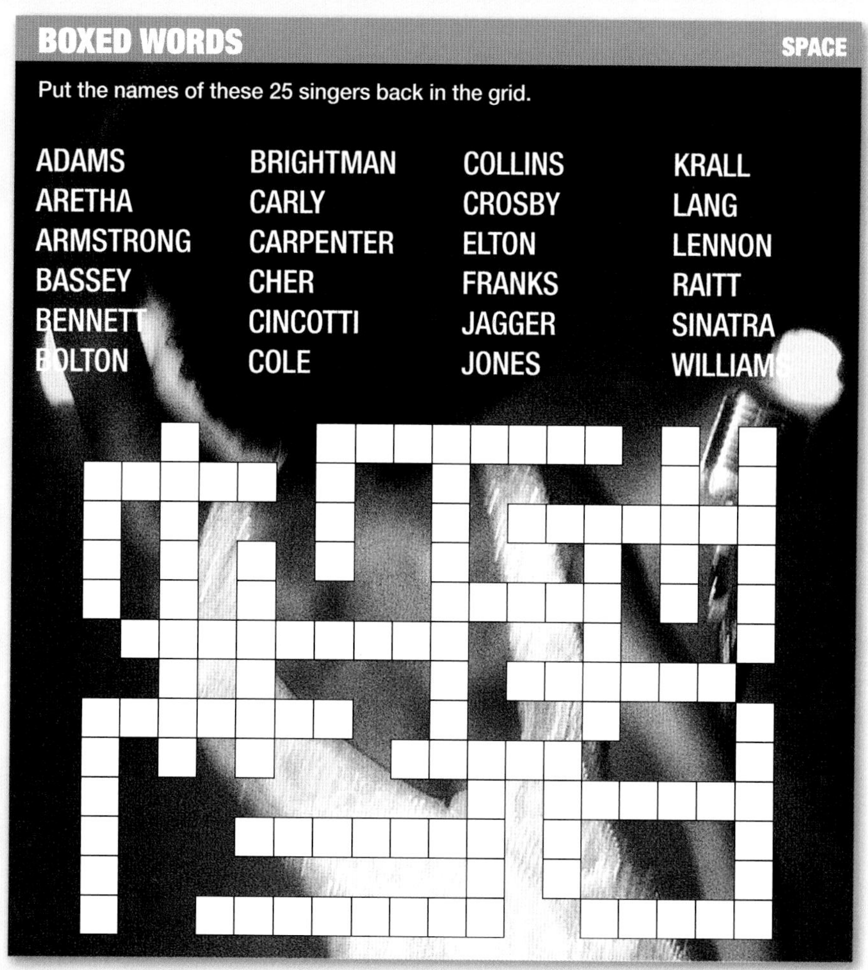

CROSSWORD PUZZLE

Complete the crossword puzzle with the help of the following clues.

Across

I. Charged (7).
5. Ledge (5).
8. Aestivate (9).
9. One quarter of eight (3).
10. Hinder growth (5).
12. One tenth of one thousand (7).
13. Purchased (6).
14. Body of land surrounded by water (6).
17. Not aligned (7).
19. Possessed (5).
21. Sick (3).
22. Acrobatic (9).
24. North East African country (5).
25. Places of learning (7).

Down

1. Fire residues (5).
2. A young lion (3).
3. To extend (7).
4. An apothecary unit: one eighth of an ounce (6).
5. Strict (5).
6. To amuse (9).
7. Inundated (7).
11. Uncommonly (9).
13. It is burned in the open air (7).
15. One of your digestive organs (7).
16. Ascends (6).
18. Correct (5).
20. It shortens the tail (5).
23. Also (3).

PERFECT COPIES?

CONCENTRATION

Which two of these maps are absolutely identical?

A

B

C

D

E

F

GENERAL KNOWLEDGE

PROBLEM

LOGIC

Coquettishly, a certain lady refuses to divulge her age. Finally, tired of being hassled by government departments, she sends the following riddle to the importunate questioners.

'I am between 50 and 80 years old, and each of my children has as many children of his or her own as he or she has brothers and sisters. If you want to know my age, it's easy: it's the same as the number of my descendants.'

How many children and grandchildren does she have, and how many candles will she have to blow out on her next birthday?

CUBES

STRUCTURE

Make three words with Roman Catholic connotations by taking one letter from each side of each cube.

1. .... 2. .... 3. ....

PARONYMS

LANGUAGE

Find the pair of paronyms (for example, collision and collusion) that complete the following sentences in a meaningful way.

1. Her frequent _ _ _ _ _ _ to famous people created the _ _ _ _ _ _ _ _ _ that she mixed in their circles.
2. _ _ _ _ _ _ _ John, who now seems to be her close friend, several other boys have sat _ _ _ _ _ _ _ Mary, the most beautiful girl in the class.
3. Now that we have had a stop for water, we may _ _ _ _ _ _ _ _ _ with our walk, and this time you may _ _ _ _ _ _ _ _ me.
4. Since they come with such high qualifications, we can _ _ _ _ _ _ _ _ _ all the applicants for this job, _ _ _ _ _ _ _ _ _ one, who seems not even to know how to spell his name!

ANAGRAMS

STRUCTURE

The following 10 words are anagrams of units of measurement. Can you identify them?

1. CHIN ....
2. LEAST ....
3. LIME ....
4. MINUET ....
5. NEMESIS ....
6. NOT ....
7. RACE ....
8. NOTES ....
9. RELIT ....
10. TEACHER ....

KNOW YOUR WORLD

SPACE

Make use of the following clues and positions marked on the map to find the names of these 20 cities or geographical features in Africa. Include the name of the country as well, for greater precision.

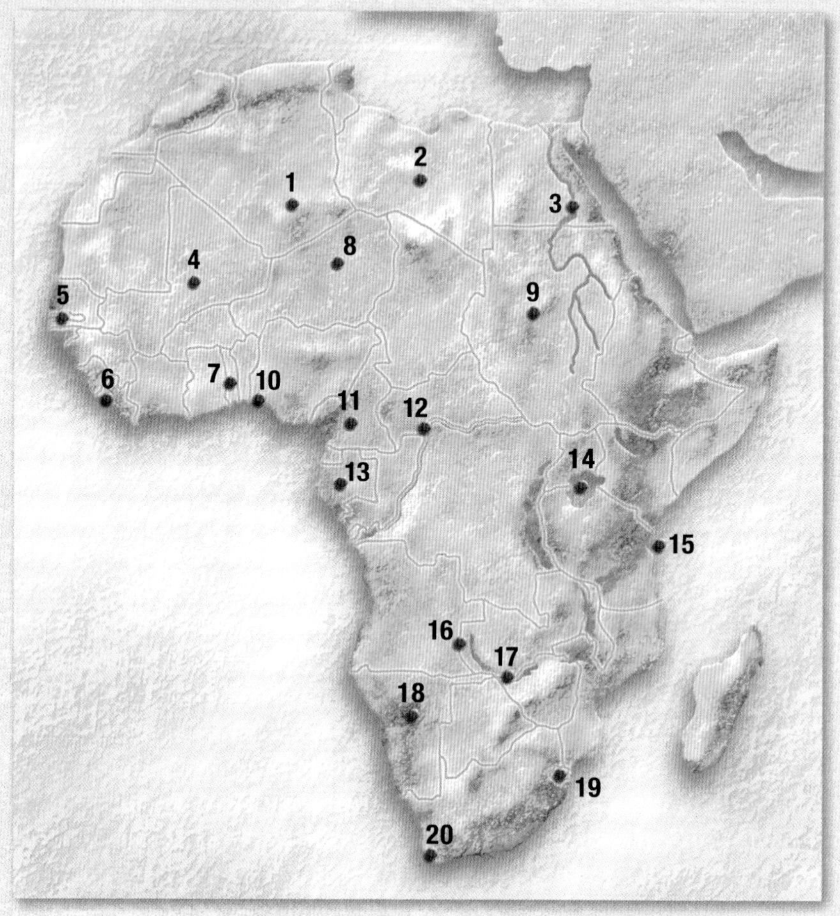

1. I am a volcanic massif inhabited by Tuaregs. I am in the country where Constantine is situated; my highest point is 2918 metres and my principal city is Tamanrasset.
2. My main regions are Tripolitania, Fezzan and Cyrenaica.
3. I am a city on the Nile and a dam (one of the biggest in the world) responsible for filling the reservoir of Lake Nasser.
4. I am a city in the north of a country whose capital is Bamako, and I used to be an important religious and intellectual centre.
5. I am the smallest country on the African continent, my currency is the dalasi and I am situated south of Senegal. My capital is Banjul.
6. I am the capital of a country whose name recalls the history of slavery and whose revenue is drawn largely from the lease of its flag (it possesses the second largest fleet in the world). I was named after an American president.
7. I am a country that is a narrow strip of land opening on to the Gulf of Guinea. My capital, Lomé, is situated on the coast.
8. I am situated in a country in turmoil whose president, Bare Mainsarra, was assassinated in 1999. This area of the Sahara desert is popular with rally enthusiasts and lovers of the desert.
9. A country crossed by the Blue Nile, I include the Nubian Desert in the north and the mountains of Darfur in the west.
10. I am the old capital of my country, and its main port. I was supplanted by Abuja.
11. I have been a member of the Commonwealth since 1995, and my name recalls that of a type of biscuit.
12. I am a river in central Africa and I flow through a capital that has the same name as mine minus the first two letters.
13. I am a country situated on the Atlantic coast, and was probably originally inhabited by Pygmies. My most notable political figure is Omar Bongo and the name of my capital, founded in 1849, recalls my past history as a French colony.
14. I am a large lake and source of the River Nile. Seen from far, I look pink because of the flamingos that gather here in great numbers.
15. I am an island in the Indian Ocean near Pemba. My incorporation into Tanganyika in 1964 gave rise to the name of the country to which I now belong.
16. I am the border between two countries whose names begin with the letters at both ends of the alphabet.
17. A raging river at times during its 2 660 km journey, the Zambezi is strewn with waterfalls. I am one of them, 108 metres high, found on the border of the countries whose capital cities are Lusaka and Harare.
18. My capital is Windhoek and the Gariep (Orange) River marks my border with South Africa. I became independent in 1990.
19. I am a kingdom of 17 000 km^2; my capital is Mbabane and my currency the lilangeni.
20. I am the cape at the southern tip of Africa, discovered by Bartholomew Dias in 1488 and rounded by Vasco da Gama in 1497. My old name was Cape of Storms.

MIXED PROVERBS — GENERAL KNOWLEDGE

The words making up three proverbs have been mixed up. It's up to you to disentangle them and find the originals.

MASTER TRADES NONE
MAKES OF HEART
GROW OF FONDER
ABSENCE JACK THE
KNOWLEDGE ALL
IS POWER

1. ....
....
....
....

2. ....
....
....
....

3. ....
....
....
....

ESCALETTERS — STRUCTURE

Add the letters provided one at a time to form new words.

ALE

+ **B** _ _ _ _
+ **M** _ _ _ _ _
+ **C** _ _ _ _ _ _
+ **I** _ _ _ _ _ _ _
+ **A** _ _ _ _ _ _ _ _
+ **N** _ _ _ _ _ _ _ _ _

MATCHING UP — ASSOCIATION

Pair each writer with his or her own quotation.

Dorothy Parker	A	A.........	1	Great thoughts, like great deeds, need no trumpet.
Coleridge	B	B.........	2	Memory is the treasury and guardian of all things.
Gracian	C	C.........	3	All the world's a stage.
Sophocles	D	D.........	4	Of all noises, I think music is the least disagreeable.
Stephen King	E	E.........	5	Wise-cracking is simply callisthenics with words.
Shakespeare	F	F.........	6	Poetry: the best words in the best order.
Samuel Johnson	G	G.........	7	Good things, when short, are twice as good.
Emily Dickinson	H	H.........	8	Fiction is the truth inside the lie.
Cicero	I	I.........	9	A short saying often contains much wisdom.
Philip Bailey	J	J.........	10	Success is counted sweetest by those who ne'er succeed.

ONE WORD TOO MANY — LOGIC

In each of the following series of words cross out the one that doesn't have the same property as the others. Look carefully at the letters that make up each word, and at possible additions or substitutions.

1. **Symbol – Reaching – Sighted – Flung – Fetched – Out**

2. **Achromatic – Beech – Chamber – Dutch – Hatch – Matching**

3. **Blood – Wine – Face – Grass – Light – Hair**

MIXED QUOTES — GENERAL KNOWLEDGE

The words making up three quotations about evil have been mixed up. Untangle them to find the original quotations.

1. ....
....
....

2. ....
....
....

3. ....
....
....

HISTORICAL LANDMARKS — TIME

Pair up these actors and actresses. The rule is that they were both born in the same year. Then try to classify them chronologically from the oldest to the youngest.

Alec Baldwin	A	1. .... and ....
Cameron Diaz	B	
William Hurt	C	2. .... and ....
Russell Crowe	D	
Wayne Brady	E	3. .... and ....
Juliette Binoche	F	
Charlotte Rampling	G	4. .... and ....
Tom Selleck	H	
Christian Slater	I	5. .... and ....
Sharon Stone	J	
Julie Walters	K	6. .... and ....
Renee Zellweger	L	

CLOSE-UP — CONCENTRATION

Identify the object, animal or person shown in this close-up.

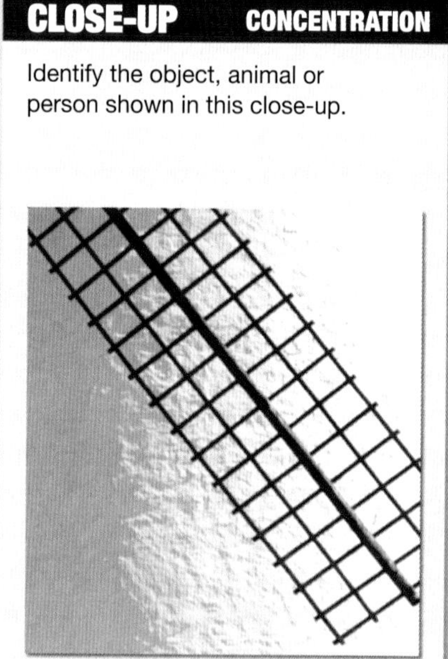

CUBES — STRUCTURE

Make three names of plants used in herbal teas by taking one letter from each side of each cube.

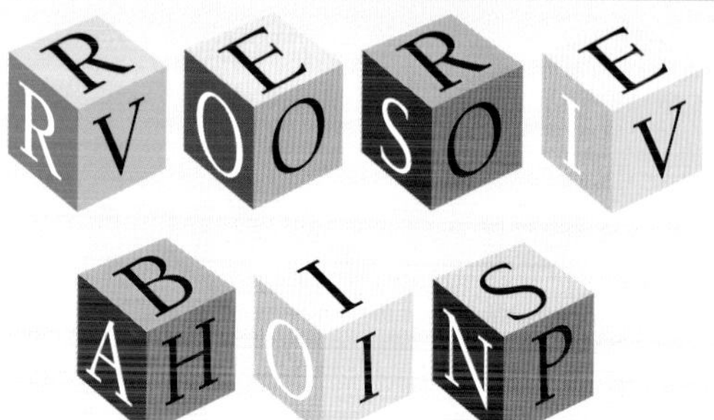

1. .... 2. .... 3. ....

PROBLEM — LOGIC

Ronald has lost plenty of money at poker this year and he now has to pay his friends back. If he divides the sum due by 2, 3, 4, 5, 6, 7, 8, 9 or 10, he never gets the right amount and is always left with one dollar over after the division. Taking this as an omen, he goes to play this fictive remaining dollar at the casino and miraculously wins back all he had lost.
What is the minimum amount that Ronald lost before his fantastic stroke of luck?

ODD ONE OUT — LOGIC

Find the odd one out in each of these series of diagrams, that is, the only one that doesn't share certain elements found in all the others.

A

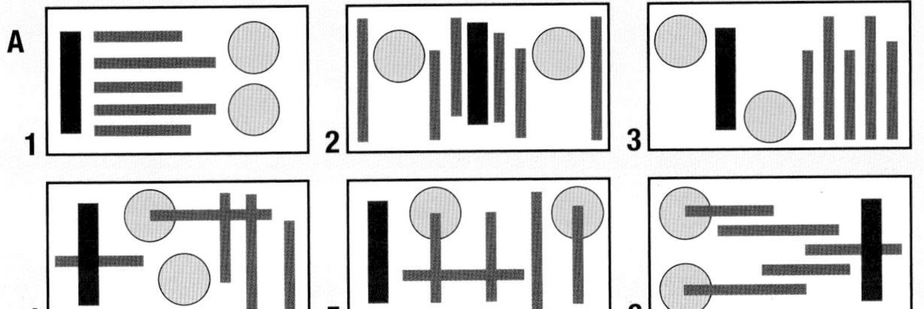

B

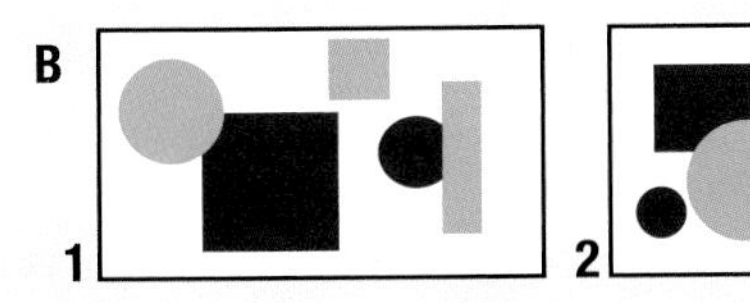

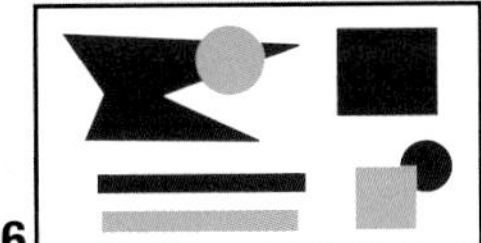

C

D

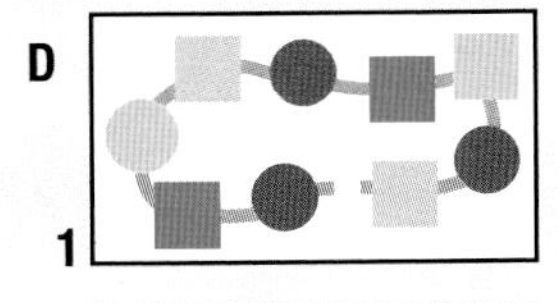

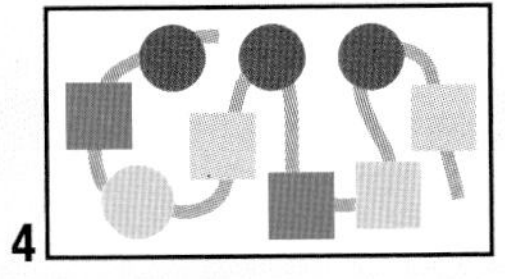

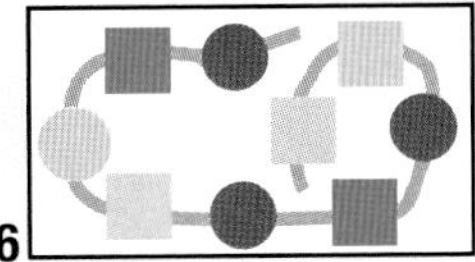

E

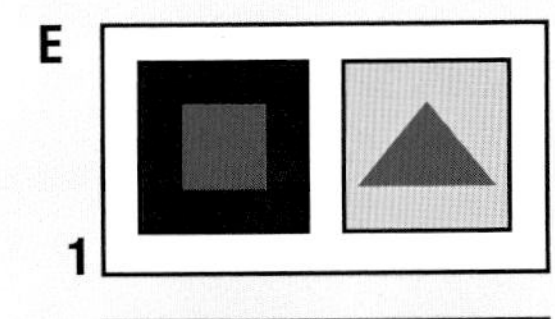

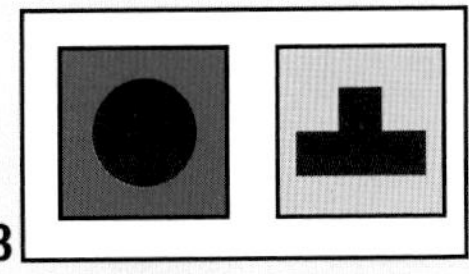
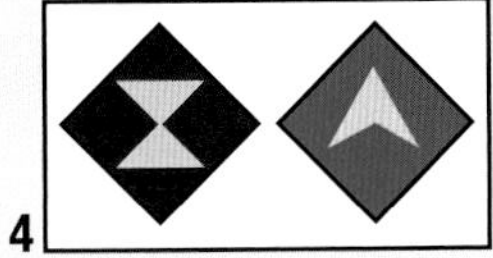
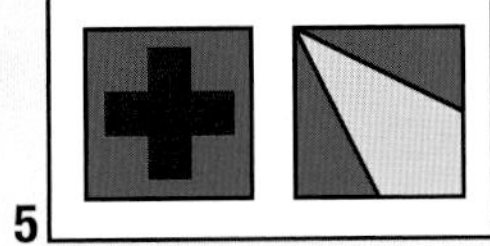
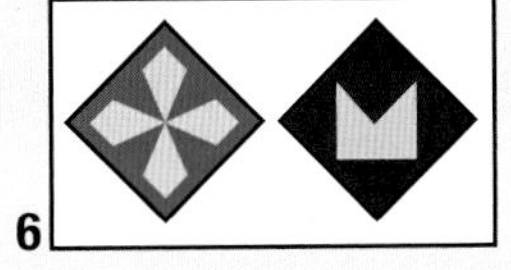

HOMOPHONES — LANGUAGE

Find homophones (words that sound the same but differ in meaning) to complete the meaning of the following sentences.

1. *The seeds that are to be ____ have been ____ into a sack for sale.*

2. *I ___ that the bird could ____ for hours without developing ____ muscles.*

3. *She had only a few _____ and she had the good _____ not to waste her money on costly ______.*

4. *A person who takes self-defence _______ probably _______ his or her chances of being robbed in the street.*

SPEED LIMIT OF 90! — LOGIC

Using these 16 numbers, reach a total of 90, no more, in all possible directions (even diagonally) by placing each one in a box identical to the shape it is written in.

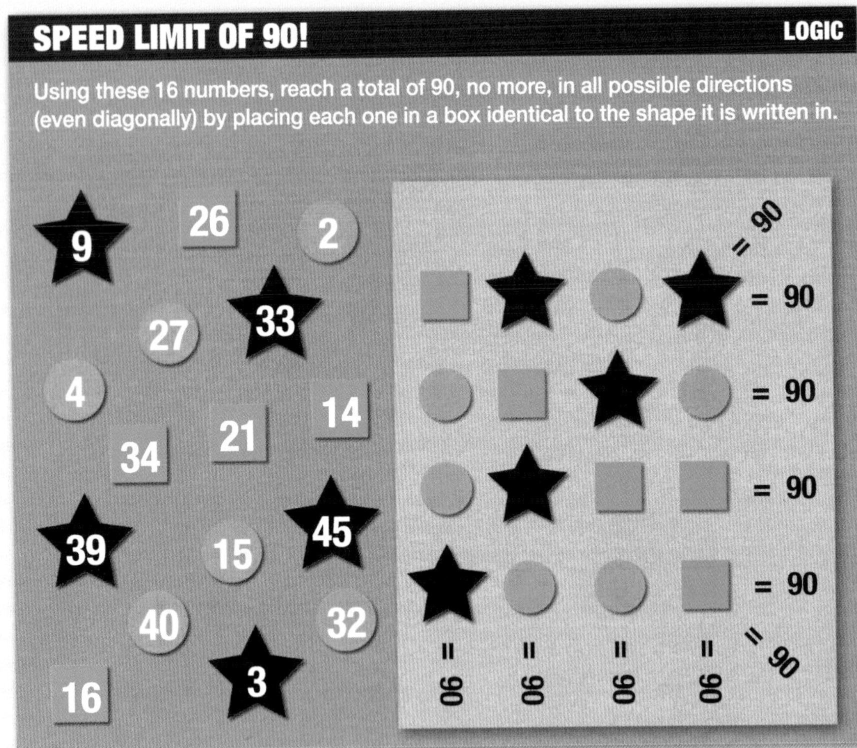

WORD HOLES — LANGUAGE

Fill the gaps in the following words to transform the proper nouns into common nouns.

1. _ P A _ U L _
2. _ _ L U C _ _ _ Y
3. I _ V _ _ A _ _ _ N
4. J _ _ _ _ E _ _ A N
5. M A _ _ R _ T I _ N
6. R _ _ _ O G _ _ _ _ E R

PUZZLE — SPACE

Look at this figure.

Which four numbered pieces do we need to make figure A? (Do not superimpose the pieces or rotate them).

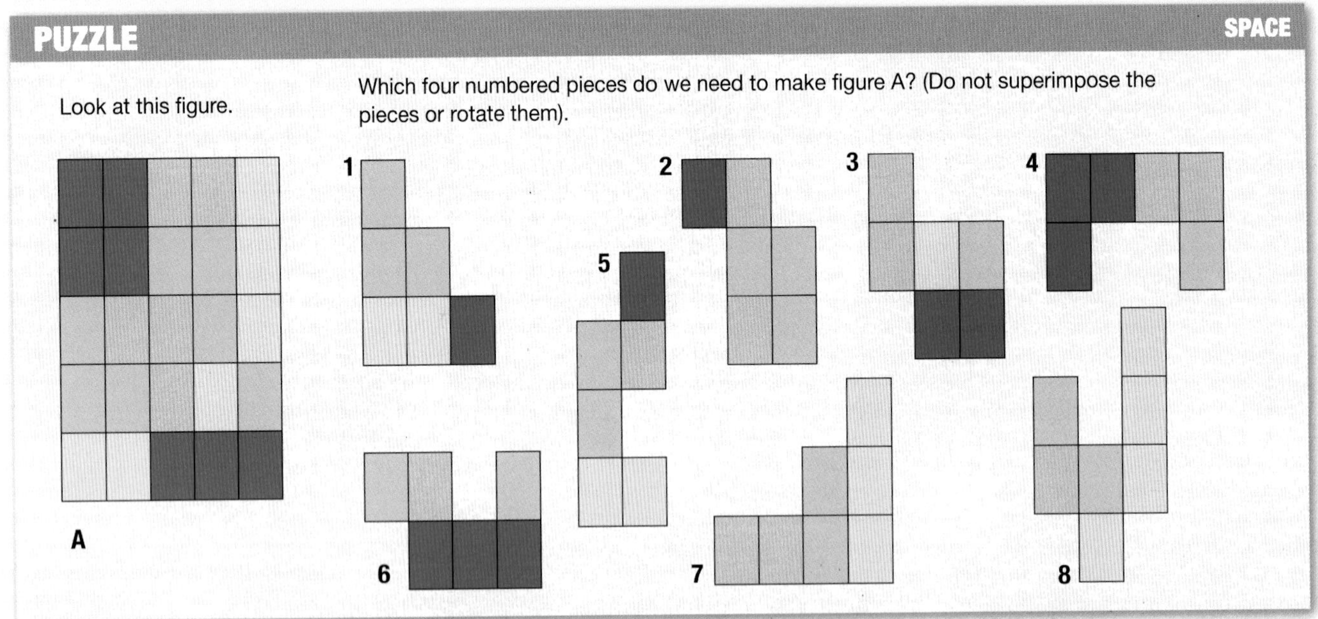

ONE WORD TOO MANY — LOGIC

In each of the following series of words, cross out the one that does not have the same property as the others. Pay special attention to the letters of which each word is composed.

1. Bake – Gin – King – Mite – Ram – Row
2. Abcess – Indefinite – Afghan – Narghile – Somnolence – Retro
3. Casting – Fleeting – Martinets – Stand – Penitent – Trick

WHICH COMES NEXT? LOGIC

1. Find the number that follows logically in this sequence:

4 | 32 | 256 | 2 048 | 16 384 | 131 072 | ?

2. Find the numbers that complete the molecules in the centre.

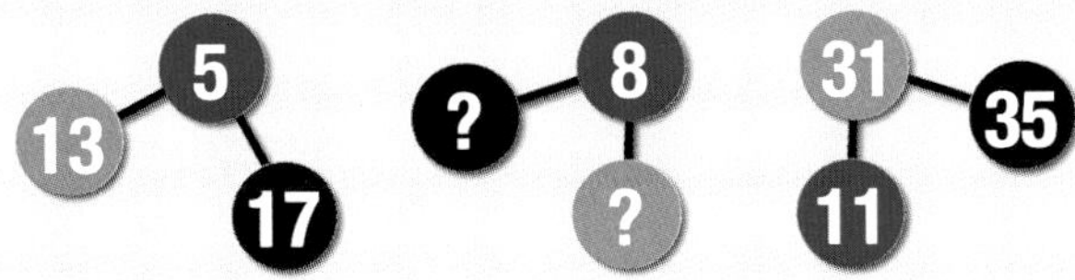

3. Find the line that continues the following logical sequence:

1
1 1
2 1
1 2 1 1
1 1 1 2 2 1
3 1 2 2 1 1
1 3 1 1 2 2 2 1
1 1 1 3 2 1 3 2 1 1
? ? ? ? ? ? ? ? ? ? ? ? ? ?

LADDER STRUCTURE

Use the eight crosspieces to reconstruct the ladder in such a way that words suggesting two American holidays can be read vertically. Certain letters are missing in the crosspieces, and you have to find them.

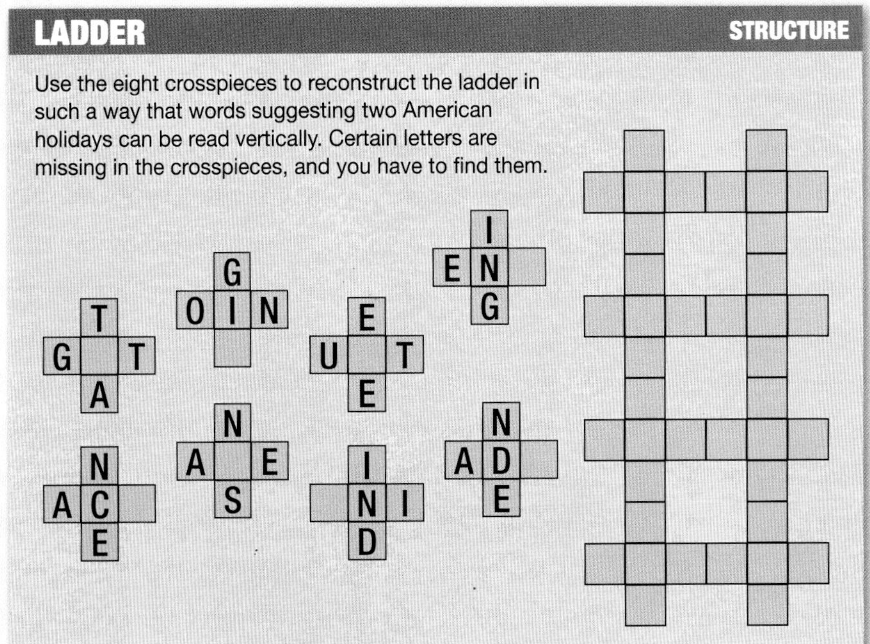

SANDWICH STRUCTURE

A well-known quote from a soliloquy in one of Shakespeare's plays can be found in the middle column of this puzzle. Find it by completing the five-letter words read horizontally. Several possibilities may present themselves at times, but only one will lead to the right solution.

S	A		E	D
F	L		W	S
C	U		E	D
K	E		P	S
S	P		K	E
F	I		E	S
S	O		A	R
H	O		K	S
D	A		E	S
D	E		E	R
M	O		S	E
C	A		L	E
F	E		D	S
V	O		E	R
O	T		E	R
F	L		T	S
H	O		E	L
B	L		N	D
B	A		E	D
B	I		E	S
A	C		E	D
B	R		A	D
P	I		U	E
D	R		G	S
F	R		E	D
L	O		E	R
R	A		I	O
D	R		F	T
C	O		P	S
B	O		E	S

THEMATIC CROSSWORD

GENERAL KNOWLEDGE

Using the following clues – nationality, title of work and year, fill in the names of winners of the Nobel Prize for Literature.

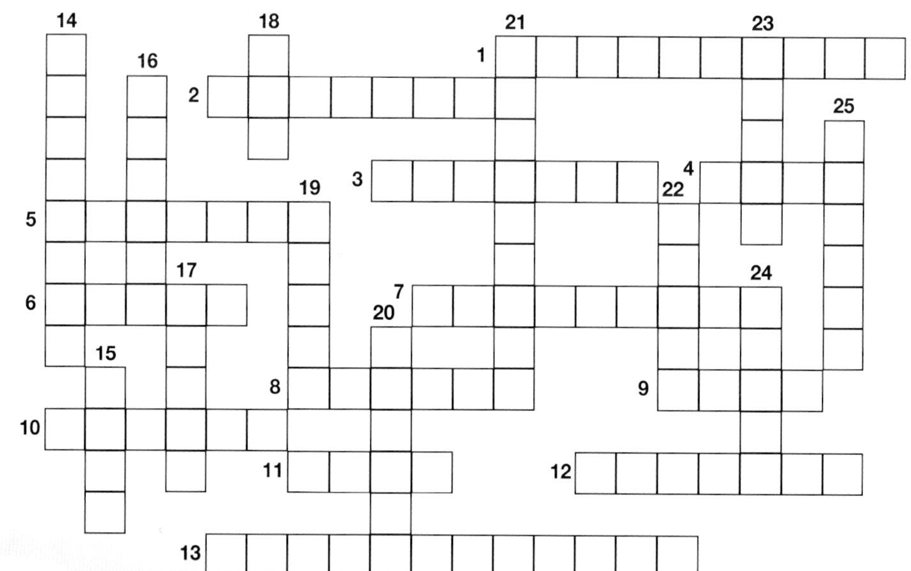

Across:

1. Italian, *Six Characters in search of an Author*, Nobel 1934.
2. American, *Sanctuary*, Nobel 1949.
3. British, *Lord of the Flies*, Nobel 1983.
4. German, *The Train was on Time,* Nobel 1972.
5. French, *Thérèse Desqueyroux*, Nobel 1952.
6. German, *The Tin Drum*, Nobel 1999.
7. American, *The Old Man and the Sea*, Nobel 1954.
8. French, *Nausea*, Nobel refused in 1964.
9. Irish, *Arms and the Man*, Nobel 1925.
10. Polish, naturalised American, *Poem on Time Frozen*, Nobel 1980.
11. German, *Death in Venice*, Nobel 1929.
12. French, *Creative Evolution*, Nobel 1927.
13. Russian, *Gulag Archipelago*, Nobel 1970.

Down:

14. Portuguese, *The One-Armed God*, Nobel 1998.
15. French, *The Immoralist*, Nobel 1947.
16. Chilean, *Canto general*, Nobel 1971.
17. French *The Georgics*, Nobel 1985.
18. Mexican, *The Monkey Grammarian*, Nobel 1990.
19. French, *The Plague*, Nobel 1957.
20. French, *At the Sign of the Web-Footed Queen*, Nobel 1921.
21. French, *Solitude*, Nobel 1901.
22. American, with the first name Sinclair, *Babbitt*, Nobel 1930.
23. British of American origin, *Murder in the Cathedral*, Nobel 1948.
24. Irish, *Deirdre*, Nobel 1923.
25. Greek, *Sun, the First*, Nobel 1979.

RECITATION

GENERAL KNOWLEDGE

Find the missing words of the first three verses of this poem by Robert Louis Stevenson, from the columns to the right.

The Dumb Soldier

When the grass was closely	**a.** *grown*	**b.** *mown*	**c.** *sown*
Walking on the lawn	**a.** *with Joan:*	**b.** *alone:*	**c.** *and stone:*
In the turf a hole I	**a.** *found.*	**b.** *ground.*	**c.** *pound.*
And hid a soldier	**a.** *in the ground.*	**b.** *in a mound.*	**c.** *underground.*
Spring and daisies came	**a.** *apace;*	**b.** *to the surface;*	**c.** *with haste;*
Grasses hide my	**a.** *soldier's face;*	**b.** *hiding place;*	**c.** *naughty trace;*
Grasses run like a	**a.** *rippling sea,*	**b.** *golden prairie,*	**c.** *green sea*
O'er the lawn up to	**a.** *me.*	**b.** *my knee.*	**c.** *Joan and me.*
Under grass alone	**a.** *he lies,*	**b.** *he sighs,*	**c** *he dies,*
Looking up with	**a.** *sad, sad eyes,*	**b.** *leaden eyes,*	**c.** *glazed eyes,*
Scarlet coat and	**a** *pointed gun,*	**b.** *trousers dun,*	**c.** *colours run,*
To the stars and to	**a.** *my Mum.*	**b.** *the sun.*	**c.** *some fun.*

POINTS IN COMMON — ASSOCIATION

In each of these series, find a word that has a direct connection with all three words.

1. **sun – break – light** ....
2. **sleep – jay – stick** ....
3. **on – cabin – ship's** ....
4. **pleat – bread – edge** ....
5. **period – down – circle** ....
6. **clippers – hammer – brush** ....

LOOPY LETTERS — STRUCTURE

Find the right order in which to place these dominoes so that the names of two countries in the northern hemisphere can be read horizontally, one from right to left and the other from right to left. Two dominoes have been swapped between lines to make your task more difficult.

ONE TOO MANY — CONCENTRATION

Look at this fish tank for a few minutes and then cover it.

Which fish did not feature in the fish tank before?

LOTTO — LOGIC

Get a total of 49 in all directions by using 16 lotto numbers that you have crossed out and placed in a box identical to that in which they were written.

★ 24	■ 32	★ 12	● 3
● 19	● 1	■ 16	■ 5
★ 22	■ 2	● 9	★ 6
■ 10	● 4	★ 8	● 23

●	■	★	■	= 49
★	●	■	●	= 49
●	■	★	★	= 49
■	★	●	●	= 49
= 49	= 49	= 49	= 49	= 49

(Diagonals: = 49)

MYSTERY WORDS

The following clues will enable you to identify the places in question. Try to use as few clues as possible by uncovering them one at a time.

MYSTERY PLACE 1

1. I am the land of the Red Dragon and the locals call me Cymru.
2. Portmeirion, an unusual village conceived by an eccentric architect, Williams-Ellis, is situated here.
3. In 1967 I provided the setting for *The Prisoner*, which became a cult television series.
4. Lewis Carroll apparently met Alice in one of my seaside resorts, Llandudno.
5. I am part of the United Kingdom.
6. My capital is Cardiff.

MYSTERY PLACE 2

1. In an Amerindian language my name means 'meeting place'.
2. I am a cosmopolitan city on the continent of America and my inhabitants call me the Liveable Metropolis.
3. I am also called the Great City of the Lakes.
4. In 1615, a French trapper, Etienne Brule, founded a trading post on this site to store his furs before sending them to Quebec on the St Lawrence.
5. My name is composed of only four letters, which are used once or several times: N, O, R and T.
6. I am one of the main cities of Canada, situated 40km from the Niagara Falls.

MYSTERY PLACE 3

1. I am an island as large as France and Belgium combined.
2. In 1960, I proclaimed my independence, putting an end to 75 years as a French protectorate.
3. I am situated on the tropic of Capricorn.
4. The Seychelles separated themselves from me a long time ago.
5. The N4 and N7 link my capital Antananarivo to the Mozambique Channel.
6. My inhabitants are the Malagasies.

A. ....

B. ....

C. ....

WORDS IN THE PICTURE

LANGUAGE

Find at least 20 words beginning with the letters Fl that are illustrated literally or figuratively in this picture.

GENERAL KNOWLEDGE

MYSTERY PLACE 4

1. I am made up of 118 islands ...
2. ... separated by 160 canals ...
3. ... crossed by more than 400 bridges.
4. I established my supremacy in the Adriatic and then in the whole Mediterranean area one thousand years ago ...
5. ... until continental trade took over from maritime trade.
6. I am still the love capital of Venetia.

D. ....

MYSTERY PLACE 5

1. When it is midday in London, it is 17 h here.
2. Lumphini Park, where fierce boxing matches are held, is situated here.
3. In one of my suburbs you can visit Jim Thompson's house, a marvellous structure made entirely of teak.
4. I am the capital of a kingdom whose kings are called Rama.
5. I am criss-crossed with canals, the 'khlongs', which give great pleasure to tourists – for only about 500 baht.
6. The Chao Phraya flows through me and I am the capital of a country formerly known as Siam.

E. ....

NUMBER PYRAMID — LOGIC

Each brick in a number pyramid is the sum of the two bricks just below it. Fill in all the spaces on this pyramid, taking note of the numbers already in place and observing the following rules:

- all the numbers at the base are positive integers.
- **a** is a multiple of 7, **c** is a multiple of 5 and **e** is a multiple of 11.

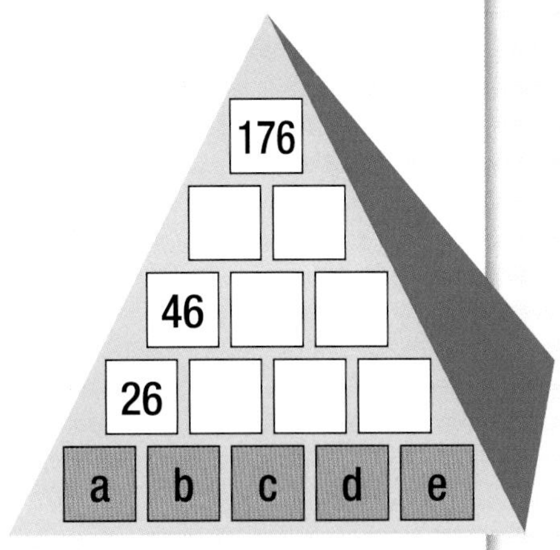

ROSETTE — STRUCTURE

Fill the rosette by forming words out of the letters below. Always write your answers by starting from the outside and going towards the centre of the rosette. Note that in certain series several anagrams are possible but only one will enable you to complete the grid by crossing words in both directions.

Clockwise

A. OUNTC
B. SOGOE
C. ASKCM
D. ANLIE
E. BEKAR
F. RSEPS
G. LASGS
H. CPLAS
I. FALTS
J. CANER
K. SWORD
L. EGINB
M. FNTLI
N. SSSIW
O. INTYG
P. DNGOI
Q. NMUOD
R. CNGLI

Anticlockwise

1. CLNGU
2. NGGOI
3. SDOUN
4. AGMON
5. BSTLA
6. PCERI
7. RKEEG
8. CEANL
9. LFSAK
10. SCLSA
11. PWRAS
12. STOAB
13. RFENS
14. SEDLI
15. ITNSW
16. YINDG
17. SOITM
18. CNSOI

KNOW YOUR WORLD

SPACE

Identify these 20 volcanoes with the help of the following clues and their position as given on the map. To help you, the letters comprising their names are given at the beginning of each clue.

1. (BEERSU) It reaches a height of 3 794 m on Ross Island, 1 380 km from the South Pole. It is almost permanently active. It has a lake of lava and spews out gold!
2. (ABINOPTU) In 1991, the lahars (mudslides) resulting from volcanic activity here caused 875 deaths and left 300 000 homeless. The dust cloud that belched out went right round the world in 10 days.
3. (EEELMNOPT) During its eruption in 1902, a nuée ardente (cloud of gas at a very high temperature) engulfed the town of Saint Pierre. Moving at 600 kph, it left no survivors among its 28 000 inhabitants.
4. (EEFIORRSU) At 1467 m, this Old Lady, whose first eruption dates back to 1696, is the highest peak in the Lesser Antilles.
5. (AAFIJMUY) This mountain, 3 776 m, situated in the middle of Honshu Island, has been venerated in the Land of the Rising Sun since the beginning of the eighth century.
6. (ACEELOOPPPTT) The only major eruption of this 5 465 m volcano took place around 1530. This increase in activity caused the fusion of the glacier found at the summit.
7. (AAAKKORT) In 1883, it destroyed two thirds of the island on which it is situated, created a depression of 300 m in the ocean and caused the death of more than 36 000 people. The explosion was heard four hours later nearly 5 000 km away.
8. (AINNORST) This volcano is situated in the Cycladic archipelago where an eruption in 1 500 BC probably gave rise to the legend of Atlantis.
9. (AENT) Situated on the east coast of Italy, this is the largest active volcano in Europe. Its highest point is at 3 350 m.
10. (AABMORT) At the centre of this enormous volcano, which is 60 km across, there is a caldera 600 m deep with a diameter of 6 km, formed during the cataclysmic eruption of 1815.
11. (BILMOORST) Described by Homer, this volcano is the lighthouse of the Mediterranean. It is always active but does not pose any danger.
12. (SEVUISUV) Its eruption in AD 79 destroyed Pompeii and Herculaneum and buried them under ash. Pliny the Younger's letters to Tacitus are a precious historical record of this event.
13. (AAALMNOU) This volcano, which emerged 500 000 years ago, forms the principal backbone of Hawaii, with an area of more than 5 000 km ^{2}. It is the largest volcano in the world.
14. (AAILLM) Situated in Conguillio Park, at 3 125 m, this volcano is popular with visitors because it offers many high altitude hikes close to the snows of the Sierra Nevada. It erupts frequently but is not dangerous.
15. (ABEIMNNYYZ) After a long period of dormancy lasting about 1 000 years, this Russian volcano became active again in 1955. The eruption of 1956 resulted in the most violent explosion of the 20th century.
16. (AEEHILNNSST) In 1980, after more than a century of dormancy, this volcano came to life and a small crater was formed at the summit. On May 18, it erupted. In a few seconds, the whole northern flank of the volcano collapsed, causing an avalanche of debris to spread over 2 km^2.
17. (ADDEEILNORUVZ)) In 1985, the eruption of this volcano resulted in 25 000 deaths, even though it had been forecast by vulcanologists. The village of Armero was engulfed.
18. (AAAMS) In 1783, a nuée ardente and lahars caused the death of more than 1 500 people and resulted in a serious famine in the north of the country. With the eruption of another volcano in Iceland the same year, this was said to be responsible for cooling the climate in the northern hemisphere.
19. (CCEHHILNO) In 1982, two eruptions resulted in thousands of people killed or reported missing, and caused the greatest emission of ash since 1912.
20. (AADIIJKLMNOR) This volcano, known today as Uhuru (Liberty), is the highest mountain in Africa at 5 895 m. Situated close to the Kenyan border, this volcano, so beloved of Hemingway, can be found to the east of the tectonic depression of the Great Rift Valley.

MATCHING UP — ASSOCIATION

Try to match the following writers with one of the pseudonyms they used in the course of their literary career.

Barbara Grasemann	A	A.........	1	George Orwell
Charles Dickens	B	B.........	2	George Eliot
Charlotte Bronte	C	C.........	3	George Sand
Charles Dodgson	D	D.........	4	Currer Bell
Amandine Dupin	E	E.........	5	Lewis Carroll
Mary Westmacott	F	F.........	6	Mark Twain
Eric Blair	G	G.........	7	Ralph Iron
Mary Ann Evans	H	H.........	8	Boz
Samuel Clemens	I	I.........	9	Agatha Christie
Olive Schreiner	J	J.........	10	Ruth Rendell

PROVERB — LANGUAGE

What proverb/expression does this picture represent?

SUPERIMPOSITION — CONCENTRATION

Which numbered pieces can be superimposed on grid A (without reconstructing it entirely, however)? The pieces must be used as they are, without being rotated.

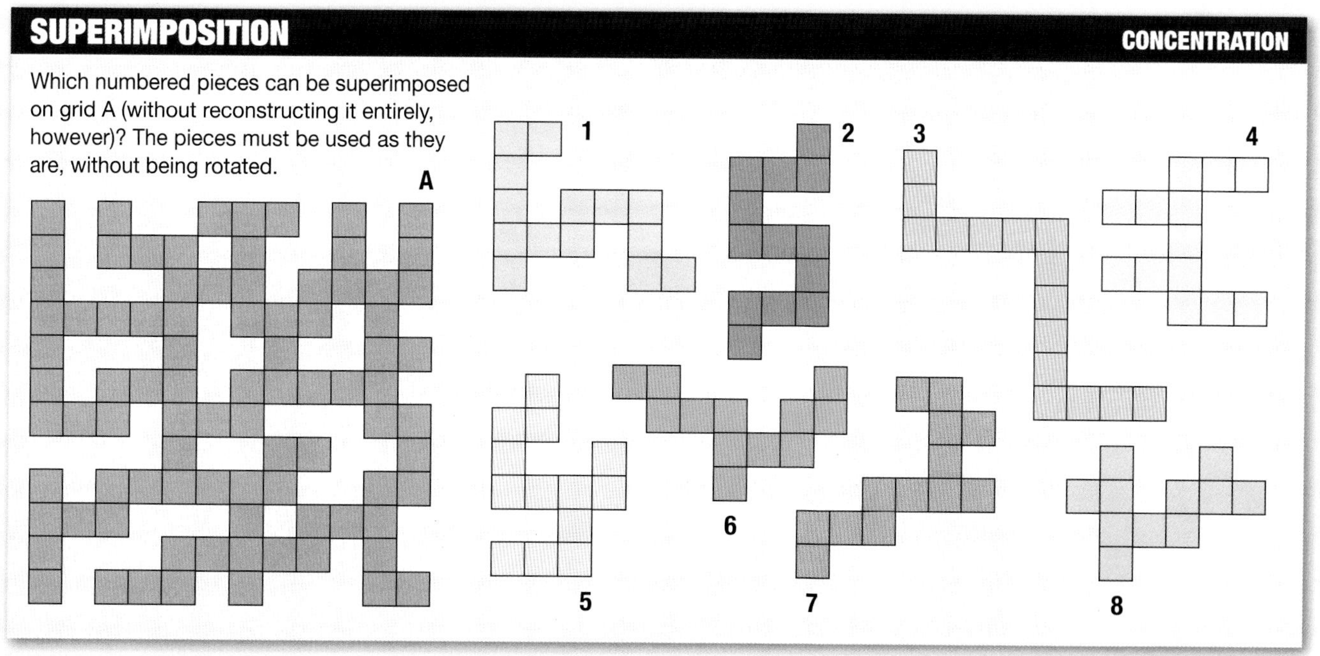

MATCHES — LOGIC

Move the three matches making up this little house to create eight triangles.

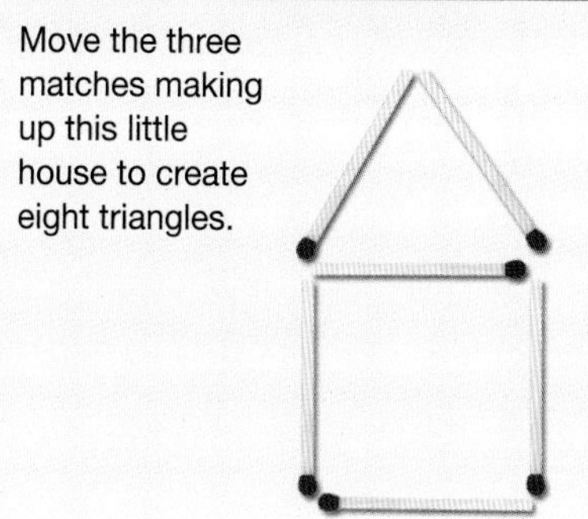

PROBLEM — LOGIC

Mr Douglas wants to change his car. He knows that a Porsche is worth 102 000 euros. He goes to see a car dealer, who tells him quite simply: 'For the price of 11 Ladas and five BMWs, you can have two Porsches, whereas one Porsche is worth as much as four BMWs plus two Ladas.'

What are one BMW and one Lada worth?

MIXED PROVERBS

GENERAL KNOWLEDGE

The words making up three proverbs have been mixed up. Untangle them to find the original proverbs.

THAN GATHERS NO ROLLING IS

WORDS WEAKEST ITS LOUDER

ACTIONS SPEAK MOSS THAN STONE A

LINK STRONGER A CHAIN NO

1. ....
2. ....
3. ....

THEMATIC CROSSWORD

GENERAL KNOWLEDGE

Atchooo! Oops Ahhh Grrrr... Smack Smack

With the help of the following clues, fill in the words of this crossword puzzle whose theme revolves around the subject of comic strips and cartoons.

Across

1/2. Superman's alias (5, 4).
4. A film was made about this superheroine, starring Halle Berry (8).
7. Mickey Mouse's dog.
9. Batman's home city (6).
10. Dagwood's boss (7).
13. A comic strip created by Young & Lebrun (7).
15. The flying superhero from Planet Krypton (8).
17. Blondie's husband (7).
18. Disney's famous duck (6).
20. See 22.
22/20. A hero created by Hal Foster (6,7).
23. A character created by Yates & Casson (6).
24. This famous mouse was first called Mortimer (6).
25 Mr. Wilson's worst nightmare (6).
26. This cat is as well known as Garfield (5).

Down

1. See 21.
2. See 1 Across.
3. A superhero, also known as Peter Parker (9).
5. He lives next door to Dennis the Menace (6).
6. The surname of Dagwood & Blondie (8).
8. Superman's lady friend (5,4).
11. Batman's loyal assistant (5).
12. See 14.
14/12. His kite always gets eaten by a tree (7,5).
15. The name of Charlie Brown's dog (6).
16. A cartoon book series featuring ancient Romans and a village of indomitable Gauls (7).
19. The blanket-carrying character in Charlie Brown (5).
21/1. He spends more time in the pub than at work (4, 4).

CROSSWORD

GENERAL KNOWLEDGE

Use the following definitions to fill in all the words in this grid.

Across

1. A curved support over an opening (4).
3. A stroke (8).
9. An oval, orange-coloured fruit (7).
10. A junction (5).
11. It's used to eat desserts with (12).
13. An announcement (6).
15. To stick (6).
17. A German dark bread, slightly bitter, made of coarse rye flour (12).
20. A thin, crisp cake or biscuit (5).
21. To remove the glossy surface of something (7).
22. A type of game bird (8).
23. An aromatic plant used for flavouring (4).

Down

1. A culinary term describing a dish prepared with almonds (8).
2. The thick part of coagulated milk (5).
4. An edible tuber favoured by the Irish (6).
5. The original form of Christmas cake (4, 8).
6. An ideal example (7).
7. To pull suddenly (4).
8. Places where exhibitions of physics and chemistry are held (7,5).
12. Said of someone who is determined to do something (4-4).
14. An edible fungus that grows underground and which is dug up by pigs (7).
16. The first ever poet laureate (6).
18. The cloth that is used for military uniforms (5).
19. To barter (4).

PUZZLE

SPACE

Look at this picture.

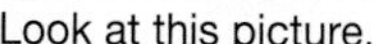

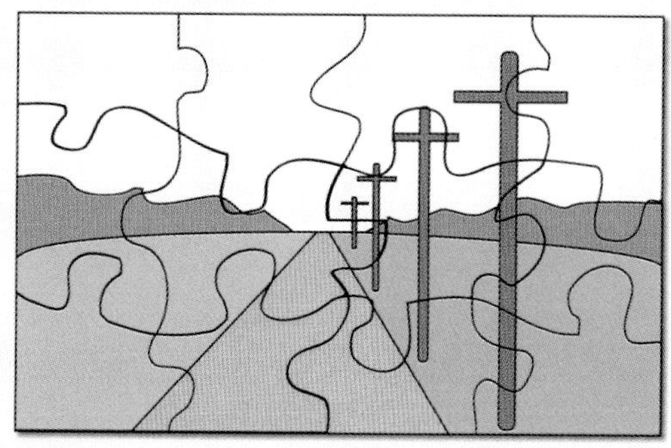

A

Picture A can be reconstructed using 12 of the 13 pieces provided below. Which one is superfluous? (The pieces are not represented on the same scale as the model).

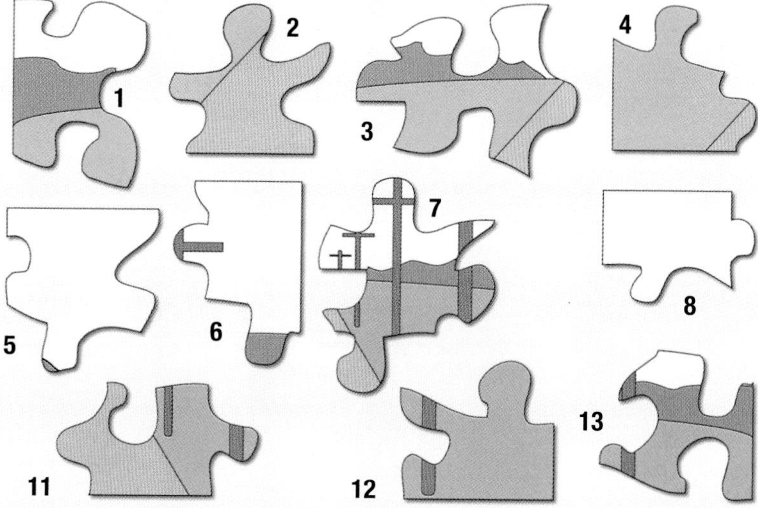

MYSTERY WORDS

Uncover the identity of each mystery character using the clues in the given order one at a time, trying to use as few clues as possible.

MYSTERY CHARACTER 1

1. I was born in Paris in 1893, but spent my childhood in Britain and Italy.
2. I was a nurse on the Italian Front during World War I.
3. I studied Arabic and worked in Baghdad on the *Baghdad Times*.
4. I was one of the first women explorers, travelling throughout the Middle East where few explorers had previously dared to go.
5. My travels resulted in at least 30 books, the first of which, in 1928, was *The Valley of the Assassins*.
6. I died at the age of 100.

MYSTERY CHARACTER 2

1. I was a Phrygian king of the 7th century BC.
2. My kingdom was completely destroyed by the Cimmerians.
3. I was selected as a judge in a music competition.
4. I preferred the flute played by the satyr Marsyas to that of the god Apollo.
5. The latter made ass's ears grow on my head to punish me.
6. According to legend, Dionysus gave me the power to transform all I touched into gold.

MYSTERY CHARACTER 3

1. My surname is shared by two painters, one very famous, whose works included exotic landscapes.
2. I am a writer with a double-barrel name, and you can see my portrait, painted by Quentin de la Tour, at the Louvre, in Paris.
3. I was motherless, and died at Ermenonville in 1778.
4. I wrote *A Discourse on the Arts and Sciences*.
5. My central tenet was that man is naturally good but is corrupted by living in society.
6. My principal works are *Emile, or On Education* and *A Treatise on the Social Contract*.

A. ....

B. ....

C. ....

STICK-ON WORDS — STRUCTURE

Use the following four-letter words to form 12 new words of 12 letters each (group in threes).

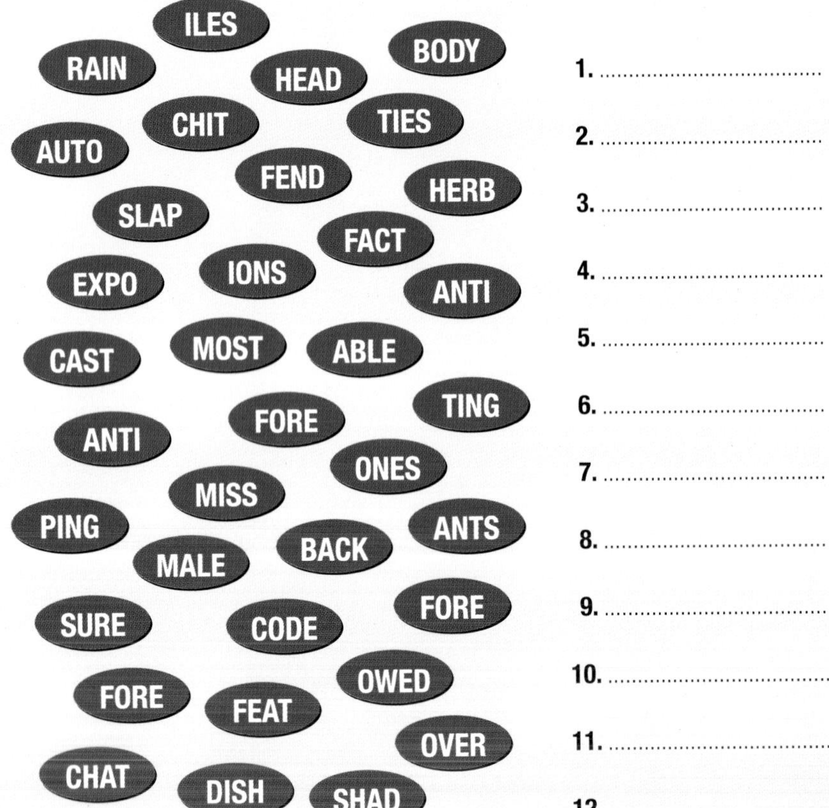

1. ....
2. ....
3. ....
4. ....
5. ....
6. ....
7. ....
8. ....
9. ....
10. ....
11. ....
12. ....

PROBLEM — LOGIC

'Look after my fish tank,' said Leo before going away for the weekend. 'You must give my fish, Arthur, exactly 6 g of daphnia every day, no more, no less. Use the measuring glasses!' So Pierre was duly given his instructions. When Pierre arrives, there are only two measuring glasses near the fish tank: the one can hold 5 g, the other 7 g. They are both empty, but a large test tube contains 12 g.

How can Pierre proceed without killing Arthur? How can he prepare two doses of exactly 6 g for the two days?

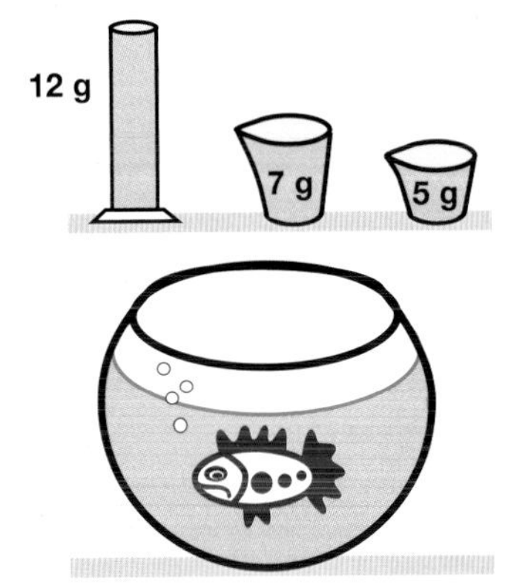

GENERAL KNOWLEDGE

MYSTERY CHARACTER 4

1. I am a Roman emperor who founded the Flavian dynasty.
2. My reign restored peace after the civil war that followed the death of Nero.
3. I started the construction of the Coliseum and reconstructed the Capitol.
4. For the sake of justice and peace, I favoured the participation of people from the provinces in the Senate.
5. I consolidated Roman rule, particularly in Germany and Britain.
6. The person next to my name in the dictionary discovered the New World, which was given his first name, Amerigo.

D. ....

MYSTERY CHARACTER 5

1. I was born in about AD 570 or 580 and died in AD 632.
2. My parents were nomads and my wife Khadija was a rich widow.
3. It was the angel Gabriel who gave me a divine mission.
4. My preaching led me to flee in 622 to Medina, where I died.
5. |By the time of my death, the people of Arabia had been converted to Islam.
6. I am the prophet of spiritual renewal and the founder of the Muslim religion.

E. ....

WORD HOLES

LANGUAGE

Fill the gaps below to find the words that contain the following items of clothing.

1. B _ _ _ E L _ T
2. D _ _ R E _ S _ S
3. S _ O C K _ _ _ S
4. _ P A _ _ _ _ _ N _ _ T S
5. _ S _ _ H I _ _ R _ _ T
6. _ _ _ V E _ S _ T _

HISTORICAL LANDMARKS

TIME

These 16 events can be coupled according to the year in which they took place. Can you pair them correctly?

A	Lenin is exiled to Siberia at the age of 27.	I	Bonaparte seizes the Arcole bridge from the Austrians.	.... and ....
B	Christopher Columbus discovers America.	J	Publication of *Alice in Wonderland*, by Lewis Carroll.	.... and ....
C	The American Congress votes for the abolition of slavery.	K	800 000 Spanish Jews expelled by King Ferdinand II of Aragon.	.... and ....
D	Atahualpa – the last of the Incas – dies, strangled by order of Pizarro.	L	Beethoven and Haydn perform together at a concert in Vienna.	.... and ....
E	Opening of the seventh Olympic Games in Paris.	M	Publication of *Robinson Crusoe*, by Daniel Defoe.	.... and ....
F	Birth of Van Dyck, painter of the Flemish school.	N	First gold rush in the Klondike.	.... and.........
G	First recorded observation of an aurora borealis.	O	The astrophysicist Hubble announces the existence of galaxies similar to our own.	.... and ....
H	Birth of the Spanish painter Velasquez.	P	Ivan the Terrible, the future Tsar, becomes Grand Prince of Russia.	.... and ....

ROSETTE — STRUCTURE

Fill the rosette by forming words out of the letters below. Always write your answers from the outside of the flower in towards the centre. Note that in some cases several anagrams can be made but only one will allow you to complete the grid with words crossing in both directions.

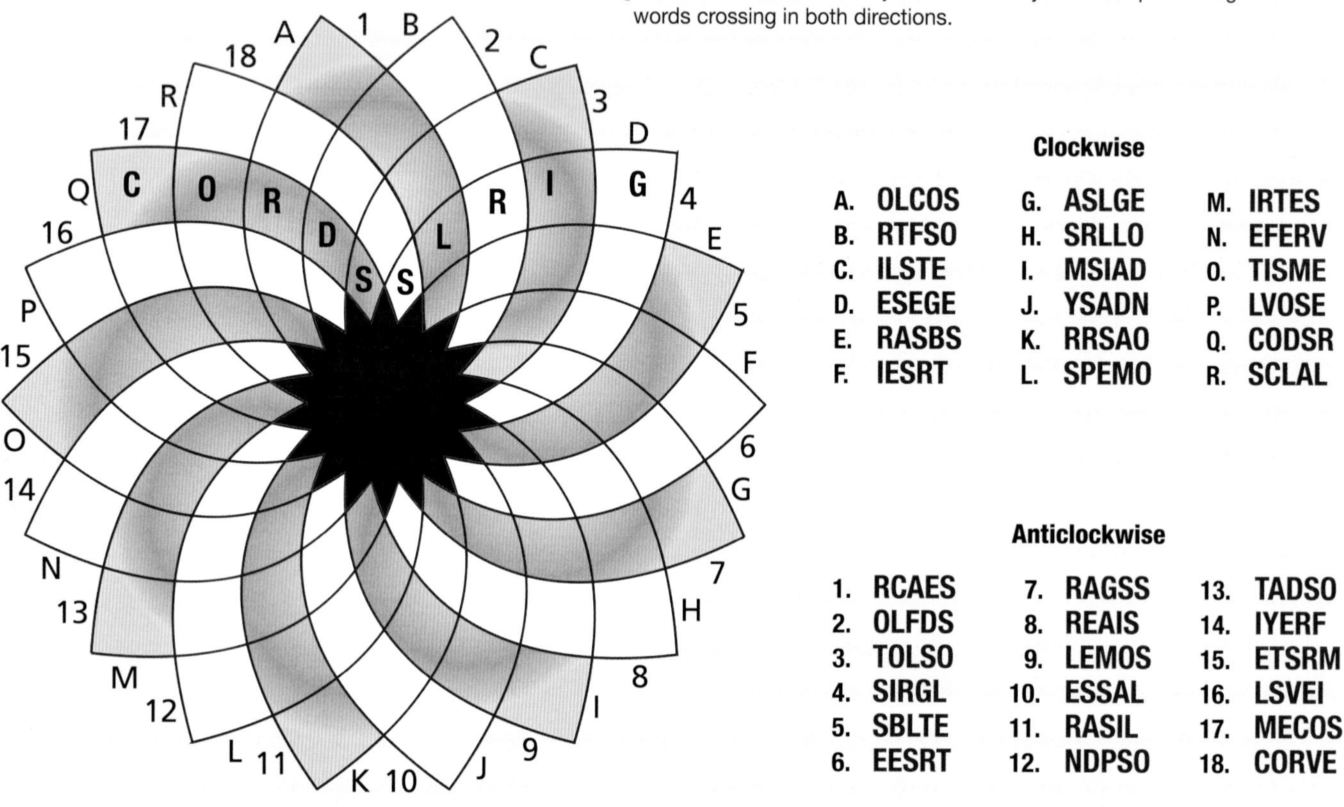

Clockwise

A. OLCOS
B. RTFSO
C. ILSTE
D. ESEGE
E. RASBS
F. IESRT
G. ASLGE
H. SRLLO
I. MSIAD
J. YSADN
K. RRSAO
L. SPEMO
M. IRTES
N. EFERV
O. TISME
P. LVOSE
Q. CODSR
R. SCLAL

Anticlockwise

1. RCAES
2. OLFDS
3. TOLSO
4. SIRGL
5. SBLTE
6. EESRT
7. RAGSS
8. REAIS
9. LEMOS
10. ESSAL
11. RASIL
12. NDPSO
13. TADSO
14. IYERF
15. ETSRM
16. LSVEI
17. MECOS
18. CORVE

PROBLEM — LOGIC

With the help of the following clues, work out what is in each box.

- The box of staples is touching only one box, the one containing bolts.
- The box of washers is touching two boxes: the one containing nuts and the one containing hooks.
- The box of bolts is touching three other boxes, including the one that contains nuts.
- The box of screws is right at the bottom and is not touching the box of hooks.
- The box of nails and the box of bolts are touching.
- One box is empty.

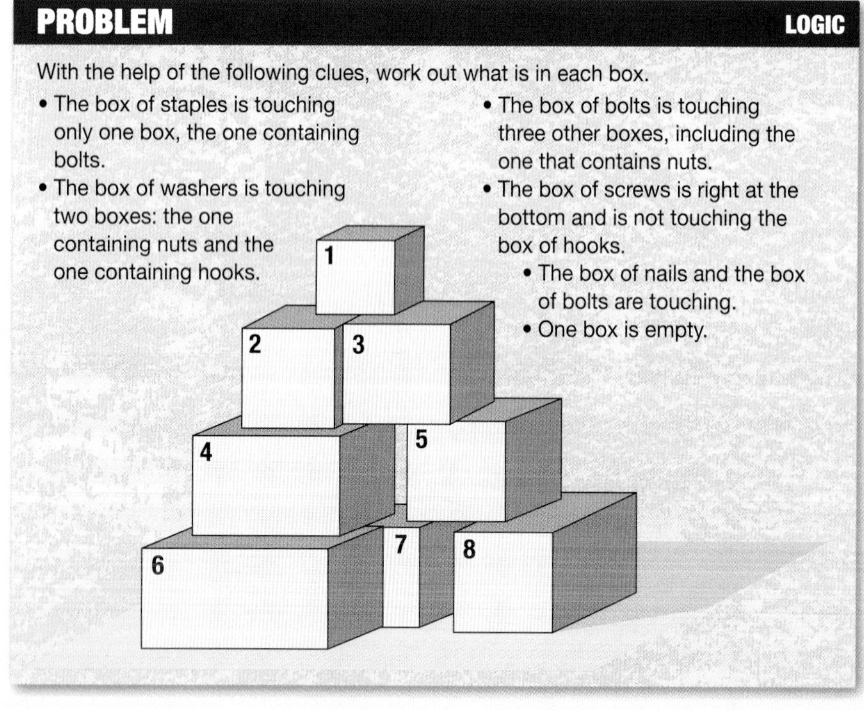

BOXED WORDS

Place the names of these tennis players in the grid.

AGASSI
AMAYA
CHANG
CONNORS
COURIER
DAVIS
EVERT
FRY
GRAF
HINGIS
KING
KORDA
LACOSTE
LECONTE
NASTASE
NOAH
PIERCE
PIOLINE
RIOS
SABATINI
SAFIN
SAMPRAS
STICH
WADE
WILANDER
WILLIAMS

NUMBER PYRAMID LOGIC

Each brick in the number pyramid is the sum of the two bricks immediately below it. Fill in all the missing numbers, taking into account the number already in place and observing the following rules:

- a, b, c, d and e are positive integers.
- a + b = c + d = e.
- b + c = d.

100

a b c d e

TRUE OR FALSE GENERAL KNOWLEDGE

Try to work out if the following statements about the ladies of the French Court are true or false. Write down the letters that appear in the boxes you tick, True or False, and you will have the name of the title given to the daughters of the king of France and of the Dauphin after the 17th century.

	True	False
1. Mme de Pompadour, the favourite of Louis XIV, was implicated in a matter of poisoning.	S	M
2. Mme de Maintenon, the widow Scarron, was a favourite of Louis XV.	I	A
3. Henri II offered Chenonceaux to Diane de Poitiers.	D	L
4. It was Mme Du Barry to whom Louis XV offered Louveciennes.	A	O
5. La Grande Mademoiselle was Mme Montespan.	D	M
6. Mme du Barry was sometimes called the countess of foie gras.	Y	E

BRAIN TEASER LOGIC

Three of the following six dogs are pedigrees, recognised breeds that win prizes at dog shows, and the three others are merely charming mongrels that are just as beloved by their owners.

Identify the pedigreed dogs with the help of the following clues:

- Two of the pedigreed dogs have a bow on their heads.
- Two of the pedigreed dogs are wearing a collar.
- Two of the pedigreed dogs are wearing a little red jacket.

1 2 3 4 5 6

SPACE

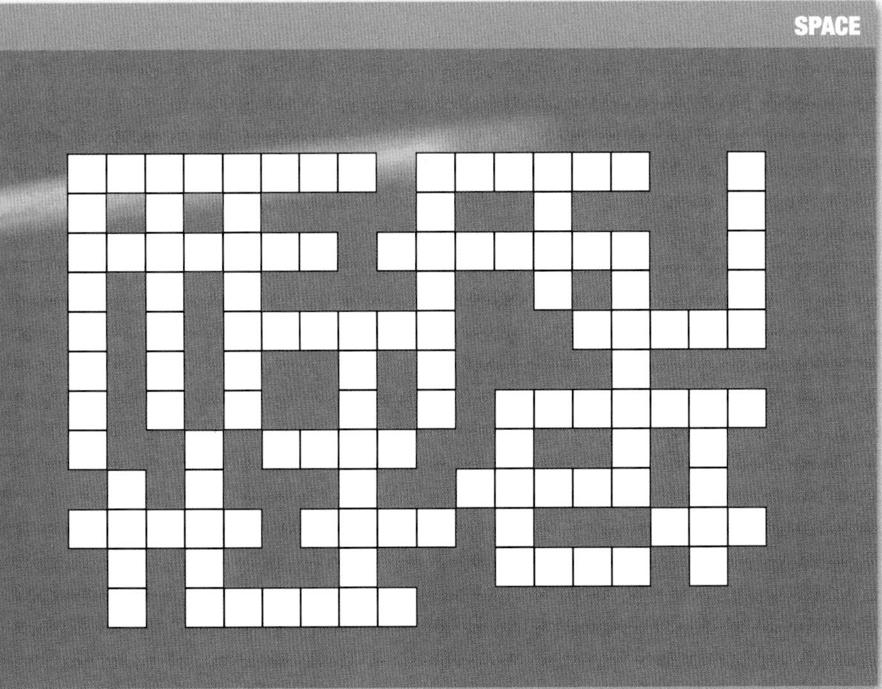

JUMBLED WORDS STRUCTURE

Untangle the letters of the names of six male writers whose names have been mixed up, two names in one.

WORDS IN THE PICTURE

LANGUAGE

Find at least 20 words beginning with the letter C that represent, literally or figuratively, something to be found in this picture.

ITINERARY

STRUCTURE

Complete, horizontally, the names of the following towns, to form, vertically, in the first and last columns, the capital of a country adjacent to France and a town close to Paris.

	U	N	S	T	E	
	J	A	C	C	I	
	E	N	I	Z	L	
	I	O	R	G	E	
	Q	U	I	T	O	
	O	M	R	E	M	

BONUS LETTERS

STRUCTURE

Using the letters of the word provided, add the bonus letter (in this case, C) and mix the letters to form a new word in accordance with the clue.

Starting word	+ C	New word	Clue
1. HOE	+ C	....	Reverberates
2. SAFE	+ C	....	Looks towards
3. SPEAR	+ C	....	Abrade
4. THAWED	+ C	....	Observed
5. DELETES	+ C	....	Chose
6. ENGRAVES	+ C	....	Carrion feeder

ZIGZAG WORDS

STRUCTURE

The names of important cities of the world hidden in this grid can be found in any direction: read horizontally or vertically, from top to bottom or bottom up, from left to right or the opposite. The words go round corners but never cross, and each letter can be used only once (watch out for multiple directions). With the letters remaining you can make the name of a major landmark in New York.

ALGIERS	BARCELONA	CAPE TOWN	JOHANNESBURG	MADRID	NAPLES
AMSTERDAM	BELGRADE	CHICAGO	LAGOS	MANILA	NASSAU
ANKARA	BOGOTA	DUBLIN	LISBON	MIAMI	NEW YORK
ATHENS	BOMBAY	DURBAN	LONDON	MOSCOW	ODESSA
BANGKOK	BRUSSELS	HANOI	MADRAS	MUNICH	OSAKA
					OTTAWA
					PARIS
					PERTH
					PHILADELPHIA
					REYKJAVIK
					ROME
					SEOUL
					SYDNEY
					TOKYO

J	O	O	O	N	I	E	N	R	K	B	A	A	R	A	K	N	A
L	H	L	D	F	G	R	E	O	T	H	R	C	E	L	O	N	A
O	A	O	N	A	L	S	W	Y	A	E	P	Y	S	U	R	B	T
T	N	N	E	S	B	U	R	G	S	N	H	A	S	E	L	S	D
T	I	C	A	D	A	L	E	D	A	L	I	B	N	A	B	R	U
A	W	A	P	U	M	P	H	I	A	B	O	M	M	A	N	I	L
B	O	G	E	B	S	T	E	R	D	A	M	E	M	A	I	M	A
A	T	O	T	L	I	N	J	A	V	I	K	O	I	R	U	M	S
S	O	M	O	R	E	Y	K	E	A	K	A	S	C	I	N	N	S
C	S	E	W	O	H	O	N	R	O	M	E	Y	H	S	S	A	A
O	E	D	N	G	A	B	O	U	P	A	R	I	S	A	U	D	R
W	L	A	C	A	N	S	E	L	U	P	E	S	E	D	O	I	D
A	P	R	I	L	O	I	S	T	H	T	R	S	K	A	D	R	A
N	B	G	H	A	I	L	Y	D	N	E	Y	A	O	M	A	T	M
B	E	L	C	G	O	S	S	O	Y	K	O	T	K	G	N	A	B

ITINERARY

STRUCTURE

Complete the names of the following places, written horizontally, so as to find, in the first and sixth columns, the name of a city on the east coast of the United States, renowned for its tea party, and a capital city in Africa.

	R	A	Z	I	
	A	M	A	R	
	A	N	T	O	
	O	P	E	K	
	L	E	N	E	
	E	V	A	D	

PROVERB

LANGUAGE

What proverb does this image represent?

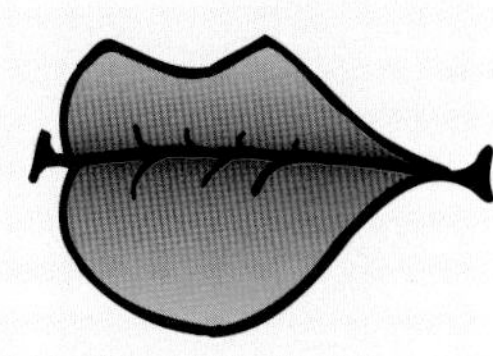

NUMBER PYRAMID

LOGIC

Each brick in a number pyramid is the sum of the two bricks immediately below. Fill in all the missing numbers, taking into account the numbers already in place. All the numbers are positive decimals. The number represented by aa,bb is a number where b = a + 1 such as 11,22 or 22,33 or 77,88.

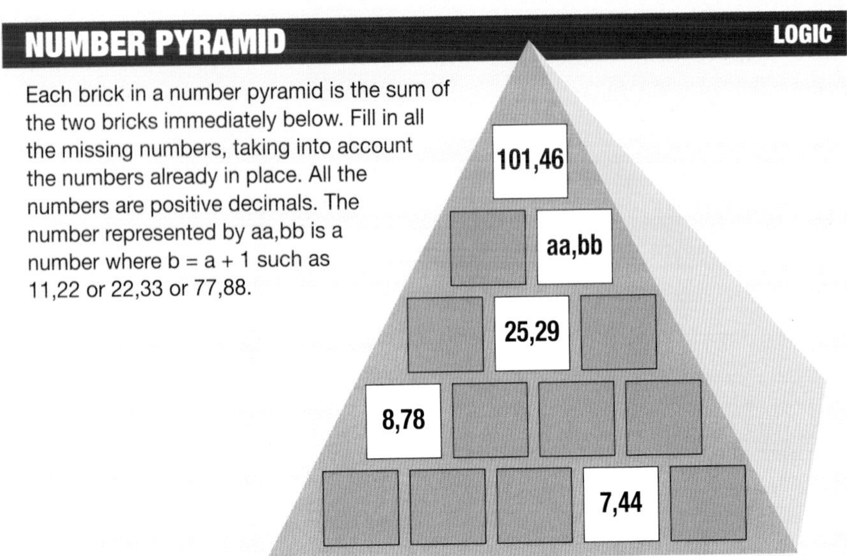

THEMATIC CROSSWORD

The words in this grid all contain at least one letter Q. Certain key letters have been positioned to guide you. Can you identify all these words and put them in the right place?

LOGIGRAM

LOGIC

COME AND JOIN THE CIRCUS

The manager of Stars of the Circus has spotted four Russian artistes whose performance was outstanding. Wanting to invite them to a gala event in which the best circus artist in the world will be chosen, he is trying to remember the first names of the four stars, their speciality and the circus they belong to. With the help of the following six pieces of information, try to help him identify what Igor, Piotr, Sacha and Vassili do – who is the acrobat, the clown, the trainer, and the juggler, and in which circus: Bouglione, Cirque du Soleil, Grüss or Zavatta.

Solution grid
When a statement allows you to eliminate an alternative, put N in the relevant place and Y if the opposite holds.

		Circus				Profession			
		Bouglione	Soleil	Grüss	Zavatta	Acrobat	Clown	Trainer	Juggler
Artist	Igor								
	Piotr								
	Sacha								
	Vassili								
Profession	Acrobat								
	Clown								
	Trainer								
	Juggler								

Clues

1. The trainer is not called Piotr and is not with Zavatta.
2. The acrobat doesn't work for Bouglione or Zavatta.
3. Neither Igor nor Vassili comes from the Cirque du Soleil and neither of them is a clown.
4. Piotr is neither an acrobat nor a clown.
5. Igor is not a trainer.
6. You will not see Sacha at the Zavatta circus.

Table of answers

Artist	Igor	Piotr	Sacha	Vassili
Profession				
Circus				

GENERAL KNOWLEDGE

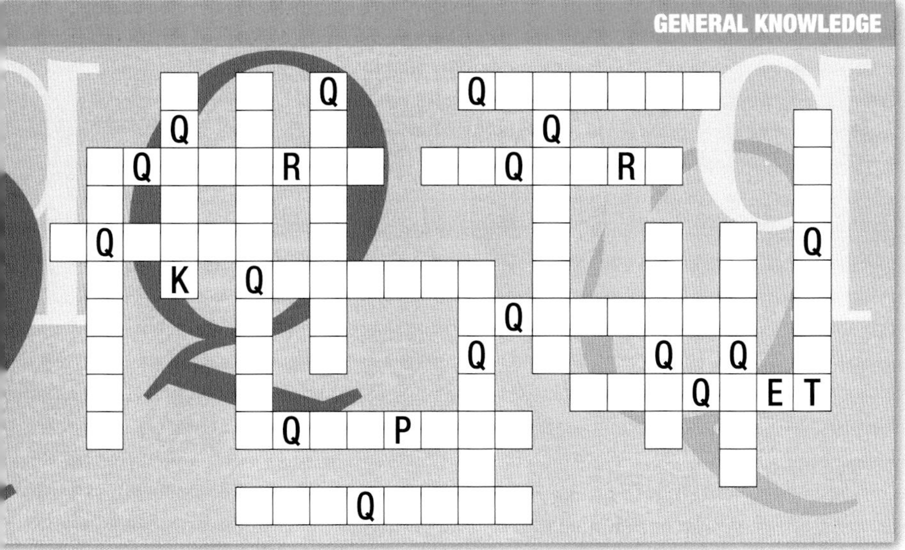

JUMBLED WORDS — STRUCTURE

PUZZLE — SPACE

In order to change structure A into a cube of 4 X 4 X 4 small cubes, you have to add a certain number of small cubes. In which numbered pile will you find the exact number of small cubes? Is there more than one pile that will fit the purpose?

A

1

2

3

4

5

CATERPILLAR — STRUCTURE

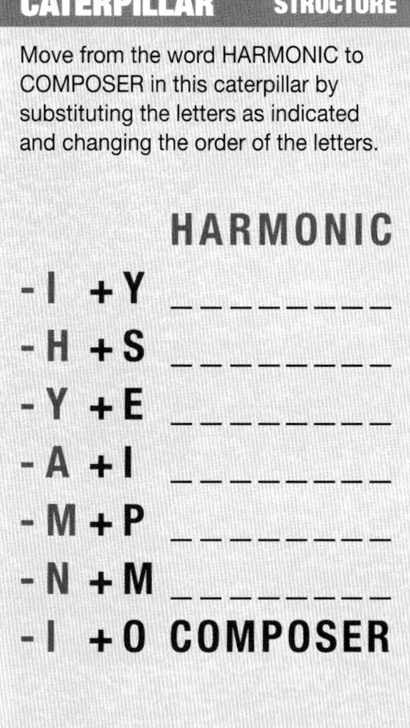

LOOPY LETTERS — STRUCTURE

Find the right order for these dominoes to read, horizontally, two words concerning air travel. One reads from left to right and the other from right to left. Two of the letters have been switched between lines to make the task more complicated.

MYSTERY WORDS

Discover, using the clues one by one and in order, the identity of the mystery object. Try to use as few clues as possible.

MYSTERY 1

1. I mark paper money.
2. I am the logic in a thought.
3. Despite being very thin, I hold things together.
4. If I am worn, a screw is useless.
5. In Greek mythology, I am your life spun, measured and cut by the Fates.
6. Ariane used me to guide Theseus through the labyrinth.

MYSTERY 2

1. I represent emptiness.
2. I can be a hiding place.
3. Even so I can be very unattractive.
4. I am a sum that is missing from the till.
5. I can be nine or 18 in a sport played with a club and a ball.
6. Black, I am a region in space from which nothing escapes.

MYSTERY 3

1. I am a partner promised in marriage.
2. I gave my name to an artistic movement initiated by the Italian painter Marinetti.
3. I am sometimes called perfect.
4. I was returned to three times in films by Robert Zemeckis.
5. I am a moment in time.
6. I am what is to come…

A. ....

B. ....

C. ....

SPOT THE 7 DIFFERENCES

CONCENTRATION

There are seven differences between these two photographs. Can you find them?

LADDER

STRUCTURE

With the aid of eight crosspieces, reconstruct the ladder by forming, vertically, words to do with knowledge. Certain letters are missing in the crosspieces – try to find them.

- O / S P _ / E
- I / I N E / _
- N / S C _ / E
- Y / I _ I / L
- _ / E N _ / C
- I / N G _ / E
- E / C _ E / L
- D / F I A / _

GENERAL KNOWLEDGE

MYSTERY 4

1. A leader bears me.
2. So does a person who is passionately in love.
3. I describe a song about romance.
4. I am also an instrument of hate, used to burn property.
5. I am a symbol of enlightenment...
6. ...because I am a source of light.

D. ....

MYSTERY 5

1. I offer the possibility of expressing an opinion.
2. I am equally a verb and the subject that performs the action.
3. Collectively, I can be one.
4. When you lose me you cannot be heard.
5. I can be in your head and in your heart.
6. I am the collection of sounds emitted by a human being.

E. ....

IDIOMATIC TRIPLETS

LANGUAGE

Find the word that fits perfectly with the three words in each line to form expressions commonly used.

1. **hand, feather, happiness**
   ....
2. **mice, east, packages**
   ....
3. **hands, slip, called**
   ....
4. **live, always, bitten**
   ....
5. **take, thing, devil**
   ....
6. **gift, water, flog**
   ....

THEMATIC CROSSWORD

GENERAL KNOWLEDGE

The words in this grid all contain at least one letter Z. Certain key letters have been placed to guide you. Can you succeed in identifying all the words and placing them in their correct places in the grid?

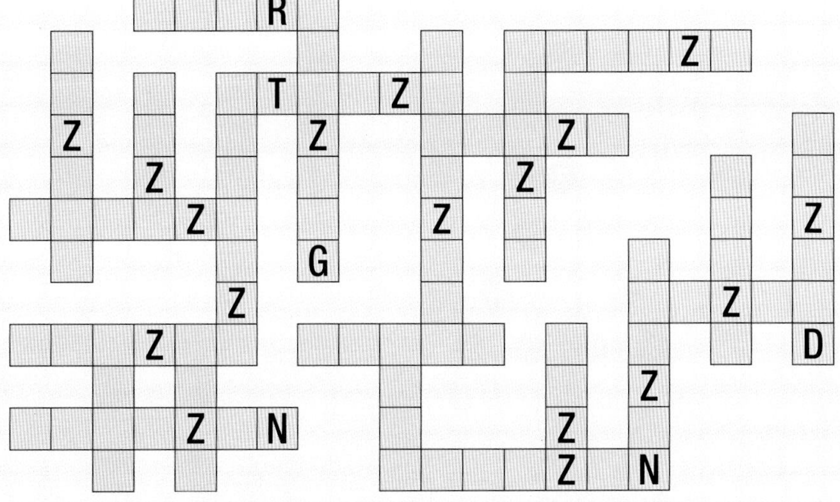

PROBLEM

LOGIC

To fill his piggy bank, Nicholas has permission to claim all the 50-cent coins left in the household change jar. Starting on January 1, Nicholas manages each month to save exactly 11 more coins than the month before. His piggy bank now contains 543 dollars. Can you say how many coins he saved during the month of December?

CUT-UP LETTERS

STRUCTURE

Cross out one letter in each of the nine words in the grid so that the letters remaining still spell an existing word. Place the letter crossed out at the end of the line to form the name, read vertically, of someone who lives on the banks of the Nile.

E	N	T	E	R	I	N	G	
E	S	C	A	R	G	O	T	
Y	E	A	R	N	I	N	G	
S	P	I	N	N	E	R	S	
T	E	R	M	I	N	A	L	
S	T	E	A	L	I	N	G	
H	E	A	V	I	E	S	T	
M	E	R	C	H	A	N	T	

ESCALETTERS

STRUCTURE

Add the letters indicated one by one to the root word to form a new words each time.

S I N

+ **E** _ _ _ _
+ **M** _ _ _ _ _
+ **O** _ _ _ _ _ _
+ **T** _ _ _ _ _ _ _
+ **O** _ _ _ _ _ _ _ _
+ **C** _ _ _ _ _ _ _ _ _

Solutions

Pages 244-245

Pages 246-247

MIXED PROVERBS

1. Let sleeping dogs lie.
2. Don't look a gift horse in the mouth.
3. A poor workman blames his tools.

BRAIN TEASER

1 and 5 : Basil with Frances
4 and 6 : Erwan with Betty
2 and 3 : Frank with Edith

CATERPILLAR

```
C R O U P I E R
S U P E R I O R
P O S T U R E R
T O R T U R E S
U T T E R E R S
S E C U R E S T
L E C T U R E S
R E S O L U T E
R O U L E T T E
```

HISTORICAL LANDMARKS

1. George Washington (1732-99)
2. Thomas Jefferson (1743-1826)
3. Abraham Lincoln (1809-1865)
4. Theodore Roosevelt (1858-1919)
5. Harry S. Truman (1884-1972)
6. Dwight D. Eisenhower (1890-1969)
7. John F. Kennedy (1917-1963)
8. Lyndon B. Johnson (1908-1973)
9. Ronald Reagan (1911-2004)
10. Bill Clinton (1946-)

SYNONYMS

1. Blemish
2. Defect
3. Shortcoming
4. Mar
5. Foible
6. Fault
7. Failing
8. Imperfection

MAGIC SQUARE

The sum of each line or diagonal is 260. The sum of each of the internal squares of four numbers is 130. The square is thus:

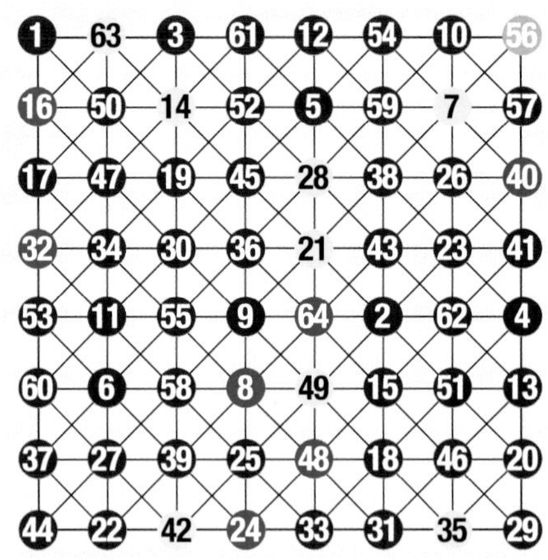

MAGIC TRIANGLE

You are looking for the possible combinations of four integers from 1 to 9 with a total of 20: (1, 2, 8, 9) (1, 3, 7, 9) (1, 4, 6, 9) (1, 4, 7, 8) (1, 5, 6, 8) (2, 3, 6, 9) (2, 3, 7, 8) (2, 4, 5, 9) (2, 4, 6, 8) and (2, 5, 6, 7). When checking the sum of the squares, notice that only (1, 5, 6, 8) (2, 3, 7, 8) and (2, 4, 5, 9) give you 126 (1 x 1+ 5 x 5 + 6 x 6 + 8 x 8, etc.) In these three combinations, 2, 5 and 8 appear twice. So you place them at the apexes to obtain the triangle.

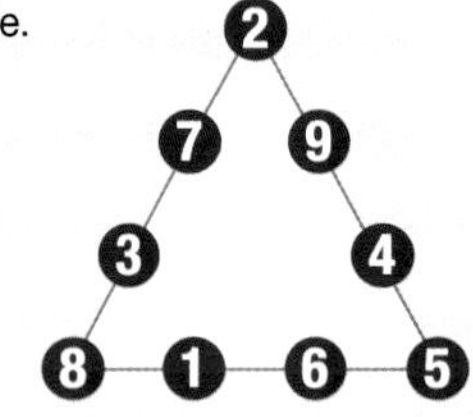

Pages 248-249

HIDDEN WORDS

The remaining letters make the name of the actor Sylvester Stallone.

STICK-ON TITLES

1. *She's got you.*
2. *Back in baby's arms.*
3. *I fall to pieces.*
4. *Walkin' after midnight.*

BROKEN SEQUENCES

Parmesan – Concerto – Reserved – Manitou – Avalanche – Puberty

HISTORICAL LANDMARKS

1. True: from 1412 to 1431.
2. True: Da Vinci 1452-1519, and Columbus 1450-1506.
3. False: it was built as a tomb by Shah Jehan for his wife Mumtaz.
4. False: It was built about 700 years ago, long after the Egyptians.
5. False: She married John Rolfe.
6. False: the battle of Trafalgar took place in 1806, and the battle of Waterloo in 1815.

CLOSE-UP

A starfish.

BRAIN TEASER

Richard: bowler hat. Victor: woollen hat. Matthew: cowboy hat. Steven: cap.
Since the cap doesn't belong to Victor (1), the bowler hat doesn't belong to Steven. So the woollen hat belongs to neither Richard nor Matthew (5), and the bowler doesn't belong to Matthew (3). That leaves only Richard for the bowler. Richard doesn't have the cap, and the cowboy hat goes to Matthew (2). The cap doesn't belong to Richard or Matthew (see above), or Victor. So it belongs to Steven, which leaves Victor with the woollen hat.

TRUE OR FALSE

1. False (L).
2. False: the principle was known c.3 000 BC by the Egyptians and the Greeks (O).
3. True; but mutton fat is of better quality (T).
4. True (L).
5. False (A).
6. True (W).

The letters produced make the word TALLOW.

PROGRESSIVE QUIZ

1. Alfred Nobel.
2. 1901.
3. Swedish.
4. Dynamite.
5. Five.
6. Economics.
7. Nelson Rolihlala Mandela and Fredrik Willem de Klerk.
8. Marie Curie: 1903 – Physics; 1911 – Chemistry.
9. December 10.
10. The anniversary of Nobel's death.

Pages 250-251

ANAGRAMS

1. Lead
2. Formalin
3. Nitrate
4. Reaction
5. Mineral
6. Reduction
7. Argon
8. Proton
9. Potash
10. Ferrous

WHICH COMES NEXT?

The 9 of diamonds.
The cards from 7 to ace (all values of a game of 32 cards) are arranged in a circle, leaving out two cards each time. The cards opposite each other are the same colour.

CHALLENGE

If you have remembered half the words or more, one minute afterwards, you have an excellent score. If you remembered less than five, try practising with shorter lists of easier words. Most of these words belong to a vocabulary little used in our everyday lives, and it would be better to concentrate on a few of them rather than try to remember them all.

LOOPY LETTERS

By inversing T-S you get the names of Mantegna and Masaccio.

ANAPHRASES

1. Compiled, complied
2. Resident, inserted
3. Desecration, considerate

MATCHING UP

A9 – B4 – C7 – D6 – E8 – F3 – G5 – H10 – I1 – J2

PROBLEM

In the church, there are three men, nine women, 81 cats (nine per woman), hence 93 living creatures who have just come in – plus the narrator, praying.
So the answer is 94.

STICK-ON TITLES

1. *Lawrence of Arabia.*
2. *Bridge on the River Kwai.*
3. *A Passage to India.*
4. *Brief Encounter.*

Pages 252-253

MOCK EXAM

BA Bangui, Balzac, Baker, Balthus, bad-mouth, basil, badabing-badaboom …
RA Rabat, Ransome, Raft, Raphael, raggle-taggle, radish, rattle…
PR Pretoria, Proust, Price, Preston, pro forma, primula, prittle-prattle…
DA Dakar, Davies, Dance, Dali, dab hand, dahlia, dabble…
CO Conakry, Coetzee, Cook, Constable, copycat, cotton, cooeee…
BR Brazzaville, Bronte, Brown, Bruegel, bric-à-brac, briar, Bravo…

CATERPILLAR

M A T A D O R
S T A R D O M
R O A S T E D
A D O P T E R
P A R O T I D
P I C A D O R
C O R R I D A

BRAIN TEASER

ARTHUR	BLAISE
L	W

CARLA	DAMIAN
W	L

EDWARD	ARTHUR
L	W

BLAISE	CARLA
W	L

DAMIAN	EDWARD
L	W

ARTHUR	CARLA
D	D

BLAISE	DAMIAN
W	L

CARLA	EDWARD
L	W

ARTHUR	DAMIAN
D	D

BLAISE	EDWARD
W	L

Blaise was victorious every time. Arthur, Carla, Damian and Edward were therefore beaten by Blaise. Edward never drew a match, and Damian never won, so Edward beat Damian, and so on.

MIXED PROVERBS

1. Pride comes before a fall.
2. Curiosity killed the cat.
3. All that glitters is not gold.

ITINERARY

Greece – Alaska

CUBES

Beowulf – Ulysses – Theseus

THE RIGHT SUM

MAGIC SQUARE

Each horizontal line, vertical column or diagonal equals 310.

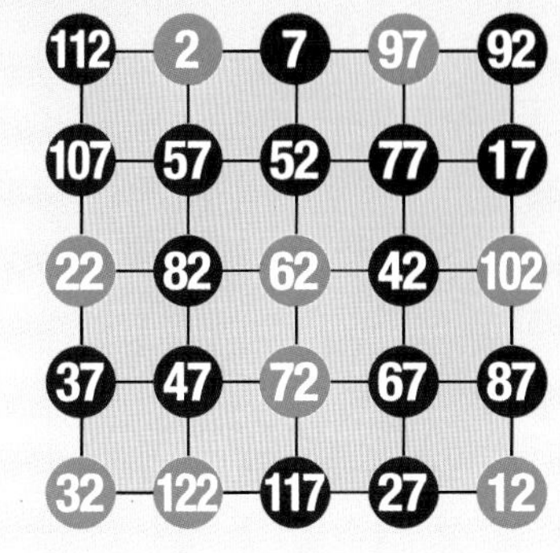

Pages 254-255

ZIGZAG WORDS

Cabaret

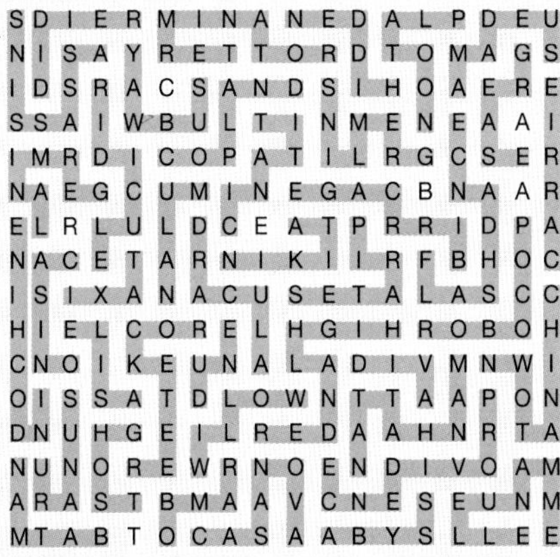

PROBLEM

The third scale is also balanced. One green cube = two pink; one mauve cube = three pink. We have the equivalent of six pink cubes on each side.

TWO MAKE A PAIR

1. Celadon
2. Orthodontist
3. Hedonism
4. Donatello
5. London
6. Dong
7. Bandoneon
8. Chardonnay
9. Belladonna lily
10. Iguanadon

MATCHES

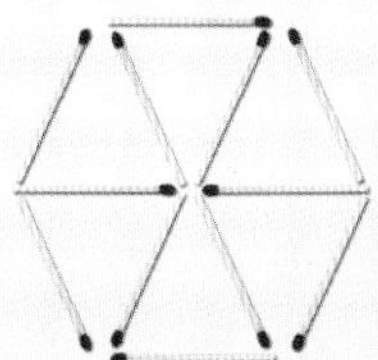

ANAGRAMS

1. Brush
2. Painter
3. Gallery
4. Icon
5. Pastel
6. Realism
7. Plaster
8. Pictures
9. Intaglio
10. Easel

HOMOGRAPHS
1. Left; **2.** Bored
3. Cross; **4.** Light

Pages 256-257

LOGIGRAM
Friends of Exotic Pets
Boa, like Tarantula, sells or refuses (clue 8). But Tarantula doesn't sell (clue 1), so Tarantula refuses and Boa sells. He sells four, according to clue 2. They are not tarantulas, housed (clue 3), nor crocodiles, who go in eights (clue 7), nor monitors, six (clue 6). **So Boa sells four boas.** What does Tarantula refuse? Not crocodiles (clue 4) and not tarantulas (clue 3). Thus Tarantula refuses monitors. How many? Six, according to clue 6. Crocodile doesn't appear in the same sentence as boas (because Boa sells four boas), monitors (because Tarantula refuses six monitors) or tarantulas (clue 5). And Crocodile has something to do with crocodiles! Eight of them (clue 7). By deduction, Monitor has something to do with tarantulas, which he houses (clue 3). You can therefore conclude that **Monitor houses three tarantulas** and that **Crocodile feeds eight crocodiles.**

Table of answers

	Sentence 1	Sentence 2	Sentence 3	Sentence 4
Word 1	Boa	Crocodile	Tarantula	Monitor
Word 2	Sells	Feeds	Refuses	Houses
Word 3	Four	Eight	Six	Three
Word 4	Boas	Crocodiles	Monitors	Tarantulas

ANAPHRASES
1. Impression, permission
2. Unclear, nuclear

TWO MAKE A PAIR
1. Alligator
2. Frigate
3. Bagatelle
4. Abnegation
5. Purgatory
6. Nougat
7. Gatecrasher
8. Gatwick
9. Vulgate
10. Gathering

MAGIC NUMBER
You can carry out the same operation with all the numbers and you will always get 6174 after a few stages!
Take 8493. 9843-3489 = 6354; 6543-3456 = 3087; 8730-0378 = 8352; 8532-2358 = 6174

HIDDEN WORDS
The word to find is MEMBRANOPHONE.

WORD PAIRS
1. Perversion – **2.** Conversion – **3.** Rawness – **4.** None – the word on the list is recreation – **5.** None – the word is originator. **6.** Star and stardom.

POINTS IN COMMON
1. Telephone; **2.** Glasses; **3.** Book; **4.** Case; **5.** Hand; **6.** Paper

Pages 258-259

HISTORICAL LANDMARKS
B (– 1250) ; G (– 1236) ; C (– 814) ; D (– 753) ; H (– 399) ; F (– 218) ; E (– 44) ; A (41)

PROBLEM
If Virgil misses the target only once (he shoots wide), he hits target A 11 times and target B 58 times to get 70 shots. He thus has (58 x 3) = (11 x 1) – (1 x 2) = 183 dollars. If he misses another shot, the bonus is only (56 x 3) + (12 x 1) = 176 dollars. So each miss costs 7 dollars. 20 more misses produce a gain of 36 dollars (176 – 7 x 20) for Virgil. So he missed the target 22 times, hit target A 32 times and target B 16 times (70 – 22 – 32).

POINTS IN COMMON
1. Moon
2. Press
3. Night
4. Cold
5. Sand
6. Pin

BROKEN SEQUENCES
1. Mediocrity
2. Incensed
3. Saccharine
4. Hybridise
5. Aviary
6. Forfeited

CATERPILLAR
W O R D S
W A R D S
D A W N S
W I N D S
W I N G S
K I N G S
S I N K S
S I N G S
S O N G S

WHICH COMES NEXT?
A. Figure 5: the shape that appears most frequently, with the colour that appears most frequently.
B. Figure 3: the shape that has the most sides, with the colour of the shape that has the least sides.
C. Figure 4: reproduction of the green shape, reduced, and in brown, as many times as there are shapes in the whole rectangle.
D. Figure 2: the missing shape; its absence results in each shape not appearing three times, twice in the same colour and once in a different colour.
E. Figure 1: the shape that has as many sides as there are different figures in the rectangle, with the colour that appears as many times as there are sides.

SANDWICH
A fool and his money are soon parted.

Pages 260-261

MIXED QUOTES
1. Imperialism is a paper tiger.
2. Women hold up half the sky.
3. Revolution is not a dinner party.

WHICH COMES NEXT?
1. It is based on the sequence of decimals of the number pi.
2. Each number is the sum of the squares of the numbers making up the preceding: 2 x 2 + 5 x 5 = 29; 2 x 2 + 9 x 9 = 85 … so the last number will be 2 x 2 + 0 x 0 = 4.
3. These are subdivisions of time … 60 seconds in one minute, 60 minutes in an hour, 24 hours in a day, so what is missing is 7 for 7 days of the week, 52 weeks in the year, 100 years per century, 10 centuries per millennium.
4. The numbers add up alternately to 10 and 5, starting with the lowest digits. So the missing number is 46.

ITINERARY

Dublin – Sydney

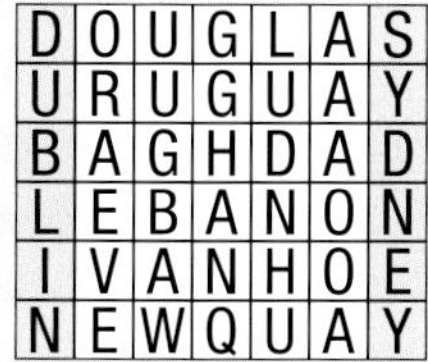

ESCALETTERS

```
       R E D
+ U    R U D E
+ N    U N D E R
+ E    E N D U R E
+ T    D E N T U R E
+ V    V E N T U R E D
+ A    A D V E N T U R E
```

IDIOMATIC TRIPLETS

1. Teeth
2. Every
3. Money
4. Love
5. Time
6. Two

STICK-ON WORDS

Candidates – Deathknell – Demonstrate – Depthgauge – Detergents – Fieldstone – Heartbreak – Knockkneed – Metropolis – Nightshirt – Pitchblack – Wristwatch

NUMBER PYRAMID

At the apex, A = a + 4b + 6c + 4d + e. Taking the rules into account, you'll find that:
A = a + 4b + 6(b + 1) + 4(b – 1) + a = 2a + 14b + 2.
So A, the sum of even numbers, is an even number. Hence A = 90. Then 2a + 14b + 2 = 90, that is, a + 7b = 44 (or else a = 44 – 7b).
We also know that b > a. Thus b > 44 – 7b or 8b > 44 and so b > 5,5.
The only solution, seeing that all the numbers are positive integers, is
b = 6 and
a = 44 – 7 x 6 = 2.

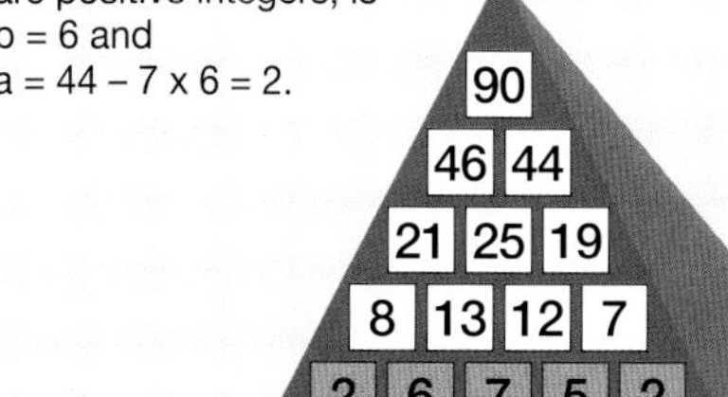

BOXED WORDS

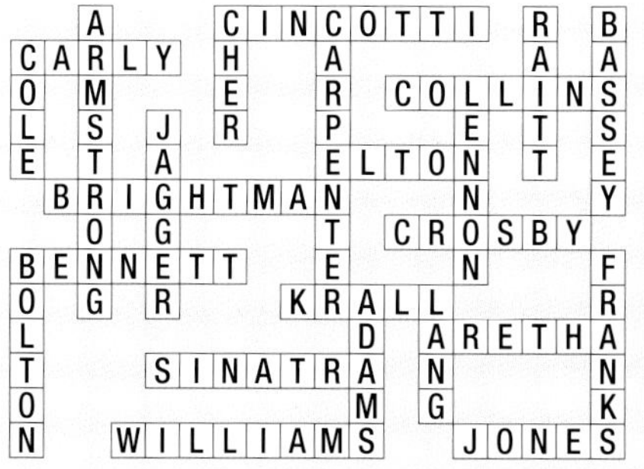

Pages 262-263

CROSSWORD PUZZLE

PERFECT COPIES?

B and D

CUBES

Apostle – Vespers – Vatican

PARONYMS

1. allusion, illusion
2. besides, beside
3. proceed, precede
4. accept, except

PROBLEM

Let N be the number of children belonging to the coquettish lady. Each of them has N-1 children. Her descendants therefore number N children + N x (N-1) grandchildren, that is, N + N2- N = N2, which is the lady's age. Her age is therefore 8 x 8 = 64 (7 x 7 = 49 < 50 and 9 x 9 = 81> 80. She has eight children, 56 grandchildren and her next birthday cake will have … 65 candles!

ANAGRAMS

1. Inch
2. Tesla
3. Mile
4. Minute
5. Siemens
6. Ton
7. Acre
8. Stone
9. Litre
10. Hectare

Pages 264-265

KNOW YOUR WORLD

1. The Hoggar plateau, in Algeria. **2.** Libya. **3.** Aswan, in Egypt. **4.** Timbuctu, in Mali. **5.** Gambia. **6.** Monrovia, in Liberia, named in honour of James Monroe. **7.** Togo. **8.** Ténéré, in Niger. **9.** Sudan. **10.** Lagos, in Nigeria. **11.** Cameroon. **12.** The Oubangui, which passes through Bangui, in the Central African Republic. **13.** Gabon (Libreville). **14.** Lake Victoria (Kenya, Uganda, Tanzania). **15.** Zanzibar, in Tanzania (Tan for Tanganyika, Zan for Zanzibar). **16.** Angola and Zambia. **17.** Victoria Falls. **18.** Namibia. **19.** Swaziland. **20.** The Cape of Good Hope, in South Africa.

MIXED PROVERBS

1. Jack of all trades, master of none.
2. Knowledge is power.
3. Absence makes the heart grow fonder.

ESCALETTERS

```
       A L E
+ B    A B L E
+ M    A M B L E
+ C    B E C A L M
+ I    A L E M B I C
+ A    A M I C A B L E
+ N    I M B A L A N C E
```

MATCHING UP

A5 – B6 – C7 – D9 – E8 – F3 – G4 – H10 – I2 – J1

ONE WORD TOO MANY

1. Each word can be preceded with the suffix 'far' – far-reaching, far-sighted, far-flung, far-fetched, far-out – all except SYMBOL.
2. You can remove CH from each word to create another, existing word (aromatic, bee, amber, hat, mating), except for DUTCH.
3. Each word correlates to the word 'red': red blood, red wine, red face, red light, red hair – except for GRASS.

Pages 266-267

MIXED QUOTES

1. The spread of evil is the symptom of a vacuum (Ayn Rand).
2. Evil is obvious only in retrospect (Gloria Steinem).
3. Evil draws men together (Aristotle).

HISTORICAL LANDMARKS

1. H and G: Selleck and Rampling (1945)
2. K and C: Walters and Hurt (1950)
3. J and A: Stone and Baldwin (1958)
4. D and F: Crowe and Binoche (1964)
5. I and L: Slater and Zellweger (1969)
6. B and E: Diaz and Brady (1972)

CLOSE-UP
A windmill

CUBES
Rosehip – Rooibos – Vervain

PROBLEM
Let P be the amount lost. We know that P-1 is a multiple of 2, 3, 4, 5, 6, 7, 8 and 9. Look for the smallest common multiple: it is 8 x 9 x 7 x 5 = 2 520 dollars. Ronald therefore owed 2 521 dollars or any multiple of 2 520 plus 1.

ODD ONE OUT

- **A. Figure 2:** all the figures include five mauve bars, one thick red bar and two yellow circles, except for number 2, which has six mauve bars.
- **B. Figure 5:** in all the figures, green covers red, except in number 5, where it is the opposite.
- **C. Figure 1:** all the figures consist of shapes with the same number of sides, except number 1, where we find shapes with four, five and six sides.
- **D. Figure 6:** The shapes and colours, like beads on a string, always occur in the same order, except in number 6, where the mauve circle and the yellow square are reversed.
- **E. Figure 2 :** each rectangle contains two figures, the first with several axes of symmetry, the second with only one. The exception to this rule is rectangle number 2, where the two shapes have more than one axis of symmetry (consider carefully the entire shape and not only the internal form).

HOMOPHONES

1. sown, sewn
2. saw, soar, sore
3. cents, sense, scents
4. lessons, lessens

Pages 268-269

SPEED LIMIT OF 90!

WORD HOLES

1. Spatula
2. Unluckily
3. Invitation
4. Journeyman
5. Maceration
6. Radiographer

PUZZLE
Pieces 4, 5, 6 and 8

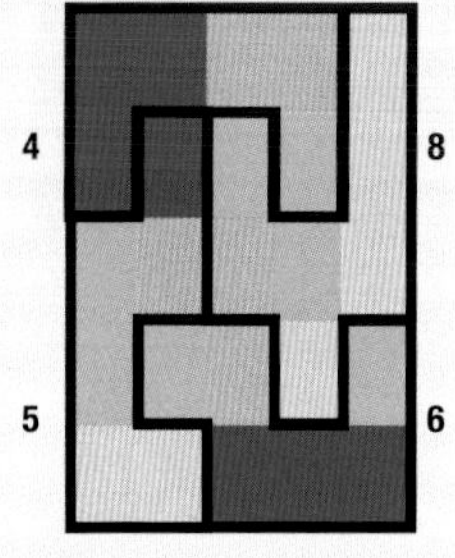

ONE WORD TOO MANY

1. You can add the word 'mar' to the start of each of these words to make new words – margin, marking, marmite, marram, marrow, except for BAKE.
2. The first five words contain consecutive letters of the alphabet (abc, def, fgh, ghi, mno), except for RETRO.
3. You can remove the letter T from each word to make a new word (casing, fleeing, marines, sand, rick), except for PENITENT.

WHICH COMES NEXT?

1. Each of the numbers is multiplied by 8, so 4 x 8 = 32, 32 x 8 = 256, etc. The missing number is therefore 131 072 x 8 = 1 048 576.
2. In each of these molecules, the sum of the pink and green atoms equals six times that of the blue, and the pink is equal to four times more than the green. You are therefore looking for two numbers, for which the sum is 6 x 8 = 48 and with the difference being 4. The numbers you are looking for are 22 for the green and 26 for the pink.
3. Each line describes what you read from the line above. The first line is a 1, so the second line reads 1 1 (one 1 on the first line). On the second line, there are two 1s, so you write 2 1 on the third line. You therefore have one 2 and one 1, so you write 1 2 1 1 on the fourth line … and so on. The last line will therefore represent three 1s, one 3, one 2, one 1, one 3 one 2 and two 1s, that is 3 1 1 3 1 2 1 1 1 3 1 2 2 1.

LADDER

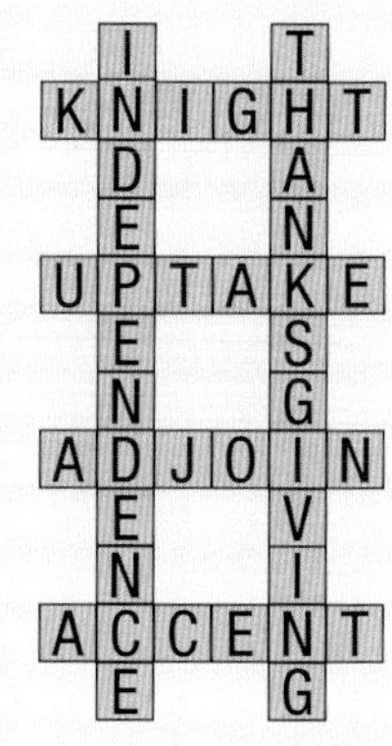

SANDWICH
To be or not to be, that is the question.

Pages 270-271

THEMATIC CROSSWORD

RECITATION

a. grown; **b.** alone; **a.** found; **c.** underground; **a.** apace; **a.** soldier's face; **c.** green sea; **b.** my knee; **a.** he lies; **b.** leaden eyes; **a.** pointed gun; **b.** the sun.

POINTS IN COMMON

1. Day
2. Walking
3. Log
4. Knife
5. Dress
6. Nail

LOOPY LETTERS

In exchanging M-N and L-K, you get Pakistan and Mongolia.

ONE TOO MANY

LOTTO

Pages 272-273

MYSTERY WORDS

A. Wales
B. Toronto
C. Madagascar
D. Venice
E. Bangkok

NUMBER PYRAMID

Since a + b equals 26, the possibilities are a = 7 and b = 19; a = 14 and b = 12; a = 21 and b = 5. We also know that b + c = 46 – 26 = 20. Now c is a multiple of 5. Thus, since b + c is also a multiple of 5, b is also a multiple of 5. Thus a = 21 and b = 5 is the right hypothesis, and consequently c = 15. So, you fill the base of the pyramid with 21; 5; 15; d; e. At the apex, you get 131 + 4d + e, which must equal 176. That means that 4d + e = 45. But a is a multiple of 11. If you try successively 11; 22; 33; 44, you'll find that the only solution that works is e = 33. Consequently, 4d = 45 – 33, so 4d = 12 and d = 3.

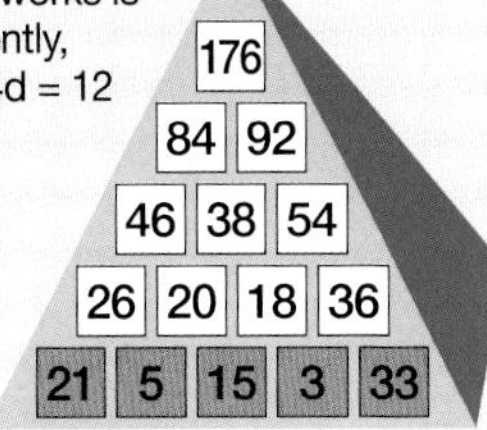

WORDS IN THE PICTURE

Here are some: filament (the bulb), Finland (the poster), filled (wine glasses), figurine (on the TV), film, finish, finance, fig (in the picture), fiacre (the toy), files, filter (coffee machine), fiancés, fidelity, finial, fife, ficus, finch, fingers, fir, fish…

ROSETTE

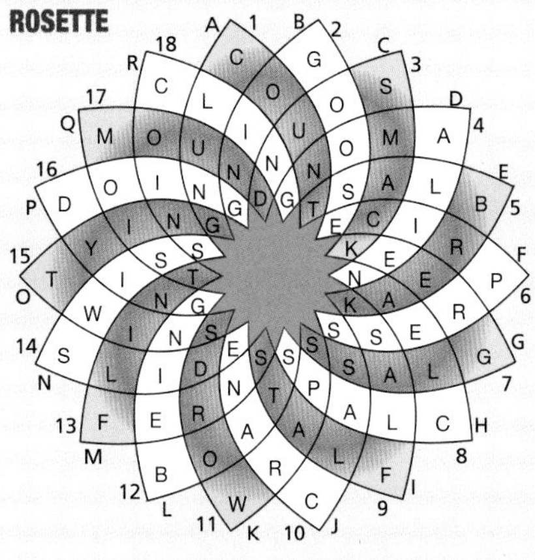

Pages 274-275

KNOW YOUR WORLD

1. Mount Erebus, in Antarctica.
2. Mount Pinatubo, in the Philippines.
3. Mont Pelée, in Martinique.
4. Mount Soufrière, in Guadeloupe.
5. Fuji-Yama, in Japan.
6. Popocatepetl, in Mexico.
7. Krakatoa, in Indonesia.
8. Santorini, in Greece.
9. Etna, in Italy.
10. Tambora, in Indonesia.
11. Stromboli, in Italy.
12. Vesuvius, in Italy.
13. Mauna Loa, in Hawaii.
14. Llaima, in Chile.
15. Bezymianny, in the Kamtchatka.
16. Mount Saint Helens, in Washington State.
17. Nevado del Ruiz, in Colombia.
18. Asama, in Japan.
19. El Chichon, in Mexico.
20. Kilimanjaro, in Tanzania.

MATCHING UP

A10 – B8 – C4 – D5 – E3 – F9 – G1 – H2 – I6 – J7

PROVERB

It's no use crying over spilt milk.

SUPERIMPOSITION

2, 3, 4, 7 and 8

MATCHES

Keep the roof as the base of the construction, then move the matches as illustrated to form six small triangles and two large ones.

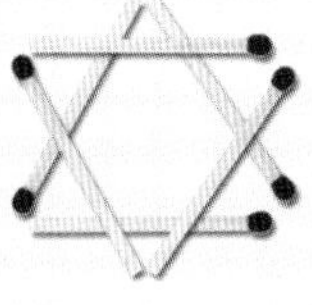

PROBLEM

Two Ladas and four BMWs are worth 102 000 euros all told. So one Lada and two BMWs cost 51 000 euros. Thus 11 Ladas and 22 BMWs are worth 561 000 euros (11 x 51 000). Now 11 Ladas and 5 BMWs are together worth 204 000 euros (2 x 102 000). So 17 BMWs (22-5) are worth 357 000 euros (561 000-204 000).
One BMW is therefore worth 21 000 euros and one Lada 9 000 euros.

Pages 276-277

MIXED PROVERBS

1. Actions speak louder than words.
2. A chain is no stronger than its weakest link.
3. A rolling stone gathers no moss.

THEMATIC CROSSWORD

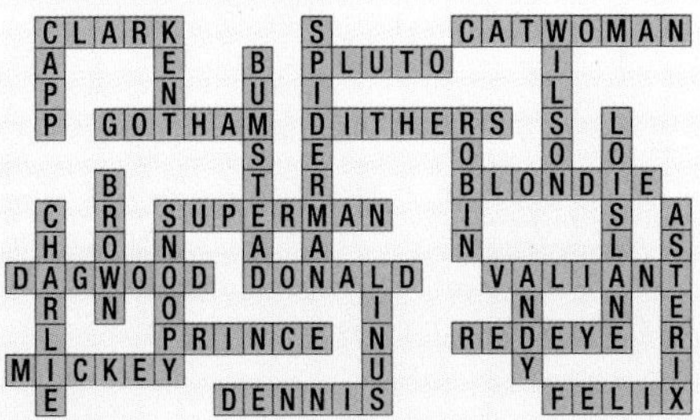

PUZZLE

Piece no. 3

CROSSWORD

Pages 278-279

MYSTERY WORDS

A. Dame Freya Stark
B. Midas
C. Jean-Jacques Rousseau
D. Vespasian
E. Mohammed

STICK-ON WORDS

Antimissiles – Autoantibody – Backslapping – Chitchatting – Codefendants – Dishonesties – Featherbrain – Forecastable – Foreshadowed – Headforemost – Malefactions – Overexposure.

PROBLEM

A represents the contents of the test tube, B the contents of the large measuring glass and C that of the small measuring glass. So to start with, you have 12g; 0g; 0g.
This is how to proceed to obtain two doses of 6g. Empty the contents of the test tube into the small measuring jug (7; 0; 5), empty the small jug into the large one (7; 5; 0), the test tube into the small measuring jug again (2; 5; 5), fill the large jug with the small one (2; 7; 3), empty the large jug into the test tube (9; 0; 3) empty the small jug into the large one (9; 3; 0), fill the small jug with the test tube (4; 3; 5) fill the large jug with the small one (4; 7; 1), empty the large jug into the test tube (11; 0; 1), empty the small jug into the large one (11; 1; 0), fill the small jug with the test tube (6; 1; 5) and finally empty the small jug into the large one (6; 6; 0) to obtain the right doses to assure Arthur's survival.

WORD HOLES

1. Bracelet
2. Decreases
3. Stockings
4. Spaceblankets
5. Psychiatrist
6. University

HISTORICAL LANDMARKS

1. 1492 B/K (Columbus, Jews expelled from Spain)
2. 1533 D/P (Incas, Ivan le Terrible)
3. 1599 F/H (Van Dyck, Velasquez)
4. 1719 G/M (Aurora, Robinson Crusoe)
5. 1796 I/L (Arcole, Beethoven and Haydn)
6. 1865 C/J (abolition of slavery in the United States, *Alice in Wonderland*)
7. 1897 A/N (Lenin, Klondike)
8. 1924 E/O (Paris Olympics, Hubble).

Pages 280-281

ROSETTE

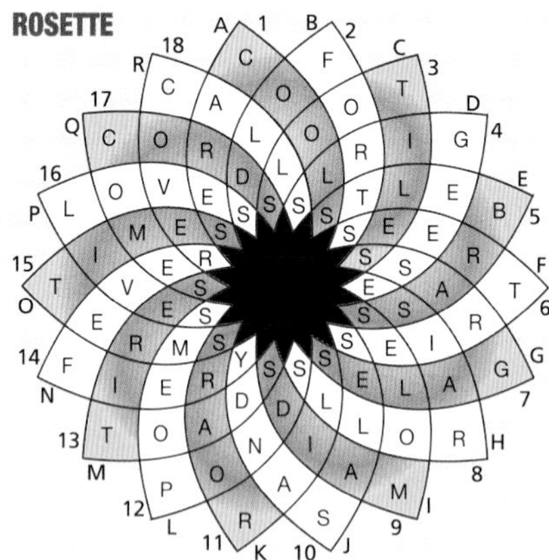

PROBLEM

1. Washers
2. Hooks
3. Nuts
4. Empty
5. Bolts
6. Screws
7. Nails
8. Staples

BOXED WORDS

NUMBER PYRAMID

Start by filling in each level of the number pyramid.
Second level: a + b = e ; b + c = d ; c + d = e; d + e.
Third level: d + e ; d + e and d + 2e.
Fourth level: 2d + 2e and 2d + 3e.
Apex: 4d = 5 e = 100.
Since 100 is also a multiple of 5 and 5e, 4d must also be a multiple of 5 in terms of this equation. Thus d can take the values of 5, 10, 15 or 20 here. And e could be equal to 16, 12, 8 and 4 respectively.
Study these pairs:
- d = 5 and e = 16: since c + d = e, the value of c is 11, but b + c = d is impossible because c must be equal to -6.
- d = 10 and e = 12: since c + d = e, c = 2. Since b + c = d, b equals 8.
And since a + b = c + d = e, a equals 4.
- d = 15 and e = 8: c must be negative so that c + d = e.
The same problem arises if d = 20 and e = 4.
Thus the only solution is:
a = 4; b = 8; c = 2;
d = 10 and e = 12.

TRUE OR FALSE

1. False: it was Mme Montespan (M).
2. False: Louis XIV (A).
3. True (D).
4. True (A).
5. False: it was Mme Montpensier (M).
6. False (E).
They called them MADAME.

BRAIN TEASER

There are two pedigreed dogs among the dogs with a bow on their heads: 2, 4 and 6; two also among the dogs wearing a collar: 1, 3 and 4; another two among the dogs wearing a small red jacket: 3, 5 and 6. The pedigreed dogs are those that appear twice among those mentioned. The pedigreed dogs are thus dog number 3 (no bow on the head, collar, little red jacket), dog number 4 (bow on the head, collar, no little red jacket) and dog number 6 (bow on the head, no collar, little red jacket).

JUMBLED WORDS

1. Capote, Mailer
2. Steinbeck, Irving
3. Caldwell, Isherwood

Pages 282-283

WORDS IN THE PICTURE

Here are a few examples: collie, cobra, conch shells, cocoon, cocktail, cookies, chicken, cat, crack, can, cups, collection, colours, cornice, corner, compass, cone, conserve, chart, column, Concorde, cucumber…

ITINERARY

Madrid – Roissy

BONUS LETTERS

1. Echo
2. Faces
3. Scrape
4. Watched
5. Selected
6. Scavenger

ZIGZAG WORDS

Statue of Liberty

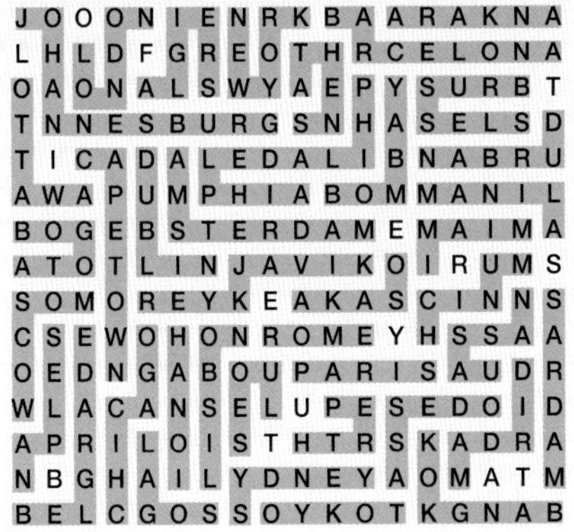

ITINERARY

Boston – Lusaka

B	R	A	Z	I	L
O	A	M	A	R	U
S	A	N	T	O	S
T	O	P	E	K	A
O	L	E	N	E	K
N	E	V	A	D	A

PROVERB

There's many a slip 'twixt cup and lip.

Pages 284-285

NUMBER PYRAMID

Considering the numbers at the second and third levels, the number aa,bb can only be 44,55 or 55,66. Try the two possibilities. If you put 44,55 in place and fill in the pyramid, you get a negative number at the base. So the right solution is 55, 66.

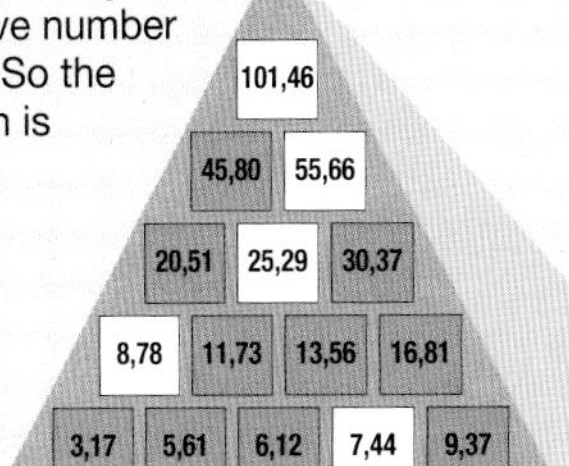

LOGIGRAM

Come and join the circus

Thanks to clues 1 and 4, we know that Piotr is a juggler. Since neither Igor nor Vassili are clowns (clue 3), Sacha must be one. Igor is not a trainer (clue 5), so he must be an acrobat. By a process of elimination, Vassili is a trainer. Sacha is not with Zavatta (clue 6), nor is Vassili (trainer) according to clue 1, nor is the acrobat Igor according to clue 2. It is therefore Piotr who works at Zavatta. According to clue 3, it is Sacha who is at Cirque du Soleil. Igor the acrobat must therefore be at Grüss, according to clue 2, and consequently Vassili works at Bouglione.

Table of answers

Artist	Igor	Piotr	Sacha	Vassili
Profession	Acrobat	Juggler	Clown	Trainer
Circus	Grüss	Zavatta	Soleil	Bouglione

THEMATIC CROSSWORD

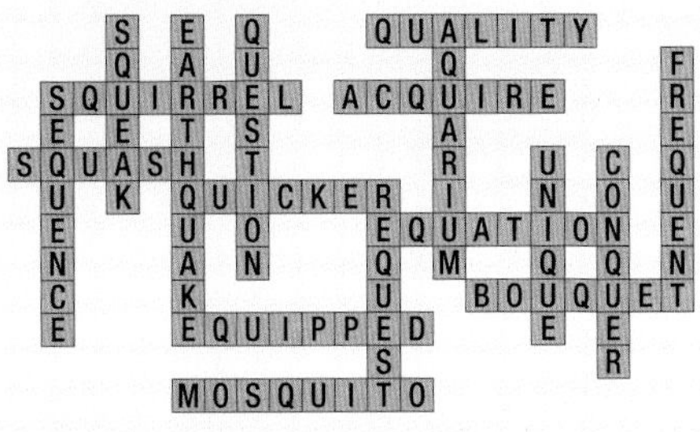

JUMBLED WORDS

1. Edison, Fleming
2. Galois, Pasteur
3. Rutherford, Marconi

PUZZLE

Pile number 2.

Structure A consists of 41 cubes, so there are 23 missing. Pile number 2 is the only one with this number. Number 1 has 24, number 3 has 22, number 4 has 24 and number 5 has 22.

CATERPILLAR

```
H A R M O N I C
M O N A R C H Y
A C R O N Y M S
R O M A N C E S
S E R M O N I C
C O N S P I R E
C O M P R I S E
C O M P O S E R
```

LOOPY LETTERS

By exchanging B and C you get Jumbo jet and Concorde.

J U M B O J E T
E D R O C N O C

Pages 286-287

WHAT AM I?

A. Thread
B. A hole
C. The future
D. Torch
E. Voice

SPOT THE 7 DIFFERENCES

LADDER

THEMATIC CROSSWORD

CUT-UP LETTERS

You can remove:
E (Renting) – G (Coasters) – Y (Earning) – P (Sinners) – T (Mineral) – I (Tangles) – A (Thieves) – N (Rematch): EGYPTIAN.

IDIOMATIC TRIPLETS

1. Bird – 2. Best – 3. Many – 4. Once – 5. Give – 6. Horse

PROBLEM

If he had one coin in January, at the end of the year he would have 1 + 12 + 23 + 34 + 45 + 56 + 67 + 78 + 89 + 100 + 111 + 122 = 738, that is 369 dollars. But he has 1 086 (543 dollars). Thus he collected 1 086 – 738 = 348 more during the 12 months. That is 348/ 12 = 29 per month (30 in January, 41 in February …). In December, Nicholas has thus added 122 + 29 = 151 coins to his money box.

ESCALETTERS

```
      S I N
+ E   S I N E
+ M   M I N E S
+ O   M O N I E S
+ T   M O I S T E N
+ O   E M O T I O N S
+ C   E C O N O M I S T
```

My memory and my life

Memory and lifestyle

A healthy lifestyle is vital for sound brain function, and therefore for the memory. It is essential to adopt brain-friendly habits (a balanced diet, regular sleep, daily exercise) and to avoid what could be detrimental (certain medicines, stimulants – tobacco, alcohol, coffee, etc – excessive stress …).

A healthy diet

There is no diet specifically designed to promote good memory function, nor is there any 'memory food' as such. Nevertheless, to function well, your brain, like your whole body, needs a balanced and varied diet, one that provides you with sufficient nourishment.

The brain consumes a great deal of glucose, which is supplied by the blood vessels. So you **must look after your circulatory system** and avoid unhealthy practices such as over-eating, or indulging in excessive sweets, fats and alcoholic beverages, which have a deleterious effect on the circulatory system. On the other hand, certain dietary deficiencies – in fibre, vitamins and protein – can adversely affect both your concentration and memory.

Eat three meals a day, maintaining a good **balance between proteins, lipids (fats) and carbohydrates** and ensuring you have an **adequate intake of vitamins, minerals and fibre**. If you don't feel inspired to cook, make use of home-delivery services (restaurants, caterers, etc).

You are strongly advised to eat meat, fish or eggs (for protein and iron) at least once a day; fruits and vegetables (fresh or frozen), which are rich in vitamins, fibre and minerals, several times a day. In addition, eat foods rich in calcium, such as dairy products. And drink **one and a half to two litres of water** or any other non-alcoholic beverage every day. It is important to **drink regularly,** without waiting to feel thirsty. Some people, especially the elderly, don't necessarily experience thirst.

Remember to weigh yourself every month. Consult your doctor if you detect a marked change in your weight, and **never go on diet without first seeking medical advice.**

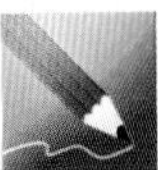

Food and your memory

Test your knowledge of the effects of diet on the health of the brain and sound memory function. Cover the answers and commentary that follow.

	TRUE	FALSE		TRUE	FALSE
1. Iron is useful for the brain.			**6.** We can do without meat.		
2. Spinach is an important source of iron.			**7.** Vitamin deficiencies can lead to serious mental problems.		
3. The brain can store the glucose that it needs.			**8.** Alcohol can have a devastating effect on the brain.		
4. High cholesterol levels adversely affect the sound functioning of the brain.			**9.** After the age of 60, we can decrease our daily food ration (do with less food).		
5. Certain fats contribute to the sound functioning of cells in the brain.			**10.** Certain foods help to develop the memory.		

1. TRUE.
Iron facilitates the circulation of oxygen throughout the body by contributing to the synthesis of the haemoglobin of red cells, which carries the oxygen molecules. To ensure proper oxygenation of the brain it is thus vital to have an adequate intake of iron. One woman in four suffers from iron deficiency and must therefore increase her intake of iron-rich foods or take iron supplements.

2. FALSE.
There are many other good sources of iron, including red meat, eggs, leafy green vegetables and pulses.

3. FALSE.
The brain uses glucose as it needs it, drawing it from the bloodstream. Because this is its only source of energy, a constant supply of glucose is thus indispensable to a well-functioning brain. The more intense the cerebral activity, the higher the energy consumption.

4. TRUE.
Excess cholesterol in the body results in sclerosis of blood vessels such as the arteries, which obstructs and so restricts the supply of oxygen and nutrients. High cholesterol therefore increases the risk of vascular problems and cerebral dysfunction.

5. TRUE.
The body can't by itself synthesise certain fatty acids (essential fatty acids) that play an important part in the sound functioning of the nerve cells and the protection of the arteries. It is thus necessary to consume them regularly, especially in the form of vegetable oils (sunflower, rape, olive and soya). These oils contain vitamin E which fights the free radicals that attack the membranes of the nerve cells.

6. TRUE.
But meat contains protein which is vital for the maintenance of the tissues. If you don't eat meat, you must consume protein in another form, such as eggs, fish, dairy products, nuts,

eeds and certain cereals. As you age, your ody's speed of protein renewal slows down. ou should therefore not decrease your onsumption of protein, but rather increase it.

'. TRUE.

'itamins are essential for the growth and good ondition of body tissue. Your body can't roduce vitamins itself. They have to be upplied by good nutrition. Among the itamins that are essential for good brain unction are vitamins B^1 (found in starches, uit and milk), B^{12} (liver, kidneys, yeast), B^6 dairy products, cereals, green vegetables), B^9 iver, yeast, potato). We know that a leficiency in vitamin B^9 or B^{12} can lead to eurological problems. But such deficiencies re rare in developed countries.

. TRUE.

aken in small quantities, alcohol stimulates he nerve cells, but a large amount of alcohol lulls them. Excessive alcohol consumption eads to the irreversible damage of a large umber of nerve cells which has a negative ffect on the memory.

. TRUE.

f you become less physically active, it is not ecessary to eat as much. On the other hand, f you maintain your level of physical activity, lo not decrease your daily intake of food. In oth cases, maintain a balanced diet.

10. FALSE.

o develop your memory to its fullest capacity, is most important to vary your diet and eat a noderate amount of everything. There is no niracle food: to function well on a long-term asis, the various parts of the brain need a ood nutritional balance.

Tasty national dishes

A balanced diet is not always in evidence in certain dishes or regional specialities, but what flavours! Allocate the following specialities to the eight countries or regions from which they originate (four dishes per country or region).

Great Britain
Germany
Eastern Europe
France
Spain
Portugal
Italy
Greece
North Africa

Solution p.341

Bacalão ....
Beef Wellington ....
Blanquette de veau ...
Blini ....
Boeuf bourguignonne ....
Borscht ....
Bouillabaisse ....
Bratwurst ....
Chorizo ....
Cock-a-leekie ....
Colcannon ....
Coq au vin ....
Couscous ....
Dolmades ....
Eisbein ....
Ful Midames ....
Gazpacho ....
Goulash ....
Harira ....
Keftedes ....
Moussaka ....
Osso buco ....
Paella ....
Pierogi ....
Pizza ....
Risotto ....
Sauerkraut ....
Spaghetti bolognese ....
Stollen ....
Tagine ....
Tzatziki ....
Yorkshire pudding ....

The calorie table

Calories are a measure of the energy value of food.
Try to find the right calorie count for the same quantity (100g or 100ml) of each of the following foodstuffs. Watch out, certain foods can be deceptive!

a. 100g pear
b. 100g cooked pasta
c. 100g pork casserole
d. 100g salad leaves
e. 100g pizza
f. 100g hamburger
g. 100g ham sandwich
h. 100ml soda water
i. 100g couscous
j. 100g apple
k. 100g steak
l. 100ml wine, 12% a/c
m. 100g egg

...... / 18 kcal
...... / 44 kcal
...... / 52 kcal
...... / 61 kcal
...... / 67 kcal
...... / 90 kcal
...... / 160 kcal
...... / 200 kcal
...... / 200 kcal
...... / 255 kcal
...... / 430 kcal
...... / 575 kcal
...... / 610 kcal

Solution p.341

Italian delights
Complete this little crossword puzzle by filling in the names of some Italian gastronomic specialities.

Solution p.341

My memory and...
bouts of insomnia

You can use occasional episodes of insomnia productively rather than worrying about them. Make the most of this time of rest to relax, sort out your problems calmly or think of pleasant projects for the future. Avoid any strain on your memory or mental faculties or any activity demanding an alert state of mind – doing your accounts, for example! Banish all cares, remain in a warm, comfortable place and insomnia will become a positive time that no longer holds any fears for you ... on condition, of course, that it is not too prolonged and remains only an occasional occurrence. As soon as fatigue once more overcomes you, that is a sign that your body wishes to rest. Don't try to resist ...

Regular, quality sleep

A healthy lifestyle also implies getting enough sleep. You sleep for about one third of your life because sleep is indispensable for the **restoration of your physical and psychological wellbeing.** People who are lacking sleep or sleep badly can be irritable and have difficulty concentrating.

A night's sleep is made up of four to six cycles on average, each lasting an hour-and-a-half to two hours. In the course of one night you therefore go through the same cycles several times. Each cycle comprises two main phases: one phase of slow sleep and another of so-called paradoxical sleep.

Slow sleep – so called because the electrical waves emitted by the brain at this time are slow and calm – is itself sub-divided into four mini-phases: very light sleep, light sleep, deep sleep and very deep sleep. Slow sleep **enables your body to recover from physical fatigue.** It is during this sleep that you 'recharge your batteries' and your tissues are restored.

During **paradoxical sleep,** the waves emitted by the brain are rapid and nervous, and the body makes small jerky movements. It is as though the brain is being overcharged. Paradoxical sleep **enables you to recover from mental fatigue**. It is also at this time that you dream. During this phase of sleep all you have learned during the day is also fixed in your memory and your memories are consolidated. But at the same time what is not worth retaining is eliminated – it is as though your brain is engaged in a sorting-out process.

What can you do to improve the quality of your sleep? You should, at any age, try to keep regular hours, going to bed and getting up at the same time each day; have a shorter siesta, if you regularly have one; exercise for at least half an hour every day (but not just before going to bed); relax before going to bed and try to eliminate any stress; limit your consumption of alcohol, coffee or tea; avoid eating copious meals and overheating your bedroom; finally, ensure that your room is quiet.

Sleep: watch out for these mistakes!
Here are several everyday behaviour patterns that can either encourage or hinder the process of falling asleep or even prevent you from sleeping well. Find five mistakes you should avoid.

Test How good is the quality of your sleep?

What difficulties have you experienced in this last month? Write down your replies on the scale below, and then add up your total number of points.

Never **0 points**
Less than once a week: **1 point**
Once a week: **2 points**
Several times a week: **3 points**
Every day: **4 points**

	Never	Less than once a week	Once a week	Several times a week	Every day
1. I take a long time to fall asleep.					
2. When I am asleep, the slightest sound wakes me.					
3. I wake up at least once during the night.					
4. If I am woken during the night, I find it difficult to go back to sleep					
5. I wake up very early in the morning and can't go back to sleep.					
6. I take sleeping pills.					
7. I am tired when I wake up.					
8. Worries prevent me falling asleep.					
9. I take long siestas.					
10. I drink a great deal of coffee or tea.					
Total per column					

Your score:

Less than 10 points
There is no doubt you enjoy good-quality sleep. If you have memory problems, they do not stem from lack of sleep. Many people would envy you ...

From 11 to 20 points
The temporary problems you experience are probably connected with your present preoccupations. They could cause some anxiety and problems of concentration. Once the situation has been sorted out everything should return to normal. Be careful of stimulants of any kind, because they affect sleep.

More than 20 points
You frequently experience problems with sleep, either in falling asleep, during the night, or in the early morning. It is therefore to be expected that in the course of the day you sometimes feel tired or even irritable. These disrupted sleep patterns will inevitably have an adverse effect on the attention you can devote to events and people around you, and on your ability to retain and retrieve information. Perhaps you are going through a difficult time. It is essential to get enough sleep – your quality of life depends on it. If you can't solve these problems on your own, speak to your doctor about them.

6. Eat a large dinner.

7. Take a bath before going to bed.

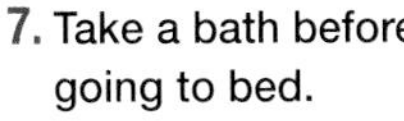

8. Sleep in a cool room (19°C).

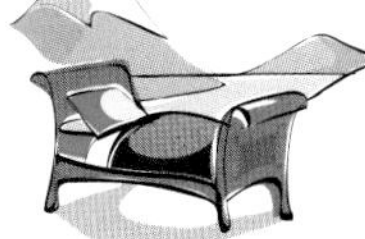

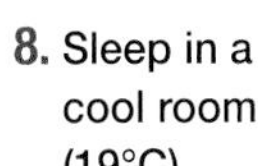

9. Switch off mentally.

10. Read.

11. Drink coffee or tea after 4pm.

12. Drink herbal tea (linden, verbena, orange blossom, camomile or rooibos) before going to bed.

13. Massage your feet and hands, or get someone to massage them for you.

14. Sleep on a firm mattress.

15. Arrange your bedroom so that it is a place of relaxation.

16. Drink plenty of alcohol.

5 errors not to commit:

Solution p.341

....

Real illnesses demand real remedies

Dietary deficiencies and sleep deprivation are not the only causes of problems to do with concentration and memory function. **Stress and anxiety** also have a deleterious effect on concentration. Excessive use of **stimulants such as alcohol and tobacco** can also impair cerebral functioning. Nicotine blocks the action of cerebral neurotransmitters as well as that of nicotinic receptors, which results in lesions and degeneration of the tissues. Alcohol slows down synaptic connections.

When problems concerning attention and concentration become chronic, medical intervention can become necessary – in the form of medicine and/or psychotherapy. **Be careful – sleeping pills and certain traditional tranquillisers** affect memory function. But there is now a new range of tranquillisers without any known side-effects. Discuss this with your doctor, always keep to the prescribed dosage and never stop the treatment without prior discussion with him or her. Any medicine that has an affect on cerebral function should be used with caution.

Herbal medicine, relaxation and yoga can also help you. Ginseng and ginkgo biloba, which have anti-oxidant properties, can stimulate the brain cells and improve circulation and oxygenation of the brain, thus indirectly promoting concentration and hence memorisation.

My memory and... my doctor

Sometimes general practitioners downplay the memory problems of their patients who nevertheless feel they have good reason to be worried. You could find yourself in this position, not knowing which specialist to consult for information or even reassurance about your condition. Tests on 'memory' can now be done in most large cities, especially in a hospital environment, but you often have a long wait before getting an appointment. You could also consult a local neurologist or a gerontologist. These specialists know all about the pathology of the memory and will listen to you. With the aid of quick, precise and painless tests they will provide you with information and frequently with reassurance concerning your condition.

Medicinal plants

Here are 15 complaints and 15 names of common plants. See if you can relate the two lists and find which plant is used to treat which complaint.

Stress, asthenia ....
Painful periods ....
Loss of appetite ....
Eczema ....
Loss of memory ....
Hoarseness ....
Inflammation of the joints ....
Minor sleep problems ....
Nasal congestion ....
Intestinal worms ....
Digestive problems ....
Constipation ....
Toothache ....
Fatigue ....
Nausea, vomiting ....

Solution p.341

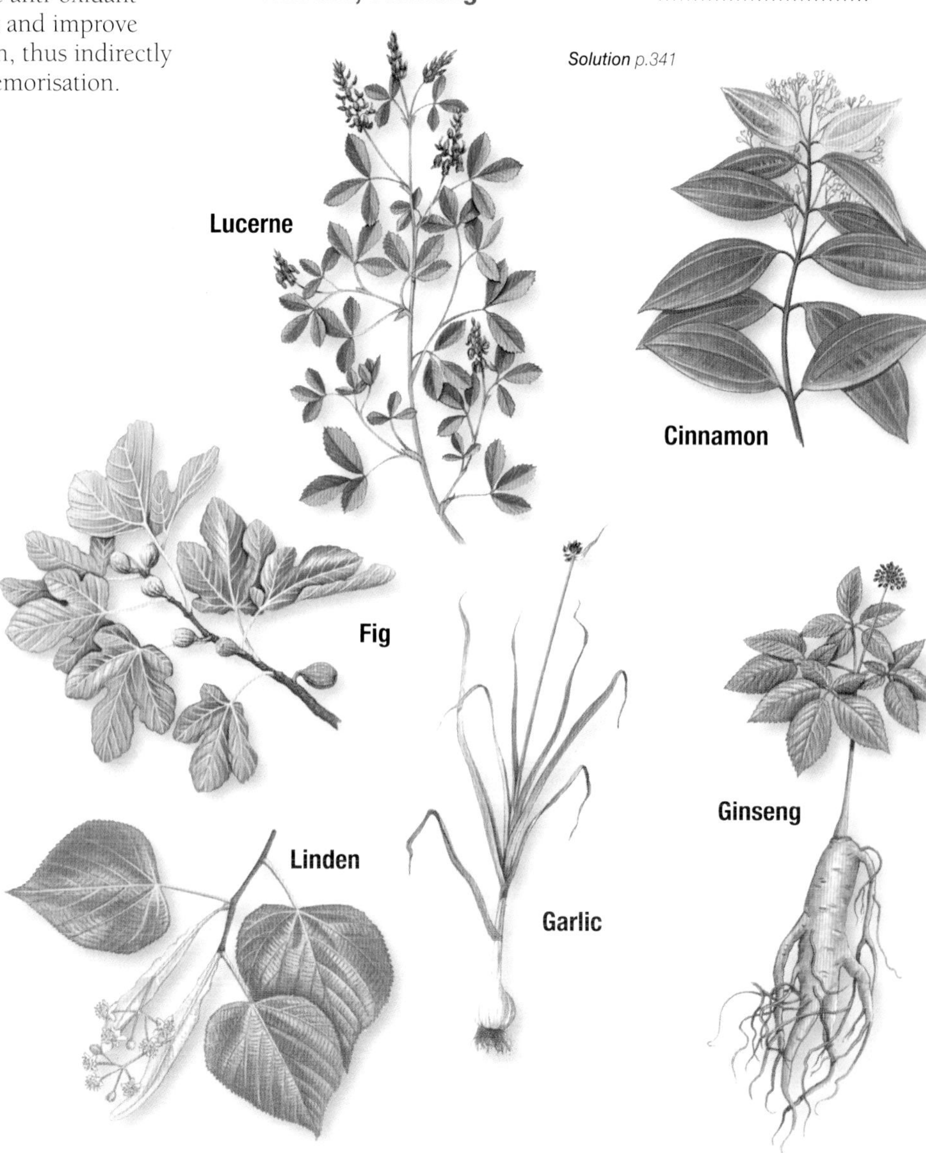

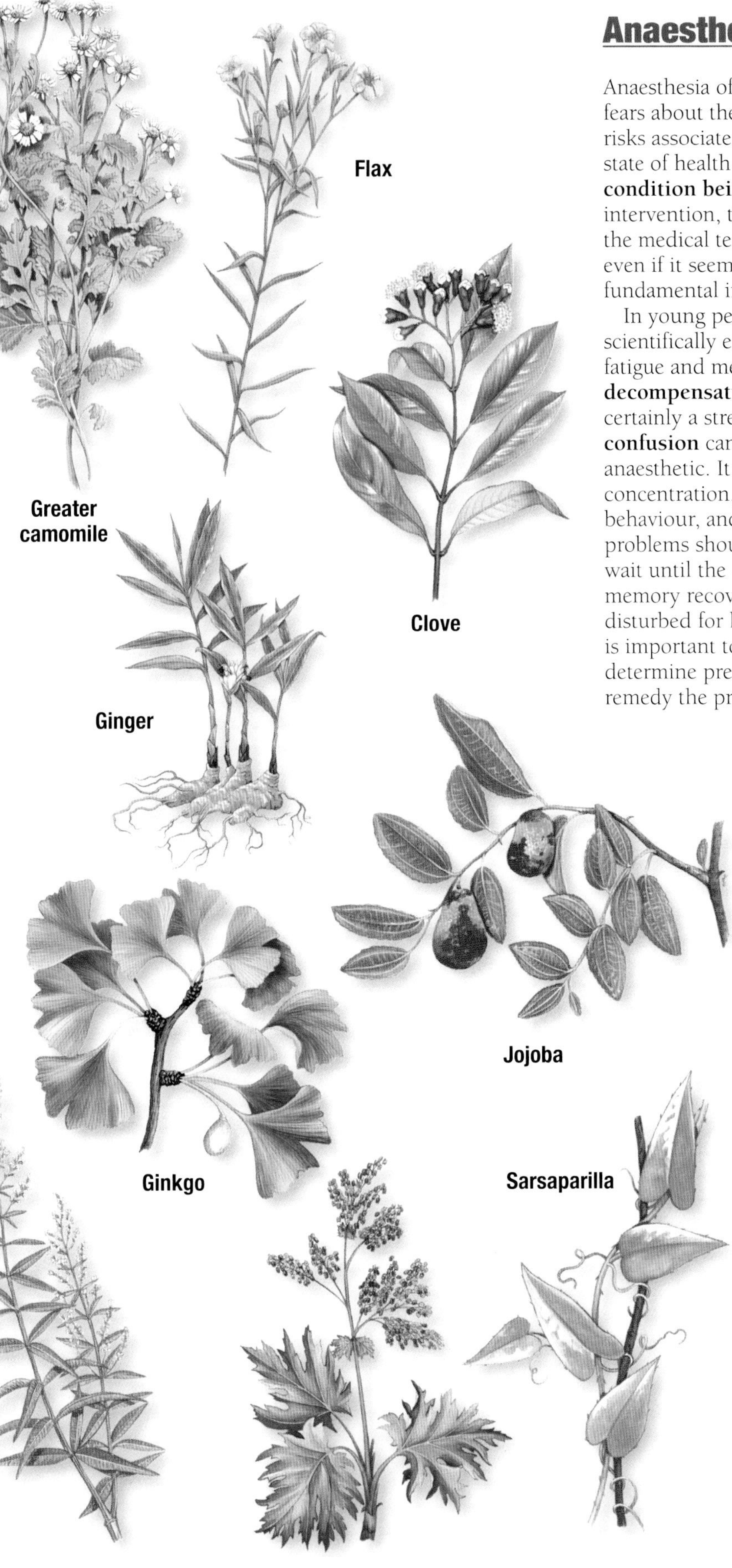

Anaesthesia and memory

Anaesthesia often arouses a lot of apprehension, especially fears about the possible impairment of the memory. The risks associated with anaesthesia depend on the general state of health of the patient – **physical and psychological condition being more important than age –**, the kind of intervention, the technique used and the professionalism of the medical team. The role of the pre-operative check-up, even if it seems to be tiresomely exhaustive, is of fundamental importance to the success of the procedure.

In young people, no definite connection has ever been scientifically established between a general anaesthetic, fatigue and memory lapses. These should rather be seen as **decompensation linked to stress** – an operation is certainly a stressful experience. In older people, **a state of confusion** can be observed for a few hours after the anaesthetic. It is accompanied by reduced powers of concentration, temporary disturbance of the memory or behaviour, and temporal and spatial disorientation. These problems should disappear after a few days. You need only wait until the effects of the medication wear off before the memory recovers. In certain people, this faculty can remain disturbed for longer. If the recovery really takes too long, it is important to consult a neurologist immediately to determine precisely what the cause is and find ways to remedy the problem.

My memory and… my convalescence

You can always keep your memory in good shape during convalescence:

- Keep a small photo album with you – with pictures of your family, holiday snaps, etc – to enable your memory to retain, or quickly recover, those familiar points of reference it needs.
- Play. Give priority to word games of all kinds, including crossword puzzles, cryptic crosswords, anagrams, scrabble, find-the-word, etc. These games can be found in large print for people with impaired vision. They enable you to exercise your vocabulary and preserve your linguistic skills.
- Re-read a book you liked, so that you can enjoy following the story without too much effort. This will provide the necessary stimulation of your powers of concentration.
- Read a new book if you are up to it and as long as the subject interests you. Be careful though – do not read for too long or you will get tired.

Memory and stages of life

In your youth, you adapt to an ever-changing environment by accumulating knowledge. As an adult you continue to accumulate and store information, but also make use of the knowledge you have already acquired. When you reach maturity, your memory attempts to extract some sort of significant pattern in your life. Then you begin to reminisce and reflect on the past: memories of your past experiences come to the fore again.

The golden triangle: body, mind and environment

Memory, like the individual, is a complex affair and its sound functioning depends on the interaction of three equally important factors – biological, psychological and environmental. Any difficulty, however minor, in one of these areas will inevitably have repercussions on the other two and hence on the memory itself.

Biological factors, the most vital, are the precondition for the other two. Memory can function really well only in the absence of problems with its vital functions. That is why it is so important to have a healthy lifestyle and to find the right balance for maintaining your physical health. Your physical state affects your psychological wellbeing – your outlook on life, personality, emotional state, your internal conflicts – and your state of mind in turn influences your physical health.

The influence of **psychological factors** on the memory is well recognised. Lack of interest or attentiveness associated with depression is the main cause of difficulty in remembering. The effort involved in memorising or retrieving memories is dependent on the degree of your motivation and mood at the time. Your brain is able to filter elements in accordance with your state of mind, so if you are sad, negative memories come more easily to mind and you remember depressing facts more readily. Conversely, when you feel euphoric, your memory stores or recalls positive images much more easily.

The **environmental factor** has two components. The one is material, relying on basic comfort, because the sense of security stemming from being in comfortable circumstances plays a part in your experience of events. The other is social, and although you can't always control this element you can influence it by making opportunities for meeting people and exchanging ideas, and participating in the life of your community. When your material needs are satisfied and you enjoy a variety of enriching social relationships, your environment can play a part in stimulating your memories. When the opposite holds, it becomes a great obstacle.

The proportional weight given to these three factors can vary from person to person and from one stage of life to the next. You probably have a greater need of emotional security in childhood, whereas your need for material comfort increases as you grow older. But memory should always be seen in the context of adaptation to the environment.

Different stages of my life

With the aid of the following questions, which you might have to adapt to your own circumstances – recall and describe episodes from your past. Try also, where possible, to link these episodes with one or more visual images. This questionnaire is not exhaustive, so add as many other memories as you like.

My childhood (from 3 to 10 years)

I remember ...

- the faces of three friends in Grade 1;
- the names and faces of three teachers;
- the name of one of the places I went to on holiday;
- relatives whom I saw regularly.

My adolescence (from 11 to 18 years)

I remember ...

- the names and faces of three friends;
- most of my teachers' names;
- the face of the first person I kissed on the mouth;
- my favourite holiday spot;
- the names and surnames of singers that I liked at that time;
- the day I tried to smoke my first cigarette;
- the first (and last) time I drank too much alcohol;
- the title of a book that I found particularly moving.

From 18 years onwards

I remember ...

- the names of my most important colleagues at work, and those of friends or acquaintances who played an important part in my life;
- my first romantic involvement;
- the day I went to see my first apartment and the day when I moved in *(try to describe this place)*;
- my wedding *(what in particular do you remember about it?)*;
- the few hours preceding the birth of my children;
- the first names and surnames of my children's teachers, and the names of teachers who had the most influence on their schooling.

Youth – adapting to the environment

We sometimes feel nostalgic when we remember how easily we used to learn things by heart – the poems of our childhood, all those lecture notes, all the material we had to cope with throughout our scholastic and academic career. Children are amazingly adept at repeating something they have heard only once, and they assimilate information very quickly. Why? Because **it is of vital importance for a child to remember.**

The primary function of this activity, which is regarded as cognitive, is in fact to develop forms of behaviour aimed at self-preservation. When a toddler accidentally touches the hot oven door, he or she retains a vivid memory of this incident that subsequently acts as a warning not to get too close to hot ovens. In all areas of activity, the main purpose is to accumulate a great deal of information that will help the child to survive and make it more independent. All experiences are important in the process of growing up because they help the child adapt to the demands of the environment and find his or her place in it. Everything new arouses the curiosity of children. Their motivation to learn is constantly stimulated by the various situations they find themselves in.

The accumulation of knowledge in your youth is therefore a **specific way of using your memory in response to the vital necessity to adapt** to a world still largely unknown. Children don't have time to get stuck in the rut of a humdrum, routine way of using the memory – which is what adults, more set in their ways, tend to do.

Mirror images

The fine psychomotor ability that we constantly use in childhood and while we are growing up decreases progressively as the years pass, partly because we don't practise this ability and partly because of ageing muscles. Copy these six drawings as faithfully as possible, but as mirror images – you might even revive an interest in drawing. Besides, practising this fine motor coordination will help you preserve your good handwriting and keep the capacity for fine sensation at your fingertips.

Solution p.341

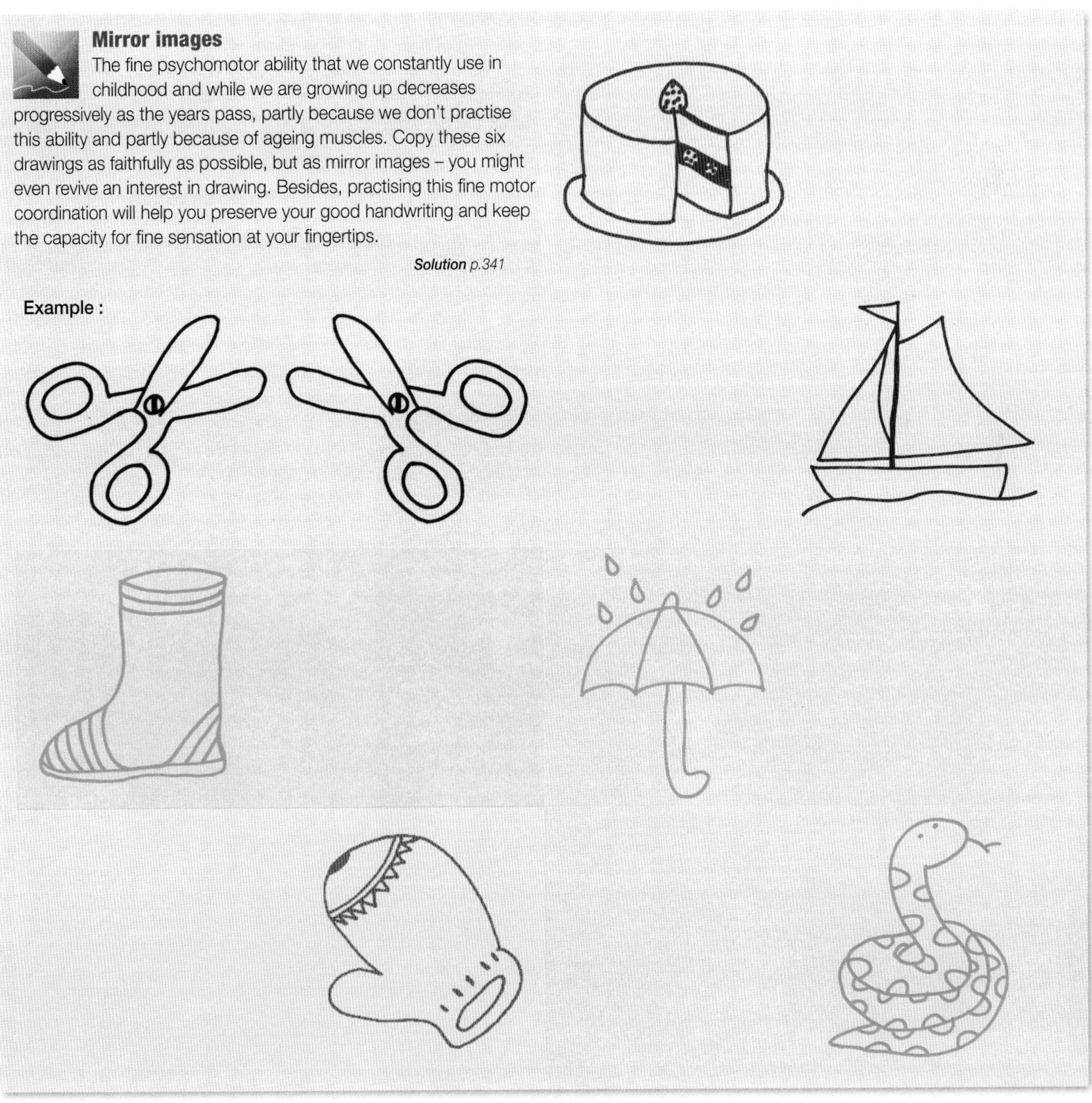

The Fox and the Crow

Mistress Crow perched high in a ....
Held in her beak a piece of ....
Master Reynard drawn by the ....
Wondered what cunning .... to tell.
'Good day, Mistress Crow, without a .... ,
You are the most .... bird I spy,
What glossy plumage, what lustrous .... ,
I've heard too you can really .....'
The Crow could not .... her pride
And opened her .... , and dropped her prize,
The .... fell into the Fox's maw
Once swallowed he allowed himself a ....
'Dear Crow, the .... of this tasty tale?
Trust not the .... deceiving veil.'
The ...., ashamed and mightily confused,
Vowed never again to fall for that ..... .

Aesop

A well-known fable

In your youth, you probably learned this short fable, much loved by teachers for its moral lesson. Try to fill in the missing words. Take your time, relax, and you will probably identify the missing words without much difficulty.

Solution p.341

Whose call is that?

The animal world forms an important part of childhood experience. One of the favourite games of children is to imitate the sounds made by certain animals. Draw on your memories, and your knowledge, to find the right term to describe the call of the following animals.
Example : the pigeon coos.

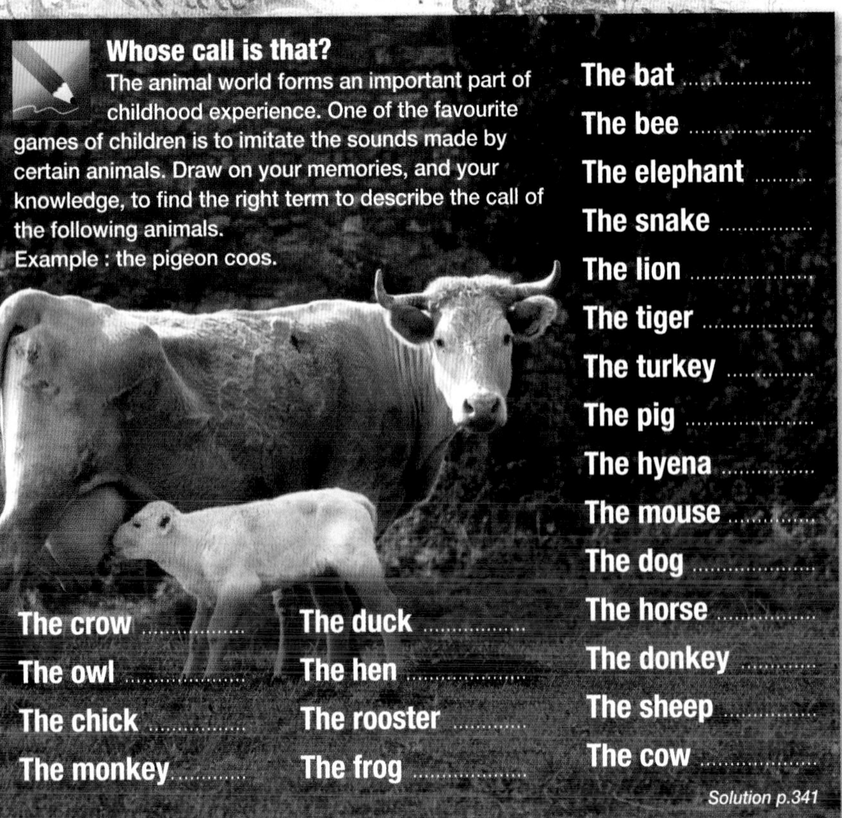

The crow ....
The owl ....
The chick ....
The monkey..............
The duck ....
The hen ....
The rooster ....
The frog ....
The bat ....
The bee ....
The elephant ....
The snake ....
The lion ....
The tiger ....
The turkey ....
The pig ....
The hyena ....
The mouse ....
The dog ....
The horse ....
The donkey ....
The sheep ....
The cow ....

Solution p.341

My memory and...
generational words

There is sometimes a yawning chasm between the language of adolescents and that of their parents or grandparents, which means they may have great difficulty communicating with each other. Try asking the person you're talking to what the unfamiliar words you hear mean, and then use them later when talking to him or her. You will probably make that person smile, but you will be putting your memory to work! It's an interesting phenomenon, too, that as people grow up, they stop using slang and revert to more conventional speech.

Adulthood: learning and using your knowledge

The more I put my memory to work the better I can adjust to my responsibilities as an adult.

Adulthood (25-50 years) is still a **time of learning.** You accumulate knowledge in response to the expectations of society (in your professional situation, family life, etc). But during this phase you also start using another aspect of your ability to remember, in that you **rely more on the knowledge you have already acquired.** In this way you can more easily adapt to the new responsibilities that appear at this time of life.

After the age of 40, you will probably notice a slight drop in your ability to concentrate, and it becomes more difficult to learn new skills quickly. So to learn as an adult you have to **make the best use of your powers of concentration,** be more attentive in a learning situation and **avoid distractions** as far as possible. Give priority to the techniques of repetition and the creation of triggers and mental images.

Travel broadens the mind ...

You have probably already travelled to or spent a holiday in a foreign country. Choose a stimulating trip that made demands on your ability to absorb new information rapidly, and think about the way in which you adapted to this new situation.

These few questions could serve to guide you.

Where were you staying?

Who were you with?

What was the weather like?

What was the time difference?

How far from home were you?

What language was spoken?

What local dishes did you discover?

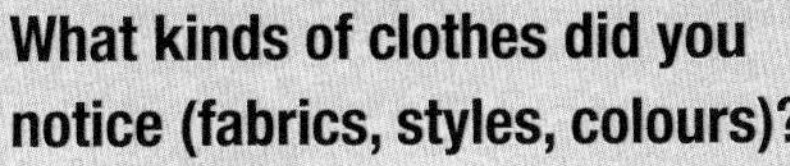

What kinds of clothes did you notice (fabrics, styles, colours)?

Did you notice any special customs?

Who did you get on well with? Can you recall their names?

What places did you visit? Name them and say where they are situated.

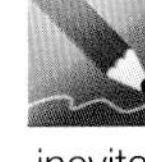

A gastronomic tour of the world

Exploring the world as an adult inevitably involves making gastronomic detours. Test your knowledge by trying to link each country with its culinary speciality.

Country	Culinary speciality
1. Austria	A. Anticuchos
3. Belgium	B. Apfelstrudel
4. Bulgaria	C. Balkenbrij
5. China	D. Braised endives
6. Finland	E. Cocido
7. India	F. Colcannon
8. Indonesia	G. Cold cucumber soup
9. Ireland	H. Enchiladas
10. Japan	I. Gado gado
11. Lebanon	J. Glögg
12. Malaysia	K. Hundred-year-old eggs
13. Mexico	L. Imam bayildi
14. Netherlands	M. Kibbeh
15. Peru	N. Miso soup
16. Senegal	O. Murgh masala
17. Thailand	P. Pumpkin pie
18. Turkey	Q. Sayur Lemak
19. USA	R. Tom Chien Dua
20. Vietnam	S. Tom Yam Gai
	T. Yassa

1.	11. ....
2.	12. ....
3.	13. ....
4.	14. ....
5.	15. ....
6.	16. ....
7.	17. ....
8.	18. ....
9.	19. ....
10.	20. ....

Solution p.341

Here's to marriage!

'Marriage should be a constant celebration' ... Utopia or reality? Whatever the case, a wedding anniversary is celebrated once a year. Do you know the accepted terms for particular wedding anniversaries?

Example: we celebrate the cotton anniversary after one year of marriage.

1. 5 years	**A. silver**
2. 10 years	**B. wood**
3. 15 years	**C. oak**
4. 20 years	**D. crystal**
5. 25 years	**E. diamond**
6. 30 years	**F. emerald or ruby**
7. 40 years	**G. tin**
8. 50 years	**H. gold**
9. 60 years	**I. pearl**
10. 70 years	**J. platinum**
11. 80 years	**K. porcelain**

1.	**7.** ....
2.	**8.** ....
3.	**9.** ....
4.	**10.** ....
5.	**11.** ....
6.	

Solution *p.342*

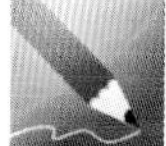

Colourful expressions

In adulthood, having lived a bit and having some experience of the behaviour of our fellow creatures, we are in a good position to make use of our knowledge of language and appreciate all its subtleties.

You have three minutes in which to find 10 expressions describing human behaviour in terms of comparisons with animals.

Example: as frightened as a rabbit

You could also make this a group activity: each person takes a turn to give an expression until you run out of inspiration (there are a fair number of expressions of this type).

Solution *p.342*

Maturity: time to revisit the past

My memories are unique, and they are the basis of my identity.

With the onset of maturity at about 50 years, many people feel that it marks a time in their life to take stock and to draw meaningful conclusions from their experiences and the knowledge they have acquired. It is also the time when they **reconsider their past in the light of the course their lives have taken and try to discern some kind of pattern that could give their lives meaning.** In a sense, we relive the events of our lives in thinking about them and trying to understand what has happened, trying to make them part of a continuum where everything will fall into place.

We all, at this time, find the same questions recurring: 'Who am I? How have the events of my life made me into what I am today? What have I gained from my experience?' This search for identity makes the memory a unique place where each person can be sure of finding what he or she really is.

The age of maturity is also when we question ourselves about the wisdom of the choices we have made, as decisions are not readily reversible at this stage. And if we have to make new decisions, such as starting another family or making a job change, doubts and questions come to the fore more strongly.

How do we learn in our mature years? We must not lose confidence in our memory but simply realise that it **takes longer to mobilise our attention.** At the same time it gets more difficult to pay attention. We need to avoid distractions as far as possible. Don't forget that the brain always tries to use as little energy as it can, and so the memory tends to save energy by working according to a set routine. We must therefore introduce minor behaviour changes into our lives from time to time so we can cope with variety and novelty without much difficulty.

My memory and... tattoos

Tattooing has become quite a craze in our society, as a fashion gimmick or badge of belonging. This indelible mark is in some ways similar to a memory. A tattoo is a sign of its time, and expresses a thought or a desire. And its owner, depending on his or her mood and psychological development, will treat it just as he or she would a memory, something to be shown (remembering it), hidden (suppressing it) or even removed through cosmetic surgery (erasing it completely).

Test

Are you set in your ways?

	Sometimes	Often	Always
1. I prepare the same meals repeatedly.			
2. I go back to the same authors whenever I choose a book.			
3. I prefer to watch one kind of film only (action film, comedy, science fiction, etc).			
4. I always buy the same make of car.			
5. I always go to the same bakery.			
6. I always buy the same shampoo.			
7. I always buy the same wine when I entertain.			

Most of your replies are sometimes: you like surprises even though you do rely on the security of a certain routine and habits.

Most of your replies are often: a certain apprehension in the face of the unknown makes you favour your habitual way of doing things and avoid learning situations.

Most of your replies are always: you don't like being confronted with novelty or variety. Be careful – this attitude to life, although respectable in itself, is a threat to your memory function. If it isn't stimulated, it will rarely be put to work.

Some tips on how to avoid falling into a rut

- If you always take the same route when going to do your shopping, take another, even if it is a little longer.
- If the meals you eat all taste the same, try some of the more exotic dishes that are sold ready prepared at supermarkets or delicatessens.
- If you like coffee, change the brand you normally use and discover other flavours.
- If you listen to only one kind of music, don't necessarily change it but embark on the discovery of new composers and performers: you have some surprises in store!
- If you enjoy reading, explore the works of new authors.
- If you belong to a library, make the most of it by exploring a new theme each week
- Start learning a new language, using a modern, more practical approach

But if you really don't want to embark on new activities and prefer to stick to your favourite round of interests, don't feel guilty! What is important is to keep your curiosity and enthusiasm alive so that you can continue to explore, to make new discoveries and feed your memory.

Your path through life

Imagine life as a road marked out into different stages. Draw yours on a piece of paper. It could be a straight or winding road, which you will mark out as you choose, marking different stages with relevant captions in large letters. Start with memories that come to mind first, leaving spaces for related memories that will come later, especially those that are more deeply

buried. The road will start with your birth and make its way towards your present situation. Use a pencil and an eraser, as you will probably have to make several changes. If you want to do this exercise in greater depth, note the places where different stages were based. Use different colours to evoke and link your perceptions of each phase (for example, blue for happy times and grey for difficult times), use tiny figures to represent significant encounters with people of importance in your life, and use crosses to show the loss of such people.

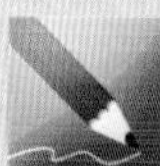

Out of the mouths of babes

Contact with children always provides plenty of surprises. Try to recall some of the words they use, or examples of their idiosyncratic pronunciation, which you found amusing or touching.

'pestacles' for **'spectacles',**

'flutterby' for **'butterfly',**

'spillage' for **'spinach',**

'capitaller' for **'caterpillar',**

'toggoban' for **'toboggan'...**

Recalling happy moments without being overcome by nostalgia for what is no more is one of the positive aspects of immersion in your memories. Generally speaking, any time spent reliving the past is in your interest only if it is done in a well-considered and positive way. In doing this, we are often motivated by the desire to avoid repeating mistakes that have been injurious to us in the past. You must accept that you can't necessarily find an explanation for everything, that you mustn't focus on what is in the past but rather be conscious of what the present still has to offer. But if this approach is not conducive to a sense of wellbeing, and does not open up new prospects or pleasant possibilities in the future, it would be better not to dwell on it.

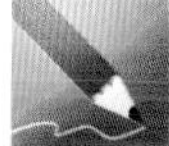

Are you movie-mad?

Film enthusiasts, it's your turn! Here is a list of legendary films and the names of their directors. Match each film with the right director.

1. Apocalypse Now
2. Breakfast at Tiffany's
3. Doctor Zhivago
4. Aguirre, Wrath of God
5. La Dolce Vita
6. Gone with the Wind
7. E.T., The Extra-Terrestrial
8. Shirley Valentine
9. Rio Bravo
10. Citizen Kane
11. Some Like it Hot
12. Remains of the Day
13. Yellow Earth
14. Moby Dick
15. Rear Window
16. The Great Dictator
17. The Quiet Man
18. Annie Hall
19. Chess Players
20. Women in Love

Lost works of art

Return each painting to its creator.

Solution p.34

1. Botticelli
2. Mary Cassatt
3. Edgar Degas
4. Frida Kahlo
5. Gustav Klimt
6. Edvard Munch
7. Pablo Picasso
8. Rembrandt
9. Henri de Toulouse-Lautrec
10. Leonardo da Vinci
11. Van Gogh
12. Andy Warhol

My memory and...
my daily rhythm

Keeping your mind and memory active depends to some extent on having a regular pace of life: enough sleep, three meals a day, an afternoon nap if possible (or short time of rest when necessary). Not letting anyone rush or hassle you in your activities and taking time to think before acting will also be beneficial. To establish whether your pace of life suits you, make sure that you are not tired on waking in the morning, that you are fairly even-tempered and that your weight remains more or less constant.

DOCTOR
HIVAGO

Scream	....
rnica	....
ilyn	....
Moulin-Rouge, la Goulue	....
flowers	....
her and Child	....
f-Portrait with Monkey	....
ration of the Magi	....
Kiss	....
Birth of Venus	....
Night Watch	....
cers at the barre	....

A. Woody Allen
B. Charles Chaplin
C. Francis Ford Coppola
D. Blake Edwards
E. Federico Fellini
F. Victor Fleming
G. John Ford
H. Lewis Gilbert
I. Howard Hawks
J. Werner Herzog
K. Alfred Hitchcock
L. John Huston
M. James Ivory
N. Chen Kaige
O. David Lean
P. Satyajit Ray
Q. Ken Russell
R. Steven Spielberg
S. Orson Welles
T. Billy Wilder

Solution p.342

1.	**11.** ....
2.	**12.** ....
3.	**13.** ....
4.	**14.** ....
5.	**15.** ....
6.	**16.** ....
7.	**17.** ....
8.	**18.** ....
9.	**19.** ....
10.	**20.** ....

The age of maturity is also when you at last have a little time for yourself. And this is when you can again spend time on cultural activities you had to neglect previously due to lack of time, or acquire new skills that were inaccessible to you for the same reason. A thirst for knowledge is characteristic of this time of life. You only need to think of the way people of mature age flock to cultural events and participate in adult education courses.

Advancing in age: repeating to perpetuate

If the elderly repeat themselves, it's because they feel they are not really being heard.

We often surprise ourselves by remarking to our elders, with a certain amount of irritation, 'You've already told us that a hundred times!' But what we take to be a turning in on themselves or else a lack of openness to life around them is in fact an expression of a fundamental need: that of inscribing the self in a continuum that is both personal and collective. Repetition is a means of sharing, the expression of a desire to pass on our own experience and view of the world. It is also a form of response to one of the fundamental questions that arise with advancing age: 'What image of myself will I leave when I die?' There are also other factors accounting for the tendency to repetition prevalent among people older than 70 whom we too readily describe as confused or 'rambling'.

- **Fatigue or lack of attentiveness** sometimes leads to people repeating the same thing to their immediate circle – something that can happen to anyone.
- Some elderly people often recount episodes in their lives that had a profound influence on them or shocked them. **They need to go over and over the experience of this shock,** in an attempt to alleviate the effect it had on them.
- People sometimes repeat things if they have **the impression that they have not been heard.** This can continue until the person concerned is sure that what he or she has said has indeed been taken into account. This happens especially in families where not much consideration is given to what individual members of the family say. If what they say is heard, it is not necessarily acknowledged. People then have to repeat themselves in an effort to make others listen to them. This often happens at a time of life when we lack confidence and self-assurance, during a bout of depression, for example.
- On the more general level of society at large something comparable can be observed: the opinions of the elderly, traditionally regarded by the young as a source of wisdom, are no longer respected and valued. The important discourse today is that of youth discovering life's pleasures and adults who are socially active and influential. **The elderly are confronted with a series of stereotypes:** 'they are losing their memory'; 'they ramble on and repeat themselves'. As what they say has little influence on those around them, it's understandable that they tend to repeat themselves, so exposing themselves once again to the prejudice of which they are the victims. So a vicious circle is set up with a divisive effect on the different generations, separating them even further.

In fact, we are still capable of learning at this stage of life. Not only do the neurons create new connections to compensate for the loss of certain others, but it has recently been proved that new neurons from the cell source in the hippocampus can also appear. But for that to happen, they must be stimulated. **So the key word here is stimulation!** That means being exposed to novelty, variety, and seeking opportunities for new learning situations. We must realise that **the memory will require more concentration and alertness,** that it will be more easily distracted and that it will work less rapidly. But it is still perfectly possible to learn a foreign language, for example, at an advanced age!

Young words

The creation of new words enriches our language and ensures that it remains alive. The language generated by the young is constantly incorporated into our speech and becomes part of our linguistic heritage. This evolution is reflected in the dictionary. Bring your vocabulary up to date by guessing the meaning of the following words or phrases.

Bluejacking

Metrosexual

Identity theft

The triple bottom line

Zorbing

Pharming

Downshifter

Screenager

Green accounting

Blogger

Solution p.342

Say it with flowers...

The increasing variety of flower species has consigned to oblivion the traditional language of flowers. Would you be able to each of these flowers with what it symbolises? It is often easy to guess what is symbolises from the very appearance of the flower.

1. Camellia	Jealousy ....
2. Crocus	Constancy ....
3. Gentian	Trial ....
4. Hydrangea	Love and beauty ....
5. Laurel	Suspicion ....
6. Lily-of-the-valley	Coldness ....
7. Peony	Glory ....
8. Rose	Confusion ....
9. Snowdrop	Happiness ....

Solution p.342

Who sings what ?

In the last 50 years or so a great variety of singers, presenting a great diversity of singing styles, have made their appearance. The first lines of some of these songs will have remained in your memory. Put the right singer or group with the right line and try to remember the song title.

1. ABBA	A. You walked into the party
2. Louis Armstrong	B. You must understand that the touch of your hand
3. Beatles	C. You've painted up your lips
4. The Bee Gees	D. I waited 'til I saw the sun
5. Tony Bennett	E. No more carefree laughter
6. Blondie	F. I see trees of green
7. Marvin Gaye	G. Close your eyes and I'll kiss you
8 Enrique Iglesias	H. When I was small
9. Norah Jones	I. The way you wear your hat
10. Carole King	J. Once I had a love and it was a gas
11. Freddie Mercury	K. Ooh I bet you're wondrin' how I knew
12. Police	L. Would you dance if I asked you to dance?
13. Elvis Presley	M. When you're down and troubled
14. Kenny Rogers	N. Is this the real life, is this just fantasy?
15. Carly Simon	O. I've known a few guys who thought they were smart
16. Barbra Streisand	P. Giant steps are what you take
17. Tina Turner	Q. Well it's one for the money
18. Shania Twain	R. Life is a moment in space

Solution p.342

Memory and life events

Memory doesn't function in a vacuum, it is a system of vital interactions. The key precondition for an active memory is a strong, constant connection with the environment. When a crisis arises, the usual memory stimulants no longer play their part. Adapting to the situation and re-establishing the lost links with life around you then becomes an indispensable prerequisite for restoring good memory function.

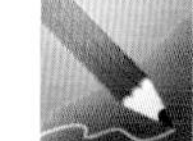

What are your memory triggers?
Your whole physical environment, from household objects to the landmarks surrounding you, can remind you of important moments that stimulated you mentally and generated memories. Pick up your last birthday present, for example. Doesn't it remind you of the person who gave it to you, what you said to each other, what you felt when you received it?

Environment and triggers

Every intensely experienced moment of my life stimulates my memory and helps construct my personality.

In the course of your life you are confronted with different environments. Each of these – family, professional circle, daily contacts, your circle of friends, and further afield, your socio-cultural milieu – provides the framework for important events and significant meetings, **crucial moments in your relation with the world** that represent so many stimulators indispensable for memory function. They are in a sense the food with which your memories are nourished, much as glucose and oxygen are necessary to feed the brain. These **external triggers** are an integral part of your personality. They have played a part in making you what you are. In addition, you have so-called **inner or subjective triggers** – curiosity, interest, desire, will, as well as projects and plans, everything that motivates you to learn, experiment, or act – that stimulate your memory to get to work.

External triggers start working in your early childhood. Talking, toilet training, washing yourself unaided, eating correctly and learning good table manners – all these learning processes were introduced and reinforced by your parents and teachers to enable you as a child to adapt to life in society.

School is the next powerful source of memory triggers. Your emotional environment is suddenly expanded, with a large new circle of acquaintances, and many new things to learn that are essential for the development of your personality. These include rules regulating the relations between children, which will subsequently influence their relations with others; handling those first emotional attachments, or even first love relationships; accepting the authority of the teachers, which will often serve later as a model of the relations between you as an adult and other authority figures; adjusting to the rules and constraints imposed by being a member of a community; and finally the scholastic learning situation itself, with the whole paraphernalia and stress of evaluation and competition, which will influence your future behaviour in your professional career.

My first photos

- What kind of baby was I?
- What happened at mealtime with my parents?
  – What tricks did they use to make me eat (one spoon for Mommy, etc)?
  – What rules did they enforce most frequently (don't play with your food, take your elbows off the table ...)?
  At mealtimes, a child has to face the expectations of his or her parents and this can lead to drama. For some, it becomes a trial of strength. Whatever the situation, this time of conviviality brings family relations into play and remains engraved on the memory.
- What happened at bedtime?
  – Who took me to bed?
  – What nursery rhymes, poems or stories were read to me at this time?
  – Was I afraid of a bogeyman, a ghost, or any other fantastic creation?

The family situation (both the home you come from and the one you will start yourself later) serves as a particularly important trigger. Everything that concerns family relations triggers an even more vivid process of remembering because its emotional impact is already in place. This explains, moreover, why certain unhappy events that are hushed up by families cause virtual memory blackouts. These gaps in the continuum of family history can later rouse one of the family members into undertaking an avid search for information, or it can be expressed in the form of psychosomatic symptoms.

Finally, the **workplace** can be a great source of triggers. Here your memory uses its 'fund of knowledge' while

My primary school photos

- What were the names of my teachers?
  - Do I have pleasant memories of them?
  - What did they teach me?
- What were the names of the children who were top of the class?
- What subject was I best at? And which one did I struggle most with?
- What was my favourite game at playtime?
  - What were the rules?
  - How many players were there?
  - Who usually won?

My family photos

- Where did I get married?
  - Where was the building?
  - What was the name of the officiator?
  - Who were my witnesses?
- Where was the reception held? What do I remember about that day?
- Who was the first person I told about it?
- What were the first words of my children?
  - When and where did they pronounce them?
  - Who did I tell first?
- When did I change my hairstyle?
  - How many times have I changed it
  - With which stages of my life are the different hairstyles associated?

My important documents

- Who gave me my first payslip?
  - What did my work entail?
  - Who were my colleagues?
  - What kind of relations did I have with them?
- From what organisation did I receive my other payslips? What memories do they evoke?
- With whom did I sign my first lease agreement? And my first agreement to buy?

bringing it up to date through acquiring yet more knowledge – of new people, new techniques and new work processes. In this unstable world, resistance to change is common. People don't abandon their established habits and skills without a certain reluctance, which is increased tenfold by fear of the unknown. (This attitude arises from the same mental indolence that makes us take the same routes or use the same products.) Forgetting what we have learned, in a sense, while making an effort to learn anew by facing the challenge of novelty, demands a great deal of energy. This can be an unsettling experience, particularly for those who are wedded to routine, and can cause problems, especially where memory is concerned.

Famous monuments

In 10 minutes, link each monument to one of these cities *Solution p.342*

1. Agra	**a. Westminster Abbey**
2. Barcelona	**b. The Hermitage Palace**
3. Beijing	**c. The Brandenburg Gate**
4. Berlin	**d. The Sagrada Familia**
5. Copenhagen	**e. Sigismond's column**
6. Florence	**f. Hagia Sophia**
7. Istanbul	**g. La Sainte-Chapelle**
8. Lhasa	**h. The Little Mermaid**
9. London	**i. Independence Hall**
10. Paris	**j. The Taj Mahal**
11. Philadelphia	**k. The Summer Palace**
12. Saint-Petersburg	**l. The Duomo**
13. San Francisco	**m. Golden Gate Bridge**
14. Venice	**n. The Potala**
15. Warsaw	**o. The Rialto Bridge**

The presence of a famous monument, especially one that is visually impressive and of great historical interest, often makes you remember the city as a whole. In the same way, at different times in your life, something that is striking or highly unusual makes you remember both it and its surroundings.

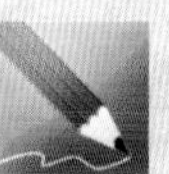

Top Hits

Do you recognise these songs from the 70s, 80s and 90s? Put each song title with the name of the right singer or singers.

1. ....
2. ....
3. ....
4. ....
5. ....
6. ....
7. ....
8. ....
9. ....
10. ....
11. ....
12. ....

1. Nothing compares to you	**a. ABBA**
2. YMCA	**b. Kim Carnes**
3. Beat it	**c. Cher**
4. The way we were	**d. Celine Dion**
5. I will always love you	**e. Whitney Houston**
6. Me and Bobby McGee	**f. Michael Jackson**
7. Bette Davis Eyes	**g. Janis Joplin**
8. Because you loved me	**h. Madonna**
9. Careless whisper	**i. Sinead O'Connor**
10. Dancing queen	**j. Barbra Streisand**
11. Believe	**k. Village People**
12. Like a virgin	**l. Wham!**

You will remember these songs only if there is the right combination of lyrics you can identify with, a catchy tune and a talented presenter. So liking a song is not enough to make you remember it; it also has to find a special resonance in you. There must be some correspondence between the words and an event or experience in your own life at the time, between a state of mind and a mood captured in the music, which aroused a particular emotion in you. Each time you hear the song, these associations will resurface.

After completing this game, think of all the songs that have marked stages along the path of your life, those associated with a specific place or time, or special people …

Solution p.342

When the memory triggers don't function

When I have to face difficult changes in my life, my memory can be affected.

At each stage of life, drastic changes can take place, upsetting the routine of your life and forcing you to move in new directions. You then have to undergo a major psychological readjustment to re-establish your sense of stability. Whether it be a new job, moving house, the birth of a child, a divorce, or loss of someone close to you, all these changes involve adapting to new circumstances.

The other deprivations you have to accept as you grow older – the loss of professional involvement, the departure of children, the death of parents or of a spouse, deterioration in health – sometimes lead to crises in which you have to review your situation and your relation to others, and this can affect your memory. **It is not growing older as such that affects the memory – it is the disruption of your well-established sense of stability.** When your environment changes and you lose your points of reference, your relation with the world around you is impoverished and there is nothing to serve as a memory trigger. Your internal memory triggers are also disrupted by the crisis: exhaustion or even depression bring loss of interest, of curiosity, and of plans for the future. You become distracted and unfocused, and so your memory is underutilised and unstimulated.

My memory and...
TV programmes

Are you one of those people who can never remember a film or TV programme a week after seeing it? It's probably because you allow yourself to be seduced by the sheer variety of programmes and watch TV too much. Many adults devote on average four hours a day to this activity, that is, half their leisure time. The memory of a specific programme is thus swamped in a flood of information. Your memory spontaneously selects what seems most significant, ignoring the rest. Watching TV less frequently is probably the answer if you want to remember a certain programme for a long time.

Taking retirement is a good illustration of this process. When the world of work is the only source of sustenance fed into your memory, to the exclusion of other centres of interest or activities, this change of lifestyle can result in a feeling of being at a loose end, an inability to concentrate, and memory problems. This is because the memory is no longer sufficiently well supplied or stimulated. The real difficulty then will be not so much your inability to remember as knowing what to retain in order to feed your memory appropriately.

This problem is even more serious for the unemployed. Isolation, the lack of stimulation and plans, together with the deprivation of social recognition and a poor self-image are major factors causing memory problems. In this situation, people could wonder: What is worth remembering? Why? For whom?

Memory and interpersonal relationships

If I really take an interest in other people, I feed my memory

Your memory is in good health when it is fulfilling its function of interacting with the environment, which supplies it with stimulation. Your network of personal relationships is especially important in this regard.

Use this table as a basis for thinking about your own personal network. Who are the people around you? What connection do they have with you? In what context? Take your time, letting ideas flow into your mind. Leave the table and return to it several times.

To help you visualise the possible development of your relationships, use one colour for all the people who are likely to recur under different headings. People you know in a professional context might also feature in the category Friends.

Work

Daily life (neighbours, shopkeepers, etc.)

Friends

Family

Clubs, societies (cultural, sporting, etc.)

Others

You have most probably found that you have a much more extensive relational network than you were aware of. But long-lasting relationships based on deep affinity are not necessarily abundant, and having a great number of acquaintances is not always enough to counteract a feeling of loneliness. This feeling is perfectly normal. You can nevertheless differentiate between feeling lonely and real solitude. **You are never really alone**, unless you live on a desert island. On the other hand, **you are not always able to vitalise relationships** that are still incipient or considered superficial. Are you genuinely curious about other people, do you really try to get to know the person behind the mere appearance presented to the world? In this area, curiosity is not a bad fault! It is curiosity that motivates you to draw nearer to others, and which provides you with memory triggers. We all have an underlying pool of relations that can be developed into really meaningful relationships, a source of personal enrichment and that will also provide something of value to feed into the memory.

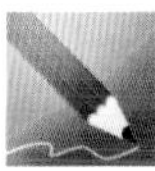

Family home

Work your way down the various storeys of this house to familiarise yourself with the family structure and then answer the questions that follow.

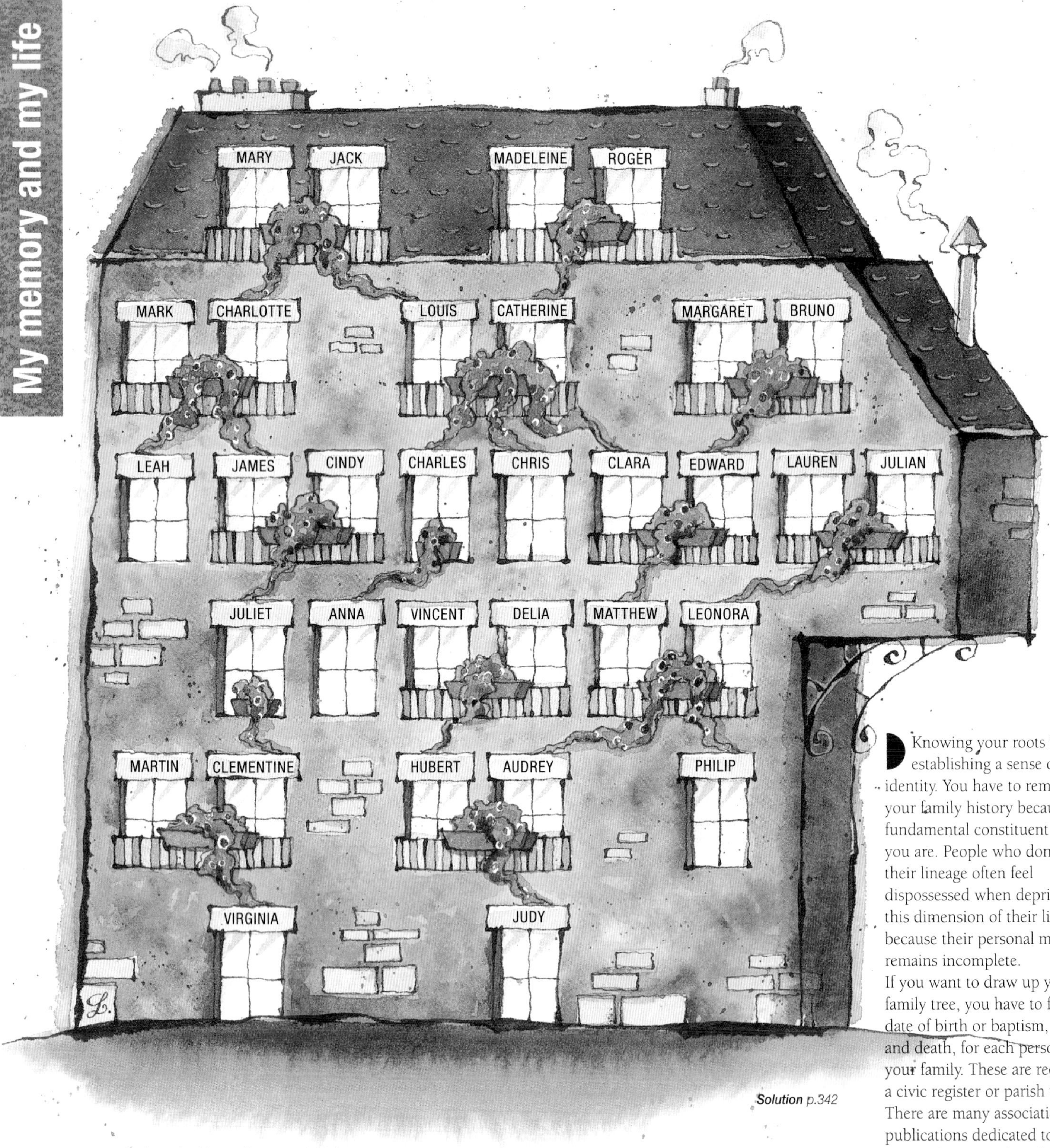

MARY JACK MADELEINE ROGER

MARK CHARLOTTE LOUIS CATHERINE MARGARET BRUNO

LEAH JAMES CINDY CHARLES CHRIS CLARA EDWARD LAUREN JULIAN

JULIET ANNA VINCENT DELIA MATTHEW LEONORA

MARTIN CLEMENTINE HUBERT AUDREY PHILIP

VIRGINIA JUDY

Solution p.342

1. How is Clara related to Judy?...

2. Who has the most descendants?..

3. Which generation produced the most children?.......................

4. All the members of this family have a second name, that of one of their grandfathers or grandmothers. What possible second names could Audrey, Chris and Judy have? ....

5. Who are Louis' great-grandchildren? ....

Knowing your roots is vital in establishing a sense of identity. You have to remember your family history because it is a fundamental constituent of what you are. People who don't know their lineage often feel dispossessed when deprived of this dimension of their lives, because their personal memory remains incomplete.

If you want to draw up your family tree, you have to find the date of birth or baptism, marriage and death, for each person in your family. These are recorded in a civic register or parish register. There are many associations and publications dedicated to helping you in this research. Of course, if your family is composed of many different nationalities your task will be somewhat more complicated!

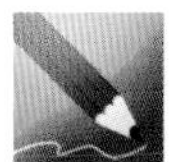

Family words

Are you familiar with the vocabulary of family relationships? Look at each of these words and write down your own definition. If there are several participants, the winner will be the one whose definition is closest to the exact meaning.

First cousin Second cousin Cognate Polyandry Dowry Affinity Consanguinity Mixed marriage

Solution p.342

Agnate Uterine

Expanding your social network

The web of relations you weave around yourself, sometimes unawares, can be expanded and improved in both quality and quantity. Any new activity has the potential to generate communication and interaction, and so lessen the feeling of loneliness. Associations, clubs and societies are interesting from this point of view. They provide ample opportunities for meeting new people and supplying your memory with the external source of stimulation that it needs.

- **Charities and activist associations or NGOs** can also provide opportunities for creating bonds of some depth with people whose aspirations and ideals you share. You must remember, however, that these groups expect dedication from their voluntary members who must above all be prepared to devote their time and energy to a common cause. You would be mistaken in expecting only social interaction and meetings from them.

Sports clubs and cultural societies aim to bring together people who share the same interests. It will be easy to find topics of conversation there and, with the help of a little curiosity to spur you on, to create stronger bonds with people who might well become real friends.

My memory and… retirement

Retirement is not always a happy time for your memory. Adapting to this change in your way of life – and pace of life – is not always easy. Some people lapse into a state of physical and mental inactivity, whereas others, conversely, fling themselves into a strange kind of hyperactivity. Whatever your way of life might be, remember that your memory needs a well-ordered rhythm of life that must be as structured as it was during your active working life. Any form of excess in this area will unsettle your memory.

Your centres of interest

Write your activities down in blue, use red for those you would like to do but haven't yet tried, and green for those you have given up. Ask yourself what you really want – do you really want to be part of a group, for example?

Arts and crafts
Sporting activities
NGOs or activist organisations
Games and recreational activities
Cultural activities

This table will enable you to visualise both your centres of interest and your ability or opportunity to put them into practice. How can you manage to develop your potential in these areas and reduce the presence of red and green? First of all, find in the telephone book (or get from an information office) the address and telephone numbers of clubs or centres where these activities take place locally. The Internet is also a good tool to use for obtaining information quickly. If you want to participate in a sport, for example, you will find there the addresses of most of the sports clubs in your area.

Memory, stress and anxiety

We all lead lives punctuated by crises, and we must constantly adapt to new changes that can cause stress and anxiety or even bouts of depression. Your ability to remember is always affected by such changes. It is therefore vital to learn how to manage stress and how to relax.

Tests How do you handle stress?

This questionnaire is designed to help you determine how you react in stressful situations. In responding to the questions, choose the answer that corresponds most closely to your own position.

1. When you are criticised at work, how do you usually respond?

a. You react coolly. ☐
b. You are angry. ☐
c. You respond calmly to criticism. ☐

2. When you wish to buy a home, how do you go about it?

a. You start setting the process in motion as soon as you have a gap in your timetable. ☐
b. You rush off to view possible homes whenever you can manage to squeeze this into your timetable. ☐
c. You plan to set aside a month for this process – arranging appointments with estate agents, getting all the relevant details, viewing, etc – without overloading your day. ☐

3. You find yourself in a tricky emotional relationship; how do you react?

a. You feel you have reached a deadlock and don't know how to get out of it. ☐
b. You express your feelings without considering the consequences. ☐
c. You take a humorous view of the situation and try to downplay it. ☐

4. In the morning, you prefer to ...

a. Get up very early to ensure you won't be late, and are prepared to arrive early. ☐
b. Wait until the last moment before getting up and having a rushed breakfast. ☐
c. Give yourself enough time to wake up and have a leisurely breakfast. ☐

5. When people around you offer to help you complete a task, how do you take it?

a. You prefer to manage on your own rather than bother others. ☐
b. You think that it will only be done properly if you do it yourself. ☐
c. You accept the help of others, even if different approaches might produce a less than perfect result. ☐

6. In your work you tend to be ...

a. Ultraperfectionist. ☐
b. Dissatisfied. ☐
c. Someone who tries to do their best with the means at their disposal. ☐

7. You are going through a bad patch ...

a. You become withdrawn. ☐
b. You tend to become aggressive towards those around you. ☐
c. You discuss it with people you trust and take note of their reaction. ☐

Count your a's, b's and c's.

Mostly a
You are one of those people who don't like bothering others and prefer to do everything themselves, even at the risk of psychological exhaustion. You strive incessantly to 'do more, do better', without always being aware of it. Perhaps you should try to be a little kinder to yourself, to have confidence in people around you rather than wanting to control everything.

Mostly b
You lead a very hectic life, and when confronted with tricky situations you tend to rush headlong into things. The results are sometimes good but can also be catastrophic. Try to protect yourself by taking time to think. You have plenty of strings to your bow – make the most of that and relax!

Mostly c
You are one of those people who stand back and give themselves time to weigh the pros and cons. You try to have a positive influence on things. You must be a pleasure to have as a colleague.

Good and bad stress

Stressed? A little – no problem.
Terribly – here comes trouble!

The word 'stress' has invaded our vocabulary and has been widely used in the media, in current expressions such as 'the stress of modern life' or 'stress in the workplace'. But what exactly is stress, really?

According to current usage, stress is equated with any pressure or strain experienced as such. In fact, it is the **adaptive reaction of the body to any change.** Changing your job is one kind of stress. Changing your pace of life is another, but so is changing your diet, your environment, etc. Any strong emotion, whether positive or negative, is also a form of stress.

The state of stress is therefore not bad in itself – it is an alarm signal given out by the body trying to adapt to a situation – if you can quickly develop the appropriate responses. This is therefore regarded as good stress. It is something you must take note of, rather like pain that protects you from physical harm. On the physiological level, this alarm signal is manifested in a release of adrenalin and noradrenalin to provide the energy you need for an appropriate response. **Good stress is in fact a stimulant.**

When the situation generating the stress persists or is repeated at regular intervals, your body adapts by releasing cortisone – this is the so-called resistance phase – but it can also be completely overwhelmed and respond by slowing down the general metabolism. During this phase, known as exhaustion, your body becomes vulnerable. This is manifested in a heightened susceptibility to illness and lowering of immunity. **It is this repetition over time that is harmful,** and is what we call bad stress.

A state of stress can be expressed in biological symptoms that are quite incapacitating: inability to sleep well, tachycardia, respiratory problems, stomachache, etc. It can also take the form of behaviour problems, such as irritability, inattentiveness, loss of appetite (or conversely, bulimia), tobacco addiction and nail-biting.

Are you inclined to be a worrier or a depressive?

Certain states of mind or kinds of behaviour reveal a tendency to anxiety or depression that can have an adverse affect on your memory. This questionnaire will help you to identify them. Put a cross in the column corresponding to what you experience or could have experienced recently. Reply as spontaneously as you can.

	YES	SOMETIMES	NO
1. I lack energy.			
2. I am often bored.			
3. I am afraid that something awful will happen.			
4. I feel useless.			
5. I have the impression that my memory is not as good as that of my friends.			
6. I am dissatisfied with the life I am leading at the moment.			
7. I worry about trifles.			
8. I find it difficult to relax.			
9. I don't enjoy going out or meeting people.			
10. I have inexplicable panic attacks.			
11. I am often in a sullen mood.			
12. I haven't much appetite.			
13. I am tormented by what happened in the past.			
14. I struggle to get going in the morning.			
15. I get upset about nothing.			
Total of points obtained:			

Mostly NO
You are not one of those people who can be said to suffer from anxiety or depression. You know how to avoid isolation and to remain dynamic. When you have a problem, you can take the bull by the horns, which is a good safeguard against depression

You answered YES or SOMETIMES to questions 3-7-8-10-15
You are a worrier, anxious either because you are going through a difficult time, or because this is part of your nature. Whatever the reason, you must learn to relax. Anxiety is incapacitating; it can have an adverse effect on the memory and impede the smooth functioning of the process of encoding and retrieving information. Don't hesitate to seek advice.

You answered mostly YES or SOMETIMES to the other questions
You are perhaps going through a period of depression, which could be either organic or psychological in origin. It is important to discuss this with a doctor. He or she can give you medication and refer you to a psychologist who will help you at this difficult time. Don't simply ignore these symptoms. You need assistance, both physically and mentally, to restore your strength and cope with your problems. Don't become withdrawn. Be selective in your choice of obligations and relinquish some of them without feeling guilty. Rather choose activities that you enjoy.

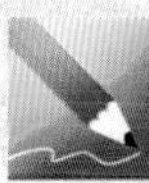

Meet your match!

Take a box of matches, the standard variety or better still, the extra-long ones that are easier to see and to manipulate.

Warming up: Using 12 matches, make the figure below: five squares, one large and four small.

First stage

Set your timer: you have five minutes to make the first two figures.

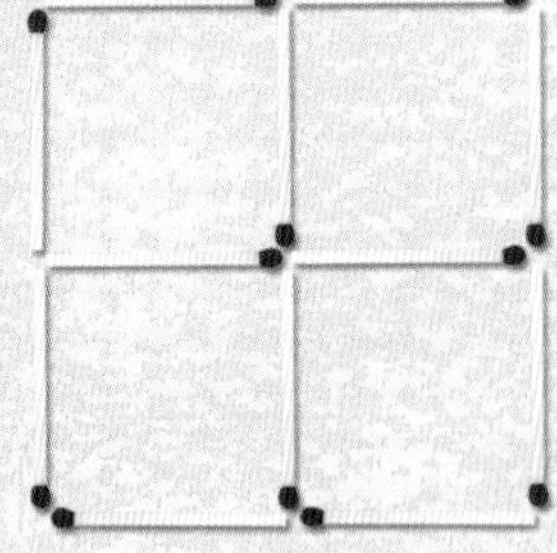

1. Remove two matches so as to form two squares.
2. Move four matches so as to form 10 squares (the matches may overlap).

Second stage

Take as much time as you need now to do the next two figures.

1. Use your 12 matches to construct the basic form opposite. Then move three matches to form three squares.
2. Construct the figure below with 16 matches, then move two matches to form four squares.

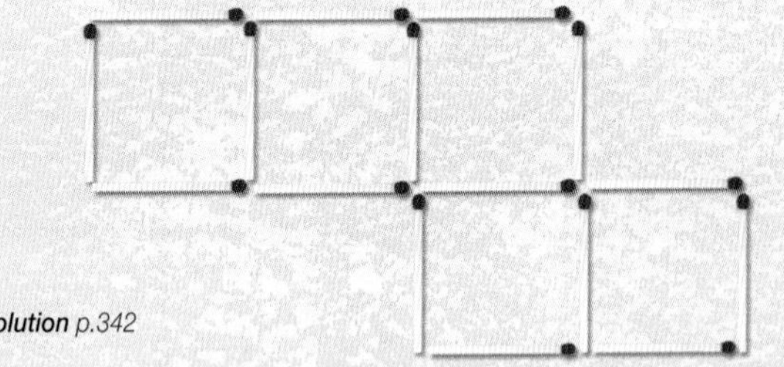

Solution p.342

Any activity involving a time limit, even a game, is a source of stress! The presence of a deadline can interfere with your ability to concentrate, and hence your performance, especially as it can have physiological side-effects – sweating, palpitations, etc – that increase as your attention is disrupted.

To concentrate effectively in such circumstances, don't be distracted by the timer, and don't take it as a personal challenge to succeed. Play for the sake of playing, in a positive spirit, and you will be able to take your time without your stress levels rising too much. Stress will then act as a stimulant without affecting your ability to organise your ideas. This classic puzzle, the game using matches, is a good way to work on your ability to concentrate and think things out. Don't hesitate to start all over again and to keep trying: it's the only method that pays off.

When the memory is disturbed

When I am pressed for time, nervous or anxious, my memory lets me down.

The emotions you generate during a state of stress adversely affect your ability to pay attention and concentrate, which is essential for any memory function. Because you are focused on whatever is disturbing you, you lose track of the information you want to remember. In 70-80 percent of cases, forgetting is due to problems with perception or attentiveness. But if the effects of stress are in evidence during the memorisation process, they are just as much of an inhibiting factor in the process of retrieval: **emotions are disruptive, and nervous tension can cause a memory block.** Who has never experienced stage fright during a public appearance? Actors know only too well that experience of having their mind go blank before a stage appearance. The fear of forgetting can create enough stress to completely paralyse all the memory circuits – but only momentarily. You only have to start up, to get the machine going again by beginning to talk, for the stage fright to disappear and your memory system to start functioning normally again.

Anxiety, which is concomitant with stress, **also disrupts the memory circuits.** We fail to live in the present because the brain functions by anticipation, seeing the future in a grimly negative light – 'and if that happens, what will I do?' Thinking about the future in that way dissociates you from your immediate environment and prevents you from absorbing new information.

More generally, **any lowering of morale has an effect on the memory.** Simply put, this is because any depressive episode entails first and foremost a drop in vital energy, and remembering – paying attention, concentrating, making associations and creating mental images, then consolidating information, repeating it, etc – requires plenty of energy. Hence the problems we have with attentiveness, concentration, and so memorisation. That is why we should not take these moments lightly. We should dismiss with contempt comments such as 'pull yourself together' and other morsels of moralising advice of that nature, and should not hesitate to seek help so as to recover the energy necessary for coping. Effective treatment is now available, based on psychological support and/or antidepressants.

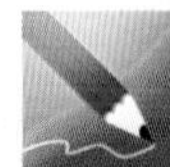

The dictionary

In eight minutes, find five words beginning with CY, SY, GEN, EQUI and HAR. *Solution p.343*

CY..................	SY..................	GEN................
CY..................	SY..................	GEN................
CY..................	SY..................	GEN................
CY..................	SY..................	GEN................
CY..................	SY..................	GEN................

Handling stress

- **Pinpoint the sources of stress in your life** and ask yourself which ones can be avoided.
- **Learn to protect yourself** (don't try to do everything yourself, let others help you).
- **Distance yourself,** don't react without due consideration, and avoid acting emotively. Whatever the task to be done, it is the way you approach things that does or does not engender a state of stress.
- **Don't keep your worries to yourself;** confide in someone you trust and who you know is kind and has a positive outlook.
- **Learn to look after yourself,** to do what you enjoy, to treat yourself to times of relaxation (beauty treatments, excursions, etc) .
- **Participate in activities that release stress, give you pleasure and revitalise you:** those involving physical movement (dance, tai-chi, hiking and sport are highly recommended).
- **Learn to unwind,** because this will rest your body as much as your spirit (try yoga, relaxation, taking siestas, going on quiet walks, etc).

Mind games have a calming effect if they include physical relaxation and make you lose track of time, while games based on manual activity can reduce stress. But note that video games can often be more stressful than relaxing! As for group games, they must produce a sense of wellbeing and promote laughter and shared amusement, without being demanding, imposing time constraints, or encouraging competitiveness. When such games involve physical activity, it is preferable for the participants to know each other well to avoid embarrassment.

My memory and... faces

Could you describe the face of one of your neighbours or friends so accurately that an identikit could be drawn up from your description? It's not so easy, as we don't readily pay close attention to physical characteristics. But we can work on the study of physiognomy and improve our ability to remember faces. Practise on your friends. Turn your back and describe in detail the faces of each in turn – the colour of their eyes, hair, skin, the shape of the nose, mouth, size of forehead, bodily proportions, etc. This will encourage you to pay more attention in future to the faces of people you meet regularly!

EQUI................. HAR.................
EQUI................. HAR.................
EQUI................. HAR.................
EQUI................. HAR.................
EQUI................. HAR.................

Time constraints and the resulting stress probably prevented you from rapidly finding the required number of words.

Put pen to paper

In these two dialogues, only one person is talking. Give the second person a voice to create two convincing scenes or exchanges.

1. Domestic dispute

Jean: Why did you pick those roses from the garden?

Julian:..

Jean: But, you silly fool, it's not today!

Julian: ....

Jean: The day you remember anything will be the day hens grow teeth!

Julian: ....

Jean: But I'm not exaggerating! If you bought a diary, you wouldn't forget things so often!

Julian: ....

Jean: Why should it always be up to me to buy you things? What a skinflint! You call yourself a husband!

2. Remembering ...

Julian Do you know what day it is today?

Jean: ....

Julian: Yes, I know, but what else?

Jean: ....

Julian: But have you already forgotten? What does this day mean to you?

Jean: ....

Julian: I'm very disappointed.

Jean: ....

Julian: So I'm the only one who remembers?

Jean: ....

Julian: Oh well, after all you've said to me, I think that you should also be worried.

Writing can be an outlet for emotions and can relieve tension, particularly when you can project yourself into a character. Many writers get rid of the stress and anxiety of their lives in this way.

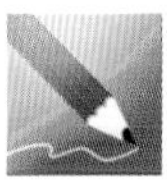

On a high note

Link the name of each composer with the title of his work.

1. Mozart	a. Parsifal	1. ....
2. Verdi	b. Carmen	2. ....
3. Rossini	c. The Marriage of Figaro	3. ....
4. Bizet	d. Tosca	4. ....
5. Puccini	e. Aïda	5. ....
6. Wagner	f. The Barber of Seville	6. ....
7. Offenbach	g. Orpheus in the Underworld	7. ....
8. Berlioz	h. Fidelio	8. ....
9. Beethoven	i. Don Quixote	9. ....
10. Massenet	j. The Damnation of Faust	10. ....

Solution p.343

The benefit of listening to music for relaxation and its calming effects is well recognised. Classical music, the blues, jazz, etc all help us to relax and go to sleep more easily. Get used to turning the volume down, though, to avoid subjecting your eardrums to too much pressure and overstimulating the neurons in this area. Listen repeatedly to tunes or songs that are beneficial in having a soothing effect on you; in this way you can create a kind of musical conditioning that is really effective in getting you to relax.

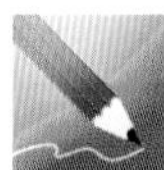

Words and states of mind

In this quaint little story key words making up four expressions that describe states of mind are embedded. Can you find them?

Leo, a fish who kept his socks on,
Went out in a storm for some action.
The waves kicked and curled,
Threw him home in a whirl
Where he landed with some satisfaction.

Solution p.343

It is sometimes awkward to discuss your fears or anxieties with others. And you rarely hear anything but 'Fine, thank you', in response to the traditional greeting of 'How are you?' Sometimes, using expressions and proverbs - which most languages have in abundance – can enable you to reveal your inner feelings without exposing yourself too much.

Tranquillising plants

Unscramble these words to find the names of seven plants used to combat stress.

1. ....
2. ....
3. ....
4. ....
5. ....
6. ....
7. ....

We often ignore the real properties of plants. Herbalists and homeopaths are trying to make their healing properties better known, and their success can also be ascribed to the fact that allopathic medicines traditionally prescribed for stress and anxiety are not without side-effects. Although the beneficial effects of plant remedies no longer have to be proven, we must nevertheless realise that they are not always a panacea.

Solution p.343

My memory and... my medication

Human beings have always used substances for stimulation or, conversely, for relaxation. Each period in history has had its 'drug'; no society has been drug-free. Although a reasonable intake of alcohol, tobacco, coffee, etc has no effect on the memory, problems can result from excessive indulgence over a long period. People who over-indulge are at risk of developing not only memory problems, but also neurological disorders.

The benefits of relaxation

Relaxation is a technique based on autosuggestion in which you direct your attention on to your bodily sensations. Focusing in this particular way, which calms and controls the constant flow of mental images and dispels negative thoughts, induces a state of relaxation. Moreover, practising relaxation regularly serves to train the mind to keep focusing on the present moment. In daily life, this approach promotes a calm state of mind, concentration and receptiveness, which are all essential factors in good memory function.

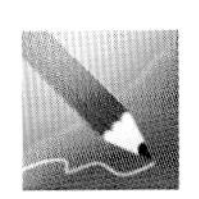

Sit and relax

1. Sit in a comfortable chair, wearing loose clothing. Place your legs slightly apart, feet – bare or in slippers – flat on the floor, pelvis slightly forward, back straight leaning against the back of the chair, head in line with the top of the spine. Rest your hands on your thighs, palms turned upwards.

2. Take your time looking around you, then close your eyes.

3. With your eyes closed, visualise the décor, and listen to the noises around you, if there are any, to include them in this moment of relaxation.

4. Pay attention to your bodily sensations. Are there any feelings of tension? Try to localise them. Then listen to the rhythm of your breathing: is it rapid, or calm and measured?

5. Next, focus your attention on the places where your body is supported by the chair – your thighs, buttocks, back – and on the ground. Let your body go, resting more heavily on these areas of support as though it needed to spread itself out to take up more space on the chair. Relax all your muscles in turn by focusing successively on the following zones: forehead, eyes, cheeks, lower jaw, scalp, neck, shoulders, arms, hands, and all the fingers. Let this relaxed feeling flow like a stream and seep into your back, torso, stomach, entire pelvic area, buttocks, and right down to your feet. Take time to experience and welcome the new sensations that appear.

6. Now switch your attention to your respiration and start breathing more slowly and deeply. With each breath, draw the air in deeply and imagine it going right down to the lower abdomen, then breathe out as though you are emptying the air out from this zone. Breathe like this six or seven times, then revert to normal breathing. Take time to experience and welcome the new sensations you feel.

7. In this relaxed state, let an image reflecting calmness and serenity come to mind. Visualise the details of this image – colours, play of light, sounds, etc. Take your time enjoying this image and the sensations accompanying it.

8. When you choose to, let this image fade slowly away, then turn your attention once more to your bodily sensations. Visualise parts of the décor around you. Start breathing more quickly, then slowly start to move your extremities, your feet, hands, head and lastly your other muscles. Stretch as though you were waking up. Finally, open your eyes.

My memory and... laughter

Laughter is the best medicine for ensuring a sense of wellbeing – this is the claim made by practitioners of laughter therapy, who also maintain that the memory functions better after a good laughing session. Laughing is certainly a good way to release tension and regulate breathing, and promotes physical and psychological relaxation. It also provides a welcome diversion from mental and physical pain and can achieve a long-lasting calming effect. The memory certainly benefits from all these positive spin-offs.

Breathing to oxygenate the brain

- Relax, following the instructions given above for relaxation in a sitting position.
- When you have reached the stage of breathing more deeply and slowly (6), imagine, with each breath, that fresh air is entering through the right nostril, going through the right cerebral hemisphere, warming up as it passes through the left hemisphere, then going out again, warmer, through the left nostril.

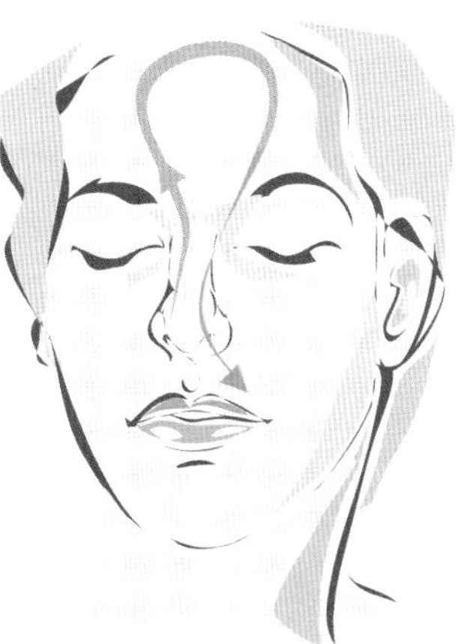

- Breathe in this way three or four times, then reverse the process: fresh air enters the left nostril, goes through the left cerebral hemisphere, warms up as it passes through the right hemisphere, and exits, much warmer, through the right nostril. Breathe in this way three or four times,then revert to normal breathing.
- Take your time experiencing and welcoming the new sensations that arise, particularly in your head.

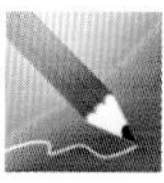

Foot massage: doing it for yourself

First bathe your feet, in cold water if you have circulatory problems.

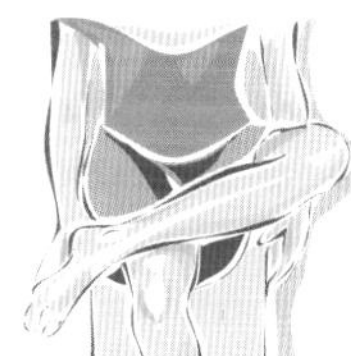

1. Rest one foot on the opposite knee so that you can manipulate it easily; find a comfortable position that does not strain your back, nicely settled in an armchair, for example. Keep a bottle of oil for massaging ready.

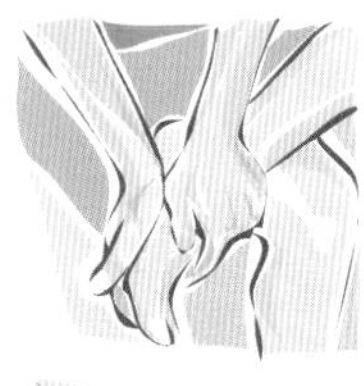

2. Carry out energetic massaging movements over your whole foot. Both hands must cover your foot at the same time. Use the whole surface of your palms, using continuous movements, without stopping.

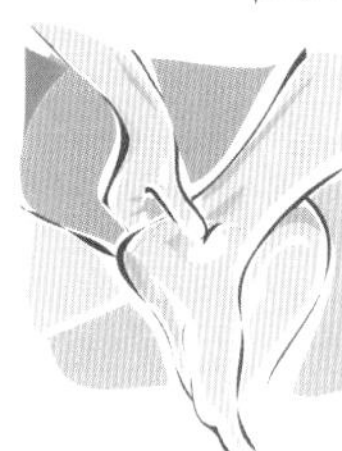

3. Take your Achilles tendon in your opposite hand, with your thumb on one side of your tendon, and the other fingers on the other side, and make circular movements over the area between the heel and the ankle bone, then do up and down movements, as though trying to lengthen or stretch the Achilles tendon.

4. Repeat the massage over the whole foot (2). Move the opposite hand for a moment, to massage the arch of your foot with the base of the palm, with circular movements, without removing your other hand

5. Massage the top of the arch of your foot with both hands, then, with the base of your palm, massage the pads of your foot, toe joints and then the toes themselves.

6. Slide your hands over each side of your foot, with your toes between your palms, then do the same thing between each toe.

7. Massage each toe with 'cork-pulling' movements, up and down. Then repeat massaging the whole foot. Next, insert your fingers between each toe.

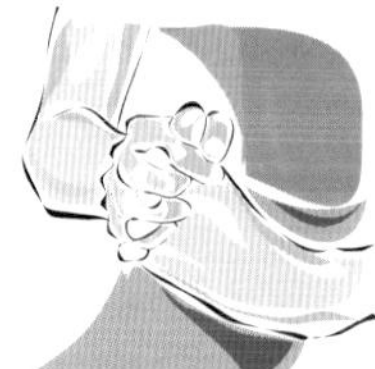

8. Keeping your fingers between the toes, do circular movements to make your ankle joint suppler.

9. Finish off by massaging the whole foot, then, holding the foot in one hand, massage the whole arch of the foot from heel to toe with your other hand, while increasing the pressure on the toes and bending them up slightly towards your leg. Repeat this procedure with your other foot.

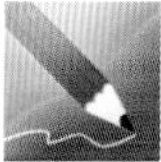

Facial massage: doing it for someone else

The person to be massaged must lie down, with her head supported on a cushion. Sit behind her head, in a position that suits your back. Touch her forehead lightly with the back of your hand.

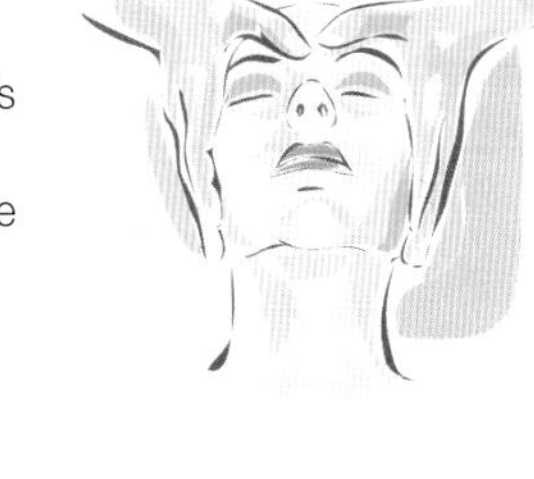

1. When she is ready, place your two thumbs in the space between her eyebrows, with your other fingers covering her forehead and temples. This is the basic starting position for this massage, with your hands enclosing the face. Apply the right pressure, which must be firm but soft, and keep it there for a few seconds.

2. Slide your thumbs and fingers towards her temples, going down as far as her ears; massage them vigorously by rolling them between your fingers. Here again, the movements must be continuous, with no stopping. Do this several times, starting from the initial position.

3. Still starting from the same position, slide your thumbs over the bridge of her nose, with your other fingers sliding along the cheeks. Your thumbs must follow the outline of her nose above her top lip. With your hands over the jaws, massage the base of the cheeks with a kind of soft kneading motion. Do this several times.

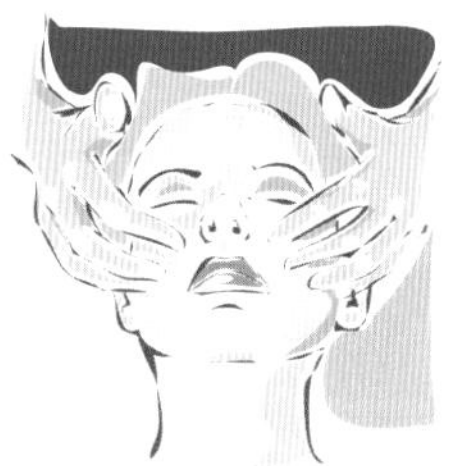

4. Using your fingertips, pat the whole surface of the cheeks very lightly, then return to the initial position.

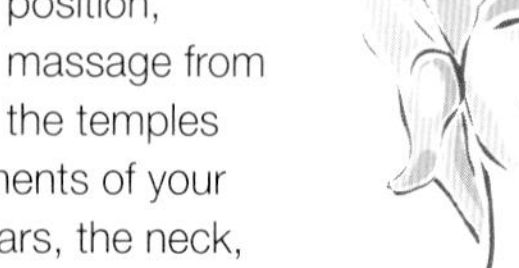

5. From the starting position, massage from the temples down with circular movements of your fingers, then behind the ears, the neck, and finally the top of the shoulders.

6. Stimulate the whole scalp by applying a kind of light scratching with the fingertips. Return to the starting position.

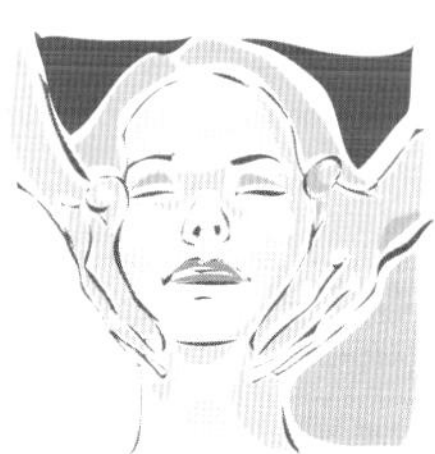

7. Put your hands around her jaw, move your hands apart while pressing softly to relax the jaws and go back over the sides of her face to the forehead. Go back through the starting position several times but then go right up to the hairline to indicate that the massage is over.

Collective memory

The memory of each individual forms part of a collective memory, which serves as a kind of memory matrix. It is a reservoir of knowledge and shared experiences, making it possible for people who don't know each other to recognise a common meeting point. It creates bonds between groups, communities and nations.

Constructing individual identity within and through a group

I exist partly through recognising myself in others.

You probably remember the day the twin towers of the World Trade Center were destroyed in 2001, and the day of the football World Cup final played between France and Brazil in 1998. These events aroused such intense emotion that many people remember exactly what they were doing at the time. This is the way in which tragic or exciting events of our time, which create opportunities for shared experience, contribute to the construction of our common past and our collective memory.

When you have the impression of sharing common ideas and similar experiences with someone, of being familiar with the same smells and tastes, when you recognise your own accent in someone else's speech, you know that you belong in some way to the same family. Culture is the word generally used to express this similarity with others. **Culture is essentially a collective memory.** It is because you have learned the same things at school, spoken with the same accent, been fed on the same food that you and others of the same culture have such a similar stock of memories.This is your common heritage. Individual identities are defined in the context of this larger pool of collective memory.

Group memory, community memory and on a larger scale, national memory, is not something acquired from books. **It is imparted automatically, by your body language, your behaviour and what is left unsaid.** Someone from a Latin country, for instance, will feel comfortable with people who express their feelings, who use their hands for gesticulating and touching each other in social interaction. This mode of communication could upset people who come from regions where they are traditionally more reserved in their interpersonal relationships.

Whereas in the past this form of memory was part of our oral memory, it is now also widely transmitted by the media, such as television. We often reflect it unawares – in the way we dress and speak, for instance. So, while you construct your own identity thanks to your collective memory, you simultaneously contribute to its development from day to day. This stems from a fundamental human need – that of belonging. It is almost as if, to know ourselves, we need to recognise ourselves in others. Collective memory thus enables you to feel less alone when you are confronting certain life events.

Popular names

Classify these 40 names (20 per sex) in terms of their popularity in specific decades: the five girls' names and boys' names found most frequently in the 1930s, in the 1950s, in the 1970s and in the new century.

Solution p.343

Boys: Brian, Charles, Christopher, Daniel, David, Donald, Gary, Harry, Jack, James, Jeffrey, Joseph, Joshua, Lewis, Mark, Michael, Richard, Robert, Thomas, William

Girls: Angela, Barbara, Betty, Charlotte, Chloe, Dorothy, Emily, Helen, Jennifer, Kimberly, Lauren, Linda, Lisa, Maria, Mary, Megan, Michelle, Patricia, Sandra, Susan

B	1930s	G
....		....
....		....
....		....
....		....
....		....

B	1950s	G
....		....
....		....
....		....
....		....
....		....

B	1970s	G
....		....
....		....
....		....
....		....
....		....

B	2000s	G
....		....
....		....
....		....
....		....
....		....

First names are always to some degree symbolic, and are also an expression of collective memory. Choosing a name is often difficult. You may want the name to be in accord with certain social conventions, or trendy, or to be a reminder of someone you like, or to be a family name, or to be a name drawn from a holy book. In short, the name you choose will always reflect something of the background of the person who bears it.

Religions of the world

Rank the following 10 great religions according to the number of their adherents (in decreasing order).

a. **Animism**
b. **Baha'i**
c. **Buddhism**
d. **Christianity**
e. **Confucianism**
f. **Hinduism**
g. **Islam**
h. **Judaism**
i. **Shintoism**
j. **Sikhism**

Solution p.343

1.	**6.** ....
2.	**7.** ....
3.	**8.** ....
4.	**9.** ....
5.	**10.** ....

There are more believers in the world than agnostics and atheists. Religions form part of the collective memory: when a certain faith is founded, it develops and spreads thanks to being preserved in the memory of a great number of people.

Using your collective memory

My memory and... commercials

Advertisers know only too well that to sell their products they need to hold the consumer's interest from the beginning to the end of a commercial. But why do we remember one commercial rather than another? Some elements in combination often ensure the success of a product: eye-catching images, rhythmic music, a short simple story – in a few sentences – repeated broadcasting and, finally, encouraging the consumer to identify with the product in some way. If you remember an advert, it's because it played on a perceived need for the product and you identified yourself with that need.

There are so many activities and interactions – including games – that rely on general knowledge or shared experience. This accumulation of knowledge and experience structures our identity as it is largely made up of our personal culture. But it is also remarkable how it draws us closer to others: using your collective memory involves communicating with other people on the same subject, reminiscing about acquaintances or common experiences, or simply doing things together. Here are some activities designed for this purpose:

- general knowledge games (like Trivial Pursuit) that make demands on our memory and are also entertaining;
- membership of cultural associations or conservation bodies dedicated to preserving our cultural heritage;
- collecting antiques;
- cultural visits or trips – there's nothing like them for sharing our knowledge with others and expanding it further;
- meetings with old people to share their knowledge of our common past, making theirs our own, and to understand their view of the present;
- regular meetings with other people to discuss current affairs; this will help us remember these events for much longer.

Remember your lines

Find the titles of the films that these lines come from.

'Frankly, my dear, I don't give a damn!' ....

'Go ahead, make my day' ....

'Of all the gin joints in all the towns in all the world, she walks into mine' ....

'Show me the money' ....

'Phone home' ....

'I'll make him an offer he can't refuse' ....

'May the force be with you' ....

'I could have made class. I could have been a contender.' ....

'Let's get out of these wet clothes and into a dry Martini' ....

'Nature, Mr Allnutt, is what we are put into this world to rise above' ....

Solution p.343

A feature-length film is often famous because of the talent of the director and actors, but this fame can also sometimes be ascribed to the quality of the dialogue. Some film fanatics can even recite the dialogues of whole scenes. Their passion for words and an unusual turn of phrase spur them on to achieve these feats of memory.

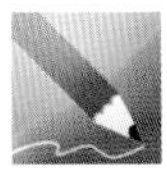

Modern inventions

Can you say when each of these objects became part of our daily lives?

credit card ....

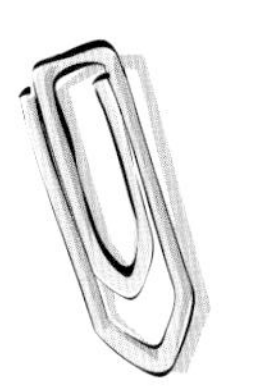

paper clip ....

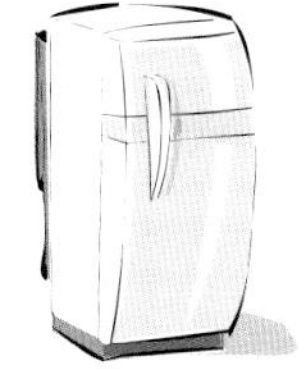

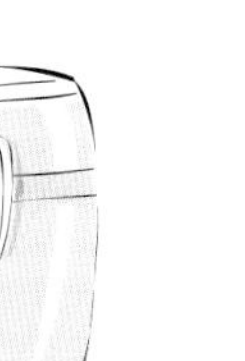

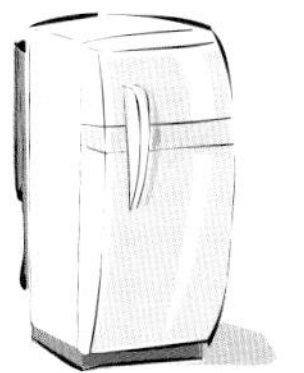

refrigerator ....

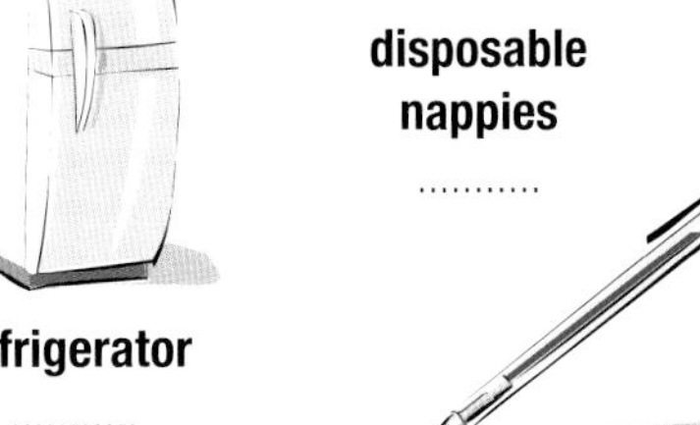

disposable nappies ....

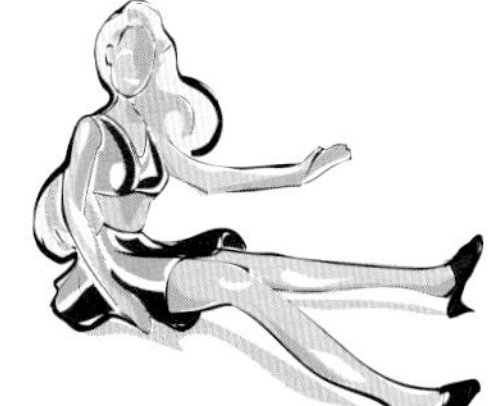

Barbie doll ....

ballpoint pen ....

Scotch tape ....

plastic bottle ....

wireless ....

computer ....

supermarket trolley ....

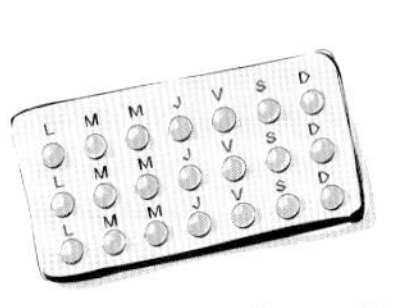

contraceptive pill ....

television ....

vegetable mill ....

mobile phone ....

household gloves ....

Solution p.343

The collective memory is also structured around progress. Improvements in the quality of our everyday lives are often associated with inventions of an apparently minor order. Thanks to photography, we are able to see what amazing technological development has occurred in the last two centuries. All this visual evidence enriches our own collective memory.

To each country its currency

Money is as much collective as individual: collective in that it is shared and used by all, individual in that we each have our own. When you have visited a country, you often remember its currency. Discover your own numismatic talents by identifying the country where each of these currencies is used.

Baht	**Lev**	**Shekel** ....
Dirham	**Rand**	**Sol** ....
Dông	**Real**	**Yuan** ....
Forint	**Rouble**	**Zloty** ....
Guarani	**Rupiah**	

Solution p.343

My memory and...
cooking recipes

Are you incapable of remembering a recipe? Whether it be fusion food or an old recipe passed down from your grandmother, the quantities may be what you have the most difficulty in remembering. This is perfectly normal, because vision is not involved: the mental image of the required quantity doesn't exist. To overcome this problem, take your recipe and read it several times, look at the weight and quantity of the ingredients and try to find a mnemonic strategy that helps.

Answers and lists

Puzzle solutions

Page 16

Brainy words jumbled up

TEDERNID: **dendrite** – GIMENNES: **meninges** – OXOTRENCE: **neocortex** – YSSAPEN: **synapse** – MADALYGA: **amygdala** – SPAPUMOCIPH: **hippocampus** – CALICOTIP: **occipital** – EROUNN: **neuron** – CIMBLI: **limbic** – OBEL: **lobe** – SHERHEPEMI: **hemisphere** – EPTARILA: **parietal.**

Rebus

Our brains need glucose.

Page 17

Famous doctors

S				F				K	O	C	H			J
C				L							I			E
H	A	R	V	E	Y			S	I	M	P	S	O	N
W				M			B				P			N
E				I			A				O			E
I		H	U	N	T	E	R				C			R
T				G			N				R		A	
Z							A				A		S	
E						W	R	I	G	H	T		C	
R							D		A		E		L	
	P								L	I	S	T	E	R
	L								E				P	
L	I	V	I	N	G	S	T	O	N	E			I	
	N												U	
	Y			P	A	R	A	C	E	L	S	U	S	

The name that doesn't appear on the grid is Charcot.

Page 18

Rebus

The right half controls the left half of the body.

Page 19

In the labyrinth of the brain

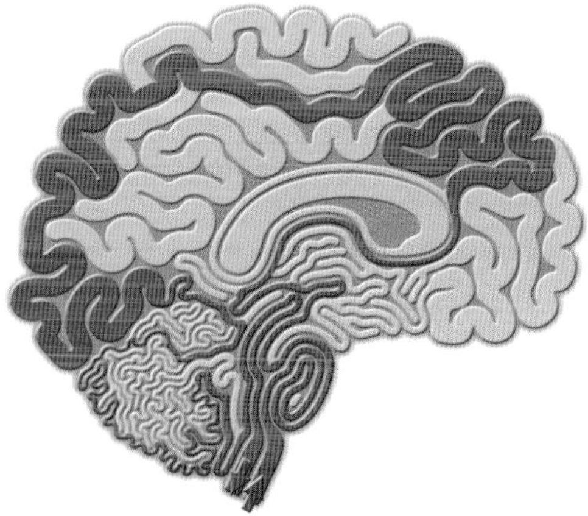

Page 22

Sounds that surround us

1. Birdsong – **2.** A bicycle bell – **3.** A glass breaking – **4.** A coffee grinder – **5.** A cellphone ringing – **6.** A door slamming – **7.** A motorbike accelerating – **8.** The roar of an aircraft.

Spot the 7 differences

Page 23

Touch and sensation

Soft: cashmere, a baby's skin, a rose petal, rice flour, a duvet... – **Textured:** skin of an orange, a clam shell, the skin of an avocado, a rock... – **Rough:** Velcro, a cat's tongue, sandpaper, coir... – **Slimy:** pulp, a snail, dishwashing liquid, oil, a frog... – **Smooth:** glass, satin, lacquered wood, a billiard ball, coated paper...

A world of flavours

Cinnamon: spice cake – **Saffron:** paella – **Basil:** pesto – **Garlic:** aioli – **Nutmeg:** Béchamel sauce – **Cumin:** couscous – **Chilli:** quesadillas – **Coriander:** Thai green curry – **Paprika:** goulash – **Tarragon:** Béarnaise sauce – **Oregano:** pizza.

Page 24

Touché!

Stay in touch – Be out of touch – Get under your skin – Skin-tight – Beauty is only skin deep – To be touched by something/someone – By the skin of your teeth – Jump out of your skin – Risk your skin – Her affection is touching.

Page 27

Poem with holes

The Walrus and the Carpenter

*The **sun** was shining on the sea,*
*Shining with all his **might***
*He did his very best to **make***
*The billows smooth and **bright** –*
*And this was **odd**, because it was*
*The **middle** of the night.*

*The **moon** was shining sulkily,*
Because she thought the sun
*Had got no **business** to be there,*
*After the **day** was done –*
*'It's very **rude** of him,' she said*
*'To come and spoil the **fun**!'*

*The **sea** was wet as wet could be,*
*The **sands** were dry as dry.*
*You could not see a **cloud**, because*
*There was no **cloud** in the sky:*
*No **birds** were flying overhead –*
*There were no **birds** to fly.*

The Walrus and the Carpenter
*Were walking close at **hand***
*They **wept** like anything to see*
*Such quantities of **sand.***
*'If this were only **swept** away,'*
*They said, 'it would be **grand**!'*

*'If seven **maids** with seven mops*
***Swept** it for half a year,*
*Do you suppose,' the Walrus **said**,*
*'That they could get it **clear**?'*
'I doubt it,' said the Carpenter,
*And shed a **bitter** tear.*

A tasty puzzle

Page 29

Monuments in mirror image

Pages 30–31

The weight of words, the impact of pictures

Because I'm worth it (**L'Oreal,** cosmetics) – Vorsprung durch Technik (**Audi** cars) – Put a tiger in your tank (**Esso**) – Kills Bugs Dead (**Raid** insecticide) – Coffee at its best (**Nescafe** instant coffee) – It's the real thing (**Coca-Cola** soft drink) – Sch ... you know who (**Schweppes** soft drinks) – Let your fingers do the walking (**Yellow Pages**) – 57 varieties (**Heinz** baked beans) – They're grrr–eat! (**Kelloggs** Frosties cereal) – All the news that's fit to print (**New York Times** daily newspaper) – Don't leave home without it (**American Express** credit card)

Page 31

We remember them still

1. Bicorn hat: **Napoleon** –
2. Glasses–nose–moustache: **Groucho Marx** –
3. Harley Davidson: **James Dean** – 4. Electric guitar: **Jimi Hendrix** – 5. Cane and hat: **Charlie Chaplin** –
6. Little red book: **Mao Zedong** – 7. Cigar: **Winston Churchill, Fidel Castro** – 8. Bikini briefs: **Madonna** – 9. Black gloves: **Rita Hayworth** *(Gilda)* – 10.Elephant: **Hannibal.**

Page 32

The letter chase

Post: past – **Hallow:** callow – **Fixed:** mixed – **Gullet:** mullet – **Gross:** cross – **Fern:** tern – **Pure:** pare – **Main:** maid – **Circus:** cirrus – **True:** trug – **Grand:** grid – **Lathe:** lithe – **Cruet:** cruel – **Marinate:** marinade – **Turner:** burner – **Vest:** vast – **Suite:** smite – **Latin:** satin – **Ooze:** doze – **Crude:** prude – **Miscount:** discount – **Button:** mutton – **Cream:** dream – **Invert:** invest – **Tickle:** tackle – **Wallet:** ballet – **Dally:** rally – **Indent:** intent – **Port:** sort – **Painting:** fainting – **Hominy:** homily – **Attitude:** aptitude – **Pose:** rose – **Hollow:** follow – **Mouth:** south – **Flower:** blower – **Pest:** vest – **Collusion:** collision – **Forewind:** forewing – **Scarf:** scare – **Mission:** fission – **Provision:** prevision – **Forage:** borage – **Infect:** infest – **Induct:** induce – **Break:** creak – **Friction:** fraction – **Bout:** tout – **Access:** abcess – **Deride:** derive – **Prone:** prune – **Elope:** slope – **Canal:** banal – **Implore:** implode – **Dotage:** dosage – **Cortex:** vortex – **Harp:** carp – **Revere:** revert – **Ramble:** rumble – **Concert:** convert – **Dough:** cough – **Place:** plane – **Quite:** quote – **Revel:** bevel – **Cling:** clang – **Verge:** merge

Page 33

Mock exam

Name
Alexandra
Alfred
Amelia
Anthony
Anne
Emily
Ellen
Elaine
Estelle
Eric
Margaret
Mary
Marion
Miriam
Mathilda
Patricia
Penelope
Patrick
Pablo
Paul

Plant
Aster
Arum
Apricot
Acacia
Anemone
Edelweiss
Elm
Eucalyptus
Echinacea
Erica
Marguerite
Myrtle
Magnolia
Mallow
Marjoram
Petunia
Pine
Protea
Primula
Peach

Animal
Aardvark
Addax
Anteater
Antelope
Alligator
Egret
Eagle
Emu
Elephant
Echidna
Macaque
Meerkat
Marmot
Mandrill
Mongoose
Porcupine
Petrel
Platypus
Polecat
Penguin

Country
Austria
Azerbaijan
Argentina
Australia
Angola
Egypt
El Salvador
Ethiopia
Eritrea
Estonia
Mozambique
Morocco
Mauritania
Mexico
Madagascar
Peru
Philippines
Pakistan
Paraguay
Papua-New Guinea

Town
Addis-Ababa
Athens
Avignon
Alexandria
Ankara
Erfurt
Entebbe
Edinburgh
Eindhoven
Edmonton
Marseille
Madrid
Malmö
Macao
Manchester
Paris
Prague
Pisa
Pamplona
Pittsburgh

Celebrity
Attila
Allende (Salvador)
Archimedes
Amundsen (Roald)
Armstrong (Neil)
Erasmus
Eisenhower (Dwight)
Elizabeth II
Engels (Friedrich)
Einstein (Albert)
Magellan
Macmillan (Harold)
Machiavelli
Mandela (Nelson)
Mao Zedong
Pericles
Peron (Eva)
Patton (George)
Pasteur (Louis)
Polo (Marco)

The four basic operations

1 536 + 541 = 2 077
18 659 + 3 874 = 22 533
59 246 + 66 666 + 8 756 = 134 668
589 – 821 = -232
5 896 – 4 172 = 1 724
698 324 – 8 753 = 689 571
147 x 654 = 96 138
5 891 x 258 = 1 519 878
47 985 x 4 658 = 223 514 130
583 : 52 = 11,211
4 627 : 111 = 41,684
31 772 : 32,5 = 977,6

Stick-on syllables

Cormorant – pelican – guineafowl – budgerigar – gallinule – woodpecker – canary – pipit – francolin – moorhen – peacock – seagull – phalarope – sandpiper – pigeon

Page 39

Know your herbs

1. basil – **2.** coriander – **3.** parsley – **4.** flat-leafed parsley – **5.** mint – **6.** rocket

Misleading numbers

The number 6.

Missing letters

Square no. 4.

Page 40

Hotchpotch

1. 20 triangles – 5 squares – 14 rectangles.
2. 0 – 1 – 3 – 7 – 8.
3. 26 squares.

Answers and lists

Spot the 7 differences

Page 42

The letter E
The letter E occurs 113 times.

Police mystery
The third man is lying. If he had really been there for 20 minutes, his beer would have had very little foam left and so he wouldn't have had any on his lips. The bar owner had just given it to him. So he had actually been in the bar for barely five minutes.

Page 43

Watch those letters!
1. R, A, C, T, T: tract
2. O, B, E, L, W: below, or elbow

Page 49

Searching for small words
37 commas – 36 articles – 30 conjunctions.

Watch those shapes!
20 crossed out – 15 underlined – 12 circled

Page 50

The pull of the black hole

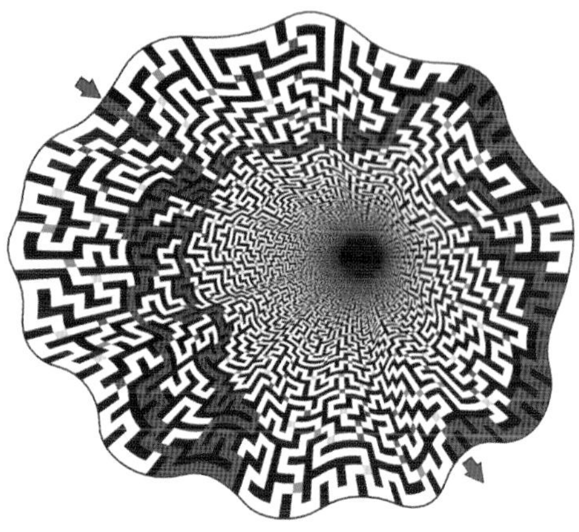

Page 51

Odd one out
The cherries are the only fruit with a single seed.

Dining with friends
Vincent: asparagus – **Laura:** chicken – **Paul:** soufflé – **Sophie:** grilled cheese – **Matthew:** chocolate eclairs – **Charlotte:** sweets.

Page 52

The letter chase

CARE	CAPE	BIND	BIRD
DISH	FISH	ALOUD	CLOUD
SOCKS	ROCKS	PLANT	PLANE
LATER	WATER	GUN	SUN
BENCH	BEACH	MOAN	MOON

Family problems
First generation: **6** – Second generation: **13** – Third genration: **18** – Fourth generation: **36.**

Close-up
Drops of water on a spider's web.

Caterpillar

	CAPABLE
–B + S	PALACES
– A + U	CAPSULE
– P + S	CLAUSES
– L + R	SAUCERS
– C + D	ASSURED
– R + M	ASSUMED
– U + A	AMASSED
– D + G	MASSAGE
– A + E	**MESSAGE**

Page 116

To the tune of rock 'n roll
Beach Boys: *Good Vibrations* – **Beatles:** *Help!* – **Chuck Berry:** *Roll Over Beethoven* – **Bee Gees:** *Massachusetts* – **Louis Prima:** *I'm Just a Gigolo* – **Rolling Stones:** *Satisfaction* – **Fats Domino:** *Blueberry Hill* – **Doors:** *Light My Fire* – **Elvis Presley:** *Love Me Tender* – **Police:** *Roxanne* – **Pink Floyd:** *Another Brick In The Wall* – **Bob Dylan:** *Blowing In The Wind* – **Simon and Garfunkel:** *Mrs Robinson* – **Bill Haley:** *Rock Around The Clock.*

The right definition
A 2 – **B** 3 – **C** 2 – **D** 3 – **E** 2 – **F** 1.

Page 117

Changing words
Regime: emigre – **Space:** capes – **Amend:** named – **Pier:** ripe – **Part:** rapt – **Dire:** ride – **Rage:** gear – **Drain:** nadir – **Cause:** sauce – **Renal:** learn – **Eager:** agree.

Street scene
Market; marketplace; mackerel; macaw; marigold; magenta; mailbox; mail; maize; male; man; mamma; mammal; mane; manners; mannequin; mare; marked down; marlin; marrow; material; mauve; matron …

Page 119

Memory of spaces
1. The medal

2. The ladybird

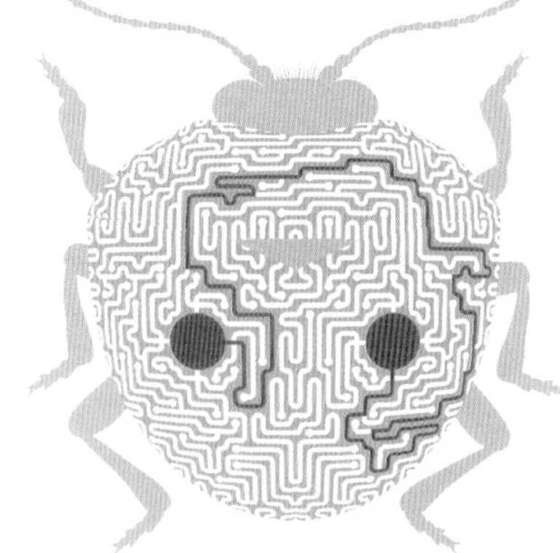

3. The maze

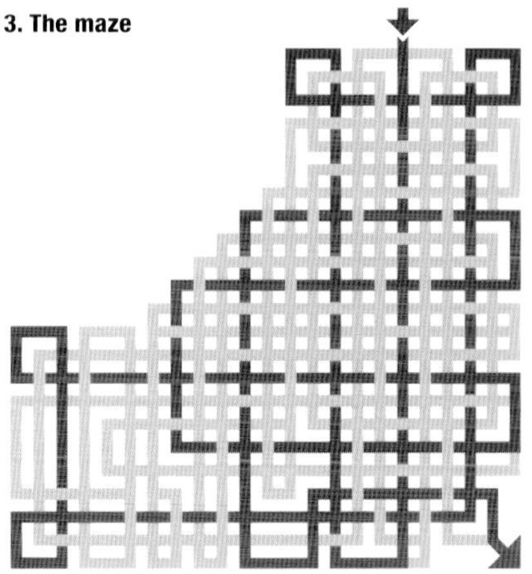

Page 120

One line is enough

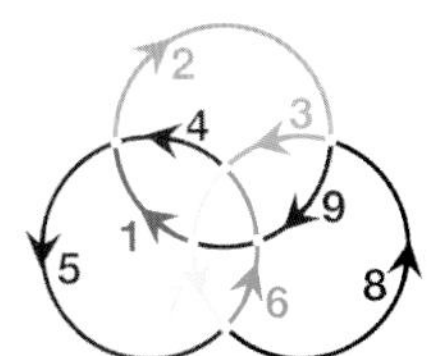

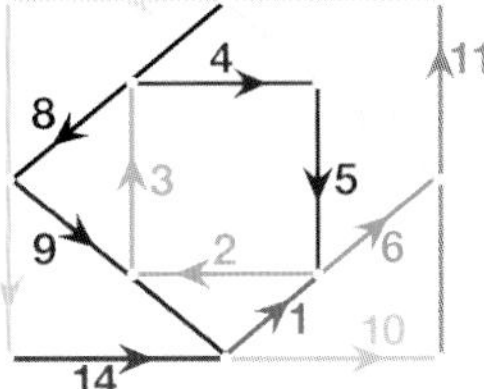

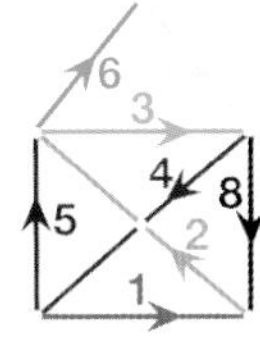

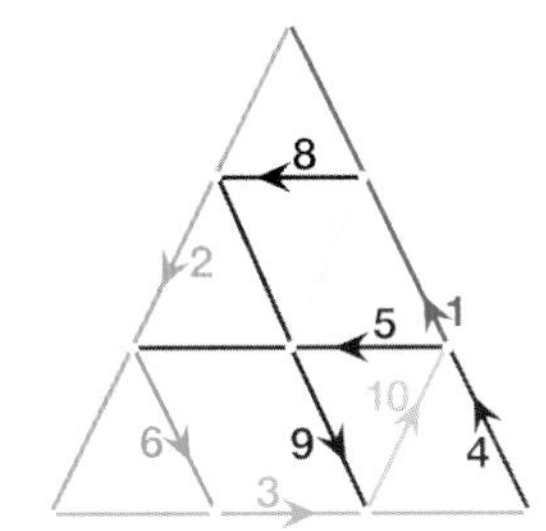

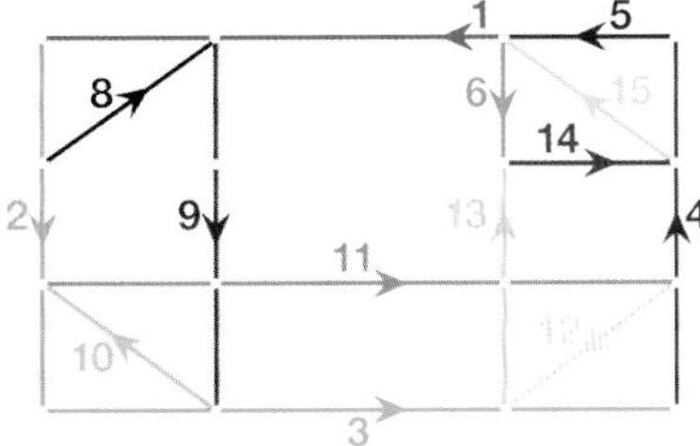

The right reflection

The right reflection is that of silhouette no. 1.

Page 121

The Chinese puzzle

The square

The egg

Pages 122–123

The big quiz

History and geography

1. c) Hannibal – **2. c)** Pompeii – **3. c)** Emily Pankhurst – **4. b)** Anne Frank – **5. d)** Aristotle – **6. c)** The Red Cross – **7. d)** Roosevelt – **8. c)** St Helena – **9. a)** *Enola Gay* – **10. b)** Michel Debré – **11. c)** Istanbul – **12. a)** Upper Volta – **13. d)** In the Czech Republic – **14. b)** Angel Falls – **15. a)** In Mexico.

Art and literature

16. d) Henri Cartier-Bresson – **17. b)** Alfred Hitchcock – **18. c)** Charlie Chaplin – **19. b)** Daniel Radcliffe – **20. c)** J R Tolkien – **21. b)** *Mona Lisa* – **22. b)** Monet – **23. c)** Whistler – **24. b)** Michelangelo – **25. b)** *The philosopher's brothel* – **26. b)** The 'Heroic symphony' – **27. a)** *Dallas* – **28. b)** The Beatles – **29. c)** Jean-Paul Sartre – **30. b)** Patrick White – **31. a)** Hamlet – **32. c)** *The Mysterious Affair of Styles* – **33. a)** George Orwell – **34. b)** Virginia Woolf – **35. a)** Emily Bronte – **36. a)** *In Remembrance of Things Past* – **37. c)** Winston Churchill.

Science and technology

38. a) Nicéphore Niépce – **39. d)** MRI – **40. a)** Archimedes – **41. a)** Nicolas Copernicus – **42. c)** Rudolph Diesel – **43. a)** 1933 – **44. c)** Robert Koch – **45. b)** Isaac Newton – **46. a)** 2 – **47. b)** Bauxite – **48. d)** 9 – **49. b)** Chloroform – **50. b)** Christiaan Barnard.

Page 125

Poly-? Ante-? Semi-? Pre-?

Poly-

Polyandry – polychrome – polycotton – polyculture – polygamy – polyglot – polygon – polymath – polyphony – polystyrene – polythene ...

Ante-

Antebellum – antecedent – antediluvian – anteater – antelope – antenatal – antenna – antenuptial – anterior – anteroom ...

Semi-

Semiarid – semicircle – semicolon – semiconductor – semidetached – semifinal – seminal – seminary – semiotics – semiquaver ...

Pre-

Precaution – precedent – precinct – precise – predate – predict – predilection – prejudice – premise – premium ...

Page 126

Cities of Britain

1. PLYMOUTH – **2.** EXETER – **3.** PORTSMOUTH – **4.** BRISTOL – **5.** SWANSEA – **6.** GLOUCESTER – **7.** OXFORD – **8.** LONDON – **9.** CAMBRIDGE – **10.** BIRMINGHAM – **11.** LIVERPOOL – **12.** MANCHESTER – **13.** YORK – **14.** EDINBURGH – **15.** NEWCASTLE – **16.** ABERDEEN.

Synonyms

Goodness

Altruism, generosity, integrity, kindness, piety, virtue ...

Apogee

Apotheosis, culmination, nadir, peak, top, zenith ...

Convulsion

Agitation, contraction, shaking, spasm, upheaval, upset ...

Enthusiasm

Ardour, dynamism, exaltation, fascination, liveliness, passion ...

Partisan

Adept, adherent, ally, devotee, member, supporter ...

Pages 126–127

Mystery words

A. A match
B. A grain
C. A phone card
D. An Oscar
E. A shadow
F. An alarm clock
G. A secret
H. A key

Page 127

The flags of Europe

1. Iceland – **2.** Yugoslavia – **3.** Switzerland – **4.** Russia – **5.** Romania – **6.** Poland – **7.** Greece – **8.** Hungary – **9.** Luxembourg – **10.** Ireland – **11.** Portugal – **12.** Denmark – **13.** Norway – **14.** Austria – **15.** Estonia – **16.** Netherlands – **17.** Italy – **18.** Spain – **19.** Finland – **20.** Turkey – **21.** Czech Republic – **22.** Bulgaria – **23.** Belgium – **24.** Sweden – **25.** Ukraine.

History and chronology

First flight by the Wright brothers (1904)
San Francisco Earthquake (1911)
The Great Flu Epidemic (1917–18)
The Wall Street Crash (1929).
Winston Churchill became Prime Minister (1941)
Bay of Pigs invasion (1961)
First man on the Moon (1969)
Fall of the Berlin Wall (1989)
Return of Hong Kong to China (1997)
First and last flights of Concorde (1969/2004)

Page 129

Well-known TV programmes

3. *Coronation Street* (1960) – **16.** *Charlie's Angels* (1976) – **10.** *The Muppet Show* (1977) – **7.** *Dallas* (1978) – **15.** *Cheers* (1982) - **13.** *The Late Show with David Letterman* (1982) – **9.** *The Oprah Winfrey Show* (1985) – **12.** *Baywatch* (1989) – **5.** *Seinfeld* (1989) – **8.** *Absolutely Fabulous* (1992) – **2.** *Frasier* (1993) – **1.** *Friends* (1994) – **18.** *Everybody loves Raymond* (1996) – **4.** *Sex and the City* (1998) – **17.** *Will and Grace* (1998) – **14.** *Who wants to be a Millionaire?* (1999) – **11.** *Big Brother* (2000) – **6.** *The Weakest Link* (2000).

Two comic actors and their films

Peter Sellers

1. *Dr Strangelove* (1963) – **2.** *The Pink Panther* (1963) – **6.** *What's new Pussycat?* (1965) – **8.** *The Party* (1968) – **10.** *The Fiendish Plot of Dr Fu Manchu* (1980).

Robin Williams

3. *Dead Poets' Society* (1989) – **4.** *The Fisher King* (1991) – **5.** *Good Morning Vietnam* (1987) – **7.** *Aladdin* (1992) – **9.** *Mrs Doubtfire* (1993).

Page 130

A habit doesn't make a monk

1. b. Spectacles (1280, Salvino degli Armati)

2. c. The necktie (about 1650, it appeared in France worn by the Croatian soldiers of the Royal-Cravate regiment)

3. l. The macintosh (1830s, Charles Macintosh)

4. f. Rubber boots (1853, Abraham Hutchinson)

5. h. The tailored suit (about 1880, John Redfern)

6. k. The zip (1890, Elias Howe)

7. e. The bracelet watch (1904, Louis Cartier for Cartier and Hans Wilsdorf for Rolex)

8. j. Blue jeans (Oscar Levi-Strauss, 1908)

9. m. Briefs (1918, Étienne Valton for Petit Bateau)

10. i. Nail polish (1932, Charles and Joseph Revson, Charles Lachman for Revlon)

11. n. Nylon stockings (1938, Wallace H. Carothers for DuPont of Nemours)

12. o. The bikini (1946, Louis Réard)

13. d. Stiletto heels (Roger Vivier, 1954)

14. a. The miniskirt (1965, Mary Quant and Courrèges)

15. g. The disposable razor (1975, Bic).

Page 132

Details that jar your senses

1. Missing shelf – **2.** Shoes in the bookcase – **3.** Door handle on the wall – **4.** Flower hanging from the ceiling – **5.** Laptop on the wall – **6.** Upside-down picture – **7.** Goldfish in the fireplace – **8.** Drawers in the wall – **9.** Date on the calendar (February 31) – **10.** Inverted catch – **11.** Umbrellas in a vase – **12.** Book in the form of a chairback – **13.** Rolling pin in the form of a chair leg – **14.** Tap on the table – **15.** Upside-down glasses of wine – **16.** Table without legs.

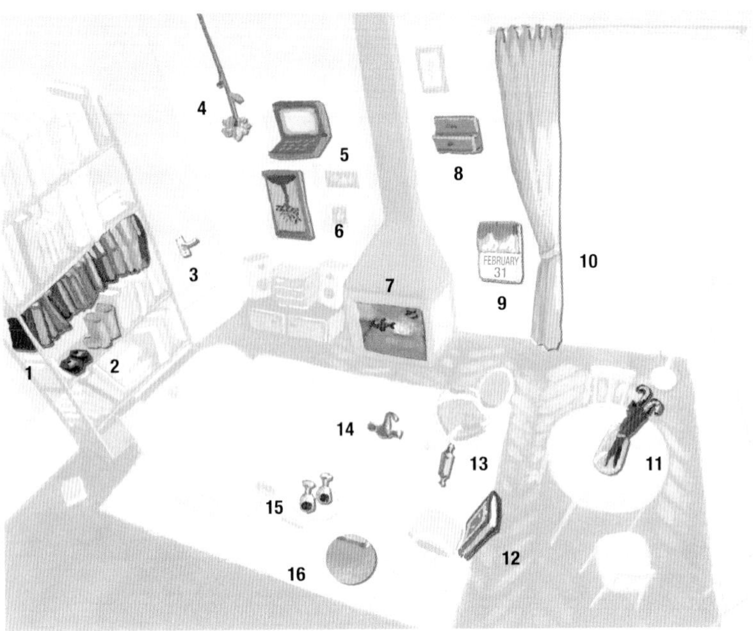

Page 133

Cryptogram

First proverb:

The early bird catches the worm.

Second proverb:

The grass is always greener on the other side.

Page 134

Mental arithmetic

769 + 586 = **1 355**
698 + 524 = **1 222**
587 + 269 + 874 = **1 730**
356 + 587 + 214 = **1 157**
1 005 + 33 + 646 = **1 684**
994 + 136 + 428 = **1 558**
650 + 123 + 541 = **1 314**
421 + 789 + 666 = **1 876**

Page 135

The Owl and the Pussy-cat

The Owl and the Pussy-cat went to **sea**
In a beautiful pea-green **boat**
They took some **honey**
and plenty of money
Wrapped up in a **five-pound** note
The Owl looked up to the **stars** above
And **sang** to a small guitar,
'O **lovely** Pussy! O Pussy, my love,
What a **beautiful** Pussy you are,
You are, You are!
What a **beautiful** Pussy you are!'

Pussy said to the **Owl** ,
'You elegant **fowl**!
How charmingly **sweet** you sing!
O let us be **married**! too long we have **tarried**:
But what shall we do for a **ring**?'
They **sailed** away for a year and a day
To the land where the **Bong Tree** grows
And there in a wood a **Piggy-Wig** stood
With a **ring** at the end of his nose,
His nose, His nose,
With a **ring** at the end of his nose.

'Dear Pig, are you **willing** to sell for a **shilling**
Your ring?' Said the Piggy, '**I will.**'
So they took it away,
and were **married** next day
By the **turkey** who lives on the **hill**
They dined on **mince** and slices of **quince**
Which they ate with a **runcible** spoon
And hand in hand, on the edge of the **sand**
They danced by the light of the moon,
The moon, The moon,
They danced by the light of the moon.

Page 136

Songs and words

Paris: *I love Paris in the springtime – April in Paris – Free man in Paris – Moonlight over Paris ...*
The sun: *Here comes the sun – You are my sunshine – Under the Sun – A Place in the Sun ...*
Love: *All you need is love – Love me tender – Love is a many-splendoured thing – Love to love you baby – Love, love me do ...*
Colours: *The colours of the wind – Love is blue – Black magic woman – Mellow yellow ...*
Names of cities: *Autumn in New York – Chicago – San Francisco – In the port of Amsterdam – One night in Bangkok – Rio de Janeiro blues ...*

Perfume, hippopotamus, catastrophe and nectarine

Per: peril – period – perform – perceive – perch ...
Hippo: Hippocratic – hippodrome – hippogriff – hippocampus – hippocras ...
Cata: cataclysm – catacomb – catalepsis – catalogue – catalyst ...
Nec: necessity – neck – necropolis – necrosis – nectar ...

A hairy story

Blond hair: Marilyn Monroe, Grace Kelly, Brigitte Bardot, Robert Redford, Claudia Schiffer ...
Red hair: Rita Hayworth, Nicole Kidman, Jasper Carrott, Lucille Ball, Rupert Grint ...
Black hair: Cleopatra, Louise Brooks, Charlie Chaplin, Clark Gable, Snow White ...

Footloose

Put your foot in your mouth, foot-and-mouth disease, foot of a hill, have a heavy foot, a foot soldier, one foot in the door, start off on the wrong foot, be wrong-footed, travel on foot, one foot in the grave, set out on foot, foot the bill, put a foot wrong, put your best foot forward, get under someone's feet, follow in someone's footsteps ...

Page 137

European currencies

Austria: the schilling – **Belgium:** the Belgian franc – **Cyprus:** the Cyprus pound – **Czech Republic:** the Czech koruna – **Denmark:** the Danish krone – **Estonia:** the kroon – **Finland:** the Finnish mark – **France:** the French franc – **Germany:** the Deutschmark – **Greece:** the drachma – **Hungary:** the forint – **Ireland:** the Irish punt – **Italy:** the lira – **Latvia:** santimi and lats – **Lithuania:** litas – **Luxembourg:** the Luxembourg franc – **Malta:** Maltese lira – **The Netherlands:** the Dutch florin – **Poland:** zloty – **Portugal:** the escudo – **Slovakia:** the Slovak Koruna – **Slovenia:** the tolar – **Spain:** the peseta – **Sweden:** the Swedish krona – **United Kingdom:** the British pound.
The United Kingdom, Denmark and Sweden have not as yet adopted the euro.

Great rivers of the world

1. c. Amazon (7 000 km) – **2. f.** Nile (6 700 km) – **3. b.** Mississippi–Missouri (6 210 km) – **4. g.** Yangzi Jiang – (5 980 km) – **5. d.** Congo (4 800 km) – **6. e.** Amur (4 440 km) – **7. h.** Mekong (4 025 km) – **8. a.** Ganges (3 090 km)

Page 138

Words ending in -tle, words ending in -oot

Words ending in -tle: apostle, battle, beetle, cattle, fettle, kettle, mettle, nestle, prattle, rattle
Words ending in -oot: boot, cheroot, foot, loot, moot, offshoot, reboot, root, soot, toot.

Page 139

Who am I?

Figaro: Wolfgang Amadeus Mozart – **Flying machine:** Leonardo da Vinci – **Freedom:** Nelson Mandela – **Stratford:** Shakespeare – **Polonium:** Marie Curie – **Surrealism:** Salvador Dalí – **Gettysburg:** Abraham Lincoln – **Dr Gachet:** Vincent Van Gogh – **Mazurka:** Frédéric Chopin.

Pages 140–141

The calendar crutch

New Year's day: January 1 – **St Valentine's day:** February 14 – **Workers' day:** May 1 – **Good Friday:** March/April – **Easter Sunday:** March/April – **Pesach:** April – **Ascension day:** May 20 – **Independence Day** (US): July 4 – **Ramadan:** October/November – **Hallowe'en:** October 31 – **All Saints eve:** November 1 – **Day of the dead:** November 2 – **Guy Fawkes**: November 5 – **Armistice day:** November 11 – **Thanksgiving** – fourth Thursday of November in the US; second Monday of October in Canada – **Christmas day:** December 25 – **Boxing day:** December 26.
Diwali, Eid-ul Fitr and **Hannukah** fall on various dates according to different calendars and phases of the moon.

Pages 142–143

The states of India

1. Jammu and Kashmir – **2.** Himachal Pradesh – **3.** Punjab – **4.** Haryana – **5.** Uttar Pradesh – **6.** Delhi – **7.** Rajasthan – **8.** Sikkim – **9.** Arunachal Pradesh – **10.** Assam – **11.** Nagaland – **12.** Meghalava – **13.** Manipur – **14.** Tripur – **15.** Mizoram – **16.** Bihar – **17.** Madhya Pradesh – **18.** Gujarat – **19.** West Bengal – **20.** Orissa – **21.** Maharashtra – **22.** Andhra Pradesh – **23.** Karnataka – **24.** Tamil Nadu – **25.** Kerala – **26.** Goa – **27.** Pondicherry.

Page 143

Hidden objects

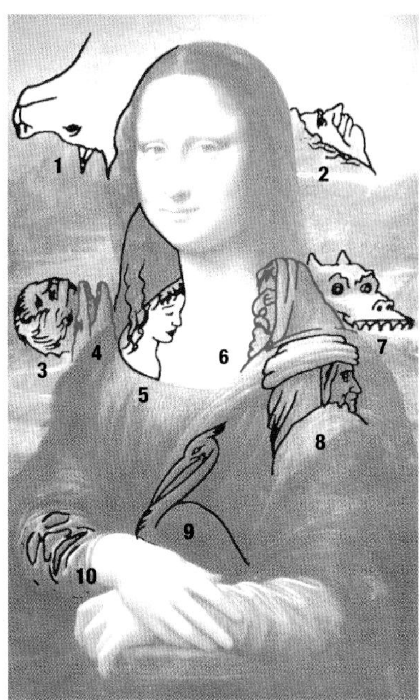

1. Dog's head – **2.** Man's profile –**3.** Lion's head – **4.** Crocodile's head – **5.** Woman's profile – **6.** Old man's profile – **7.** Dragon's head – **8.** Man's profile – **9.** Heron's head – **10.** Mask.

Page 147

Wright or wrong?

1. dynamite – **2.** receive – **3.** separate – **4.** definitely – **5.** hopeful – **6.** truly – **7.** biceps – **8.** therefore – **9.** psychology – **10.** epitome – **11.** apostrophe – **12.** vacillate

Page 206

Points in common

1. Shoe-chair = **foot** – windmill-yacht = **wind** – zebra-op art = **stripes** – duvet-bird = **feather** – spectacles-astronomy = **lenses** – hair-tree = **root** – carpet-sheep = **wool** – steps-mountain = **climb.**
2. Disinfectant-apéritif = **alcohol** – banana-press = **yellow** – crab-salt = **pinch** – bicycle-cheese = **wheel** – cock-mountain = **crest** – fish-caterpillar = **butterfly** – shoe-steak = **leather** – food-multiplication = **table.**
3. Computer-brain= **memory** – phrase-money = **coin** – palm-calendar = **date** – butterfly-tank = **caterpillar** – peak-syringe = **needle** – ear-carpenter = **hammer** – elbow-thief = **crook.**

Page 207

Hotchpotch of letters

Red: CABIN – **Green:** CRUISE – **Pink:** BRIDGE – **Orange:** ANCHOR – **Blue:** CAPTAIN.

Colourful images

White: wedding dress, milk, teeth, salt, lily, snow, noise; as white as snow, to bleed someone white, to have a reputation that is whiter than white.
Red: blood, rubies, nose, fire engine, strawberry, tomato, card; to be in the red, to see red, a red–letter day.
Yellow: gold, sunflower, sun, lemon, canary, butter, jersey; to be a yellow-belly, yellow journalism, to have a yellow streak.
Green: emerald, grass, leaf, cucumber, olive, salad, wood; to have green fingers, the green-eyed monster, to greenlight a project.
Black: night, coal, comedy, future, pirate flag, dress, heart; to be in the black, to see things in black and white, to be in someone's black book.
Blue: sky, turquoise, bluebell, jeans, sea, moon, note; her blue-eyed boy; a blue-riband event, came at her out of the blue.

Page 210

The apartment

1. Displaced objects
The trophy: from the bookshelf to the cabinet beneath the picture – The cup: from the kitchen counter to the table – The ball: from the carpet in the dining area to the room at the back – The round carpet: from the entrance to the space in front of the TV – The cocktail glass: from the coffee table to the counter.
2. Added objects
A lemon-squeezer on the counter – A green plant behind the blue armchair – A vase on the television – A painting on the right wall – A book on the sofa.
3. Removed objects
The sculpture on the blue cabinet –The salt cellar on the counter – The flowerpot on the table – The measuring jug under the counter – The side table next to the sofa.

Pages 212–213

Matching the diagram

Diagram 3.

Disks

2 – 3 – 5.

Pages 214–215

The dance of the cubes

Shape 1: 14 cubes – **Shape 2:** 8 cubes – **Shape 3:** 13 cubes – **Shape 4:** 12 cubes – **Shape 5:** 9 cubes – **Shape 6:** 11 cubes.

The dance of the letters

1. Adelaide – Brisbane – Canberra
2. Apple/Banana – Apricot/Pawpaw – Pear/Peach – Mango/Orange.

The animal world

Eric: the wolf – **Lee:** the elephant – **Mark:** the lion – **Lucy:** the giraffe – **Charles:** the polar bear – **Justine:** the seal.

Logical sequences

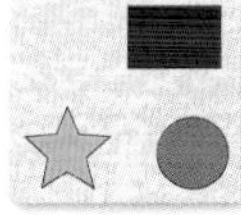

1. The star and the rectangle are always diagonally opposite.
2. The sum of the two first numbers gives the third number.
The sum of the three first numbers gives the fourth number.
The sum of the four first numbers gives the fifth number.
The sum of the five first numbers gives the last number.
The sixth number has no connection with the logical sequence.
3. 1. C (add 3 letters, subtract 2 letters, etc.).
2. S (add 1 letter, add 2 letters, etc.).
3. S (subtract 1 letter each time).
4. I (add 4 letters each time).
5. D (add 4 letters, subtract 3 letters, etc.).
6. O (add 4 letters, subtract 2 letters, add 3 letters, etc.).

Page 216

From jumbled words to a sentence

Indifferent to the winds, which rarely abated, the old fortified village sat in the shadow of the castle from which projected a gigantic and no doubt very ancient tower, from the top of which you could scan the whole horizon.

Page 217

Jigsaw puzzle

Piece no. 7 does not belong to the puzzle.

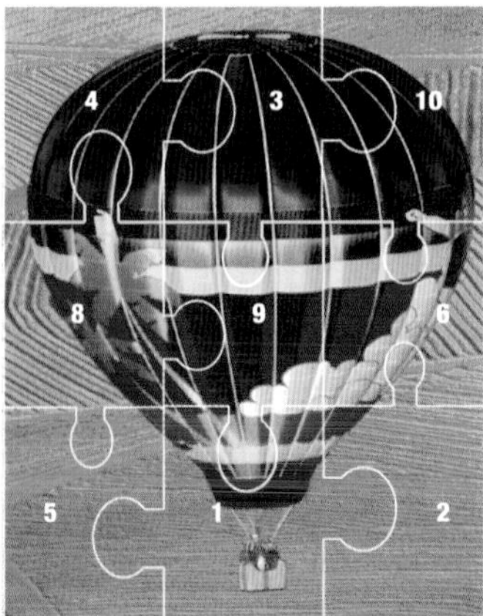

Page 218

Number sequences

1. A gap of six digits separates the first two numbers. The gaps that follow are, in succession, 8 (6+2), 10 (8+2), 12 (10+2), 14 (12+2), 16 (14+2). You add 16 to the sixth number to get the seventh, which is 77.
2. The number 215. Each time you have to multiply the number by 3 and add 2.
3. Number A = 33 – Number B = 35.
You have to add 6 to each number when you move to the right and subtract 6 when you move to the left. You add 2 for each move towards the bottom and subtract 2 for each move towards the top.
4. The digit 5. This square has to be divided into four other squares containing four boxes each. In each of these squares, the biggest number is the sum of the three others (here, 9 + 2 + 5 = 16).

Shape sequences

1.

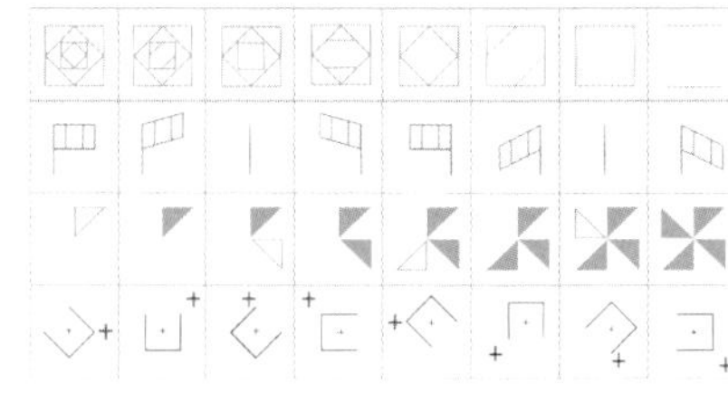

2. Card no. 2.

Palindromes

Common nouns: kayak – madam – rotor...
Verbs: gag – level – pull up – put up – repaper...
Names: Anna – Ava – Elle – Hannah – Otto...
Towns: Akasaka (Tokyo) – Glenelg (Scotland) – Kanatanak (Alaska) – Kinikinik (Alberta) – Qaanaaq (Greenland) ...
Phrases: A Toyota's a Toyota – Boston did not sob – Do geese see God? ...
Dates: 10.01.1001 – 13.11.1131 ...

Page 219

Film sequence

Star Wars (George Lucas, United States, 1977) – *Elephant Man* (David Lynch, United States, 1980) – *Out of Africa* (Sydney Pollack, United States, 1986) – *Love Story* (Arthur Hiller, United States, 1970) – *Gone with the Wind* (Victor Fleming, United States, 1939) – *The Magnificent Seven* (John Sturges, United States, 1960) – *Ginger and Fred* (Federico Fellini, Italy, 1985) – *When Harry met Sally* (Rob Reiner, United States, 1989) – *Monsoon Wedding* (Mira Nair, India, 2001) – *La Dolce Vita* (Federico Fellini, Italy, 1960). The film that is not American or European is *Monsoon Wedding*, which was an Indian production.

The sound of music...

1st group: the Jacobs contained 7 musicians.
2nd group: the Funnies contained 5 musicians.
3rd group: the Cats contained 4 musicians.
4th group: the Rockers contained 6 musicians.

Page 220

What a story!

Mr X booked a seat on the plane by phone, to Fort-de-France (4). He packed his suitcase (6). At the airport, having chatted up a very attractive stewardess (12), he left Paris (1). As they were landing, Mr X realised that he had boarded a plane bound for Greenland (9). He shivered with cold at the open door (2). But his suitcase was waiting for him at Fort-de-France (8). Mr X tried to move heaven and earth to leave Greenland the same day (10), and the hostess did her best (11), without success. Mr X was forced to spend a night in a hotel (3) while waiting for the next flight to Martinique. He took off eventually (13) and reached his intended destination (7). Mr X appeared at the door of the aircraft dressed in an anorak which he had had to buy as a result of the cold (5).

Page 221

A zoo let loose

Page 222

In the car

– the engine: starter, carburettor, spark plugs, oil, petrol, battery, cylinder head, cylinder head joint, connecting rods, air filter, oil filter, petrol filter, gear box… ;

– the body: shock absorbers, brakes, brake pads, brake liquid, front wing, rear wing, doors, roof, convertible roof, bonnet, boot, bumper, windscreen, lights, indicator, hazard lights, brake lights, foglamps, windscreen wipers, wheels,wheel rims, hub caps, tyres, locks… ;

– interior fittings: seats, rearview mirror, upholstery, headrest, steering wheel, pedals, gear stick, glove compartment, dashboard, lighter, horn, carpets… ;

– safety features: seatbelt, headrest, airbags… ;

– accessories: cupholders, inteior deodorant, arm rests, sun visors, radio/CD player, speakers, air-conditioner…

Pages 223

Points in common

The 7 groups of 4 categories have a common theme.

Cooking: ladle – cake – electric beater – chef's hat

Religion: menorah – rosary – gong – bishop's crosier

Recreation: deckchair – tent – swimsuit – camera

Arts: violin – palette – clapperboard – bust

Technology: computer mouse – satellite dish – transistor – mobile phone

Odour: skunk – ether – atomiser – cheese

Red: lipstick – ladybird – cherry – poppy

Page 225

Initials

Some suggestions:

1. Low Pressure Valve Stops Mudslide
Lax Plumbers Violate Safety Measures
Loud Percussion Vibrations Shatter Moonstone

2. Mondays Catch Everyone Down, Right?
My Chocolate Egg Drips Readily
Mary Calls Ed Daily, Remember?

3. Lemon Tarts Easily Require Sugar
Left Totally Enraged, Rowena Screamed
Leafy Trees Epitomise Residential Streets

4. Let's Munch Delicious Nutritious Carrots
Lara Mackintosh's Dog Nipped Charlie
Lean Mean Dogs Need Chow

Stringing along

Suggestions:

CELL-PHONE/**PHONE**-TIC
BUT-TER/**TER**-RIFIC
CRI-ME/**ME**-NACE
CAR-PET/**PET**-ULANT
GAR-DEN/**DEN**-IZEN
LEAD-EN/**EN**-UNCIATE
EN-TRAP/**TRAP**-PINGS
PA-PER/**PER**-FECT
BE-FORE/**FORE**-CAST
PRO-TECT/**TECT**–ONIC
ME-TAL/**TAL**-LY
SUB-TEXT/**TEXT**-URE
MAM-MAL/**MAL**-IGN
AN-CHOR/**CHOR**-AL
NUM-BER/**BER**-RY
PLA-CARD/**CARD**-IGAN
CUR-RENT/**RENT**-AL
BO-TOX/**TOX**-IC

Page 226

World tour *(see bottom of page)*

Page 228

The correct distances

In France

1. Paris–Lille: 207 km
2. Paris–Nantes: 343 km
3. Paris–Lyon: 391 km
4. Paris–Strasbourg: 400 km
5. Paris–Bordeaux: 500 km
6. Paris–Marseille: 662 km
7. Paris–Nice: 687 km
8. Paris–Toulon: 694 km
9. Paris–Ajaccio: 921 km

In Europe

1. Paris–Brussels: 265 km
2. Paris–London: 343 km
3. Paris–Zurich: 491 km
4. Paris–Dublin: 780 km
5. Paris–Berlin: 881 km
6. Paris–Prague: 885 km
7. Paris–Copenhagen: 1 028 km
8. Paris–Madrid: 1 050 km
9. Paris–Rome: 1 117 km
10. Paris–Stockholm: 1 549 km
11. Paris–Helsinki: 1 911 km
12. Paris–Athens: 2 093 km

Page 226

Around the world

1. Paris–Algiers: 1 373 km
2. Paris–Marrakech: 2 081 km
3. Paris–Istanbul: 2 263 km
4. Paris–Moscow: 2 494 km
5. Paris–Cairo: 3 222 km
6. Paris–Baghdad: 3 875 km
7. Paris–Dakar: 4 224 km
8. Paris–Washington: 6 177 km
9. Paris–Rio de Janeiro: 9 146 km
10. Paris–Cape Town: 9 293 km
11. Paris–Saigon: 10 147 km
12. Paris–Sydney: 16 966 km

Page 229

Stick-on words

KNOCK–TURN: **nocturne** – PURR–FORM: **perform** – LAY–BELL: **label** – DAY–LEA: **daily** – SIGH–CLICK: **cyclic** – CREW–SIBYL: **crucible** – BOY–ANT: **buoyant** – OR–ROCK: **auroch** – ADD–DOOR: **adore** – NIGHT–RATE: **nitrate** – CHASE–SUN: **chasten** – MATCH–OH: **macho** – WRECK–ORDER: **recorder** – REEF–FINE: **refine** – REAP–LIE: **reply** – SEE–PIER: **sepia.**

Page 230

Happy endings

Doctor: medicine – **Tree:** pine – **Jump:** trampoline – **Read:** magazine – **Dye:** aniline – **Mountain:** alpine – **Poverty:** breadline – **Coffee:** caffeine – **Swimming:** chlorine – **Dog:** canine – **Factory:** machine – **Together:** combine – **Principal:** main – **Agony:** pain – **Landscape:** terrain – **Locomotive:** train – **Teetotaller:** abstain – **Reach:** attain – **Cheap:** bargain – **Hook:** Captain – **Keep:** maintain – **Arrest:** detain.

Two images, one word

1. Mushroom – foot: **fungus**
2. Empty pocket – shoe: **shoestring**
3. King – tooth: **crown**
4. Sun – dancer: **star**
5. Italy – eagle: **Rome**
6. Cannes – hand: **Palme d'Or**
7. Musket – fireworks: **gunpowder**
8. Hair – tie: **knot**
9. Church tower – horse race: **steeplechase**
10. Beer – bread: **yeast**
11. Coconut – cow: **milk**
12. Chignon – slipper: **ballet dancer**

Page 231

To each its own references

Taxi

– Transport, meter, rank, train station, plane (a plane taxis on the runway) ...

– The yellow taxis of New York, *Taxi Driver* (a film by Martin Scorsese), Vanessa Paradis (who sang the hit song *Joe le taxi) ...*

Nose

– Smell, nostrils, running, handkerchief ...

– Detective (has a nose for the truth), irritation (to get up someone's nose), Cleopatra, Sphinx, wine (it has a good nose), *Cyrano de Bergerac* (a book by Edmond Rostand, about a big-nosed hero) ...

Bicycle

– Wheel, tandem, Tour de France ...

– *Bicycle Thieves* (a film by Vittorio de Sica), the song *Daisy Daisy* ('on a bicycle made for two') ...

Phantom

– white, sheet, haunted house, pregnancy, limb ...

– *Phantom of the Opera* (a film, remade several times, and a musical by Andrew Lloyd Webber) ...

Sun

– Moon, holidays, umbrellas, sunglasses, sunblock, solstice ...

– Louis XIV (the Sun King), Incas (Temple of the Sun), *Here comes the sun* (Beatles), *Sunset Boulevard* (a film by Billy Wilder) ...

Gold

– Silver, ring, marriage, bullion, mines ...

– Age (the golden years), goodness (a heart of gold), romance (a golden moment), silence (silence is golden), *Goldfinger* (a James Bond movie, starring Sean Connery) ...

Mouse

– Rat, cat, cheese, computer, trap, squeak ...

– *Hickory dickory dock* (nursery rhyme), *Of Mice and Men* (a book by John Steinbeck), Walt Disney (Mickey Mouse), *Maus* (a comic strip by Art Spiegelman) ...

Night

– Black, stars, sleep, pyjamas, moth, club ...

– *Night Watch* (a painting by Rembrandt), *Nightmare on Elm Street* (at least 5 sequels in this horror series) ...

Plane

– Flight, airport, runway, supersonic, stewardess ...

– Kamikaze, *Airport* (series of films spawned by Arthur Hailey's bestseller), Lindbergh, *Spirit of Saint Louis ...*

Page 232

Memorising the right definition

Blenny: n. a fish of the family Blenniidae, found in coastal waters.

Drosometer: n. An instrument which measures the amount of dew deposited on a surface.

Galatea: n. A strong, cotton fabric of twill weave, used for clothing.

Koan: n. A problem or riddle, in Zen Buddhism, which has no logical solution.

Periapt: n. A charm, or amulet.

Ramstam: adv. Headlong, or hastily.

Sciamachy: n. A fight with an imaginary enemy.

Tetrarch: n. The ruler of one quarter of a country.

Ventifact: n. A pebble shaped by windblown sand.

Zetetic: adj. As of an inquiry, investigating.

Leapfrogging over sheep

In 2 stages

Tea kettle steam **locomotive**
Car wheel carousel **funfair**
Telephone wire cut **surgery**
Coffee ground sand **beach**

In 3 stages

Telescope lens glass flute **champagne**
Hairdresser cut scissors secateurs **gardening**
Make-up cleanser soap Marseille **bouillabaisse**
Computer printer paper tree **cherry tree**

In 4 stages

Savanna Africa desert oasis ombre **silhouette**
Wrist bracelet watch hour time **climate**
Bird feather quill ink squid **sea**
News magazine articles words speech **promise**

In 5 stages

Ball basket shoe foot onion soup **kitchen**
Door key music chamber bed duvet **feather**
Circle ring marriage ties rope knot **sailor**
Animal vegetable nature landscape painting artist **selfportrait**

Page 239

The causes of the war of Rion

1. **Who?** Orus, prince of Olys.
2. **What?** To kidnap the beautiful Persephone.
3. **Where?** From Rion.
4. **When?** In 9600.
5. **How?** By trickery, during the absence of King Taramac.
6. **What for?** To make her queen of Olys.
7. **Why?** Because she had been promised to him by the goddess Amoria.

Page 242

Words, words, words...

1. GOSSIP – **2.** CHATTER – **3.** CHINWAG – **4.** NEGOTIATE – **5.** MURMUR – **6.** MONOLOGUE – **7.** CONVERSE – **8.** COMMUNICATE – **9.** TRANSMIT – **10.** CONFER – **11.** PARLEY.

Page 243

Little scraps of paper

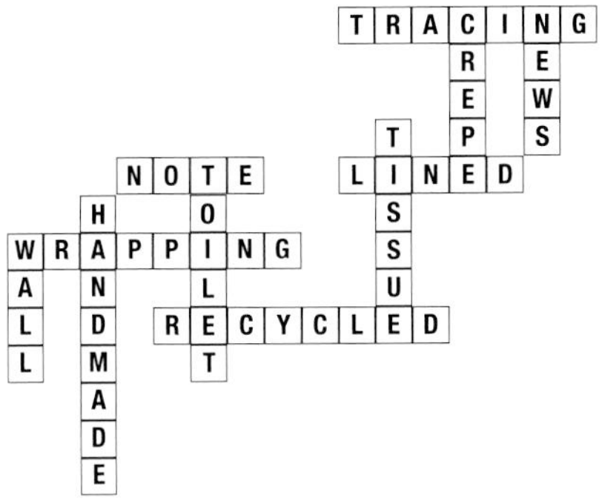

Page 299

Tasty national dishes

Eastern Europe: Blini, Borscht, Goulash, Pierogi.
France: Blanquette de veau, Boeuf bourguignonne, Bouillabaisse, Coq au vin.
Germany: Bratwurst, Eisbein, Sauerkraut, Stollen.
Great Britain: Beef Wellington, Cock–a–leekie, Colcannon, Yorkshire pudding.
Greece: Dolmades, Keftedes, Moussaka, Tzatziki.
Italy: Osso buco, Pizza, Risotto, Spaghetti bolognese.
North Africa: Couscous, Ful Midames, Harira, Tagine.
Spain and Portugal: Bacalão, Chorizo, Gazpacho, Paella.

The calorie table

d. 100g salad leaves**:** 18 kcal.
h. 100ml soda water**:** 44 kcal.
j. 100g apple**:** 52 kcal.
a. 100g pear**:** 61 kcal.
l. 100ml wine,12% a/c: 67 kcal.
b. 100g cooked pasta**:** 90 kcal.
m. 100g egg: 160 kcal.
k. 100g steak: 200 kcal.
e. 100g pizza: 200 kcal.
f. 100g hamburger: 255 kcal.
g. 100g ham sandwich**:** 430 kcal.
i. 100g couscous: 575 kcal.
c. 100g pork casserole: 610 kcal.

Page 300

Italian delights

Sleep: watch out for these mistakes !

Five errors not to commit.

1. It is preferable to go to sleep calm and relaxed.
4. It is better to rest your body for two hours before going to bed.
6. On the contrary, a light meal aids a good sleep.
11. If you are sensitive to caffeine, it is better not to drink anything containing it after 4pm.
16. To think that a large consumption of alcohol will help you sleep is a big mistake. Alcohol puts the senses to sleep for a short while, but it is after all a stimulant. In addition, it can induce nightmares.

Page 302

Medicinal plants

Chinese rhubarb: constipation – **Cinnamon:** loss of appetite – **Clove:** toothache – **Fig:** digestive problems – **Flax:** inflammation of the joints – **Garlic:** intestinal worms – **Greater camomile:** painful periods – **Ginger:** nausea and vomiting – **Ginkgo:** loss of memory – **Ginseng:** stress, asthenia – **Jojoba:** hoarseness – **Lemon verbena:** nasal congestion – **Linden:** minor sleep problems – **Lucerne:** fatigue – **Sarsaparilla:** eczema

Page 305

Mirror images

Page 306

A well-known fable

The Fox and the Crow

Mistress Crow perched high in a tree
Held in her beak a piece of cheese
Master Reynard drawn by the smell
Wondered what cunning tale to tell.
'Good day, Mistress Crow, without a lie,
You are the most beautiful bird I spy,
What glossy plumage, what lustrous wing,
I've heard too you can really sing.'
The Crow could not contain her pride
And opened her beak, and dropped her prize,
The cheese fell into the Fox's maw
Once swallowed he allowed himself a guffaw
'Dear Crow, the moral of this tasty tale?
Trust not the flatterer's deceiving veil.'
The Crow, ashamed and mightily confused,
Vowed never again to fall for that ruse.

Whose call is that?

The crow **caws** – The owl **hoots** – The chick **cheeps** – The monkey **chatters** – The duck **quacks** – The hen **clucks** – The rooster **crows** – The frog **croaks** – The bat **squeaks** – The bee **buzzes** – The elephant **trumpets** – The snake **hisses** – The lion **roars** – The tiger **growls** – The turkey **gobbles** – The pig **oinks** – The hyena **laughs** – The mouse **squeaks** – The dog **barks** – The horse **whinnies** – The donkey **brays** – The sheep **bleats** – The cow **moos.**

Page 307

A tasty tour of the world

Austria: apfelstrudel (an apple pie) – **Belgium:** braised endives – **Bulgaria:** cold cucumber soup – **China:** hundred-year-old eggs (duck eggs preserved for about three months in mud and chalk) – **Finland:** glögg (spiced hot wine) – **India:** murgh masala (chicken cooked with spices) – **Indonesia:** gado gado (salad with bean sprouts and a peanut dressing) – **Ireland:** colcannon (mashed potatoes and cabbage) – **Japan:** miso soup – **Lebanon:** kibbeh (meat balls with a cracked wheat coating) – **Malaysia:** sayur lemak (a spicy chicken, vegetable and coconut soup) – **Mexico:** enchiladas (maize tortillas rolled and stuffed) – **Netherlands:** balkenbrij (pork-head pudding) – **Peru:** anticuchos (beef chunks marinated and cooked on a skewer) – **Senegal:** yassa (marinated meat or fish) – **Thailand:** tom yam gai (hot and sour chicken soup) **Turkey:** imam bayildi (aubergine stuffed with onions, tomato, pinenuts and raisins) – **United States:** pumpkin pie – **Vietnam:** tom chien dua (coconut-flavoured prawns on skewers).

Page 308

Here's to marriage!

5 years: wood – **10 years:** tin – **15 years:** porcelain – **20 years:** crystal – **25 years:** silver – **30 years:** pearl – **40 years:** emerald or ruby – **50 years:** gold – **60 years:** diamond – **70 years:** platinum – **80 years:** oak.

Colourful expressions

Eat like a **pig** – Swim like a **fish** – As quiet as a **mouse** – As blind as a **bat** – As slow as a **snail** – As proud as a **peacock** – When the **cat** is away, the **mice** will play – To have a **bird** brain – To put the **cat** among the **pigeons** – Put the cart before the **horse** – To be like a **bull** in a china shop – To get on your high **horse – Horses** for courses – Get a **bee** in your bonnet – To have a **flea** in your ear **...**

Page 310

Are you movie mad?

Apocalypse Now: **Francis Ford Coppola** – *Breakfast at Tiffany's:* **Blake Edwards** – *Doctor Zhivago:* **David Lean** – *Aguirre, Wrath of God:* **Werner Herzog** – *La Dolce Vita:* **Federico Fellini** – *Gone with the Wind:* **Victor Fleming** – *E.T., The Extra-Terrestrial:* **Steven Spielberg** – *Shirley Valentine:* **Lewis Gilbert** – *Rio Bravo:* **Howard Hawks** – *Citizen Kane:* **Orson Welles** – *Some Like it Hot:* **Billy Wilder** – *Remains of the Day:* **James Ivory** – *Yellow Earth:* **Chien Kaige** – *Moby Dick:* **John Huston** – *Rear Window:* **Alfred Hitchcock** – *The Great Dictator:* **Charles Chaplin** – *The Quiet Man:* **John Ford** – *Annie Hall:* **Woody Allen** – *Chess Players:* **Satyajit Ray** – *Women in Love:* **Ken Russell.**

Lost works of art

Botticelli: *The birth of Venus* – **Mary Cassatt:** *Mother and Child* – **Edgar Degas:** *Dancers at the barre* – **Frida Kahlo:** *Self-portrait with Monkey* – **Gustav Klimt:** *The Kiss* – **Edvard Munch:** *The Scream* – **Pablo Picasso:** *Guernica* – **Rembrandt:** *The Night Watch* – **Henri de Toulouse-Lautrec:** *Au Moulin-Rouge, la Goulue* – **Leonardo da Vinci:** *The Adoration of the Magi* – **Vincent van Gogh:** *Sunflowers* – **Andy Warhol:** *Marilyn.*

Page 312

Young words

Bluejacking: when a nearby owner of a bluetooth radio communication system (as on a mobile) detects another owner nearby and sends them an unexpected message on their mobile – **Blogger:** a person who keeps a weblog (a 'blog'), a website on a particular subject to which people can add their comments – **Downshifter:** a person who opts for a simpler, less well-paid lifestyle – **Green accounting:** a system of accounting that considers the effects of production and consumption on the environment – **Identify theft:** electronic data theft – **Metrosexual:** an urban young man concerned with fashion and male grooming, not necessarily homosexual – **Pharming:** the genetic manipulation of plants and animals with genes from other organisms, which are then 'milked' to harvest pharmaceutical drugs against certain diseases – **Screenager:** a young person brought up in the age of TV and computers – **Triple bottom line:** a measure of economic success that takes into account profit, environmental sustainability and social responsibility – **Zorbing:** an extreme sport in which the participant is harnessed inside a large rubber ball which is then pushed off a cliff.

Page 313

Say it with flowers ...

Camellia: constancy – **Crocus:** jealousy – **Gentian:** suspicion – **Hydrangea:** coldness – **Laurel:** glory – **Lily-of-the-valley:** happiness – **Peony:** confusion – **Rose:** love and beauty – **Snowdrop:** trial.

Who sings what?

ABBA: E. *Knowing me, knowing you* – **Louis Armstrong:** F. *What a Wonderful World* – **Beatles:** G. *All My Loving* – **The Bee Gees:** H. *First of May* – **Tony Bennett:** I. *They Can't Take That Away from Me* – **Blondie:** J. *Heart of Glass* – **Marvin Gaye:** K. *I Heard it through the Grapevine* – **Enrique Iglesias:** L. *Hero* – **Norah Jones:** D. *Don't Know Why* – **Carole King:** M. *You've Got a Friend* – **Freddie Mercury:** N. *Bohemian Rhapsody* – **Police:** P. *Walking on the Moon* – **Elvis Presley:** Q. *Blue Suede Shoes* – **Kenny Rogers:** C. *Ruby Don't Take your Love to Town* – **Carly Simon:** A. *You're so Vain* – **Barbra Streisand:** R. *Woman in Love* – **Tina Turner:** B. *What's Love got to do with it?* – **Shania Twain:** O. *That Don't Impress me Much.*

Page 315

Famous monuments

Agra (India): Taj Mahal – **Barcelona:** The Sagrada Familia – **Beijing:** The Summer Palace – **Berlin:** The Brandenburg Gate – **Copenhagen:** The Little Mermaid – **Florence:** The Duomo – **Istanbul:** Hagia Sophia – **Lhasa** (Tibet): The Potala (palace of the Dalai Lama) – **London:** Westminster Abbey – **Paris:** La Sainte-Chapelle – **Philadelphia:** Independence Hall – **St Petersburg:** The Hermitage Palace – **San Francisco:** Golden Gate bridge – **Venice:** The Rialto bridge – **Warsaw:** Sigismond's column.

Page 316

Top Hits

1970s

Me and Bobby McGee: Janis Joplin – *The Way we Were:* Barbra Streisand – *YMCA:* Village People – *Dancing Queen:* ABBA

1980s

Bette Davis Eyes: Kim Carnes – *Beat it:* Michael Jackson – *Like a Virgin:* Madonna – *Careless Whisper:* Wham!

1990s

Nothing Compares to You: Sinead O'Connor – *I will Always Love You:* Whitney Houston – *Because you Loved Me:* Celine Dion – *Believe:* Cher.

Page 318

The family home

1. Her great-grandmother.
2. Mary and Jack have the most descendants (15).
3. The second generation.
4. Audrey: Clara or Lauren – Chris: Jack or Roger – Judy: Delia or Leonora.
5. Audrey and Philip.

Page 319

Family words

Affinity: (n) a relationship by marriage or adoption, in other words, by means other than blood.
Agnate: (n) related to a common male ancestor.
Cognate: (n) related to a common female ancestor.
Dowry: (n) the property or money given by a woman, in some cultures, and by a man in others, to the new partner in marriage.
First cousin: (n) the son or daughter of one of your parent's siblings.
Mixed marriage: (n) marriage between people of different religion, race or nationality.
Polyandry: (n) the marriage of one woman to several men at the same time.
Second cousin: the child of a first cousin of either of your parents.
Uterine: (adj) said of two children who have the same mother but not the same father .
Consanguinity: (n) a relationship by blood.

Page 322

Meet your match!

First step

1.

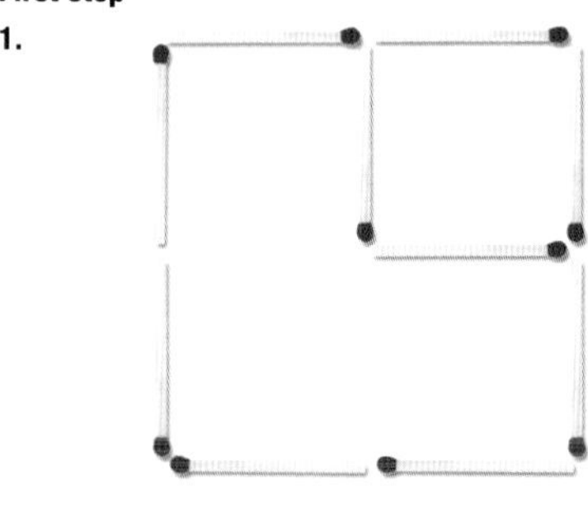

2.

Second step

1

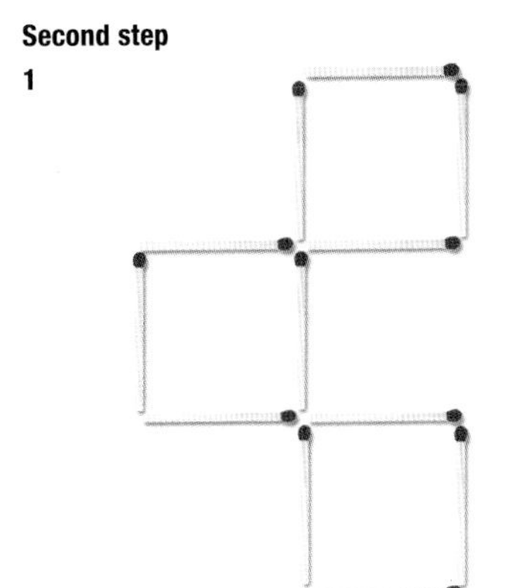

2

The dictionary

CY: cyanide, cyberspace, cycle, cylinder, cypress …
SY: syllable, symbolic, sympathy, synagogue, system …
GEN: gender, general, generate, generous, genteel …
EQUI: equidistant, equine, equipment, equivalent, equivocal …
HAR: harass, harbinger, harbour, harmful, harmony …

Page 324

On a high note

1. The Marriage of Figaro – **2.** Aïda – **3.** The Barber of Seville – **4.** Carmen – **5.** Tosca – **6.** Parsifal – **7.** Orpheus in the Underworld – **8.** The Damnation of Faust – **9.** Fidelio – **10.** Don Quixote.

Words and states of mind

Kept his socks on (to keep calm).
In a storm (to be raging mad about something).
Threw him in a whirl (confused or unsettled him).
Satisfaction.

Tranquillising plants

1. Valerian – **2.** Linden – **3.** Lemon balm – **4.** St John's wort – **5.** Passionflower – **6.** Hops – **7.** Orange blossom.

Page 327

Popular names

1930s:
Robert – Richard – James – William – Donald
Mary – Betty – Dorothy – Helen – Barbara
1950s:
All the above, plus:
Charles, Gary, Michael, David, Thomas
Linda, Patricia, Susan, Maria, Sandra
1970s:
Brian, Christopher, Jeffrey, Joseph, Mark
Angela, Jennifer, Kimberly, Lisa, Michelle
2000:
Daniel, Harry, Jack, Joshua, Lewis
Charlotte, Chloe, Emily, Lauren, Megan

Page 328

Religions of the world

1. Christianity – **2.** Islam – **3.** Hinduism – **4.** Buddhism – **5.** Animism – **6.** Sikhism – **7.** Judaism – **8.** Baha'i– **9.** Confucianism – **10.** Shintoism.

Remember your lines

1. *Gone with the Wind* – **2.** *Sudden Impact* – **3.** *Casablanca* – **4.** *Jerry Maguire* – **5.** *E.T., the Extra-Terrestrial* – **6.** *The Godfather* – **7.** *Star Wars* – **8.** *On the Waterfront* – **9.** *Every Day's a Holiday* – **10.** *The African Queen.*

Page 329

Modern inventions

Paper clip: 1900 – **Wireless:** 1910 – **Refrigerator:** 1913 – **Television:** 1923 – **Scotch tape:** 1925 – **Vegetable mill:** 1932 – **Supermarket trolley:** 1934 – **Ballpoint pen:** 1943 – **Household gloves:** 1948 – **Computer:** 1948 – **Credit card:** 1950 – **Contraceptive pill:** 1954 – **Disposable nappies:** 1956 – **Barbie doll:** 1959 – **Plastic bottle:** 1963 – **Mobile phone:** 1979.

To each country its currency

Baht: Thailand – **Dirham:** Morocco – **Dông:** Vietnam – **Forint:** Hungary – **Guarani:** Paraguay – **Lev:** Bulgaria – **Rand:** South Africa – **Real:** Brazil – **Rouble:** Russia – **Rupiah:** Indonesia – **Shekel:** Israel – **Sol:** Peru – **Yuan:** China – **Zloty:** Poland.

Lists of games and exercises

By category

Space

Structure

Time

By type

By theme or title

Tests

Personal questionnaires and exercises

Relaxation exercises

List of 'My memory and ...' boxes

General index

The page numbers in bold (**234**) refer to the extended treatment of subjects; the headings and numbers in italic (*310*) refer to the games, tests and exercises related to the categories beneath which they appear; and the asterisks (209*) indicate the boxed texts on an orange panel that occur throughout the book.

A

B-C

D

E

F

G

H-I

J-K

L

M

N-O

P

Useful web pages

There are many web sites that offer information on the medical and psychological aspects of memory, as well as those that give tips for improving your memory and those that will help with the word exercises and crossword puzzles in this book. Most local or national health centres, community centres and pensioners' associations will be able to give you further information on medical experts and support groups near you as well as on activities and interest groups you could get involved with in order to stimulate your memory.

Serious stuff

Bupa
www.bupa.co.uk/health_information/asp/your_health/factsheets/
This UK private-health site contains a clear and concise A to Z of downloadable health information, reviewed and approved by relevant healthcare professionals, including doctors, dentists, nurses, physios, exercise physiologists and dietitians.

Butler Hospital Memory & Aging Program
www.memorydisorder.org
The Butler Hospital is affiliated with the Brown Medical School in Providence, Rhode Island, USA. Its Memory & Aging Program provides a state-of-the-art assessment and treatment of memory disorders and is dedicated to developing new treatments for Alzheimer's disease and other types of dementia. The site contains information on the causes and treatment of memory loss.

Dementia.com
www.dementia.com/index.jhtml?source=google
Once you have registered with this site, which costs nothing, you will have access to articles, literature and news about the various types of dementia.

Full Circle of Care
http://www.fullcirclecare.org/alzheimers/welcome.htm
A US site, this nonetheless contains very good information for caregivers the world over on taking care of people with Alzheimer's disease.

Learning & Memory
www.learnmem.org/
This academic journal provides articles and papers online, covering the scientific study of the brain and its learning and memory capacity.

Mayo Clinic, Jacksonville, Florida
www.mayoclinic.org/memorydisorders jax/
A state-designated memory clinic, it offers its services to all residents of Florida, regardless of their ability to pay. The web site includes details on support groups, a description of a memory disorder evaluation and what to bring to one, information on clinical trials and research and on other web resources.

Medline Plus
www.nlm.nih.gov/medlineplus/memory.html
This service of the US National Library of Health and the National Institutes of Health provides articles on many aspects of memory, as well as on diagnosis, clinical trials, and descriptions of particular disorders.

New York Memory and Healthy Aging Services
www.nymemory.org/services.html
A neurologist and a psychiatrist run this organisation dedicated to the diagnosis and management of memory disorders. They have recently done a study of memory and menopause, which you will find on their web site, as well as information on drugs used to treat memory disorders.

Out of memory
library.thinkquest.org/~C0110291/disorder/index.php
Memory basics, tricks, disorders, the latest research on memory, the purpose of memory and mnemonics ... all are covered on this site, written for the layperson. It includes a useful glossary.

The Ribbon
www.theribbon.com
The Ribbon Online is a website inspired by The Ribbon Newsletter, created to provide information for caregivers who are dealing with Alzheimer's and dementia. It has a biweekly newsletter, chat room and discussion forum.

Fun stuff

AllWords.Com
www.allwords.com
A thesaurus, dictionary and word-puzzle aid all in one, this site enables you to look up the meaning of words in alphabetical order, find words starting or ending with certain letters and words that match. Slang, puns and word games test your lexical skills.

LyricFind.com
www.lyricfind.com
You will find the lyrics of many familiar songs in English here, searchable by artist, song name and lyrics.

Memory
www.exploratorium.edu/memory
An exhibition on Memory, at the Exploratorium in San Francisco, has been placed indefinitely online. It covers articles and lectures on memory, memory games, a brain dissection, a guestbook of earliest memories and droodles – a combination of a doodle and a riddle.

Mind Tools
www.mindtools.com/memory.html
You will find here tips on memory techniques, remembering simple and long lists, long numbers and grouped information, using aide-memoires, learning a foreign language and remembering information for exams.

Risa Song Lyrics Archive
www.risa.co.uk/sla/
Rediscover the words of your favourite songs in this archive, which organises the lyrics of pop songs in English by performer, title and first line.

The Word Spy
www.wordspy.com
A website that focuses on what it calls 'lexpionage' – 'the sleuthing of new words and phrases' which have appeared in print and on other web sites – this site is your guide to the very latest words in the English language.

Wikipedia
en.wikipedia.org/wiki/Main_Page
This free encyclopedia, which you can select in many languages, covers a vast array of subjects organised with links to related subjects. Look up a date to find what happened around the world on that day, find out about a famous person, the meaning of a word, and the details on a particular subject.

World Wide Words
www.worldwidewords.org/index.htm
A site giving English words and phrases, their origin and evolution and what they mean.

Credits

PHOTOS
AKG IMAGES PARIS: 240, 241, 243l. **Pete BOSMAN**: 39, 183. **COLLECTION PARTICULIÈRE/X, D.R.**: 134r. **CONSEIL DE L'EUROPE**: 8, 137. **CORBIS ROYALTY-FREE**: 9, 65, 85b, 93cr, 93tl, 93ctr, 98t, 104cl, 155, 214r, 217, 280, 307, 338. **COSMOS/SPL**: 18t, 19b. **DAGLI ORTI**: 310. **© DIGITAL VISION**: 52t, 188, 219, 261, 334t. **GETTY IMAGES/PHOTODISC**: 17t, 22, 28/29b, 29tr, 29tr, 29cl, 29cr, 29b, 40/41, 58/59, 59bl, 63, 64, 66, 70, 77bl, 81, 82, 93trc, 93cl, 93lc, 99, 104tc, 104ctl, 104bl, 104cb and cr, 104bc, 105bl, 111cl, 151, 152b, 154ctl and bcr, 154ctr and bl, 154bc, 156, 157br, 158, 163b, 167, 168, 180, 181bl, 191, 194, 196c, 199cl, 199cb and br, 249t, 250, 252b, 255, 256, 257, 263, 266, 270b, 283, 284, 286, 288t, 292, 295, 313b, 328, 329b, 332, 333tl, 333tr, 333cl, 333cr, 333b, 334. **GOODSHOOT.COM**: 33, 83, 85t, 91, 93ctl, 93c, 104ctr and c, 154tl and cr ,154tc and br, 154tr and cl, 178, 198, 221, 225. **INPRA:** film posters, 187, 310/311. **© ICONOTEC/Atamu Rahi:** 93tlc, 104tl and tr. **READER'S DIGEST Assoc. Inc./GID/c, l, t, 2003/NIGTG**: 313t. **RMN/G. Blot/**Georges de La Tour, *The Cardsharp:* 78; **RMN/H. Lewandowski/**Camille Alfred Pabst, *The Spouse's Ransom or Alsatian Wedding*/musée d'Orsay: 86. **Isabelle ROZENBAUM and Frédéric CIROU/PhotoAlto**: 23, 27, 51t, 51t, 51b, 98b, 110br, 154tcr and br, 298, 299tl, 299ctl, 299cr, 299br, 300. **Isabelle ROZENBAUM/PhotoAlto**: 51tr, 93c, 93rc, 104ctc, 104rb and bl, 163t. **Marcel STIVE**: 88. **SRD/A. Grégoire**: 315cl; **SRD/A. Nouri**: 93bl, 153t, 190/191t, 192, 252t ; **SRD/D. Pavois**: 154tc, 243r, 249, 249b, 315tl, 315bl, 315b; **SRD/J.-P. Delagarde**: 71, 72, 270t, 277; **SRD/J.-P. Germain/**musée Jean de La Fontaine, Château-Thierry: 152t, 306t.

ARTWORK
Laurent AUDOUIN: 6ct, 6b, 7ct, 60/61, 148/149, 172, 176, 244/245, 282. **Emmanuel BATISSE**: 50t, 64, 178cl, 209, 210. **Pete BOSMAN**: 235, 329. **Philippe BUCAMP**: 94/95. **Jacqueline CAULET**: 22, 25, 26/27, 31tl, 36/37, 42, 53, 56/57, 57tr, 82,83,91,100cr, 130, 138l, 154, 175, 179, 189, 223/224, 230/231, 239, 242/243, 276b, 281, 300, 301, 309b, 325, 326. **Adam CARNEGIE**: 16b, 18b, 35cr, 57br, 76b, 77tl, 117b, 129r, 139b, 162t, 171, 230/231, 272, 275, 316t. **Marc DONON**: 15b, 16h, 21. **Philippe FASSIER**: 19t, 50b, 79, 96, 107, 110, 119, 167l, 182, 196br, 199ct, 332, 334. **Steven FELMORE**: 63b, 69, 126, 142/143, 157, 178cl, 299. **William FRASCHINI**: 73, 101t, 103, 162b, 187b, 188, 302/303, 324t. **Sylvie GUERRAZ**: 43, 45, 55, 67b, 68, 76t, 80, 95b, 124, 129bl, 130br, 166, 174, 207, 219, 222r, 227cr, 242tl, 254t, 264, 274. **Sylvie GUERRAZ-Jacqueline CAULET**: 216/217. **Nicolas JARREAU**: 133. **Jean-Pierre LAMERAND**: 67, 81, 99tl, 120, 143, 153, 162cr, 196bl, 206, 220/221, 337. **Patrick LESTIENNE**: 14t, 17b, 24, 26b, 28, 31br, 47, 52b, 54, 114, 131, 136br, 138br, 142, 147, 227tl, 238, 308/309, 316b, 318, 321, 323, 324b. **Coll. D. PAVOIS**: 115. **D. PAVOIS**: 222tl, 271, 293. **Claude QUIEC**: 35b, 100cl, 117cr, 139, 140/141, 159, 232/233. **Carine SANSON**: cover, 3, 6tl, 6cb, 7tr, 7cb, 7b, 12/13, 84, 112/113, 132, 136l, 202/203, 228, 296/297, 336, 342/343.

TEXTS
'Because I'm worth it' is a patented slogan, property of **l'Oréal**: 30/31b. 'The Lady is a Tramp', Lorenz Hart/Richard Rodgers **© Gallo Music Publishers**: 57. Isabella Gardner, *Summer Remembered* (excerpt) from *The Collected Poems.* Copyright © 1990 by The Estate of Isabella Gardner. Reprinted with the permission of BOA Editions, Ltd: 58

101 Ways to Improve your Memory
is published by The Reader's Digest Association Far East Ltd
Printed in Hong Kong